CLASSICAL SOCIOLOGICAL THEORY

THIRD EDITION

George Ritzer
University of Maryland

Boston   Burr Ridge, IL   Dubuque, IA   Madison, WI   New York   San Francisco
St. Louis   Bangkok   Bogotá   Caracas   Lisbon   London   Madrid   Mexico City
Milan   New Delhi   Seoul   Singapore   Sydney   Taipei   Toronto

McGraw-Hill Higher Education
*A Division of The **McGraw-Hill** Companies*

CLASSICAL SOCIOLOGICAL THEORY

This book is printed on acid-free paper.

1 2 3 4 5 6 7 8 9 0   DOC/DOC   9 0 9 8 7 6 5 4 3 2 1 0

ISBN 0-07-229606-2

Editorial director: *Phillip A. Butcher*
Sponsoring editor: *Sally Constable*
Developmental editor: *Katherine Blake*
Marketing manager: *Leslie A. Kraham*
Project manager: *Carrie Sestak*
Production supervisor: *Rose Hepburn*
Freelance design coordinator: *Gino Cieslik*
Photo research coordinator: *Sharon Miller*
Photo researcher: *Sarah Evertson*
Compositor: *GAC Indianapolis*
Typeface: *10/12 Times Roman*
Printer: *R. R. Donnelly & Sons Company*

Library of Congress Cataloging-in-Publication Data

Ritzer, George
   Classical sociological theory / George Ritzer. — 3rd ed.
       p.   cm.
   Includes bibliographical references and indexes.
   ISBN 0-07-229606-2 (acid-free paper)
       1. Sociology — History.   2. Sociology — Methodology — History
   3. Sociologists — Biography.   I. Title.
   HM19.R48 2000
   301'.09 21—dc21   99-045912

http://www.mhhe.com

PERMISSIONS ACKNOWLEDGMENTS

Chapter Two James Coleman excerpt from a review of Harold Garfinkel's *Studies in Ethnomethodology* from *American Sociological Review* 33 (1968). © 1968 by the American Sociological Association. Reprinted with the permission of the author and the American Sociological Association. • Steven Seidman, excerpt from "Symposium: Queer Theory/Sociology: A Dialogue" from *Sociological Theory* 12 (1994). © 1994 by the American Sociological Association. Reprinted with the permission of the author and the American Sociological Association.

Chapter Three Auguste Comte, excerpts from *A General View of Positivism,* translated by J. H. Bridges. © 1957. Reprinted with the permission of Robert Speller & Sons, Publishers.

Chapter Five Karl Marx, excerpts from *Capital: A Critique of Political Economy, Volume I.* © 1967. Reprinted with the permission of International Publishers. • Karl Marx, excerpts from *The Economic and Philosophic Manuscripts of 1844,* edited by Dirk J. Struik. © 1932, © 1964. Reprinted with the permission of International Publishers.

Chapter Six Emile Durkheim, excerpts from *The Elementary Forms of Religious Life,* translated by Joseph Ward Swain. © 1965 by the Free Press. Reprinted with the permission of The Free Press, a division of Simon & Schuster, Inc. • Steven Lukes, excerpts from *Emile Durkheim: His Life and Work* (New York: Harper & Row, 1972). © 1972 by Steven Lukes. Reprinted with the permission of Sterling Lord Literistic, Inc. • Whitney Pope, Jere Cohen and Lawrence E. Hazelrigg, excerpt from "On the Divergence of Weber and Durkheim: A Critique of Parsons' Convergence Thesis" from *American Sociological Review* 40 (1975). © 1975 by the American Sociological Association. Reprinted with the permission of the authors and the American Sociological Association. • Lisa Ann Tole, excerpt from "Durkheim on Religion and Moral Community in Modernity" from *Sociological Inquiry* 63 (1993). © 1993 by the University of Texas Press. Reprinted with the permission of the author and the University of Texas Press.

Chapter Seven Mary Fulbrook, excerpt from "Max Weber's 'Interpretive Sociology'" from *British Journal of Sociology* 29 (1978). Reprinted with the permission of Routledge. • Max Weber, excerpts from *Economy and Society, 2 vols.,* ed by Guenther Roth and Claus Wittich, tr. by the editors and others © 1978 by The Regents of the University of California. Reprinted with the permission of the University of California Press.

Chapter Eight Birgitta Nedelman, excerpt from "Individualization, Exaggeration and Paralyzation: Simmel's Three Problems of Culture" from *Theory, Culture and Society* 8 (1991). © 1991 by Sage Publications, Ltd. Reprinted with the permission of the publishers. • Georg Simmel, excerpts from *The Philosophy of Money,* edited and translated by Tom Bottomore and David Frisby. © 1978 by Routledge & Kegan Paul, Ltd. Reprinted with the permission of Routledge.

Chapter Eleven Karl Mannheim, excerpts from *Ideology and Utopia,* translated by Louis Wirth and Edward Shils (New York: Harcourt Brace, 1936). Reprinted with the permission of Routledge. • Karl Mannheim, excerpts from *Man and Society in an Age of Reconstruction,* translated by Edward Shils (New York: Harcourt Brace, 1940). Reprinted with the permission of Routledge.

Chapter Twelve George Herbert Mead, excerpts from *Mind, Self and Society: From the Standpoint of a Social Behaviorist.* © 1934 by The University of Chicago, renewed © 1962 by Charles W. Morris. Reprinted with the permission of The University of Chicago Press.

Chapter Thirteen Robert Bierstedt, excerpt from "The Common Sense World of Alfred Schutz" from *Social Research* 30 (1963). © 1963. Reprinted with the permission of the publishers. • Robert A. Gorman, excerpt from "Alfred Schutz: An Exposition and Critique" from *British Journal of Sociology* 26 (1975). Reprinted with the permission of Routledge. • Alfred Schutz, excerpts from *Collected Papers I: The Problems of Social Reality,* 1973. Edited by Maurice Natanson. Reprinted with the permission of Kluwer Academic Publishers, The Netherlands.

Chapter Fourteen Robert K. Merton, excerpts from "Remembering the Young Talcott Parsons" from *American Sociologist* 15 (1980). © 1980 by the American Sociological Association. Reprinted with the permission of the author and the American Sociological Association. • Robert K. Merton, excerpts from "Remembering the Young Talcott Parsons" from *American Sociologist* 15 (1980). © 1979 by the American Sociological Association. Reprinted with the permission of the author the American Sociological Association. • Figures 14.1 and 14.3: "Structure of the General Action System" and "Society, Its Subsystems and the Functional Imperatives" from Talcott Parsons and Gerald Platt, *The American University.* © 1973 by The President and Fellows of Harvard College. Reprinted with the permission of the Harvard University Press. • Figure 14.2: "Parson's Action Schema" adapted from Talcott Parsons, *Societies: Evolutionary and Comparative Perspectives.* © 1966. Adapted with the permission of Prentice-Hall, Inc., Upper Saddle River, NJ.

Appendix Thomas L. Hankin, excerpt from "In Defense of Biography: The Use of Biography in the History of Science" from *History of Science* 17 (1979). © 1979. Reprinted with the permission of the author. • Reba Rowe Lewis, excerpt from "Forging New Syntheses: Theories and Theorists" from *American Sociologist* (Fall/Winter 1991). © 1991 by the American Sociological Association. Reprinted with the permission of the author and the American Sociological Association.

Photo Credits 10 Culver Pictures 30 Corbis 48 Courtesy of the University of Chicago 56 Courtesy of the American Sociological Association 62 Brown Brothers 92 Culver Pictures 118 Culver Pictures 152 The Granger Collection 188 Corbis 218 The Granger Collection 260 The Granger Collection 293 Culver Pictures 298 Culver Pictures 303 Culver Pictures 313 Oberlin College Archives 313 Library of Congress 338 Courtesy of the University of Chicago Library 362 Courtesy of Mrs. J. Molncar Piliszanska 390 Courtesy of the University of Chicago 410 Courtesy estate of Alfred Schutz 434 The Granger Collection 462 Courtesy of George Ritzer

ABOUT
THE AUTHOR

GEORGE RITZER is Professor of Sociology at the University of Maryland. His major areas of interest are sociological theory and the sociology of consumption. He has served as Chair of the American Sociological Association's Sections on Theoretical Sociology (1989–1990) and Organizations and Occupations (1980–1981). Professor Ritzer has been Distinguished Scholar-Teacher at the University of Maryland and has been awarded a Teaching Excellence award. He has held the UNESCO Chair in Social Theory at the Russian Academy of Sciences and a Fulbright-Hays Fellowship. He has been Scholar-in-Residence at the Netherlands Institute for Advanced Study and the Swedish Collegium for Advanced Study in the Social Sciences.

Dr. Ritzer's main theoretical interests lie in metatheory as well as applied social theory. In metatheory, his contributions include *Metatheorizing in Sociology* (Lexington Books, 1991), *Sociology: A Multiple Paradigm Science* (Allyn and Bacon, 1975, 1980), and *Toward an Integrated Sociological Paradigm* (Allyn and Bacon, 1981). His major works in the application of social theory, especially to consumption, include *The McDonaldization of Society* (Pine Forge Press, 1993, 1996), *Expressing America: A Critique of the Global Credit Card Society* (Pine Forge Press, 1995), *The McDonaldization Thesis* (Sage, 1998), and *Enchanting a Disenchanted World: Revolutionizing the Means of Consumption* (Pine Forge Press, 1999). Professor Ritzer's work has been translated into many different languages; there are a dozen translations of *The McDonaldization of Society* alone.

In 1997 McGraw-Hill published the first edition of Professor Ritzer's *Postmodern Social Theory*. In 2000 McGraw-Hill will publish the fifth editions of Dr. Ritzer's *Sociological Theory* and the fifth edition of his *Modern Sociological Theory*.

TO MOTHER,
with Appreciation
and Love

CONTENTS

LIST OF BIOGRAPHICAL AND AUTOBIOGRAPHICAL SKETCHES xvii
PREFACE xviii

PART 1 INTRODUCTION 1

1 A HISTORICAL SKETCH OF SOCIOLOGICAL THEORY: THE EARLY YEARS 3

INTRODUCTION 4
SOCIAL FORCES IN THE DEVELOPMENT OF SOCIOLOGICAL THEORY 6
    Political Revolutions 6
    The Industrial Revolution and the Rise of Capitalism 8
    The Rise of Socialism 8
    Feminism 9
    Urbanization 9
    Religious Change 10
    The Growth of Science 11
INTELLECTUAL FORCES AND THE RISE OF SOCIOLOGICAL THEORY 11
    The Enlightenment 11
    The Conservative Reaction to the Enlightenment 12
    The Development of French Sociology 14
    The Development of German Sociology 19
    The Origins of British Sociology 29
    The Key Figure in Early Italian Sociology 34
    Turn-of-the-Century Developments in European Marxism 35
THE CONTEMPORARY RELEVANCE OF CLASSICAL SOCIOLOGICAL
    THEORY 36

2 A HISTORICAL SKETCH OF SOCIOLOGICAL THEORY: THE LATER YEARS 39

EARLY AMERICAN SOCIOLOGICAL THEORY 40
    Politics 40
    Social Change and Intellectual Currents 40

The Chicago School   46
WOMEN IN EARLY SOCIOLOGY   52
SOCIOLOGICAL THEORY TO MID-CENTURY   53
    The Rise of Harvard, the Ivy League, and
        Structural Functionalism   53
    The Chicago School in Decline   58
    Developments in Marxian Theory   59
    Karl Mannheim and the Sociology of Knowledge   60
SOCIOLOGICAL THEORY FROM MID-CENTURY   61
    Structural Functionalism: Peak and Decline   61
    Radical Sociology in America: C. Wright Mills   63
    The Development of Conflict Theory   64
    The Birth of Exchange Theory   65
    Dramaturgical Analysis: The Work of Erving Goffman   66
    The Development of Sociologies of Everyday Life   67
    The Rise and Fall (?) of Marxian Sociology   71
    The Challenge of Feminist Theory   72
    Structuralism and Poststructuralism   74
RECENT DEVELOPMENTS IN SOCIOLOGICAL THEORY   75
    Micro-Macro Integration   75
    Agency-Structure Integration   76
    Theoretical Syntheses   77
THEORIES OF MODERNITY AND POSTMODERNITY   78
    The Defenders of Modernity   78
    The Proponents of Postmodernity   79
THEORIES TO WATCH IN THE EARLY TWENTY-FIRST CENTURY   80
    Multicultural Social Theory   80
    Postmodern and Post-Postmodern Social Theories   81
    Theories of Consumption   82
    Others   83

PART 2   CLASSICAL SOCIOLOGICAL THEORY   85

     3   AUGUSTE COMTE   87

COMTE'S PROFOUND AMBITIONS   88
    Positivism: The Search for Invariant Laws   88
    Law of the Three Stages   90
    Positivism: The Search for Order and Progress   91
COMTE'S SOCIOLOGY   94
    Social Statics   94
    Social Dynamics   98
THEORY AND PRACTICE   101
    Who Will Support Positivism?   101

COMTE'S PLANS FOR THE FUTURE 105
COMTE: A CRITICAL ASSESSMENT 106
    Positive Contributions 107
    Basic Weaknesses in Comte's Theory 108

4   HERBERT SPENCER 113

SPENCER AND COMTE 114
GENERAL THEORETICAL PRINCIPLES 115
    Evolutionary Theory 118
SOCIOLOGY 119
    Defining the Science of Sociology 119
    Sociological Methods 122
THE EVOLUTION OF SOCIETY 125
    Simple and Compounded Societies 128
    Militant and Industrial Societies 128
THE EVOLUTION OF SOCIETAL INSTITUTIONS 130
    Domestic Institutions 130
    Ceremonial Institutions 133
    Political Institutions 134
    Ecclesiastical Institutions 136
    Professional Institutions 138
    Industrial Institutions 139
ETHICS AND POLITICS 141

5   KARL MARX 147

INTRODUCTION 147
    Is Marx's Theory Outmoded? 148
    Was Marx a Sociologist? 149
    Early and Late Marxian Theory 150
THE DIALECTIC 150
HUMAN POTENTIAL 156
    Powers and Needs 157
    Consciousness 157
    Human Potential and Nature 159
    Activity 160
    Sociability 161
    Unanticipated Consequences 162
ALIENATION 162
    Components of Alienation 163
    Distortions Resulting from Alienation 164
    Emancipation 166
THE STRUCTURES OF CAPITALIST SOCIETY 167
    Commodities 168
    Capital 169

Private Property 171
Division of Labor 171
Social Class 172
CULTURAL ASPECTS OF CAPITALIST SOCIETY 173
Class Consciousness and False Consciousness 174
Ideology 175
MARX'S ECONOMICS: A CASE STUDY 176

6   EMILE DURKHEIM 181

SOCIAL FACTS 183
External and Coercive 183
Material and Nonmaterial 184
Levels of Social Reality 184
THE DIVISION OF LABOR IN SOCIETY 185
Dynamic Density 186
Law 187
Anomie 190
Collective Conscience 190
Collective Representations 191
SUICIDE AND SOCIAL CURRENTS 192
The Four Types of Suicide 194
A Group Mind? 196
RELIGION 198
Sacred and Profane 199
Totemism 199
Collective Effervescence 200
SOCIAL REFORMISM 201
Occupational Associations 201
Cult of the Individual 202
THE ACTOR IN DURKHEIM'S THOUGHT 203
Assumptions about Human Nature 204
Socialization and Moral Education 206
Dependent Variables 208
Weaknesses in Durkheim's Microsociology 210
EARLY AND LATE DURKHEIMIAN THEORY 211

7   MAX WEBER 215

METHODOLOGY 216
History and Sociology 216
Verstehen 219
Causality 221
Ideal Types 222
Values 225
SUBSTANTIVE SOCIOLOGY 227
What Is Sociology? 228

Social Action   229
Class, Status, and Party   230
Structures of Authority   231
Rationalization   239
Religion and the Rise of Capitalism   249

8   GEORG SIMMEL   259

PRIMARY CONCERNS   259
Levels and Areas of Concern   261
Dialectical Thinking   262
INDIVIDUAL CONSCIOUSNESS   265
SOCIAL INTERACTION ("ASSOCIATION")   266
Interaction: Forms and Types   267
SOCIAL STRUCTURES   271
OBJECTIVE CULTURE   272
THE PHILOSOPHY OF MONEY   274
Money and Value   275
Money, Reification, and Rationalization   276
Negative Effects   278
Tragedy of Culture   279
SECRECY: A CASE STUDY IN SIMMEL'S SOCIOLOGY   282
Secrecy and Social Relationships   283
Other Thoughts on Secrecy   285

**9   EARLY WOMEN SOCIOLOGISTS AND CLASSICAL
      SOCIOLOGICAL THEORY: 1830–1930**
By Patricia Madoo Lengermann and Jill Niebrugge-Brantley   289

HARRIET MARTINEAU (1802–1876)   291
CHARLOTTE PERKINS GILMAN (1860–1935)   296
JANE ADDAMS AND THE WOMEN OF CHICAGO   302
Jane Addams (1860–1935)   304
The Women of Chicago   309
ANNA JULIA COOPER (1859–1964) AND IDA WELLS-BARNETT
(1862–1931)   312
MARIANNE SCHNITGER WEBER (1870–1954)   316
BEATRICE POTTER WEBB (1858–1943)   318

10   THORSTEIN VEBLEN   323

INTELLECTUAL INFLUENCES   323
Marxian Theory   324
Evolutionary Theory   325
Economic Theory   327
BASIC PREMISES   328
Human Nature   329

The Industrial Arts 330
Cultural Lag 331
Cultural Borrowing 331
SUBSTANTIVE ISSUES 333
Theory of the Leisure Class 333
Business versus Industry 337
Higher Learning 345
Politics 349

11   KARL MANNHEIM 353

THE SOCIOLOGY OF KNOWLEDGE 354
The Sociology of Knowledge and the Theory of Ideology ... 354
A Sociological Approach 356
IDEOLOGY AND UTOPIA 365
Ideology 365
Utopia 367
CONSERVATISM 370
RATIONALITY AND THE IRRATIONALITY OF THE TIMES 372
Types of Rationality and Irrationality 373
PLANNING AND SOCIAL RECONSTRUCTION IN THE
MODERN WORLD 376
A CRITICAL ANALYSIS OF MANNHEIM'S WORK 380

12   GEORGE HERBERT MEAD 385

INTELLECTUAL ROOTS 385
Behaviorism 385
Pragmatism 387
Dialectics 388
THE PRIORITY OF THE SOCIAL 388
THE ACT 389
Stages 389
Gestures 392
Significant Symbols 393
MENTAL PROCESSES AND THE MIND 395
Intelligence 395
Consciousness 396
Mind 397
SELF 398
Child Development 399
Generalized Other 400
"I" and "Me" 401
SOCIETY 402
EVOLUTION 404
DIALECTICAL THINKING 405

13   ALFRED SCHUTZ   409

INTERPRETATIONS OF SCHUTZ'S WORK   409
THE IDEAS OF EDMUND HUSSERL   412
SCIENCE AND THE SOCIAL WORLD   414
    Life-World versus Science   414
    Constructing Ideal Types   416
TYPIFICATIONS AND RECIPES   417
THE LIFE-WORLD   419
INTERSUBJECTIVITY   420
    Knowledge   421
    Private Components of Knowledge   421
REALMS OF THE SOCIAL WORLD   422
    Folgewelt and *Vorwelt*   422
    Umwelt and We Relations   423
    Mitwelt and They Relations   425
CONSCIOUSNESS, MEANINGS, AND MOTIVES   426
INTERPRETING SCHUTZIAN THEORY   429

14   TALCOTT PARSONS   431

PARSONS'S INTEGRATIVE EFFORTS   432
GENERAL PRINCIPLES   433
    Philosophical and Theoretical Roots   433
    Action Theory   435
    The Turn Away from Action Theory   437
    Pattern Variables   440
    AGIL   441
    Consistency in Parsonsian Theory: Integration and Order   442
THE ACTION SYSTEM   443
    Social System   445
    Cultural System   448
    Personality System   449
    Behavioral Organism   450
CHANGE AND DYNAMISM IN PARSONSIAN THEORY   451
    Evolutionary Theory   451
    Generalized Media of Interchange   452

APPENDIX   SOCIOLOGICAL METATHEORIZING AND A METATHEORETICAL SCHEMA FOR ANALYZING SOCIOLOGICAL THEORY   455

METATHEORIZING IN SOCIOLOGY   455
    Pierre Bourdieu's Reflexive Sociology   459
THE IDEAS OF THOMAS KUHN   460
SOCIOLOGY: A MULTIPLE-PARADIGM SCIENCE   462
TOWARD A MORE INTEGRATED SOCIOLOGICAL PARADIGM   464

Levels of Social Analysis: An Overview   465
Levels of Social Analysis: A Model   467
REFERENCES   473
INDEXES   535
    Name Index   535
    Subject Index   539

LIST OF BIOGRAPHICAL AND AUTOBIOGRAPHICAL SKETCHES

Abdel Rahman Ibn-Khaldun	10
Sigmund Freud	30
Robert Park	48
Pitirim A. Sorokin	56
C. Wright Mills	62
Auguste Comte	92
Herbert Spencer	118
Karl Marx	152
Emile Durkheim	188
Max Weber	218
Georg Simmel	260
Harriet Martineau	293
Charlotte Perkins Gilman	298
Jane Addams	303
Anna Julia Cooper	313
Ida Wells-Barnett	313
Thorstein Veblen	338
Karl Mannheim	362
George Herbert Mead	390
Alfred Schutz	410
Talcott Parsons	434
George Ritzer: Autobiography as a Metatheoretical Tool	462

PREFACE

With this third edition, *Classical Sociological Theory* moves into its second decade *and* its second century. In preparing this revision I have, once again, been impressed with the continued relevance of classical theorists and the importance of the continuing work devoted to them and their ideas.

The biggest change in this edition is the addition of a chapter (Chapter 10) devoted to Thorstein Veblen. Veblen had a grand theory of the relationship between business and industry that rivals in scope and ambition the other grand theories of classical theory. However, his work is made even more important by the fact that he also was able to avoid the "productivist" bias of most classical social theorists and to develop a theory of consumption that is of growing importance in a society in which consumption shows every sign of becoming more important than production. It is in his thinking on consumption that one finds the ideas—especially conspicuous leisure and conspicuous consumption—for which he is so famous.

Beyond the new chapter, there are innumerable minor changes to the text designed either to bring it up to date or to clarify an argument. And many recent citations have been added to the text (and bibliography) so that the book reflects the latest scholarship.

However, with the book already well over 500 pages, the goal here has not been so much to expand the text (although that has occurred in some places), but to prevent it from growing too much longer and perhaps even to shorten it a bit. I'm not sure I've succeeded in the latter, but there have been substantial cuts throughout the text. I have also tried to make the book easier to read, primarily by adding many headings and subheadings.

Once again, I want to thank Patricia Lengermann and Jill Niebrugge-Brantley for revising their important Chapter 9: Early Women Sociologists and Classical Sociological Theory: 1830–1930. That chapter not only has made this book much stronger, but has laid the groundwork for their recently published text/reader, *The Women Founders: Sociology and Social Theory, 1830–1930* (McGraw-Hill, 1998). Thanks also to a long list of reviewers—Maboud Ansari, David Ashley, J. I. ("Hans") Bakker, Keith Gotham, Peter Kivisto, J. Knotterus, James Marshall, Neil McLaughlin, Martin Orr, Robert Perrin, Jane A. Rinehart, Susan Roxburgh, Teresa L. Schied, and Peter Singelmann.

I would also like to thank a number of people at McGraw-Hill including Sally Constable, Kathy Blake, and Carrie Sestak. Thanks, also, to my assistants, Jan Geesin and Zinnia Cho, who did the library work that made this book possible.

George Ritzer

PART ONE

INTRODUCTION

1

A HISTORICAL SKETCH OF SOCIOLOGICAL THEORY: THE EARLY YEARS

INTRODUCTION

SOCIAL FORCES IN THE DEVELOPMENT
OF SOCIOLOGICAL THEORY
  Political Revolutions
  The Industrial Revolution and the Rise of Capitalism
  The Rise of Socialism
  Feminism
  Urbanization
  Religious Change
  The Growth of Science

INTELLECTUAL FORCES AND THE RISE
OF SOCIOLOGICAL THEORY
  The Enlightenment
  The Conservative Reaction to the Enlightenment
  The Development of French Sociology
  The Development of German Sociology
  The Origins of British Sociology
  The Key Figure in Early Italian Sociology
  Turn-of-the-Century Developments in European Marxism

THE CONTEMPORARY RELEVANCE OF CLASSICAL
SOCIOLOGICAL THEORY

This book is designed as an introduction to the work of the classical sociological theorists, and we begin with one-sentence statements that get to the essence of the theories to be covered in these pages:

- We are evolving in the direction of a world dominated by science. (*Auguste Comte*)
- The world is moving in the direction of increasing order and harmony. (*Herbert Spencer*)
- Capitalism is based on the exploitation of the workers by the capitalists. (*Karl Marx*)
- The modern world offers less moral cohesion than earlier societies did. (*Emile Durkheim*)

3

- The modern world is an iron cage of rational systems from which there is no escape. (*Max Weber*)
  - The city spawns a particular type of person. (*Georg Simmel*)
  - Gender inequality explains most of the ills in society, individual experience, and history. (*Charlotte Perkins Gilman*)
  - People engage in conspicuous consumption. (*Thorstein Veblen*)
  - Knowledge is shaped by the social world. (*Karl Mannheim*)
  - People's minds and their conceptions of themselves are shaped by their social experiences. (*George Herbert Mead*)
  - In their social relationships, people often rely on tried and true "recipes" for how to handle such relationships. (*Alfred Schutz*)
  - Society is an integrated system of social structures and functions. (*Talcott Parsons*)

This book is devoted to helping the reader to better understand these theoretical ideas, as well as the larger theories from which they are drawn, within the context of the life-work of the classical theorists.

INTRODUCTION

By *classical* sociological theory we mean theories of great scope and ambition that either were created during sociology's classical age in Europe (roughly the early 1800s through the early 1900s) or had their roots in that period and culture. The theories of Comte, Spencer, Marx, Durkheim, Weber, Simmel, and Mannheim were produced during the classical age largely in France, England, and Germany. The theories of Veblen, Mead, Schutz, and Parsons were largely produced later and mainly in the United States, but they had most of their sources in the classical age and in European intellectual traditions.

The work of these theorists is discussed in this book for two basic reasons. First, in all cases their work was important in its time and played a central role in the development of sociology in general and sociological theory in particular. Second, their ideas continue to be relevant to, and read by, contemporary sociologists, although this is less true of the work of Comte and Spencer (who are of more historical significance) than it is of the others.

This book does not deal with all sociological theory but rather with classical theory. However, in order to better understand the ideas of the classical theorists to be discussed in depth throughout this book, we begin with two chapters that offer an overview of the entire history of sociological theory. Chapter 1 deals with the early years of sociological theory, while Chapter 2 brings that history up to the present day and to the most recent developments in sociological theory. Taken together, these two chapters offer the context within which the work of the classical theorists is to be understood. The two introductory chapters are animated by the belief that it is important to understand not only the historical sources of classical theories but also their later impact. More generally, the reader should have a broad sense of sociological theory before turning to a detailed discussion of the classical theorists. The remainder of the body of this book (Chapters 3 through 14) deals with the ideas of the major classical theorists. Thus, the ideas of the major classical theorists will be discussed twice. They will be introduced very briefly in either the first or second chapter in their historical context, and they will be discussed in great depth in the chapter devoted to each of the theorists.

Why focus on these theorists and not the innumerable others whose names and ideas will arise in the course of these first two chapters? The simplest answer to this question is that space limitations make it impossible to deal with all classical theorists. Beyond that, many theorists are not given full-chapter treatment because their theories do not *belong to, or have centrally important roots in, the classical age*. Furthermore, to be discussed in depth, theories must meet a series of other criteria. That is, to be included, theories must have a *wide range* of application, must deal with *centrally important social issues,* and must have stood up well under the *test of time* (that is, they must continue to be read and to be influential).[1] Thus, a number of theorists who are briefly discussed in this chapter (for example, Louis DeBonald) will not be discussed in detail later because their ideas do not meet one or more of the criteria listed above, especially the fact that their theories have not stood the test of time. A number of the more contemporary theorists discussed in Chapter 2 (for example, Erving Goffman and Harold Garfinkel) are not discussed further later in the book because they are associated more with the modern era than with classical sociological theory.

Our focus is on the important classical theoretical work of *sociologists,* as well as on work which has been done by those who are often associated with other fields (for example, Karl Marx and his association with the field of economics) but which has come to be *defined as important in sociology.* To put it succinctly, this is a book about the "big ideas" in the history of sociology, ideas that deal with major social issues and are far-reaching in their scope.

In addition to the theorists mentioned above, Chapter 9 is devoted to a number of early female theorists—especially, Harriet Martineau, Charlotte Perkins Gilman, Jane Addams, Ann Julia Cooper, Ida Wells-Barnett, Marianne Weber, and Beatrice Potter Webb. Because their contributions are only now being recognized, they do not fit fully the profile of classical sociological theory outlined in the last few paragraphs. On the one hand, they are clearly classical thinkers who worked in the same time frame as the male theorists previously mentioned. In the main, their theories have a wide range of application and have certainly addressed centrally important issues. They were either sociologists or nonsociologists whose work is coming to be seen as important in sociology. On the other hand, one cannot say that their work has stood the test of time. The fact is that as a result of discrimination against women, they were not widely read or highly influential in their own time, let alone ours. Nevertheless, they are included in this book because of the belief that as their work is rediscovered and read, their influence will

---

[1] These four criteria constitute our definition of (classical) *sociological theory.* Such a definition stands in contrast to the formal, "scientific" definitions that are often used in theory texts of this type. A scientific definition might be that a theory is a set of interrelated propositions that allows for the systematization of knowledge, explanation, and prediction of social life and the generation of new research hypotheses (Faia, 1986). Although such a definition has a number of attractions, it simply does not fit many of the idea systems to be discussed in this book. In other words, most classical (and contemporary) theories fall short on one or more of the formal components of theory, but they are nonetheless considered theories by most sociologists.

grow in future years. As with the male theorists, these female theorists have produced a set of "big ideas."

Presenting a history of sociological theory is an important task (S. Turner, 1998), but because we devote only the first two chapters to it, what we offer is a highly selective historical sketch.[2] The idea is to provide the reader with a scaffolding which should help in putting the later detailed discussions of classical theorists in a larger context. As the reader proceeds through the later chapters, it will prove useful to return to these two overview chapters and place the discussions in that context. (It would be especially useful to glance back occasionally to Figures 1.1 and 2.1, which are schematic representations of the histories covered in those chapters.)

One cannot establish the precise date when sociological theory began. People have been thinking about, and developing theories of, social life since early in history. But we will not go back to the early historic times of the Greeks or Romans or even to the Middle Ages. We will not even go back to the seventeenth century, although Olson (1993) has traced the sociological tradition to the mid-1600s and the work of James Harrington on the relationship between the economy and the polity. This is not because people in those epochs did not have sociologically relevant ideas, but because the return on our investment in time would be small; we would spend a lot of time getting very few ideas that are relevant to modern sociology. In any case, none of the thinkers associated with those eras thought of themselves, and few are now thought of, as sociologists. (For discussion of one exception, see the biographical sketch of Ibn-Khaldun.) It is only in the 1800s that we begin to find thinkers who can be clearly identified as sociologists. These are the classical sociological thinkers we shall be interested in (Camic, 1997; for a debate over what makes theory classical, see Connell, 1997; Collins, 1997b), and we begin by examining the main social and intellectual forces that shaped their ideas.

SOCIAL FORCES IN THE DEVELOPMENT OF SOCIOLOGICAL THEORY

All intellectual fields are profoundly shaped by their social settings. This is particularly true of sociology, which is not only derived from that setting but takes the social setting as its basic subject matter. We will focus briefly on a few of the most important social conditions of the nineteenth and early twentieth centuries, conditions that were of the utmost significance in the development of sociology. We also will take the occasion to begin introducing the major figures in the history of sociological theory.

Political Revolutions

The long series of political revolutions ushered in by the French Revolution in 1789 and carrying over through the nineteenth century was the most immediate factor in the rise of sociological theorizing. The impact of these revolutions on many societies was enormous, and many positive changes resulted. However, what attracted the attention of many early theorists was not the positive consequences, but the negative effects of such

[2]For a much more detailed historical sketch see, for example, Szacki (1979).

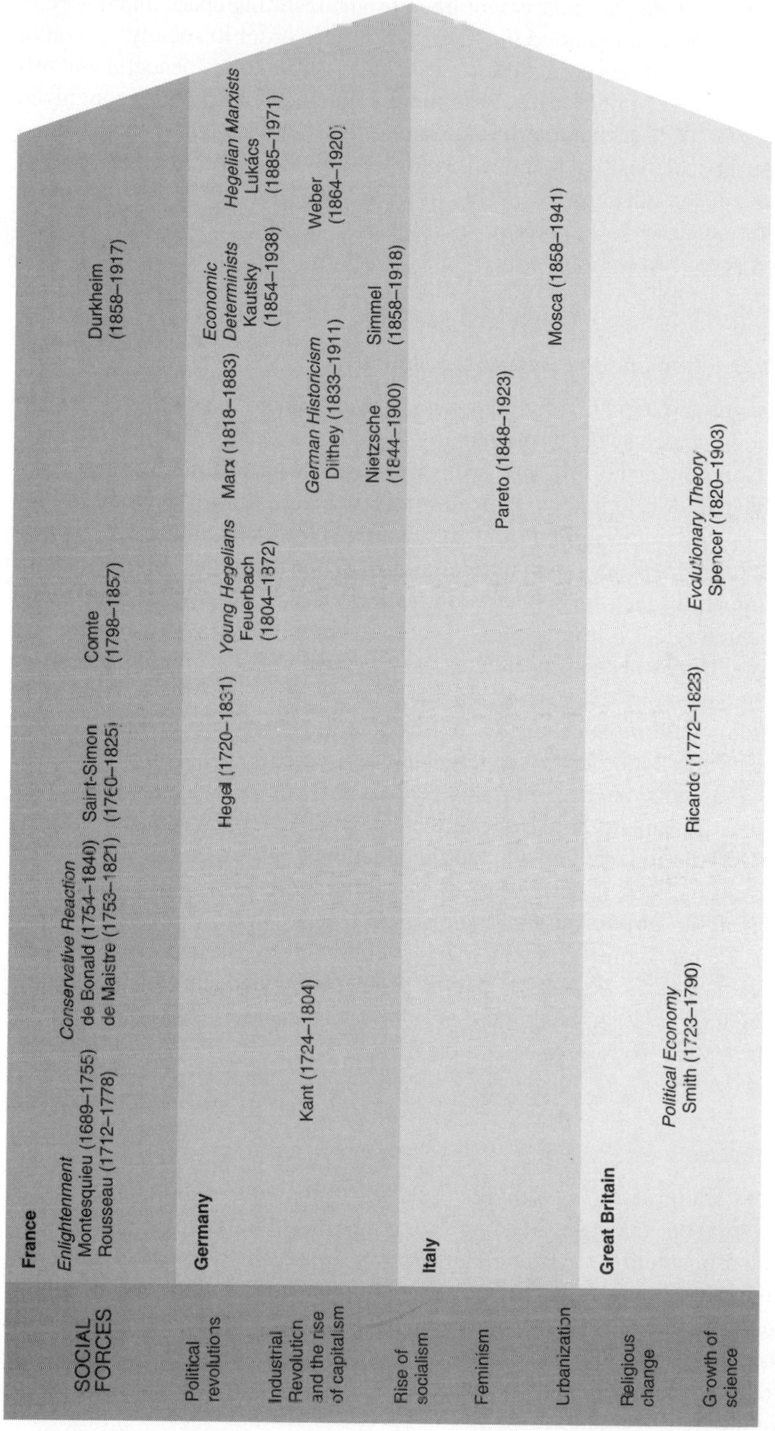

SOCIAL FORCES

Political revolutions
Industrial Revolution and the rise of capitalism
Rise of socialism
Feminism
Urbanization
Religious change
Growth of science

France

Enlightenment Montesquieu (1689–1755) Rousseau (1712–1778)

Conservative Reaction de Bonald (1754–1840) de Maistre (1753–1821)

Saint-Simon (1760–1825)

Comte (1798–1857)

Durkheim (1858–1917)

Germany

Kant (1724–1804)

Hegel (1770–1831)

Young Hegelians Feuerbach (1804–1872)

Marx (1818–1883)

German Historicism Dilthey (1833–1911)

Nietzsche (1844–1900)

Economic Determinists Kautsky (1854–1938)

Simmel (1858–1918)

Weber (1864–1920)

Hegelian Marxists Lukács (1885–1971)

Italy

Pareto (1848–1923)

Mosca (1858–1941)

Great Britain

Political Economy Smith (1723–1790)

Ricardo (1772–1823)

Evolutionary Theory Spencer (1820–1903)

FIGURE 1.1
Sociological Theory: The Early Years

changes. These writers were particularly disturbed by the resulting chaos and disorder, especially in France. They were united in a desire to restore order to society. Some of the more extreme thinkers of this period literally wanted a return to the peaceful and relatively orderly days of the Middle Ages. The more sophisticated thinkers recognized that social change had made such a return impossible. Thus they sought instead to find new bases of order in societies that had been overturned by the political revolutions of the eighteenth and nineteenth centuries. This interest in the issue of social order was one of the major concerns of classical sociological theorists, especially Comte, Durkheim, and Parsons.

The Industrial Revolution and the Rise of Capitalism

At least as important as political revolution in the shaping of sociological theory was the Industrial Revolution, which swept through many Western societies, mainly in the nineteenth and early twentieth centuries. The Industrial Revolution was not a single event but many interrelated developments that culminated in the transformation of the Western world from a largely agricultural to an overwhelmingly industrial system. Large numbers of people left farms and agricultural work for the industrial occupations offered in the burgeoning factories. The factories themselves were transformed by a long series of technological improvements. Large economic bureaucracies arose to provide the many services needed by industry and the emerging capitalist economic system. In this economy, the ideal was a free marketplace where the many products of an industrial system could be exchanged. Within this system, a few profited greatly while the majority worked long hours for low wages. A reaction against the industrial system and against capitalism in general followed and led to the labor movement as well as to various radical movements aimed at overthrowing the capitalist system.

The Industrial Revolution, capitalism, and the reaction against them all involved an enormous upheaval in Western society, an upheaval that affected sociologists greatly. Five major figures in the early history of sociological theory—Karl Marx, Max Weber, Emile Durkheim, Georg Simmel, and Thorstein Veblen—were preoccupied, as were many lesser thinkers, with these changes and the problems they created for society as a whole. They spent their lives studying these problems, and in many cases they endeavored to develop programs that would help solve them.

The Rise of Socialism

One set of changes aimed at coping with the excesses of the industrial system and capitalism can be combined under the heading "socialism." Although some sociologists favored socialism as a solution to industrial problems, most were personally and intellectually opposed to it. On the one side, Karl Marx was an active supporter of the overthrow of the capitalist system and its replacement by a socialist system. Although he did not develop a theory of socialism per se, he spent a great deal of time criticizing various aspects of capitalist society. In addition, he engaged in a variety of political activities that he hoped would help bring about the rise of socialist societies.

However, Marx was atypical in the early years of sociological theory. Most of the early theorists, such as Weber and Durkheim, were opposed to socialism (at least as it was envisioned by Marx). Although they recognized the problems within capitalist society, they sought social reform within capitalism rather than the social revolution argued for by Marx. They feared socialism more than they did capitalism. This fear played a far greater role in shaping sociological theory than did Marx's support of the socialist alternative to capitalism. In fact, as we will see, in many cases sociological theory developed in reaction *against* Marxian and, more generally, socialist theory.

Feminism

In one sense there has always been a feminist perspective. Wherever women are subordinated—and they have been subordinated almost always and everywhere—they seem to have recognized and protested that situation in some form (Lerner, 1993). While precursors can be traced to the 1630s, high points of feminist activity and writing occurred in the liberationist moments of modern Western history; a first flurry of productivity in the 1780s and 1790s with the debates surrounding the American and French revolutions; a far more organized, focused effort in the 1850s as part of the mobilization against slavery and for political rights for the middle class; and the massive mobilization for women's suffrage and for industrial and civic reform legislation in the early twentieth century, especially the Progressive Era in the United States.

All of this had an impact on the development of sociology, in particular on the work of a number of women in or associated with the field—Harriet Martineau, Charlotte Perkins Gilman, Jane Addams, Florence Kelley, Anna Julia Cooper, Ida Wells-Barnett, Marianne Weber, and Beatrice Potter Webb, to name just a few. But their creations were, over time, pushed to the periphery of the profession, annexed or discounted or written out of sociology's public record by the men who were organizing sociology as a professional power base. Feminist concerns filtered into sociology only on the margins, in the work of marginal male theorists or of the increasingly marginalized female theorists. The men who assumed centrality in the profession—from Spencer, through Weber and Durkheim—made basically conservative responses to the feminist arguments going on around them, making issues of gender an inconsequential topic to which they responded conventionally rather than critically in what they identified and publicly promoted as sociology. They responded in this way even as women were writing a significant body of sociological theory. The history of this gender politics in the profession, which is also part of the history of male response to feminist claims, is only now being written (for example, see Deegan, 1988; Fitzpatrick, 1990; Gordon, 1994; Lengermann and Niebrugge-Brantley, 1998; Rosenberg, 1982).

Urbanization

Partly as a result of the Industrial Revolution, large numbers of people in the nineteenth and twentieth centuries were uprooted from their rural homes and moved to urban settings. This massive migration was caused, in large part, by the jobs created by the industrial system in the urban areas. But it presented many difficulties for those people

---

ABDEL RAHMAN IBN-KHALDUN: A Biographical Sketch

There is a tendency to think of sociology as exclusively a comparatively modern, Western phenomenon. In fact, however, scholars were doing sociology long ago and in other parts of the world. One example is Abdel Rahman Ibn-Khaldun.

Ibn-Khaldun was born in Tunis, North Africa, on May 27, 1332 (Faghirzadeh, 1982). Born to an educated family, Ibn-Khaldun was schooled in the Koran (the Muslim holy book), mathematics, and history. In his lifetime, he served a variety of sultans in Tunis, Morocco, Spain, and Algeria as ambassador, chamberlain, and member of the scholar's council. He also spent two years in prison in Morocco for his belief that state rulers were not divine leaders. After approximately two decades of political activity, Ibn-Khaldun returned to North Africa, where he undertook an intensive five-year period of study and writing. Works produced during this period increased his fame and led to a lectureship at the center of Islamic study, Al-Azhar Mosque University in Cairo. In his well-attended lectures on society and sociology, Ibn-Khaldun stressed the importance of linking sociological thought and historical observation.

By the time he died in 1406, Ibn-Khaldun had produced a corpus of work that had many ideas in common with contemporary sociology. He was committed to the scientific study of society, empirical research, and the search for causes of social phenomena. He devoted considerable attention to various social institutions (for example, politics, economy) and their interrelationships. He was interested in comparing primitive and modern societies. Ibn-Khaldun did not have a dramatic impact on classical sociology, but as scholars in general, and Islamic scholars in particular, rediscover his work, he may come to be seen as being of greater historical significance.

---

who had to adjust to urban life. In addition, the expansion of the cities produced a seemingly endless list of urban problems—overcrowding, pollution, noise, traffic, and so forth. The nature of urban life and its problems attracted the attention of many early sociologists, especially Max Weber and Georg Simmel. In fact, the first major school of American sociology, the Chicago school, was in large part defined by its concern for the city and its interest in using Chicago as a laboratory in which to study urbanization and its problems.

Religious Change

Social changes brought on by political revolutions, the Industrial Revolution, and urbanization had a profound effect on religiosity. Many early sociologists came from religious backgrounds and were actively, and in some cases professionally, involved in religion (Hinkle and Hinkle, 1954). They brought to sociology the same objectives as they had in their religious lives. They wished to improve people's lives (Vidich and Lyman, 1985). For some (such as Comte), sociology was transformed into a religion. For others, their sociological theories bore an unmistakable religious imprint. Durkheim wrote one of his major works on religion. Morality played a key role not only in Durkheim's sociology but also in the work of Talcott Parsons. A large portion of Weber's work also was devoted to the religions of the world. Marx, too, had an interest in religiosity, but his orientation was far more critical. Spencer discussed religion ("eccelesiastical institutions") as a significant component of society.

The Growth of Science

As sociological theory was being developed, there was an increasing emphasis on science, not only in colleges and universities but in society as a whole. The technological products of science were permeating every sector of life, and science was acquiring enormous prestige. Those associated with the most successful sciences (physics, biology, and chemistry) were accorded honored places in society. Sociologists (especially Comte, Durkheim, Spencer, Mead, and Schutz) from the beginning were preoccupied with science, and many wanted to model sociology after the successful physical and biological sciences. However, a debate soon developed between those who wholeheartedly accepted the scientific model and those (such as Weber) who thought that distinctive characteristics of social life made a wholesale adoption of a scientific model difficult and unwise (Lepenies, 1988). The issue of the relationship between sociology and science is debated to this day, although even a glance at the major journals in the field indicates the predominance of those who favor sociology as a science.

INTELLECTUAL FORCES AND THE RISE OF SOCIOLOGICAL THEORY

Although social factors are important, the primary focus of this chapter is the intellectual forces that played a central role in shaping sociological theory. In the real world, of course, intellectual factors cannot be separated from social forces. For example, in the discussion of the Enlightenment that follows, we will find that that movement was intimately related to, and in many cases provided the intellectual basis for, the social changes discussed above.

The many intellectual forces that shaped the development of social theories are discussed within the national context where their influence was primarily felt (Levine, 1995). We begin with the Enlightenment and its influences on the development of sociological theory in France.

The Enlightenment

It is the view of many observers that the Enlightenment constitutes a critical development in terms of the later evolution of sociology (Hawthorn, 1976; Hughes, Martin, and Sharrock, 1995; Nisbet, 1967; Zeitlin, 1981, 1990, 1994, 1996). The Enlightenment was a period of remarkable intellectual development and change in philosophical thought.[3] A number of long-standing ideas and beliefs—many of which related to social

---

[3]This section is based on the work of Irving Zeitlin (1981, 1990, 1994, 1996). Although Zeitlin's analysis is presented here for its coherence, it has a number of limitations: there are better analyses of the Enlightenment, there are many other factors involved in shaping the development of sociology, and Zeitlin tends to overstate his case in places (for example, on the impact of Marx). But on the whole, Zeitlin provides us with a useful starting point, given our objectives in this chapter.

life—were overthrown and replaced during the Enlightenment. The most prominent thinkers associated with the Enlightenment were the French philosophers Charles Montesquieu (1689–1755) and Jean Jacques Rousseau (1712–1778). The influence of the Enlightenment on sociological theory, however, was more indirect and negative than it was direct and positive. As Irving Zeitlin puts it, "Early sociology developed as a reaction to the Enlightenment" (1981:10).

The thinkers associated with the Enlightenment were influenced, above all, by two intellectual currents—seventeenth-century philosophy and science.

Seventeenth-century philosophy was associated with the work of thinkers such as René Descartes, Thomas Hobbes, and John Locke. The emphasis was on producing grand, general, and very abstract systems of ideas that made rational sense. The later thinkers associated with the Enlightenment did not reject the idea that systems of ideas should be general and should make rational sense, but they did make greater efforts to derive their ideas from the real world and to test them there. In other words, they wanted to combine empirical research with reason (Seidman, 1983:36–37). The model for this was science, especially Newtonian physics. At this point, we see the emergence of the application of the scientific method to social issues. Not only did Enlightenment thinkers want their ideas to be, at least in part, derived from the real world, but they also wanted them to be useful to the social world, especially in the critical analysis of that world.

Overall, the Enlightenment was characterized by the belief that people could comprehend and control the universe by means of reason and empirical research. The view was that because the physical world was dominated by natural laws, it was likely that the social world was, too. Thus it was up to the philosopher, using reason and research, to discover these social laws. Once they understood how the social world worked, the Enlightenment thinkers had a practical goal—the creation of a "better," more rational world.

With an emphasis on reason, the Enlightenment philosophers were inclined to reject beliefs in traditional authority. When these thinkers examined traditional values and institutions, they often found them to be irrational—that is, contrary to human nature and inhibitive of human growth and development. The mission of the practical and change-oriented philosophers of the Enlightenment was to overcome these irrational systems. The theorist who was most directly and positively influenced by Enlightenment thinking was Karl Marx, but he formed his early theoretical ideas in Germany.

The Conservative Reaction to the Enlightenment

On the surface, we might think that French classical sociological theory, like Marx's theory, was directly and positively influenced by the Enlightenment. French sociology became rational, empirical, scientific, and change-oriented, but not before it was also shaped by a set of ideas developed in reaction to the Enlightenment. In Seidman's view, "The ideology of the counter-Enlightenment represented a virtual inversion of Enlightenment liberalism. In place of modernist premises, we can detect in the Enlightenment critics a strong anti-modernist sentiment" (1983:51). As we will see, sociology in general, and French sociology in particular, has from the beginning been an uncomfortable mix of Enlightenment and counter-Enlightenment ideas.

The most extreme form of opposition to Enlightenment ideas was French Catholic counterrevolutionary philosophy, as represented by the ideas of Louis de Bonald (1754–1840) and Joseph de Maistre (1753–1821) (Reedy, 1994). These men were reacting against not only the Enlightenment but also the French Revolution, which they saw partly as a product of the kind of thinking characteristic of the Enlightenment. De Bonald, for example, was disturbed by the revolutionary changes and yearned for a return to the peace and harmony of the Middle Ages. In this view, God was the source of society; therefore, reason, which was so important to the Enlightenment philosophers, was seen as inferior to traditional religious beliefs. Furthermore, it was believed that because God had created society, people should not tamper with it and should not try to change a holy creation. By extension, de Bonald opposed anything that undermined such traditional institutions as patriarchy, the monogamous family, the monarchy, and the Catholic Church.

Although de Bonald represented a rather extreme form of the conservative reaction, his work constitutes a useful introduction to its general premises. The conservatives turned away from what they considered to be the "naive" rationalism of the Enlightenment. They not only recognized the irrational aspects of social life but also assigned them positive value. Thus they regarded such phenomena as tradition, imagination, emotionalism, and religion as useful and necessary components of social life. In that they disliked upheaval and sought to retain the existing order, they deplored developments such as the French Revolution and the Industrial Revolution, which they saw as disruptive forces. The conservatives tended to emphasize social order, an emphasis that became one of the central themes of the work of several sociological theorists.

Zeitlin (1981) outlined ten major propositions that he sees as emerging from the conservative reaction and providing the basis for the development of classical French sociological theory.

1 Whereas Enlightenment thinkers tended to emphasize the individual, the conservative reaction led to a major sociological interest in, and emphasis on, society and other large-scale phenomena. Society was viewed as something more than simply an aggregate of individuals. Society was seen as having an existence of its own with its own laws of development and deep roots in the past.

2 Society was the most important unit of analysis; it was seen as more important than the individual. It was society that produced the individual, primarily through the process of socialization.

3 The individual was not even seen as the most basic element within society. A society consisted of such component parts as roles, positions, relationships, structures, and institutions. The individuals were seen as doing little more than filling these units within society.

4 The parts of society were seen as interrelated and interdependent. Indeed, these interrelationships were a major basis of society. This view led to a conservative political orientation. That is, because the parts were held to be interrelated, it followed that tampering with one part could well lead to the undermining of other parts and, ultimately, of the system as a whole. This meant that changes in the social system should be made with extreme care.

5 Change was seen as a threat not only to society and its components but also to the individuals in society. The various components of society were seen as satisfying people's needs. When institutions were disrupted, people were likely to suffer, and their suffering was likely to lead to social disorder.

6 The general tendency was to see the various large-scale components of society as useful for both society and the individuals in it. As a result, there was little desire to look for the negative effects of existing social structures and social institutions.

7 Small units, such as the family, the neighborhood, and religious and occupational groups, also were seen as essential to individuals and society. They provided the intimate, face-to-face environments that people needed in order to survive in modern societies.

8 There was a tendency to see various modern social changes, such as industrialization, urbanization, and bureaucratization, as having disorganizing effects. These changes were viewed with fear and anxiety, and there was an emphasis on developing ways of dealing with their disruptive effects.

9 While most of these feared changes were leading to a more rational society, the conservative reaction led to an emphasis on the importance of nonrational factors (ritual, ceremony, and worship, for example) in social life.

10 Finally, the conservatives supported the existence of a hierarchical system in society. It was seen as important to society that there be a differential system of status and reward.

These ten propositions, derived from the conservative reaction to the Enlightenment, should be seen as the immediate intellectual basis of the development of sociological theory in France. Many of these ideas made their way into early sociological thought, although some of the Enlightenment ideas (empiricism, for example) were also influential.[4]

The Development of French Sociology

We turn now to the actual founding of sociology as a distinctive discipline—specifically, to the work of three French thinkers, Claude Saint-Simon, Auguste Comte, and especially Emile Durkheim.

Claude Henri Saint-Simon (1760–1825)   Saint-Simon was older than Auguste Comte, and in fact Comte, in his early years, served as Saint-Simon's secretary and disciple. There is a very strong similarity between the ideas of these two thinkers, and yet a bitter debate developed between them that led to their eventual split (Pickering, 1993; Thompson, 1975).

The most interesting aspect of Saint-Simon was his significance to the development of *both* conservative (like Comte's) and radical Marxian theory. On the conservative side, Saint-Simon wanted to preserve society as it was, but he did not seek a return to

---

[4]Although we have emphasized the discontinuities between the Enlightenment and the counter-Enlightenment, Seidman makes the point that there also are continuities and linkages. First, the counter-Enlightenment carried on the scientific tradition developed in the Enlightenment. Second, it picked up the Enlightenment emphasis on collectivities (as opposed to individuals) and greatly extended it. Third, both had an interest in the problems of the modern world, especially its negative effects on individuals.

life as it had been in the Middle Ages, as did de Bonald and de Maistre. In addition, he was a *positivist* (Durkheim, 1928/1962:142), which meant that he believed that the study of social phenomena should employ the same scientific techniques as were used in the natural sciences. On the radical side, Saint-Simon saw the need for socialist reforms, especially the centralized planning of the economic system. But Saint-Simon did not go nearly as far as Marx did later. Although he, like Marx, saw the capitalists superseding the feudal nobility, he felt it inconceivable that the working class would come to replace the capitalists. Many of Saint-Simon's ideas are found in Comte's work, but Comte developed them in a more systematic fashion (Pickering, 1997).

   Auguste Comte (1798–1857)   Comte (see Chapter 3) was the first to use the term *sociology* (Pickering, forthcoming).[5] He had an enormous influence on later sociological theorists (especially Herbert Spencer and Emile Durkheim). And he believed that the study of sociology should be scientific, just as many classical theorists did and most contemporary sociologists do (Lenzer, 1975).

   Comte was greatly disturbed by the anarchy that pervaded French society and was critical of those thinkers who had spawned both the Enlightenment and the revolution. He developed his scientific view, "positivism," or "positive philosophy," to combat what he considered to be the negative and destructive philosophy of the Enlightenment. Comte was in line with, and influenced by, the French counterrevolutionary Catholics (especially de Bonald and de Maistre). However, his work can be set apart from theirs on at least two grounds. First, he did not think it possible to return to the Middle Ages; advances of science and industry made that impossible. Second, he developed a much more sophisticated theoretical system than his predecessors, one that was adequate to shape a good portion of early sociology.

   Comte developed *social physics,* or what in 1839 he called *sociology* (Pickering, forthcoming). The use of the term *social physics* made it clear that Comte sought to model sociology after the "hard sciences." This new science, which in his view would ultimately become *the* dominant science, was to be concerned with both social statics (existing social structures) and social dynamics (social change). Although both involved the search for laws of social life, he felt that social dynamics was more important than social statics. This focus on change reflected his interest in social reform, particularly reform of the ills created by the French Revolution and the Enlightenment. Comte did not urge revolutionary change, because he felt the natural evolution of society would make things better. Reforms were needed only to assist the process a bit.

   This leads us to the cornerstone of Comte's approach—his evolutionary theory, or the *law of the three stages.* The theory proposes that there are three intellectual stages through which the world has gone throughout its history. According to Comte, not only does the world go through this process, but groups, societies, sciences, individuals, and even minds go through the same three stages. The *theological* stage is the first, and it characterized the world prior to 1300. During this period, the major idea system

---

   [5]While he recognizes that Comte created the label "sociology," Eriksson (1993) has challenged the idea that Comte is the progenitor of modern, scientific sociology. Rather, Eriksson sees people like Adam Smith and more generally the Scottish Moralists, as the true source of modern sociology. See also, L. Hill (1996) on the importance of Adam Ferguson; and Ullmann-Margalit (1997) on Ferguson and Adam Smith.

emphasized the belief that supernatural powers, religious figures, modeled after humankind, are at the root of everything. In particular, the social and physical world is seen as produced by God. The second stage is the *metaphysical* stage, which occurred roughly between 1300 and 1800. This era was characterized by the belief that abstract forces like "nature," rather than personalized gods, explain virtually everything. Finally, in 1800 the world entered the *positivistic* stage, characterized by belief in science. People now tended to give up the search for absolute causes (God or nature) and concentrated instead on observation of the social and physical world in the search for the laws governing them.

It is clear that in his theory of the world Comte focused on intellectual factors. Indeed, he argued that intellectual disorder was the cause of social disorder. The disorder stemmed from earlier idea systems (theological and metaphysical) that continued to exist in the positivistic (scientific) age. Only when positivism gained total control would social upheavals cease. Because this was an evolutionary process, there was no need to foment social upheaval and revolution. Positivism would come, although perhaps not as quickly as some would like. Here Comte's social reformism and his sociology coincide. Sociology could expedite the arrival of positivism and hence bring order to the social world. Above all, Comte did not want to seem to be espousing revolution. There was, in his view, enough disorder in the world. In any case, from Comte's point of view, it was intellectual change that was needed, so there was little reason for social and political revolution.

We have already encountered several of Comte's positions that were to be of great significance to the development of classical sociology—his basic conservatism, reformism, and scientism, and his evolutionary view of the world. Several other aspects of his work deserve mention because they also were to play a major role in the development of sociological theory. For example, his sociology does *not* focus on the individual but rather takes as its basic unit of analysis larger entities such as the family. He also urged that we look at *both* social structure and social change. Of great importance to later sociological theory, especially the work of Spencer and Parsons, is Comte's stress on the systematic character of society—the links among and between the various components of society. He also accorded great importance to the role of consensus in society. He saw little merit in the idea that society is characterized by inevitable conflict between workers and capitalists. In addition, Comte emphasized the need to engage in abstract theorizing and to go out and do sociological research. He urged that sociologists use observation, experimentation, and comparative historical analysis. Finally, Comte believed that sociology ultimately would become the dominant scientific force in the world because of its distinctive ability to interpret social laws and to develop reforms aimed at patching up problems within the system.

Comte was in the forefront of the development of positivistic sociology (Bryant, 1985; Halfpenny, 1982). To Jonathan Turner, Comte's positivism emphasized that "the social universe is amenable to the development of abstract laws that can be tested through the careful collection of data," and "these abstract laws will denote the basic and generic properties of the social universe and they will specify their 'natural relations'" (1985:24). As we will see, a number of classical theorists (especially Spencer and Durkheim) shared Comte's interest in the discovery of the laws of social life. While positivism remains important in contemporary sociology, it has come under attack from a number of quarters (Morrow, 1994).

Even though Comte lacked a solid academic base on which to build a school of Comtian sociological theory, he nevertheless laid a basis for the development of a significant stream of sociological theory. But his long-term significance is dwarfed by that of his successor in French sociology and the inheritor of a number of its ideas, Emile Durkheim. (For a debate over the canonization of Durkheim, as well as other classical theorists discussed in this chapter, see Parker, 1997; Mouzelis, 1997.)

Emile Durkheim (1858–1917)   Although for Durkheim, as for Comte, the Enlightenment was a negative influence, it also had a number of positive effects on his work (for example, the emphasis on science and social reformism). However, Durkheim is best seen as the inheritor of the conservative tradition, especially as it was manifested in Comte's work. But whereas Comte had remained outside of academia, Durkheim developed an increasingly solid academic base as his career progressed. Durkheim legitimized sociology in France, and his work ultimately became a dominant force in the development of sociology in general and of sociological theory in particular.

Durkheim was politically liberal, but he took a more conservative position intellectually. Like Comte and the Catholic counterrevolutionaries, Durkheim feared and hated social disorder. His work was informed by the disorders produced by the general social changes discussed earlier in this chapter, as well as by others (such as industrial strikes, disruption of the ruling class, church–state discord, the rise of political anti-Semitism) more specific to the France of Durkheim's time (Karady, 1983). In fact, most of his work was devoted to the study of social order. His view was that social disorders were *not* a necessary part of the modern world and could be reduced by social reforms. Whereas Marx saw the problems of the modern world as inherent in society, Durkheim (along with most other classical theorists) did not. As a result, Marx's ideas on the need for social revolution stood in sharp contrast to the reformism of Durkheim and the others. As classical sociological theory developed, it was the Durkheimian interest in order and reform that came to dominate, while the Marxian position was eclipsed.

Social Facts   Durkheim developed a distinctive conception of the subject matter of sociology and then tested it in an empirical study. In *The Rules of Sociological Method* (1895/1964), Durkheim argued that it is the special task of sociology to study what he called *social facts*. He conceived of social facts as forces (Takla and Pope, 1985) and structures that are external to, and coercive of, the individual. The study of these large-scale structures and forces—for example, institutionalized law and shared moral beliefs—and their impact on people became the concern of many later sociological theorists (Parsons, for example). In *Suicide* (1897/1951), Durkheim reasoned that if he could link such an individual behavior as suicide to social causes (social facts), he would have made a persuasive case for the importance of the discipline of sociology. But Durkheim did not examine why individual A or B committed suicide; rather, he was interested in the causes of differences in suicide rates among groups, regions, countries, and different categories of people (for example, married and single). His basic argument was that it was the nature of, and changes in, social facts that led to differences in suicide rates. For example, a war or an economic depression would create a collective mood of depression that would in turn lead to increases in suicide rates. As we will see in Chapter 6, there is much more to be said on this subject, but the key point for our purposes here is that Durkheim developed a distinctive view of sociology and sought to demonstrate its usefulness in a scientific study of suicide.

In *The Rules of Sociological Method,* Durkheim differentiated between two types of social facts—material and nonmaterial. Although he dealt with both in the course of his work, his main focus was on *nonmaterial social facts* (for example, culture, social institutions) rather than *material social facts* (for example, bureaucracy, law). This concern for nonmaterial social facts was already clear in his earliest major work, *The Division of Labor in Society* (1893/1964). His focus there was a comparative analysis of what held society together in the primitive and modern cases. He concluded that earlier societies were held together primarily by nonmaterial social facts, specifically, a strongly held common morality, or what he called a strong *collective conscience.* However, because of the complexities of modern society, there had been a decline in the strength of the collective conscience. The primary bond in the modern world was an intricate division of labor, which tied people to others in dependency relationships. However, Durkheim felt that the modern division of labor brought with it several "pathologies"; it was, in other words, an inadequate method of holding society together. Given his conservative sociology, Durkheim did not feel that revolution was needed to solve these problems. Rather, he suggested a variety of reforms that could "patch up" the modern system and keep it functioning. Although he recognized that there was no going back to the age when a powerful collective conscience predominated, he did feel that the common morality could be strengthened in modern society and that people thereby could cope better with the pathologies that they were experiencing.

Religion In his later work, nonmaterial social facts occupied an even more central position. In fact, he came to focus on perhaps the ultimate form of a nonmaterial social fact—religion—in his last major work, *The Elementary Forms of Religious Life* (1912/1965). Durkheim examined primitive society in order to find the roots of religion. He believed that he would be better able to find those roots in the comparative simplicity of primitive society than in the complexity of the modern world. What he found, he felt, was that the source of religion was society itself. Society comes to define certain things as religious and others as profane. Specifically, in the case he studied, the clan was the source of a primitive kind of religion, *totemism,* in which things like plants and animals are deified. Totemism, in turn, was seen as a specific type of nonmaterial social fact, a form of the collective conscience. In the end, Durkheim came to argue that society and religion (or, more generally, the collective conscience) were one and the same. Religion was the way society expressed itself in the form of a nonmaterial social fact. In a sense, then, Durkheim came to deify society and its major products. Clearly, in deifying society, Durkheim took a highly conservative stance: one would not want to overturn a deity *or* its societal source. Because he identified society with God, Durkheim was not inclined to urge social revolution. Instead, he was a social reformer seeking ways of improving the functioning of society. In these and other ways, Durkheim was clearly in line with French conservative sociology. The fact that he avoided many of its excesses helped make him the most significant figure in French sociology.

These books and other important works helped carve out a distinctive domain for sociology in the academic world of turn-of-the-century France, and they earned Durkheim the leading position in that growing field. In 1898, Durkheim set up a scholarly journal devoted to sociology, *L'année sociologique* (Besnard, 1983a). It became a powerful force in the development and spread of sociological ideas. Durkheim was intent on fostering the growth of sociology, and he used his journal as a focal point for the development of a group of disciples. They would later extend his ideas and carry them to many other locales and into the study of other aspects of the social world (for example, sociology of law and sociology of the city) (Besnard, 1983a:1). By 1910, Durkheim had established a strong center of sociology in France, and the academic institutionalization of sociology was well under way in that nation (Heilbron, 1995).

The Development of German Sociology

Whereas the early history of French sociology is a fairly coherent story of the progression from the Enlightenment and the French Revolution to the conservative reaction and to the increasingly important sociological ideas of Saint-Simon, Comte, and Durkheim, German sociology was fragmented from the beginning. A split developed between Marx (and his supporters), who remained on the edge of sociology, and the early giants of mainstream German sociology, Max Weber and Georg Simmel.[6] However, although Marxian theory itself was deemed unacceptable, its ideas found their way in a variety of positive and negative ways into mainstream German sociology.

The Roots and Nature of the Theories of Karl Marx (1818–1883) The dominant intellectual influence on Karl Marx was the German philosopher G. W. F. Hegel (1770–1831).

Hegel According to Ball, "it is difficult for us to appreciate the degree to which Hegel dominated German thought in the second quarter of the nineteenth century. It was largely within the framework of his philosophy that educated Germans—including the young Marx—discussed history, politics and culture" (1991:25). Marx's education at the University of Berlin was shaped by Hegel's ideas as well as by the split that developed among Hegel's followers after his death. The "Old Hegelians" continued to subscribe to the master's ideas, while the "Young Hegelians," although still working in the Hegelian tradition, were critical of many facets of his philosophical system.

Two concepts represent the essence of Hegel's philosophy—the dialectic and idealism (Hegel, 1807/1967, 1821/1967). The *dialectic* is both a way of thinking and an image of the world. On the one hand, it is a way of thinking that stresses the importance of processes, relations, dynamics, conflicts, and contradictions—a dynamic rather than a static way of thinking about the world. On the other hand, it is a view that the *world* is made up not of static structures but of processes, relationships, dynamics, conflicts, and contradictions. Although the dialectic is generally associated with Hegel, it certainly predates him in philosophy. Marx, trained in the Hegelian tradition, accepted the significance of the dialectic. However, he was critical of some aspects of the way Hegel used it. For example, Hegel tended to apply the dialectic only to ideas, whereas Marx felt that it applied as well to more material aspects of life, for example, the economy.

---

[6]For an argument against this and the view of continuity between Marxian and mainstream sociology, see Seidman (1983).

Hegel is also associated with the philosophy of *idealism*, which emphasizes the importance of the mind and mental products rather than the material world. It is the social definition of the physical and material worlds that matters most, not those worlds themselves. In its extreme form, idealism asserts that *only* the mind and psychological constructs exist. Some idealists believed that their mental processes would remain the same even if the physical and social worlds no longer existed. Idealists emphasize not only mental processes but also the ideas produced by these processes. Hegel paid a great deal of attention to the development of such ideas, especially to what he referred to as the "spirit" of society.

In fact, Hegel offered a kind of evolutionary theory of the world in idealistic terms. At first, people were endowed only with the ability to acquire a sensory understanding of the world around them. They could understand things like the sight, smell, and feel of the social and physical world. Later, people developed the ability to be conscious of, to understand, themselves. With self-knowledge and self-understanding, people began to understand that they could become more than they were. In terms of Hegel's dialectical approach, a contradiction developed between what people were and what they felt they could be. The resolution of this contradiction lay in the development of an individual's awareness of his or her place in the larger spirit of society. Individuals come to realize that their ultimate fulfillment lies in the development and the expansion of the spirit of society as a whole. Thus, individuals in Hegel's scheme evolve from an understanding of things to an understanding of self to an understanding of their place in the larger scheme of things.

Hegel, then, offered a general theory of the evolution of the world. It is a subjective theory in which change is held to occur at the level of consciousness. However, that change occurs largely beyond the control of actors. Actors are reduced to little more than vessels swept along by the inevitable evolution of consciousness.

Feuerbach   Ludwig Feuerbach (1804–1872) was an important bridge between Hegel and Marx. As a Young Hegelian, Feuerbach was critical of Hegel for, among other things, his excessive emphasis on consciousness and the spirit of society. Feuerbach's adoption of a materialist philosophy led him to argue that what was needed was to move from Hegel's subjective idealism to a focus not on ideas but on the material reality of real human beings. In his critique of Hegel, Feuerbach focused on religion. To Feuerbach, God is simply a projection by people of their human essence onto an impersonal force. People set God over and above themselves, with the result that they become alienated from God and project a series of positive characteristics onto God (that He is perfect, almighty, and holy), while they reduce themselves to being imperfect, powerless, and sinful. Feuerbach argued that this kind of religion must be overcome and that its defeat could be aided by a materialist philosophy in which people (not religion) became their own highest object, ends in themselves. Real people, not abstract ideas like religion, are deified by a materialist philosophy.

Marx, Hegel, and Feuerbach   Marx was simultaneously influenced by, and critical of, *both* Hegel and Feuerbach. Marx, following Feuerbach, was critical of Hegel's adherence to an idealist philosophy. Marx took this position not only because of his adoption of a materialist orientation but also because of his interest in practical activities. Social facts like wealth and the state are treated by Hegel as ideas rather than as real, material entities. Even when he examined a seemingly material process like labor, Hegel was looking only at abstract mental labor. This is very different from Marx's interest in the labor of real, sentient people. Thus Hegel was looking at the wrong issues as far as Marx was concerned. In addition, Marx felt that Hegel's idealism led to a very conservative political orientation. To Hegel, the process of evolution was occurring beyond the control of people and their activities. In any case, in that people seemed to be moving toward greater consciousness of the world as it could be, there seemed no need for any revolutionary change; the process was already moving in the "desired" direction. Whatever problems did exist lay in consciousness, and the answer therefore seemed to lie in changing thinking.

Marx took a very different position, arguing that the problems of modern life can be traced to real, material sources (for example, the structures of capitalism) and that the solutions, therefore, can be found *only* in the overturning of those structures by the collective action of large numbers of people (Marx and Engels, 1845/1956:254). Whereas Hegel "stood the world on its head" (that is, focused on consciousness, not the real material world), Marx firmly embedded his dialectic in a material base.

Marx applauded Feuerbach's critique of Hegel on a number of counts (for example, its materialism and its rejection of the abstractness of Hegel's theory), but he was far from fully satisfied with Feuerbach's own position (Thomson, 1994). For one thing, Feuerbach focused on the religious world, whereas Marx believed that it was the entire social world, and the economy in particular, that had to be analyzed. Although Marx accepted Feuerbach's materialism, he felt that Feuerbach had gone too far in focusing one-sidedly, nondialectically, on the material world. Feuerbach failed to include the most important of Hegel's contributions, the dialectic, in his materialist orientation, particularly the relationship between people and the material world. Finally, Marx argued that Feuerbach, like most philosophers, failed to emphasize praxis—practical activity—in particular, revolutionary activity. As Marx put it, "The philosophers have only *interpreted* the world, in various ways; the point, however, is to *change* it" (cited in Tucker, 1970:109).

Marx extracted what he considered to be the two most important elements from these two thinkers—Hegel's dialectic and Feuerbach's materialism—and fused them into his own distinctive orientation, *dialectical materialism*, which focuses on dialectical relationships within the material world.

Political Economy   Marx's materialism and his consequent focus on the economic sector led him rather naturally to the work of a group of *political economists* (for example, Adam Smith and David Ricardo). Marx was very attracted to a number of their positions. He lauded their basic premise that labor was the source of all wealth. This ultimately led Marx to his *labor theory of value,* in which he argued that the profit of the capitalist was based on the exploitation of the laborer. Capitalists performed the rather simple trick of paying the workers less than they deserved, because they received less pay than the value of what they actually produced in a work period. This *surplus value,* which was retained and reinvested by the capitalist, was the basis of the entire capitalist system. The capitalist system grew by continually increasing the level of exploitation of the workers (and therefore the amount of surplus value) and investing the profits for the expansion of the system.

Marx also was affected by the political economists' depiction of the horrors of the capitalist system and the exploitation of the workers. However, whereas they depicted the evils of capitalism, Marx criticized the political economists for seeing these evils as inevitable components of capitalism. Marx deplored their general acceptance of capitalism and the way they urged people to work for economic success within it. He also was critical of the political economists for failing to see the inherent conflict between capitalists and laborers and for denying the need for a radical change in the economic order. Such conservative economics was hard for Marx to accept, given his commitment to a radical change from capitalism to socialism.

Marx and Sociology   Marx was not a sociologist and did not consider himself to be one. Although his work is too broad to be encompassed by the term *sociology,* there is a sociological theory to be found in Marx's work. From the beginning, there were those who were heavily influenced by Marx, and there has been a continuous strand of Marxian sociology, primarily in Europe. But for the majority of early sociologists, his work was a negative force, something against which to shape their sociology. Until very recently, sociological theory, especially in America, has been characterized by either hostility to or ignorance of Marxian theory. This has, as we will see in Chapter 2, changed dramatically, but the negative reaction to Marx's work was a major force in the shaping of much of sociological theory (Gurney, 1981).

The basic reason for this rejection of Marx was ideological. Many of the early sociological theorists were inheritors of the conservative reaction to the disruptions of the Enlightenment and the French Revolution. Marx's radical ideas and the radical social changes he foretold and sought to bring to life were clearly feared and hated by such thinkers. Marx was dismissed as an ideologist. It was argued that he was not a serious sociological theorist. However, ideology per se could not have been the real reason for the rejection of Marx, because the work of Comte, Durkheim, and other conservative thinkers was also heavily ideological. It was the nature of the ideology, not the existence of ideology as such, that put off many sociological theorists. They were ready and eager to buy conservative ideology wrapped in a cloak of sociological theory, but not the radical ideology offered by Marx and his followers.

There were, of course, other reasons why Marx was not accepted by many early theorists. He seemed to be more an economist than a sociologist. Although the early sociologists would certainly admit the importance of the economy, they would also argue that it was only one of a number of components of social life.

Another reason for the early rejection of Marx was the nature of his interests. Whereas the early sociologists were reacting to the disorder created by the Enlightenment, the French Revolution, and later the Industrial Revolution, Marx was not upset by these disorders—or by disorder in general. Rather, what interested and concerned Marx most was the oppressiveness of the capitalist system that was emerging out of the Industrial Revolution. Marx wanted to develop a theory that explained this oppressiveness and that would help overthrow that system. Marx's interest was in revolution, which stood in contrast to the conservative concern for reform and orderly change.

Another difference worth noting is the difference in philosophical roots between Marxian and conservative sociological theory. Most of the conservative theorists were heavily influenced by the philosophy of Immanuel Kant. Among other things, this led them to think in linear, cause-and-effect terms. That is, they tended to argue that a change in *A* (say, the change in ideas during the Enlightenment) leads to a change in *B* (say, the political changes of the French Revolution). In contrast, Marx was most heavily influenced, as we have seen, by Hegel, who thought in dialectical rather than cause-and-effect terms. Among other things, the dialectic attunes us to the ongoing reciprocal effects of social forces. Thus, a dialectician would reconceptualize the example discussed above as a continual, ongoing interplay of ideas and politics.

Marx's Theory   To oversimplify enormously (see Chapter 5 for a much more detailed discussion), Marx offered a theory of capitalist society based on his image of the basic nature of human beings. Marx believed that people are basically productive; that is, in order to survive, people need to work in, and with, nature. In so doing, they produce the food, clothing, tools, shelter, and other necessities that permit them to live. Their productivity is a perfectly natural way by which they express basic creative impulses. Furthermore, these impulses are expressed in concert with other people; in other words, people are inherently social. They need to work together to produce what they need to survive.

Throughout history this natural process has been subverted, at first by the mean conditions of primitive society and later by a variety of structural arrangements erected by societies in the course of history. In various ways, these structures interfered with the natural productive process. However, it is in capitalist society that this breakdown is most acute; the breakdown in the natural productive process reaches its culmination in capitalism.

Basically capitalism is a structure (or, more accurately, a series of structures) that erects barriers between an individual and the production process, the products of that process, and other people; ultimately, it even divides the individual himself or herself. This is the basic meaning of the concept of *alienation:* it is the breakdown of the natural interconnection between people and between people and what they produce. Alienation occurs because capitalism has evolved into a two-class system in which a few capitalists own the production process, the products, and the labor time of those who work for them. Instead of naturally producing for themselves, people produce unnaturally in capitalist society for a small group of capitalists. Intellectually, Marx was very concerned with the structures of capitalism and their oppressive impact on actors. Politically, he was led to an interest in emancipating people from the oppressive structures of capitalism.

Marx actually spent very little time dreaming about what a utopian socialist state would look like (Lovell, 1992). He was more concerned with helping to bring about the demise of capitalism. He believed that the contradictions and conflicts within capitalism would lead dialectically to its ultimate collapse, but he did not think that the process was inevitable. People had to act at the appropriate times and in the appropriate ways for socialism to come into being. The capitalists have great resources at their disposal to forestall the coming of socialism, but they could be overcome by the concerted action of a class-conscious proletariat. What would the proletariat create in the process? What is socialism? Most basically, it is a society in which, for the first time, people could approach Marx's ideal image of productivity. With the aid of modern technology, people could interact harmoniously with nature and other people to create what they needed to survive. To put it another way, in socialist society, people would no longer be alienated.

The Roots and Nature of the Theories of Max Weber (1864–1920) and Georg Simmel (1858–1918)   Although Marx and his followers in the late nineteenth and early twentieth centuries remained outside mainstream German sociology, to a considerable extent early German sociology can be seen as developing in opposition to Marxian theory.

Weber and Marx   Albert Salomon, for example, claimed that a large part of the theory of the early giant of German sociology, Max Weber, developed "in a long and intense debate with the ghost of Marx" (1945:596). This is probably an exaggeration, but in many ways Marxian theory did play a negative role in Weberian theory. In other ways, however, Weber was working *within* the Marxian tradition, trying to "round out" Marx's theory. Also, there were many inputs into Weberian theory other than Marxian theory (Burger, 1976). We can clarify a good deal about the sources of German sociology by outlining each of these views of the relationship between Marx and Weber (Antonio and Glassman, 1985; Schroeter, 1985). It should be borne in mind that Weber was not intimately familiar with Marx's work (much of it was not published until after Weber's death) and that Weber was reacting more to the work of the Marxists than to Marx's work itself (Antonio, 1985:29; Turner, 1981:19–20).

Weber *did* tend to view Marx and the Marxists of his day as economic determinists who offered single-cause theories of social life. That is, Marxian theory was seen as tracing all historical developments to economic bases and viewing all contemporaneous structures as erected on an economic base. Although this is not true of Marx's own theory (as we will see in Chapter 5), it was the position of many later Marxists.

One of the examples of economic determinism that seemed to rankle Weber most was the view that ideas are simply the reflections of material (especially economic) interests, that material interests determine ideology. From this point of view, Weber was supposed to have "turned Marx on his head" (much as Marx had inverted Hegel). Instead of focusing on economic factors and their effect on ideas, Weber devoted much of his attention to ideas and their effect on the economy. Rather than seeing ideas as simple reflections of economic factors, Weber saw them as fairly autonomous forces capable of profoundly affecting the economic world. Weber certainly devoted a lot of attention to ideas, particularly systems of religious ideas, and he was especially concerned with the impact of religious ideas on the economy. In *The Protestant Ethic and the Spirit of Capitalism* (1904–05/1958), he was concerned with Protestantism, mainly as a system of ideas, and its impact on the rise of another system of ideas, the "spirit of capitalism," and ultimately on a capitalist economic system. Weber had a similar interest in other world religions, looking at how their nature might have obstructed the development of capitalism in their respective societies. On the basis of this kind of work, some scholars came to the conclusion that Weber developed his ideas in opposition to those of Marx.

A second view of Weber's relationship to Marx, as mentioned earlier, is that he did not so much oppose Marx as try to round out his theoretical perspective. Here Weber is seen as working more within the Marxian tradition than in opposition to it. His work on religion, interpreted from this point of view, was simply an effort to show that not only do material factors affect ideas but ideas themselves affect material structures.

A good example of the view that Weber was engaged in a process of rounding out Marxian theory is in the area of stratification theory. In this work on stratification, Marx focused on social *class,* the economic dimension of stratification. Although Weber accepted the importance of this factor, he argued that other dimensions of stratification were also important. He argued that the notion of social stratification should be extended to include stratification on the basis of prestige (*status*) and *power.* The inclusion of these other dimensions does not constitute a refutation of Marx but is simply an extension of his ideas.

Both of the views outlined above accept the importance of Marxian theory for Weber. There are elements of truth in both positions; at some points Weber *was* working in opposition to Marx, while at other points he *was* extending Marx's ideas. However, a third view of this issue may best characterize the relationship between Marx and Weber. In this view, Marx is simply seen as only one of many influences on Weber's thought.

Other Influences   We can identify a number of sources of Weberian theory, including German historians, philosophers, economists, and political theorists. Among those who influenced Weber, the philosopher Immanuel Kant (1724–1804) stands out above all the others.   But we must not overlook the impact of Friedrich Nietzsche (1844–1900)—especially his emphasis on the hero—on Weber's work on the need for individuals to stand up to the impact of bureaucracies and other structures of modern society.

The influence of Immanuel Kant on Weber and on German sociology generally shows that German sociology and Marxism grew from different philosophical roots. As we have seen, it was Hegel, not Kant, who was the important philosophical influence on Marxian theory. Whereas Hegel's philosophy led Marx and the Marxists to look for relations, conflicts, and contradictions, Kantian philosophy led at least some German sociologists to take a more static perspective. To Kant the world was a buzzing confusion of events that could never be known directly. The world could only be known through thought processes that filter, select, and categorize these events. The content of the real world was differentiated by Kant from the forms through which that content can be comprehended. The emphasis on these forms gave the work of those sociologists within the Kantian tradition a more static quality than that of the Marxists within the Hegelian tradition.

Weber's Theory   Whereas Karl Marx offered basically a theory of capitalism, Weber's work was fundamentally a theory of the process of rationalization (Brubaker, 1984; Kalberg, 1980, 1990, 1994). Weber was interested in the general issue of why institutions in the Western world had grown progressively more rational while powerful barriers seemed to prevent a similar development in the rest of the world.

Although rationality is used in many different ways in Weber's work, what interests us here is a process involving one of four types identified by Kalberg (1980, 1990, 1994; see also Brubaker, 1984; Levine, 1981a), *formal rationality.* Formal rationality involves, as was usually the case with Weber, a concern for the actor making choices of means and ends. However, in this case, that choice is made in reference to universally applied rules, regulations, and laws. These, in turn, are derived from various large-scale structures, especially bureaucracies and the economy. Weber developed his theories in the context of a large number of comparative historical studies of the West, China, India, and many other regions of the world. In these studies, he sought to delineate the factors that helped bring about or impede the development of rationalization.

Weber saw the bureaucracy (and the historical process of bureaucratization) as the classic example of rationalization, but rationalization is perhaps best illustrated today by the fast-food restaurant (Ritzer, 1996). The fast-food restaurant is a formally rational system in which people (both workers and customers) are led to seek the most rational means to ends. The drive-through window, for example, is a rational means by which workers can dispense, and customers can obtain, food quickly and efficiently. Speed and efficiency are dictated by the fast-food restaurants and the rules and regulations by which they operate.

Weber embedded his discussion of the process of bureaucratization in a broader discussion of the political institution. He differentiated among three types of authority systems—traditional, charismatic, and rational-legal. Only in the modern Western world can a rational-legal authority system develop, and only within that system does one find the full-scale development of the modern bureaucracy. The rest of the world remains dominated by traditional or charismatic authority systems, which generally impede the development of a rational-legal authority system and modern bureaucracies. Briefly, *traditional* authority stems from a long-lasting system of beliefs. An example would be a leader who comes to power because his or her family or clan has always provided the group's leadership. A *charismatic* leader derives his or her authority from extraordinary abilities or characteristics, or more likely simply from the *belief* on the part of followers that the leader has such traits. Although these two types of authority are of historical importance, Weber believed that the trend in the West, and ultimately in the rest of the world, is toward systems of *rational-legal* authority. In such systems, authority is derived from rules legally and rationally enacted. Thus, the president of the United States derives his authority ultimately from the laws of society. The evolution of rational-legal authority, with its accompanying bureaucracies, is only one part of Weber's general argument on the rationalization of the Western world.

Weber also did detailed and sophisticated analyses of the rationalization of such phenomena as religion, law, the city, and even music. But we can illustrate Weber's mode of thinking with one other example—the rationalization of the economic institution. This discussion is couched in Weber's broader analysis of the relationship between religion and capitalism. In a wide-ranging historical study, Weber sought to understand why a rational economic system (capitalism) had developed in the West and why it had failed to develop in the rest of the world. Weber accorded a central role to religion in this process. At one level, he was engaged in a dialogue with the Marxists in an effort to show that, contrary to what many Marxists of the day believed, religion was not merely an epiphenomenon. Instead, it had played a key role in the rise of capitalism in the West and in its failure to develop elsewhere in the world. Weber argued that it was a distinctively rational religious system (Calvinism) that played the central role in the rise of capitalism in the West. In contrast, in the other parts of the world that he studied, Weber found more irrational religious systems (for example, Confucianism, Taoism, Hinduism), which helped to inhibit the development of a rational economic system. However, in the end, one gets the feeling that these religions provided only temporary barriers, for the economic systems—indeed, the entire social structure—of these societies ultimately would become rationalized.

Although rationalization lies at the heart of Weberian theory, it is far from all there is to the theory. But this is not the place to go into that rich body of material. Instead, let us return to the development of sociological theory. A key issue in that development is. Why did Weber's theory prove more attractive to later sociological theorists than Marxian theory?

The Acceptance of Weber's Theory   One reason is that Weber proved to be more acceptable politically. Instead of espousing Marxian radicalism, Weber was more of a liberal on some issues and a conservative on others (for example, the role of the state). Although he was a severe critic of many aspects of modern capitalist society and came to many of the same critical conclusions as did Marx, he was not one to propose radical solutions to problems (Heins, 1993). In fact, he felt that the radical reforms offered by many Marxists and other socialists would do more harm than good.

Later sociological theorists, especially Americans, saw their society under attack by Marxian theory. Largely conservative in orientation, they cast about for theoretical alternatives to Marxism. One of those who proved attractive was Max Weber. (Durkheim and Vilfredo Pareto were others.) After all, rationalization affected not only capitalist but also socialist societies. Indeed, from Weber's point of view, rationalization constituted an even greater problem in socialist than in capitalist societies.

Also in Weber's favor was the form in which he presented his judgments. He spent most of his life doing detailed historical studies, and his political conclusions were often made within the context of his research. Thus they usually sounded very scientific and academic. Marx, although he did much serious research, also wrote a good deal of explicitly polemical material. Even his more academic work is laced with acid political judgments. For example, in *Capital* (1867/1967), he described capitalists as "vampires" and "werewolves." Weber's more academic style helped make him more acceptable to later sociologists.

Another reason for the greater acceptability of Weber was that he operated in a philosophical tradition that also helped shape the work of later sociologists. That is, Weber operated in the Kantian tradition, which meant, as we have seen, that he tended to think in cause-and-effect terms. This kind of thinking was more acceptable to later sociologists, who were largely unfamiliar and uncomfortable with the dialectical logic that informed Marx's work.

Finally, Weber appeared to offer a much more rounded approach to the social world than Marx. Whereas Marx appeared to be almost totally preoccupied with the economy, Weber was interested in a wide range of social phenomena. This diversity of focus seemed to give later sociologists more to work with than the apparently more single-minded concerns of Marx.

Weber produced most of his major works in the late 1800s and early 1900s. Early in his career, Weber was identified more as a historian who was concerned with sociological issues, but in the early 1900s his focus grew more and more sociological. Indeed, he became the dominant sociologist of his time in Germany. In 1910, he founded (with, among others, Georg Simmel, whom we discuss below) the German Sociological Society (Glatzer, 1998). His home in Heidelberg was an intellectual center not only for sociologists but for scholars from many fields. Although his work was broadly influential in Germany, it was to become even more influential in the United States, especially after Talcott Parsons introduced Weber's ideas (and those of other European theorists, especially Durkheim) to a large American audience. Although Marx's ideas did not have a significant positive effect on American sociological theorists until the 1960s, Weber was already highly influential by the late 1930s.

Simmel's Theory   Georg Simmel was Weber's contemporary and a cofounder of the German Sociological Society. Simmel was a somewhat atypical sociological theorist (Frisby, 1981; Levine, Carter, and Gorman, 1976a, 1976b). For one thing, he had an immediate and profound effect on the development of American sociological theory, whereas Marx and Weber were largely ignored for a number of years. Simmel's work helped shape the development of one of the early centers of American sociology—the University of Chicago—and its major theory, symbolic interactionism (Jaworski, 1995; 1997). The Chicago school and symbolic interactionism came, as we will see, to dominate American sociology in the 1920s and early 1930s (Bulmer, 1984). Simmel's ideas were influential at Chicago mainly because the dominant figures in the early years of Chicago, Albion Small and Robert Park, had been exposed to Simmel's theories in Berlin in the late 1800s. Park attended Simmel's lectures in 1899 and 1900, and Small carried on an extensive correspondence with Simmel during the 1890s. They were instrumental in bringing Simmel's ideas to students and faculty at Chicago, in translating some of his work, and in bringing it to the attention of a large-scale American audience (Frisby, 1984:29).

Another atypical aspect of Simmel's work is his "level" of analysis, or at least that level for which he became best known in America. Whereas Weber and Marx were preoccupied with large-scale issues like the rationalization of society and a capitalist economy, Simmel was best known for his work on smaller-scale issues, especially individual action and interaction. He became famous early for his thinking, derived from Kantian philosophy, on *forms* of interaction (for example, conflict) and *types* of interactants (for example, the stranger). Basically, Simmel saw that understanding interaction among people was one of the major tasks of sociology. However, it was impossible to study the massive number of interactions in social life without some conceptual tools. This is where forms of interaction and types of interactants came in. Simmel felt that he could isolate a limited number of forms of interaction that could be found in a large number of social settings. Thus equipped, one could analyze and understand these different interaction settings. The development of a limited number of types of interactants could be similarly useful in explaining interaction settings. This work had a profound effect on symbolic interactionism, which, as the name suggests, was focally concerned with interaction. One of the ironies, however, is that Simmel also was concerned with large-scale issues similar to those that obsessed Marx and Weber. However, this work was much less influential than his work on interaction, although there are contemporary signs of a growing interest in the large-scale aspects of Simmel's sociology.

It was partly Simmel's style in his work on interaction that made him accessible to early American sociological theorists. Although he wrote heavy tomes like those of Weber and Marx, he also wrote a set of deceptively simple essays on such interesting topics as poverty, the prostitute, the miser and the spendthrift, and the stranger. The brevity of such essays and the high interest level of the material made the dissemination of Simmel's ideas much easier. Unfortunately, the essays had the negative effect of obscuring Simmel's more massive works (for example, *Philosophy of Money,* translated in 1978; see Poggi, 1993), which were potentially as significant to sociology. Nevertheless, it was partly through the short and clever essays that Simmel had a much more significant effect on early American sociological theory than either Marx or Weber did.

We should not leave Simmel without saying something about *Philosophy of Money,* because its English translation made Simmel's work attractive to a whole new set of theorists interested in culture and society. Although a macro orientation is clearer in *Philosophy of Money,* it always existed in Simmel's work. For example, it is clear in his famous work on the dyad and the triad. Simmel thought that some crucial sociological developments take place when a two-person group (or *dyad*) is transformed into a *triad* by the addition of a third party. Social possibilities emerge that simply could not exist in a dyad. For example, in a triad, one of the members can become an arbitrator or mediator of the differences between the other two. More important, two of the members can band together and dominate the other member. This represents on a small scale what can happen with the emergence of large-scale structures that become separate from individuals and begin to dominate them.

This theme lies at the base of *Philosophy of Money.* Simmel was concerned primarily with the emergence in the modern world of a money economy that becomes separate from the individual and predominant. This theme, in turn, is part of an even broader and more pervasive one in Simmel's work, the domination of the culture as a whole over the individual. As Simmel saw it, in the modern world, the larger culture and all its various components (including the money economy) expand, and as they expand, the importance of the individual decreases. Thus, for example, as the industrial technology associated with a modern economy expands and grows more sophisticated, the skills and abilities of the individual worker grow progressively less important. In the end, the worker is confronted with an industrial machine over which he or she can exert little, if any, control. More generally, Simmel thought that in the modern world, the expansion of the larger culture leads to the growing insignificance of the individual.

Although sociologists have become increasingly attuned to the broader implications of Simmel's work, his early influence was primarily through his studies of small-scale social phenomena, such as the forms of interaction and types of interactants.

The Origins of British Sociology

We have been examining the development of sociology in France (Comte, Durkheim) and Germany (Marx, Weber, and Simmel). We turn now to the parallel development of sociology in England. As we will see, Continental ideas had their impact on early British sociology, but more important were native influences.

Political Economy, Ameliorism, and Social Evolution   Philip Abrams (1968) contended that British sociology was shaped in the nineteenth century by three often conflicting sources—political economy, ameliorism, and social evolution.[7] Thus when the Sociological Society of London was founded in 1903, there were strong differences over the definition of *sociology.* However, there were few who doubted the view that sociology could be a science. It was the differences that gave British sociology its distinctive character, and we will look at each of them briefly.

---

[7]For more recent developments in British sociology, see Abrams et al. (1981).

SIGMUND FREUD: A Biographical Sketch

Another leading figure in German social science in the late 1800s and early 1900s was Sigmund Freud. Although he was not a sociologist, Freud influenced the work of many sociologists (for example, Talcott Parsons and Norbert Elias) and continues to be of relevance to social theorists (Brennan, 1997; Carveth, 1982; Kaye, 1991; Kurzweil, 1995).

Sigmund Freud was born in the Austro-Hungarian city of Freiberg on May 6, 1856 (Puner, 1947). In 1859, his family moved to Vienna, and in 1873, Freud entered the medical school at the University of Vienna. Freud was more interested in science than in medicine and took a position in a physiology laboratory. He completed his degree in medicine, and after leaving the laboratory in 1882, he worked in a hospital and then set up a private medical practice with a specialty in nervous diseases.

Freud at first used hypnosis in an effort to deal with a type of neurosis known as *hysteria*. He had learned the technique in Paris from Jean Martin Charcot in 1885. Later he adopted a technique, pioneered by a fellow Viennese physician, Joseph Breuer, in which hysterical symptoms disappeared when the patient talked through the circumstances in which the symptoms first arose. By 1895, Freud had published a book with Breuer with a series of revolutionary implications: that the causes of neuroses like hysteria were psychological (not, as had been believed, physiological) and that the therapy involved talking through the original causes. Thus was born the practical and theoretical field of *psychoanalysis*. Freud began to part company with Breuer as he came to see sexual factors, or more generally the *libido,* at the root of neuroses. Over the next several years, Freud refined his therapeutic techniques and wrote a great deal about his new ideas.

By 1902, Freud began to gather a number of disciples around him, and they met weekly at his house. By 1903 or 1904, others (like Carl Jung) began to use Freud's ideas in their psychiatric practices. In 1908, the first Psychoanalytic Congress was held, and the next year a periodical for disseminating psychoanalytic knowledge was formed. As quickly as it had formed, the new field of psychoanalysis became splintered as Freud broke with people like Jung and they went off to develop their own ideas and found their own groups. World War I slowed the development of psychoanalysis, but it expanded and developed greatly in the 1920s. With the rise of Nazism, the center of psychoanalysis shifted to the United States, where it remains to this day. But Freud remained in Vienna until the Nazis took over in 1938, despite the fact that he was Jewish and the Nazis had burned his books as early as 1933. On June 4, 1938, only after a ransom had been paid and President Roosevelt had interceded, Sigmund Freud left Vienna. Freud had suffered from cancer of the jaw since 1923, and he died in London on September 23, 1939.

Political Economy   We have already touched on *political economy,* which was a theory of industrial and capitalist society traceable in part to the work of Adam Smith (1723–1790).[8] As we saw, political economy had a profound effect on Karl Marx. Marx studied political economy closely, and he was critical of it. But that was not the direction taken by British economists and sociologists. They tended to accept Smith's idea

---

[8]Smith is usually included as a leading member of the Scottish Enlightenment (Chitnis, 1976) and as one of the Scottish Moralists (Schneider, 1967:xi), who were seeking to establish the basis for sociology.

that there was an "invisible hand" that shaped the market for labor and goods. The market was seen as an independent reality that stood above individuals and controlled their behavior. The British sociologists, like the political economists and unlike Marx, saw the market as a positive force, as a source of order, harmony, and integration in society. Because they saw the market, and more generally society, in a positive light, the task of the sociologist was not to criticize society but simply to gather data on the laws by which it operated. The goal was to provide the government with the facts it needed to understand the way the system worked and to direct its workings wisely.

The emphasis was on facts, but which facts? Whereas Marx, Weber, Durkheim, and Comte looked to the structures of society for their basic facts, the British thinkers tended to focus on the individuals who made up those structures. In dealing with large-scale structures, they tended to collect individual-level data and then combine them to form a collective portrait. In the mid-1800s it was the statisticians who dominated British social science, and this kind of data collection was deemed to be the major task of sociology. The objective was the accumulation of "pure" facts without theorizing or philosophizing. These empirical sociologists were detached from the concerns of social theorists. Instead of general theorizing, the "emphasis settled on the business of producing more exact indicators, better methods of classification and data collection, improved life tables, higher levels of comparability between discrete bodies of data, and the like" (Abrams, 1968:18).

It was almost in spite of themselves that these statistically oriented sociologists came to see some limitations in their approach. A few began to feel the need for broader theorizing. To them, a problem such as poverty pointed to failings in the market system as well as in the society as a whole. But most, focused as they were on individuals, did not question the larger system; they turned instead to more detailed field studies and to the development of more complicated and more exact statistical techniques. To them, the source of the problem had to lie in inadequate research methods, *not* in the system as a whole. As Philip Abrams noted, "Focusing persistently on the distribution of individual circumstances, the statisticians found it hard to break through to a perception of poverty as a product of social structure. . . . They did not and probably could not achieve the concept of structural victimization" (1968:27). In addition to their theoretical and methodological commitments to the study of individuals, the statisticians worked too closely with government policy makers to arrive at the conclusion that the larger political and economic system was the problem.

Ameliorism   Related to, but separable from, political economy was the second defining characteristic of British sociology—*ameliorism*, or a desire to solve social problems by reforming individuals. Although British scholars began to recognize that there were problems in society (for example, poverty), they still believed in that society and wanted to preserve it. They desired to forestall violence and revolution and to reform the system so that it could continue essentially as it was. Above all, they wanted to prevent the coming of a socialist society. Thus, like French sociology and some branches of German sociology, British sociology was conservatively oriented.

Because the British sociologists could not, or would not, trace the source of problems such as poverty to the society as a whole, the source had to lie within the individuals themselves. This was an early form of what William Ryan (1971) later called "blaming the victim." Much attention was devoted to a long series of individual problems—

"ignorance, spiritual destitution, impurity, bad sanitation, pauperism, crime, and intemperance—above all intemperance" (Abrams, 1968:39). Clearly, there was a tendency to look for a simple cause for all social ills, and the one that suggested itself before all others was alcoholism. What made this perfect to the ameliorist was that this was an individual pathology, not a social pathology. The ameliorists lacked a theory of social structure, a theory of the social causes of such individual problems.

Social Evolution But a stronger sense of social structure was lurking below the surface of British sociology, and it burst through in the latter part of the nineteenth century with the growth of interest in *social evolution*. One important influence was the work of Auguste Comte, part of which had been translated into English in the 1850s by Harriet Martineau (Hoecker-Drysdale, forthcoming). Although Comte's work did not inspire immediate interest, by the last quarter of the century, a number of thinkers had been attracted to it and to its concern for the larger structures of society, its scientific (positivistic) orientation, its comparative orientation, and its evolutionary theory. However, a number of British thinkers sharpened their own conception of the world in opposition to some of the excesses of Comtian theory (for example, the tendency to elevate sociology to the status of a religion).

In Abrams's view, the real importance of Comte lay in his providing one of the bases on which opposition could be mounted against the "oppressive genius of Herbert Spencer" (Abrams, 1968:58). In both a positive and a negative sense, Spencer was a dominant figure in British sociological theory, especially evolutionary theory (J. Turner, forthcoming).

Herbert Spencer (1820–1903) In attempting to understand Spencer's ideas (see Chapter 4), it is useful to compare and contrast them with Comtian theory.

Spencer and Comte Spencer is often categorized with Comte in terms of their influence on the development of sociological theory, but there are some important differences between them. For example, it is less easy to categorize Spencer as a conservative. In fact, in his early years, Spencer is better seen as a political liberal, and he retained elements of liberalism throughout his life. However, it is also true that Spencer grew more conservative during the course of his life and that his basic influence, as was true of Comte, was conservative.

One of his liberal views, which coexisted rather uncomfortably with his conservatism, was his acceptance of a laissez-faire doctrine: he felt that the state should not intervene in individual affairs, except in the rather passive function of protecting people. This meant that Spencer, unlike Comte, was not interested in social reforms; he wanted social life to evolve free of external control.

This difference points to Spencer as a *Social Darwinist* (G. Jones, 1980). As such, he held the evolutionary view that the world was growing progressively better. Therefore, it should be left alone; outside interference could only worsen the situation. He adopted the view that social institutions, like plants and animals, adapted progressively and positively to their social environment. He also accepted the Darwinian view that a process of natural selection, "survival of the fittest," occurred in the social world. (Interestingly, it was Spencer who coined the phrase "survival of the fittest" several years *before* Charles Darwin's work on natural selection.) That is, if unimpeded by external intervention, people who were "fit" would survive and proliferate whereas the "unfit" would eventually die out. Another difference was that Spencer emphasized the individual, whereas Comte focused on larger units such as the family.

Comte and Spencer shared with Durkheim and others a commitment to a science of sociology (Haines, 1992), which was a very attractive perspective to early theorists. Another influence of Spencer's work, shared with both Comte and Durkheim, was his tendency to see society as an *organism*. In this, Spencer borrowed his perspective and concepts from biology. He was concerned with the overall structure of society, the interrelationship of the *parts* of society, and the *functions* of the parts for each other as well as for the system as a whole.

Most important, Spencer, like Comte, had an evolutionary conception of historical development. However, Spencer was critical of Comte's evolutionary theory on several grounds. Specifically, he rejected Comte's law of the three stages. He argued that Comte was content to deal with evolution in the realm of ideas, in terms of intellectual development. Spencer, however, sought to develop an evolutionary theory in the real, material world.

Evolutionary Theory   It is possible to identify at least two major evolutionary perspectives in Spencer's work (Haines, 1988; Perrin, 1976).

The first of these theories relates primarily to the increasing *size* of society. Society grows through both the multiplication of individuals and the union of groups (compounding). The increasing size of society brings with it larger and more differentiated social structures, as well as the increasing differentiation of the functions they perform. In addition to their growth in terms of size, societies evolve through compounding, that is, by unifying more and more adjoining groups. Thus, Spencer talks of the evolutionary movement from simple to compound, doubly-compound, and trebly-compound societies.

Spencer also offers a theory of evolution from *militant* to *industrial* societies. Earlier, militant societies are defined by being structured for offensive and defensive warfare. While Spencer was critical of warfare, he felt that in an earlier stage it was functional in bringing societies together (for example, through military conquest) and in creating the larger aggregates of people necessary for the development of industrial society. However, with the emergence of industrial society, warfare ceases to be functional and serves to impede further evolution. Industrial society is based on friendship, altruism, elaborate specialization, recognition for achievements rather than the characteristics one is born with, and voluntary cooperation among highly disciplined individuals. Such a society is held together by voluntary contractual relations and, more important, by a strong common morality. The government's role is restricted and focuses only on what people ought not to do. Obviously, modern industrial societies are less warlike than their militant predecessors. Although Spencer sees a general evolution in the direction of industrial societies, he also recognizes that it is possible that there will be periodic regressions to warfare and more militant societies.

In his ethical and political writings, Spencer offered other ideas on the evolution of society. For one thing, he saw society as progressing toward an ideal, or perfect, moral state. For another, he argued that the fittest societies survive, while unfit societies should be permitted to die off. The result of this process is adaptive upgrading for the world as a whole.

Thus Spencer offered a rich and complicated set of ideas on social evolution. As we will see, his ideas first enjoyed great success, then were rejected for many years, and more recently have been revived with the rise of neoevolutionary sociological theories (Buttel, 1990).

The Reaction against Spencer in Britain   Despite his emphasis on the individual, Spencer was best known for his large-scale theory of social evolution. In this, he stood in stark contrast to the sociology that preceded him in Britain. However, the reaction against Spencer was based more on the threat that his idea of survival of the fittest posed to the ameliorism so dear to most early British sociologists. Although Spencer later repudiated some of his more outrageous ideas, he *did* argue for a survival-of-the-fittest philosophy and against government intervention and social reform:

> Fostering the good-for-nothing at the expense of the good, is an extreme cruelty. It is a deliberate stirring-up of miseries for future generations. There is no greater curse to posterity than that of bequeathing to them an increasing population of imbeciles and idlers and criminals. . . . The whole effort of nature is to get rid of such, to clear the world of them, and make room for better. . . . If they are not sufficiently complete to live, they die, and it is best they should die.
>
> (Spencer, cited in Abrams, 1968:74)

Such sentiments were clearly at odds with the ameliorative orientation of the British reformer-sociologists.

The Key Figure in Early Italian Sociology

We close this sketch of early, primarily conservative, European sociological theory with a brief mention of one Italian sociologist, Vilfredo Pareto (1848–1923). Pareto was influential in his time, but his contemporary relevance is minimal (for one exception, see Powers, 1986). There was a brief outburst of interest in Pareto's (1935) work in the 1930s, when the major American theorist, Talcott Parsons, devoted as much attention to him as he gave to Weber and Durkheim. However, in recent years, except for a few of his major concepts, Pareto also has receded in importance and contemporary relevance (Femia, 1995).

Zeitlin argued that Pareto developed his "major ideas as a refutation of Marx" (1981:171). In fact, Pareto was rejecting not only Marx but also a good portion of Enlightenment philosophy. For example, whereas the Enlightenment philosophers emphasized rationality, Pareto emphasized the role of nonrational factors such as human instincts. This emphasis also was tied to his rejection of Marxian theory. That is, because nonrational, instinctual factors were so important *and* so unchanging, it was unrealistic to hope to achieve dramatic social changes with an economic revolution.

Pareto also developed a theory of social change that stood in stark contrast to Marxian theory. Whereas Marx's theory focused on the role of the masses, Pareto offered an elite theory of social change, which held that society inevitably is dominated by a small elite that operates on the basis of enlightened self-interest. It rules over the masses of people, who are dominated by nonrational forces. Because they lack rational capacities, the masses, in Pareto's system, are unlikely to be a revolutionary force. Social change occurs when the elite begins to degenerate and is replaced by a new elite derived from the nongoverning elite or higher elements of the masses. Once the new elite is in power, the process begins anew. Thus, we have a cyclical theory of social change instead of the directional theories offered by Marx, Comte, Spencer, and others. In addition, Pareto's theory of change largely ignores the plight of the masses. Elites come and go, but the lot of the masses remains the same.

This theory, however, was not Pareto's lasting contribution to sociology. That lay in his scientific conception of sociology and the social world: "My wish is to construct a system of sociology on the model of celestial mechanics [astronomy], physics, chemistry" (cited in Hook, 1965:57). Briefly, Pareto conceived of society as a system in equilibrium, a whole consisting of interdependent parts. A change in one part was seen as leading to changes in other parts of the system. Pareto's systemic conception of society was the most important reason Parsons devoted so much attention to Pareto's work in his 1937 book, *The Structure of Social Action,* and it was Pareto's most important influence on Parsons's thinking. Fused with similar views held by those who had an organic image of society (Comte, Durkheim, and Spencer, for example), Pareto's theory played a central role in the development of Parsons's theory and, more generally, in structural functionalism.

Although few modern sociologists now read Pareto's work, it can be seen as a rejection of the Enlightenment and of Marxism and as offering an elite theory of social change that stands in opposition to the Marxian perspective.

Turn-of-the-Century Developments in European Marxism

While many nineteenth-century sociologists were developing their theories in opposition to Marx, there was a simultaneous effort by a number of Marxists to clarify and extend Marxian theory. Between roughly 1875 and 1925, there was little overlap between Marxism and sociology. (Weber is an exception to this.) The two schools of thought were developing in parallel fashion with little or no interchange between them.

After the death of Marx, Marxian theory was first dominated by those who saw in his theory scientific and economic determinism. Wallerstein calls this the era of "orthodox Marxism" (1986:1301). Friedrich Engels, Marx's benefactor and collaborator, lived on after Marx's death and can be seen as the first exponent of such a perspective. Basically, this view was that Marx's scientific theory had uncovered the economic laws that ruled the capitalist world. Such laws pointed to the inevitable collapse of the capitalist system. Early Marxian thinkers, like Karl Kautsky, sought to gain a better understanding of the operation of these laws. There were several problems with this perspective. For one thing, it seemed to rule out political action, a cornerstone of Marx's position. That is, there seemed no need for individuals, especially workers, to do anything. In that the system was inevitably crumbling, all they had to do was sit back and wait for its demise. On a theoretical level, deterministic Marxism seemed to rule out the dialectical relationship between individuals and larger social structures.

These problems led to a reaction among Marxian theorists and to the development of "Hegelian Marxism" in the early 1900s. The Hegelian Marxists refused to reduce Marxism to a scientific theory that ignored individual thought and action. They are labeled *Hegelian Marxists* because they sought to combine Hegel's interest in consciousness (which some, including the author of this text, view Marx as sharing) with the determinists' interest in the economic structures of society. The Hegelian theorists were significant for both theoretical and practical reasons. Theoretically, they reinstated the importance of the individual, consciousness, and the relationship between thought and action. Practically, they emphasized the importance of individual action in bringing about a social revolution.

The major exponent of this point of view was Georg Lukács (Fischer, 1984). According to Martin Jay, Lukács was "the founding father of Western Marxism" and his work *Class and Class Consciousness* is "generally acknowledged as the charter document of Hegelian Marxism" (1984:84). Lukács had begun in the early 1900s to integrate Marxism with sociology (in particular, Weberian and Simmelian theory). This integration was soon to accelerate with the development of critical theory in the 1920s and 1930s.

THE CONTEMPORARY RELEVANCE OF CLASSICAL SOCIOLOGICAL THEORY

Classical sociological theories are important not only historically (Camic, 1997), but also because they are living documents with contemporary relevance to both modern theorists and today's social world. Tiryakian (1994) has outlined three criteria for judging a sociological work a classic. First, it is "must reading" for beginners because it demonstrates "the power and imagination of sociological analysis" (Tiryakian, 1994:4). Second, it is useful to both contemporary theorists and researchers. That is, new theories are built on the shoulders of the classic theorists and their work generates hypotheses to be tested empirically by modern researchers. Third, it is of sufficient richness and depth that it is worth rereading at a later point in a sociologist's career.

The works of the theorists discussed at least in some depth in this chapter qualify as classics in terms of these criteria. More specifically, the work of the classic thinkers continues to inspire modern sociologists in a variety of different ways. Let us look briefly at just a few examples of this kind of work.

While Durkheim has usually been seen as a political conservative, some recent commentators have tended to see a more radical, even revolutionary, strand in Durkheimian theory (Gane, 1992; Pearce, 1989). In fact, Pearce's major theme is "that the development of many of Durkheim's concepts can be used to help specify a realistic set of socialist goals" (1989:10). Alexander (1988b) has used some of Durkheim's ideas on culture and religion to analyze the Watergate scandal, for example, the ritualistic aspects of the Watergate hearings and other aspects of the scandal. Mestrovic (1992:158) has addressed Durkheim's work in light of the contemporary conflict between modern and postmodern thinkers and has concluded that Durkheimian theory provides the seeds of a perspective that is preferable to either of the others: "Durkheim was seeking a new world order that would preserve . . . progress and capitalist efficiency [the modern viewpoint], but that would be balanced with . . . mystic sympathy and sense of international social solidarity [a more postmodern viewpoint]." Lehmann (1993a) has used a key tool of the postmodernists, "deconstruction," to analyze Durkheim's work. (Lehmann [1993b] has also been in the forefront of studying Durkheim's ideas in light of feminist theory.) Specific aspects of Durkheim's work have also spawned a great deal of contemporary thought and research, but none more than his work on suicide and its various correlates (Skog, 1991).

Similarly, Weinstein and Weinstein (1993) have presented a "postmodernized" version of Simmelian theory to complement the well-known modern side of Simmel's perspective. Ritzer (1995) has used aspects of Simmel's theory to highlight many of the central problems associated with the increasingly global credit card society, especially the "temptation to imprudence," fraud, and threats to privacy.

The challenge in interpreting Marx's theory is the recent failure of communist nations ostensibly built on his principles. However, many Marxists feel that those nations were highly distorted versions of Marx's communist vision, and with those distortions out of the way it will now be possible to gain a clearer sense of Marx's ideas. As Graham says, "the enterprise of assessing Marx seems to me to be in its infancy" (1992:165). Thus, rather than being a dusty historical figure, Graham contends that "Marx is our contemporary" (1992:165).

On the contemporary relevance of Weber, Goldman argues that "there is continuity between many of Weber's concerns and the concerns of contemporary sociology . . . Weber still has much to contribute to the development of contemporary sociology" (1993:859). Said Collins, "Reading Weber, for some of us, is at least as worthwhile as reading contemporary writers on the same topics, if not more so. Weber is deeper, more analytical, more comprehensive . . . Weber in many respects is still the state of the art" (1993a:861). Examinations of the success of the Japanese (Ritzer and LeMoyne, 1991), and more generally a number of Asian (Biggart 1991), economies have been based on Weberian theory. As mentioned earlier, Ritzer (1996) has used Weber's rationalization theory to analyze the McDonaldization of society and more specifically the McDonaldization of credit through the widespread dissemination of credit cards (Ritzer, 1995: chapter 6). More specifically, Weber's most famous book, *The Protestant Ethic and the Spirit of Capitalism,* has over the years spawned an enormous body of work, and such work continues (Davies, 1992; Silber, 1993).

Of notable interest in this context is the work of the early women sociologists to be discussed in Chapter 9. In many cases their work has been, or is just now being, rediscovered (Rogers, 1998). Thus, we are at the very early stages of the exploration of the contemporary relevance of the ideas of the classic female sociological thinkers. We can expect the list of contemporary effects to grow exponentially in the coming years.

SUMMARY

This chapter sketches the early history of sociological theory. The first, and much briefer, section deals with the various social forces involved in the development of sociological theory. Although there were many such influences, we focus on how political revolution, the Industrial Revolution, and the rise of capitalism, socialism, feminism, urbanization, religious change, and the growth of science affected sociological theory. The second part of the chapter examines the influence of intellectual forces on the rise of sociological theory in various countries. We begin with France and the role played by the Enlightenment, stressing the conservative and romantic reaction to it. It is out of this interplay that French sociological theory developed. In this context, we examine the major figures in the early years of French sociology—Claude Henri Saint-Simon, Auguste Comte, and Emile Durkheim.

Next we turn to Germany and the role played by Karl Marx in the development of sociology in that country. We discuss the parallel development of Marxian theory and sociological theory and the ways in which Marxian theory influenced sociology, both positively and negatively. We begin with the roots of Marxian theory in Hegelianism, materialism, and political economy. Marx's theory itself is touched upon briefly. The discussion then shifts to the roots of German sociology. Max Weber's work is examined in order to show the diverse sources of German sociology. Also discussed are some of the reasons that Weber's theory proved more acceptable to later sociologists than did Marx's ideas. This section closes with a brief discussion of Georg Simmel's work.

The rise of sociological theory in Britain is considered next. The major sources of British sociology were political economy, ameliorism, and social evolution. In this context, we touch on the work of Herbert Spencer as well as on some of the controversy that surrounded it.

This discussion is followed by a brief discussion of Italian sociological theory, in particular the work of Vilfredo Pareto, and the turn-of-the-century developments in European Marxian theory, primarily economic determinism and Hegelian Marxism. Finally, there is a brief discussion of the contemporary relevance of classical sociological theory.

This concludes our review of the early history of sociological theory. In this chapter, we have already discussed, in historical context, the work of six theorists who will later receive full-chapter treatment—Comte, Spencer, Marx, Durkheim, Weber, and Simmel. We will also touch on these theorists in the next chapter in terms of their influence on later sociological theory. Chapter 2 will also include a brief discussion, within the historical context of more recent theoretical developments, of the work of other theorists defined here as classical thinkers and treated in depth later in the book—Veblen, Mead, Mannheim, Schutz, and Parsons.

Finally, while we have mentioned feminist theory and the early women sociological theorists in this chapter, we have not had much to say about the nature and impact of their work. That is because, as we will see in Chapter 9, their work was largely excluded from mainstream sociological thinking and had little impact on its development. Chapter 9 can be viewed as a first effort to help rectify this omission and exclusion.

2

A HISTORICAL SKETCH OF SOCIOLOGICAL THEORY: THE LATER YEARS

EARLY AMERICAN SOCIOLOGICAL THEORY
  Politics
  Social Change and Intellectual Currents
  The Chicago School
WOMEN IN EARLY SOCIOLOGY
SOCIOLOGICAL THEORY TO MID-CENTURY
  The Rise of Harvard, the Ivy League, and Structural Functionalism
  The Chicago School in Decline
  Developments in Marxian Theory
  Karl Mannheim and the Sociology of Knowledge
SOCIOLOGICAL THEORY FROM MID-CENTURY
  Structural Functionalism: Peak and Decline
  Radical Sociology in America: C. Wright Mills
  The Development of Conflict Theory
  The Birth of Exchange Theory
  Dramaturgical Analysis: The Work of Erving Goffman
  The Development of Sociologies of Everyday Life
  The Rise and Fall (?) of Marxian Sociology
  The Challenge of Feminist Theory
  Structuralism and Poststructuralism
RECENT DEVELOPMENTS IN SOCIOLOGICAL THEORY
  Micro-Macro Integration
  Agency-Structure Integration
  Theoretical Syntheses
THEORIES OF MODERNITY AND POSTMODERNITY
  The Defenders of Modernity
  The Proponents of Postmodernity
THEORIES TO WATCH IN THE EARLY TWENTY-FIRST CENTURY
  Multicultural Social Theory
  Postmodern and Post-Postmodern Social Theories
  Theories of Consumption
  Others

It is difficult to give a precise date for the founding of sociology in the United States. There was a course in social problems taught at Oberlin as early as 1858, Comte's term *sociology* was used by George Fitzhugh in 1854, and William Graham Sumner taught social science courses at Yale beginning in 1873. During the 1880s, courses specifically bearing the title "Sociology" began to appear. The first department with *sociology* in its title was founded at the University of Kansas in 1889. In 1892, Albion Small moved to the University of Chicago and set up the new department of sociology. The Chicago department became the first important center of American sociology in general and of sociological theory in particular (F. Matthews, 1977).

EARLY AMERICAN SOCIOLOGICAL THEORY

Politics

Schwendinger and Schwendinger (1974) argue that the early American sociologists are best described as political liberals and not, as was true of most early European theorists, as conservatives. The liberalism characteristic of early American sociology had basically two elements. First, it operated with a belief in the freedom and welfare of the individual. In this belief, it was influenced far more by Spencer's orientation than by Comte's more collective position. Second, many sociologists associated with this orientation adopted an evolutionary view of social progress (Fine, 1979). However, they split over how best to bring about this progress. Some argued that steps should be taken by the government to aid social reform, while others pushed a laissez-faire doctrine, arguing that the various components of society should be left to solve their own problems.

Liberalism, taken to its extreme, comes very close to conservatism. The belief in social progress—in reform or a laissez-faire doctrine—and the belief in the importance of the individual both lead to positions supportive of the system as a whole. The overriding belief is that the social system works or can be reformed to work. There is little criticism of the system as a whole; in the American case this means, in particular, that there is little questioning of capitalism. Instead of imminent class struggle, the early sociologists saw a future of class harmony and class cooperation. Ultimately this meant that early American sociological theory helped to rationalize exploitation, domestic and international imperialism, and social inequality (Schwendinger and Schwendinger, 1974). In the end, the political liberalism of the early sociologists had enormously conservative implications.

Social Change and Intellectual Currents

In their analyses of the founding of American sociological theory, Roscoe Hinkle (1980) and Ellsworth Fuhrman (1980) outline several basic contexts from which that body of theory emerged. Of utmost importance are the social changes that occurred in American society after the Civil War (Bramson, 1961). In Chapter 1, we discussed an array of factors involved in the development of European sociological theory; several of these factors (such as industrialization and urbanization) were also intimately involved in the development of theory in America. In Fuhrman's view, the early American sociologists saw the positive possibilities of industrialization, but they were also well aware of its dangers. Although these early sociologists were attracted to the ideas generated by the labor movement and socialist groups about dealing with the dangers of industrialization, they were not in favor of radically overhauling society.

Arthur Vidich and Stanford Lyman (1985) make a strong case for the influence of Christianity, especially Protestantism, on the founding of American sociology. American sociologists retained the Protestant interest in saving the world and merely substituted one language (science) for another (religion). "From 1854, when the first works in sociology appeared in the United States, until the outbreak of World War I, sociology was a moral and intellectual response to the problems of American life and thought, institutions, and creeds" (Vidich and Lyman, 1985:1). Sociologists sought to define, study, and help solve these social problems. While the clergyman worked within religion to help improve it and people's lot within it, the sociologist did the same within society. Given their religious roots, and the religious parallels, the vast majority of sociologists did not challenge the basic legitimacy of society.

Another major factor in the founding of American sociology discussed by both Hinkle and Fuhrman is the simultaneous emergence in America, in the late 1800s, of academic professions (including sociology) and the modern university system. In Europe, in contrast, the university system was already well established *before* the emergence of sociology. Although sociology had a difficult time becoming established in Europe, it found the going easier in the more fluid setting of the new American university system.

Another characteristic of early American sociology (as well as other social science disciplines) was its turn away from a historical perspective and in the direction of a positivistic, or "scientistic," orientation. As Ross puts it, "The desire to achieve universalistic abstraction and quantitative methods turned American social scientists away from interpretive models available in history and cultural anthropology, and from the generalizing and interpretive model offered by Max Weber" (1991:473). Instead of interpreting long-term historical changes, sociology had turned in the direction of scientifically studying short-term processes.

Still another factor was the impact of established European theory on American sociological theory. European theorists largely created sociological theory, and the Americans were able to rely on this groundwork. The Europeans most important to the Americans were Spencer and Comte. Simmel was of some importance in the early years, but the influence of Durkheim, Weber, and Marx was not to have a dramatic effect for a number of years. As an illustration of the impact of early European theory on American sociology, the history of the ideas of Herbert Spencer is interesting and informative.

Herbert Spencer's Influence on Sociology   Why were Spencer's ideas so much more influential in the early years of American sociology than those of Comte, Durkheim, Marx, and Weber? Hofstadter (1959) offered several explanations. To take the easiest first, Spencer wrote in English, while the others did not. In addition, Spencer

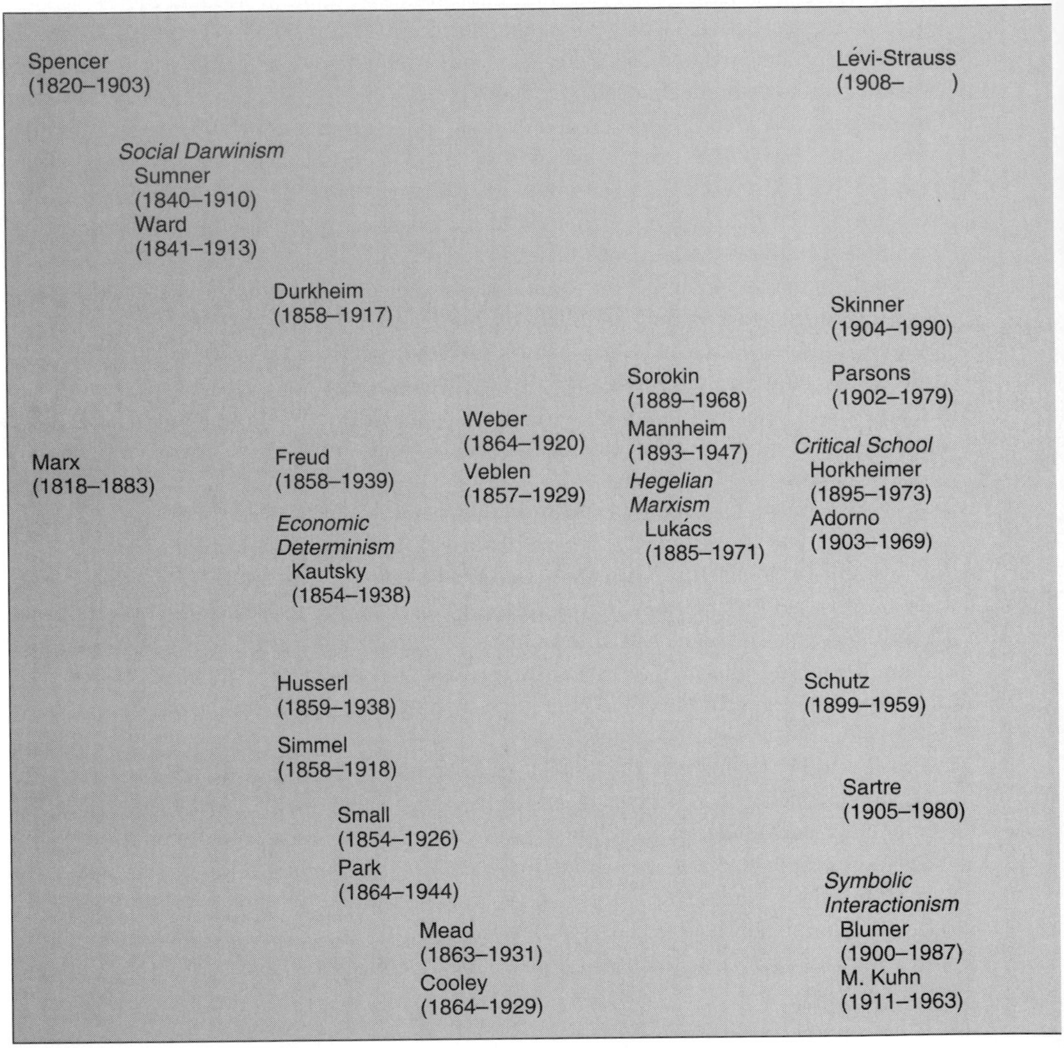

Spencer
(1820–1903)

Lévi-Strauss
(1908–   )

Social Darwinism
Sumner
(1840–1910)
Ward
(1841–1913)

Durkheim
(1858–1917)

Skinner
(1904–1990)

Sorokin
(1889–1968)

Parsons
(1902–1979)

Weber
(1864–1920)

Mannheim
(1893–1947)

Marx
(1818–1883)

Freud
(1858–1939)

Veblen
(1857–1929)

Critical School
Horkheimer
(1895–1973)

*Hegelian
Marxism*

*Economic
Determinism*
Kautsky
(1854–1938)

Lukács
(1885–1971)

Adorno
(1903–1969)

Husserl
(1859–1938)

Schutz
(1899–1959)

Simmel
(1858–1918)

Small
(1854–1926)
Park
(1864–1944)

Sartre
(1905–1980)

*Symbolic
Interactionism*
Blumer
(1900–1987)
M. Kuhn
(1911–1963)

Mead
(1863–1931)
Cooley
(1864–1929)

FIGURE 2.1
Sociological Theory: The Later Years

Structuralism

Poststructuralism
Foucault (1926–1984)

Network Theory
Rational Choice Theory
Coleman
(1926–1995)

Exchange Theory
Blau
(1918–   )
Emerson
(1925–1982)

Homans
(1910–1989)

Postmodern
Social Theory
Baudrillard
(1929–   )

Structural Functionalism
Merton
(1910–   )

Neofunctionalism
Alexander
(1947–   )

Systems Theory
Luhmann
(1927–1998)

Post-Postmodern
Social Theory

Radical Sociology
Mills
(1916–1962)

Conflict Theory
Dahrendorf
(1929–   )

Structural Marxism
Althusser
(1918–1990)

Feminist
Sociological Theory

Micro-Macro and
Agency Structure
Integration Theory

Economic Marxism
Sweezy
(1910–   )
Braverman
(1920–1976)

Habermas
(1929–   )

Synthetic
Theory

Theories of
Consumption

Multiculturalism

Historical Marxism
Wallerstein
(1930–   )

Phenomenological
Sociology
Berger
(1929–   )
Luckmann
(1927–   )

Theories of
Modernity
Giddens
(1938–   )

Ethnomethodology
Garfinkel
(1929–   )

Existential Sociology
Goffman
(1922–1982)

wrote in nontechnical terms, thereby making his work broadly accessible. Indeed, some have argued that the lack of technicality is traceable to Spencer's *not* being a very sophisticated scholar. But there are other, more important reasons for Spencer's broad appeal. He offered a scientific orientation that was attractive to an audience becoming enamored of science and its technological products. He offered a comprehensive theory that seemed to deal with the entire sweep of human history. The breadth of his ideas, as well as the voluminous work he produced, allowed his theory to be many different things to many different people. Finally, and perhaps most important, his theory was soothing and reassuring to a society undergoing the wrenching process of industrialization—society was, according to Spencer, steadily moving in the direction of greater and greater progress.

Spencer's most famous American disciple was William Graham Sumner, who accepted and expanded upon many of Spencer's Social Darwinist ideas. Spencer also influenced other early American sociologists, among them Lester Ward, Charles Horton Cooley, E. A. Ross, and Robert Park.

By the 1930s, however, Spencer was in eclipse in the intellectual world in general, as well as in sociology. His Social Darwinist, laissez-faire ideas seemed ridiculous in the light of massive social problems, a world war, and a major economic depression. In 1937 Talcott Parsons announced Spencer's intellectual death for sociology when he echoed historian Crane Brinton's words of a few years earlier, "Who now reads Spencer?" Today Spencer is of little more than historical interest, but his ideas *were* important in shaping early American sociological theory. Let us look briefly at the work of two American theorists who were influenced, at least in part, by Spencer's work.

William Graham Sumner (1840–1910)   William Graham Sumner was the person who taught the first course in the United States that could be called sociology. Sumner contended that he had begun teaching sociology "years before any such attempt was made at any other university in the world" (Curtis, 1981:63).

Sumner was the major exponent of Social Darwinism in the United States, although he appeared to change his view late in life (N. Smith, 1979). The following exchange between Sumner and one of his students illustrates his "liberal" views on the need for individual freedom and his position against government interference:

> "Professor, don't you believe in any government aid to industries?"
>   "No! It's root, hog, or die."
>   "Yes, but hasn't the hog got a right to root?"
>   "There are no rights. The world owes nobody a living."
>   "You believe then, Professor, in only one system, the contract-competitive system?"
>   "That's the only sound economic system. All others are fallacies."
>   "Well, suppose some professor of political economy came along and took your job away from you. Wouldn't you be sore?"
>   "Any other professor is welcome to try. If he gets my job, it is my fault. My business is to teach the subject so well that no one can take the job away from me."
>   (Phelps, cited in Hofstadter, 1959:54)

Sumner basically adopted a survival-of-the-fittest approach to the social world. Like Spencer, he saw people struggling against their environment, and the fittest were those who would be successful. Thus Sumner was a supporter of human aggressiveness and competitiveness. Those who succeeded deserved it, and those who did not succeed deserved to fail. Again like Spencer, Sumner was opposed to efforts, especially government efforts, to aid those who had failed. In his view such intervention operated against the natural selection that, among people as among lower animals, allowed the fit to survive and the unfit to perish. As Sumner put it, "If we do not like the survival of the fittest, we have only one possible alternative, and that is survival of the unfittest" (Curtis, 1981:84). This theoretical system fit in well with the development of capitalism because it provided theoretical legitimacy for the existence of great differences in wealth and power.

Sumner is of little more than historical interest for two main reasons. First, his orientation and Social Darwinism in general have come to be regarded as little more than a crude legitimation of competitive capitalism and the status quo. Second, he failed to build a solid enough base at Yale to build a school of sociology with many disciples. That kind of success was to occur some years later at the University of Chicago (Heyl and Heyl, 1976). In spite of success in his time, "Sumner is remembered by few today" (Curtis, 1981:146).

Lester F. Ward (1841–1913)   Lester Ward had an unusual career in that he spent most of it as a paleontologist working for the federal government. During that time, Ward read Spencer and Comte and developed a strong interest in sociology. He published a number of works in the late 1800s and early 1900s in which he expounded his sociological theory. As a result of the fame that this work achieved, in 1906 Ward was elected the first president of the American Sociological Society. It was only then that he took his first academic position, at Brown University, a position that he held until his death.

Ward, like Sumner, accepted the idea that people had evolved from lower forms to their present status. He believed that early society was characterized by its simplicity and its moral poverty, whereas modern society was more complex, happier, and offered greater freedom. One task of sociology, *pure sociology,* was to study the basic laws of social change and social structure. But Ward was not content simply to have sociology study social life. He believed that sociology should have a practical side; there should also be an *applied sociology.* This applied sociology involved the conscious use of scientific knowledge to attain a better society. Thus, Ward was not an extreme Social Darwinist; he believed in the need for and importance of social reform.

Although of historical importance, Sumner and Ward have not been of long-term significance to sociological theory. We turn now, however, first briefly to a theorist of the time, Thorstein Veblen, who has been of long-term significance and whose influence today in sociology is increasing, and then to a group of theorists, especially Mead, and to a school, the Chicago school, that came to dominate sociology in America. The Chicago school was unusual in the history of sociology in that it was one of the few (the Durkheimian school in Paris was another) "collective intellectual enterprises of an integrated kind" in the history of sociology (Bulmer, 1984:1). The tradition begun at the University of Chicago is of continuing importance to sociology and its theoretical (and empirical) status.

Thorstein Veblen (1857–1929)   Veblen, who was not a sociologist but mainly held positions in economics departments, and even in economics was a marginal figure, nonetheless produced a body of social theory that is of enduring significance to those in a number of disciplines, including sociology. The central problem for Veblen was the clash between "business" and "industry." By business, Veblen meant the owners, leaders, "captains" of industry who focused on the profits of their own companies, but to keep prices and profits high, often engaged in efforts to limit production. In so doing they obstructed the operation of the industrial system and adversely affected society as a whole (through higher rates of unemployment, for example), which is best served by the unimpeded operation of industry. Thus, business leaders were the source of many problems within society, which, Veblen felt, should be led by people (e.g., engineers) who understood the industrial system and its operation and were interested in the general welfare.

Most of Veblen's importance today is traceable to his book *The Theory of the Leisure Class* (1899/1994). Veblen is critical of the leisure class (which is closely tied to business) for its role in fostering wasteful consumption. To impress the rest of society, the leisure class engaged in both "conspicuous leisure" (the nonproductive use of time) and "conspicuous consumption" (spending more money on goods than they are worth). Those in all other social classes are influenced by this example and seek, directly and indirectly, to emulate the leisure class. The result is a society characterized by the waste of time and money. What is of utmost importance about this work is that unlike most other sociological works of the time (as well as most of Veblen's other works), *The Theory of the Leisure Class* focuses on consumption rather than production. Thus, it anticipated the current shift in social theory away from a focus on production toward a focus on consumption (Slater, 1997; Ritzer, 1999).

The Chicago School[1]

The department of sociology at the University of Chicago was founded in 1892 by Albion Small. Small's intellectual work is of less contemporary significance than the key role he played in the institutionalization of sociology in the United States (Faris, 1970; Matthews, 1977). He was instrumental in creating a department at Chicago that was to become the center of the discipline in the United States for many years. Small collaborated on the first textbook in sociology in 1894. In 1895 he founded the *American Journal of Sociology,* a journal that to this day is a dominant force in the discipline. In 1905, Small cofounded the American Sociological Society, *the* major professional association of American sociologists to this date (Rhoades, 1981). (The embarrassment caused by the initials of the American Sociological Society, ASS, led to a name change in 1959 to the American Sociological Association—ASA.)

Early Chicago Sociology   The early Chicago department had several distinctive characteristics. For one thing, it had a strong connection with religion. Some members were ministers themselves, and others were sons of ministers. Small, for example,

---

[1]See Bulmer (1985) for a discussion of what defines a school and why we can speak of the "Chicago school." Tiryakian (1979, 1986) also deals with schools in general, and the Chicago school in particular, and emphasizes the role played by charismatic leaders as well as methodological innovations. See also Amsterdamska (1985). For a discussion of this school within the broader context of developments within American sociological theory, see Hinkle (1994).

believed that "the ultimate goal of sociology must be essentially Christian" (Matthews, 1977:95). This opinion led to a view that sociology must be interested in social reform, and this view was combined with a belief that sociology should be scientific.[2] Scientific sociology with an objective of social amelioration was to be practiced in the burgeoning city of Chicago, which was beset by the positive *and* negative effects of urbanization and industrialization.

W. I. Thomas (1863–1947)   In 1895, W. I. Thomas became a fellow at the Chicago department, where he wrote his dissertation in 1896. Thomas's lasting significance was in his emphasis on the need to do scientific research on sociological issues (Lodge, 1986). Although he championed this position for many years, its major statement came in 1918 with the publication of *The Polish Peasant in Europe and America,* which Thomas coauthored with Florian Znaniecki. Martin Bulmer sees it as a "landmark" study because it moved sociology away from "abstract theory and library research and toward the study of the empirical world utilizing a theoretical framework" (1984:45). Norbert Wiley sees *The Polish Peasant* as crucial to the founding of sociology in the sense of "clarifying the unique intellectual space into which this discipline alone could see and explore" (1986:20). The book was the product of eight years of research in both Europe and the United States and was primarily a study of social disorganization among Polish migrants. The data were of little lasting importance. However, the methodology was significant. It involved a variety of data sources, including autobiographical material, paid writings, family letters, newspaper files, public documents, and institutional letters.

Although *The Polish Peasant* was primarily a macrosociological study of social institutions, over the course of his career Thomas gravitated toward a microscopic, social-psychological orientation. He is best known for the following social-psychological statement (made in a book coauthored by Dorothy Thomas): "If men define situations as real, they are real in their consequences" (Thomas and Thomas, 1928:572). The emphasis was on the importance of what people think and how this affects what they do. This microscopic, social-psychological focus stood in contrast to the macroscopic, social-structural and social-cultural perspectives of such European scholars as Marx, Weber, and Durkheim. It was to become one of the defining characteristics of Chicago's theoretical product—symbolic interactionism (Rock, 1979:5).

Robert Park (1864–1944)   Another figure of significance at Chicago was Robert Park (Shils, 1996). Park had come to Chicago as a part-time instructor in 1914 and quickly worked his way into a central role in the department. Park's importance for the development of sociology lay in several areas. First, he became the dominant figure in the Chicago department, which, in turn, dominated sociology into the 1930s. Second, Park had studied in Europe and was instrumental in bringing Continental thinkers to the attention of Chicago sociologists. Park had taken courses with Simmel, and Simmel's ideas, particularly his focus on action and interaction, were instrumental in the development of the Chicago school's theoretical orientation (Rock, 1979:36–48). Third, prior to becoming a sociologist, Park had been a reporter, and this experience gave him a

---

[2]As we will see, however, the Chicago school's conception of science was to become too "soft," at least in the eyes of the positivists who later came to dominate sociology.

ROBERT PARK: A Biographical Sketch

Robert Park did not follow the typical career route of an academic sociologist—college, graduate school, professorship. Instead, he led a varied career before he became a sociologist late in life. Despite his late start, Park had a profound effect on sociology in general and on theory in particular. Park's varied experiences gave him an unusual orientation to life, and this view helped to shape the Chicago school, symbolic interactionism, and, ultimately, a good portion of sociology.

Park was born in Harveyville, Pennsylvania, on February 14, 1864 (Matthews, 1977). As a student at the University of Michigan, he was exposed to a number of great thinkers, such as John Dewey. Although he was excited by ideas, Park felt a strong need to work in the real world. As Park said, "I made up my mind to go in for experience for its own sake, to gather into my soul . . . 'all the joys and sorrows of the world'" (1927/1973:253). Upon graduation, he began a career as a journalist, which gave him this real-world opportunity. He particularly liked to explore ("hunting down gambling houses and opium dens" [Park, 1927/1973:254]). He wrote about city life in vivid detail. He would go into the field, observe and analyze, and finally write up his observations. In fact, he was already doing essentially the kind of research ("scientific reporting") that came to be one of the hallmarks of Chicago sociology—that is, urban ethnology using participant observation techniques (Lindner, 1996).

Although the accurate description of social life remained one of his passions, Park grew dissatisfied with newspaper work, because it did not fulfill his familial or, more important, his intellectual needs. Furthermore, it did not seem to contribute to the improvement of the world, and Park had a deep interest in social reform. In 1898, at age thirty-four, Park left newspaper work and enrolled in the philosophy department at Harvard. He remained there

sense of the importance of urban problems and of the need to go out into the field to collect data through personal observation (Lindner, 1996; Strauss, 1996). Out of this emerged the Chicago school's substantive interest in urban ecology (Gaziano, 1996; Maines, Bridger and Ulmer, 1996; Perry, Abbott and Hutter, 1997). Fourth, Park played a key role in guiding graduate students and helping develop "a cumulative program of graduate research" (Bulmer, 1984:13). Finally, in 1921, Park and Ernest W. Burgess published the first truly important sociology textbook, *An Introduction to the Science of Sociology.* It was to be an influential book for many years and was particularly notable for its commitments to science, to research, and to the study of a wide range of social phenomena.

Beginning in the late 1920s and early 1930s, Park began to spend less time in Chicago. Finally, his lifelong interest in race relations (he had been secretary to Booker T. Washington before becoming a sociologist) led him to take a position at Fisk University (a black university) in 1934. Although the decline of the Chicago department was not caused solely or even chiefly by Park's departure, its status began to wane in the 1930s. But before we can deal with the decline of Chicago sociology and the rise of

for a year but then decided to move to Germany, at that time the heart of the world's intellectual life. In Berlin he encountered Georg Simmel, whose work was to have a profound influence on Park's sociology. In fact, Simmel's lectures were the *only* formal sociological training that Park received. As Park said, "I got most of my knowledge about society and human nature from my own observations" (1927/1973:257). In 1904, Park completed his doctoral dissertation at the University of Heidelberg. Characteristically, he was dissatisfied with his dissertation: "All I had to show was that little book and I was ashamed of it" (Matthews, 1977:57). He refused a summer teaching job at the University of Chicago and turned away from academe as he had earlier turned away from newspaper work.

His need to contribute to social betterment led him to become secretary and chief publicity officer for the Congo Reform Association, which was set up to help alleviate the brutality and exploitation then taking place in the Belgian Congo. During this period, he met Booker T. Washington, and he was attracted to the cause of improving the lot of black Americans. He became Washington's secretary and played a key role in the activities of the Tuskegee Institute. In 1912 he met W. I. Thomas, the Chicago sociologist, who was lecturing at Tuskegee. Thomas invited him to give a course on "the Negro in America" to a small group of graduate students at Chicago, and Park did so in 1914. The course was successful, and he gave it again the next year to an audience twice as large. At this time, he joined the American Sociological Society, and only a decade later he became its president. Park gradually worked his way into a full-time appointment at Chicago, although he did not get a full professorship until 1923, when he was fifty-nine years old. Over the approximately two decades that he was affiliated with the University of Chicago, he played a key role in shaping the intellectual orientation of the sociology department.

Park remained peripatetic even after his retirement from Chicago in the early 1930s. He taught courses and oversaw research at Fisk University until he was nearly eighty years old. He traveled extensively. He died on February 7, 1944, one week before his eightieth birthday.

other departments and theories, we need to return to the early days of the school and the two figures whose work was to be of the most lasting theoretical significance—Charles Horton Cooley and, most important, George Herbert Mead.[3]

Charles Horton Cooley (1864–1929)   The association of Cooley with the Chicago school is interesting in that he spent his career at the University of Michigan. But Cooley's theoretical perspective was in line with the theory of symbolic interactionism that was to become Chicago's most important product.

Cooley received his Ph.D. from the University of Michigan in 1894. He had developed a strong interest in sociology, but there was as yet no department of sociology at Michigan. As a result, the questions for his Ph.D. examination came from Columbia University, where sociology had been taught since 1889 under the leadership of Franklin Giddings. Cooley began his teaching career at Michigan in 1892 before completion of his doctorate.

[3]There were many other significant figures associated with the Chicago School, including Everett Hughes (Chapoulie, 1996; Strauss, 1996).

Although Cooley had a wide range of views, he is remembered today mainly for his insights into the social-psychological aspects of social life. His work in this area is in line with that of George Herbert Mead, although Mead was to have a deeper and more lasting effect on sociology than Cooley had. Cooley had an interest in consciousness, but he refused (as did Mead) to separate consciousness from the social context. This is best exemplified by a concept of his that survives to this day—the *looking-glass self*. By this concept, Cooley understood that people possess consciousness and that it is shaped in continuing social interaction.

A second basic concept that illustrates Cooley's social-psychological interests, and which is also of continuing interest and importance, is that of the primary group. *Primary groups* are intimate, face-to-face groups that play a key role in linking the actor to the larger society. Especially crucial are the primary groups of the young—mainly the family and the peer group. Within these groups, the individual grows into a social being. It is basically within the primary group that the looking-glass self emerges and that the ego-centered child learns to take others into account and, thereby, to become a contributing member of society.

Both Cooley (Winterer, 1994) and Mead rejected a *behavioristic* view of human beings, the view that people blindly and unconsciously respond to external stimuli. They believed that people had consciousness, a self, and that it was the responsibility of the sociologist to study this aspect of social reality. Cooley urged sociologists to try to put themselves in the place of the actors they were studying, to use the method of *sympathetic introspection,* in order to analyze consciousness. By analyzing what they as actors might do in various circumstances, sociologists could understand the meanings and motives that are at the base of social behavior. The method of sympathetic introspection seemed to many to be very unscientific. In this area, among others, Mead's work represents an advance over Cooley's. Nevertheless, there is a great deal of similarity in the interests of the two men, not the least of which is their shared view that sociology should focus on such social-psychological phenomena as consciousness, action, and interaction.

George Herbert Mead (1863–1931) *The* most important thinker associated with the Chicago school and symbolic interactionism was not a sociologist but a philosopher, George Herbert Mead.[4] Mead started teaching philosophy at the University of Chicago in 1894, and he taught there until his death in 1931 (G. Cook, 1993). He is something of a paradox, given his central importance in the history of sociological theory, both because he taught philosophy, not sociology, and because he published comparatively little during his lifetime. The paradox is, in part, resolved by two facts. First, Mead taught courses in social psychology in the philosophy department, and they were taken by many graduate students in sociology. His ideas had a profound effect on a number of them. These students combined Mead's ideas with those they were getting in the sociology department from people like Park and Thomas. Although at the time there was no theory known as symbolic interactionism, it was created by students out of these various inputs. Thus Mead had a deep, personal impact on the people who were later to develop symbolic interactionism. Second, these students put together their notes on Mead's courses and published a posthumous volume under his name. The work, *Mind,*

---

[4]For a dissenting view, see Lewis and Smith (1980).

Self and Society (Mead, 1934/1962), moved his ideas from the realm of oral to that of written tradition. Widely read to this day, this volume forms the main intellectual pillar of symbolic interactionism.

We deal with Mead's ideas in Chapter 12, but it is necessary at this point to underscore a few points in order to situate him historically. Mead's ideas need to be seen in the context of psychological behaviorism. Mead was quite impressed with this orientation and accepted many of its tenets. He adopted its focus on the actor and his behavior. He regarded as sensible the behaviorists' concern with the rewards and costs involved in the behaviors of the actors. What troubled Mead was that behaviorism did not seem to go far enough. That is, it excluded consciousness from serious consideration, arguing that it was not amenable to scientific study. Mead vehemently disagreed and sought to extend the principles of behaviorism to an analysis of the "mind." In so doing, Mead enunciated a focus similar to that of Cooley. But whereas Cooley's position seemed unscientific, Mead promised a more scientific conception of consciousness by extending the highly scientific principles and methods of psychological behaviorism.

Mead offered American sociology a social-psychological theory that stood in stark contrast to the primarily societal theories offered by most of the major European theorists. The most important exception was Simmel. Thus symbolic interactionism was developed, in large part, out of Simmel's interest in action and interaction and Mead's interest in consciousness. However, such a focus led to a weakness in Mead's work, as well as in symbolic interactionism in general, at the societal and cultural levels.

The Waning of Chicago Sociology   Chicago sociology reached its peak in the 1920s, but by the 1930s, with the death of Mead and the departure of Park, the department had begun to lose its position of central importance in American sociology (Cortese, 1995). Fred Matthews (1977; see also Bulmer, 1984) pinpoints several reasons for the decline of Chicago sociology, two of which seem of utmost importance.

First, the discipline had grown increasingly preoccupied with being scientific—that is, using sophisticated methods and employing statistical analysis. However, the Chicago school was viewed as emphasizing descriptive, ethnographic studies (Prus, 1996), often focusing on their subjects' personal orientations (in Thomas's terms, their "definitions of the situation"). Park came progressively to despise statistics (he called it "parlor magic") because it seemed to prohibit the analysis of subjectivity, of the idiosyncratic, and of the peculiar. The fact that important work in quantitative methods was done at Chicago (Bulmer, 1984:151–189) tended to be ignored in the face of its overwhelming association with qualitative methods.

Second, more and more individuals outside Chicago grew increasingly resentful of Chicago's dominance of both the American Sociological Society and the *American Journal of Sociology.* The Eastern Sociological Society was founded in 1930, and eastern sociologists became more vocal about the dominance of the Midwest in general and Chicago in particular (Wiley, 1979:63). By 1935, the revolt against Chicago led to a non-Chicago secretary of the association and the establishment of a new official journal, the *American Sociological Review* (Lengermann, 1979). According to Wiley, "the Chicago school had fallen like a mighty oak" (1979:63). This signaled the growth of other power centers, most notably Harvard and the Ivy League in general. Symbolic interactionism was largely an indeterminate, oral tradition and as such eventually lost ground to more explicit and codified theoretical systems like the structural functionalism associated with the Ivy League (Rock, 1979:12).

WOMEN IN EARLY SOCIOLOGY

Simultaneously with the developments at the University of Chicago described in the previous section, even sometimes in concert with them, and at the same time that Durkheim, Weber, and Simmel were creating a European sociology, and sometimes in concert with them as well, a group of women who formed a broad and surprisingly connected network of social reformers were also developing pioneering sociological theories. These women included Jane Addams (1860–1935), Charlotte Perkins Gilman (1860–1935), Anna Julia Cooper (1858–1964), Ida Wells-Barnett (1862–1931), Marianne Weber (1870–1954), and Beatrice Potter Webb (1858–1943); with the possible exception of Cooper, they can all be connected through their relationship to Jane Addams. That they are not today known or recognized in conventional histories of the discipline as sociologists or as sociological theorists is a chilling testimony to the power of gender politics within the discipline of sociology and to sociology's essentially unreflective and uncritical interpretation of its own practices. While the sociological theory of each of these women is a product of individual theoretical effort, when they are read collectively they represent a coherent and complementary statement of early feminist sociological theory.

The chief hallmarks of their theories, hallmarks which may in part account for their being passed over in the development of professional sociology, include: (1) an emphasis on women's experience and women's lives and works' being equal in importance to men's; (2) an awareness that they spoke from a situated and embodied standpoint and therefore, for the most part, not with the tone of imperious objectivity that male sociological theory would come to associate with authoritative theory making; (3) the idea that the purpose of sociology and sociological theory is social reform—that is, the end is to improve people's lives through knowledge; and (4) the claim that the chief problem for amelioration in their time was inequality. What distinguishes these early women most from each other is the nature of and the remedy for the inequality on which they focused—gender, race, or class, or the intersection of these. But all these women translated their views into social and political activism that helped to shape and change the North Atlantic societies in which they lived, and this activism was as much a part of their sense of doing sociology as creating theory was. They believed in social science research as part of both their theoretical and activist enactments of sociology and were highly creative innovators of social science method.

As the developing discipline of sociology marginalized these women as sociologists and sociological theorists, it often incorporated their research methods into its own practices, while using their activism as an excuse to define these women as "not sociologists." Thus they are remembered as social activists and social workers rather than sociologists. Their heritage is a sociological theory that is a call to action as well as to thought.

SOCIOLOGICAL THEORY TO MID-CENTURY

The Rise of Harvard, the Ivy League, and Structural Functionalism

We can trace the rise of sociology at Harvard from the arrival of Pitirim Sorokin in 1930 (Johnston, 1995). When Sorokin arrived at Harvard, there was no sociology department, but by the end of his first year one had been organized, and he had been appointed its head. Although Sorokin was a sociological theorist, and he continued to publish into the 1960s, his work is surprisingly little cited today. His theorizing has not stood the test of time very well. Sorokin's long-term significance may well have been in the creation of the Harvard sociology department and the hiring of Talcott Parsons (who had been an instructor of economics at Harvard) for the position of instructor of sociology. Parsons became *the* dominant figure in American sociology for introducing European theorists to an American audience, for his own sociological theories, and for his many students who themselves became major sociological theorists.

Pitirim Sorokin (1889–1968)   Sorokin developed a theory that, if anything, surpassed Parsons's in scope and complexity. The most complete statement of this theory is contained in the four-volume *Social and Cultural Dynamics,* published between 1937 and 1941. In it, Sorokin drew on a wide range of empirical data to develop a general theory of social and cultural change. In contrast to those who sought to develop evolutionary theories of social change, Sorokin developed a cyclical theory. He saw societies as oscillating among three different types of mentalities—sensate, ideational, and idealistic. Societies dominated by *sensatism* emphasize the role of the senses in comprehending reality; those dominated by a more transcendental and highly religious way of understanding reality are *ideational;* and *idealistic* societies are transitional types balancing sensatism and religiosity.

The motor of social change is to be found in the internal logic of each of these systems. That is, they are pressed internally to extend their mode of thinking to its logical extreme. Thus a sensate society ultimately becomes so sensual that it provides the groundwork for its own demise. As sensatism reaches its logical end point, people turn to ideational systems as a refuge. But once such a system has gained ascendancy, it too is pushed to its end point, with the result that society becomes excessively religious. The stage is then set for the rise of an idealistic culture and, ultimately, for the cycle to repeat itself. Sorokin not only developed an elaborate theory of social change, but he also marshaled detailed evidence from art, philosophy, politics, and so forth to support his theory. It was clearly an impressive accomplishment.

There is much more to Sorokin's theorizing, but this introduction should give the reader a feeling for the breadth of his work. It is difficult to explain why Sorokin has fallen out of favor in sociological theory. Perhaps it is the result of one of the things that Sorokin loved to attack, and in fact wrote a book about, *Fads and Foibles in Modern Sociology and Related Sciences* (1956). It may be that Sorokin will be rediscovered by a future generation of sociological theorists. At the moment, his work remains outside the mainstream of modern sociological theorizing.

Talcott Parsons (1902–1979)   Although he published some early essays, Parsons's major contribution in the early years was in his influence on graduate students who themselves were to become notable sociological theorists. The most famous was Robert Merton, who received his Ph.D. in 1936 and soon became a major theorist and the heart of Parsonsian-style theorizing at Columbia University. In the same year (1936), Kingsley Davis received his Ph.D., and he, along with Wilbert Moore (who received his Harvard degree in 1940), wrote one of the central works in structural-functional theory, the theory that was to become the major product of Parsons and the Parsonsians. But Parsons's influence was not restricted to the 1930s. Remarkably, he produced graduate students of great influence well into the 1960s.

The pivotal year for Parsons and for American sociological theory was 1937, the year in which he published *The Structure of Social Action.* This book was of significance to sociological theory in America for four main reasons. First, it served to introduce grand European theorizing to a large American audience. The bulk of the book was devoted to Durkheim, Weber, and Pareto. His interpretations of these theorists shaped their images in American sociology for many years.

Second, Parsons devoted almost no attention to Marx (or to Simmel [Levine, 1991a]), although he emphasized the work of Durkheim and Weber and even Pareto. As a result, Marxian theory continued to be largely excluded from legitimate sociology.

Third, *The Structure of Social Action* made the case for sociological theorizing as a legitimate and significant sociological activity. The theorizing that has taken place in the United States since then owes a deep debt to Parsons's work.

Finally, Parsons argued for specific sociological theories that were to have a profound influence on sociology. At first, Parsons was thought of, and thought of himself, as an action theorist. He seemed to focus on actors and their thoughts and actions. But by the close of his 1937 work and increasingly in his later work, Parsons sounded more like a structural-functional theorist focusing on large-scale social and cultural systems. Although Parsons argued that there was no contradiction between these theories, he became best known as a structural functionalist, and he was the primary exponent of this theory, which gained dominance within sociology and maintained that position until the 1960s. Parsons's theoretical strength, and that of structural functionalism, lay in delineating the relationships among large-scale social structures and institutions (see Chapter 14).

Parsons's major statements on his structural-functional theory came in the early 1950s in several works, most notably *The Social System* (1951 [Barber, 1994]). In that work and others, Parsons tended to concentrate on the structures of society and their relationship to each other. These structures were seen as mutually supportive and tending toward a dynamic equilibrium. The emphasis was on how order was maintained among the various elements of society (Wrong, 1994). Change was seen as an orderly process, and Parsons (1966, 1971) ultimately came to adopt a neoevolutionary view of social change. Parsons was concerned not only with the social system per se but also with its relationship to the other *action systems,* especially the cultural and personality systems. But his basic view on intersystemic relations was essentially the same as his view of intrasystemic relations, that is, that they were defined by cohesion, consensus, and order. In other words, the various *social structures* performed a variety of positive *functions* for each other.

It is clear, then, why Parsons came to be defined primarily as a *structural functional-ist*. As his fame grew, so did the strength of structural-functional theory in the United States. His work lay at the core of this theory, but his students and disciples also con-centrated on extending both the theory and its dominance in the United States.

Although Parsons played a number of important and positive roles in the history of sociological theory in the United States, his work also had negative consequences. First, he offered interpretations of European theorists that seemed to reflect his own theoretical orientation more than theirs. Many American sociologists were initially ex-posed to erroneous interpretations of the European masters. Second, as already pointed out, early in his career Parsons largely ignored Marx, with the result that Marx's ideas continued for many years on the periphery of sociology. Third, his own theory as it developed over the years had a number of serious weaknesses. However, Parsons's pre-eminence in American sociology served for many years to mute or overwhelm the crit-ics. Not until much later did the weaknesses of Parsons's theory, and more generally of structural functionalism, receive a full airing.

But we are getting too far ahead of the story, and we need to return to the early 1930s and other developments at Harvard. We can gain a good deal of insight into the devel-opment of the Harvard department by looking at it through an account of its other ma-jor figure, George Homans.

George Homans (1910–1989)   A wealthy Bostonian, George Homans received his bachelor's degree from Harvard in 1932 (Homans, 1962, 1984; see also Bell, 1992). As a result of the Great Depression, he was unemployed but certainly not penniless. In the fall of 1932, L. J. Henderson, a physiologist, was offering a course in the theories of Vil-fredo Pareto, and Homans was invited to attend and accepted. (Parsons also attended the Pareto seminars.) Homans's description of why he was drawn to and taken with Pareto says much about why American sociological theory was so highly conservative, so anti-Marxist:

> I took to Pareto because he made clear to me what I was already prepared to believe . . . Someone has said that much modern sociology is an effort to answer the arguments of the revolutionaries. As a Republican Bostonian who had not rejected his comparatively wealthy family, I felt during the thirties that I was under personal attack, above all from the Marxists. I was ready to believe Pareto because he provided me with a defense.
>
> (Homans, 1962:4)

Homans's exposure to Pareto led to a book, *An Introduction to Pareto* (coauthored with Charles Curtis), published in 1934. The publication of this book made Homans a soci-ologist even though Pareto's work was virtually the only sociology he had read up to that point.

In 1934 Homans was named a junior fellow at Harvard, a program started to avoid the problems associated with the Ph.D. program. In fact, Homans never did earn a Ph.D. even though he became one of the major sociological figures of his day. Homans was a junior fellow until 1939, and in those years he absorbed more and more sociology. In 1939 Homans was affiliated with the sociology department, but the connection was broken by the war.

PITIRIM A. SOROKIN: A Biographical Sketch

Pitirim Sorokin was born in a remote village in Russia on January 21, 1889 (Johnston, 1995). In his teenage years, and while a seminary student, Sorokin was arrested for revolutionary activities and spent four months in prison. Eventually, Sorokin made his way to St. Petersburg University and interspersed diligent studies, teaching responsibilities, and revolutionary activities that once again landed him in prison briefly. Sorokin's dissertation was scheduled to be defended in March 1917, but before his examination could take place, the Russian Revolution was under way. Sorokin was not able to earn his doctorate until 1922. Active in the revolution, but opposed to the Bolsheviks, Sorokin took a position in Kerensky's provisional government. But when the Bolsheviks emerged victorious, Sorokin once again found himself in prison, this time at the hands of the Bolsheviks. Eventually, under direct orders from Lenin, Sorokin was freed and allowed to return to the university and pick up where he had left off. However, his work was censored, and he was harassed by the secret police. Sorokin finally was allowed to leave Russia, and, after a stay in Czechoslovakia, he arrived in the United States in October 1923.

At first, Sorokin gave lectures at various universities, but eventually he obtained a position at the University of Minnesota. He soon became a full professor. Sorokin already had published several books in Russia, and he continued to turn them out at a prodigious rate in the United States. Of his productivity at Minnesota, Sorokin said, "I knew it exceeded the lifetime productivity of the average sociologist" (1963:224). Books such as *Social Mobility* and *Contemporary Sociological Theories* gave him a national reputation, and by 1929 he was offered (and accepted) the first chair at Harvard University in sociology. The position was placed in the department of economics because there was not yet a sociology department at Harvard.

Soon after his arrival at Harvard, a separate department of sociology was created, and Sorokin was named as its first chairman. In that position, Sorokin helped build the most important sociology department in the United States. During this period, Sorokin also completed what would become his best-known work, *Social and Cultural Dynamics* (1937–41).

Pitirim Sorokin has been described as "the Peck's bad boy and devil's advocate of American sociology" (R. Williams, 1980b:100). Blessed with an enormous ego, Sorokin seemed critical of almost everyone and everything. As a result, Sorokin and his work were the subject of much critical analysis. All of this is clear in an excerpt from a letter he wrote to the editor of the *American Journal of Sociology:*

> The strongly disparaging character of the reviews is a good omen for my books because of a high correlation between the damning of my books . . . and their subsequent career.

By the time Homans had returned from the war, the Department of Social Relations had been founded by Parsons at Harvard, and Homans joined it. Although Homans respected some aspects of Parsons's work, he was highly critical of Parsons's style of theorizing. A long-running exchange began between the two men that later manifested itself publicly in the pages of many books and journals. Basically, Homans argued that

> The more strongly they have been damned (and practically all my books were damned by your reviewers), the more significant and successful were my damned works.
>
> (Sorokin, 1963:229)

One of Sorokin's more interesting and long-running feuds was with Talcott Parsons. Parsons had been appointed at Harvard as an instructor of sociology when Sorokin was chairman of the department.   Under Sorokin's leadership, Parsons made very slow career progress at Harvard. Eventually, however, he emerged as the dominant sociologist at Harvard and in the United States. The conflict between Sorokin and Parsons was heightened by the extensive overlap between their theories. Despite the similarities, Parsons's work attracted a far wider and far more enduring audience than did Sorokin's. As the years went by, Sorokin developed a rather interesting attitude toward Parsons's work, which was reflected in several of his books. On the one hand, he was inclined to criticize Parsons for stealing many of his best ideas. On the other hand, he was severely critical of Parsonsian theory.

Another tension in their relationship was over graduate students. One of the great achievements of the early Harvard department was its ability to attract talented graduate students like Robert Merton. Although these students were influenced by the ideas of both men, Parsons's influence proved more enduring than Sorokin's. Merton was Sorokin's graduate assistant, but he did not accept Sorokin's theoretical orientation. When Merton submitted a paper laying out his preliminary thoughts on his dissertation, Sorokin responded: "As a term paper—it is O.K. You will get something like A—. But, from a deeper and the only important standpoint, I have to make several—and sharp—criticisms of your paper" (cited in Merton, 1989:293).

Parsons replaced Sorokin as chairman of the sociology department and transformed it into the Department of Social Relations. Of that, Sorokin said:

> So I am not responsible for whatever has happened to the department since, either for its merging with abnormal and social psychology and cultural anthropology to form a "Department of Social Relations," or for the drowning of sociology in an eclectic mass of the odds and ends of these disciplines. . . . The Department of Social Relations . . . has hardly produced as many distinguished sociologists as the Department of Sociology did . . . under my chairmanship.
>
> (Sorokin, 1963:251)

Sorokin was eventually isolated in the Harvard department, relegated to a "desolate looking" office, and reduced to putting a mimeographed statement under the doors of departmental offices claiming that Parsons had stolen his ideas (Coser, 1977:490).

Sorokin died on February 11, 1968.

Parsons's theory was not a theory at all but rather a vast system of intellectual categories into which most aspects of the social world fit. Further, Homans believed that theory should be built from the ground up on the basis of careful observations of the social world. Parsons's theory, however, started on the general theoretical level and worked its way down to the empirical level.

In his own work, Homans amassed a large number of empirical observations over the years, but it was only in the 1950s that he hit upon a satisfactory theoretical approach with which to analyze these data. That theory was psychological behaviorism, as it was best expressed in the ideas of his colleague at Harvard, the psychologist B. F. Skinner. On the basis of this perspective, Homans developed his exchange theory. We will pick up the story of this theoretical development later in the chapter. The crucial point here is that Harvard and its major theoretical product, structural functionalism, became preeminent in sociology in the late 1930s, replacing the Chicago school and symbolic interactionism.

The Chicago School in Decline

We left the Chicago department in the mid-1930s on the wane with the death of Mead, the departure of Park, the revolt of eastern sociologists, and the founding of the *American Sociological Review*. But the Chicago school did not disappear. Into the early 1950s it continued to be an important force in sociology. Important Ph.D.s were still produced there, such as Anselm Strauss and Arnold Rose. Major figures remained at Chicago, such as Everett Hughes (Faught, 1980), who was of central importance to the development of the sociology of occupations.

However, the central figure in the Chicago department in this era was Herbert Blumer (1900–1987) (*Symbolic Interaction,* 1988). He was a major exponent of the theoretical approach developed at Chicago out of the work of Mead, Cooley, Simmel, Park, Thomas, and others. In fact, it was Blumer who coined the phrase *symbolic interactionism* in 1937. Blumer played a key role in keeping this tradition alive through his teaching at Chicago. He wrote a number of essays that were instrumental in keeping symbolic interactionism vital into the 1950s. Blumer was also important because of the organizational positions he held in sociology. From 1930 to 1935, he was the secretary-treasurer of the American Sociological Society, and in 1956 he became its president. More important, he held institutional positions that affected the nature of what was published in sociology. Between 1941 and 1952, he was editor of the *American Journal of Sociology* and was instrumental in keeping it one of the major outlets for work in the Chicago tradition in general and symbolic interactionism in particular.

While the East Coast universities were coming under the sway of structural functionalism, the Midwest remained (and to some degree to this day remains) a stronghold of symbolic interactionism. In the 1940s, major symbolic interactionists fanned out across the Midwest—Arnold Rose was at Minnesota, Robert Habenstein at Missouri, Gregory Stone at Michigan State, and, most important, Manford Kuhn (1911–1963) at Iowa.

A split developed between Blumer at Chicago and Kuhn at Iowa; in fact, people began to talk of the differences between the Chicago and the Iowa schools of symbolic interactionism. Basically, the split occurred over the issue of science and methodology. Kuhn accepted the symbolic-interactionist focus on actors and their thoughts and actions, but he argued that they should be studied more scientifically—for example, by using questionnaires. Blumer was in favor of "softer" methods such as sympathetic introspection and participant observation.

Despite this flurry of activity, the Chicago school was in decline, especially given the movement of Blumer in 1952 from Chicago to the University of California at Berkeley.

Gary Alan Fine (1995) has written of the development of a "second" Chicago school emerging in the post–World War II years, but while Chicago continued to have a strong department, it did not have the strong and coherent focus on interactionism and observational research that had characterized the original Chicago school. Nonetheless, that focus was strong enough to have a profound effect on later work of this type. Whatever the state of the Chicago school, the Chicago tradition has remained alive to this day with major exponents dispersed throughout the country and the world. To take one recent example, Fine (1996) has done an observational study of restaurants from the point of view of the interaction that takes place in them and the order that is created.

Developments in Marxian Theory

From the early 1900s to the 1930s, Marxian theory had continued to develop largely independently of mainstream sociological theory. At least partially, the exception to this was the emergence of the critical, or Frankfurt, school out of the earlier Hegelian Marxism.

The idea of a school for the development of Marxian theory was the product of Felix J. Weil. The Institute of Social Research was officially founded in Frankfurt, Germany, on February 3, 1923 (Bottomore, 1984; Wiggershaus, 1994). Over the years, a number of the most famous thinkers in Marxian theory were associated with the critical school—Max Horkheimer, Theodor Adorno, Erich Fromm, Herbert Marcuse, and, more recently, Jurgen Habermas.

The Institute functioned in Germany until 1934, but by then things were growing increasingly uncomfortable under the Nazi regime. The Nazis had little use for the Marxian ideas that dominated the Institute, and their hostility was heightened because many of those associated with it were Jewish. In 1934 Horkheimer, as head of the Institute, came to New York to discuss its status with the president of Columbia University. Much to Horkheimer's surprise, he was invited to affiliate the Institute with the university, and he was even offered a building on campus. And so *a* center of Marxian theory moved to *the* center of the capitalist world. The Institute stayed there until the end of the war, but after the war, pressure mounted to return it to Germany. In 1949, Horkheimer did return to Germany, and he brought the Institute with him. Although the Institute itself moved to Germany, many of the figures associated with it took independent career directions.

It is important to underscore a few of the most important aspects of critical theory. In its early years, those associated with the Institute tended to be fairly traditional Marxists devoting a good portion of their attention to the economic domain. But around 1930, a major change took place as this group of thinkers began to shift its attention from the economy to the cultural system, which it came to see as the major force in modern capitalist society. This was consistent with, but an extension of, the position taken earlier by Hegelian Marxists like Georg Lukács. To help them understand the cultural domain, the critical theorists were attracted to the work of Max Weber. The effort to combine

Marx and Weber and thereby create "Weberian Marxism"[5] (Dahms, 1997; Lowy, 1996) gave the critical school some of its distinctive orientations and served in later years to make it more legitimate to sociologists who began to grow interested in Marxian theory.

A second major step taken by at least some members of the critical school was to employ the rigorous social-scientific techniques developed by American sociologists to research issues of interest to Marxists. This, like the adoption of Weberian theory, made the critical school more acceptable to mainstream sociologists.

Third, critical theorists made an effort to integrate individually oriented Freudian theory with the societal- and cultural-level insights of Marx and Weber. This seemed to many sociologists to represent a more inclusive theory than that offered by either Marx or Weber alone. If nothing else, the effort to combine such disparate theories proved stimulating to sociologists and many other intellectuals.

The critical school has done much useful work since the 1920s, and a significant amount of it is of relevance to sociologists. However, the critical school had to await the late 1960s before it was "discovered" by large numbers of American theorists.

Karl Mannheim and the Sociology of Knowledge

Brief mention should be made at this point of the work of Karl Mannheim (1893–1947) (Kettler and Meja, 1995). Born in Hungary, Mannheim was forced to move first to Germany and later to England. Influenced by the work of Marx on ideology, as well as that of Weber, Simmel, and the neo-Marxist Georg Lukács, Mannheim is best known for his work on systems of knowledge (for example, conservatism). In fact, he is almost single-handedly responsible for the creation of the contemporary field known as the sociology of knowledge. Also of significance is his thinking on rationality, which tends to pick up themes developed in Weber's work on this topic but deals with them in a far more concise and a much clearer manner (Ritzer, 1998).

From a base in England starting in the 1930s, Karl Mannheim was busy creating a set of theoretical ideas that provided the foundation for an area of sociology—the sociology of knowledge—that continues to be important to this day (McCarthy, 1996). Mannheim, of course, built on the work of many predecessors, most notably Karl Marx (although Mannheim was far from being a Marxist). Basically, the sociology of knowledge involves the systematic study of knowledge, ideas, or intellectual phenomena in general. To Mannheim, knowledge is determined by social existence. For example, Mannheim seeks to relate the ideas of a group to their position in the social structure. Marx did this by relating ideas to social classes, but Mannheim extends this perspective by linking ideas to a variety of different positions within society (for example, differences between generations).

In addition to playing a major role in creating the sociology of knowledge, Mannheim is perhaps best known for his distinction between two idea systems— *ideology* and *utopia* (B. Turner, 1995). An ideology is an idea system that seeks to conceal and conserve the present by interpreting it from the point of view of the past.

---

[5]This label fits some critical theorists better than others and it also applies to a wide range of other thinkers (Agger, 1998).

A utopia, in contrast, is a system of ideas that seeks to transcend the present by focusing on the future. Conflict between ideologies and utopias is an ever-present reality in society.

SOCIOLOGICAL THEORY FROM MID-CENTURY

Structural Functionalism: Peak and Decline

The 1940s and 1950s were paradoxically the years of greatest dominance and the beginnings of the decline of structural functionalism. In these years, Parsons produced his major statements that clearly reflected his shift from action theory to structural functionalism. Parsons's students had fanned out across the country and occupied dominant positions in many of the major sociology departments (for example, Columbia and Cornell). These students were producing works of their own that were widely recognized contributions to structural-functional theory. For example, in 1945 Kingsley Davis and Wilbert Moore published an essay analyzing social stratification from a structural-functional perspective. It was one of the clearest statements ever made of the structural-functional view. In it, they argued that stratification was a structure that was functionally necessary for the existence of society. In other words, in ideological terms they came down on the side of inequality.

In 1949 Merton (1949/1968) published an essay that became *the* program statement of structural functionalism. In it, Merton carefully sought to delineate the essential elements of the theory and to extend it in some new directions. He made it clear that structural functionalism should deal not only with positive functions but also with negative consequences (dysfunctions). Moreover, it should focus on the net balance of functions and dysfunctions or whether a structure is overall more functional or more dysfunctional.

However, just as it was gaining theoretical hegemony, structural functionalism came under attack, and the attacks mounted until they reached a crescendo in the 1960s and 1970s. The Davis-Moore structural-functional theory of stratification was attacked from the start, and the criticisms persist to this day. Beyond that, a series of more general criticisms received even wider recognition in the discipline. There was an attack by C. Wright Mills on Parsons in 1959, and other major criticisms were mounted by David Lockwood (1956), Alvin Gouldner (1959/1967, 1970), and Irving Horowitz (1962/1967). In the 1950s, these attacks were seen as little more than "guerrilla raids," but as sociology moved into the 1960s, the dominance of structural functionalism was clearly in jeopardy.

George Huaco (1986) linked the rise and decline of structural functionalism to the position of American society in the world order. As America rose to world dominance after 1945, structural functionalism achieved hegemony within sociology. Structural functionalism supported America's dominant position in the world in two ways. First, the structural-functional view that "every pattern has consequences which contribute to the preservation and survival of the larger system" was "nothing less than a celebration of the United States and its world hegemony" (Huaco, 1986:52). Second, the structural-functional emphasis on

C. WRIGHT MILLS: A Biographical Sketch

C. Wright Mills was born on August 28, 1916, in Waco, Texas. He came from a conventional middle-class background; his father was an insurance broker and his mother a housewife.   He attended the University of Texas and by 1939 had obtained both a bachelor's and a master's degree.   He was quite an unusual student who, by the time he left Texas, already had published articles in the two major sociology journals. Mills did his doctoral work at, and received a Ph.D. from, the University of Wisconsin (Scimecca, 1977). He took his first job at the University of Maryland but spent the bulk of his career, from 1945 until his death, at Columbia University.

Mills was a man in a hurry (Horowitz, 1983). By the time he died at forty-five from his fourth heart attack, Mills had made a number of important contributions to sociology.

One of the most striking things about C. Wright Mills was his combativeness; he seemed to be constantly at war. He had a tumultuous personal life, characterized by many affairs, three marriages, and a child from each marriage. He had an equally tumultuous professional life. He seemed to have fought with and against everyone and everything. As a graduate student at Wisconsin, he took on a number of his professors. Later, in one of his early essays, he engaged in a thinly disguised critique of the ex-chairman of the Wisconsin department. He called the senior theorist at Wisconsin, Howard Becker, a "real fool" (Horowitz, 1983). He eventually came into conflict with his coauthor, Hans Gerth, who called Mills "an excellent operator, whippersnapper, promising young man on the make, and Texas cowboy á la ride and shoot" (Horowitz, 1983:72). As a professor at Columbia, Mills was isolated and estranged from his colleagues. Said one of his Columbia colleagues:

> There was no estrangement between Wright and me. We began estranged. Indeed, at the memorial services or meeting that was organized at Columbia University at his death, I seemed to be the only person who could not say: 'I used to be his friend, but we became somewhat distant.' It was rather the reverse.
>
> (cited in Horowitz, 1983:83)

Mills was an outsider and he knew it: "I am an outlander, not only regionally, but down deep and for good" (Horowitz, 1983:84). In *The Sociological Imagination* (1959), Mills challenged not only the dominant theorist of his day, Talcott Parsons, but also the dominant methodologist, Paul Lazarsfeld, who also happened to be a colleague at Columbia.

Mills, of course, was at odds not only with people; he was also at odds with American society and challenged it on a variety of fronts. But perhaps most telling is the fact that when Mills visited the Soviet Union and was honored as a major critic of American society, he took the occasion to attack the censorship in the Soviet Union with a toast to an early Soviet leader who had been purged and murdered by the Stalinists: "To the day when the complete works of Leon Trotsky are published in the Soviet Union!" (Tilman, 1984:8)

C. Wright Mills died in Nyack, New York, on March 20, 1962.

equilibrium (the best social change is no change) meshed well with the interests of the United States, then "the wealthiest and most powerful empire in the world." The decline of U.S. world dominance in the 1970s coincided with structural functionalism's loss of its preeminent position in sociological theory.

Radical Sociology in America: C. Wright Mills

As we have seen, although Marxian theory was largely ignored or reviled by mainstream American sociologists, there were exceptions, the most notable of which is C. Wright Mills (1916–1962). Mills is noteworthy for his almost single-handed effort to keep a Marxian tradition alive in sociological theory. Modern Marxian sociologists have far outstripped Mills in theoretical sophistication, but they owe him a deep debt nonetheless for the personal and professional activities that helped set the stage for their own work (Alt, 1985–86). Mills was not a Marxist, and he did not read Marx until the mid-1950s. Even then he was restricted to the few available English translations, because he could not read German. Because Mills had published most of his major works by then, his work was not informed by a very sophisticated Marxian theory.

Mills published two major works that reflected his radical politics as well as his weaknesses in Marxian theory. The first was *White Collar* (1951), an acid critique of the status of a growing occupational category, white-collar workers. The second was *The Power Elite* (1956), a book that sought to show how America was dominated by a small group of businessmen, politicians, and military leaders. Sandwiched in between was his most theoretically sophisticated work, *Character and Social Structure* (Gerth and Mills, 1953), coauthored with Hans Gerth (H. Gerth, 1993). Ironically, considering Mills's major role in the history of Marxian sociological theory, this book was stronger in Weberian and Freudian theory than in Marxian theory. Nevertheless, the book is a major theoretical contribution, though it is not widely read today—possibly because it did not seem to fit well with Mills's best-known radical works. In fact, it was heavily influenced by Hans Gerth, who had a keen interest in Weberian theory.

In the 1950s, Mills's interest moved more in the direction of Marxism and in the problems of the Third World. This interest resulted in a book on the communist revolution in Cuba, *Listen, Yankee: The Revolution in Cuba* (1960), and another book, entitled *The Marxists* (1962). Mills's radicalism put him on the periphery of American sociology. He was the object of much criticism, and he, in turn, became a severe critic of sociology. The critical attitude culminated in *The Sociological Imagination* (1959). Of particular note is Mills's severe criticism of Talcott Parsons and his practice of grand theory. In fact, many sociologists were more familiar with Mills's critique than they were with the details of Parsons's work.

The Sociological Imagination is also noted for its distinction between personal troubles and public issues, as well as the objective of linking the two. This approach is reminiscent, within the realm of social problems, of the focus of *Character and Social Structure*: the relationship between "the private and the public, the innermost acts of the individual with the widest kinds of socio-historical phenomena" (Gerth and Mills, 1953:xvi). The issue of personal troubles and public issues, and their relationship, has been extraordinarily influential in sociology (see, for example, Ritzer, 1995).

Mills died in 1962, an outcast in sociology. However, before the decade was out, both radical sociology and Marxian theory were to begin to make important inroads into the discipline.

The Development of Conflict Theory

Another precursor to a true union of Marxism and sociological theory was the development of a conflict-theory alternative to structural functionalism. As we have just seen, structural functionalism had no sooner gained leadership in sociological theory than it came under increasing attack. The attack was multifaceted: structural functionalism was accused of such things as being politically conservative, unable to deal with social change because of its focus on static structures, and incapable of adequately analyzing social conflict.

One of the results of this criticism was an effort on the part of a number of sociologists to overcome the problems of structural functionalism by integrating a concern for structure with an interest in conflict. This work constituted the development of *conflict theory* as an alternative to structural-functional theory. Unfortunately, it often seemed little more than a mirror image of structural functionalism with little intellectual integrity of its own.

The first effort of note was Lewis Coser's (1956) book on the functions of social conflict (Jaworski, 1991). This work clearly tried to deal with social conflict from within the framework of a structural-functional view of the world. Although it is useful to look at the functions of conflict, there is much more to the study of conflict than an analysis of its positive functions.

Other people sought to reconcile the differences between structural functionalism and conflict theory (Coleman, 1971; Himes, 1966; van den Berghe, 1963). Although these efforts had some utility, the authors were generally guilty of papering over the major differences between the two theoretical alternatives (A. Frank, 1966/1974).

The biggest problem with most of conflict theory was that it lacked what it needed most—a sound basis in Marxian theory. After all, Marxian theory was well developed outside of sociology and should have provided a base on which to develop a sophisticated sociological theory of conflict. The one exception here is the work of Ralf Dahrendorf (born 1929).

Dahrendorf is a European scholar who is well versed in Marxian theory. He sought to embed his conflict theory in the Marxian tradition. However, in the end his conflict theory looked more like a mirror image of structural functionalism than like a Marxian theory of conflict. Dahrendorf's major work, *Class and Class Conflict in Industrial Society* (1959), was the most influential piece in conflict theory, but that was largely because it sounded so much like structural functionalism that it was palatable to mainstream sociologists. That is, Dahrendorf operated at the same level of analysis as the structural functionalists (structures and institutions) and looked at many of the same issues. (In other words, structural functionalism and conflict theory are part of the same paradigm; see Appendix.) Dahrendorf recognized that although aspects of the social system could fit together rather neatly, there also could be considerable conflict and tension among them.

In the end, conflict theory should be seen as little more than a transitional development in the history of sociological theory. It failed because it did not go far enough in the direction of Marxian theory. It was still too early in the 1950s and 1960s for American sociology to accept a full-fledged Marxian approach. But conflict theory was helpful in setting the stage for the beginning of that acceptance by the late 1960s.

We should note the contribution to conflict theory by Randall Collins (1975, 1990, 1993). On the one hand, Collins's effort suffers from the same weakness as the other works in the conflict tradition: it is relatively impoverished in terms of Marxian theory. On the other, Collins did identify another weakness in the conflict tradition, and he attempted to overcome it. The problem is that conflict theory generally focuses on social structures; it has little or nothing to say about actors and their thoughts and actions. Collins, schooled in the phenomenological-ethnomethodological tradition (which will be discussed shortly), attempted to move conflict theory in this direction.

The Birth of Exchange Theory

Another important theoretical development in the 1950s was the rise of exchange theory. The major figure in this development is George Homans, a sociologist whom we left earlier, just as he was being drawn to B. F. Skinner's psychological behaviorism. Skinner's behaviorism is a major source of Homans's, and sociology's, exchange theory.

Dissatisfied with Parsons's deductive strategy of developing theory, Homans was casting about for a workable alternative for handling sociological theory inductively. Further, Homans wanted to stay away from the cultural and structural foci of Parsonsian theory and wanted to concentrate instead on people and their behavior. With this in mind, Homans turned to the work of his colleague at Harvard, B. F. Skinner. At first, Homans did not see how Skinner's propositions, developed to help explain the behavior of pigeons, might be useful for understanding human social behavior. But as Homans looked further at data from sociological studies of small groups and anthropological studies of primitive societies, he began to see that Skinner's behaviorism was applicable and that it provided a theoretical alternative to Parsonsian-style structural functionalism. This realization led to an article entitled "Social Behavior as Exchange" in 1958 and in 1961 to a full-scale, book-length statement of Homans's theoretical position, *Social Behavior: Its Elementary Forms*. These works represented the birth of exchange theory as an important perspective in sociology. Since then exchange theory has attracted a good deal of attention, both positive and negative.

Homans's basic view was that the heart of sociology lies in the study of individual behavior and interaction. He was little interested in consciousness or in the various kinds of large-scale structures and institutions that were of concern to most sociologists. His main interest was rather in the reinforcement patterns, the history of rewards and costs, that lead people to do what they do. Basically, Homans argued that people continue to do what they have found to be rewarding in the past. Conversely, they cease doing what has proved to be costly in the past. In order to understand behavior, we need to understand an individual's history of rewards and costs. Thus, the focus of sociology should not be on consciousness or on social structures and institutions but on patterns of reinforcement.

As its name suggests, exchange theory is concerned not only with individual behavior but also with interaction between people involving an exchange of rewards and costs. The premise is that interactions are likely to continue when there is an exchange of rewards. Conversely, interactions that are costly to one or both parties are much less likely to continue.

Another major statement in exchange theory is Peter Blau's *Exchange and Power in Social Life,* published in 1964. Blau basically adopted Homans's perspective, but there was an important difference. Whereas Homans was content to deal mainly with elementary forms of social behavior, Blau wanted to integrate this with exchange at the structural and cultural levels, beginning with exchanges among actors, but quickly moving on to the larger structures that emerge out of this exchange. He ended by dealing with exchanges among large-scale structures. This approach is very different from the exchange theory envisioned by Homans. In some senses, it represents a return to the kind of Parsonsian-style theorizing that Homans found so objectionable. Nevertheless, the effort to deal with both small- and large-scale exchange in an integrated way proved a useful theoretical step.

Although he was eclipsed for many years by Homans and Blau, Richard Emerson (1981) has emerged as a central figure in exchange theory (Cook and Whitmeyer, forthcoming; Molm and Cook, 1995). He is noted particularly for his effort to develop a more integrated micro-macro approach to exchange theory. Exchange theory has now developed into a significant strand of sociological theory, and it continues to attract new adherents and to take new directions (Cook, O'Brien, and Kollock, 1990; Szmatka and Mazur, 1996; see also the ensuing discussion).

Dramaturgical Analysis: The Work of Erving Goffman

Erving Goffman (1922–1982) is often thought of as the last major thinker associated with the original Chicago school (Travers, 1992; Tseelon, 1992); Fine and Manning (forthcoming) see him as arguably the most influential twentieth-century American sociologist. He received his Ph.D. from Chicago in 1953, one year after Herbert Blumer (who had been Goffman's teacher) had left Chicago for Berkeley. Soon after, Goffman joined Blumer at Berkeley, where they were able to develop something of a center of symbolic interactionism. However, it never became anything like what Chicago had been. Blumer was past his organizational prime, and Goffman did not become a focus of graduate-student work. After 1952 the fortunes of symbolic interactionism declined, although it continues to be a prominent sociological theory.

In spite of the decline of symbolic interactionism in general, Goffman carved out a strong and distinctive place for himself in contemporary sociological theory (Manning, 1992). Between the 1950s and the 1970s, Goffman published a series of books and essays that gave birth to dramaturgical analysis as a variant of symbolic interactionism. Although Goffman shifted his attention in his later years, he remained best known for his *dramaturgical theory.*

Goffman's best-known statement of dramaturgical theory, *Presentation of Self in Everyday Life,* was published in 1959. To put it simply, Goffman saw much in common between theatrical performances and the kinds of "acts" we all put on in our day-to-day actions and interactions. Interaction is seen as very fragile, maintained by social performances. Poor performances or disruptions are seen as great threats to social interaction just as they are to theatrical performances.

Goffman went quite far in his analogy between the stage and social interaction. In all social interaction there is a *front region,* which is the parallel of the stage front in a theatrical performance. Actors both on the stage and in social life are seen as being interested in appearances, wearing costumes, and using props. Furthermore, in both there is a *back region,* a place to which the actors can retire to prepare themselves for their performance. Backstage or offstage, in theater terms, the actors can shed their roles and be themselves.

Dramaturgical analysis is clearly consistent with its symbolic-interactionist roots. It has a focus on actors, action, and interaction. Working in the same arena as traditional symbolic interactionism, Goffman found a brilliant metaphor in the theater to shed new light on small-scale social processes (Manning, 1991, 1992).

Goffman's work is widely read today and acknowledged for its originality and its profusion of insights (R. Collins, 1986b; Ditton, 1980). However, there are several general criticisms of this work. First, Goffman is seen as having been interested in somewhat esoteric topics rather than the truly essential aspects of social life. Second, he was a micro theorist in an era in which the great rewards have gone to macro theorists. As Randall Collins says, "The more we look at this [Goffman's] work . . . the more he emerges as the leading figure in the microsociology of our times" (1981c:6). Third, he attracted few students who were able to build theoretically upon his insights; indeed, some believe that it is impossible to build upon Goffman's work. It is seen as little more than a series of idiosyncratic bursts of brilliant insight. Finally, little theoretical work has been done by others in the dramaturgical tradition (one exception is Lyman and Scott [1970]).

The one area in which Goffman's work has proved fruitful is in empirical research utilizing his dramaturgical approach (Meyrowitz, 1995; Shirazi-Mahajan, 1995; Sijuwade, 1995).

The Development of Sociologies of Everyday Life

The 1960s and 1970s witnessed a boom (Ritzer, 1975a,b) in several theoretical perspectives that can be lumped together under the heading of sociologies of everyday life (J. Douglas, 1980; Weigert, 1981).

Phenomenological Sociology and the Work of Alfred Schutz (1899–1959)   The philosophy of phenomenology, with its focus on consciousness, has a long history, but the effort to develop a sociological variant of phenomenology can be traced to the publication of Alfred Schutz's *The Phenomenology of the Social World* in Germany in 1932. However, it was not translated into English until 1967, with the result that it has only recently had a dramatic effect on American sociological theory. Schutz arrived in the United States in 1939 after fleeing the Nazis in Austria. Shortly after, he took a position at the New School for Social Research in New York, from which he was able to influence the development of phenomenological, and later ethnomethodological, sociology in the United States.

As we will see in Chapter 13, Schutz took the phenomenological philosophy of Edmund Husserl, which was aimed inward toward an understanding of the transcendental ego, and turned it outward toward a concern for intersubjectivity (Rogers, forthcoming). Schutz was focally concerned with the way in which people grasp the consciousness of others while they live within their own stream of consciousness. Schutz also used intersubjectivity in a larger sense to mean a concern with the social world, especially the social nature of knowledge.

Much of Schutz's work focuses on an aspect of the social world called the *life-world,* or the world of everyday life. This is an intersubjective world in which people both create social reality and are constrained by the preexisting social and cultural structures created by their predecessors. While much of the life-world is shared, there are also private (biographically articulated) aspects of that world. Within the life-world, Schutz differentiated between intimate face-to-face relationships ("we-relations") and distant and impersonal relationships ("they-relations"). While face-to-face relations are of great importance in the life-world, it is far easier for the sociologist to study more impersonal relations scientifically. Although Schutz turned away from consciousness and to the intersubjective life-world, he did offer insights into consciousness, especially in his thoughts on meaning and people's motives.

Overall, Schutz was concerned with the dialectical relationship between the way people construct social reality and the obdurate social and cultural reality that they inherit from those who preceded them in the social world.

The mid-1960s were crucial in the development of phenomenological sociology. Not only was Alfred Schutz's major work translated and his collected essays published, but Peter Berger and Thomas Luckmann collaborated to publish a book, *The Social Construction of Reality* (1967), that became one of the most widely read theory books of the time. It made at least two important contributions. First, it constituted an introduction to Schutz's ideas that was written in such a way as to make it available to a large American audience. Second, it presented an effort to integrate Schutz's ideas with those of mainstream sociology.

Ethnomethodology   Although there are important differences between them, ethnomethodology and phenomenology are often seen as closely aligned (Langsdorf, 1995). One of the major reasons for this association is that the creator of this theoretical perspective, Harold Garfinkel, was a student of Alfred Schutz at the New School. Interestingly, Garfinkel had previously studied under Talcott Parsons, and it was the fusion of Parsonsian and Schutzian ideas that helped give ethnomethodology its distinctive orientation.

Hilbert (1992) has recently shed new light on the origins of Garfinkel's ideas and of ethnomethodology. While Garfinkel was a student of Parsons, he rejected the latter's structural-functional perspective and, in the process, rediscovered (accidentally) classical sociological ideas embedded in the work of Durkheim and Weber (Hilbert, 1992). Specifically, while he accepted basic themes in Parsons's work such as the importance of normative prescriptions and shared understandings, Garfinkel rejected Parsons's fundamental premise that the normative order is separate from and controls (through socialization) the behavioral order. Instead of Parsonsian theoretical abstractions,

Garfinkel's focus was empirical studies of the everyday world. Thus, Garfinkel continued to work with the Parsonsian issues of order and society not theoretically, but rather in the "details of their workings . . . in their achievement" (Button, 1991:6–7). In these studies, Garfinkel discovered a variety of sociological principles that are consistent with the work of Durkheim and Weber. For one thing, Garfinkel found that the social world was not reified. This stood in contrast to Parsons's tendency to reify the cultural (and social) system but was consistent with Weber's refusal to reify social structure and with Durkheim's orientation to study, not reify, external and coercive social facts. For another, Garfinkel's commitment to empirical research stood in contrast to Parsons's propensity for grand theory and was more consistent with the empirical bent of both Weber and Durkheim.

After receiving his Ph.D. from Harvard in 1952, Garfinkel settled at the University of California at Los Angeles (Heritage, 1984; Rawls, forthcoming). It was there that ethnomethodology was developed by Garfinkel and his graduate students. Over the years a number of major ethnomethodologists emerged from this milieu. Geographically, ethnomethodology was the first distinctive theoretical product of the West Coast, and it remained centered there for a long time. Today, ethnomethodologists are also found throughout the rest of the United States, as well as in other parts of the world, especially Great Britain.

Ethnomethodology began to receive a wide national audience with the publication in 1967 of Garfinkel's *Studies in Ethnomethodology*. Although written in a difficult and obscure style, the book elicited a lot of interest. The fact that this book came out at the same time as the translation of Schutz's *The Phenomenology of the Social World* and the publication of Berger and Luckmann's *The Social Construction of Reality* seemed to indicate that sociologies of everyday life were coming of age.

Basically, *ethnomethodology* is the study of "the body of common-sense knowledge and the range of procedures and considerations [the methods] by means of which the ordinary members of society make sense of, find their way about in, and act on the circumstances in which they find themselves" (Heritage, 1984:4). Writers in this tradition are heavily tilted in the direction of the study of everyday life. While phenomenological sociologists tend to focus on what people think, ethnomethodologists are more concerned with what people actually do. Thus, ethnomethodologists devote a lot of attention to the detailed study of conversations. Such mundane concerns stand in stark contrast to the interest of many mainstream sociologists in such abstractions as bureaucracies, capitalism, the division of labor, and the social system. Ethnomethodologists might be interested in the way a sense of these structures is created in everyday life; they are not interested in such structures as phenomena in themselves.

Ethnomethodology is determinedly empirical in its orientation. Ethnomethodologists generally decline to theorize about the social world, preferring instead to go out and study it. This calls into question the inclusion of ethnomethodology in a book like this one. Says Button, "Ethnomethodology . . . never bought into the business of theorising," or "The idea that ethnomethodology is *theory* . . . would perplex many ethnomethodologists" (1991:4, 9). But ethnomethodology *is* treated in this book, and for at least two reasons. First, its basic premises constitute an attack on much of sociological theory, and we learn much about ethnomethodology (and traditional theory) from those attacks. Second, the findings of ethnomethodological studies are used to create theories of everyday life (as we will see in the work of Anthony Giddens, to take one example).

There was clearly something about ethnomethodology that was threatening to mainstream sociologists who were still in control of the discipline. In fact, both phenomenology and, more important, ethnomethodology have been subjected to some brutal attacks by mainstream sociologists. Here are two examples. The first is from a review of Garfinkel's *Studies in Ethnomethodology* by James Coleman:

> Garfinkel simply fails to generate any insights at all from the approach. . . .
> Perhaps the program would be more fertile in the hands of someone more carefully observant but it is strangely sterile here. . . .
> . . . this chapter appears to be not only an ethnomethodology disaster in itself but also evidence of the more general inadequacies of ethnomethodology . . .
> . . . this chapter is another major disaster, combining the rigidities of the most mathematically enraptured technicians with the technical confusions and errors of the soft clinician and without the insights or the technical competence of the creative and trained sociologist.
> Once again, Garfinkel elaborates very greatly points which are so commonplace that they would appear banal if stated in straightforward English. As it is, there is an extraordinarily high ratio of reading time to information transfer, so that the banality is not directly apparent upon a casual reading.

> (Coleman, 1968:126–130)

The second example is Lewis Coser's 1975 presidential address to the American Sociological Association. Coser saw few redeeming qualities in ethnomethodology and subjected it to a savage attack, engaging in a great deal of name-calling, labeling ethnomethodology "trivial," "a massive cop-out," "an orgy of subjectivism," and a "self-indulgent enterprise." The bitterness of these and other attacks is an indication of the degree to which ethnomethodology represented a threat to the establishment in sociology.

Today, ethnomethodology has overcome a significant part of the early opposition and has, to a large degree, become an accepted part of sociological theory. For example, it is now quite routine to see works by ethnomethodologists appearing in the major mainstream sociology journals such as *The American Sociological Review* (for example, Greatbatch and Dingwall, 1997). However, that acceptance is far from complete, as Pollner (1991:370) humorously points out: Few sociologists "want their children to marry an ethnomethodologist, much less to be one—and rarely to hire one. Nevertheless, the discipline recognizes and begins to incorporate the contributions of what was once regarded as a pariah." Other ethnomethodologists lament how their orientation is put upon, marginalized, and misunderstood (Button, 1991).

In the last few pages, we have dealt with several micro theories—exchange theory, phenomenological sociology, and ethnomethodology. Although the last two theories share a sense of a thoughtful and creative actor, such a view is not held by exchange theorists. Nevertheless, all three theories have a primarily micro orientation to actors and their actions and behavior. In the 1970s, such theories grew in strength in sociology and threatened to replace more macro-oriented theories (such as structural functionalism, conflict theory, neo-Marxian theories) as the dominant theories in sociology (Knorr-Cetina, 1981a; Ritzer, 1985).

The Rise and Fall (?) of Marxian Sociology

The late 1960s were the point at which Marxian theory finally began to make significant inroads into American sociological theory (Cerullo, 1994; Jay, 1984). There are a number of reasons for this. First, the dominant theory (structural functionalism) was under attack for a number of things, including being too conservative. Second, Mills's radical sociology and conflict theory, although not representing sophisticated Marxian theory, had laid the groundwork for an American theory that was true to the Marxian tradition. Third, the 1960s was the era of black protests, the reawakening of the women's movement, the student movement, and the anti–Vietnam War movement. Many of the young sociologists trained in this atmosphere were attracted to radical ideas. At first, this interest was manifest in what was called in those days "radical sociology" (Colfax and Roach, 1971). Radical sociology was useful as far as it went, but like Mills's work, it was rather weak on the details of Marxian theory.

It is hard to single out one work as essential to the development of Marxian sociology in America, but one that did play an important role was Henri Lefebvre's *The Sociology of Marx* (1968). It was important for its essential argument, which was that although Marx was not a sociologist, there was a sociology in Marx. An increasing number of sociologists turned to Marx's original work, as well as to that of many Marxists, for insights that would be useful in the development of a Marxian sociology. At first this simply meant that American theorists were finally reading Marx seriously, but later there emerged many significant pieces of Marxian scholarship by American sociologists.

American theorists were particularly attracted to the work of the critical school, especially because of its fusion of Marxian and Weberian theory. Many of the works have been translated into English, and a number of scholars have written books about the critical school (for example, Jay, 1973, 1986; Kellner, 1993).

Along with an increase in interest came institutional support for such an orientation. Several journals devoted considerable attention to Marxian sociological theory, including *Theory and Society, Telos,* and *Marxist Studies.* A section on Marxist sociology was created in the American Sociological Association in 1977. Not only did the first generation of critical theorists become well known in America, but second-generation thinkers, especially Jurgen Habermas, received wide recognition.

Of considerable importance was the development of significant pieces of American sociology done from a Marxian point of view. One very significant strand is a group of sociologists doing historical sociology from a Marxian perspective (for example, Skocpol, 1979; Wallerstein, 1974, 1980, 1989). Another is a group analyzing the economic realm from a sociological perspective (for example, Baran and Sweezy, 1966; Braverman, 1974; Burawoy, 1979). Still others are doing fairly traditional empirical sociology, but work that is informed by a strong sense of Marxian theory (Kohn, 1976, for example).

However, with the disintegration of the Soviet Union and the fall of Marxist regimes around the world, Marxian theory fell on hard times in the 1990s. Some people remain unreconstructed Marxists; others have been forced to develop modified versions of Marxian theory (see the discussion below of the post-Marxists; there is also a journal entitled *Rethinking Marxism*). Still others have come to the conclusion that Marxian theory must be abandoned. Representative of the latter position is Ronald Aronson's book *After Marxism* (1995). The very first line of the book tells the story: "Marxism is over, and we are on our own" (Aronson, 1995:1). This from an avowed Marxist! While Aronson recognizes that some will continue to work with Marxian theory, he cautions that they must recognize that it is no longer part of the larger Marxian project of social transformation. That is, Marxian theory is no longer related, as Marx intended, to a program aimed at changing the basis of society; it is theory without practice. One-time Marxists are on their own in the sense that they can no longer rely on the Marxian project, but rather must grapple with modern society with their "own powers and ener-gies" (Aronson, 1995:4).

Aronson is among the more extreme critics of Marxism from within the Marxian camp. Others recognize the difficulties, but seek in various ways to adapt some variety of Marxian theory to contemporary realities (Brugger, 1995; Kellner, 1995). Neverthe-less, larger social changes have posed a grave challenge for Marxian theorists, who are desperately seeking to adapt to these changes in a variety of ways. Whatever else can be said, the "glory days" of Marxian social theory appear to be over. Marxian social theorists of various types will survive, but they are not likely to approach the status and power of their predecessors in the recent history of sociology.

The Challenge of Feminist Theory

Beginning in the late 1970s, precisely at the moment that Marxian sociology gained sig-nificant acceptance from American sociologists, a new theoretical outsider issued a challenge to established sociological theories—and even to Marxian sociology itself. This latest brand of radical social thought is contemporary feminist theory, which has continued to grow in range and complexity and will influence sociology into the twenty-first century.

In Western societies, one can trace the record of critical feminist writings back almost 500 years (Donovan, 1985; Lerner, 1993; A. Rossi, 1974; Spender, 1982), and there has been an organized political movement by and for women for more than 150 years (Ban-ner, 1984; Bolt, 1993; Carden, 1974; Chafetz and Dworkin, 1986; Deckard, 1979; Flexner, 1959; Giddings, 1984; Kandal, 1988; G. Matthews, 1992; O'Neill, 1971; M. Ryan, 1990). In America in 1920, the movement finally won the right for women to vote, fifty-five years after that right had been constitutionally extended to all men. Ex-hausted and to a degree satiated by victory, the American women's movement over the next thirty years weakened in both size and vigor, only to spring back to life, fully reawakened, in the 1960s. Three factors helped create this new wave of feminist ac-tivism: the general climate of critical thinking that characterized the period; the anger of women activists who flocked to the antiwar, civil rights, and student movements only to encounter the sexist attitudes of the liberal and radical men in those movements (Densi-more, 1973; Evans, 1980; Morgan, 1970; Shreve, 1989; Snitow, Stansell, and Thomp-son, 1983); and women's experience of prejudice and discrimination as they moved in ever larger numbers into wage work and higher education (Bookman and Morgen, 1988; Caplan, 1993; Garland, 1988; MacKinnon, 1979). For these reasons, particularly the last, the women's movement continued into the 1990s, even though the activism of many other 1960s movements has faded. Moreover, during these years activism by and for women became an international phenomenon, drawing in women from many societies and from most stratificational locations in North America. Feminist writing has now entered its "third wave" in the writings of women who will spend most of their adult lives in the twenty-first century (C. Bailey, 1997; Orr, 1997).

A major feature of this international women's movement has been an explosively growing new literature on women that makes visible all aspects of women's hitherto unconsidered lives and experiences. This literature, which is popularly referred to as *women's studies* or the *new scholarship on women,* is the work of an international and interdisciplinary community of writers, located both within and outside universities and writing for both the general public and specialized academic audiences. In what must be one of the more impressive examples of sustained intellectual work in recent times, feminist scholars have launched a probing, multifaceted critique that makes visible the complexity of the system that subordinates women.

Feminist theory is the theoretical strand running through this literature: sometimes implicit in writings on such substantive issues as work (Daniels, 1988; DeVault, 1991; Hochschild, 1989, 1997; Kanter, 1977; Pierce, 1995; Rollins, 1985) or rape (Sanday, 1990, 1996; Scully, 1990) or popular culture (McCaughey, 1997; Radway, 1984); sometimes centrally and explicitly presented, as in the analyses of motherhood by Adrienne Rich (1976), Nancy Chodorow (1978), and Jessica Benjamin (1988); and increasingly the sole, systematic project of a piece of writing. Of this recent spate of wholly theoretical writing, certain statements have been particularly salient to sociology because they are directed to sociologists by people well versed in sociological theory (Chafetz, 1984; P. Collins, 1990, 1998; Lengermann and Niebrugge-Brantley, 1990; Lengermann and Niebrugge, 1995; D. Smith, 1979, 1987, 1990a, 1990b, 1992, 1993; Stacey and Thorne, 1985; Wallace, 1989). Journals that bring feminist theory to the attention of sociologists include *Signs, Feminist Studies, Sociological Inquiry,* and *Gender & Society,* as does the professional association Sociologists for Women in Society (SWS) and the National Women's Studies Association (NWSA).

Feminist theory looks at the world from the vantage points of a hitherto unrecognized and invisible minority, women, with an eye to discovering the significant but unacknowledged ways in which the activities of women—subordinated by gender and variously affected by other stratificational practices, such as class, race, age, enforced heterosexuality, and geosocial inequality—help to create our world. This viewpoint dramatically reworks our understanding of social life. From this base, feminist theorists have begun to challenge sociological theory.

Those issuing this challenge argue that sociologists have persistently refused to incorporate the insights of the new scholarship on women into their discipline's understanding of the social world. Instead, feminist sociologists have been segregated from the mainstream, and feminism's comprehensive theory of social organization has been reduced to a single research variable, sex, and a simple social role pattern, gender (Alway, 1995; Laslett and Thorne, 1992; Lemert, 1992b; D. Smith, 1990b; Stacey and Thorne, 1985, 1996; R. Wallace, 1989; Yeatman, 1987). To date, these charges seem valid. Reasons for sociology's avoidance of feminist theory may include deep antiwoman, antifeminist prejudices, suspicion of the scientific credentials of a theory so closely associated with political activism, and caution born of half-recognition of the profoundly radical implications of feminist theory for sociological theory and method.

Yet these feminist writings now assume a critical mass in sociology. They offer an exciting paradigm for the study of social life. And those whose experiences and perceptions make them a receptive audience for this theory—women in general and both women and men affected by feminism in particular—may now constitute a numerical majority in the sociological community. For all these reasons, implications of feminist theory are moving increasingly into the mainstream of the discipline, engaging all its subspecialties, influencing many of its long-established theories, both macro and micro, and interacting with the new poststructuralist and postmodernist developments described below.

Structuralism and Poststructuralism

One development that we have said little about up to this point is the increase in interest in *structuralism* (Lemert, 1990). Usually traced to France (and often called *French structuralism* [Clark and Clark, 1982; Kurzweil, 1980]), structuralism has now become an international phenomenon. Although its roots lie outside sociology, structuralism clearly has made its way into sociology. The problem is that structuralism in sociology still is so undeveloped that it is difficult to define with any precision. The problem is exacerbated by structuralism's more or less simultaneous development in a number of fields; it is difficult to find one single coherent statement of structuralism. Indeed, there are significant differences among the various branches of structuralism.

We can get a preliminary feeling for structuralism by delineating the basic differences that exist among those who support a structuralist perspective. There are those who focus on what they call the "deep structures of the mind." It is their view that these unconscious structures lead people to think and act as people do. The work of the psychoanalyst Sigmund Freud might be seen as an example of this orientation. Then there are structuralists who focus on the invisible larger structures of society and see them as determinants of the actions of people as well as of society in general. Marx is sometimes thought of as someone who practiced such a brand of structuralism, with his focus on the unseen economic structure of capitalist society. Still another group sees structures as the models they construct of the social world. Finally, a number of structuralists are concerned with the dialectical relationship between individuals and social structures. They see a link between the structures of the mind and the structures of society. The anthropologist Claude Lévi-Strauss is most often associated with this view.

As structuralism grew within sociology, outside sociology a movement was developing beyond the early premises of structuralism: *poststructuralism* (Lemert, 1990). The major representative of poststructuralism is Michel Foucault (J. Miller, 1993). In his early work, Foucault focused on structures, but he later moved beyond structures to focus on power and the linkage between knowledge and power. More generally, poststructuralists accept the importance of structure but go beyond it to encompass a wide range of other concerns.

Poststructuralism is important not only in itself, but also because it is often seen as a precursor to postmodern social theory (to be discussed later in this chapter). In fact, it is difficult, if not impossible, to draw a clear line between poststructuralism and postmodern social theory. Thus Foucault, a poststructuralist, is often seen as a postmodernist, while Jean Baudrillard (1972/1981), who is usually labeled a postmodernist, certainly did work, especially early in his career, that is poststructuralist in character.

RECENT DEVELOPMENTS IN SOCIOLOGICAL THEORY

While many of the developments discussed in the preceding pages continued to be important in the late twentieth century, in this section we will deal with three broad movements that were of utmost importance—micro-macro integration, agency-structure integration, and theoretical syntheses.

Micro-Macro Integration

A good deal of the most recent work in American sociological theory has been concerned with the linkage between micro and macro theories and levels of analysis. In fact, I argued that micro-macro linkage emerged as the central problematic in American sociological theory in the 1980s and it continued to be of focal concern in the 1990s (Ritzer, 1990a). (An important precursor to contemporary American work on the micro-macro linkage is the contribution of the European sociologist Norbert Elias [1939/1994] to our understanding of the relationship between micro-level manners and the macro-level state.)

There are a number of examples of efforts to link micro-macro levels of analysis and/or theories. In my own work (Ritzer, 1979, 1981a), I have sought to develop an integrated sociological paradigm that integrates micro and macro levels in both their objective and subjective forms. Thus, in my view, there are four major levels of social analysis that must be dealt with in an integrated manner—macro subjectivity, macro objectivity, micro subjectivity, and micro objectivity. Jeffrey Alexander (1982–83) has created a "multidimensional sociology" which deals, at least in part, with a model of levels of analysis that closely resembles my model. Alexander (1987) develops his model based on the problem of order, which is seen as having individual (micro) and collective (macro) levels, and on the problem of action, which is viewed as possessing materialist (objective) and idealist (subjective) levels. Out of these two continuua, Alexander develops four major levels of analysis—collective-idealist, collective-materialist, individual-idealist, individual-materialist. While the overall model developed by Alexander is strikingly similar to mine, Alexander accords priority to the collective-idealist level, while I insist that we be concerned with the dialectical relationship among all levels. Another kindred approach has been developed by Norbert Wiley (1988), who also delineates four very similar major levels of analysis—self or individual, interaction, social structure, and culture. However, while both Alexander and I focus on both objective and subjective levels, Wiley's levels are purely subjective. James Coleman (1986) has concentrated on the micro-to-macro problem, while Allen Liska (1990) has extended Coleman's approach to deal with the macro-to-micro problem as well. Coleman (1990) has extended his micro-to-macro model and developed a much more elaborate theory of the micro-macro relationship based on a rational choice approach derived from economics (see below).

Agency-Structure Integration

Paralleling the growth in interest in the United States in micro-macro integration, has been a concern in Europe for agency-structure integration (Sztompka, 1994). Just as I saw the micro-macro issue as the central problem in American theory, Margaret Archer (1988) sees the agency-structure topic as the basic concern in European social theory. While there are many similarities between the micro-macro and agency-structure literatures (Ritzer and Gindoff, 1992, 1994), there are also substantial differences. For example, while agents are usually micro-level actors, collectivities like labor unions can also be agents. And while structures are usually macro-level phenomena, we also find structures at the micro level. Thus, we must be careful in equating these two bodies of work, and much care needs to be taken in trying to interrelate them.

There are four major efforts in contemporary European social theory that can be included under the heading of agency-structure integration. The first is Anthony Giddens's (1984) structuration theory. The key to Giddens's approach is that he sees agency and structure as a "duality." That is, they cannot be separated from one another: agency is implicated in structure and structure is involved in agency. Giddens refuses to see structure as simply constraining (as, for example, does Durkheim), but sees structure as both constraining *and* enabling. Margaret Archer (1982) rejects the idea that agency and structure can be viewed as a duality, but rather sees them as a dualism. That is, agency and structure can and should be separated. In distinguishing them, we become better able to analyze their relationship to one another. Archer (1988) is also notable for extending the agency-structure literature to a concern for the relationship between culture and agency and more recently developing a more general agency-structure theory (Archer, 1995).

While both Giddens and Archer are British, the third major contemporary figure involved in the agency-structure literature is Pierre Bourdieu from France (Bourdieu, 1977; Bourdieu and Wacquant, 1992; Swartz, 1997). In Bourdieu's work, the agency-structure issue translates into a concern for the relationship between habitus and field. *Habitus* is an internalized mental, or cognitive, structure through which people deal with the social world. The habitus both produces, and is produced by, the society. The *field* is a network of relations among objective positions. The structure of the field serves to constrain agents, be they individuals or collectivities. Overall, Bourdieu is concerned with the relationship between habitus and field. While the field conditions the habitus, the habitus constitutes the field. Thus, there is a dialectical relationship between habitus and field.

The final major theorist of the agency-structure linkage is the German social thinker Jurgen Habermas. We have already mentioned Habermas as a significant contemporary contributor to critical theory. Habermas (1987a) has also dealt with the agency-structure issue under the heading of "the colonization of the life-world." The life-world is a micro world where people interact and communicate. The system has its roots in the life-world, but it ultimately comes to develop its own structural characteristics. As these structures grow in independence and power, they come to exert more and more control over the life-world. In the modern world, the system has come to "colonize" the life-world, that is, to exert control over it.

The theorists discussed in this section not only are the leading theorists on the agency-structure issue, but they are arguably (especially Bourdieu, Giddens, and Habermas) the leading theorists in the world today. After a long period of dominance by American theorists (Mead, Parsons, Merton, Homans, and others), the center of social theory seems to be returning to its birthplace—Europe. Furthermore, Nedelmann and Sztompka have argued that with the end of the Cold War and the fall of communism, we are about to "witness another Golden Era of European Sociology" (1993:1). This seems to be supported by the fact that today the works that catch the attention of large numbers of the world's theorists are European in origin. One example is Ulrich Beck's *Risk Society: Towards a New Modernity* (1992), in which he discusses the unprecedented risks facing society today. It is clear that, at least for now, the center of sociological theory *has* shifted back to Europe.

Theoretical Syntheses

The movements toward micro-macro and agency-structure integration began in the 1980s, and both continued to be strong in the 1990s. They set the stage for the broader movement toward theoretical syntheses which began at about the beginning of the 1990s. Lewis (1991) has suggested that the relatively low status of sociology may be the result of excessive fragmentation and that the movement toward greater integration may enhance the status of the discipline. What is involved here is a wide-ranging effort to synthesize two or more different theories (for example, structural functionalism and symbolic interactionism). Such efforts have occurred throughout the history of sociological theory (Holmwood and Stewart, 1994). However, there are two distinctive aspects of the new synthetic work in sociological theory. First, it is very widespread and not restricted to isolated attempts at synthesis. Second, the goal is generally a relatively narrow synthesis of theoretical ideas, and not the development of a grand synthetic theory that encompasses all of sociological theory.

These synthetic works are occurring within and among many of the theories (and theorists; see, for example, Levine's [1991a] call for a synthesis of the ideas of Simmel and Parsons) discussed in this chapter as well as in and among some theories we have yet to mention. Examples include neofunctionalism (Alexander, 1998a; Alexander and Colomy, 1985, 1990a) which seeks to overcome many of the limitations of structural-functionalism by integrating ideas from a wide range of theories; symbolic interactionism which has "cobbled a new theory from the shards of other theoretical approaches [e.g. feminist and exchange theory]" (Fine, 1990:136–137); exchange theory which has sought to synthesize ideas derived from such sources as symbolic interactionism and network theory (Cook, O'Brien, and Kollock, 1990); post-Marxists who have sought to integrate mainstream ideas into Marxian theory (Elster, 1985; Mayer, 1994; Roemer, 1986c); and postmodern Marxists who, as the name suggests, have attempted to bring postmodern ideas into Marxian theory (Harvey, 1989; Jameson, 1984; Laclau and Mouffe, 1985).

Then there are efforts to bring perspectives from outside sociology into sociological theory. There have been works oriented to bringing biological ideas into sociology in an effort to create sociobiology (Crippen, 1994; Maryanski and Turner, 1992). Rational choice theory is based in economics, but it has made inroads into a number of fields including sociology (Coleman, 1990). Systems theory has its roots in the hard sciences, but in the late twentieth century Niklas Luhmann (1982) made a powerful effort to develop a system theory that could be applied to the social world.

THEORIES OF MODERNITY AND POSTMODERNITY

As we begin the twenty-first century, social theorists[6] have become increasingly preoccupied with whether society, as well as theories about it, has undergone a dramatic transformation. On one side is a group of theorists (for example, Jurgen Habermas and Anthony Giddens) who believe that we continue to live in a society that can still best be described as modern and about which we can theorize in much the same way that social thinkers have long contemplated society. On the other side is a group of thinkers (for example, Jean Baudrillard, Jean-François Lyotard, Fredric Jameson, and Arthur Kroker) who contend that society has changed so dramatically that we now live in a qualitatively different, postmodern society. Furthermore, they argue that this new society needs to be thought about in new and different ways.

The Defenders of Modernity

All the great classical sociological theorists (Marx, Weber, Durkheim, and Simmel) were concerned, in one way or another, with the modern world and its advantages and disadvantages. Of course, the last of these (Weber) died in 1920, and the world has changed dramatically since then. While all contemporary theorists recognize these dramatic changes, there are some who believe that there is more continuity than discontinuity between the world today and the world that existed around the last *fin de siecle*.

Mestrovic (1998:2) has labeled Anthony Giddens "the high priest of modernity." Giddens (1990, 1991, 1992) uses terms like "radical," "high," or "late" modernity to describe society today and to indicate that while it is not the same society as the one described by the classical theorists, it is continuous with that society. Giddens sees modernity today as a "juggernaut" that is, at least to some degree, out of control. Ulrich Beck (1992) contends that while the classical stage of modernity was associated with industrial society, the emerging new modernity is best described as a "risk society." While the central dilemma in classical modernity was wealth and how it ought to be distributed, the central problem in new modernity is the prevention, minimization, and channeling of risk (from, for example, a nuclear accident). Jurgen Habermas (1981, 1987b) sees modernity as an "unfinished project." That is, the central issue in the modern world continues, as it was in Weber's day, to be rationality. The utopian goal is still the maximization of the rationality of both the "system" and the "life-world." I (Ritzer, 1996) also see rationality as the key process in the world today. However, I pick up on Weber's focus on the problem of the increase in formal rationality and the danger

---

[6]I am using the term "social" rather than "sociological" theorist here to reflect the fact that many contributors to the recent literature are not sociologists, although they are theorizing about the social world.

of an "iron cage" of rationality. While Weber focused on the bureaucracy, today I see the paradigm of this process as the fast-food restaurant, and I describe the increase in formal rationality as the McDonaldization of society.

Not only do these and other theorists (for example, Touraine, 1995; Wagner, 1994) persist in seeing the world in modern terms, but they continue to think about it using modern tools. Basically, they are standing back and apart from society, rationally and systematically analyzing and describing it, and portraying it using grand narratives, albeit in more self-conscious ways than their forebears did. Modernity as a juggernaut, the transition from industrial to risk society, the rationalization of life-world and system, and the McDonaldization of society are far more similar to the grand narratives of the classical theorists of modernity than they are at variance with them.

The Proponents of Postmodernity

Postmodernism is hot (Kellner, 1989a; Ritzer, 1997; Seidman, 1994a), indeed it is so hot, it is discussed so endlessly in many fields including sociology, that it may already be in the process of burning out (Lemert, 1994b). We need to differentiate, at least initially, between postmodernity and postmodern social theory (Best and Kellner, 1991). *Postmodernity* is a new historical epoch that is supposed to have succeeded the modern era, or modernity. *Postmodern social theory* is a new way of thinking about postmodernity; the world is so different that it requires entirely new ways of thinking. Postmodernists would tend to reject the theoretical perspectives outlined in the previous section, as well as the ways in which the thinkers involved created their theories.

There are probably as many portrayals of postmodernity as there are postmodern social theorists. To simplify things, we will summarize some of the key elements of a depiction offered by one of the most prominent postmodernists, Fredric Jameson (1984, 1991). First, postmodernity is a depthless, superficial world; it is a world of simulation (for example, a jungle cruise at Disneyland rather than the real thing). Second, it is a world that is lacking in affect and emotion. Third, there is a loss of a sense of one's place in history; it is hard to distinguish past, present, and future. Fourth, instead of the explosive, expanding, productive technologies of modernity (for example, automobile assembly lines), postmodern society is dominated by implosive, flattening, reproductive technologies (television, for example). In these and other ways, postmodern society is very different from modern society.

Such a different world requires a different way of thinking. Rosenau (1992; Ritzer, 1997) defines the postmodern mode of thought in terms of the things that it opposes, largely characteristics of the modern way of thinking. First, postmodernists reject the kind of grand narratives that characterize much of classical sociological theory. Instead, postmodernists prefer more limited explanations, or even no explanations at all. Second, there is a rejection of the tendency to put boundaries between disciplines—to engage in something called sociological (or social) theory that is distinct from, say, philosophical thinking or even novelistic storytelling. Third, postmodernists are often more interested in shocking or startling the reader than they are in engaging in careful, reasoned academic discourse. Finally, instead of looking for the core of society (say rationality, or capitalistic exploitation), postmodernists are more inclined to focus on more peripheral aspects of society.

Clearly, much is at stake in the debate between the modernists and the postmodernists, including the future of sociological theory. If the modernists win out, sociological theory in the first decade of the twenty-first century will look much like it always has, but if the postmodernists emerge victorious, the world, and social theories of that world, will be very different. The most likely scenario, however, is that the world will be composed of some combination of modern and postmodern elements and the social theorists of each persuasion will continue to battle it out for hegemony.

THEORIES TO WATCH IN THE EARLY TWENTY-FIRST CENTURY

It is impossible to predict the directions that sociological theory will take, but in this section we discuss several approaches that are likely to attract considerable attention and undergo substantial development.

Multicultural Social Theory

A recent development, closely tied to postmodernism—especially its emphasis on the periphery and its tendency to level the intellectual playing field—is the rise of multicultural social theory (Lemert, 1993; Rogers, 1996a). This rise of multicultural theory was foreshadowed by the emergence of feminist sociological theory in the 1970s. The feminists complained that sociological theory had been largely closed to women's voices; in the ensuing years many minority groups echoed the feminists' complaints. In fact, minority women (for example, African Americans and Latinas) began to complain that feminist theory was restricted to white, middle-class females and had to be more receptive to many other voices. Today, feminist theory has become far more diverse, as has sociological theory.

A good example of the increasing diversity of sociological theory is the rise of "queer" sociological theory (Morton, 1996; Warner, 1993). Seidman (1994b) documents the silence of classical sociological theory on sexuality in general and homosexuality in particular. He finds it striking that while the classical theorists were dealing with a wide range of issues relating to modernity, they had nothing to say about the making of modern bodies and modern sexuality. While the silence was soon to be broken, it was not until the work of Michel Foucault (1980) on the relationships among power, knowledge, and sexuality that the postmodern study of sexuality in general, and homosexuality in particular, began. What emerged was the sense of homosexuality as both a subject and an identity paralleling the heterosexual self and identity.

Seidman has argued, however, that what distinguishes queer theory is a rejection of any single identity, including homosexuality, and the argument that all identities are multiple or composite, unstable and exclusionary. Thus, at any given time each of us is a composite of a series of identity components (for example, "sexual orientation, race, class, nationality, gender, age, ableness" [Seidman, 1994b:173]), and these components can be combined and recombined in many different ways. As a result, Seidman rejects the homosexual-heterosexual dichotomy and seeks to move queer theory in the direction of a more general social theory:

Queer theorists shift their focus from an exclusive preoccupation with the oppression and liberation of the homosexual subject to an analysis of the institutional practices and discourses producing sexual knowledges and how they organize social life, with particular attention to the way in which these knowledges and social practices repress differences. In this regard, queer theory is suggesting . . . the study . . . of those knowledges and social practices which organize "society" as a whole by sexualizing—heterosexualizing or homosexualizing—bodies, desires, acts, identities, social relations, knowledges, cultures, and social institutions. Queer theory aspires to transform homosexual theory into a general social theory or one standpoint from which to analyze whole societies.

(Seidman, 1994b:174)

Thus, queer theory is put forth as but one of what have been called "standpoint theories," that is, theories that view the social world from a specific vantage point (much as Marx viewed capitalism from the standpoint of the proletariat). We can expect to see a burgeoning of such multicultural, standpoint theories as the twenty-first century unfolds.

Multicultural theory has taken a series of diverse forms beyond that of a more variegated feminist theory. Examples include Afrocentric theory (Asante, 1996), Appalachian studies (Banks, Billings, and Tice, 1996), Native American theory (Buffalohead, 1996), and even theories of masculinity (Connell, 1996; Kimmel, 1996). Among the things that characterize multicultural theory are the following:

• A rejection of universalistic theories that tend to support those in power; multicultural theories seek to empower those who lack clout.

• Multicultural theory seeks to be inclusive, to offer theory on the behalf of many disempowered groups.

• Multicultural theorists are not value free; they often theorize on behalf of those without power and to work in the social world to change social structure, culture, and the prospects for individuals.

• Multicultural theorists seek to disrupt not only the social world but the intellectual world; they seek to make it far more open and diverse.

• There is no effort to draw a clear line between theory and other types of narratives.

• There is ordinarily a critical edge to multicultural theory; it is both self-critical and critical of other theories and, most importantly, of the social world.

• Multicultural theorists recognize that their work is limited by the particular historical, social, and cultural context in which they happen to live (Rogers, 1996b:11–16).

Postmodern and Post-Postmodern Social Theories

It is safe to assume that postmodern social theories will continue to be important in sociology and many other fields. In fact, sociology has been slow to pick up on postmodern theory and there continues to be considerable hostility toward it in the discipline. However, the theory is too powerful and too well entrenched in many other fields to be largely ignored in sociology. Thus, postmodern social theory will attract more adherents (and detractors) in sociology in the years to come.

At the same time, there is already well established, primarily in France (the center of theoretical movements like postmodernism), a body of work that can best be thought of as post-postmodernism. For example, postmodern social theory is associated with a critique of a liberal, humanistic perspective and a shift away from a concern with the human subject. However, Ferry and Renaut (1985/1990) seek to rescue humanism and subjectivity and Lilla (1994:20) offers a defense of human rights. Manent (1994/1998) self-consciously analyzes modernity and the human subject. Lipovetsky (1987/1994) attacks the tendency of postmodern social theorists to be hypercritical of the contemporary world by defending the importance of fashion. He argues, for example, that fashion enhances rather than detracts from individuality. Thus, just as postmodern social theory is likely to thrive in the coming years, so too are theories that constitute a reaction against it and a return to more modern concerns. Postmodern social theory is not only important in itself, but also for its stimulation of reactions against it. Sociology, and sociological theory in particular, is likely to be revived by postmodern social theory and the challenges it poses (Owen, 1997).

Theories of Consumption

Coming of age during the Industrial Revolution, and animated by its problems and prospects, sociological theory has long had a "productivist bias." That is, theories have tended to focus on industry, industrial organizations, work, and workers. This is most obvious in Marxian and neo-Marxian theory, but it is found in many other theories such as Durkheim's thinking on the division of labor, Weber's work on the rise of capitalism in the West and the failure to develop it in other parts of the world, Simmel's analysis of the tragedy of culture produced by the proliferation of human products, the interest of the Chicago school in work, the concern in conflict theory with relations between employers and employees, leaders and followers, and so on. Much less attention has been devoted to consumption and the consumer. There are exceptions such as Thorstein Veblen's (1899/1994) famous work on "conspicuous consumption" and Simmel's thinking on money and fashion, but in the main social theorists have had far less to say about consumption than production.

Postmodern social theory has tended to define postmodern society as a consumer society with the result that consumption plays a central role in that theory. Most notable is Jean Baudrillard's (1970/1998) *Consumer Society*. Lipovetsky's post-postmodern work on fashion is reflective of the growing interest in and out of postmodern social theory in consumption. Since consumption is likely to continue to grow in importance, especially in the West, and production is likely to decline, it is safe to assume that we will see a dramatic increase in theoretical (and empirical) work on consumption (for an overview of extant theories of consumption, see Slater, 1997). To take one example, we are witnessing something of an outpouring of theoretically based work on the settings in which we consume, such as *Consuming Places* (Urry, 1995), *Enchanting a Disenchanted World: Revolutionizing the Means of Consumption* (Ritzer, 1999), and *Shelf Life: Supermarkets and the Changing Cultures of Consumption* (Humphery, 1998). We are likely to see much more work on such settings, as well as on consumers, consumer goods, and the process of consumption.

Others

Beyond the previous generalizations, it is difficult to foresee the future of sociological theory. For one thing, it is possible that new theories will burst upon the scene and attract adherents. It is also possible that what is today a minor theory will vault to prominence. Some of today's most important theories may grow less attractive. However, it is safe to assume that most, if not all, the theories singled out for discussion in this chapter will continue to be important. It is likely that some (feminist, multicultural, rational choice) will increase in importance while others (neofunctionalism) will experience a decline. One things seems sure—the landscape of social theory is likely to be dotted with more theories, none of which is likely to gain hegemony in the field. Postmodernists have criticized the idea of "totalizations," or overarching theoretical frameworks. It seems unlikely that social theory will come to be dominated by a single totalization. Rather, we are likely to see a field with a proliferating number of perspectives that have some supporters and that help us to understand part of the social world. Sociological theory will not be a simple world to understand and to use, but it will be an exciting world that offers a plethora of old and new ideas.

SUMMARY

This chapter picks up where Chapter 1 left off and deals with the history of sociological theory since the beginning of the twentieth century. We begin with the early history of American sociological theory, which was characterized by its liberalism, by its interest in Social Darwinism, and consequently by the influence of Herbert Spencer. In this context, the work of the two early sociological theorists, Sumner and Ward, is discussed. However, they did not leave a lasting imprint on American sociological theory. In contrast, the Chicago school, as embodied in the work of people like Small, Park, Thomas, Cooley, and especially Mead, did leave a strong mark on sociological theory, especially on symbolic interactionism.

While the Chicago school was still predominant, a different form of sociological theory began to develop at Harvard. Pitirim Sorokin played a key role in the founding of sociology at Harvard, but it was Talcott Parsons who was to lead Harvard to a position of preeminence in American theory, replacing Chicago's symbolic interactionism. Parsons was important not only for legitimizing "grand theory" in the United States and for introducing European theorists to an American audience but also for his role in the development of action theory and, more important, structural functionalism. In the 1940s and 1950s, structural functionalism was furthered by the disintegration of the Chicago school that began in the 1930s and was largely complete by the 1950s.

The major development in Marxian theory in the early years of the twentieth century was the creation of the Frankfurt, or critical, school. This Hegelianized form of Marxism also showed the influence of sociologists like Weber and of the psychoanalyst Sigmund Freud. Marxism did not gain a widespread following among sociologists in the early part of the century.

Structural functionalism's dominance within American theory in mid-century was rather short-lived. Although traceable to a much earlier date, phenomenological sociology, especially the work of Alfred Schutz, began to attract significant attention in the 1960s. Marxian theory was still largely excluded from American theory, but C. Wright Mills kept a radical tradition alive in America in the 1940s and 1950s. Mills also was one of the leaders of the attacks on structural functionalism, attacks that mounted in intensity in the 1950s and 1960s. In light of some of these attacks, a conflict-theory alternative to structural functionalism emerged in this period. Although influenced by Marxian theory, conflict theory suffered from an inadequate integration of Marxism. Still another alternative born in the 1950s was exchange theory, and it continues to attract a small but steady number of followers. Although symbolic interactionism lost some of its steam, the work of Erving Goffman on dramaturgical analysis in this period gained a following.

Important developments took place in other sociologies of everyday life (symbolic interactionism can be included under this heading) in the 1960s and 1970s, including some increase in interest in phenomenological sociology and, more important, an outburst of work in ethnomethodology. During this period Marxian theories of various types came into their own in sociology, although those theories have been seriously compromised by the fall of the Soviet Union and other communist regimes in the late 1980s and early 1990s. Also of note during this period was the growing importance of structuralism and then poststructuralism, especially in the work of Michel Foucault. Of overwhelming significance was the explosion of interest in feminist theory, an outpouring of work that continues apace as we move beyond the year 2000.

In addition to those just mentioned, three other notable developments occurred in the 1980s and continued into the 1990s. First was the rise in interest in the United States in the micro-macro link. Second was the parallel increase in attention in Europe to the relationship between agency and structure. Third was the growth, especially in the 1990s, of a wide range of synthetic efforts.

The chapter concludes with a discussion of some theories to watch as we enter the twenty-first century. Multicultural theories of various types are likely to flourish. Postmodern social theories will continue to develop, but so will reactions against them, including those we can think of as post-postmodern social theories. Relating to postmodern theory, but also a reflection of changes in society and a reaction against the productivist bias that has dominated sociological theory since its inception, theories of consumption will attract attention. Whatever theories come to flower, it seems clear that a single theoretical perspective will be unlikely to dominate the discipline.

From the point of view of the remainder of this book, this chapter has played two major roles. First, it demonstrated that the classical theorists introduced in Chapter 1—Comte, Spencer, Marx, Durkheim, Weber, and Simmel—influenced the later development of sociological theory in a variety of direct and indirect ways. Second, it allowed us to introduce, within their historical context, the other classical theorists who will be discussed in detail later in this book—the founding "mothers," Veblen, Mannheim, Mead, Schutz, and Parsons.

PART **TWO**

CLASSICAL SOCIOLOGICAL THEORY

3

AUGUSTE COMTE

COMTE'S PROFOUND AMBITIONS
    Positivism: The Search for Invariant Laws
    Law of the Three Stages
    Positivism: The Search for Order and Progress
COMTE'S SOCIOLOGY
    Social Statics
    Social Dynamics
THEORY AND PRACTICE
    Who Will Support Positivism?
COMTE'S PLANS FOR THE FUTURE
COMTE: A CRITICAL ASSESSMENT
    Positive Contributions
    Basic Weaknesses in Comte's Theory

Alfred North Whitehead said: "A science which hesitates to forget its founders is lost" (1917/1974:115). Practitioners in an advanced science like physics *have* forgotten the field's founders, or at least they have relegated them to works on the history of the field. A student in physics does not ordinarily read about the work of Isaac Newton but rather about the contemporary state of knowledge on the issues that Newton, and other classic physicists, first addressed. The state of knowledge in contemporary physics has far outstripped that of Newton; hence there is no need for a student to learn about his ideas. Newton's still useful ideas have long since been integrated into the knowledge base of physics. According to Whitehead, physics is *not* lost; it has (largely) forgotten Isaac Newton and the other important figures in the early history of the field.

Why then are students in sociology being asked to read about the work of an early nineteenth-century thinker like Auguste Comte (1798–1857)? The fact is that in spite of a variety of weaknesses, a number of Comte's ideas (e.g., positivism) continue to be important in contemporary sociology. More importantly, many more of his ideas were important in their time and had a significant impact on the development of sociology and sociological theory. While sociological theory has progressed far beyond many of Comte's ideas, sociology is not yet (and some say it will never be) in the position of physics, able to forget the work of its founders.

COMTE'S PROFOUND AMBITIONS

Positivism: The Search for Invariant Laws

Comte is remembered to this day in sociology for his championing of *positivism* (Half-penny, 1982; Scharff, 1995; J. Turner, 1985a, 1990a). While this term has a multitude of meanings, it is usually used to mean the search for invariant laws of both the natural and the social world. In Comte's version of positivism these laws can be derived from doing research on the social world and/or from theorizing about that world. Research is needed to uncover these laws, but in Comte's view the facts derived from research are of secondary importance to sound speculation. Thus Comte's positivism involves empirical research, but that research is subordinated to theory.

Comte's thinking is premised on the idea that there is a real world (for example, biological, sociological) out there and that it is the task of the scientist to discover and report on it. Because of this view, Comte is what we would now call a *realist*. Here is the way Comte put the issue: "Positive philosophers . . . approach the questions with the simple aim of ascertaining the true state of things, and reproducing it with all possible accuracy in their theories" (1830–42/1855:385). Later, Comte argued that positivist philosophy (or any philosophy) "can only be valid insofar as it is an exact and complete representation of the relations naturally existing" (1851/1957:8–9). (This is sometimes called the "copy theory" of truth.)

There are two basic ways of getting at the real world that exists out there—doing research and theorizing. As we saw above, while Comte recognized the importance of research, he emphasized the need for theory and speculation. In emphasizing theory and speculation, Comte was at variance with what has now come to be thought of as positivism, especially pure empiricism through sensory observations and the belief in quantification. As Pickering puts it, "Comte would not recognize the mutilated version of positivism that exists today" (1993:697).

While there are many contemporary sociologists who think of themselves as positivists, positivism has come under severe attack in recent years. Considerable work in the philosophy of science has cast doubt on whether positivism fits the natural sciences, and this tends to raise even greater doubts about the possibility of positivistic sociology. Some sociologists (interpretationists) never accepted a positivist approach, and others who did have either totally abandoned it or adopted a modified positivist perspective (for example, Collins, 1989a). Positivism has not disappeared from sociology, but it seems clear that sociology now finds itself in a postpositivist age (Shweder and Fiske, 1986).

Comte's interest in positivism is intimately related to his interest in sociology. Comte "discovered" sociology in 1839. Consistent with his commitment to positivism, he defined *sociology* as a positivistic science. In fact, in defining *sociology,* Comte related it to one of the most positivistic sciences, physics: "Sociology . . . is the term I may be allowed to invent to designate social physics" (1830–42/1855:444).

Comte (1830–42/1855) developed a hierarchy of the positivistic sciences—mathematics, astronomy, physics, biology (physiology), chemistry, and at the pinnacle (at least in his early work)—sociology.[1] (It is interesting to note that Comte leaves no place for psychology, which would seem to be reduced to a series of biological instincts.) This hierarchy descends from the sciences that are the most general, abstract, and remote from people to those that are the most complex, concrete, and interesting to people (Heilbron, 1990). Sociology builds upon the knowledge and procedures of the sciences that stand beneath it, but in Comte's view sociology is "the most difficult and important subject of all" (1851/1968:31). Given his high estimation of sociology, it is easy to see why Comte has long been esteemed by sociologists. And given the fact that as a positivist, Comte viewed theorizing as the ultimate activity, it is clear why he has had such high status among theorists.

Comte explicitly identified three basic methods for sociology—three basic ways of doing social research in order to gain empirical knowledge of the real social world. The first is *observation,* but Comte is quick to reject isolated, atheoretical observations of the social world. Without theory we would not know what to look for in the social world and we would not understand the significance of what we find. Observations should be directed by some theory, and when made, they should be connected to some law. The second of Comte's methods is the *experiment,* but this method is better suited to the other sciences than it is to sociology. It is obviously virtually impossible to interfere with, and to attempt to control, social phenomena. The one possible exception would be a natural experiment in which the consequences of something that happens in one setting (for example, a tornado) are observed and compared to the conditions in settings in which such an event did not occur. Finally, there is *comparison,* which Comte divides into three subtypes. First, we can compare humans to lower animal societies. Second, we can compare societies in different parts of the world. Third, we can compare the different stages of societies over time. Comte found this last subtype particularly important; in fact, he labeled it the "chief scientific device" of sociology (1830–42/55:481). It is so important that we separate it from the other comparative methods and accord it independent status as Comte's fourth major methodology—*historical research.* In fact, John Stuart Mill sees this as one of Comte's most important contributions in placing the "necessity of historical studies as the foundation of sociological speculation" (1961:86). In his own work, Comte used the historical method almost exclusively, although, as we will see, there are very real questions about how well he actually used this methodology.

Although Comte wrote about research, he most often engaged in speculation or theorizing in order to get at the invariant laws of the social world. He did not derive these laws inductively from observations of the social world; rather, he deduced them from his general theory of human nature. (A critic might ask questions like: How did Comte derive his theory of human nature? Where did he get it from? How can we ascertain whether or not it is true?) In this way Comte (1891/1973:302–304) created a number of general positivistic laws, laws which he applied to the social world.

---

[1]In his later work, Comte added a seventh science that ranked above sociology—morals. We will have more to say about this later.

Law of the Three Stages

Comte's most famous law is the *Law of the Three Stages.* Comte identified three basic stages and proceeded to argue that the human mind, people through the maturation process, all branches of knowledge, and the history of the world (and even, as we will see later, his own mental illness) *all* pass successively through these three stages. Each stage involves the search by human beings for an explanation of the things around them.

1. **The Theological Stage**   Comte saw the theological stage as the first stage and the necessary point of departure for the other two stages. In this stage, the human mind is searching for the essential nature of things, particularly their origin (where do they come from?) and their purpose (why do they exist?). What this comes down to is the search for absolute knowledge. It is assumed that all phenomena are created, regulated, and given their purposes by supernatural forces or beings (gods). While Comte includes *fetishism* (the worship of an object such as a tree) and *polytheism* (the worship of many gods) in the theological stage, the ultimate development in this stage is *monotheism,* or the worship of a single divinity which explains everything.

2. **The Metaphysical Stage**   To Comte this stage is the least important of the three stages. It is a transitional stage between the preceding theological stage and the ensuing positivistic stage. It exists because Comte believes that an immediate jump from the theological to the positivistic stage is too abrupt for people to handle. In the metaphysical stage, abstract forces replace supernatural beings as the explanation for the original causes and purposes of things in the world. For example, mysterious forces such as "nature" are invoked to explain why things are the way they are ("it was an act of nature"). Mill gives as an example of a metaphysical perspective Aristotle's contention that the "rise of water in a pump is attributed to nature's horror of a vacuum" (1961:11). Or to take a more social example, we could say that an event occurred because it was the "will of the people." While numerous entities can be seen as causes in the metaphysical stage, its ultimate point is reached when one great entity (for example, nature) is seen as the cause of everything.

3. **The Positivist Stage**   This, of course, is the final and most important stage in Comte's system. At this point people give up their vain search for original causes or purposes. All we can know are phenomena and the relations among them, not their essential nature or their ultimate causes. People drop such nonscientific ideas as supernatural beings and mysterious forces. Instead, they look for the invariable natural laws that govern *all* phenomena. Examinations of single phenomena are oriented toward linking them to some general fact. The search for these laws involves both doing empirical research and theorizing. Comte differentiated between concrete and abstract laws. Concrete laws must come inductively from empirical research, while abstract laws must be derived deductively from theory. Comte was much more interested in creating abstract laws than in creating concrete ones. While positivism can be characterized by many different laws, he sees it ultimately gravitating toward a smaller and smaller number of general abstract laws.

Although Comte recognized an inevitable succession through these three stages, he also acknowledged that at any given point in time all three might be operant. What he envisioned in the future of the world was a time when the positivistic stage would be complete and we would see the elimination of theological or metaphysical thinking.

Comte applied the Law of the Three Stages in a number of different arenas. He saw people going through the three stages and viewed the child as a theologian, the adolescent as a metaphysician, and the adult as a positivist.[2] He also saw all the sciences in his hierarchy going through each of these stages. (Because it was a new science in Comte's time, sociology had not yet gone through the positivistic stage. Comte devoted much of his life to the development of positivistic sociology.) And he saw the history of the world in these terms. The early history of the world was the theological stage; the world next went through the metaphysical stage; and during Comte's lifetime the world was entering the last, or positivistic, stage. He believed that in the positivistic stage people would come to better understand the invariant laws that dominate them and would be able to adapt to these laws "with fewer difficulties and with greater speed" (Comte, 1852/1968:383). These laws would also guide people in making choices that could expedite the emergence, but not alter the course, of inevitable social developments.

Positivism: The Search for Order and Progress

While Comte used the term *positivism* in the sense of a science committed to the search for invariant laws, he also used it in another way— as the opposite of the negativism that, in his view, dominated the social world of his day. More specifically, that negativity was the moral and political disorder and chaos that occurred in France, and throughout Western Europe, in the wake of the French Revolution of 1789 (Levy-Bruhl, 1903/1973). Among the symptoms of this malaise were intellectual anarchy, political corruption, and incompetence of political leaders. Comte's positive philosophy was designed to counter the negative philosophy and its symptoms that he found all around him.

But while Comte placed great blame on the French Revolution, he found the major source of the disorder to be intellectual anarchy. "The great political and moral crisis that societies are now undergoing is shown by a rigid analysis to arise out of intellectual anarchy" (Comte, 1830–42/1855:36). Comte traced that intellectual anarchy to the coexistence during his lifetime of all three "incompatible" philosophies—theological, metaphysical, and positivistic. Not only did all three exist at one time, but none of them at that point was very strong. Theology and metaphysics were in decay, in a "state of imbecility," and positivism as it relates to the social world (sociology) was as yet unformed. The conflict among, and weaknesses of, these three intellectual schemes allowed a wide variety of "subversive schemes" to grow progressively more dangerous. The answer to this intellectual chaos clearly lay in the emergence of any one of them as preeminent, and given Comte's law, the one that was destined to emerge supreme was positivism. Positivism had already become preeminent within the sciences (except sociology) and had brought order to each, where previously there was chaos. All that was

---

[2]Comte came to associate the history of the world with these life stages—infancy (theological), adolescence (metaphysical), and maturity (positivist).

AUGUSTE COMTE: A Biographical Sketch

Auguste Comte was born in Montpelier, France, on January 19, 1798 (Pickering, 1993:7). His parents were middle class and his father eventually rose to the position of official local agent for the tax collector. Although a precocious student, Comte never received a college-level degree. He and his whole class were dismissed from the Ecole Polytechnique for their rebelliousness and their political ideas. This expulsion had an adverse effect on Comte's academic career. In 1817 he became secretary (and "adopted son" [Manuel, 1962:251]) to Claude Henri Saint-Simon, a philosopher forty years Comte's senior. They worked closely together for several years and Comte acknowledged his great debt to Saint-Simon: "I certainly owe a great deal intellectually to Saint-Simon . . . he contributed powerfully to launching me in the philosophic direction that I clearly created for myself today and which I will follow without hesitation all my life" (Durkheim, 1928/1962:144). But in 1824 they had a falling out because Comte believed that Saint-Simon wanted to omit Comte's name from one of his contributions. Comte later wrote of his relationship with Saint-Simon as "catastrophic" (Pickering, 1993:238) and described him as a "depraved juggler" (Durkheim, 1928/1962:144). In 1852, Comte said of Saint-Simon, "I owed nothing to this personage" (Pickering, 1993:240).

Heilbron (1995) describes Comte as short (perhaps 5 feet, 2 inches), a bit cross-eyed, and very insecure in social situations, especially involving women. He was also alienated from society as a whole. These facts may help account for the fact that Comte married Caroline Massin (the marriage lasted from 1825 to 1842). She was an illegitimate child who Comte later called a "prostitute," although that label has been questioned recently (Pickering, 1997:37). Comte's personal insecurities stood in contrast to his great security about his own intellectual capacities, and it appears as if this self-esteem was well founded:

> Comte's prodigious memory is famous. Endowed with a photographic memory he could recite backwards the words of any page he had read but once. His powers of concentration were such that he could sketch out an entire book without putting pen to paper. His lectures were all delivered without notes. When he sat down to write out his books he wrote everything from memory.   (Schweber, 1991:134)

needed was for positivism to bring social phenomena within its domain. Furthermore, Comte saw this as the way to end the revolutionary crisis that was tormenting France and the rest of Western Europe.

Comte also put this issue in terms of two of his great concerns—order and progress. From his point of view, theology offered a system of order, but without progress; it was a stagnant system. Metaphysics offered progress without order; he associated it with the anarchy of his day, in which things were changing in a dizzying and disorderly way. Because of the coexistence of theology and metaphysics (as well as positivism), Comte's time was marked by *dis*order and a *lack* of progress. Positivism was the only system which offered both order *and* progress. On the one hand, positivism would bring order through the restraint of intellectual and social disorder. On the other hand, it would bring

In 1826, Comte concocted a scheme by which he would present a series of seventy-two public lectures (to be held in his apartment) on his philosophy. The course drew a distinguished audience, but it was halted after three lectures when Comte suffered a nervous breakdown. He continued to suffer from mental problems, and once in 1827 he tried (unsuccessfully) to commit suicide by throwing himself into the Seine River.

Although he could not get a regular position at the Ecole Polytechnique, Comte did get a minor position as a teaching assistant there in 1832. In 1837, Comte was given the additional post of admissions examiner, and this, for the first time, gave him an adequate income (he had often been economically dependent on his family until this time). During this period, Comte worked on the six-volume work for which he is best known, *Cours de Philosophie Positive,* which was finally published in its entirety in 1842 (the first volume had been published in 1830). In that work Comte outlined his view that sociology was the ultimate science. He also attacked the Ecole Polytechnique, and the result was that in 1844 his assistantship there was not renewed. By 1851 he had completed the four-volume *Systeme de Politique Positive,* which had a more practical intent, offering a grand plan for the reorganization of society.

Heilbron argues that a major break took place in Comte's life in 1838 and it was then that he lost hope that anyone would take his work on science in general, and sociology in particular, seriously. It was also at that point that he embarked on his life of "cerebral hygiene"; that is, Comte began to avoid reading the work of other people, with the result that he became hopelessly out of touch with recent intellectual developments. It was after 1838 that he began developing his bizarre ideas about reforming society that found expression in *Systeme de Politique Positive.* Comte came to fancy himself as the high priest of a new religion of humanity; he believed in a world that eventually would be led by sociologist-priests. (Comte had been strongly influenced by his Catholic background.) Interestingly, in spite of such outrageous ideas, Comte eventually developed a considerable following in France, as well as in a number of other countries.

Auguste Comte died on September 5, 1857.

progress through an increase in knowledge and through perfection of the relationship among the parts of the social system so that society would move nearer, although never fully attain, its determinate end (the gradual expansion of human powers). Thus, positivism is the only stage in the history of humankind that offers us both order *and* progress.

Comte saw order and progress in dialectical terms, and in this sense he offered a perspective close to that of Marx (see Chapter 5). This means that Comte refused to see order and progress as separate entities but viewed them as mutually defining and interpenetrating. "Progress may be regarded simply as the development of Order; for the order of nature necessarily contains within itself the germ of all positive progress. . . . Progress then is in its essence identical with Order, and may be looked upon as Order made manifest" (Comte, 1851/1957:116).

It is interesting and important to underscore the fact that in Comte's view the crisis of his time was a *crisis of ideas* and that this crisis could be resolved only by the emergence of a preeminent idea (positivism). In fact, Comte often described positivism as a "spirit." In this sense, Comte is an idealist: "Ideas govern the world" (1830–42/1855:36). On this issue, rather than being in accord with Marx, he stands in stark contrast to Marx (a materialist). Marx saw the capitalist crisis as stemming from the material conflict between capitalists and the proletariat, and he believed that its solution lay in a material revolution in which the economic system of capitalism would be overthrown and replaced by a communist system. Marx scoffed at the idea that he was dealing with a crisis of ideas that could be solved in the ideational realm. Marx was distancing himself from the idealism of Hegel; Comte, in contrast, had adopted a viewpoint that resembled, at least in a few respects, Hegelian idealism.

COMTE'S SOCIOLOGY

We turn now more directly to Comte's sociology, or his thoughts about the social world. Here we begin with another of Comte's lasting contributions—his distinction between *social statics* and *social dynamics*. While we do not use those terms today, the basic distinction remains important in the differentiation between social structure and social change. (By the way, Comte believed that all sciences, not just sociology, are divided into statics and dynamics.)

Social Statics

Comte defines the sociological study of social statics as "the investigation of the laws of action and reaction of the different parts of the social system" (1830–42/55:457). Contrary to what one might think, the laws of the ways in which parts of the social system interact (social statics) are *not* derived from empirical study. Rather, they are "deduced from the laws of human nature" (Comte, 1852/1968:344–345). Here, again, we see Comte's preference for theory over empirical research.

In his social statics, Comte was anticipating many of the ideas of later structural functionalists (see Chapter 14, on Parsons). Deriving his thoughts from biology (Levine, 1995), Comte developed a perspective on the parts (or *structures*) of society, the way in which they *function,* and their (functional) relationship to the larger social system. Comte also saw the parts and the whole of the social system in a state of harmony. The idea of harmony was later transformed by structural functionalists into the concept of equilibrium. Methodologically, Comte recommended that since we know about the whole, we start with it and then proceed to the parts. (Later structural functionalists also came to grant priority to the whole [the "social system"] over the parts [the "subsystems"].) For these and many other reasons Comte is often seen as a forerunner of structural functionalism.

Comte argues that "in Social Statics we must neglect all questions of time, and conceive the organism of society in its fullness. . . . Our ideal" (1852/1968:249). In other words, to use a concept developed by Weber (see Chapter 7), *social statics* describes an "ideal-typical" society. The system of social statics conceived by Comte never really existed; it was an idealized model of the social world at a given point in time. In order to construct such a model, the sociologist must, at least for the purposes of analysis, hold time still.

At a manifest level, Comte is doing a *macro*sociology of social statics (and dynamics), since he is looking at the interrelationship among the parts and the whole of the social system. Indeed, Comte explicitly defined *sociology* as the macro-level study of "collective existence" (1891/1973:172).

The Individual in Comte's Theory   However, Comte's isolated thoughts on micro-level individuals are important not only for understanding his social statics but also for comprehending many other aspects of his work. For example, the individual is a major source of energy in his social system. It is the preponderance of affect or emotion in individuals that gives energy and direction to people's intellectual activities. It is the products of those intellectual activities that lead to changes in the larger social system.

More important for understanding his social statics, as well as his overall view of the world, is the fact that Comte sees the individual as imperfect, dominated by "lower" forms of egoism rather than "higher," more social forms of altruism. In fact, Comte sees this dominance of egoism as rooted in the brain, which is viewed as having both egoistic and altruistic regions. Egoism is seen as having higher energy, thereby helping to ensure the "natural feebleness" of altruism (Comte, 1852/1968:139). Putting egoism and altruism in slightly different terms, Comte argues: "Self-love . . . when left to itself is far stronger than Social Sympathy" (1851/1957:24–25). To Comte (1852/1968:122), the chief problem of human life is the need for altruism to dominate egoism. He sees all the social sciences as being concerned with this problem and with the development of various solutions to it.

Thus, left to themselves, people will, in Comte's view, act in a selfish manner. If we are to hope to be able to create a "better" world, the selfish motives of individuals must be controlled so that the altruistic impulses will emerge. Since egoism cannot be controlled from within the individual, the controls must come from outside the individual, from society. "The higher impulses within us are brought under the influence of a powerful stimulus from without. By its means they are enabled to control our discordant impulses" (Comte, 1851/1957:25–26). Thus Comte, like Durkheim (see Chapter 6), his successor within French sociology, saw people as a problem (egoism was a central concern to both) that could be handled only through external control over people's negative impulses. In terms almost identical to those later used by Durkheim, Comte argues that "true liberty is nothing else than a rational submission to the . . . laws of nature" (1830–42/1855:435). Without such external controls,

> our intellectual faculties, after wasting themselves in wild extravagancies, would sink rapidly into incurable sloth; our nobler feelings would be unable to prevent the ascendancy of the lower instincts; and our active powers would abandon themselves to purposeless agitation. . . . Our propensities are so heterogeneous and so deficient in elevation, that there would be no fixity or consistency in our conduct . . . without them [external restrictions] all its [reason's] deliberations would be confused and purposeless.
> (Comte, 1851/1957:29–30)

Thus Comte concludes: "This need of conforming our Acts and our Thoughts to a Necessity without us, far from hampering the real development of our nature, forms the first general condition of progress towards perfection in man" (1852/1968:26).

Not only does Comte have a highly negative view of people and their innate propensity to egoism, but he also has a very limited view of the creative capacities of individuals. "We are powerless to create: all that we can do in bettering our condition is to modify an order in which we can produce no radical change" (Comte, 1851/1957:30). Thus, Comte's actors are not only egoistic but also weak and powerless. In a very real sense, people do not create the social world; rather, the social world creates people, at least those animated by the nobler altruistic motives.

Comte addresses this issue in another way, in terms of the relationship between what he calls the "subjective" and "objective" principles. The subjective principle involves "the subordination of the intellect to the heart," while the objective principle entails "the immutable Necessity of the external world . . . actually existing without us"[3] (Comte, 1851/1957:26–27). Given the preceding discussion, it should be clear why Comte argues that the subjective principle must be subordinated to the objective principle. The "heart" (especially its egoism), which dominates the intellect, must be subordinated to external societal constraints so that another aspect of the "heart," altruism, can emerge triumphant.

Comte had other, more specific things to say about the individual. For example, he distinguished among four basic categories of instincts—nutrition, sex, destruction and construction, and pride and vanity (Comte, 1854/1968:249–252). Clearly, all but the constructive instinct are in need of external control. While Comte does attribute other, more positive instincts to people (attachment to others, veneration of predecessors), it is the instincts in need of external control that define to a great degree his thoughts on the larger society. Larger social structures like the family and society are needed to restrain individual egoism and to help bring forth individual altruism.

Collective Phenomena   In spite of his clear ideas on the individual, Comte's sociology overtly begins at a more macro level, with the family, which Comte labels the "fundamental institution." The family, *not* the individual, is the building block of Comte's sociology, as he explains: "As every system must be composed of elements of the same nature with itself, the scientific spirit forbids us to regard society as composed of individuals. The true social unit is certainly the family" (1830–42/1855:502). Comte clearly believes that individuals constitute a different "level" of analysis than families (and society), which are, after all, "nothing but our smallest society" (1852/1968:161). These "smaller societies" form the natural building blocks of the larger society. Methodologically, Comte argues that "a system can only be formed out of units similar to itself and differing only in magnitude" (1852/1968:153). Individuals constitute different (microscopic) units, and (macroscopic) society cannot be formed out of them. Families are similar, albeit smaller, macroscopic units, and therefore they *can* be the

---

[3]It is the kind of viewpoint that leads us, once again, to think of Comte as a social realist; there is a real world out there.

basis of the larger society. In fact, Comte traces a progression whereby out of families tribes emerge and from tribes come nations. The family is the "true germ of the various characteristics of the social organism" (Comte, 1830–42/1855:502). The family not only is the building block of society but also serves to integrate the individual and society, since it is through the family that people learn to be social; the family is the "school" of society. Thus, it is the family that must play a crucial role in the control of egoistic impulses and the emergence of individual altruism. Furthermore, if we are ever to improve society significantly, a change in the family will be the fundamental basis of any such alteration. Since the family is such a pivotal institution, a change in it will have profound effects on both individuals and the larger society.

While the family is the most basic and most pivotal institution, the most important institution to Comte is religion, "the universal basis of all society" (1852/1968:7). Doing a kind of structural-functional analysis, Comte identifies two major functions of religion. First, it serves to regulate individual life, once again primarily by subduing egoism and elevating altruism. Second, it has the more macroscopic function of fostering social relationships among people, thereby providing the basis for the emergence of large-scale social structures.

Another important social institution to Comte is language. Language is profoundly social; it is what allows people to interact with one another. Thus, language helps promote unity among people. It connects people not only with their contemporaries but also with their predecessors (we can read their ideas) and their successors (they can read our ideas). Language is also crucial to religion in that it permits the formation, transmission, and application of religious ideas.

Another element of society that serves to hold people together is the division of labor[4] (a view very much like that of Durkheim; see Chapter 6). Social solidarity is enhanced in a system in which individuals are dependent upon others. Society should have a division of labor so that people can occupy the positions for which they qualify on the basis of their abilities and training. Conversely, society should not force people into positions for which they are either underqualified or overqualified (Durkheim calls this the "forced division of labor"). While Comte argues for the need for a division of labor, he is very concerned here, as he is elsewhere, about the dangers of excessive specialization in work in general and in intellectual work in particular. He worries about the tendency in society toward overspecialization and argues that the government should intervene to emphasize the good of the whole.

The government, in Comte's view, is based on force. While force can hold society together, if the use of force gets out of hand, the government will be more of a destructive than an integrative factor in society. To prevent this from occurring, the government needs to be regulated by a "broader and higher society. . . . This is the mission of true Religion" (Comte, 1852/1968:249). Comte clearly did not have a high regard for government, and he felt that religion was needed "to repress or to remedy the evils to which all governments are prone" (1852/1968:252).

---

[4]Or what Comte calls the "division of employments."

Social Dynamics

While Comte does have other things to say about social statics, he devoted more attention to social dynamics. He felt that less was known about social statics than about
social dynamics. Furthermore, the topic of social dynamics was, in his opinion, more
interesting and of far greater importance than social statics. However, one may question
these contentions. How is it that Comte knew more about the history of the world than
he did about the nature of his own society? Why is the past (and future) more interesting
than the present? In response to these questions, and contrary to Comte, it can be clearly
argued that we always know more about the present than the past (or certainly the future)
and that the here and now is far more interesting and far more important than the past (or
future). Nevertheless, it is on the basis of his beliefs on these issues that Comte abbrevi-
ates his discussion of social statics and moves on to the study of social dynamics.

The goal of Comte's social dynamics is to study the laws of succession of social phenomena. Society is always changing, but the change is ordered and subject to social
laws. There is an evolutionary process in which society is progressing in a steady fashion to its final harmonious destiny under the laws of positivism: "We are always
becoming more intelligent, more active, and more loving" (Comte, 1853/1968:60). Al-
ternatively, Comte labels *social dynamics* the "theory of the Natural Progress of Human
Society" (1830–42/1855:515). Overall, Comte sees us evolving toward our "noblest
dispositions," toward the dominance of altruism over egoism. Comte also offers a
somewhat more specific view of this future state toward which we are evolving:

> The individual life, ruled by personal instincts; the domestic, by sympathetic instincts;
> and the social, by the special development of intellectual influences, prepare for the states
> of human existence which are to follow: and that which ensues is, first, personal moral-
> ity, which subjects the preservation of the individual to a wise discipline; next, domestic
> morality, which subordinates selfishness to sympathy; and lastly, social morality, which
> directs all individual tendencies by enlightened reason, always having the general econ-
> omy in view, so as to bring into concurrence all the faculties of human nature, according
> to their appropriate laws.
>
> (Comte, 1830–42/1855:515)

In his view, society invariably follows this law of progressive development; only its
speed from one time period, or one society, to another may vary.

Because invariant laws are controlling this process of change, there is relatively little
that people can do to affect the overall direction of the process. Nevertheless, people
can make a difference by acting "upon the intensity and secondary operation of
phenomena, but without affecting their nature or their filiation" (Comte,
1830–42/1855:470). People can modify (for example, speed up) only what is in accord
with existing tendencies; that is, people are able to bring about only things that would
have happened in any event. It is the fact that people can affect the development of society, if only marginally, that led Comte to his ideas on changing society and his
thoughts on the relationship between theory and practice. We will have much more to
say about this issue later in this chapter. However, it should be pointed out here that the
idea that people can have only a minimal impact did not prevent Comte from developing grandiose plans for the future, positivistic society.

Comte's theory of the evolution of society is based on his theory of the evolution of the mind through the three stages described above. He contends that he himself has "tested" this law by means of all the major methods—observation, experiment, comparison, historical research—and found it "as fully demonstrated as any other law admitted into any other department of natural philosophy" (Comte, 1830–42/1855:522).

Having derived this social law theoretically (from the laws of human nature), he turns to a "study" of the history of the world to see whether the "data" support his abstract theory. However, Comte's use of the words *study* and *data* is misleading, since his methods did not incorporate the criteria that we usually associate with a research study and the data derived from it. For one thing, if Comte's findings contradicted the basic laws of human nature, he would conclude that the research was wrong rather than question the theory (Mill, 1961:85). Comte did no systematic study of the history of the world (how could one systematically study such a vast body of material?), and he did not produce data about that history (he merely provided a series of broad generalizations about vast periods of history). In other words, Comte did not do a research study in the positivistic sense of the term. In fact, Comte acknowledges this by saying that all he is offering is an abstract history; science is not yet ready for a concrete history of the world.

As he had in other areas of his work, Comte offered a dialectical sense of the history of the world. What this meant, in particular, was that he saw the roots of each succeeding stage in history in its prior stage or stages. In addition, each stage prepared the ground for the next stage or stages. In other words, each stage in history is dialectically related to past and future stages. A similar viewpoint is offered by Marx (see Chapter 5), who sees capitalism as being dialectically related to previous economic systems (for example, feudalism) as well as to the future communist society. Although on this point, and on several others, Comte's ideas resemble those of Marx, the reader should bear in mind that the differences between the two thinkers far exceed their similarities. This difference will be clearest when we discuss Comte's conservative views about the future of the world, which are diametrically opposed to Marx's radical communist society.

Never humble, Comte *began* his analysis of social dynamics by asserting, "My principle of social development . . . affords a *perfect* interpretation of the past of human society—at least in its principal phases" (1830–42/1855:541; italics added). Similarly, at the close of the historical discussion briefly outlined below, Comte concluded, "The laws originally deduced from an abstract examination of human nature have been demonstrated to be real laws, *explaining the entire course of the destinies of the human race*" (1853/1968:535; italics added).

History   Comte limited his study to Western Europe (and the "white race") because it had evolved the most and because it was, in his view, the "elite" of humanity. We need not go into great detail here about his historical theory because it is of little lasting significance. Furthermore, because it is more central to Comte's underlying theory, we will focus on the changing nature of ideas rather than on more material transformations (for example, Comte sees society as evolving from the warfare characteristic of the theological stage to industry, which was to dominate the positivist stage). Comte begins with the theological stage, which he traces to antiquity. He divides the theological stage into three succeeding periods—fetishistic, polytheistic, and monotheistic. In the early fetishistic stage, people personify external objects (for example, a tree), give them lives like their own, and then deify those objects. Much later, polytheism in Egypt, Greece, and Rome developed. Finally, Comte analyzes the rise of monotheism, especially Roman Catholicism, in the Middle Ages. Although all of these are part of the theological stage, Comte is careful to show that they also possess the germs of the positivism that was to emerge at a much later point in history.

Comte sees the fourteenth century as a crucial turning point, as theology began a long period of enfeeblement and decline. More specifically, Catholicism was undermined and eventually replaced by Protestantism, which Comte sees as nothing more than a growing protest against the old social order's intellectual basis (theology). This, for Comte, represents the beginning of the negativity that he sought to counteract with his positivism, a negativity which did not begin to be systematized into a doctrine until the mid-seventeenth century. Protestantism laid the groundwork for this negativity by encouraging unlimited free inquiry. This change in ideas, the development of a negative philosophy, led to a corresponding negativity in the social world and to the social crisis that obsessed Comte. This negative doctrine was developed by French thinkers like Voltaire (1649–1778) and Jean-Jacques Rousseau (1712–1778), whom Comte did not see as systematic thinkers; as a result, he believed they were incapable of producing coherent speculations. Nevertheless, these incoherent theories gained a following among the masses because they appeared at a time when theology was greatly weakened and positivism was not yet ready to take its place. Most generally, this entire period was the transitional period, the metaphysical stage, between theology and positivism.

Comte himself was writing during what he believed to be the close of the metaphysical stage: "We find ourselves therefore living at a period of confusion, without any general view of the past, or sound appreciation of the future, to enlighten us for the crisis prepared by the whole progress yet achieved" (Comte, 1830–42/1855:738–739). Negativity had far outstripped positivity, and there was, as yet, no available intellectual means to reorganize society. Everywhere Comte turned there was crisis—art was "adrift," science was suffering from overspecialization, and philosophy had fallen into "nothingness." Overall, Comte describes the situation as "the philosophical anarchy of our time" (1830–42/1855:738). This philosophical anarchy prepared the way for social revolution, especially the French Revolution, which while negative in many senses, was salutary in that it paved the way for the positivistic reorganization of society. As a social event it demonstrated "the powerlessness of critical principles to do anything but destroy" (Comte, 1830–42/1855:739).

Not only was France the site of the major political revolution, but it was to take the lead in the reorganization of Western Europe. It had the most advanced negative ideas and developments, *and* it had gone farthest in positive directions. In terms of the latter, its industrial activity was most "elevated," its art was most advanced, it was "foremost" in science, and it was closer to the new, positive philosophy (and, of course, his eminence, Auguste Comte, lived there). While Comte saw signs during this period of the development of positivism, he recognized that in the short run metaphysics (and the metaphysical stage) had won out. He described the effort in France to develop a constitutional government as being based on metaphysical principles, and he felt that at a philosophical level Rousseau's "retrograde" philosophy had won out. He felt that Rousseau sought to emulate older societies, in which people were freer and more natural, rather than provide a basis for modern society. While this negative development held sway for half a century in France, Comte also saw within it positive developments in industry, art, science, and philosophy.

Comte saw this period as dominated by a focus on the individual and the metaphysical notion of individual rights. Concern for the individual led only to disorder; in its place, Comte, as we have seen, urged a focus on collective phenomena like the family and society. In addition, a focus on individual rights furthered the tendency toward disorder and chaos; Comte sought a society based on what he viewed as the positive idea of *duties* rather than on individual rights. The idea of duties was seen as a positive notion both because it was more scientific (for example, more "precise") and because it had a "calming" influence on people's egoism as well as on the rampant negativity of the day. Instead of focusing on their individual rights, people were urged to concentrate on their duties to the larger society. This emphasis on duties would enable society to control individual egoism and to better bring out the altruism innate in people. These new duties were to help form the basis of a new spiritual authority that would help regenerate society and morality. This new spiritual authority was, of course, positivism.

THEORY AND PRACTICE

The discussion of the previous section, in broad outline, is Comte's theory of social dynamics. Yet Comte (like Marx) wanted to do more than theorize. He wanted his theoretical ideas to lead to practical social changes; he explicitly and self-consciously sought the "connection between theory and practice" (Comte, 1851/1968:46). To this end, Comte sees two objectives for positivism. The first, covered in the preceding sections, is to generalize scientific conceptions—in other words, to advance the science of humanity. The second, covered in this section, is to systematize the art and practice of life (Comte, 1851/1957:3). Thus, positivism is *both* a scientific philosophy and a political practice; the two "can never be dissevered" (Comte, 1851/1968:1).

Who Will Support Positivism?

One of the first political questions addressed by Comte is: Which social groups are likely to support the new doctrine of positivism? It was assumed by Comte that many philosophers would be ardent supporters of this new set of ideas, but philosophers are limited in terms of their ability to implement their ideas. What of the groups of people who are more actively engaged in the social world?

Comte begins by excluding the upper classes because they are in the thrall of metaphysical theories, are too self-seeking, occupy positions too overly specialized to understand the total situation, are too aristocratic, are absorbed in fighting over remnants of the old system, and are blinded by their educational experiences. Overall, he sees the wealthy as more likely than other social groups to be characterized by "avarice, ambition, or vanity" (Comte, 1851/1957:144). Comte also did not expect too much help from the middle classes because they are too busily involved in trying to move into the upper classes.

Comte did expect help from three groups: in addition to the philosophers, who would supply the intellect, the working class would bring the needed action and women would provide the required feeling. The philosophers, especially those attracted to positivistic ideas, would be involved, but the major agents of political change would be women and members of the working class: "It is among women, therefore, and among the working classes that the heartiest supporters of the new doctrine will be found" (Comte, 1851/1957:4). Both groups are generally excluded from government positions and thus will be more likely to see the need for political change. Furthermore, discrimination against them in the educational system ("the present worthless methods of instruction by words and entities" [Comte, 1851/1957:142]) is less likely to blind them to the need for such change. Comte also sees both women and the working class as possessing "strong social instincts" and "the largest stock of good sense and good feeling" (1851/1957:142).

The Working Class   In Comte's view, the members of the working class are better able to think during the workday because their jobs are not as fully absorbing as those of people in the higher social classes. Presumably this means that the working class has more time and energy to reflect on the benefits of positivism than do the upper classes. The working class is superior not only intellectually, at least in the sense discussed above, but also morally. Comte offers a highly romanticized view of the morality of the working class: "The life of the workman . . . is far more favourable to the development of the nobler instincts" (1851/1957:144–145). More specifically, Comte attributes a long series of traits to members of the working class, including more affectionate ties at home; the "highest and most genuine types of friendship"; "sincere and simple respect for superiors"; experience with life's miseries, which stimulates them to nobler sympathies; and a greater likelihood of engaging in "prompt and unostentatious self-sacrifice at the call of a great public necessity" (Comte, 1851/1957:145–146).

Comte sees the spread of communism among the working classes in his day as evidence that the trend toward social revolution is focusing in on moral issues. But Comte reinterprets communism as a moral rather than an economic movement so that it fits into his scheme. He argues that communism must be separated from the "numerous extravagant schemes" (presumably Saint-Simon's socialism or Marx's call for a communist revolution) that were being discussed at the time (Comte, 1851/1957:167). To Comte, communism was "a simple assertion of the paramount importance of Social Feeling" (1851/1957:169). To show how far he is willing to water down the idea of communism, Comte argues that "the word *Republican* expresses the meaning as well, and without the same danger" (1851/1957:169). Clearly, this is a very different meaning of the term *communism* than the one used by Marx (see Chapter 5) and by most other thinkers who have employed the term.

Comte sees positivism as *the* alternative to communism: positivism is the "only doctrine which can preserve Western Europe from some serious attempt to bring Communism into practical operation" (1851/1957:170). Comte offers a number of contrasts between positivism and communism. First, positivism focuses on moral responses rather than on political responses and economic issues. (Here Comte clearly recognizes that communism, at least as it was being practiced in his time, was an economic and political, rather than a moral, system). Second, communism seeks to suppress individuality, whereas positivism seeks both individuality and cooperation among independent individuals. Third, communism seeks the elimination of the leaders of industry, whereas positivism sees them as essential. (Thus, while the leaders of industry cannot play a role in the positivist revolution, they do play, as we will see later, a central role, along with bankers, in Comte's vision of the revamped positivist society.) Fourth, communism seeks to eliminate inheritance, while positivism sees inheritance as important because it provides for historical continuity from generation to generation. In spite of his rejection of communism, Comte sees it as important as another, largely negative, force providing the groundwork for the emergence of positivism.

Women   Comte's interest in the working class as a revolutionary force is not unusual, but his attraction to women as such a group is. Comte had some extraordinary views about women. His major position was that women brought to politics the needed subordination of intellect to social feeling. And Comte came to believe that feeling was preeminent, far more important than intellect or action: feeling is "the predominating principle, the motive power of our being, the only basis on which the various parts of our natures can be brought into unity" (1851/1957:227). Women are "the best representatives of the fundamental principle on which Positivism rests, the victory of social over selfish affections" (Comte, 1851/1957:232). Comte sometimes gushes with his admiration for women in general (as he did more specifically for his beloved "Saint" Clotilde).[5] "Morally . . . she merits always our loving veneration, as the purest and simplest impersonation of Humanity, who can never be adequately represented in any masculine form" (1851/1957:234). Or even more strongly, "Woman is the spontaneous priestess of Humanity" (Comte, 1851/1957:253). (Of course, this means that men in general, and Comte in particular, are the priests of humanity.) Nevertheless, in spite of his admiration for women, he clearly sees men as superior practically and intellectually. On the intellectual issue Comte contends, "Women's minds no doubt are less capable than ours of generalizing very widely, or of carrying on long processes of deduction . . . less capable than men of abstract intellectual exertion" (1851/1957:250). Because of their intellectual and practical superiority, it is men who are to take command in the actual implementation of positivism.

On the one hand, Comte clearly admired the moral and affectual aspects of women, and as a result, he was willing to accord them a key revolutionary role. On the other hand, he felt that men excelled in intellect and action, and he tended to demean the intellectual and active capacities of women. In terms of implementing their role in the positivist revolution, women were supposed to alter the educational process within the family and to form "salons" to disseminate positivistic ideas. In spite of his veneration of women, Comte did not believe in equality: "Equality in the position of the two sexes is contrary to their nature" (1851/1957:275). He defended this view on the basis of the fact that positivism has *discovered* the following "axiom": "Man should provide for Woman" (Comte, 1851/1957:276). More practically, positivism would institute a new doctrine: "Worship of Woman, publicly and privately" (Comte, 1851/1957:283).

[5]In fact, Comte thanks Clotilde for helping him come to understand the importance of affection.

Thoughts, Feelings, and Actions   Comte's focus on women, and his emphasis on their capacity for feeling, represented a general change in perspective from his earlier positions. As we have seen, Comte emphasized order in social statics and progress in social dynamics. To order and progress he now added the importance of feeling (love), which he associated with women. As a result he came to proclaim the "positivist motto, *Love, Order, Progress*" (Comte, 1851/1957:7). Positivism was no longer important just intellectually but morally as well. Similarly, Comte added the emotional element to his previous commitment to thought and action by arguing that positive philosophy represented a comprehensive perspective encompassing "Thoughts, Feelings, and Actions" (1851/1957:8).

Comte went further than simply according feeling equal status with thought and action; he gave feeling the preeminent place in his system. Feeling was to direct the intellect as well as practical activity. In particular, Comte argued that "individual happiness and public welfare are far more dependent upon the heart than upon the intellect" (1851/1957:15). It is this kind of viewpoint that led the champion of positivist intellectual life to the anti-intellectualism that is one of the problems we will discuss later in this chapter.

The emphasis on feeling and love led Comte in his later work to add the science of morality (the study of sentiment) to his list of sciences. "Morals is the most *eminent* of the Sciences" (Comte, 1853/1968:41). Morality was a science which in his system exceeded even sociology. "The field of Morals is at once more *special,* more *complex,* and more *noble* than that of Sociology" (Comte, 1853/1968:40). Not only was morality the most important science, but it was also crucial in giving direction to political changes. In Comte's terms, morality is "the ultimate object of all Philosophy, and the starting point of all Polity" (1851/1957:101). In other words, morality lies at the center of the relationship between theory and practice. Comte sees a natural morality in the world, and it is the task of the positivist to discover its laws. It is these underlying laws of morality that guide our intellectual thoughts and our political actions. Comte concludes, "It is henceforth a fundamental doctrine of Positivism, a doctrine of as great political as philosophical importance, that the Heart preponderates over the Intellect" (1851/1957:18).

Having added morality to the list of his major concerns, Comte returns to his Law of the Three Stages to look at each stage from the point of view of thoughts, feelings, and actions. He sees the theological stage as being dominated by feeling and imagination, with only slight restraint from reason. Theology operated on a purely subjective level, with the result that it was out of touch with the objectivity of practice in the real world. "Theology asserted all phenomena to be under the dominion of Wills more or less arbitrary," but in the real world people were, of course, led by "invariable laws" (Comte, 1851/1957:10). The transitional metaphysical stage continued to be dominated by feeling, was muddled in its thoughts, and was even less able to deal with the practical world. However, positivism finally offered the unity and harmony of thought, feeling, and action. The ideas of positivism are derived from the practical world and are certainly a monumental intellectual achievement. And positivism also came to comprehend the moral sphere. Only when positivism incorporates morality "can the claims of theology be finally set aside" (Comte, 1851/1957:13). Among other things, morality (feeling) is important for giving direction to thought and action. For example, without the direction of morality, positivism is prone to be too specialized and to deal with "useless or insolvable questions" (Comte, 1851/1957:21). Under the guidance of morality, positivism comes to focus on the broadest, most important, most pressing, and most solvable problems of the day.

With morality added to positivism, it is but a short step for Comte to declare positivism a religion: "Thus Positivism becomes, in the true sense of the word, a Religion; the only religion which is real and complete; destined therefore to replace all imperfect and provisional systems resting on the primitive basis of Theology" (1851/1957:365). And this means that Comte and his principal followers become priests of humanity, with far greater influence than any other previous priesthood. In fact, Comte, with customary humility, declared himself the "founder of the Religion of Humanity" (1853/1968:x). The object of worship in the new religion of positivism is not a god or gods but humanity, or what Comte later referred to as the "Great Being," that is, "the whole constituted by the beings [including animals], past, future, and present, which co-operate willingly in perfecting the order of the world" (1854/1968:27). The Great Being lies at the base of the positivist religion: "The Positive Religion inspires all the servants of the Great Being with a sacred zeal to represent that Being as fully as possible" (Comte, 1852/1968:65).

COMTE'S PLANS FOR THE FUTURE

Given Comte's exaggerated conception of positivism, as well as of his own position in it, it should come as little surprise that he ultimately conceived a grand visionary plan for the future of the world. It is here that we find most of Comte's most outrageous and ridiculous ideas. (It might be that one should take his earlier theories more seriously than his later vision of the future.) Standley calls Comte's vision of the future a "Memorable Fancy" (1981:158). We do not want to go into too much detail, so we will merely suggest the lengths to which Comte went in proposing ways of implementing his positivistic ideas.

For example, he suggested a new positivistic calendar which was to be composed of thirteen months, each divided into twenty-eight days. He created a large number of public holidays to reaffirm positivism, its basic principles, and its secular heroes. He even got into the question of the design of new positivistic temples. He specified the number of priests and vicars required in each temple. Forty-two of the vicars were to be chosen as the priests of humanity, and from that group the high priest ("the Pontiff") of positivism was to be chosen (as opposed to the Catholic pontiff, who resided in Italy, the positivist pontiff was normally supposed to reside in Paris). (Comte saw himself as the current pontiff and worried over the fact that there was no clear successor on the horizon.) All these religious figures were to be freed of material cares and therefore were to be supported by the bankers! Comte even specified incomes for religious figures—240 pounds for vicars, 480 pounds for priests, and 2400 pounds for the high priest. Given Comte's views on the positive influence of women, all the priests were to be married so that "they may be under the full influence of affection" (Comte, 1854/1968:224). However, in spite of his high esteem for women, they were not permitted to serve as priests, vicars, or the pontiff. These positions were reserved for men.

While he did not see them as revolutionary forces, Comte eventually accorded members of the upper class, such as bankers and industrialists, central roles in the new positivist society. It was specified that Western Europe was to have "two thousand bankers, a hundred thousand merchants, two hundred thousand manufacturers, and four hundred thousand agriculturists" (Comte, 1854/1968:269). Merchants, manufacturers, and industrialists were to be apportioned an adequate number of members of the proletariat. Bankers would be both the centers of the commercial world and the suppliers of required funds to the positivist priesthood. Furthermore, from those bankers who are most distinguished for "breadth of thought and generosity of feeling" would be derived the supreme triumvirate (bankers representing merchants, manufacturers, and agriculturalists), which was to handle governmental functions (Comte, 1854/1968:301). However, overseeing and directing the operation of this government would be the pontiff and his priests, armed with the religion of positivism.

Turning to other matters, Comte urged the adoption of a positivist library of 100 titles (already specified by him). Additional reading was to be discouraged because it hampered meditation. This, too, is reflective of Comte's growing anti-intellectualism (see the next section).

Given Comte's negative views on individual passion, he urged chastity within the positivist family. He felt that positivism would "discredit and repress the most troublesome of the egoistic instincts [sex!]" (Comte, 1854/1968:251). To deal with the problem of sex, Comte espoused virgin birth. While he did not yet know how virgin birth was to be accomplished (could he have anticipated artificial insemination?), he seemed confident that others would be able to solve the problem eventually. He also favored eugenics, in which only the "higher types" of people (women) would be allowed to reproduce. Such a plan "would improve the human race" (Comte, 1854/1968:244). He said that we should devote "the same attention to the propagation of our species as to that of the more important domestic animals" (Comte, 1891/1973:222).

The positive family was to be composed of a husband, a wife, ordinarily three children, *and* the husband's parents. The latter were included to bring the wisdom of the past into the family of the present. The mother of the husband, possessing not only the wisdom of advanced age but also the feeling inherent in the female sex, would become the "goddess" of the positivist family.

These are just a few of the myriad of highly detailed proposals Comte put forth on the basis of his positivist theory. He was careful to point to a division of labor in the development of these guidelines. The positivist philosopher was to come up with the ideas, but he was not to intervene himself in the social world. Such interventions are left to the politician, guided, of course, by the positivist priesthood.

COMTE: A CRITICAL ASSESSMENT

From the previous discussion of a few of Comte's ideas about the future, the reader might conclude that Comte ought to be dismissed out of hand. In fact, it might even be asked once again why a chapter on Comte is included in this book. Thus, we will begin this concluding section with an overview of Comte's most important contributions to sociology. Later we will turn to the far more numerous weaknesses in Comte's work— weaknesses which lead us to conclude that it is safe for the science of sociology to forget much of Comte's work and get on with its own development, which has forged far ahead of Comte's ideas.

Positive Contributions

First, of course, Comte was the first thinker to use the term *sociology;* he can be seen as the "founder" of sociology. While it is certainly the case that thinkers throughout the course of human history have dealt with sociological issues, Comte was the first to make such a focus explicit and to give it a name.

Second, Comte defined *sociology* as a positivistic science. While this is, as we will see later, a mixed blessing, the fact is that the majority of contemporary sociologists continue to see sociology as a positivistic science. They believe that there are invariant laws of the social world and that it is their task to discover those laws. Many search for such laws empirically, while others (for example, J. Turner, 1985a) follow Comte's model and go about the search for such laws theoretically. Much of contemporary empirical sociology, and a significant segment of sociological theory, continues to accept Comte's positivistic model of sociology.

Third, Comte articulated three major methods for sociology—observation, experiment, and comparison (the historical comparative method is sufficiently important to be distinguished as a fourth methodology)—which continue to be widely used in sociology. While Comte's work is badly dated in most respects, it is surprisingly contemporary in terms of its methodological pronouncements. For example, there has been a substantial resurgence of interest in historical studies in contemporary sociology (see, for example, Mann, 1986; Wallerstein, 1989).

Fourth, Comte differentiated in sociology between social statics and social dynamics. This continues to be an important differentiation in sociology, but the concepts are now called *social structure* and *social change*. Sociologists continue to focus on society as it is presently constituted as well as on its changing nature.

Fifth, although again a mixed blessing, Comte defined *sociology* in macroscopic terms as the study of collective phenomena. This was to take clearer form in the work of Durkheim, who defined *sociology* as the study of social facts (see Chapter 6). More specifically, many of Comte's ideas played a key role in the development of a major contemporary sociological theory—structural functionalism (see Chapter 14).

Sixth, Comte stated clearly his basic ideas about the domination of human nature, if left on its own, by egoism. Because he is clear about such basic views, the reader gets a sound understanding of where Comte's thoughts on the larger structures of society come from. Basically, those larger structures are needed to control individual egoism and to permit the emergence of individual altruism.

Seventh, Comte offered a dialectical view of macro structures. He saw contemporary macro structures as being the product of past structures and as possessing the seeds of future structures. This view gave his work a strong sense of historical continuity. His dynamic, dialectical view of social structure is superior to positions taken by many later, even contemporary, theorists of social structure who have tended to adopt static, ahistorical perspectives.

Eighth, Comte was not content with simply developing abstract theory but was interested in integrating theory and practice. While this ambition was marred by some of his ludicrous ideas for the future society, the integration of theory and practice remains a cherished objective among contemporary sociologists. In fact, there is a growing interest in what is now called *applied* sociology, and the American Sociological Association has a section on sociological practice.

Basic Weaknesses in Comte's Theory

We can begin the discussion of Comte's specific weaknesses with a quotation from one of his severest critics, Isaiah Berlin:

> His grotesque pedantry, the unreadable dullness of his writing, his vanity, his eccentricity, his solemnity, the pathos of his private life, his insane dogmatism, his authoritarianism, his philosophical fallacies . . . [his] obstinate craving for unity and symmetry at the expense of experience . . . with his fanatically tidy world of human beings joyfully engaged in fulfilling their functions, each within his own rigorously defined province, in the rationally ordered, totally unalterable hierarchy of the perfect society.
>
> (Berlin, 1954:4–5, 22)

One is hard-pressed to think of a more damning critique of any social theorist, yet much of it is warranted. The issue here is: Where and how did Comte go wrong in his social theorizing?

First, Comte's theory was overly influenced by the trials and tribulations of his own life. For one thing, very much ignored in his lifetime, Comte became increasingly grandiose in his theoretical and practical ambitions. For another, his largely unfulfilled relationships with women, especially his beloved Clotilde, led him to a series of outrageous ideas about women and their role in society. This problem was amplified by a sexism that led him to accord feelings to women, while men were given intellectual capacities and political and economic power. Then we must add the fact that Comte was deeply troubled psychologically; one often feels, especially in regard to the later works, that one is reading the rantings of a lunatic.

Second, Comte seemed to fall increasingly out of touch with the real world. After *Positive Philosophy,* his theories were characterized by a spinning out of the internal logic of his own ideas. One reason is that despite his claims, Comte actually did no real empirical research. His idea of doing empirical research was to offer gross generalities about the historical stages, and the evolution, of the world. Comte's looseness about data analysis is reflected in the following statement: "Verification of this theory may be found *more or less distinctly* in every period of history" (1851/1957:240; italics added). Had Comte been a better data analyst, and had he been more generally in touch with the historical and contemporary worlds, his theories might not have become so outrageous.

Third, Comte also grew progressively out of touch with the intellectual work of his time. Indeed, he is famous for practicing cerebral hygiene rather early in his life. He systematically avoided reading newspapers, periodicals, and books (except for a few favorite poems) and thereby sought to keep the ideas of others from interfering with his own theorizing. In effect, Comte was increasingly anti-intellectual. This ultimately became manifest in his substantive work, in which he urged such things as the abolition of the university and the withdrawal of economic support for science and scientific societies. It is also manifest in his positivist reading list of 100 books. Presumably, this limited list meant that all other books did not need to be read and could be safely burned. Comte's anti-intellectualism is also found in other aspects of his substantive work. For example, in making the case that strong affect helps lead to important scientific findings, Comte downgrades the importance of rigorous scientific work: "Doubtless, the method of pure science leads up to it also; but only by a long and toilsome process, which exhausts the power of thought, and leaves little energy for following out the new results to which this great principle gives rise" (1851/1957:243). The clear lesson of Comte's errors is that a theorist must remain in touch with *both* the empirical and the intellectual worlds.

Fourth, he failed as a positivist, both in his empirical and in his theoretical work. As to his empirical work, we have seen that he did woefully little of it and that the work he did was really little more than a series of gross generalizations about the course of world history. There was certainly little or no induction from data derived from the real world. Regarding his theoretical work, it is hard even to think of many of his bizarre generalizations about the social world as sociological laws. Even if we take Comte's word that these were, in fact, laws, it remains the case that few, if any, social thinkers have confirmed the existence of these invariant laws. While Comte argued that his laws should be reflections of what actually transpired in the social world, the fact is that he most often seemed to impose his vision on the world.

Fifth, while Comte is credited with creating sociology, there is very little actual sociology in his work. His sketchy overviews of vast sweeps of history hardly qualify as historical sociology. His admittedly weak statements on a few elements of social statics contributed little or nothing to our understanding of social structure. Thus, little, if any, of Comte's substantive sociology survives to this day. John Stuart Mill was quite right when he argued, "Comte has not, in our opinion, created sociology . . . he has, for the first time, made the creation possible" (1961:123–124). Comte's lasting legacy is that he created some domains—sociology, positivist sociology, social statics, social dynamics—which his successors have filled in with some genuine substantive sociology.

Sixth, it can be argued that Comte really made no original contributions.[6] Mill clearly minimizes Comte's contribution in this domain: "The philosophy called Positive is not a recent invention of M. Comte, but a simple adherence to the traditions of all the great scientific minds whose discoveries have made the human race what it is" (1961:8–9; see also Heilbron, 1990). Mill also argues that Comte was well aware of his lack of originality: "M. Comte claims no originality for his conception of human

---

[6]Heilbron (1990:155) disagrees, arguing that Comte's original contribution lies in his *"historical and differential theory of science."* (This theory is discussed early in this chapter.)

knowledge" (1961:6). Comte readily acknowledged his debt to such renowned positivists as Bacon, Descartes, and Galileo. A similar point could be made about Comte's contribution to sociology. Comte clearly recognized important forerunners in sociology, such as Charles de Montesquieu (1689–1755) and Giovanni Vico (1668–1774). While he may have invented the term *sociology,* he certainly did not create the practice of sociology.

Seventh, whatever sociology Comte did have to offer was distorted by a primitive organicism (Levine, 1995b), in which he saw strong similarities between the workings of the human and the social body. For example, Comte argues that composite groups like social classes and cities are "the counterpart of animal tissues and organs in the organisation of the Great Being" (1852/1968:153). Later, he contends that the family is the social counterpart of cells in an organism. Furthermore, Comte sees an analogy between social disorder and disease in organisms. Just as medicine deals with physical diseases, it "is left for Positivism to put an end to this long disease [social anarchy]" (Comte, 1852/1968:375). This kind of organicism has long been eliminated from sociology.

Eighth, Comte tended to develop theoretical ways of thinking and theoretical tools that he then imposed on whatever issue he happened to be analyzing. For example, Comte seemed to be fond of things that came in threes, and many of his theoretical ideas had three components. In terms of theoretical tools, he was not content to apply his Law of the Three Stages to social history; he also applied it to the history of sciences, the history of the mind, and the development of individuals from infancy through adulthood. A particularly bizarre example of this tendency to apply the Law of the Three Stages to anything and everything is Comte's application of it to his own mental illness:

> I will confine myself to recording here the valuable phenomena I was able to observe in the case of my own cerebral malady in 1826. . . . The complete course . . . enabled me to verify twice over my then recently discovered Law of the Three Stages; for while I passed through those stages, first *inversely,* then *directly,* the order of their succession never varied.
>
> During the three months in which the medical treatment aggravated my malady, I descended gradually from positivism to fetishism, halting first at monotheism, and then longer at polytheism. In the following five months . . . I reascended slowly from fetishism to polytheism, and from that to monotheism, whence I speedily returned to my previous positivism . . . thus furnishing me with a decisive confirmation of my fundamental Law of the Three Stages.
>
> (Comte, 1853/1968:62–63)

Ninth, Comte's "outrageous," "colossal" self-conceit (Mill, 1961) led him to make a series of ridiculous blunders. On the one hand, his never powerful theoretical system grew progressively weak as he increasingly subordinated the intellect to feeling. One manifestation of this is his unrealistic and highly romanticized view of the working class and women as agents of the positivist revolution. This decline in intellect is also manifest in his practice of cerebral hygiene as well as in his limiting of the number of positive books. On the other hand, and more important, his oversized ego led him to suggest a series of social changes, many of which, as we have seen, are ludicrous.

Tenth, Comte seemed to sacrifice much of what he stood for in his later turn toward positivist religion. In the framing of this religion, Comte seemed to be most influenced by the structure of Catholicism. In fact, T. H. Huxley called Comte's system "Catholicism minus Christianity" (cited in Standley, 1981:103). Comte acknowledged his debt to Catholicism when he argued that positivism is "more coherent, as well as more progressive, than the noble but premature attempt of medieval Catholicism" (1851/1957:3). His positivist religion mirrored Catholicism with its priests, vicars, and even its pontiff. Clearly, positivist religion has had no lasting impact, and it certainly served to subvert Comte's scientific pretensions.

Finally, there is the issue of the totalitarian implications of Comte's plans for the future. For one thing, these were highly detailed plans in which Comte personally sought to dictate what the various agents in his system would do. For another, his plans even extended to specific institutions such as the family. Particularly notable here are his ideas on the application of the principles of animal husbandry to humans. Ultimately, of course, his plans encompassed religion, with his notion of a supreme pontiff who would rule over the positivist empire.

SUMMARY

This is not an unbiased presentation of Comte's ideas. It is clear that contemporary sociology has moved far beyond Comtian theory, and this chapter underscores that point. While there are a number of useful derivatives from Comte's theory, the main point is that there are innumerable weaknesses in that theory. This chapter is concerned with the limited number of positive derivatives from Comte's theories and, more important, the negative lessons that can be of utility to the modern sociologist.

On the positive side, Comte offers us a positivist perspective, and many contemporary sociologists continue to accept the idea of the search for invariant social laws. Comte has also given us the term *sociology,* and his focus within that field on social statics and social dynamics remains a viable distinction. His basic methods of social research—observation, experimentation, comparison, and historical research—remain major methods of social research. Within his work on social statics, he made a number of contributions (a focus on structures, functions, equilibrium) that were important in the development of the contemporary theory of structural functionalism. Also within social statics, it is to Comte's credit that he laid out a detailed view of human nature on which he then erected his macrosociological theory. At the macro level, Comte offers a dialectical sense of structural relations, and his social realism anticipates that of Durkheim and many other later theorists. His work on social dynamics was relevant to later evolutionary theorists. Finally, Comte was not content simply to speculate, but was interested in linking theory and practice.

While these are important accomplishments, there are far more things to be critical of in Comte's work. He allowed his theoretical work to be distorted by his personal experiences. He lost touch with both the social and intellectual worlds. His empirical and theoretical work was lacking, given his own positivistic standard. There is really little substantive sociology in his work, and that which he offers is distorted by a primitive organicism. There is little in his work that was new at the time. Comte tended to impose his theoretical schemes on anything and everything, no matter how good the fit. His oversized ego led him to a number of outrageous theoretical blunders as well as many ludicrous suggestions for reforming the social world. His reform proposals were further undermined by his increasing preoccupation with positivism as a religion and his role as the pontiff of this new religion. Finally, his blueprint for the future positivist society had many totalitarian implications.

4

HERBERT SPENCER

SPENCER AND COMTE
GENERAL THEORETICAL PRINCIPLES
   Evolutionary Theory
SOCIOLOGY
   Defining the Science of Sociology
   Sociological Methods
THE EVOLUTION OF SOCIETY
   Simple and Compounded Societies
   Militant and Industrial Societies
THE EVOLUTION OF SOCIETAL INSTITUTIONS
   Domestic Institutions
   Ceremonial Institutions
   Political Institutions
   Ecclesiastical Institutions
   Professional Institutions
   Industrial Institutions
ETHICS AND POLITICS

In the theoretical ideas of Herbert Spencer (1820–1903) we see a considerable advance over those of Auguste Comte. Not only was Spencer's work important in the development of sociological theory, but many of his theoretical ideas stand up well from the vantage point of contemporary sociological theory. In spite of this, Jonathan Turner (1985b), who is strongly in sympathy with many of Spencer's ideas, has pointed out that modern sociological theorists have been disinclined to take Spencer seriously, relegating him, like Comte, to the "dustbin" of history. (Actually, in superheated terms, Turner argues that contemporary social theorists have been inclined to "spit on the grave of Spencer" [1985b:71].) This negativity is, to a large extent, traceable to Spencer's highly conservative libertarian (*not* liberal) politics and to his belief in a sociological version of survival of the fittest. While I do not fully share Turner's enthusiasm for Spencer, there is much of merit in Spencer's work. It will be demonstrated that a number of Spencer's theoretical ideas continue to be important and relevant to sociological theory. However, there are also serious problems with Spencer's theory which lead to the conclusion that while it represents an advance over Comtian theory, it is not quite up to the standard of the other major early theorists—Marx, Durkheim, Weber, and Simmel—to be discussed in the ensuing four chapters.

SPENCER AND COMTE

A useful starting point for this discussion is the relationship between Spencer's ideas and those of Auguste Comte. While the lives of Spencer and Comte overlapped, the two men were separated by the English Channel (Spencer was British, while Comte was French) and there was a substantial difference in their ages (Comte was twenty-two years old when Spencer was born, and Spencer lived for forty-six years after Comte's death and into the twentieth century). Thus, Comte had completed most of his work before Spencer published his first book, *Social Statics,* in 1850. However, almost as soon as Spencer had published *Social Statics,* comparisons began to be made between his theories and those of Comte. There are a number of seeming similarities between the work of the two men, but Spencer most often felt the need to distinguish his theories from those of Comte.

Spencer commented on Comte's work in various places and even felt compelled to write an essay entitled "Reasons for Dissenting from the Philosophy of M. Comte" (1864/1883/1968). Spencer began with great, if only obligatory, praise for Comte's work: "In working out this conception [of positivism] he has shown remarkable breadth of view, great originality, immense fertility of thought, unusual powers of generalization" (1864/1883/1968:118). In spite of such an encomium, Spencer was concerned mainly with positioning himself as one of Comte's "antagonists" and with distinguishing his own ideas from those of Comte because their work was "so utterly different in nature" (Spencer, 1904a:414).

Spencer did acknowledge his terminological debt to Comte by admitting, "I also adopt his word, Sociology" (1864/1883/1968:130). Both derived the terms *structure* and *function* largely from biology, and they tended to use them in similar ways. In utilizing these terms, and the perspective they imply, both Spencer and Comte played key historic roles in the development of structural functionalism. However, regarding another set of terms, *social statics* and *social dynamics,* there are important differences between the two men. While Spencer uses these terms, he denies that they are drawn from or resemble Comte's identical terms. In his autobiography, Spencer contends that when *Social Statics* (1850/1954) was published, he "knew nothing more of Auguste Comte, than that he was a French philosopher" (1904a:414). For Comte, these terms refer to all types of societies, while Spencer relates them specifically to his future ideal society. Spencer defines *social statics* as dealing with "the equilibrium of a perfect society" and *social dynamics* as relating to "the forces by which society is advanced toward perfection" (1850/1954:367). Thus, for Spencer the terms *social statics* and *social dynamics* are normative, while for Comte they are descriptive.

Spencer classifies himself, like Comte, as a positivist interested in the discovery of the invariant laws of the social world, but he hastens to add that positivism was not invented by Comte. While Spencer sees himself as a positivist, he does not accept Comte's version of positivism, especially Comte's sense of a positivist religion. Spencer, like Comte, dealt with a wide range of sciences, but unlike Comte, he argued that "the sciences cannot be rightly placed in any linear order whatever" (1883:185). Rather, Spencer viewed the sciences as being interconnected and interdependent. Another major distinction made by Spencer was between Comte's subjectivity (his concern with ideas) and Spencer's objectivity (his concern with things):

What is Comte's professed aim? To give a coherent account of the progress of *human conceptions*. What is my aim? To give a coherent account of the progress of the *external world*. Comte proposes to describe the necessary, and the actual, filiation of *ideas*. I propose to describe the necessary, and actual, filiation of *things*. Comte professes to interpret the genesis of *our knowledge of nature*. My aim is to interpret, as far as it is possible, the genesis of the *phenomena which constitute nature*. The one end is *subjective,* the other is *objective*.

(Spencer, 1904b:570)

Thus, although both Spencer and Comte were concerned with the evolution of the world, Comte was mainly interested in the evolution of ideas, while Spencer focused on structural (and functional) evolution.

Finally, there are powerful political differences between Spencer and Comte. As we saw in the last chapter, Comte wanted to construct a society, even a world, dominated by a positivistic religion of humanity and led by the high priests of positivism. Spencer countered that Comte's faith that "the 'Religion of Humanity' will be the religion of the future is a belief countenanced neither by induction nor by deduction" (1873/1961:283). In addition, Spencer had little regard for centralized control, which he felt would do far more harm than good. Thus, Spencer's ideal is a society in which the government is reduced to a minimum and individuals are allowed maximum freedom. We will return to Spencer's political ideas later in the chapter, but suffice it to say that they are radically different from Comte's politics. Spencer was led to muse on how "profoundly opposed" were Comte's and his "avowed or implied ideals of human life and human progress" (1904a:414).

Comte believed that individuals could be taught morality, largely through the positivist religion, but Spencer ridiculed the idea that morality could be taught in any fashion and by any means. Spencer believed that moral ideas emerge from individual action. In arriving at this conclusion, Spencer used here, as he did in many other places in his work, a survival-of-the-fittest perspective. In this specific case, the requirements of an orderly life will force people to act on the basis of their higher moral sentiments and repress their lower sentiments; in other words, people will be rewarded for moral behavior and penalized for immoral behavior. To put it another way, moral actions are likely to survive, while immoral actions are not. Spencer concludes that this "natural selection" of moral actions "alone is national education" (1873/1961:340).

In sum, while Spencer and Comte shared concerns with sociology, structures and functions, social statics and social dynamics, positivism, the relationships among the sciences, the evolution of the world, the future ideal society, and morality, there are profound differences in their views on most of these topics as well as in their overall theories. Given this relationship—or, more accurately, this lack of a strong relationship—we turn to a discussion of Spencer's sociological theory.

GENERAL THEORETICAL PRINCIPLES

Spencer's thoughts on the social world are based on a series of general theoretical principles. He begins by arguing that in the early history of humankind religion and science were unified in their efforts to analyze and understand the world (Spencer, 1902/1958).

HERBERT SPENCER: A Biographical Sketch

Herbert Spencer was born in Derby, England, on April 27, 1820. He was not schooled in the arts and humanities, but rather in technical and utilitarian matters. In 1837 he began work as a civil engineer for a railway, an occupation he held until 1846. During this period, Spencer continued to study on his own and began to publish scientific and political works.

In 1848 Spencer was appointed an editor of *The Economist,* and his intellectual ideas began to solidify. By 1850, he had completed his first major work, *Social Statics.* During the writing of this work, Spencer first began to experience insomnia, and over the years his mental and physical problems mounted. He was to suffer a series of nervous breakdowns throughout the rest of his life.

In 1853 Spencer received an inheritance that allowed him to quit his job and live for the rest of his life as a gentleman scholar. He never earned a university degree or held an academic position. As he grew more isolated, and physical and mental illness mounted, Spencer's productivity as a scholar increased. Eventually, Spencer began to achieve not only fame within England but also an international reputation. As Richard Hofstadter put it: "In the three decades after the Civil War it was impossible to be active in any field of intellectual work without mastering Spencer" (1959:33). Among his supporters was the important industrialist Andrew Carnegie, who wrote the following to Spencer during the latter's fatal illness of 1903:

> Dear Master Teacher . . . you come to me every day in thought, and the everlasting "why" intrudes—Why lies he? Why must he go? . . . The world jogs on unconscious of its greatest mind. . . . But it will wake some day to its teachings and decree Spencer's place is with the greatest.   (Carnegie, cited in Peel, 1971:2)

But that was not to be Spencer's fate.

Gradually, the two begin to separate, with religion coming to focus on the unknowable and science on that which can be known. However, this differentiation is far from complete, even in the modern era, so religion and science continue to overlap and to conflict. In fact, Spencer sees his own work as involving elements of science (intelligence) and religion (morals).

Spencer's main concern was with the knowable world and was therefore much more scientific than it was religious. (This is another contrast to Comte, whose later work became far more religious than scientific.) Science could never know the ultimate nature of things, but it could strive for the highest possible degree of knowledge. Before we can get to his thoughts on science, we first need to deal with his philosophy, which Spencer sees as transcending the sciences in the search for the complete unification of knowledge, for "truths which unify concrete phenomena belonging to all divisions of

One of Spencer's most interesting characteristics, one that was ultimately to be the cause of his intellectual undoing, was his unwillingness to read the work of other people. In this, he resembled another early giant of sociology, Auguste Comte, who practiced "cerebral hygiene." Of the need to read the works of others, Spencer said: "All my life I have been a thinker and not a reader, being able to say with Hobbes that 'if I had read as much as other men I would have known as little'" (Wiltshire, 1978:67). A friend asked Spencer's opinion of a book, and "his reply was that on looking into the book he saw that its fundamental assumption was erroneous, and therefore did not care to read it" (Wiltshire, 1978:67). One author wrote of Spencer's "incomprehensible way of absorbing knowledge through the powers of his skin . . . he never seemed to read books" (Wiltshire, 1978:67).

If he didn't read the work of other scholars, where, then, did Spencer's ideas and insights come from? According to Spencer, they emerged involuntarily and intuitively from his mind. He said that his ideas emerged "little by little, in unobtrusive ways, without conscious intention or appreciable effort" (Wiltshire, 1978:66). Such intuition was deemed by Spencer to be far more effective than careful study and thought: "A solution reached in the way described is more likely to be true than one reached in the pursuance of a determined effort [which] causes perversion of thought" (Wiltshire, 1978:66).

Spencer suffered because of his unwillingness to read seriously the works of other people. In fact, if he read other work, it was often only to find confirmation for his own, independently created ideas. He ignored those ideas that did not agree with his. Thus, his contemporary, Charles Darwin, said of Spencer: "If he had trained himself to observe more, even at the expense of . . . some loss of thinking power, he would have been a wonderful man" (Wiltshire, 1978:70). Spencer's disregard for the rules of scholarship led him to a series of outrageous ideas and unsubstantiated assertions about the evolution of the world. For these reasons, sociologists in the twentieth century came to reject Spencer's work and to substitute for it careful scholarship and empirical research.

Spencer died on December 8, 1903.

Nature" (1902/1958:277). In this section we will discuss Spencer's "general philosophy," in which he deals with "universal truths" for all the world, while later we will analyze his "special philosophies" and the narrower, but still universal, truths of specific areas, especially those relating to the *social* world. In emphasizing the overarching character of philosophy, Spencer rejects the positivistic idea that the goal of science is the reduction of an array of complex laws to a simple law and accepts, instead, the goal of knowledge integrated from a range of specific scientific fields.

Spencer articulates a series of general truths about the world, including the facts that matter is indestructible, that there is continuity of motion and persistence of force, that the relations among forces persist, and that matter and motion are continually redistributed. By a process of *deduction* from these general laws, Spencer articulates a series of ideas that constitute his general *evolutionary theory.*

Evolutionary Theory

Spencer believes that all inorganic, organic, and superorganic (societal) phenomena undergo evolution and devolution, or dissolution. That is, phenomena undergo a process of evolution whereby matter becomes integrated and motion tends to dissipate. Phenomena also undergo a process of devolution in which motion increases and matter moves toward disintegration. Having deduced these general principles of evolution and dissolution from his overarching principles, Spencer then turns to specific areas in order to show that his theory of evolution (and devolution) holds inductively, that is, that "all orders *do* exhibit a progressive integration of Matter and concomitant loss of Motion" (1902/1958:308).

The combination of induction and deduction leads Spencer to his "final" evolutionary formula:

> Evolution is an integration of matter and concomitant dissipation of motion; during which the matter passes from an indefinite, incoherent homogeneity to a definite, coherent, heterogeneity; and during which the retained motion undergoes a parallel transformation.
> (Spencer, 1902/1958:394)

Let us decompose this general perspective and examine each of the major elements of Spencer's evolutionary theory.

First, evolution involves progressive change from a less coherent to a more coherent form; in other words, it involves increasing *integration*. Second, accompanying increasing integration is the movement from homogeneity to more and more heterogeneity; in other words, evolution involves increasing *differentiation*. Third, there is a movement from confusion to order, from indeterminacy to determined order, "an increase in the distinctness with which these parts are marked off from one another" (Spencer, 1902/1958:361); in other words, evolution involves movement from the *indefinite to the definite*. (In Chapter 14 we will see that Parsons developed a similar evolutionary theory in his later work.)

Thus, the three key elements of evolution are increasing integration, heterogeneity, and definiteness. More specifically, Spencer is concerned with these elements, and his general theory of evolution, as they apply to both *structures* and *functions*. At the most general level, Spencer associates structures with "matter" and sees them growing more integrated, heterogeneous, and definite. Functions are linked to "retained motion," and they, too, are seen as growing increasingly integrated, heterogeneous, and definite. We will have occasion to deal with Spencer's more concrete thoughts on the evolution of functions and structures in his work on society.

Having outlined his general theory of evolution, Spencer turns to the issue of the reasons for the occurrence of evolution. First, Spencer argues that homogeneous phenomena are inherently unstable: "the absolutely homogeneous must lose its equilibrium; and the relatively homogeneous must lapse into the relatively less homogeneous" (1902/1958:426). One reason for this instability is the fact that the different parts of a homogeneous system are constantly subjected to different forces, which tend to differentiate them from one another. Changes in one part of the once homogeneous system will inevitably result in changes in other parts, leading, in turn, to greater multiformity. A second factor in sequence, but not in importance, is the multiplication of effects. In

Spencer's view, the multiplication of effects proceeds in a geometric manner. In other words, a small change in a once homogeneous system has increasingly ramifying effects. Thus, over time, the once homogeneous system grows increasingly heterogeneous. Third, Spencer discusses the effects of segregation on evolution. A sector becomes segregated from the others because of a likeness among its components, which are different from the components of other sectors. This segregation serves to maintain differences among the sectors, and this, in turn, furthers the multiplication of effects when one sector is exposed to, and incorporates, the distinguishing characteristics of other sectors.

Given that evolution is an inevitable process, the issue becomes: Where is evolution headed? While en route to their end state, phenomena move through a series of transitional states that can be described as "moving equilibria," while the end state of the process is a new equilibrium. It could be argued that we are moving to "a state of quiescence," and it could then be asked: "Are we not manifestly progressing toward omnipresent death" through the dissipation of moving forces? (Spencer, 1902/1958:508). Spencer responds negatively to this question, arguing that we are moving toward universal life through new stages in the evolutionary process. He does, however, posit an end state of the evolutionary process: "Evolution can end only in the establishment of the greatest perfection and the most complete happiness" (Spencer, 1902/1958:511). Spencer obviously has great faith in the evolutionary process, and its ultimate state of perfection gives him a standard by which he can assess all other steps in the evolutionary process.

In spite of his faith in evolution, Spencer recognizes, in a dialectical fashion, that the process of dissolution complements the evolutionary process and periodically leads to its undoing. The dissolution process is likely to occur when evolution has ended and the evolved phenomenon has begun to decay.

Evolution constitutes the focus of Spencer's work in a variety of realms, but our concern is with the evolution of human societies in terms of their growth and with the evolution of structures and functions. Following Spencer's approach, we will look at the evolution of society in general as well as that of a number of specific social institutions. Spencer's rationale for devoting so much attention to the evolution of society and its institutions is his view that a fully adequate understanding of human social relations requires an understanding of their evolution (as well as their cycles and dissolution).

SOCIOLOGY

Defining the Science of Sociology

Given Spencer's focus on evolution, he defines "the study of Sociology as the study of Evolution in its most complex form" (1873/1961:350). To put it another way, sociology is "the natural history of societies" or, more specifically, "an order among those structural and functional changes which societies pass through" (Spencer, 1873/1961:63–64). However, Spencer does not restrict sociology to historical societies but also accepts the study of the ways in which *contemporary* organizations and institutions "are severally related to other phenomena of their respective times—the political institutions, the class-distinctions, the family arrangements, the modes of distribution and degrees of intercourse between localities, the amounts of knowledge, the religious beliefs, the morals, the sentiments, the customs, the ideas" (1873/1961:120). But while Spencer sanctions the need for contemporaneous research, he feels that the true meaning of his work is found only when it is placed in a historical, evolutionary context. However, whether sociological research focuses on historical or contemporary issues, it is clear that Spencer's sociology concentrates largely on macro-level social phenomena (social aggregates)—societies, social structures, social institutions—as well as the functions of each.[1]

Spencer (1873/1961:115) shares with Comte the view that sociology should deal with social questions in the same scientific manner in which we address issues in the natural sciences. Furthermore, Spencer, like Comte, sees sociology, especially in its evolutionary concerns, as the most complex of sciences.

While Spencer sees sociology as a (complex) science, he recognizes that it is not an exact science, but he rhetorically wonders how many sciences are exact sciences? To be a science, in Spencer's view, a field of study need only consist of generalizations (laws) and interpretations based on those generalizations. Sociology seeks laws of social phenomena in the same way that the natural sciences seek the laws of natural phenomena. "Either society has laws or it has not. If it has not, there can be no order, no certainty, no system in its phenomena. If it has, then are they like the other laws of the universe—sure, inflexible, ever active, and having no exceptions" (Spencer, 1850/1954:40). Although sociology and other sciences seek to make predictions about the future on the basis of laws, in most cases all sciences must be satisfied with only the most general predictions.

Legitimizing Sociology   In endeavoring to lay the groundwork for his kind of scientific sociology, Spencer confronted the problem that many other early sociologists faced—the need to legitimize the field. For example, he felt compelled to argue that laypeople lack the capacity to grasp the complex issues of concern to sociologists: one needs to be a trained sociologist in order to comprehend them. Because in their everyday lives they deal with the same issues that are of concern to sociologists, laypeople in Spencer's day, and to this day as well, are convinced, erroneously, that they can do as good a job of social analysis as trained sociologists can. Spencer also confronted the misplaced confidence of laypeople in their views and their hostility to sociologists by arguing that the incapacity of the layperson "is accompanied by extreme confidence of judgment on sociological questions, and a ridicule of those who, after long discipline, begin to perceive what there is to be understood, and how difficult is the right understanding of it" (1873/1961:115). As a result of these lay attitudes, Spencer saw many barriers to sociology's receiving the recognition it deserves. These include the fact that few laypeople will be able to grasp the complexity of sociology's subject matter, an unconsciousness on the part of laypeople that there are any such complex phenomena, the misplaced confidence of laypeople, and the fact that the minds of most laypeople are not adaptable and flexible enough to accept the new perspective offered by sociology.

---

[1]In his work, though, Spencer does offer some insightful micro accounts, especially of rituals in his discussion of ceremonies (see pages 133–134).

Spencer felt that sociologists, in contrast to laypeople, require disciplined habits of thought and that those habits are to be derived from a careful study of other sciences. This need to study other sciences is buttressed by an argument similar to one made by Comte, that is, that the science of sociology encompasses the phenomena of concern in all other sciences. Spencer gave particular importance to the need for sociologists to be familiar with the fields of biology and psychology.

Sociology and Biology   Spencer saw three basic linkages between biology and sociology. First, he believed that all social actions are determined by the actions of individuals and that those actions conform to the basic laws of life in general. Thus, to understand social actions, the sociologist must know the basic laws of life, and it is biology that helps us comprehend those laws. Second, there are powerful analogies between sociology and biology. That is, society as a whole, like the living body, is characterized by, among other things, growth, structure, and function. Thus an understanding of the biology of the living organism, which after all is far easier to study than the social organism, offers many keys to understanding society. Spencer concludes, "There can be no rational apprehension of the truths of Sociology until there has been reached a rational apprehension of the truths of Biology" (1873/1961:305). Third, a kind of natural progression and linkage exist between the two fields, since humans are the "terminal" problem for biology and the starting point for sociology.

A more specific similarity between biology and sociology is the operation of the survival-of-the-fittest process in both living and social organisms. Spencer felt that survival of the fittest occurs in both the biological and the social realms and that the lessons of biology from the natural world are that there should be no interference with this process in the social world.

Sociology and Psychology   Spencer also devoted considerable attention to psychology as another major base for sociology. He adopted the general position that "psychological truths underlie sociological truths" (Spencer, 1873/1961:348). As he saw it, psychology is the study of intelligence, feeling, and action. He believed that one of the great lessons of psychology is that feeling, *not* intelligence, is linked to action. This belief led Spencer to emphasize sentiments and to downgrade the importance of intelligence and cognition in his sociological analyses (see the preceding chapter, on Comte, for a similar view). While people throughout history have been dominated by sentiments and desires, this was especially true in primitive societies. Primitive people were inherently impulsive, and because they were "not much habituated to associated life," they were "habituated to that uncontrolled following of immediate desires" (Spencer, 1908a:64). In contrast, people in the modern world, while still dominated by feelings, emotions, and desires, are better able to control them because they are more habituated to collective life. Thus, Spencer is led to argue that primitive people are characterized by greater selfishness and that there is more altruism in the modern world. This general orientation leads Spencer to focus substantively on collective phenomena, and politically this emphasis on the importance of feelings is one of the factors causing him to oppose conscious and intelligent change of society.

While Spencer embeds his sociology in a set of assumptions about the psychological characteristics of individuals, he does *not* accept the idea that these characteristics are fixed. Rather, psychological characteristics change with the changes in society as well as with those in the larger environment.

From his study of psychology, and more generally from his basic philosophical orientation, Spencer comes to the "methodological individualist" conclusion that the units of society are individuals and that individuals are the source of social phenomena. Everything in society is derived from the motives of individuals, the combined similar motives of many individuals, or the conflict between those with one set of motives and others with another set. However, while Spencer bases his sociology on such psychological principles, he does not spend much time analyzing the ways in which these psychological phenomena lead to the development of society and its various institutions. Rather, Spencer assumes that individuals are the units, and the base, of society and institutions, and then he proceeds to the macro level to study the evolution of society and its institutions. This lack of concern (with a few exceptions; see the discussion of ceremonial institutions later in this chapter) for how macro-level phenomena (society and institutions) emerge from micro-level units (individuals and their motives) is a serious weakness in Spencer's sociological theory.

Sociological Methods

Within the context of Spencer's definition of sociology as a science, he addressed a range of methodological problems.

Difficulties Facing Sociology   Spencer attempts to show "how greatly the advance of Sociology is hindered by the nature of its subject-matter" (1873/1961:66). He believes that sociology confronts several difficulties that differentiate it from natural sciences. To begin with, there are objective difficulties that involve the intrinsic nature of the facts that sociologists must analyze. For example, social phenomena are not directly perceptible. Unlike natural phenomena, they cannot be studied and measured with such instruments as clocks, thermometers, scales, and microscopes. (Of course, modern sociology has demonstrated that at least some social phenomena *can* be studied and measured with instruments [for example, audiotapes and videotapes].) Another methodological difficulty for sociologists, in Spencer's view, is that they, unlike psychologists, cannot utilize introspection as a method; social facts cannot be studied through introspection, but psychological facts can. (Again, at least some modern sociologists [for example, phenomenologists] do use introspection as a method.)

The facts of concern to sociologists not only are different from those found in the natural sciences and psychology but also are far more complex and difficult to study. Sociologists inevitably deal with an enormous range of highly dispersed details. It is often difficult to gain a sense of what is happening, because things occur over a wide geographic area and over long periods of time. Thus, for example, Spencer contends that the increasing division of labor is very difficult to study and was under way for quite some time before its development was recognized.

Another objective difficulty facing sociology is the untrustworthiness of its data, derived from *both* past and present societies. For one thing, the data are often distorted by the subjective states of the witnesses to the events under study, but sociologists must rely on the reports of such witnesses for their data. For another, the sociological observer is often misled by superficial and trivial facts and fails to see what is truly important. Spencer offers a number of cautions to sociologists: "In every case we have to beware of the many modes in which evidence may be vitiated—have to estimate its worth when it has been discounted in various ways; and have to take care that our conclusions do not depend on any particular class of facts gathered from any particular place or time" (1873/1961:102). While Spencer recognizes that the objective difficulties are formidable, he still feels that sociology can deal scientifically with general classes of facts, although not with specific facts.

Sociologists must also confront the reality that they are the human observers of humanly created phenomena. As human beings, sociologists use modes of observation and reasoning in their daily lives, and such habits may not be useful in, or may even be impediments to, sociological study. Sociologists must be wary of assessing others on the basis of their own standards. They are likely to experience difficulties in their own society, and those difficulties are greatly magnified when sociologists examine other societies.

Biases   Sociologists also have a very different relationship to the facts they observe than do natural scientists. Sociologists' emotions may affect their judgments of social phenomena or lead them to make judgments without sufficient evidence. Spencer argues that "minds thus swayed by disproportionate hates and admirations, cannot frame those balanced conclusions respecting social phenomena which alone constitute Social Science" (1873/1961.144). In this context, Spencer deals with a number of specific emotional biases.

First, there is what Spencer calls an *educational bias*. He traces this to the fact that we live in a society that combines elements of both militant and industrial societies (which are discussed later in this chapter). The result is that we are taught a tangle of ideas derived from both systems, and this causes the sociologist to misinterpret social phenomena. The sociologist must not be biased against either militant or industrial society and must be able to study both types impartially and to recognize that both have been necessary historically. For example, as we will discuss later, Spencer, in spite of his biases against warfare, is able to see that war is functional for militant societies.

Second, there is the *bias of patriotism* (and antipatriotism). As Spencer argues: "'Our country, right or wrong,' . . . Whoever entertains such a sentiment has not that equilibrium of feeling required for dealing scientifically with social phenomena" (1873/1961:185). Sociologists must emancipate themselves from the bias of patriotism, but Spencer recognizes that such emancipation is not easy to accomplish. However, he holds out hope for the future, since he believes that the triumph of industrial society, the resulting increase in harmonious sentiments, and the decrease in hostility to societies different from our own will lead to a decline in patriotic bias and an increased capacity to be objective about our society and others, both historically and contemporaneously.

Third, there is *class bias,* found in the upper and lower classes, among employers and the employed, which Spencer regards as the most serious of the biases in sociological work. Since all sociologists come from a given class, they are likely to reflect this bias in their work. Once again, however, Spencer holds out hope for the future, in which greater societal harmony will lead to less class antagonism and to the increased ability of sociologists to come to more balanced conclusions about social phenomena. However, Spencer goes further and uses the argument about class bias to underscore his conservative orientation: "The class-bias obscures the truth, otherwise not easy to see, that the existing type of industrial organization, like the existing type of political organization, is about as good as existing human nature allows. The evils there are in it are nothing but the evils brought round on men by their own imperfections" (1873/1961:229). Spencer's conservatism, and its implications for his sociology, will be touched upon throughout this chapter.

Fourth, Spencer discusses *political bias*. The current government, its laws, and its political parties, among other political phenomena, serve to bias sociologists in their work. Not only are sociologists prone to view things the way the current political system sees them, but they are led to examine visible political forms and ignore less visible political phenomena (for example, "national character"). Furthermore, the existing political system tends to obscure the unanticipated effects of legal and other political changes. For example, the government will attune observers to acknowledge the anticipated benefits of political changes and to ignore their unanticipated evils.

Finally, Spencer looks at *theological bias*. For example, the sociologist may be led to assess things relative to the creed of a given religion rather than to the way they relate to human welfare in general. While Spencer foresees no end to religion, he does see it undergoing the evolutionary trend described earlier, and this trend will serve to mitigate theology as a source of bias in the future.

Spencer's Approach   In seeking to exclude these and other biases from sociological research, Spencer is articulating a "value-free" position for the discipline (see Chapter 7, on Weber, for a more complex view of this issue). He argues, for example, that

> in pursuing our sociological inquiries . . . we must, as much as possible, exclude whatever emotions the facts are calculated to excite . . . trustworthy interpretations of social arrangements imply an almost passionless consciousness. Though feeling cannot and ought not to be excluded from the mind when otherwise contemplating them, yet it ought to be excluded when contemplating them as natural phenomena to be understood in their causes and effects.
>
> (Spencer, 1908b:230, 232)

In his own work Spencer employed what has come to be called the *comparative-historical* method. That is, he engaged mainly in the comparative study of the different stages of societies over time as well as of various kinds of contemporary societies. His goal in this research was always to seek out, inductively, support (or, presumably, lack of support) for the theories derived deductively from his most general orientation. He was also interested in developing empirical generalizations based on his comparative, especially evolutionary, studies.

We must not close this section without mentioning the fifteen volumes of data on various societies (for example, ancient Mexicans, ancient Romans) commissioned by

Spencer but put together by others in accord with a category system developed by Spencer (J. Turner, 1985b:95–104). While these volumes have been little read or used by sociologists, and while they are almost impossible to find today, they reflect Spencer's commitment to empirical research of the comparative-historical variety in order to create a base whereby he and others could inductively support, or fail to support, theories derived deductively.

THE EVOLUTION OF SOCIETY

Spencer employs his evolutionary theory in his massive three-volume work, *The Principles of Sociology* (1908a, 1908b, 1908c). (Much of this work had been published in serial form in magazines in the late 1800s.) In his more specific focus on the evolution of society and its major institutions, Spencer employs the three general dimensions outlined earlier—increasing *integration* (increasing size and coalescence of masses of people), *heterogeneity,* and *definiteness* (clearly demarcated social institutions). In addition, he employs a fourth dimension, the *increasing coherence* of social groups (modern civilized nations hold together far longer than early wandering groups of people). Thus, he offers the following statement as his general formula of social evolution: "There is progress toward greater size, coherence, multiformity and definiteness" (Spencer, 1908a:597).

Before we go any further, it is important to make it clear that in spite of appearances, Spencer does *not* adopt an inevitable, unilinear view of social evolution. That is, evolution does not have to occur, and it does *not* always move in a single direction. Societies are constantly changing in light of changes in their environs, but these changes are not necessarily evolutionary. "Only now and then does the environing change initiate in the organism a new complication, and so produce a somewhat higher structure" (Spencer, 1908a:95–96). It is possible at any given moment for there to be no change, dissolution, *or* evolution. Not only is evolution not inevitable, but when it does occur, it does not take the form of a simple unilinear pattern; the stages do not necessarily occur in serial order.

Before getting to the actual evolution of society, we need a definition of *society.* Spencer discusses the issue of *nominalism* (society is nothing more than its component parts) versus *realism* (society is a distinct and separable entity) and comes down on the side of realism because of the "permanence of the relations among component parts which constitutes the individuality of a whole" (1908a:447). "Thus we consistently regard society as an entity, because, though formed of discrete units, a certain concreteness in the aggregate of them is implied by the general persistence of the arrangements among them throughout the area occupied" (Spencer, 1908a:448). Thus, Spencer considers society a "thing," but it is unlike any other thing except for parallel principles in the way the component parts are arranged.

It should be pointed out here that there is an uncomfortable fit between Spencer's social realism and his previously discussed methodological individualism. Methodological individualism generally leads to, and is more comfortable with, a nominalist position on society. Conversely, methodological individualism generally rules out a realist orientation to society. Spencer holds to both without telling us much about how he is able to adopt two such discordant perspectives or how they are linked to one another. In other words, how do individuals create a "real" society? Spencer begins with assumptions about individuals, imposes the existence of society, and then ends (as we will see later) with a series of concerns about the negative impact of society on individuals.

Spencer sees societies as being like organic bodies (but unlike inorganic bodies) in that they are characterized by permanent relations among the component parts (Levine, 1995b). Spencer's *organicism* led him to see a number of parallelisms between society and organic entities. Among other similarities, both entities increase in size and are subject to structural and functional differentiation. Furthermore, both are characterized by an increasing division of labor, the development of interrelated differentiations that make still other differentiations possible. The component parts of both society and an organism are interconnected and in need of each other. In addition, if the whole of society or an organism dies, parts can live on; conversely, the whole can live on even if parts die (for example, society continues even after individuals die).

One issue here is whether Spencer believed that society is an organism or that there are simply important analogies between the two. While at times Spencer discussed society as an organism, his avowed position was that there are merely important parallels between the two and that one could improve one's understanding of society by better understanding the parallelisms.

In a more concrete sense, Spencer (1908b) sees society as a gathering of people forming a group in which there is cooperation to seek common ends. Cooperation in society implies some form of organization. In Spencer's view, there are two basic types of cooperation. The first is the division of labor, which is a spontaneously and unconsciously developed system that directly serves the interests of individuals and indirectly those of society. Here we have a situation in which individuals consciously pursue their private ends and the unconsciously evolving organization is *not* coercive. The second cooperative system is the one for defense and government, that is, the political organization, which is a consciously and purposefully created system that directly serves the interests of society and indirectly those of the individual. The political system involves the conscious pursuit of public ends, and this consciously evolving organization is coercive in regard to individuals.

The first element in Spencer's work on the evolution of society is society's growth in size. In his view, societies, similar to living organisms, "begin as germs" (Spencer, 1908a:463). "Superorganic" (social) phenomena, like organisms, grow through both the multiplication of individuals and the union ("compounding") of groups (for example, tribes), both of which may go on simultaneously.

The increase in the size of society is accompanied by an increase in *structure*. Spencer defines a *structure* as "an organization" (1908c:3). Greater size requires more differentiation, a greater unlikeness of parts. In fact, Spencer argues that "to reach great size [society] must acquire great complexity" (1908a:471). More generally, he contends that "all social structures result from specializations of a relatively homogeneous mass" (Spencer, 1908c:181). The first differentiation is the emergence of one or more people claiming and/or exercising authority. This is followed soon after by the division between the *regulative* and the *sustaining* structures of society. We will have more to say about these structures later, but at this early stage the regulative structure is associated with military activities while economic activities that maintain the group are linked to the sustaining structures. At first, this differentiation is closely linked to the division of labor among the sexes, with men handling the regulative structure (the military) and women the sustaining structures. As society evolves, each of these structures undergoes further differentiation; for example, the regulative agency acquires a system of kings, local rulers, petty chiefs, and so on. Then there are differentiations of social classes as the military, the priestly, and the slave classes emerge. Further differentiations occur *within* each social class; in the priestly class, for example, sorcerers, priests, diviners, and exorcists develop. Overall, society moves toward increasing structural differentiation and complexity.

The increasing differentiation of structures is accompanied by increasingly differentiated functions. A *function* is "the need subserved" by a structure (Spencer, 1908c:3). Spencer argues that "changes of structures cannot occur without changes of functions" (1908a:485). More generally, he contends that one cannot truly understand structures without a clear conception of their functions, or the needs served by the structures. In a relatively undifferentiated state, the various parts of society can perform each other's functions. Thus, in a primitive society the male warriors could raise food and the females could fight if it became necessary. However, as society grows increasingly complex structurally, it is more and more difficult for highly specialized parts to perform each other's functions. Evolution brings functional progress along with structural progress: "With advance of organization, every part, more limited in its office, performs its office [that is, function] better, the means of exchanging benefits becomes greater; each aids all, and all aid each with increasing efficiency; and the total activity we call life, individual or national, augments" (Spencer, 1908a:489).

Having argued that societies evolve both structurally and functionally, Spencer returns to the sustaining and regulative systems mentioned above and adds a third, the *distributing* system. In the discussion of these three systems, Spencer makes great use of analogies between social systems and organisms. In both social systems and organisms the sustaining system is concerned with the *internal* matters needed to keep them alive. In the living body the sustaining system takes the form of the alimentary organs, while in the social system it adopts the form of the various elements of the industrial system. *External* matters for both social systems and organisms are handled by the regulative system. The regulative system takes the form of the neuromuscular system in organisms and the government-military apparatus in social systems. Both are concerned with warfare with other systems and conflicts with the environment. Finally, the distributive system links the sustaining and regulative organs and systems. Here Spencer sees an analogy between blood vessels (in organisms) and roads (in social systems), "channels which carry, in the one case blood-corpuscles and serum, and in the other case men and commodities" (1908a:510). In addition to describing each of these structures and the functions they perform, Spencer also demonstrates how each is undergoing a process of evolution.

Simple and Compounded Societies

On the basis of what he claims are inductions from the evolution of past and present societies, Spencer develops two different systems for classifying societies. The first, or primary, method is based on the increasing number of members of the aggregate as well as the degree to which that aggregate is *compounded*, or added to, by combining with other aggregates through such means as conquest or peaceful merger. While, as we saw above, Spencer has argued in general against a simple unilinear theory of evolution, the latter is just what he seems to offer here: "The stages of compounding and recompounding *have to be passed through in succession*. No tribe becomes a nation by simple growth; and no great society is formed by the direct union of the smallest societies" (1908a:555; italics added).

Spencer identifies four types of societies on the basis of their degree of compounding. First, there are *simple* societies, which constitute single working entities that are not connected with any other entities. These are relatively homogeneous and uncivilized societies that have not gone through a compounding process. Second, we find *compound* societies, in which there is some increase in heterogeneity. For example, here we may find the emergence of a supreme chief who rules over the chiefs of several simple groups. Obviously, since there are now several groups, some compounding has occurred either by conquest or by peaceful means. We also find in compound societies, as a result of increasing heterogeneity, an increase in the division of economic labor and in organization. Third, there are *doubly-compound* societies, formed on the basis of the recompounding of compound groups. Here we find still more heterogeneity and further advances in civilization. Thus, in the political realm we find even more developed and stable governments. Spencer describes many other advances in these societies, such as the development of an ecclesiastical hierarchy, a more complex division of economic labor, law emerging from custom, more towns and roads, and more advanced knowledge and arts. Finally, there are the *trebly-compound* societies, or the great nations of the world, which are even more advanced in the areas just mentioned, as well as in many others. Included in this category are both older societies, like the Roman Empire, and modern nations.

Militant and Industrial Societies

Spencer offers a secondary system of classifying societies, although this one became better known than his primary system of classifying societies by their degree of compounding. This is his famous distinction between *militant* and *industrial* societies and the character of societies as they oscillate between the two. Militant societies tend to be dominated by the regulative system, while industrial societies are characterized by their more highly developed sustaining systems. These are ideal types, as Spencer recognizes: "During social evolution there has habitually been a mingling of the two" (1908b:568). Spencer sees a long-term evolutionary trend from militant to industrial societies, although here he is more careful to be clear that this trend is *not* unilinear. Spencer also briefly mentions the possibility of a future, "higher" type of society characterized by intellectual and esthetic concerns (Perrin, 1976), but he has little to say of a substantive nature about the possibility of this third type of society.

Spencer goes into much more detail about militant societies than about industrial societies, and what he says about them is much clearer, because militant societies had long been in existence whereas industrial societies were still emerging in his day.

Militant societies are characterized by highly structured organizations for offensive and defensive warfare. In effect, the army and the nation are one: "The army is the nation mobilized while the nation is the quiescent army, and which, therefore, acquires a structure common to army and nation" (Spencer, 1908a:557). The militant society is dominated by its regulative system, with centralized and despotic government control, unlimited political control over personal conduct, and a rigidly controlled, disciplined, and regimented population. The cooperation that exists in society is a result of compulsion. The individual exists for the good of the collectivity: "Under the militant type the individual is owned by the state. While preservation of the society is the primary end, preservation of each member is a secondary end" (Spencer, 1908b:572). There is a rigid status hierarchy, and individual positions are fixed as to rank, occupation, and locality. Industry, such as it is, exists largely to fill the needs of the government-military.

While he is critical of warfare, and hopes for a future society in which warfare is reduced or eliminated, Spencer believes that war is useful in militant societies in producing social aggregation (by, for example, military conquest). It is also useful in laying the groundwork for industrial society: "Without war large aggregates of men cannot be formed, and . . . without large aggregates of men there cannot be a developed industrial state" (Spencer, 1873/1961:176). This attitude toward warfare is also linked to Spencer's views on survival of the fittest: "We must recognize the truth that the struggles for existence between societies have been instrumental to their evolution" (1908b:241). However, with the development of industrial society, war becomes more dysfunctional than functional, as it serves to block industrial growth, consumes needed people and materials, draws off intellectual resources, and fosters antisocial attitudes and behaviors in a society that values harmony.

As is his normal pattern, Spencer arrives at the characteristics of the militant society deductively and then demonstrates that they are supported by induction from actual militant societies. However, he is forced to deviate from his usual pattern in the case of industrial societies because their characteristics are not fully emergent and continue to be hidden by the militant characteristics of society. Therefore, in his depiction of industrial societies Spencer is forced to rely even more heavily on the deductive method, although he does find some support in data derived from societies with industrial characteristics.

The industrial society is dominated by the sustaining system, and its industrial system is more developed and diverse. The regulative control that continues to exist tends to be negative (people shall *not* do certain things) rather than positive (people must do certain things). There is no need for despotic control, and the government tends to be democratic, with representatives of the people exercising power. The control that remains tends to be much more decentralized. There is voluntary cooperation among people, and the collectivity exists to serve the welfare of the people. Individuality is protected and permitted to flourish. The military system is subordinated to the needs of the industrial system. Control is exercised by contracts voluntarily entered into by individuals. Harmony, rather than conflict and warfare, characterizes industrial societies. While militant societies are forced to be economically autonomous because of the hostility from and toward their neighbors, industrial societies are much more interdependent economically. While militant societies tend to be rather inflexible, industrial societies are much more changeable and adaptable.

Of course, these societies are ideal types that vary greatly from one setting to another. Spencer made clear the ideal-typical character of his depiction of a militant society: "Having contemplated the society *ideally* organized for war, we shall be prepared to recognize in real societies the characteristics which war has brought about" (1908b:569; italics added). Spencer details a number of factors that contribute to variation within each of these types, including racial composition, the nature of the immediately preceding society, the habitat, and surrounding societies. Spencer also discusses "hybrid societies," which are only partially militant or industrial, although he contends that hybrid societies are likely to be more like militant societies than industrial societies. In fact, he describes the society in which he lived as such a transitional hybrid—semi-militant and semi-industrial (Spencer, 1908c:551). Finally, while there is a general evolutionary trend toward industrial societies, Spencer recognizes that regression to more militant societies is possible. For example, an international conflict can cause an industrial society to grow more militant, engaging in more aggressive external acts and developing a more repressive internal government. While Spencer sees a continual threat of rebarbarization, he hopes for some sort of federation of the nations of the world that would forbid wars among member nations. Thus, in his militant-industrial categorization system Spencer does *not* offer a unilinear view of the evolution of society.

Having dealt with the evolution of society as a whole, Spencer turns to the evolution of a variety of social institutions, and we will deal with each of them in the next section. In general, Spencer takes as his objective the description of a society's "*institutions,* regulative and operative, and the ways in which *structures* and *functions* have gradually established themselves" (1873/1961:52; italics added).

THE EVOLUTION OF SOCIETAL INSTITUTIONS

Domestic Institutions

Spencer sees family (or domestic) institutions performing several important functions. First, they help to preserve the social aggregates (for example, societies) in which they occur. Different family structures exist in different societies, and that type of family which survives in any given society is viewed by Spencer as "relatively appropriate" for that society (1908a:610). (We encounter here, again, the conservative implications of Spencer's structural-functional orientation, since he seems to be offering a defense of any family structure that exists at a given point in time.) Second, a function of families is to provide society with the maximum possible number of healthy offspring raised to maturity. Third, as family structures evolve, they further more, and burden less, the interests of parents. Highly evolved family structures give parents the following advantages: longer periods before reproduction, a decreased number of offspring, an increased pleasure in child care, and a longer life span after reproduction and child rearing are completed. The last years of the parents' lives bring pleasure to both the parents and their offspring. This final phase in the evolution of the family brings biological and sociological advantages, and it is also the highest stage in an ethical sense.

In primitive (or simple) societies the family as we know it does not exist, because life is unsettled and indefinite. The relations between the sexes are unregulated by larger institutions and systems of ideas. Spencer, reflecting his Victorian biases, describes a number of "repugnant practices" in primitive societies, such as the lending of wives and incest. He describes an evolution from this "repugnant" base, but it is not a uniform, unilinear process. For example, he finds a number of "civilized" domestic customs among the primitives and some "uncivilized" domestic customs in more advanced societies. "Nevertheless, on contemplating the facts in their *ensemble,* we see that progress towards higher social types is joined with progress towards higher types of domestic institutions" (Spencer, 1908a:621–622). Spencer, in spite of his caveats, proceeds to trace the history of "successively higher forms of family structure" (1908a:622). In other words, there is a progression to more evolved family forms in terms of greater coherence, multiformity, and definiteness.

Spencer looks at this evolution from the vantage point of the various types of relations between men and women, husbands and wives. In the most primitive state he finds *promiscuity* predominant. However, in his view this incoherent and indefinite domestic form (if it can even be called that) must give way to other types of relationships between husband and wife: "As, however, under ordinary conditions the rearing of more numerous and stronger offspring must have been favoured by more regular sexual relations, there must, on the average, have been a tendency for the societies most characterized by promiscuity to disappear before those less characterized by it" (Spencer, 1908a:652). We encounter again Spencer's tendency to use the survival-of-the-fittest perspective. The irregularity of promiscuity is not suitable for the constant production of large numbers of offspring, and thus it must die out and be replaced by more regular relations between husbands and wives, which are better able to perform this function.

The next evolutionary stage is characterized by *polyandry,* in which one woman is related to several men. Polyandry constitutes an advance over promiscuity and itself undergoes a process of evolution (for example, from the case in which a woman is married to several unrelated husbands to one in which the several husbands are brothers). While polyandry may be well adapted to certain settings and may work well within them, in most settings it does not work well in terms of social preservation, the rearing of offspring, and the welfare of adults. "Other things equal, this *inferior* family-type has yielded to *superior* family-types; both because of its inferior fertility, and because of the smaller family-cohesion, and consequently smaller social cohesion, resulting from it" (Spencer, 1908a:663; italics added).

The next evolutionary stage is *polygyny,* in which one husband has a plurality of wives. Spencer sees polygyny as an advance over both promiscuity and polyandry because of the more definite relationships between husbands and wives. Further, it functions better in the sense of better fulfilling social needs by reducing the mortality of children and women. Furthermore, it fills the needs of society by contributing to social cohesion through more widely ramifying family connections. It has done this, for example, by furthering the political stability that results from an established succession of rulers in the same family line and by making possible a more developed form of ancestor worship. Such collective worship is a source of societal cohesion. However, in the end, Spencer sees polygyny as being adaptive for only "low stages of social evolution . . . it repeats within the household the barbarism characterizing the life outside the household" (1908a:678). In other words, it seems suited only to the militant stage.

Finally, there is *monogamy,* which, again from the vantage point of Spencer's Victorian England, where it was the norm, is the most advanced form of domesticity. While monogamy is found in the most primitive societies, it grows increasingly common as societies evolve. Among other things, it is the most evolved family system in terms of definiteness and the strength of the links among family members. In Spencer's view, monogamy better serves the interests of offspring, parents, and the larger society than do other types of relations. The monogamous family is best suited to the industrial-type society.

Spencer links the evolution of the family toward monogamy with improvements in the status of women and children. Women tend to be treated cruelly in militant societies, but their status increases and their treatment improves with the shift toward industrial societies and monogamy. Part of this is traceable to the increasing altruism of industrial societies, which benefits all social relationships, and part of it to the shift from the low status of women, associated with polygyny, to their higher status, associated with monogamy. There is a similar improvement in the situation of children. In early societies children are more often treated badly, and because of the need for (male) warriors, female children are treated more poorly than their male counterparts. In industrial societies there is more recognition of the rights of children and more equality in the treatment of male and female children.

In his analysis of the evolution of the family, Spencer relies mainly on a series of inductions made from empirical evidence. However, he argues that the conclusions derived from induction are in accord with his overall theory of evolution. Within the family we see movement from the "small, incoherent, and indefinite . . . to [the] most coherent, most definite, most complex" (Spencer, 1908a:757–758). More contemporary families function better than their predecessors in providing for the welfare of the species, offspring, parents, and society.

Finally, Spencer looks to the future of the family and makes it clear that he does not adopt a unilinear theory of evolution: "We must beware of supposing that developed societies [and families] will become universal" (1908a:763). "Inferior" types of societies and families will survive in "inferior" settings to which they are well adapted. He expects that the militant societies, and their attendant less developed family types, will continue to survive in some areas of the world. However, within industrial societies Spencer does adopt a unilinear view with regard to the family: "The monogamic form of the sexual relation is manifestly the ultimate form; and any changes to be anticipated must be in the direction of completion and extension of it" (1908a:764). Along with the triumph of the monogamous family will come a number of positive benefits, such as the extinguishing of promiscuity, the suppression of bigamy and adultery, a decrease in domestic dissension, an increase in altruism, and greater solicitude of children by parents and of aged parents by their children. Spencer also anticipates greater equality of the sexes in domestic life, "but it seems improbable that absolute equality with men will be reached" (1908a:768).

Ceremonial Institutions

Next Spencer turns to ceremonial institutions as structures which regulate people's lives. Actually, as Jonathan Turner (1985b:116) points out, ceremonies are preinstitutional or subinstitutional. On the one hand, they form the base of later, full-fledged religious and political institutions. On the other hand, they involve mainly more micro-level interactions among people that are the basis of later, more macro-level social institutions. (This is one of the few areas in which Spencer works at the micro level.)

In the most primitive societies ceremonies function to exert social, political, and religious control over people. But over time these forms of control differentiate, become autonomous, exert control by themselves, and develop independent ceremonies. Primitive tribes may lack political and religious regulation, but they do have an early form of social regulation through ceremonies themselves. While most social functions have correspondingly large structures, the functions of ceremonial control have minuscule correlative structures. As society evolves, large-scale political and religious structures emerge to perform these functions. But at the same time, ceremonial control grows less important as these structures exert more definite and detailed control. Indeed, ceremonies which are based largely on fear work best in militant societies and erode with the passage to the more peaceful and harmonious industrial society.

Spencer takes pains to point out that the evolution of ceremonies is not a result of individual choice or deliberate action but rather has a "natural genesis." That is, ceremonies evolve gradually. They flow naturally from the emotional characteristics of individuals. Since they develop naturally and are the products of emotions, not intellect, they should not be altered as a result of cognitive thought and conscious human action. Spencer begins his description of the evolution of ceremonies by identifying a number of components of ceremonial rule and describing how they change over time.

Trophies give their possessors status and power, but since the winning of trophies is linked to militancy, the practice diminishes with industrialism and "complete industrialism necessitates entire cessation of it" (Spencer, 1908b:51). *Mutilations,* or the cutting off of parts of the body, are also associated with militancy and also tend to disappear with the increase of industrialism. *Presents,* originally spontaneous gifts to authorities, are more likely in militant societies because of the fear of those in power. Rather than disappearing, presents become more mandatory with the development of industrialism. Presents once given to rulers eventually become political revenue, and those given to gods eventually become ecclesiastical revenue.

Unlike the ceremonies discussed above, *visits* are not usually found in simple societies. They tend to appear in compound societies in the form of visits to the chief or king. But they are associated even more with the structure of society than with size alone. That is, visits represent manifestations of obedience in militant societies and tend to become less imperative with increasing industrialism. In addition to becoming less likely as a form of obedience, visits also tend to move away from being paid exclusively to the most powerful leaders and toward being paid to less and less powerful leaders. Eventually, visits take the form of propitiations among equals. This shift from appeasement of elites to propitiation of equals is manifest in other ceremonies as well.

Obeisances are demonstrations of subjection to a master. Initially, an obeisance may take the form of prostrating oneself before a king, but later it moves to descending to one knee and still later to kissing the king's hand. Such forms of obeisance are more likely in militant societies (because of fear of the king) and are likely to decline with the movement toward industrialism. Obeisances, like visits, change over time and come to take forms such as shaking hands among equals. *Forms of address* are similar to obeisances and state in words what obeisances do in acts. They, too, are more likely in militant societies and are also likely to come to be employed by equals.

Titles, or descriptive names of honor, originate in militant societies, with those accorded titles being military leaders. In fact, even the word *God* is rooted in words expressing superiority. Titles tend to evolve during the militant period and to dissolve with the coming of industrialism:

> It is indisputable, then, that serving first to commemorate the triumphs of savages over their foes, titles have expanded, multiplied and differentiated, as conquests have formed large societies by consolidation and reconsolidation of small ones; and that, belonging to the social type generated by habitual war, they tend to lose their uses and their values, in proportion as this type is replaced by one fitted for carrying on the pursuits of peace.
>
> (Spencer, 1908b:178)

To be rich in militant societies implies that one is victorious in warfare. With the spoils of war, one is able to construct the highest and most ornate homes. However, with the evolution to industrialism, wealth and the signs of it are no longer directly traceable to being a military leader. It even becomes harder to distinguish members of the industrial elite from their subordinates, because the latter emulate their superiors in the external signs of wealth. This is like the situation in *fashion:* rather than *not* doing what the leaders do, subordinates demonstrate respect by copying what the leaders do and wear. Fashion, therefore, tends to accompany industrial, not militant, society, since it tends toward a system of greater equality. This trend toward greater equalization and individuality tends to weaken ceremonies in general.

Much of the preceding discussion relates changes in ceremonies to the evolution from militant to industrial societies. Spencer also relates this change to the simple, compound, doubly-compound, and trebly-compound growth of military (but not industrial) societies. With increasing size, there are great increases in the number of ceremonies and the degree to which they regulate all actions of life. Ceremonies take on increasingly heterogeneous forms. They also increase in definiteness, "ending . . . in fixed forms prescribed in all their details, which must not under penalty be departed from. And in sundry places . . . [they are] consolidated into coherent codes set forth in books" (Spencer, 1908b:217). Thus, ceremonies tend to evolve with the increasing size of militant societies, but this tendency is reversed when we move from militant to industrial societies. Ceremonies decline with industrialism, and when Spencer peers into the future, he anticipates further declines in ceremonies.

Political Institutions

"The political organization is to be understood as that part of social organization which constantly carries on directive and restraining functions for public ends" (Spencer, 1908b:247). Before getting to the evolution of political organizations, we must discuss the source of political power in early societies. In Spencer's view, the sole source of political power in such societies is the feeling of community. Furthermore, political organizations (as well as ceremonial and ecclesiastical organizations) "are at once the products of aggregate feeling, derive their powers from it, and are restrained by it" (Spencer, 1908b:325). Not only did public opinion control political authority in early society, but it continues to do so to a large extent in contemporary society. The power of public opinion, of course, tends to downgrade the importance of any specific political system, since all political systems derive their power from the collective feeling of the community.

There are small primitive societies without political organizations. However, as tribes grow in size, they tend to begin to develop a rudimentary political organization, as exemplified by the emergence of a chief, and later, a chief who rules over a series of minor chieftains. Such early political organizations are functional in a variety of ways, such as the removal of antagonisms that impede cooperation, the maintenance of order, the enablement of a more elaborate division of labor, and the formation of still larger aggregates. However, these political organizations can also be dysfunctional by being tyrannical, demanding excessive taxes, and exercising excessive restraints on people. In addition, as the political system grows, it can become an impediment to the further growth of society by resisting needed efforts to reorganize society and absorbing resources needed for the growth of society. Thus, there is a dialectical relationship here— political organizations are needed for growth, but they can also serve to impede growth. Overall, however, Spencer believes that the political organization is advantageous. It is a gradually and unconsciously evolved system that secures for individuals benefits they could not have achieved if they acted singly.

After growth, Spencer deals with integration in the evolution of the political system. Political integration, like all evolutionary integration, occurs when the elements of society are subjected to like forces. These forces may be external to society (for example, climate) or internal to society (for example, racial composition), but the general rule is that a common set of such forces serves to transform what was at first an incoherent political system into one which is increasingly integrated. Then there is the increasing differentiation of the political organization. The primitive, homogeneous political system tends to break down, as all homogeneous systems must. Over time, an increasingly differentiated political system evolves.

In addition to discussing the evolution of the political organization in general terms, Spencer deals with the evolution of a number of specific elements of that system, such as political heads, consultative bodies, representative bodies, ministries, local governing agencies, military systems, the judiciary, the executive, laws, and revenue. Needless to say, he finds confirmation within each for his general theory of evolution. Let us look at just a few examples:

• The despotic leader is instrumental, at least in militant societies, in advancing civilization. The despot is particularly useful in engaging in warfare that compounds societies, consolidating smaller and weaker societies into larger and more powerful ones. However, with the transition to peaceful and voluntary industrial societies, despotism ceases to be a functional form of political leadership.

- There are early manifestations of representative bodies, such as the selection of leaders by lot, but it is with the transition to industrial societies and their voluntary co-operation that the election of representatives and the formation of representative bodies become common.
- Ministries are initially formed out of the ruler's aides, and they are, at first, "vague and irregular" (Spencer, 1908b:445). With evolution, ministries grow in size and number, become better defined, develop increasingly differentiated offices (structures) and functions, grow more integrated with the various offices forming an incorporated body, and come increasingly to represent the public will rather than that of the leader.
- In early, militant societies, the military coincides with the political and economic institutions, but with evolution the military becomes a separate, differentiated entity. The military itself becomes an increasingly structured, unified, and coherent organization with increasingly centralized command.
- The judicial system is at first undifferentiated from the military, with the combined system handling both internal and external aggression. Over time, the judicial system comes to be separated and itself becomes a centralized and heterogeneous organization.
- Revenue for the government is at first very irregular and indefinite, but over time it grows more regular and definite in the form of taxation. War is the main reason for new taxes or the increasing of old taxes, and even in modern society, where war is less common, war or the threat of war is very often the source of tax increases.

Spencer closes with some thoughts on the political future. He is careful to make it clear that there is no single political future and that there will be variations from one society to another. While the same evolutionary principles that dominated in the past will continue to dominate in the future, and while industrial societies are less prone to warfare than are militant societies, one cannot predict whether or not nations will make war on one another. Spencer depicts a future political regime which is the logical extreme of the industrial-type political structure, but the "possibility of a high social state, political as well as general, fundamentally depends on the cessation of war" (1908b:663). War, as we have seen, has ceased to be functional: "From war has been gained all that it had to give" (Spencer, 1908b:664). Nevertheless, wars will continue to occur, and their frequency will affect the likelihood of the emergence of Spencer's ideal political regime.

Looking at future ideal structures first, Spencer depicts an elective headship and a representative legislature responsive to the general will. Government will grow less centralized, allowing for more local and individual control. Turning to functions, Spencer sees less need to protect members from outsiders and therefore greater attention to protecting individuals from one another. This protection will help contribute to more equitable relationships among members of society. Political activity will be more restricted, and there will be limitations on political functions. The limitations on political structures and functions will allow for more individual freedom.

Ecclesiastical Institutions

As he does with all other institutions, Spencer looks at religion from his familiar evolutionary perspective: "Ecclesiastical institutions illustrate very clearly the general law of evolution" (1908c:150). In spite of their general adherence to this law, the progress of ecclesiastical institutions, like all others, is "irregular."

Spencer sees ecclesiastical institutions as structures,[2] and he inquires, in his normal pattern, about where they come from and what needs (functions) they perform. On the first issue, Spencer makes it clear that religion is not innate in "human nature," since there are primitive societies in which no religion is found. In primitive societies in which he finds the roots of religion, he traces the phenomena to efforts to appease ghosts.

In primitive, and therefore militant, societies, medicine men predominate over priests because they are the ones who deal antagonistically with ghosts; thus, they are best fitted to the overriding hostility of a militant society. Internally and externally, primitive societies are dominated by *enmity* rather than *amity.* In the long run, however, priests are destined to win out over medicine men for a variety of reasons, but most important because amity will win out over enmity, altruism over selfishness, and industrial societies over militant ones.

At first, the priestly function is vaguely diffused throughout society. However, as a result of the law of the instability of the homogeneous, differentiation begins to occur, and one member of the group, usually the eldest male descendant, emerges as the first differentiated quasi priest. Over time, this differentiation tends to become more fixed and definite.

Spencer believes that both ecclesiastical and political institutions are derived from the same human sentiments of reverence. As a result, in primitive societies there is little distinction between the sacred and secular worlds ("originally Church and State are undistinguished" [Spencer, 1908c:125]). Thus, one person tends to be the ruler-priest. The early chief was likely to be both the best warrior *and* the priest; consequently, the chief performed *both* military and sacerdotal functions. Thus, the early priests were militant, often engaging in brutal and savage military actions. Over time, however, the priests' linkage to warfare grew more and more distant.

Differentiation is likely to occur as the two structures divide and there emerges an independent priest who intervenes with the supernatural not merely on behalf of himself or his family but for a range of unrelated persons. Once differentiated, ecclesiastical institutions grow by the subordination of other religious institutions (as a result, for example, of the conquest of neighboring societies and their religious institutions).

Ecclesiastical institutions do not evolve in isolation from the changing nature of other social institutions, especially the polity: "The component institutions of each society habitually exhibit kindred traits of structure. Where the political organization is but little developed, there is but little development of the ecclesiastical organization; while along with a centralized coercive civil rule there goes a religious rule no less centralized and coercive" (Spencer, 1908c:81). In primitive, unsettled societies with disorganized institutions, the religious institutions tend to be similarly unsettled. However, once society grows more settled, the ecclesiastical institutions tend to become more distinct and more developed.

---

[2]This is more than a little confusing, since modern sociologists distinguish between largely subjective institutions and largely objective structures (Blau, 1960).

Once ecclesiastical institutions become distinguished from political institutions, a struggle for supremacy begins between them. At first, religion has a series of advantages in this struggle. For example, as a representative of the deity, religion gives authority to the ruler; it has influence with the feared (and revered) supernatural beings; it can grant or refuse to grant forgiveness for sins; its representatives are the cultured class, and they have accumulated substantial property. As a result, spiritual power is at first predominant over temporal power.

However, in the long term, temporal power gains ascendancy over spiritual power. This change is related to the rise of industrialism. Among other things, voluntary cooperation with the state is substituted for the compulsory cooperation required by religion. The general resistance to authority in industrialism translates into a resistance to church authority. As philosophy and science advance, the increasing belief in and knowledge of natural causes replaces the religious emphasis on supernatural causation. Finally, the more general diffusion of knowledge reduces the significance and power of priestly knowledge.

While the transition to industrialism implies a decline in the importance of religion, Spencer sees religion as functional even in modern industrial societies. He argues that ecclesiastical institutions "have been indispensable components of social structures from the beginning down to the present time: groups in which they did not arise having failed to develop" (Spencer, 1908c:148). Among the many functions of religion are serving as a force of cohesion, acting as a check on warfare within society, promoting the conservation and continuity of social arrangements, functioning as a supplementary regulative system to the regulation imposed by the political system, and providing obedient individuals through both coercion by the church and self-restraint by the members. Thus, Spencer, again taking a conservative position, applauds ecclesiastical institutions for their resistance to change and their ability to hold individuals and the social aggregate together, as well as for linking both to their past. As he puts it, "Ecclesiasticism stands for the principle of social continuity. *Above all other agencies* it is that which conduces to cohesion; not only between the coexisting parts of a nation, but also between its present generation and its past generations" (Spencer, 1908c:105; italics added).

Professional Institutions

One of the distinctive aspects of Spencer's sociology is the amount of attention he devoted to the professions, a subject that became a traditional (Ritzer and Walczak, 1986) and continuing (Abbott, 1988; Dingwall and King, 1995) concern of sociologists. The professions represent for Spencer a paradigm case of his overarching perspective: "No group of institutions illustrates with greater clearness the process of social evolution; and none shows more undeniably how social evolution conforms to the law of evolution at large" (1908c:317).

Spencer begins his discussion of the professions by arguing that groups provide a variety of functions for society, including the preservation of society from destruction by its enemies, the regulation of life, and the sustaining of life. Beyond these specific functions, "there is the augmentation of life; and this function it is which the professions in general subserve" (Spencer, 1908c:180). Thus, the professions constitute a structure whose function is the *augmentation of life*. Physicians physically increase the life span, while a range of other professionals, such as composers, poets, artists, scientists, and teachers, expand upon and improve the quality of life.

Spencer traces the roots of the professions to the homogeneous political-ecclesiastical agency, but when this agency subdivides, he sees religion as the main source of the professions. The obvious reason for this is the existence of professional priests; more indirect is the connection between religion and later lawyers and teachers, which stems from the fact that the early priests are characterized by their intellectual capacity, knowledge, and power. Priests were "able to devote time and energy to that intellectual labour and discipline which are required for professional occupations as distinguished from other occupations" (Spencer, 1908c:184).

Physicians can be traced to the early medicine men, who believed diseases were the result of supernatural causes and who thus employed supernatural cures. As part of the primitive militant societies, medicine men dealt with diseases antagonistically. As a result, Spencer sees priests as a more important source of physicians, since priests attempted to deal with the supernatural sympathetically rather than antagonistically. The priest tended to see diseases as being of divine origin. Thus, the cause of epilepsy was believed to be possession by the devil, and the cure lay in exorcism. Eventually, both physicians and surgeons differentiated from the priesthood, with the early physicians continuing to be similar to the priests in dealing with physical evils supernaturally inflicted, while the surgeons came to focus on more naturally caused (and cured) physical injuries.

Over time an increasing division of labor occurs among physicians (and surgeons) as they come to focus on highly specific parts of the body or illnesses. With this increasing differentiation comes an increase in integration through, among other things, professional associations, common educational experiences, and a centralized system of licensing.

Spencer proceeds to analyses of the evolution of a wide range of specific occupations that he, sometimes questionably,[3] considers professions. For example, he details the differentiation of law from the ecclesiastical institution and then examines the process of specialization within law itself. In the end, Spencer, in his typically conservative manner, concludes that all the specific professions, as well as the professions in general, are indispensable to society.

Industrial Institutions

Industry is the final institution that Spencer examines from an evolutionary perspective. A central aspect of the industrial structure is the division of labor and the functions it performs. The *division of labor* is defined as "that specialization of functions which directly or indirectly concerns the fulfillment of material wants, and the making of material aids to mental wants" (Spencer, 1908c:340). Spencer's first concern is to find the root causes of the division of labor.

---

[3]For example, most contemporary sociologists would not agree with Spencer's categorization of orators or biographers as professionals.

He begins by examining a number of physio-psychological causes, such as differences in the natural aptitudes of individuals, social classes, and males and females. In terms of the role of gender differences in the division of labor, Spencer places much of the blame on males in "rude" (that is, primitive) societies and on their ability "to force on the females the least desirable occupations . . . to the women is deputed all drudgery not beyond their strength" (1908c:345). However, Spencer is most concerned with the inhumane way males deal with females in militant societies, but he comforts himself with the belief that such treatment becomes more humane with the evolution to industrial society. However, even though the treatment of females is more humane, a division of labor continues to exist between the sexes: "The men do the heavy, outdoor work, and the women the light, indoor work" (Spencer, 1908c:344–345). Many contemporary sociologists would be critical of this division, but Spencer reserves his criticisms for earlier, less humane systems.

Spencer sees other causes of the division of labor, such as the character of the physical environment, divisions within the same locale, divisions between locales, and differences between the productive and distributive sectors of society. Whatever the causes, evolution brings with it an ever-increasing division of labor.

The next issue is the evolution from simple acquisition of that which is needed for survival (for example, by hunting and gathering) to the production of needed commodities. Production itself goes through an evolution from the use of human power to the use of animal power and ultimately machine power. The early development of production is inhibited by the early militant societies. While such societies are conducive to some production (for example, guns), "in most respects the destroying activities have been antagonistic to the productive activities" (Spencer, 1908c:366). Thus, chronic warfare tends to destroy nascent industrial organizations and to be hostile to occupations that are not related to warfare. The progress of industry is intimately related to the decline of militancy.

Another barrier to industrial development is, interestingly, human nature. In order for industrial evolution to continue, "human nature has to be remoulded" (Spencer, 1908c:362). As we have seen, Spencer argues that human nature is not set but evolves as society evolves. Thus, the primitive character of human nature tends to inhibit industrial development. But industry does advance, albeit slowly at first because of the limitations of human nature. Changes in society like the advance of industry tend to expand human nature, permitting further industrial progress. Thus, "production increases as the desires multiply and become stronger" (Spencer, 1908c:364). There is, then, a dialectic between the advances of industry and of human nature, with advances in each furthering the other.

A necessary concomitant of the increasing division of labor and the expansion of production is the expansion of the distributive system needed to transport goods from one setting to another. Here we see the evolutionary differentiation of distributors from producers. Over time, there is expansion in the complexity of the system of distribution. Along with the evolution of the distributive system comes the need for the evolution of the system of exchange, ending in the development of paper money, which makes distribution and production easier.

Another element of the industrial system is the means of regulating labor. Initially, the regulation of labor is fused in a combined industrial-political-ecclesiastical organization. Over time, industrial control tends to differentiate, with the result that "the control of industrial activity has gradually become independent of Church and State" (Spencer, 1908c:420). Spencer traces the history of the regulation of labor from paternal regulation (father controls production) through patriarchal regulation (father and grandfather control production; ultimately a step toward communal control) and communal regulation (at first on the basis of blood ties, but expanding to the larger group) to regulation by guilds and trade unions. Guilds and unions often begin as militant organizations and continue to be militant in Spencer's day because their militancy is required in that transitional phase in order to keep opposing forces (for example, harsh employers) in check. However, they also give workers an experience of cooperation, and Spencer believes that their cooperative aspect will increase and their militant characteristics will decline as we move further away from militant societies and toward industrial societies.

Spencer also deals with slavery and serfdom as early forms of control over labor that are associated with militant societies. These inefficient and compulsory systems decline as society moves toward the voluntary cooperation of industrial society. It is free labor on the basis of contracts that fits best in the modern, industrial society.

In looking to the future of industrial systems, Spencer is not sympathetic to socialism, which he sees as fitting better in a militant society than in an industrial society characterized by voluntary cooperation (we will have more to say about his views on socialism shortly). Spencer is more concerned with the growing power of the state than he is with the expansion of socialism. He sees a trend toward state regulation of industry, and as a result, "the present voluntary industrial organization will have its place entirely usurped by a compulsory industrial organization" (Spencer, 1908c:605). He fears that ultimately there "will be established a state in which no man can do what he likes but every man must do what he is told" (Spencer, 1908c:605). In fact, he sees "statism" as standing in opposition to "individualism" (Spencer, 1892/1965). Thus, Spencer fears an evolutionary retrogression with restraint coming to replace the historic movement toward greater individual freedom.

ETHICS AND POLITICS

In his earliest book, *Social Statics* (1850/1954), and in much later books, especially his two-volume *The Principles of Ethics* (1897/1978), Spencer articulated a rather consistent ethical and political position that informs, and is informed by, his substantive work. He subtitled *Social Statics* "The conditions essential to human happiness specified, and the first of them developed," while he described *The Principles of Ethics* as a set of "rules of right conduct on a scientific basis" (Spencer, 1897/1978:xiv). We will briefly examine in this section Spencer's ethical and political ideas. A key issue is whether these ideas greatly enhanced or fatally injured his sociology.

Spencer's moral and political ideas are derived, to a large extent, from his methodological individualism. As we have seen throughout this chapter, Spencer focused on macro-level phenomena, but he did so with the view that the base of these phenomena was individual "units." This specific view of the social world is deduced, like many others, from his general principles: "As a multitude is but an assemblage of units, and as the characteristics of a multitude result from the properties of its units, so social phenomena are consequences of the natures of individual men" (Spencer, 1902/1958:8). Or, more strongly, "The properties of the units determine the properties of the aggregate" (Spencer, 1873/1961:41).[4] The characteristics of people in an associated state are derived from the inherent properties of individuals: "No phenomenon can be presented by a corporate body but what there is a preexisting capacity in its individual members for producing" (Spencer, 1850/1954:17). Just as macro-level phenomena are derived from individuals, so too is the moral law of society: "The right ruling of humanity in its state of *multitude* is to be found in humanity in its state of *unitude*" (Spencer, 1850/1954:18). Spencer believes that individuals are endowed with a moral sense that dictates their actions and ultimately the structure and functioning of society.

While individuals are the proximate cause of social morality, the more distant cause is God. The things that people come to view as moral are in line with divine rule. Spencer castigates those who "doubt the foresight and efficiency of the Divine arrangements" (1850/1954:47). He further argues that "human happiness is the divine will" (Spencer, 1850/1954:67). Thus, society is seen as evolving toward an increasing state of perfection and happiness.

Another factor in this evolution to a perfect moral state is that evil, in Spencer's view, progressively disappears. To explain this disappearance, Spencer once again employs the survival-of-the-fittest argument.[5] As he sees it, evil is a result of nonadaptation to external conditions, or "unfitness to the conditions of existence" (Spencer, 1850/1954:59). However, such nonadaptation is constantly diminishing and must ultimately disappear. More generally, Spencer argues that "all excess and all deficiency must disappear; that is, all unfitness must disappear; that is, all imperfection must disappear" (1850/1954:59). As a result of the survival-of-the-fittest argument applied to evil, Spencer concludes that "the ultimate development of the ideal man is logically certain" (1850/1954:59).

Turning the argument around, Spencer contends that human happiness comes from the satisfaction of desires and that gratification can come only from an exercise of human faculties. Thus, people must be free to exercise their faculties; that is, they must have liberty. Spencer invokes God on the side of this viewpoint as well: "God intends he [the human] should have that liberty. Therefore he has a right to that liberty" (1850/1954:69). He also embeds this argument in his methodological individualism by

---

[4]While we see here (and have seen elsewhere) that individual units lie at the base of aggregates, Spencer also recognizes a dialectic in which changes in the aggregate in turn alter the units. Spencer specifies a number of superorganic products that serve to modify the individual, including material "appliances" (for example, the steam engine), language, knowledge, science, customs and laws, esthetic products (literature), and so on.

[5]By the way, Spencer (1897/1978) later makes it clear that his ideas on evolution are *not* indebted to Charles Darwin, whose book *On the Origin of the Species* appeared in 1859, almost a decade *after* Spencer had published *Social Statics*. However, in the preface to the fourth edition of *First Principles* (1902/1958), Spencer did admit to altering some of his ideas as a result of Darwin's influence.

contending that people are endowed with "an *instinct of personal rights*" (Spencer, 1850/1954:86). Furthermore, this liberty must not be the right of just a few; since everyone has these faculties, all individuals have the right to exercise them freely.

However, there are limits on personal liberty, most important in the fact that an individual, in exercising his or her liberty, cannot be allowed to infringe on the liberty of others. However, since individuals are not endowed with the capacity to prevent their actions from infringing on the rights of others, society is needed to perform this function. This leads to Spencer's libertarian political position that there is a role for the state but it is a highly limited one. In his view the state must protect the liberty of individuals, but "it ought to do nothing more than protect" (Spencer, 1850/1954:264–265). Because he does see this limited role for the state, Spencer rejects the label "laissez-faire theorist" that some affixed to him.

Of course, such a libertarian position fits well with Spencer's views on evolution and survival of the fittest. Other than protecting individual liberty, the state is to get out of the way and allow the "law" and dynamics of evolution to work themselves out. Here is one of the ways in which Spencer describes that law:

> The well-being of existing humanity and the unfolding of it into this ultimate perfection are both secured by that same beneficent, though severe, discipline to which animate creation at large is subject: a discipline which is pitiless in the working out of good: a felicity-pursuing law which never swerves for the avoidance of partial and temporary suffering. The poverty of the incapable, the distresses that come upon the imprudent, the starvation of the idle, and those shoulderings aside of the weak by the strong, which leaves so many "in shallows and in miseries," are the decrees of a large, far-seeing benevolence.
>
> (Spencer, 1850/1954:288–289)

Thus, Spencer does not look upon such "harsh realities" as hunger and disease as evil; rather, they "are seen to be full of the highest benificence— the same benificence which brings to early graves the children of diseased parents and singles out the low-spirited, the intemperate, and the debilitated as the victims of an epidemic" (Spencer, 1850/1954:289). Similarly, and more harshly, "Society is constantly excreting its unhealthy, imbecile slow, vacillating, faithless members" (Spencer, 1850/1954:289). To put it more directly, those who are not healthy, not smart, not steadfast, and not believers in the divine should, and will, for the benefit of the larger society, die, as long as the natural process of evolution is left to operate in accord with its basic laws.

Thus we return to Spencer's libertarian politics. The state, as well as private philanthropists, is enjoined from preventing misery because to do so would cause greater misery for future generations. That is, if the unfit are allowed to survive, they will produce only similarly unfit offspring and that will only increase the magnitude of the problem for societies of the future. Those individuals, both in and out of the government, who think of themselves as doing good are in fact doing great harm to society. Interference by the state (and other agencies) serves only to encourage the multiplication of the unfit, to discourage the multiplication of the fit, and to stop the "purifying" process of natural evolution. Those who interfere "bequeath to posterity a continually increasing curse" (Spencer, 1850/1954:290).

Specifically, Spencer opposes state-administered charity (or any charity, for that matter) and state-run education. He even opposes government involvement in sanitation matters, such as garbage removal. Throughout his work Spencer often returns to the theme of the evils of state intervention. In the end, the government is to refrain from intervention not only because such interference hampers the natural process of evolution but also because it curtails individual rights: "For a government to take from a citizen more property than is needful for the efficient defense of that citizen's rights is to infringe his rights" (Spencer, 1850/1954:333). What Spencer seeks is a "society organized upon the same [evolutionary] system as an individual being" (1850/1954:403).

In his autobiography, Spencer railed against the distortion of his libertarian position ("genuine liberalism") by the "modern perversion of it which, while giving them nominal liberties in the shape of votes . . . is busily decreasing their liberties, both by the multiplication of restraints and commands, and by taking away larger parts of their incomes to be spent not as they individually like, but as public officials like" (1904a:487–488). Elsewhere, Spencer described the contrast in this way: "Liberalism habitually stood for individual freedom *versus* State-coercion" (1892/1965:5).

In response to the critics of his position, Spencer (1873/1961) expressed shock at being seen as an enemy of the poor and other unfortunate members of society. He depicts himself as more humane than that. He argues that he is not for inaction but rather for the use of "fit means" to deal with the problems of the unfortunate. Of course, one wonders about the credibility of such a position in light of views like his concern that "the diligent and provident labourer had to pay that the good-for-nothings might not suffer" (Spencer, 1892/1965:113). Obviously, Spencer had little regard for those on the public dole and wished that those who worked hard should not have to pay for the poor, with the result, presumably, that the poor would be permitted to suffer and ultimately die.

Obviously, if Spencer is opposed to state intervention, he would certainly be opposed to any radical (for example, socialist, communist) alteration of society. He believes that sociology, with its focus on the long history of unintentional evolutionary changes, will help disabuse us of the notion that "social evils admit of radical cures" (Spencer, 1873/1961:19). Societies arise by slow evolution, not by human manufacture and certainly not by human demolition and remanufacture. Spencer's fears about the controls exercised by the capitalist state were nothing in comparison to his fears about socialistic control, which he equated with slavery and tyranny. As a result of this view, Spencer associates socialism with militant societies and argues that it will "cease to be normal as fast as the society becomes predominantly industrial in its type" (1908c:577).

Spencer differentiates his own ideal society from that of socialists and communists by arguing that he is not in favor of giving people equal shares of things but rather of giving "each an opportunity of acquiring the objects he desires" (Spencer, 1850/1954:118). Spencer sees socialism as standing in opposition to the selfishness which he feels is an inherent part of human nature. It is unrealistic to expect that selfish people will voluntarily surrender their excess productivity to others; selfish people cannot produce an unselfish system. Relatedly, as we saw earlier in this chapter, Spencer views people as being endowed with an "instinct for personal rights," and one of those rights, which he sees as an element of human nature, is a desire for property. Therefore, socialism stands in opposition to this element of human nature and, as a result, cannot survive.

Spencer's opposition to socialism and communism is also related to his opposition to any abrupt or revolutionary change. This follows from his oft-stated view that evolution is, and must be, a gradual process. Not only does abrupt change violate evolution, but it also would lead to a radically altered society that would be out of harmony with human nature, which changes glacially.

The moral and political views outlined above, as well as many others, led many sociologists, as Jonathan Turner (1985b) argues, to dismiss Spencer's theoretical perspective. That is, contemporary, often liberal or radical, sociological theorists tend to reject the kind of conservative morality and politics preached by Spencer. Their rejection of his morality and politics led to a rejection of his sociological theory. I agree with Turner that this is not a good reason to reject a theory. That is, one should not reject a theory merely because one opposes the morals or politics of its creator. However, there is another reason to question Spencer's theory, and that is on the basis of the feeling that his scientific sociology is shaped and distorted by his moral and political views. From my perspective, there is a very suspicious fit between Spencer's "scientific" sociology and his moral and political views. In fact, it could be argued that Spencer's claim to being scientific is vitiated by the fact that his work is biased by his moral and political proclivities. (Of course, similar things could be said about Marx, Weber, Simmel, and many other classical theorists.) Spencer cautioned sociologists about being biased in their work, but it seems clear that Spencer's sociological theory is weakened by his own biases. Thus it is not Spencer's specific morality or politics that leads us to question his work but rather the fact that they biased and distorted his theory.

That being said, we should not lose sight of the fact that there is much more of merit in Spencer's sociological theory than he is usually given credit for today. His meritorious ideas have been analyzed and underscored throughout this chapter.

SUMMARY

Herbert Spencer has a more powerful theory, and his work has more contemporary significance, than that of the other significant figure in the "prehistory" of sociological theory, Auguste Comte. Their theories have some similarities (for example, positivism) but far more differences (for example, Comte's faith in a positivist religion and Spencer's opposition to any centralized system of control).

Spencer offers a series of general principles from which he deduces an evolutionary theory: increasing integration, heterogeneity, and definiteness of both structures and functions. Indeed, sociology, for Spencer, is the study of the evolution of societies. While Spencer sought to legitimize sociology as a science, he also felt that sociology is linked to, and should draw upon, other sciences such as biology (especially the idea of survival of the fittest) and psychology (especially the importance of sentiments). In part from his concern with psychology, Spencer developed his methodological-individualist approach to the study of society.

Spencer addresses a number of the methodological difficulties confronting sociology as a science. He is especially concerned with various biases the sociologist must overcome—educational, patriotic, class, political, and theological. In seeking to exclude these biases, Spencer articulates a "value-free" position for sociology. In much of his substantive work, Spencer employs the comparative-historical method.

The evolution of society occupies a central place in Spencer's sociology. In his analysis of societal evolution, Spencer employs the three general aspects of evolution mentioned above—increasing integration (increasing size and coalescence of masses of people), heterogeneity, and definiteness (here, clearly demarcated institutions)—as well as a fourth aspect—the increasing coherence of social groups. In his evolutionary social theory, Spencer traces, among other things, the movement from simple to compounded societies and from militant to industrial societies.

In addition to dealing with the overall evolution of society, Spencer deals in considerable detail with the evolution of a number of social institutions—domestic, ceremonial, political, ecclesiastical, professional, and industrial. In each case, he employs the elements of his general theory of evolution, and he pays special attention to the evolution of structures and functions in these institutions, as well as in the larger society.

Spencer also articulates a series of ethical and political ideals. Consistent with his methodological individualism, Spencer argues that people must be free to exercise their abilities; they must have liberty. The only role for the state is the protection of individual liberty. Such a laissez-faire political perspective fits well with Spencer's ideas on evolution and survival of the fittest. Given his perspective on the gradual evolution of society, Spencer also rejects the idea of any radical solution (for example, communism) to society's problems.

5

KARL MARX

INTRODUCTION
  Is Marx's Theory Outmoded?
  Was Marx a Sociologist?
  Early and Late Marxian Theory
THE DIALECTIC
HUMAN POTENTIAL
  Powers and Needs
  Consciousness
  Human Potential and Nature
  Activity
  Sociability
  Unanticipated Consequences
ALIENATION
  Components of Alienation
  Distortions Resulting from Alienation
  Emancipation
THE STRUCTURES OF CAPITALIST SOCIETY
  Commodities
  Capital
  Private Property
  Division of Labor
  Social Class
CULTURAL ASPECTS OF CAPITALIST SOCIETY
  Class Consciousness and False Consciousness
  Ideology
MARX'S ECONOMICS: A CASE STUDY

INTRODUCTION

There has long been an uneasy and often bizarre relationship between sociological theory and the work of Karl Marx (1818–1883). In some sectors of the world, at least until the end of the Cold War, sociological theory was virtually identical with Marxian and neo-Marxian theory, and in others (most notably the United States) Marx was virtually ignored (at least until the 1960s) as a significant sociological thinker. In Eastern Europe Marx's influence was overwhelming, with sociological theory largely reduced to various forms of traditional and neo-Marxian thinking. In Western Europe Marx's influence has been highly variable. Among some Western European sociologists, Marx

147

has had a profound positive influence; others have fashioned their sociological theory specifically *against* Marxian theory. A number of European theorists were positively influenced by Marxian theory early in their careers, but turned away from it when the abuses of Soviet-style communism became clear. In the United States sociological theorists prior to the 1960s (with a few exceptions, like C. Wright Mills) tended to ignore, be ignorant of, or even be hostile to Marx's ideas. For example, in the book that revived grand theory in the United States, Talcott Parsons (1937, 1949) dismissed Marx's work in a few pages but spent hundreds of pages on the work of Emile Durkheim, Max Weber, and the marginally significant Vilfredo Pareto.[1] Most American theorists dismissed Marx as an ideologist who had little to contribute to the development of *scientific* sociological theory. However, in the 1960s young American sociologists— at least partly because of their personal experiences in the civil-rights, anti-Vietnam War, and student-rights movements—began to give serious attention to Marx as a sociological theorist. Reflecting this change was a book by Henri Lefebvre (1968) in which he argued that, although Marx was not simply a sociologist, there is a sociology in Marx's work. From the late 1960s to the late 1980s, a serious effort was made to integrate Marxian and neo-Marxian theory into American sociological theory, while in the rest of the world Marx's influence continued strong and even grew in strength in some areas. Although resistance to Marx remains among some American sociologists, many thinkers now are willing to accord Marx his rightful place among the giants of sociological thought.

Is Marx's Theory Outmoded?

With the failure of communist societies and their turn to a more capitalistically oriented economy, it is necessary to address what this means for the role of Marxian theory within sociology (Antonio, forthcoming; Aronson, 1995; Hudelson, 1993; Manuel, 1992). On the surface it appears that these changes suggest that we will see a substantial decline in interest in Marxian theory among sociologists. In fact, this *is* likely to occur, especially as a result of the fact that new theorists are less likely to turn to Marx for answers to the problems of modern capitalistic societies. However, the retreat from Marxian sociological theory is likely to be limited for several reasons.

First, most sociologists who have adopted a Marxian perspective have a deep and long-term commitment to it that is not likely to be greatly modified by changes in societies that never really embodied Marx's principles and ideals. Marx believed that in order for society to move toward communism it had to meet certain preconditions such as "mature material conditions and . . . a mature, united and determined working class" (Graham, 1992:165). Most, if not all, of the so-called communist nations did not meet these, or other, preconditions for communism. Thus, lacking the necessary preconditions, it comes as no surprise to many Marxian theorists that these nations never came close to Marx's vision of a communist society. According to Graham, "in the long run it will be much easier to analyze and appraise Marx's programme without the distraction

---

[1]Also of significance is the fact that Parsons (1998) wrote a chapter on Simmel but because of space considerations decided not to include it (Buxton, 1998; Jaworski, 1997:46).

of a disastrously distorted model in the real world" (1992:165). Second, and relatedly, many of Marx's ideas have been integrated into various sociological perspectives (see, for example, the integrated paradigm discussed in the Appendix), and they will not be excised merely because of failures in the communist bloc. Third, and most important, it is the thesis of this chapter that Marx's *sociological* theory, not his economic theory, is of greatest importance. As we will see, Marx offered an abstract, coherent, and greatly satisfying sociological theory that can be used to analyze *any* society, not just capitalistic societies and their economic systems. Since that sociological theory was un-involved in the creation of communist societies, and in fact was contradicted by them, it is relatively unscathed by recent developments in the communist world. Sociologists will continue to be attracted to the scope and elegance of Marx's sociological theory (one recent and important example is Postone, 1993).

Was Marx a Sociologist?

Many students (and some academicians), both pro- and anti-Marx, might be surprised to find Marx mentioned as one of the major theorists in the history of the discipline. Students trained in an anti-Marxian tradition or influenced by a similarly oriented mass media are socialized to believe that Marx was a bloodthirsty radical whose ideological commitments prohibited him from producing a serious scientific theory. It is crucial to sound scholarship that this myth be dispelled, and there are two bases on which it can be attacked. Similarly, it must be demonstrated to pro-Marxian students that it is legitimate to consider Marx a sociologist.

Two basic arguments can be made to those anti-Marxists who reject Marx as a soci-ologist because of his ideological orientation. First, although it is true that Marx's ap-proach is heavily influenced by his ideology, it is important to recognize that *all* sociological theorists have an ideological bias. This is as true for Comte, Spencer, Durkheim, Weber, and Simmel as it is for Marx. There is no such thing as a "value-free" sociological theory. In theorizing about social phenomena, sociologists find it im-possible to be completely neutral, and this remains true whether or not they are willing to recognize it or to admit it. Thus it *is* true that Marx's sociological theory is ideologi-cal, but that is no reason to dismiss it, because this is also true of *all* other sociological theories. The *major* difference between Marx and other sociological theorists is that Marx made no effort to conceal the ideological character of his work; indeed, as we will see, it is built into the very structure of his theorizing.

Second, although Marx was avowedly ideological in his theorizing, the widely shared view of Marx as a blood-crazed fanatic is not admissible. As we will see throughout this chapter, Marx was a humanist who was deeply hurt by the suffering and exploitation that he witnessed among the working class under capitalism. His human-ism led him to call for a revolution that would overturn the economic system, which was exploitative of the vast majority of people, and that would lead to the creation of a more humane socialist society. Although he called for revolution, Marx did *not* believe that the change *had* to be bloody. It was possible for the transition to socialism to occur peacefully, and given Marx's humanistic proclivities, this would clearly have been the most desirable course of action to him.

Although these points might ease some of the doubts among readers with an anti-Marxian bias, they will not satisfy those who begin with a pro-Marxian orientation. Such students might object that to label Marx a "sociologist" is much too restrictive. In their view, Marx defies simple categorization, because he was also a philosopher, a revolutionary, a pamphleteer, a journalist, a political scientist, a dialectician, and so forth. It is true that Marx is a highly complex thinker whose work is attractive to people in a wide range of endeavors, but among the many labels that fit Marx *is* that of sociologist (MacCrae, 1992). We can deal with those elements of Marx's thought that are relevant to sociology as long as we recognize that he is also many other things to many other people.

Early and Late Marxian Theory

There is another debate, this one among various interpreters of Marx's work. There are a number of schools of neo-Marxian theory, and many of their differences stem from varying interpretations of Marx's theory. As Paul Thomas puts it, "We have today a galaxy of different Marxisms, within which the place of Marx's own thought is ambiguous" (1991:26). For example, some stress Marx's early work on human potential and see the rest of it as derived from, and consistent with, his earlier work (see, for example, Ollman, 1976; Wallimann, 1981; Wartenberg, 1982). Others stress Marx's later work on the structures of society, especially the economic structures, and see that work as separable, and even different, from his early, largely philosophical work on human nature (see Althusser, 1969; Gandy, 1979; McMurty, 1978). This chapter is based on the premise that there is no discontinuity or contradiction between Marx's early work on human potential and his later work on the structures of capitalist society. After a general introduction to Marx's mode of thinking (the dialectic), we will look at Marx's early work on human potential and then show its relationship to his later work on the larger structures of society.

THE DIALECTIC

Marx adopted the dialectical mode of logic from Hegel. However, whereas Hegel focused on a dialectic of ideas, Marx embedded his dialectical approach in the material world. This was a crucial transformation because it allowed Marx to move the dialectic out of the realm of philosophy and into the realm of what some consider a science of social relations grounded in the material world. It is this focus that makes Marx's work most relevant to sociology, even though the dialectical approach is very different from the mode of thinking used by most sociologists (Friedrichs, 1972a, 1972b; Ollman, 1976; Schneider, 1971).

Reciprocal Relations   The dialectical method of analysis does not see a simple, one-way, cause-and-effect relationship among the various parts of the social world. For the dialectical thinker, social influences never simply flow in one direction as they do for cause-and-effect thinkers. To the dialectician one factor may have an effect on another, but it is just as likely that the latter will have a simultaneous effect on the former. For example, the increasing exploitation of the proletariat by the capitalist may cause the workers to become increasingly dissatisfied and more militant, but the increasing militancy of the proletariat might well cause the capitalists to react by becoming even more exploitative in order to crush the resistance of the workers. This kind of thinking does not mean that the dialectician never considers causal relationships in the social world. It does mean that when dialectical thinkers talk about causality, they are always attuned to reciprocal relationships among social factors as well as to the dialectical totality of social life in which they are embedded.

Fact and Value   In dialectical analysis, especially as Marx developed it, social values are not separable from social facts. Most sociologists believe that their values can and must be separated from their study of facts about the social world. The dialectical thinker believes that it is not only impossible to keep values out of the study of the social world but also undesirable because it produces a dispassionate, inhuman sociology that has little to offer to people in search of answers to the problems they confront. Facts and values are inevitably intertwined, with the result that the study of social phenomena is value-laden. Thus to Marx, it was impossible, and even if possible, undesirable, to be dispassionate in his analysis of the two major classes within capitalist society—the bourgeoisie (also called "capitalists") and the proletariat (the workers). The bourgeoisie is defined by the fact that it owns the "means of production" (factories, tools, and so on) and the proletariat by the fact that it must sell its labor time to the bourgeoisie in order to earn a wage that allows it to survive. In *Capital* (1867/1967), for example, Marx talked about the capitalists as werewolves and vampires who suck the blood out of the workers, and he was very sympathetic to the plight of the proletariat. But Marx's emotional involvement in what he was studying did not mean that his observations were inaccurate. It could even be argued that Marx's passionate views on these issues gave him unparalleled insight into the nature of capitalist society. A less passionate student might have delved less deeply into the dynamics of the system. In fact, research into the work of scientists indicates that the idea of a dispassionate scientist is largely a myth and that the very best scientists are the ones who are most passionate about, and committed to, their ideas (Mitroff, 1974).

Dividing Lines   Both of the above characteristics of the dialectic reflect Marx's view that there are no hard-and-fast dividing lines between phenomena in the social world. Marx believed that the various components of the social world blended gradually and imperceptibly into one another. Thus, to take two of Marx's major concerns, he would argue that the capitalists and the proletariat are not clearly separated but gradually blend into one another. This means that there are a large number of people who either exist in the interstices between the two classes or move from one class to another (the successful worker who becomes a capitalist; the capitalist who fails and drops into the working class).

Relations   Dialectical thinkers also take a *relational* view of the social world (Ollman, 1976). They focus on the relations within and among various aspects of the social world. Thus, in examining a bureaucracy, they look at the social relationships that go into its construction. Relationships between individuals, between groups of

KARL MARX: A Biographical Sketch

Karl Marx was born in Trier, Prussia, on May 5, 1818. His father, a lawyer, provided the family with a fairly typical middle-class existence. Both parents were from rabbinical families, but for business reasons the father had converted to Lutheranism when Karl was very young. In 1841 Marx received his doctorate in philosophy from the University of Berlin, a school heavily influenced by Hegel and the Young Hegelians, supportive, yet critical, of their master. Marx's doctorate was a dry philosophical treatise, but it did anticipate many of his later ideas. After graduation he became a writer for a liberal-radical newspaper and within ten months had become its editor-in-chief. However, because of its political positions, the paper was closed shortly thereafter by the government. The early essays published in this period began to reflect a number of the positions that would guide Marx throughout his life. They were liberally sprinkled with democratic principles, humanism, and youthful idealism. He rejected the abstractness of Hegelian philosophy, the naive dreaming of utopian communists, and those activists who were urging what he considered to be premature political action. In rejecting these activists, Marx laid the groundwork for his own life's work:

> Practical attempts, even by the masses, can be answered with a cannon as soon as they become dangerous, but ideas that have overcome our intellect and conquered our conviction, ideas to which reason has riveted our conscience, are chains from which one cannot break loose without breaking one's heart; they are demons that one can only overcome by submitting to them.

(Marx, 1842/1977:20)

Marx married in 1843 and soon thereafter was forced to leave Germany for the more liberal atmosphere of Paris. There he continued to grapple with the ideas of Hegel and his supporters, but he also encountered two new sets of ideas—French socialism and English political economy. It was the unique way in which he combined Hegelianism, socialism, and political economy that shaped his intellectual orientation. Also of great importance at this point was his meeting the man who was to become his lifelong friend, benefactor, and collaborator—Friedrich Engels (Carver, 1983). The son of a textile manufacturer, Engels had become a socialist critical of the conditions facing the working class. Much of Marx's compassion for the misery of the working class came from his exposure to Engels and his ideas. In 1844 Engels and Marx had a lengthy conversation in a famous café in Paris and laid the groundwork for a lifelong association. Of that conversation Engels said, "Our complete agreement in all theoretical fields became obvious . . . and our joint work dates from that time" (McLellan, 1973:131). In the following year, Engels published a notable work, *The Condition of the Working Class in England*. During this period Marx wrote a number of abstruse works (many unpublished in his lifetime), including *The Holy Family* and *The German Ideology* (both coauthored with Engels), but he also produced *The Economic and Philosophic*

people, and between subunits within the organization (for example, the personnel department and the engineering department) all would come under the intense scrutiny of the dialectical thinker. In addition, a dialectician never would concentrate on one

Manuscripts of 1844, which better foreshadowed his increasing preoccupation with the economic domain.

While Marx and Engels shared a theoretical orientation, there were many differences between the two men. Marx tended to be theoretical, a disorderly intellectual, and very oriented to his family. Engels was a practical thinker, a neat and tidy businessman, and a person who did not believe in the institution of the family. In spite of their differences, Marx and Engels forged a close union in which they collaborated on books and articles and worked together in radical organizations, and Engels even helped support Marx throughout the rest of his life so that Marx could devote himself to his intellectual and political endeavors.

In spite of the close association of the names of Marx and Engels, Engels made it clear that he was the junior partner:

> Marx could very well have done without me. What Marx accomplished I would not have achieved. Marx stood higher, saw farther, and took a wider and quicker view than the rest of us. Marx was a genius.
>
> (Engels, cited in McLellan, 1973:131–132)

In fact, many believe that Engels failed to understand many of the subtleties of Marx's work (C. Smith, 1997). After Marx's death, Engels became the leading spokesperson for Marxian theory and in various ways distorted and oversimplified it, although he remained faithful to the political perspective he had forged with Marx.

Because some of his writings had upset the Prussian government, the French government (at the request of the Prussians) expelled Marx in 1845, and he moved to Brussels. His radicalism was growing, and he had become an active member of the international revolutionary movement. He also associated with the Communist League and was asked to write a document (with Engels) expounding its aims and beliefs. The result was the *Communist Manifesto* of 1848, a work that was characterized by ringing political slogans (for example, "Working men of all countries, unite!").

In 1849 Marx moved to London, and, in light of the failure of the political revolutions of 1848, he began to withdraw from active revolutionary activity and to move into more serious and detailed research on the workings of the capitalist system. In 1852, he began his famous studies in the British Museum of the working conditions in capitalism. These studies ultimately resulted in the three volumes of *Capital,* the first of which was published in 1867; the other two were published posthumously. He lived in poverty during these years, barely managing to survive on a small income from his writings and the support of Engels. In 1864 Marx became reinvolved in political activity by joining the *International,* an international movement of workers. He soon gained preeminence within the movement and devoted a number of years to it. He began to gain fame both as leader of the *International* and as the author of *Capital.* But the disintegration of the *International* by 1876, the failure of various revolutionary movements, and personal illness took their toll on Marx. His wife died in 1881, a daughter in 1882, and Marx himself on March 14, 1883.

social unit in isolation from other social units. Thus, the relationship between a given bureaucracy and various other social units in the social world would be of chief concern to the dialectician.

Past, Present, Future   Dialecticians are interested not only in the relationships of social phenomena in the *contemporary* world but also in the relationship of those contemporary realities to both *past* (Bauman, 1976:81) and *future* social phenomena. This has two distinct implications for a dialectical sociology. First, it means that dialectical sociologists are concerned with studying the historical roots of the contemporary world as Marx (1857–58/1964) did in his study of the sources of modern capitalism. In fact, dialectical thinkers are very critical of modern sociology for its failure to do much historical research. A good example of Marx's thinking in this regard is found in the following famous quotation from "The Eighteenth Brumaire of Louis Bonaparte":

> Men make their own history, but they do not make it just as they please; they do not make it under circumstances chosen by themselves, but under circumstances directly encountered from the past. The tradition of all the dead generations weighs like a nightmare on the brain of the living.
>
> (Marx, 1852/1963:15)

Second, many dialectical thinkers are attuned to the future directions of society. This interest in the future is one of the main reasons that dialectical sociology is inherently political. It has an image of the future world, and it is interested in encouraging practical activities that would bring that world into existence. In trying to grasp the nature of this future world, dialecticians believe that much is to be learned from a careful study of the contemporary world. It is their view that social change is a coming to be of what potentially is, that the sources of the future exist in the present. To take an example from Marx, the proletariat of modern capitalism, which does not own the means of production, anticipates the conditions of all in socialist society. There is to be no private ownership of the means of production in socialism. This does not mean that people will not own clothes, television sets, and cars, but rather that one class will not own and dominate the industrial and organizational structure as it does in contemporary capitalism.

No Inevitabilities   But in saying that the dialectical thinker believes that the future is the coming to be of what potentially is, we do *not* imply the deterministic view that the future course of the world is preset and unchangeable. The basic nature of the dialectic militates against a deterministic orientation. Terence Ball (1991) describes Marx as a "political possibilist" rather than a "historical inevitabilist." Because social phenomena are constantly acting and reacting, the social world defies a simple, deterministic model.[2] The future *may* be based on some contemporary model, but not inevitably. Marxists hoped and believed that the future was to be found in socialism, but the proletariat could not simply wait passively for it to arrive. They had to work for it, and there were no ironclad guarantees that it would occur.

This disinclination to think deterministically is what makes the best-known model of the dialectic—thesis, antithesis, synthesis—a gross distortion. This simple model implies that a social phenomenon will inevitably spawn an opposing form and that the clash between these two will inevitably lead to a new, synthetic social form. *But in the real world, there are no inevitabilities.* Furthermore, social phenomena are not easily

---

[2]Marx did, however, occasionally discuss the inevitability of socialism.

divided into the simple thesis, antithesis, and synthesis categories adopted by some Marxists. The dialectician is interested in the study of real relationships rather than grand abstractions. It is this disinclination to deal in grand abstractions that led Marx away from Hegel and would lead him today to reject such a great oversimplification of the dialectic as thesis, antithesis, synthesis. Marx analyzed the conflict between the capitalists and the proletariat, and although he foresaw a revolution and, ultimately, a new type of society, he did not see this as an inevitable process. The proletariat would have to work and fight for socialism if it were to occur. But even if the workers did strive for it, they were not assured that it would come to pass. Actions forced upon the capitalists have made the working class more satisfied with their lot, and this has militated against the occurrence of a working-class revolt.

Conflict and Contradiction   What is perhaps best known about the dialectic is its concern with *conflict* and *contradiction* (Elster, 1985; Wilde, 1991). This leads to a number of by-products, including a concern for the process of change as well as a political program. But what is of importance here is that the dialectic leads to an interest in the conflicts and contradictions among various levels of social reality, rather than to the more traditional sociological interest in the ways that these various levels mesh rather neatly into a cohesive whole. Although Marx was aware of how the ideologies of the capitalists mesh with their objective interests, he wanted to concentrate on issues like the conflict between the large-scale structures created by capitalists and the interests of the proletariat (Durand and Hayter, 1997).

Perhaps the ultimate contradiction within capitalism for Marx exists in the relationship between the bourgeoisie and the proletariat. In Marx's terms, the bourgeoisie produces the proletariat, and in producing and expanding that class, the capitalists are producing their own grave diggers. As capitalism expands, the number of workers exploited, and the degree of exploitation, increases. The tendency for the level of exploitation to escalate leads to more and more resistance on the part of the proletariat. Resistance begets more exploitation and oppression, and the likely result is a confrontation between the two classes, a confrontation that the proletariat, in Marx's view, is likely to win (Boswell and Dixon, 1993).

Despite the importance to Marx of the future communist society, he spent surprisingly little time depicting what this world would be like. He refused to write "recipes for the kitchens of the future" (Marx, cited in T. Ball, 1991:139). In fact, he was critical of those utopian socialists who wrote book after book on their dreamlike images of future society. To Marx, the most important task was the critical analysis of contemporary capitalist society. He believed that such criticism would help bring down capitalism and create the conditions for the rise of a new socialist world. There would be time to construct communist society once capitalism was overcome. In general, however, Marx viewed communism as a classless society.

Actors and Structures   Dialectical thinkers in general are also interested (as Marx was) in the structures of society and the actors within society, as well as with the dialectical relationship between actors and social structures. But the dialectical method is even more complex than this, because, as we have already seen, the dialectician

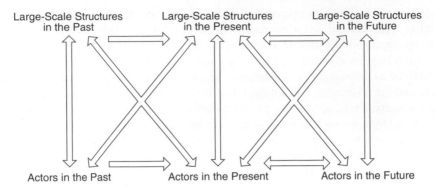

FIGURE 5.1
Schematic Representation of a Sociologically Relevant Dialectic

considers past, present, and future circumstances, and this applies to both actors and structures. Figure 5.1 is a simplified schematic representation of this enormously complex and sophisticated perspective.

Marx made it abundantly clear throughout his work that he was working with a model like that in Figure 5.1. He was attuned to the ongoing interplay among the major levels of social analysis. For example, Marx and Engels said, "Circumstances make men *just as much* as men make circumstances" (1845–46/1970:59; italics added). Lefebvre was therefore quite accurate when he argued that the heart of Marx's thought lies in the relationship between people and the large-scale structures they create (1968:8). On the one hand, these large-scale structures help people to fulfill themselves; on the other, they represent a grave threat to humanity.

Despite his general commitment to the dialectic, in particular the dialectical relationship between large-scale structures and actors, Marx came to focus more and more of his attention on the structures of capitalist society. In part, this focus is traceable to Marx's political interests, which led him to examine and criticize the structures of capitalism in order to help bring about revolutionary change. By so doing, the transition to socialism could be expedited. A good portion of this chapter will be devoted to a discussion of Marx's analysis of the structures of capitalism. But before we can analyze these, we need to begin with Marx's thoughts on the more microscopic aspects of social reality. Marx built his critical analysis of the structure of capitalist society on his premises about actors, action, and interaction.

HUMAN POTENTIAL

The basis of much of Marx's thinking lies in his ideas on the potential of human beings (or what he called *species-being*). He believed that until his time in history, people had not even begun to approach what they ultimately could become. The nature of societies prior to capitalism had been too harsh to allow people to realize their potentials. They were too busy trying merely to get enough food, shelter, and protection to develop their higher capacities. Although capitalism solved some of these problems, it was too oppressive an environment to allow most people to develop their human potential. It was Marx's hope and belief that communism would provide the kind of environment in which people could begin to express that potential fully. Thus Marx could not describe human potential in any detail, because it had yet to be allowed to develop to its fullest and to express itself adequately. Marx's critique of capitalist society was based in part on what he felt humans could become once they were freed from the shackles of capitalism and allowed to express themselves in the unfettered environment of communism.

Powers and Needs

The bases of Marx's conception of human potential were his ideas on the powers and needs of people (Heller, 1976; Ollman, 1976). *Powers* may be defined as the faculties, abilities, and capacities of people. In the Marxian system, human powers are not simply what they are now, but also what they were historically and what they can be in the future under changed social circumstances. *Needs* are the desires people feel for things that are usually not immediately available. Needs, like powers, are greatly affected by the social settings in which people exist. Even the most microscopic notions of human powers and needs cannot be discussed without taking into account the larger setting of society as a whole.

It is necessary to differentiate between natural powers and needs and species powers and needs. In brief, *natural* powers and needs are those shared with other animals, whereas *species* powers and needs are those that are uniquely human. Natural powers and needs per se are of little interest to us because, as Bertell Ollman argued, "natural" man is "*not yet a man but still an animal*" (1976:80). However, all natural powers and needs can be expressed in distinctly human ways. Sex, for example, is a behavior common to human beings and all other animals, but when it is expressed in peculiarly human ways, it moves into the category of species powers and needs.

Consciousness

The heart of the notion of human potential lies in Marx's view that people differ from animals in their possession of consciousness as well as in their ability to link this consciousness to their actions. Although borrowing from Hegel here, Marx was critical of Hegel for discussing consciousness as if it existed independently of people rather than *focusing on the consciousness of real, sentient people.* The following is the famous quotation from Marx in which he acknowledged his ties to Hegel and laid out his basic point of departure from Hegel's orientation:

> Hegel makes *the man of self-consciousness* instead of making self-consciousness the *self-consciousness of man,* of real man, man living in a real objective world and determined by that world. He stands the world *on its head* and can therefore dissolve *in the head* all the limitations which naturally remain in existence for *evil sensuousness,* for *real* man.
> (Marx and Engels, 1845/1956:254)

Thus, Marx was opposed to Hegel not only on intellectual grounds but also because his ephemeral image of self-consciousness was a barrier to the kind of political action that to Marx was imperative.

Marx went further than arguing simply in general terms that people are distinguished from other animals by their consciousness. According to Ollman (1976), Marx believed the following mental capacities set humans apart from other animals:

1 While animals just "do," people can set themselves off mentally from whatever they are doing.

2 Since they have a distinctive form of consciousness, human actors are able to choose to act or not to act. Furthermore, they are capable of choosing what kind of action to undertake.

3 The minds of human beings enable them to plan beforehand what their action is going to be.

4 Human beings possess both physical and mental flexibility.

5 Human beings are capable of giving close attention to what they are doing over a long period of time.

6 The nature of the human mind leads people to be highly social.

Consciousness is a characteristic of people, and it is shaped out of human action and interaction: "Consciousness is, therefore, from the very beginning a social product, and remains so as long as men exist at all" (Marx and Engels, 1845–46/1970:51). Out of people's activities, social relationships, and the production of material life comes an expansion of consciousness:

> Not only do the objective conditions change in the act of production . . . but the producers change, too, in that they bring out new qualities in themselves, develop themselves in production, transform themselves, develop new powers and ideas, new modes of intercourse, new needs and new language.
>
> (Marx, 1857–58/1974:494)

It is not just consciousness or self-consciousness that differentiates human beings from other animals but also the relationship of that mental capacity to the peculiar kinds of activities of which people are capable. Human beings are capable of *activity* of a distinctive kind, quality, and pace. It is the ability to control activities through consciousness that distinguishes people from animals. Marx is perfectly explicit on this point:

> The animal is immediately one with its life activity. . . . Man makes his life activity itself the object of his will and of his consciousness.
>
> (Marx, 1932/1964:113)

> A spider conducts operations that resemble those of a weaver, and a bee puts to shame many an architect in the construction of her cells. But what distinguishes the worst architect from the best of bees is this, that the architect raises his structure in imagination before he erects it in reality. At the end of every labor-process we get a result that already existed in imagination of the laborer at its commencement.
>
> (Marx, 1867/1967:178)

McMurty (1978) argues that to Marx the special property of human nature is its creative intelligence, the ability to raise a structure in one's imagination and then to erect that structure in reality. To Marx, at the most abstract level, consciousness and its ability to direct activity were the distinctive characteristics of human beings, at least potentially.

Human Potential and Nature

But the problem with this conception of human potential is that it is highly abstract, and Marx had to bring it down to the level of the real world. People, their consciousness, and their activities cannot exist in isolation; they must be related to the natural world. People require objectives for their thoughts and actions, and the most important of these objectives are other people and nature. Humans must act on something, and what they act on mainly, with all their creative powers and in interaction with other people, is nature. We can differentiate three components of the relationship between human beings and nature—perception, orientation, and appropriation.

Perception is the immediate contact that people have with nature through their senses, but a mass of unorganized perceptions is likely to leave actors quite disoriented. What is needed is a process of *orientation* that organizes, patterns, and imposes a framework on the various perceptions of the world. Once the world has been perceived and the perceptions organized, the stage is set for *appropriation,* in which actors use their creative powers on nature in order to satisfy their needs. The conscious, creative capacity of human beings makes sense in Marx's view only when it is seen in relationship to the perception, orientation, and appropriation of nature. Not only does the nature of people's powers and needs shape the form of perception, orientation, and appropriation, but the form that they take in a particular social setting affects, in turn, the nature of these powers and needs. This reciprocity reinforces the idea that for Marx human nature was not carved in stone but was very much affected by the nature of the social setting.

Following Marx, we may differentiate three basic epochs in the relationship between human potential and the processes of perception, orientation, and appropriation—primitive society, capitalism, and communism.

In *primitive society* people used natural resources to produce the things that they needed (for example, boats and shelters). Because relatively few things were produced—and those rather inefficiently—we can say that people developed their capacities to only a slight degree. Because powers were expressed to only this slight degree, the needs of people remained at a minimal level in primitive society (Ollman, 1976:91). In earliest times, people were busy desperately trying to survive and, as a result, were able to develop and express only a limited number of needs: "In lowest stages of production . . . few human needs have yet been produced, and thus few [need] to be satisfied" (Marx, 1857–58/1974:398). The ability of people to think, their consciousness, was limited and amounted to little more than animal, "sheep-like," consciousness (Marx and Engels, 1845–46/1970:51).

Capitalism is the economic system in which the bourgeoisie owns the means of production and the proletariat must sell its labor-time to the capitalist in order to survive. It was viewed by Marx as an epoch in which the creative capacity of most human beings as it is expressed in the act of appropriation is virtually eliminated. Instead, most people are reduced to wanting to make enough money to be able to *own* the commodities they desire. Thus the goal becomes ownership rather than the expression of human potential. In comparing primitive society to capitalism, Marx noted, "The ancients provide a narrow satisfaction, whereas the modern world leaves us unsatisfied, or, where it appears to be satisfied with itself, it is *vulgar* and *mean*" (1857–58/1964:85).

Communism, however, was viewed as an era in which the structural forces leading to this distortion of human nature are overthrown, and people are allowed to express their human potential in ways never before possible. The meanness of primitive life permitted only a minimal expression of that potential, and the structures of capitalism (for example, division of labor, private property, and money), while freeing people from the limitations of primitive society, represent barriers to the expression of many species powers and needs. But capitalism was seen by Marx as an important stage, because it developed the productive forces that a communist society could use, although in radically different ways, to free individuals further from the kinds of limitations encountered in primitive society and to produce unparalleled abundance. They could then express their human capacities in new and unprecedented ways. To Marx, communism is an epoch in which human beings are able to "bring their species powers out of themselves" (1932/1964:151). With a slightly different emphasis, Ollman contended that "communism is the time of full, personal appropriation" (1976:93).

Activity

Activity now can be viewed as the means by which people appropriate objects from nature. In discussing activity, we are moving out of the subjective realm of consciousness and touching on the objective realm. But because Marx's work, to its credit, is a dialectically related whole, it is virtually impossible to talk about one aspect of social reality without at least touching on the others.

It is important to note that Marx's use of activity is virtually indistinguishable from his concepts of work and creativity. Marx was most prone to use the idea of work but in a way that is much different from common usage. Ollman defined the Marxian notion of work as "conscious, purposive activity in the productive process" (1976:98). By this definition, then, work is an expression of people's distinctive abilities. In fact, work is not restricted to economic activities but encompasses all productive activities that use the creative capacities of the actor. Work, in turn, also serves to allow greater development of people's powers and needs.

Although Marx did not clearly differentiate among activity, work, and creativity, he tended to use different terms at different stages in his career. However, what is important here is that each of these terms highlights a different aspect of people's relationship to nature. *Activity* refers to the motions involved in purposeful endeavors; *work* refers to the process of production; and *creativity* refers to the ability of people to make unique products (Ollman, 1976:102). In capitalism, work tends to be separated from activity and creativity; in communism, we are likely, in Marx's view, to find a situation where as far as possible work and activity fully involve the creative capacity of human beings. That is, those who do the work jointly and democratically visualize, plan, and perform this work to realize goals which they themselves set by means which they determine.

Objectification In the activity involved in appropriating the natural world, people, according to Marx, always engage in the process of *objectification,* which means that they produce objects (food, clothes, and shelters). The process of objectification was important to Marx for several reasons. First, it reaffirmed his materialist orientation, his interest in the real world of real actors. He was not merely concerned with work in the abstract or objectification in the realm of consciousness, as was Hegel, but with objectification in the real world. Second, Marx saw objectification as the true arena in which people express their human capacities. Human potential is actualized in the objectification of products.

This process of objectification is normal and expressive of human potential if it involves certain characteristics (Israel, 1971:39). First, the activity must involve the consciousness of the actors. Second, the actors must be able to express their capabilities in a comprehensive manner. Third, they must be able to express their inherently social character in the process of objectification. Fourth, the process of objectification must not merely be a means to some other end (that is, the earning of money). In its most general sense, this means that objectification must involve the creative capacities of individuals.

Labor   In the context of this image of truly human objectification, Marx discussed work in capitalist society. For this type of society, Marx usually did not use the interrelated concepts of work, activity, and creativity. Pointedly, he was most likely to refer to *labor*. In one sense, as is clear from the following quotations, Marx used the idea of labor as an equivalent to these other concepts:

> Labor is a creator of use-value, . . . a necessary condition, independent of all forms of society, for the existence of the human race.
>
> (Marx, 1867/1967:42–43)

> Labor is . . . a process in which both man and Nature participate, and in which man of his own accord starts, regulates, and controls the material re-actions between himself and Nature. He opposes himself to Nature as one of her own forces, setting in motion arms and legs, head and hands, the natural forces of his body, in order to appropriate Nature's productions in a form adapted to his own wants. By this acting on the external world and changing it, he at the same time changes his own nature. He develops his slumbering powers and compels them to act in obedience to his sway.
>
> (Marx, 1867/1967:177)

There seems little doubt that Marx is using *labor* here to mean work, activity, and creativity. Clearly implied is appropriation, objectification, and the full expression of human potential. However, as will be made clear throughout this chapter, Marx saw labor in capitalist society as taking on some distinct and perverted forms. Instead of being an end in itself, an expression of human capabilities, labor in capitalism is reduced to a means to an end—earning money (Marx, 1932/1964:173). In capitalism, labor is *not* the equivalent of work, activity, and creativity.

Sociability

Another aspect of Marx's image of human potential is the idea that people are inherently *social*. Marx and Engels talked of "the need, the necessity, of intercourse with other men" (1845–46/1970:51). Elsewhere Marx wrote, "Man is in the most literal sense of the word a *zoon politikon,* not only a social animal, but an animal which can develop into an individual only in society" (1857–58/1964:84).

At one level, as we have already seen, this means that all other truly human capabilities make no sense in isolation; they must be related to *both* the natural and the social worlds. In Marx's view, people cannot express their humanness without nature and without other people. At another level, sociability is an integral part of human nature. That is, to Marx people are inherently social. They need to relate to other people both for the sake of relating and in order to be able to appropriate nature adequately (Mészáros, 1970:149).

Unanticipated Consequences

Finally, a little-discussed aspect of Marx's image of human nature is directly related to the development of capitalism. It addresses the issue of how people, endowed with at least potentially positive human characteristics, are able to produce a structure of capitalism that serves to distort their essential nature. This is the notion of *unanticipated consequences* (Elster, 1985:3). Although we most often associate this idea with the work of Max Weber, it seems clear that Marx too had a conception of unanticipated consequences: "Here, then, is the dialectical worm: while we are highly successful in bringing about the immediate results of our conscious intentions, we still too often fail to anticipate and forestall the undesired remoter consequences of those results themselves" (cited in Venable, 1945:76).

At the most general level, we can argue that capitalism was the unanticipated consequence of a large number of actions. People did not intend to create a structure that distorted humanity, but that is just what they did. It is also necessary to point out that the idea of unanticipated consequences, like other aspects of Marx's image of human nature, is tied to the social context. Although it is an integral part of past and present society, Marx probably would have argued (had he addressed the issue) that unanticipated consequences need not be a characteristic of society. That is, communism need not be subverted by unanticipated consequences. Yet the concept of unanticipated consequences is very useful in thinking about capitalist society. For example, capitalists believe that their actions are furthering their interests as well as the interests of the capitalist system as a whole. But as Marx believed, many of the actions of capitalists create the conditions for the system's ultimate collapse. To take only one very broad example, capitalists believe that it is in their interest as well as in the interest of the system itself to extract every last ounce of productivity from the worker. Although in the short run this may create greater profits, in the long run, in Marx's view, it creates the class that will eventually destroy the capitalist system—the proletariat.

ALIENATION

Up to this point, we have been discussing a number of components of Marx's work at the microscopic level—human potential (species-being), powers, needs, self-consciousness and consciousness, activity, work, creativity, labor, objectification, sociability, and unanticipated consequences. This discussion has been derived mainly from Marx's early work. Marx rarely allowed himself the luxury later in his life of such philosophical analyses, for it was then that he wrote about the nature of capitalist society. In his early works, Marx called the distortions of human nature that are caused by the domination of the worker by the "alien will" of the capitalist *alienation* (D. Cooper, 1991; Meisenhelder, 1991). Although he shied away from this heavily philosophical term later in his work, it remained, in a different guise, one of his main concerns. As Barbalet says, "In *Capital* Marx seldom uses the term—although he clearly employs the concept—'alienation'" (1983:95). For in the end Marx was a humanist, and even as he explored the structure of capitalist society, he never lost sight of its impact on the actor (Wartenberg, 1982).

Although it is the actor who feels alienated in capitalist society, Marx's basic analytic concern was with the structures of capitalism that cause this alienation. Thus, contrary to the view of many interpreters who argue that he takes a social-psychological approach, Marx basically offered a theory of alienation rooted in social structure. It is social structure that acts to break down the natural interconnections that characterize human nature in an ideal sense. Of crucial significance here is the two-class system in which the capitalists employ the workers (and thereby own their labor-time) and own the *means of production* (tools and raw materials) as well as the ultimate products. In order to survive and to have access to tools and nature, workers are forced to sell their labor-time to capitalists. Although the workers then use the tools and apply them to nature in order to manufacture products, the natural interrelationships are shattered.

Components of Alienation

Alienation can be seen as having four basic components. First, the workers in capitalist society are alienated from their *productive activity*. In such a society they do not work for themselves in order to satisfy their own needs. Instead, they work for capitalists, who pay them a subsistence wage in return for the right to use the workers in any way they see fit. Both workers and capitalists come to believe that the payment of a wage means that the productive activity belongs to the capitalist. Because productive activity belongs to the capitalists, and because they decide what is to be done with it, we can say that workers are alienated from that activity. Instead of being a process that is satisfying in and of itself, productive activity in capitalism is reduced, Marx argued, to an often boring and stultifying means to the fulfillment of the only end that really matters in capitalism—earning enough money to survive.

Second, the workers are alienated not only from productive activities but also from the object of those activities—the *product*. The product of their labor does not belong to the workers, to be used by them in order to satisfy basic needs. Instead, the product, like the process that resulted in its production, belongs to the capitalists, who may use it in any way they wish. This usually means that the capitalists sell it for a profit. Not only do workers not have control over the product, but they often lack detailed knowledge of aspects of the production process in which they are not personally involved. Many workers perform highly specialized tasks and as a result have little sense of their role in the total production process. For example, automobile assembly-line workers who tighten a few bolts on an engine assembly may have little feel for their role in the production of the engine, let alone for their contribution to the production of the entire car. Assembly lines often are so long and involve so many steps that individuals are reduced to insignificant roles in the overall process. Playing such small roles in the process, workers often come to feel that it is the assembly line—rather than the people who work on it—that produces the final product.

Third, the workers in capitalism are alienated from their *fellow workers.* Marx's assumption was that people basically need and want to work cooperatively in order to appropriate from nature what they require to survive. But in capitalism this cooperation is disrupted, and people, often strangers, are forced to work side by side for the capitalist. Even if the workers on the assembly line, for example, are close friends, the nature of the technology makes for a great deal of isolation. Here is the way one worker describes his social situation on the assembly line:

> You can work next to a guy for months without even knowing his name. One thing, you're too busy to talk. Can't hear. . . . You have to holler in his ear. They got these little guys coming around in white shirts and if they see you runnin' your mouth, they say, "This guy needs more work." Man, he's got no time to talk.
>
> (Terkel, 1974:165)

But this social situation is worse than simple isolation; the workers are often forced into outright competition, and sometimes conflict, with one another. In order to extract maximum productivity and to prevent the development of cooperative relationships, the capitalist pits one worker against another to see who can produce more, work more quickly, or please the boss more. The ones who succeed are given a few extra rewards; those who fail are discarded. In either case, considerable hostility is generated among the workers toward their peers. This is useful to the capitalists because it tends to deflect hostility that otherwise would be aimed at them. The isolation and the interpersonal hostility tend to make workers in capitalism alienated from fellow workers.

Finally, and most generally, workers in capitalist society are alienated from their own *human potential.* Individuals perform less and less like human beings as they are reduced in their work to animals, beasts of burden, or inhuman machines. Consciousness is numbed and, ultimately, destroyed as relations with other humans and with nature are progressively severed. The result is a mass of people who are unable to express their essential human qualities, a mass of alienated workers.

Distortions Resulting from Alienation

Alienation, then, is the structurally imposed breakdown of the interconnectedness that is, to Marx, an essential part of life, at least in an ideal sense. Communism implies the establishment of the interconnections that have been broken in capitalism. Alienation, then, can be seen as the opposite of what people can be potentially (Barbalet, 1983:53). As Elster puts it, "Marx's discussion of alienation only makes sense against the background of a normative view of what constitutes the good life for man . . . a life of all-sided creative activity" (1985:51). As a result of alienation, work in capitalism is reduced to mere labor in which the individual "does not affirm himself but denies himself, does not feel content but unhappy, does not develop freely his physical and mental energy but mortifies his body and ruins his mind" (Marx, 1932/1964:110). Labor in capitalism is therefore very different from genuine human activity.

One of Marx's most beautiful examples of the perversion of humanity by capitalism is found in his discussion of *money*. Ideally, to Marx, people can be no more or less than they actually are, but in capitalism money can bestow on people powers and abilities that they do not actually possess. The following is Marx's penetrating statement on this point:

> That which is for me through the medium of *money*—that for which I can pay (i.e., which money can buy)—that am *I*, the possessor of the money. The extent of the power of money is the extent of my power. Money's properties are my properties and essential powers—the properties and powers of its possessor. Thus, what I *am* and *am capable* of is by no means determined by my individuality. I *am* ugly, but I can buy for myself the most *beautiful* of women. Therefore I am not *ugly*, for the effect of *ugliness*—its deterrent power—is nullified by money. I, as an individual, am *lame*, but money furnishes me with twenty-four feet. Therefore I am not lame. I am bad, dishonest, unscrupulous, stupid; but money is honored, and hence its possessor. Money is the supreme good; therefore its possessor is good. Money, besides, saves me the trouble of being dishonest: I am therefore presumed honest. I am *stupid*, but money is the *real mind* of all things and how then should its possessor be stupid? Besides, he can buy talented people for himself, and is he who has power over the talented not more talented than the talented? Do not I, who thanks to money am capable of *all* that the human heart longs for, possess all human capacities? Does not money, therefore, transform all my incapacities into their contrary?
>
> (Marx, 1932/1964:167)

Although money is capable of buying virtually anything in capitalism, it cannot perform that function in a truly human world. In such a world one can, for example, "exchange love only for love" (Marx, 1932/1964:119). True wealth, and not just lots of money, is nothing but "the universality of needs, capacities, enjoyments, productive powers, etc., of individuals, produced in universal exchange. . . . What, if not the full development of human control over the forces of nature—those of his own nature—as well as those of so-called 'nature'? What, if not the absolute elaboration of his creative dispositions?" (Marx, 1857–58/1964:84–85).

The list of distortions caused by capitalist society is lengthy. First, the structure of manufacturing turns workers into "crippled monstrosities" by forcing them to work on minute details rather than allowing them to use all their capabilities (Marx, 1867/1967:360). Similarly, the natural interrelationship between head and hand is broken in capitalism so that only a few people are allowed to do headwork; most others do handwork that is devoid of mental components (Marx, 1867/1967:508). Then there is the monotony of doing the same specialized task over and over again. Engels underscored this problem: "Nothing is more terrible than being constrained to do alone one thing every day from morning to night against one's will . . . in such unbroken monotony, that this alone must make his work a torture . . . if he has the least human feeling left" (Venable, 1945:137). Then there is the point that human beings are no longer creative but are oriented solely toward owning and possessing objects. To Marx, private property makes people so "stupid and one-sided" that they feel that an object is only theirs when they possess it, that is, when it is "eaten, drunk, worn, inhabited," and so forth. For all these reasons, work in capitalism largely ceases to be an expression of human potential. In fact, in many ways it is the opposite. With human functions so highly alienating, a person is no longer able to satisfy human powers and needs and is forced to concentrate on natural powers and needs.

> As a result, therefore, man (the worker) only feels himself freely active in his animal functions—eating, drinking, procreating, or at most in his dwelling and in dressing-up, etc.; and in his human functions he no longer feels himself to be anything but an animal. What is animal becomes human and what is human becomes animal.
>
> (Marx, 1932/1964:111)

Perhaps this is the height of unanticipated consequences. People have produced a society that allows them to feel comfortable only when they function like animals.

Marx argued that capitalism is an inverted world, in which those who should be on top are relegated to the bottom, and those who deserve to be on the bottom rise to the pinnacle of society. Thus the people who are the most important to society—the proletariat—are near the bottom, generally scraping by on a subsistence wage and dominated by the capitalists. The capitalists, who simply live off the labor of the proletariat, are the dominant force in society. Also inverted is the sense of what is real in society. For example, it is people (those who sell goods, services, labor-time, and so on) who set prices, but they fail to see their essential role in this process. Rather, it appears as if it is the unreal "market" that sets prices.

Finally, the reality of life in capitalism is hidden while illusion is seen as fact. For example, from Marx's perspective, the capitalists exploit the proletariat, but the dominant belief is that the abilities of the capitalist lead to success for the worker. We shall return to this theme later in a discussion of ideology in capitalism, but the key point is that in many ways, capitalism is an inverted and distorted social system. However, Marx was not vindictive. He did not want to see the emergence of a society with the proletariat on top, but rather a society with true equality.

Emancipation

Marx's critique of capitalist society is not an end in itself, of course, but an effort to help bring about the changes needed to create a society in which human potential can be adequately expressed. We can say that the goal of Marx's sociology lies in the ultimate emancipation of humanity from the enslavement of capitalist society (Mészáros, 1970:200). As Marx put it: "Human emancipation will only be complete when the real, individual man . . . has become a *species-being*" (cited in Bender, 1970:66). Vernon Venable catches the essence of the problem and the need for reform quite well:

> Hence human activity ought to be aimed . . . at their collective rescue from the pitiable, fragmentary, self-divided, craft-idiotic, class-enslaved state in which they find themselves. It should aim, in short, at the transformation of human nature. It should make man dignified, integrated, complete and free, so that the resources and potentialities that reside in him . . . may develop, expand, and find fruitful expression.
>
> (Venable, 1945:151–152)

Thus Marx's work on human potential led him both to a critique of capitalist society and to a political program oriented to overcoming the structures of capitalism so that people can express their essential humanity (Mészáros, 1970).

The transition to socialist society and emancipation is brought about through concrete action informed by theory, or *praxis*. At one level, this concept means that we must not be content with philosophizing about capitalism but rather must develop a critical intellectual stance that will help bring about the action needed to revolutionize society. This concept also is construed to mean that capitalism can be transformed only through concrete action. Thus the proletariat must act to bring about the transition to socialism; they cannot sit back and wait for it to collapse because of internal contradictions. Marx's usage of praxis was both political and theoretical.

The communist society that would be created by praxis "does not rule over the individuals and is nothing in itself beyond the concrete individuals in their social relation to each other" (Gould, 1978:166). This would serve to eliminate alienation ("the human condition in the pre-communist stage" [Barbalet, 1983:53]) and reunite people with their products, productive activities, other people, and themselves. The goal of emancipation is *species-being*. Another way of saying this is that the goal of emancipation is communism,[3] which is "the first real emergence, the actual realization for man of man's essence and of his essence as something real" (Marx, 1932/1964:187). In Avineri's view, "Marx's postulate about the ultimate possibility of human self-emancipation must be related to his philosophical premise about the initial creation of the world by man" (1968:65). In other words, we cannot understand communism without understanding species-being.

THE STRUCTURES OF CAPITALIST SOCIETY

We have spent many pages analyzing Marx's thoughts on actors, mental processes, and action, much of which is embodied in his work on human potential and its distortion (alienation) by the structure of society, in particular the structure of capitalist society. It is time now to turn to Marx's work on those large-scale structures that are the cause of alienation in capitalist society.

The first issue to be addressed is whether Marx thought of these social structures as "things," that is, as hardened structures. Another way of putting this is to ask whether Marx adopted the position taken by Durkheim (1895/1964) that social facts should be treated as if they were "things." Marx's views on large-scale social structures were shaped by his dialectical approach, especially his tendency to focus on social relations (Ollman, 1976). Marx thought of social structures as being composed of a large number of continuing social relationships. This dynamic, or dialectical, perspective stands in sharp contrast to the view of many neo-Durkheimians, who overlook Durkheim's warning to simply *treat* social facts as things and who regard them as things *in fact*. Although he held a dynamic view of social structures, Marx did regard the set of relationships in capitalism as external to, and coercive of, actors. This is not to say that this set of relationships is inevitable or eternal, but they certainly have achieved objective reality in capitalism, and they must be overthrown in order to move on to communism. We can see how this meshed with Marx's political commitments, because this more relational view makes social structures much more changeable than would a view of them as things.

[3]According to Berki, communism is "the *only thing* that is important about Marx's thought" (1983:1).

Commodities

The basis of all of Marx's work on social structures, and the place in which that work is most clearly tied to his views on human potential, is in his analysis of *commodities,* or products of labor intended for both use and exchange. As Georg Lukács put it, "The problem of commodities is . . . the central, *structural* problem of capitalist society" (1922/1968:83).

Marx's conception of commodity was rooted in his materialist orientation, with its focus on the productive activities of actors. As we saw earlier, it was Marx's view that in their interactions with nature and with other actors, people always produce the objects that they need in order to survive; objectification is a necessary and universal aspect of human life. These objects are produced for use by oneself or by others in the immediate environment—they are *use values.* The objects are the products of human labor and cannot achieve an independent existence because they are controlled by the actors. However, in capitalism this process of objectification takes on a new and dangerous form. Instead of producing for themselves or their immediate associates, the actors produce for someone else (the capitalist). The products have *exchange values;* that is, instead of being used immediately, they are exchanged in the open market for money which is used ultimately to acquire other use values.

While people produce objects in capitalism, their role in producing commodities, and their control over them, becomes mystified. At first they are led to believe that these objects and the market for them have an independent existence, and then in fully developed capitalism this belief turns into reality as the objects and their market *do* become real, independent phenomena. The commodity becomes an independent, almost mystical external reality (Marx, 1867/1967:35).

Fetishism of Commodities   With the development of commodities comes the process Marx labeled the *fetishism of commodities* (Dant, 1996; Sherlock, 1997). The basis of this process is the labor that gives commodities their value. The fetishism of commodities involves the process by which actors fail to recognize that it is their labor that gives the commodities their value. They fetishize those commodities and come to believe that value arises from the natural properties of the things themselves. Thus the *market* takes on a function in the eyes of the actors that in Marx's view *only* actors could perform—the production of value. In Marx's terms, "A definite social relation between men . . . assumes, in their eyes, the fantastic form of a relation between things" (1867/1967:72). Granting reality to commodities and the market, the individual in capitalism progressively loses control over them.

> A commodity is therefore a mysterious thing, simply because in it the social character of men's labor appears to them as an objective character stamped upon the product of that labor: because the relations of the producers to the sum total of their own labor is presented to them as a social relation, existing not between themselves, but between the products of their labor.
>
> (Marx, 1867/1967:72)

The beauty of Marx's discussion of commodities and their fetishism is that it takes us from the level of the individual actor and action to the level of large-scale social structures. That is, people endowed with creative minds interact with other people and nature to produce objects, but this natural process results in something grotesque in capitalism. The fetishism of commodities imparts to them and to the marketplace an independent objective reality that is external to, and coercive of, the actor.

Reification   The concepts of commodities and fetishism of commodities would appear to be of limited sociological use. The concepts seem to be restricted to the economic realm—that is, to the end result of productive activity. Yet productive activity can—indeed must—be looked at more broadly if we are to grasp the whole of Marx's meaning as well as its application to sociology. We need to understand that people produce not only economic objects (food, clothing, shelters) but also social relationships and, ultimately, social structures. Looked at in this way, the fetishism of commodities is translated into the concept of reification (Lukács, 1922/1968; Sherlock, 1997). *Reification* can be thought of as "thingification," or the process of coming to believe that humanly created social forms are natural, universal, and absolute things and, as a result, that those social forms do acquire those characteristics. The concept of reification implies that people believe that social structures are beyond their control and unchangeable. This belief often comes to be a self-fulfilling prophecy. Then the structures actually *do* acquire the character people endowed them with. By using this concept, we can see that people reify the whole range of social relationships and social structures.

We can find the groundwork for the concept of reification in Marx's own discussion of labor. Basically, Marx argued that, as a *social* phenomenon, labor becomes a commodity under the peculiar circumstances of capitalism: "Labor-power can appear in the market as a commodity, only if, and so far as, its possessor, the individual whose labor-power it is, offers it for sale, or sells it, as a commodity" (1867/1967:168). Once we admit the possibility of one social phenomenon (labor) becoming reified, it becomes possible for a wide range of other social phenomena to take on the same characteristic (Lefebvre, 1968:16). Just as people reify commodities and other economic phenomena (for example, the division of labor [Rattansi, 1982; Walliman, 1981]), they also reify religious (Barbalet, 1983:147), political, and organizational structures. Marx made a similar point in reference to the state: "And out of this very contradiction between the individual and . . . the community the latter takes an independent form as the *State*, divorced from the real interests of individual and community" (cited in Bender, 1970:176).

Marx had a few things to say about the range of reified social structures, but he focused primarily on the structural components of the economy. It is these economic structures that Marx saw as causing alienation by breaking down the natural interconnectedness of people and nature.

Capital

Capital is the social relationship between the buyers and sellers of labor-power. The capitalist system is the social structure that emerges on the basis of that relationship. As an independent structure, capital (through the actors who operate in its behalf, the bourgeoisie) exploits the workers, who were and are responsible for its creation. Marx talked of the power of capital appearing "as a power endowed by Nature—a productive power that is immanent in Capital" (1867/1967:333). Thus people tend to reify capital by believing that it is natural for the capitalist system to be external to, and coercive of, them. Workers are exploited by a system that they have *forgotten* they *produced* through their labor and have the capacity to change. "By means of its conversion into an automaton, the instrument of labor confronts the laborer, during the labor-process, in the shape of capital, of dead labor, that dominates, and pumps away, living labor-power" (Marx, 1867/1967:423). This is what led Marx to conclude that capitalism is an inverted world.

Circulation of Commodities   Marx discussed not only the character of capital in general but also the character of more specific components of the capitalist system. For example, Marx examined the circulation of commodities, which he considered "the starting-point of capital" (1867/1967:146). Marx discussed two types of circulation of commodities. Both are external to, and coercive of, the actor. One of these types of circulation—Money-Commodities-(a larger sum of) Money (M_1-C-M_2)—is characteristic of capital; the other—Commodities-Money-Commodities (C_1-M-C_2)—is not.

In the simple circulation of commodities, the circuit C_1-M-C_2 predominates. An example of C_1-M-C_2 would be the fisherman who sells his catch (C_1) and then uses the money to buy bread (C_2). In a society characterized by the simple circulation of commodities, exchange is accomplished by "the conversion of the commodity into money, and the reconversion of the money into a commodity" (Marx, 1867/1967:105). This circuit, however, does not exist in isolation; it is inextricably interrelated to similar circuits involving other commodities. This type of exchange process "develops a whole network of social relations spontaneous in their growth and entirely beyond the control of the actors" (Marx, 1867/1967:112).

The simple circulation of commodities that is characterized by the circuit C_1-M-C_2 can be considered the second historical type of circulation of commodities (barter [C_1-C_2] is the first historical form). Both of these circuits eventually lead to the circulation of commodities under capitalism (M_1-C-M_2).

In the capitalist circuit, referred to by Marx as "buying in order to sell" (1867/1967:147), the individual actor buys a commodity with money and in turn exchanges it for presumably more money. Here our hypothetical fisherman buys new nets with his profits in order to increase his future profits. This circuit, similar to the circuit under the simple circulation of commodities, is characterized by two antithetical yet complementary phases. At one and the same time, one person's purchase is another's sale. The circulation of commodities under capitalism begins with a purchase (new nets) and ends with a sale (a larger catch of fish). Furthermore, the end of this circuit is not the consumption of the use value, as it is in the simple circulation of commodities. The end is money in an expanded form, money that is qualitatively identical to that at the beginning of the circuit but quantitatively different (Marx, 1867/1967:150).

The importance of the M_1-C-M_2 circuit, from our point of view, is that it is an even more abstract process than C_1-M-C_2. The "real" commodity declines in significance, with the result that the essence of capital is reduced ultimately to the "unreal" circulation of money. This greater abstractness makes reification easier, with the result that the system is even more likely to become external to, and coercive of, actors.

Private Property

Marx also analyzed the process by which *private property* becomes reified in capitalism. Most often, by private property Marx means the private ownership by the capitalist of the means of production. In his view, of course, private property, like the other structural components of capitalism, is derived from the labor of workers. "*Private property* is thus the product, the result, the necessary consequence, of *alienated labor,* of the external relation of the worker to nature and to himself" (Marx, 1932/1964:117). But workers lose sight of, and ultimately control over, this fact. Instead of controlling private property, the workers are controlled by it. As with all other structural components of Marx's work, his conception of private property was directly related to his early work on human potential and action as well as to his political goals. In relating private property to his earlier work, Marx made it clear that not only is private property the product of alienated labor, but once in existence, it in turn exacerbates alienation by imposing itself between people and the production process. If people are to realize their human potential, they must overthrow private property as well as all the other structural components of capitalist society: "The positive transcendence of *private property,* as the appropriation of *human life,* is therefore the positive transcendence of all estrangement—that is to say, the return of man from religion, family, state, etc., to his *human,* i.e., social existence" (Marx, 1932/1964:136).

Division of Labor

The division of labor is another structural component of capitalism that comes under Marx's scrutiny. Marx and Engels traced the origins of the modern division of labor to the early family, "where wife and children are the slaves of the husband" (1845–46/1970:52). Although Marx was obviously critical of these early forms of the division of labor, he was most critical of its particularly pernicious form within capitalism.

Marx's most basic view of the division of labor is set forth in his distinction between the owners of the means of production and those who must sell their labor-time to the owners in order to survive. More specifically, Marx was interested in the tendency to structure work so that people are forced to specialize in ever more minute tasks. Such specialization prevents actors from realizing and expressing their human potential (Marx, 1867/1967:350).

Marx offered a number of criticisms of the division of labor in capitalism (Venable, 1945). First, the existence of the division of labor artificially separates the individual from the community as a whole. Indeed, people come to focus almost totally on their own slots and ignore, or even fight against, the interest of the whole community. Second, the labor process is broken down so that functions that ideally would be integrated are separated. For example, intellectual functions are separated from manual tasks; work and enjoyment are separated; and the act of production is radically separated from the act of consumption. Third, the powers of the individual are reduced to simply another tool in the production process. Fourth, each person makes only a small contribution to the final product. The worker is disassociated from that product and everything that happens to it after it is produced. More generally, workers as a class lose control over *all* the things that they produce as well as the market for them. Finally, the narrow specialization has the effect on man of "stunting him, dehumanizing him, reducing him to a mere fragment of a man, a crippled monstrosity, an appendage to a machine" (Venable, 1945:124).

These criticisms of the structure of the division of labor led Marx to an inevitable political conclusion—that a society must be created in which people are *not* narrowly specialized:

> In communist society, where nobody has one exclusive sphere of activity but each can become accomplished in any branch he wishes, society regulates the general production and thus makes it possible for me to do one thing today and another tomorrow, to hunt in the morning, fish in the afternoon, rear cattle in the evening, criticize after dinner, just as I have a mind without ever becoming hunter, fisherman, shepherd or critic.
>
> (Marx and Engels, 1845–46/1970:53)

Although Marx probably never believed that such a society was totally possible, it does reflect his interest in eliminating the destructive effects of specialization. Marx was not saying that everyone can or will become good at everything. His point was that the division of labor has artificially prevented people, particularly the proletariat, from developing their abilities to the fullest. As David McLellan makes clear, Marx did not believe "that each should do the work of Raphael, but that anyone in whom there is a potential Raphael should be able to develop without hindrance. The exclusive concentration of artistic talent in particular individuals, and its suppression in the broad mass . . . is a consequence of division of labor" (1971:218). Thus in communism people will not all become, in Marx's view, poets or artists or lawyers, but the artificial barriers preventing people from developing to their fullest will be eliminated. Foremost among these barriers, and one that must be eliminated, is the division of labor.

Social Class

One other aspect of Marx's interest in social structure was social class (primarily the bourgeoisie and the proletariat). Unfortunately, while "Karl Marx frequently uses the term 'class' in his writings . . . he does not have a systematic treatment on this issue" (So, 1990:35). Various meanings of the term can be gleaned from his work, but it does seem clear, at the minimum, that he viewed social classes as structures that are external to, and coercive of, people.

Although Marx himself offered us only hints, Ollman's interpretation of Marx is quite explicit about social class. Ollman emphasized that *social classes* are "reified social relations" or "the relations between men [that] have taken on an independent existence" (1976:204–205). He also linked the emergence of social classes to the previously discussed emergence of commodities in capitalism. "*Class and commodity are brothers under the skin*" (Ollman, 1976:205; italics added). Social classes arise out of the acts of production; people come to reify classes, and as a result these classes come to have a life of their own that constrains the actor. Marx did not make this explicit, but it makes sense, given the general thrust of his arguments.

In this section, we have examined Marx's views on large-scale social structures. We saw that he tended to view them relationally rather than as real, material structures.

Nevertheless, they are external and coercive forces to Marx. All his views on such structures were rooted in his conception of commodities and the fetishism of commodities. Moving beyond the purely economic realm, Marx adopted the same view about social structures. But the bulk of Marx's work concerns the structures of the economy in capitalism—commodities, capital, private property, the division of labor, and social class. All these evolve out of the thoughts and actions of actors, and once in existence, they constrain the very processes that created them. Most of Marx's political attention was devoted to the question of how these structures could be overcome so that a communist society might be created.

CULTURAL ASPECTS OF CAPITALIST SOCIETY

Marx focused on the large-scale structures of capitalist society and their alienating impact on human beings. He did not have a great deal to say about the cultural domain, but a careful analysis indicates that he was not insensitive to the importance of this aspect of social reality. Marx's materialism led him away from a concern with culture, and it could be said that at times Marx went too far in his rejection of this domain, which he associated with the weaknesses of Hegelian philosophy. For example, in *The Critique of Political Economy* Marx wrote:

> The totality of these relations of production constitutes the *economic structure* of society, the *real foundation,* on which arises a legal and political superstructure and to which correspond definite forms of *social consciousness.* The mode of production of *material* life *conditions* the general processes of social, political, and intellectual life. It is not the consciousness of men that determines their existence, but their social existence that determines their consciousness.
>
> (Marx, 1859/1970:20–21; italics added)

Marx might be thought of here as talking about consciousness in a cultural sense (that is, talking about norms, values, or in Hegel's terms, spirit, or *Geist*) and not in the sense of mental processes and the social construction of reality. Given this interpretation, Marx seems to be relegating the cultural level to the status of an "epiphenomenon" determined by social and economic structures. This seems to be confirmed when, slightly later in the same work, Marx appears to reduce all social change to change of the material base on which is erected the cultural superstructure:

> Then begins an era of social revolution. The changes in the *economic foundation* lead sooner or later to the transformation of the whole immense *superstructure.* In studying such transformations it is always necessary to distinguish between the *material* transformation of the economic conditions of production, which can be determined with the precision of natural science, and the *legal, political, religious, artistic* or *philosophic—in short, ideological forms* in which men become *conscious* of this conflict and fight it out. *Just as one does not judge an individual by what he thinks about himself, so one cannot judge such a period of transformation by its consciousness, but on the contrary, this consciousness must be explained from the contradictions of material life.*
>
> (Marx, 1859/1970:21; italics added)

It is even clearer here that Marx is talking about the cultural level ("the legal, political, religious, artistic, philosophic—in short, ideological forms"). He even differentiates

between individual consciousness and the consciousness of a "period." We must ap-
plaud Marx for this awareness and this clear differentiation, but we also must be highly
critical of his tendency to reduce the cultural domain to an epiphenomenon, if that is in
fact what he did.

However, contrary to these words from the preface to *The Critique of Political Economy*—which is, unfortunately, one of Marx's most simplistic statements—we are led by
the thrust of his entire work and by his commitment to the dialectic to dismiss such deterministic statements. A commitment to the dialectic means a commitment to studying
the interrelationships among phenomena; it is inherently antideterministic. It could be
argued that the nature of capitalism led to the preeminence of the structural level, with
the result that the other levels are under its sway. Although this is true to Marx's char-
acterization of capitalism, he still did not simply dismiss the cultural level; he had a
number of things to offer here, particularly in his discussions of class consciousness and
false consciousness as well as ideology (Torrance, 1995).

Class Consciousness and False Consciousness

The ideas of class consciousness and false consciousness are intimately related in
Marx's work. Both refer to idea systems shared by social classes. In capitalism both
capitalists and workers have incorrect assessments of how the system works and of their
role and interest in it (*false consciousness*). In the evolution toward communism, there
is the possibility that the proletariat will develop an accurate conception of how capitalism works and how it affects them (*class consciousness*).

What is characteristic of capitalism, for *both* the proletariat and the bourgeoisie, is
false consciousness. We are not surprised to learn that workers have false consciousness, but it is sometimes startling to think of capitalists in this way. After all, they are
presumably exploiting the system, and the proletariat, to their advantage. Georg Lukács
(1922/1968), one of the foremost interpreters of Marx, pointed to a number of elements
of the false consciousness of the bourgeoisie. The bourgeoisie is unaware of its own history and the role it played in the formation of capitalism. More important, it underesti-
mates the intractability of contradictions that exist within capitalism as well as of the
role it is playing in contributing to those burgeoning contradictions. And it underesti-
mates the durability of capitalism. The bourgeoisie, like the proletariat, is unaware of
the consequences of its actions. Its idea systems contain delusions about its control over
the capitalist system. The fact is that its actions (for example, heightened exploitation)
are contributing to the ultimate demise of the system that it believes it is serving to but-
tress. The proletariat's thought system is at least as deluded as the bourgeoisie's.

There is, however, a crucial difference here between the two classes. The bourgeoisie can never transform its false consciousness into true class consciousness; this is
possible only for the proletariat. In Marx's view, the proletariat occupies this privileged
position because its lack of property is the model of the future in which all will have no
property; or to put it another way, all property will be owned collectively. At the height
of capitalism, the proletariat "is already a class in opposition to capital, but not yet a
class for itself" (McLellan, 1971:155). It is not adequate for the proletariat to be a "class

in itself"; it must become a "class for itself." If the proletariat is to take on its historic role in capitalism, "it must become a class not only 'as against capital' but also 'for itself'; that is to say, the class struggle must be raised from the level of economic necessity to the level of conscious aim and effective class consciousness" (Lukács, 1922/1968:76).

In talking about class (and false) consciousness, Marx was talking not about individual consciousness but about the consciousness of the class as a whole. Furthermore, the concepts of class consciousness and false consciousness are not, in Marx's hands, static but are rather dynamic idea systems that make sense only in terms of social change and development. False consciousness describes the situation throughout the capitalist epoch, whereas class consciousness is the condition that awaits the proletariat and that can help bring about the change from capitalist to communist society.

Ideology

The other major cultural dimension of Marx's analysis is ideology (Markus, 1991). An *ideology* can be defined as an integrated system of ideas that is external to, and coercive of, people (Lefebvre, 1968). Although Marx often talked of ideologies in the same way that he talked about class and false consciousness—that is, as mere reflections of the material base—it is clear that ideologies, too, take on an independent existence in his system. Some analysts make much of the apparent determinism of passages like the following, but it is the author's view that Marx was offering only one side of his multifaceted analysis here:

> The *ideas* [italics added] of the ruling class are in every epoch the ruling ideas, i.e., the class which is the ruling *material* force of society, is at the same time, its ruling *intellectual* force. The class, which has the means of material production at its disposal, has control at the same time over the means of mental production, so that thereby, generally speaking, the ideas of those who lack the means of mental production are subject to it. *The ruling ideas are nothing more than the ideal expression of the dominant material relationships* [italics added], the dominant material relationships grasped as ideas.
>
> (Marx and Engels, 1845–46/1970:64)

At least three basic interrelated ideas are involved in Marx's conceptualization of ideologies. First, they certainly do represent the interests of the ruling class, but that is not to say that these ideas do not have a reciprocal impact on material interests. Second, they constitute an "inverted, truncated reflection of reality" (Lefebvre, 1968:64). Third, ideologies have an independent existence that is coercive of people. Lefebvre caught the essential point for us here in discussing the effect of ideologies on members of the oppressed class: "It is the role of ideologies to secure the assent of the oppressed and exploited. Ideologies represent the latter to themselves in such a way as to wrest from them, in addition to material wealth, their spiritual acceptance of this situation, even their support" (1968:76).

An ideological system functions to alter the thoughts and actions of members of the oppressed class. In this way, ideologies serve to foster the exploitation of the proletariat. Of course, ideologies do not function in a vacuum; they operate through agents who carry out their dictates. Thus ideologies affect the actions of agents of the ruling class, who, in turn, affect the thoughts and actions of the proletariat.

MARX'S ECONOMICS: A CASE STUDY

This chapter is devoted to an analysis of Marx's sociology, but of course it is his economics for which he is far better known. Although we have touched on a number of aspects of Marx's economics, we have not dealt with it in a coherent fashion. In this closing section, we will look at Marx's economics, not as economics per se, but rather as an exemplification of his sociological theory (Mazlish, 1984).[4] There is much more to Marxian economics, but this is the most relevant way to deal with it in a book devoted to sociological theory.

A starting point for Marxian economics is in the concepts, previously touched on, of use value and exchange value. People have always created use values; that is, they have always produced things that directly satisfy their wants. A *use value* is defined qualitatively; that is, something either is or is not useful. An *exchange value,* however, is defined quantitatively, not qualitatively. It is defined by the amount of labor needed to appropriate useful qualities. Whereas use values are produced to satisfy one's own needs, exchange values are produced to be exchanged for values of another use. Whereas the production of use values is a natural human expression, the existence of exchange values sets in motion a process by which humanity is distorted. The entire edifice of capitalism, including commodities, the market, money, and so forth, is erected on the basis of exchange values.

To Marx, the basic source of any value was the amount of socially necessary labor-time needed to produce an article under the normal conditions of production and with the average degree of skill and intensity of the time. This is the well-known *labor theory of value* (Cockshott, Cottrell, and Michaelson, 1995). Although it is clear that labor lies at the base of use value, this fact grows progressively less clear as we move to exchange values, commodities, the market, and capitalism. To put it another way, "The determination of the magnitude of value by labor-time is therefore a secret, hidden under the apparent fluctuations in relative values of commodities" (Marx, 1867/1967:75). Labor, as the source of all value, is a secret in capitalism that allows the capitalists to exploit the workers.

According to Peter Worsley, Marx "put at the heart of his sociology—as no other sociology does—the theme of exploitation" (1982:115). The capitalists pay the workers *less* than the value the workers produce and keep the rest for themselves. The workers are not aware of this exploitation, and often, neither are the capitalists. The capitalists believe that this extra value is derived from their own cleverness, their capital investment, their manipulation of the market, and so on. Marx stated that "so long as trade is

---

[4]*One* way of looking at Marx's economic theory (for example, the labor theory of value) is as a specific application of his more general sociological theory. This stands in contrast to G. A. Cohen's (1978) work, in which his overriding concern is the underlying *economic* theory in Marx's work. Although Cohen sees the "economic" and the "social" as being interchangeable in Marx's work, he clearly implies that Marx's economic theory is the more general.

good, the capitalist is too much absorbed in money grubbing to take notice of this gratuitous gift of labor" (1867/1967:207). In sum, Marx said:

> The capitalist does not know that the normal price of labor also includes a definite quantity of unpaid labor, and that this very unpaid labor is the normal source of his gain. The category, surplus labor-time, does not exist at all for him, since it is included in the normal working-day, which he thinks he has paid for in the day's wages.
>
> (Marx, 1867/1967:550)

This leads us to Marx's central concept of *surplus value*. This is defined as the difference between the value of the product when it is sold and the value of the elements consumed in the formation of that product. Although means of production (raw materials and tools, the value of which comes from the labor involved in extracting or producing them) are consumed in the production process, it is labor that is the real source of surplus value. "The rate of surplus-value is therefore an exact expression for the degree of exploitation of labor-power by capital, or of the laborer by the capitalist" (Marx, 1867/1967:218). This points to one of Marx's more colorful metaphors: "Capital is dead labor, that, vampire-like, only lives by sucking living labor, and lives the more, the more labor it sucks" (1867/1967:233).

The surplus derived from this process is used by the capitalists to pay for such things as rent to landowners and interest to banks. But the most important derivation from it is profit. The capitalists can use this profit for private consumption, but that would not lead to the expansion of capitalism. Rather they expand their enterprise by converting it into a base for the creation of still more surplus value.

The desire for more profit and more surplus value for expansion pushes capitalism toward what Marx called the *general law of capitalist accumulation*. The capitalists seek to exploit workers as much as possible: "The constant tendency of capital is to force the cost of labor back towards . . . zero" (Marx, 1867/1967:600). Marx basically argued that the structure and the ethos of capitalism push the capitalists in the direction of the accumulation of more and more capital. In order to do this, given Marx's view that labor is the source of value, the capitalists are led to intensify the exploitation of the proletariat. Ultimately, however, increased exploitation yields fewer and fewer gains; an upper limit of exploitation is reached. In addition, as this limit is approached, the government is forced by pressure from the working class to place restrictions on the actions of capitalists (for example, laws limiting the length of the workday). As a result of these restrictions, the capitalists must look for other devices, and a major one is the substitution of machines for people. This substitution is made relatively easy, because the capitalists already have reduced the workers to laboring machines performing a series of simple operations. This shift to capital-intensive production is, paradoxically, a cause of the declining rate of profit since it is labor (not machines) which is the ultimate source of profit.

As mechanization proceeds, more and more people are put out of work and fall from the proletariat to the "industrial reserve army." At the same time, heightening competition and the burgeoning costs of technology lead to a progressive decline in the number of capitalists. In the end, Marx foresaw a situation in which society would be characterized by a tiny number of exploitative capitalists and a huge mass of proletarians and members of the industrial reserve army. In these extreme circumstances, capitalism would be most vulnerable to revolution. As Marx put it, the expropriation of the masses by the capitalists would be replaced by "the expropriation of a few usurpers by the mass of people" (1867/1967:764). The capitalists, of course, seek to forestall their demise. For example, they sponsor colonial adventures with the objective of shifting at least some of the burden of exploitation from the home front to the colonies. However, in Marx's view these efforts are ultimately doomed to failure, and the capitalists will face rebellion at home and abroad.

The key point about the general law of capitalist accumulation is the degree to which actors, both capitalist and proletarian, are impelled by the structure and ethos of capitalism to do what they do. Marx usually did not blame individual capitalists for their actions; he saw these actions as largely determined by the logic of the capitalist system. This is consistent with his view that actors in capitalism generally are devoid of creative independence. However, the developmental process inherent in capitalism provides the conditions necessary for the ultimate reemergence of such creative action and, with it, the overthrow of the capitalist system.

SUMMARY

Despite his overwhelming importance to sociology in both a positive and a negative sense, Karl Marx's work rarely has received its due in historical analyses of the development of sociological theory. It is one of the goals of this book to accord Marx his proper place in that history.

The chapter begins with a discussion of the dialectical approach that Marx derived from Hegel and that shapes all of Marx's work. An interest in the dialectic leads into complex philosophical issues, but our discussion concentrates on those elements of the dialectic that are most relevant to Marx's sociology and to sociological theory in general. The dialectic is contrasted with the causal logic that dominates much of sociological thinking. Among other things, the dialectic emphasizes that there are no simple cause-and-effect relationships among elements of the social world; there is no clear dividing line between fact and value; and there are no hard-and-fast dividing lines among phenomena in the social world. Further, the dialectic stresses that we should focus on social relationships; we should be oriented not only to the present but also to the past and future; we should resist the idea that there are social inevitabilities; and we should be concerned with conflicts and contradictions within the social world. Despite his political orientation toward the creation of a communist society, Marx devoted his attention to dialectical *and* critical analyses of capitalist society. It was his hope that such criticism would help bring about the overthrow of capitalist society and the coming of socialism.

In analyzing the substance of Marx's work, we begin with an analysis of the potential of human beings. This is Marx's image of human nature, but it is a human nature that is greatly affected by its social setting. Marx saw capitalism as a setting that distorts humanity, whereas communism would be a setting in which humanness would be allowed to express itself. Marx's actors are endowed with consciousness and creativity, which are expressed in various types of actions and interactions. Of utmost importance here is the need to interact with other people and with nature in order to produce the objects that people need to survive. It is significant that this natural process is subverted as a result of the unanticipated consequences of capitalism.

The distortions of humans caused by the structures of capitalism fall within the bounds of Marx's famous concept of *alienation*. People are naturally connected with their productive activity, their products, their fellow workers, and, ultimately, with themselves, with their inherent nature as human beings. But all these connections are severed by the structures of capitalism. On a political level, this led Marx to an interest in emancipating people from the oppressive structures of capitalism. On an intellectual level, it led him to examine the nature of the structures of capitalism and their oppressive impact on actors.

We examine various aspects of the structure of capitalist society. We discuss the central role played by commodities in capitalism and the way they are created by the process known as the *fetishism of commodities*. In effect, people endow commodities, and the market for them, with a life of their own. This concept is later expanded (by Lukács) to the idea of reification; that is, people make fetishes not only of commodities but also of many other structural components of capitalist society. In this context, we look at capital as the most general reified structure in capitalist society. Also, we examine a number of reified components in capitalist society, including private property, the division of labor, and social class.

Although Marx, especially in his later work, was particularly concerned with the structures of capitalism, he did have some things to say about the cultural aspects of capitalist society, especially class consciousness, false consciousness, and ideology.

We close the chapter with a discussion of Marxian economics as an illustration of Marx's overall sociological theory. Although for various reasons people have tended to ignore or denigrate it, there is a very powerful sociological theory in Marx's work.

6

EMILE DURKHEIM

SOCIAL FACTS
   External and Coercive
   Material and Nonmaterial
   Levels of Social Reality
THE DIVISION OF LABOR IN SOCIETY
   Dynamic Density
   Law
   Anomie
   Collective Conscience
   Collective Representations
SUICIDE AND SOCIAL CURRENTS
   The Four Types of Suicide
   A Group Mind?
RELIGION
   Sacred and Profane
   Totemism
   Collective Effervescence
SOCIAL REFORMISM
   Occupational Associations
   Cult of the Individual
THE ACTOR IN DURKHEIM'S THOUGHT
   Assumptions about Human Nature
   Socialization and Moral Education
   Dependent Variables
   Weaknesses in Durkheim's Microsociology
EARLY AND LATE DURKHEIMIAN THEORY

Emile Durkheim was deeply concerned with the impact of the large-scale structures of society, and society itself, on the thoughts and actions of individuals (for a very different view, see Janssen and Verheggen, 1997) His work, as interpreted by Talcott Parsons and others, was most influential in shaping structural-functional theory, with its emphasis on social structure and culture (Lehmann, 1995).

The development and use of the concept of a social fact lies at the heart of Durkheim's sociology (Gilbert, 1994). We will have a great deal to say about this concept in this chapter, but briefly and in modern terms, *social facts* are the social structures and cultural norms and values that are external to, and coercive of, actors. Students are constrained by such social structures as the university bureaucracy as well as the norms and values of American society, which place such great importance on a college education. Similar social facts constrain people in all areas of social life.

To understand why Durkheim developed the concept of social fact and what it means, we need to examine at least a few aspects of the intellectual context in which he lived.

In Durkheim's (1900/1973:3) view, sociology was born in France in the nineteenth century. He recognized its roots in the ancient philosophers (Plato, Aristotle) and more proximate sources in French philosophers such as Montesquieu and Condorcet. For example, Durkheim noted, "It is Montesquieu who first laid down the fundamental principles of social science" (1893/1960:61). However, in Durkheim's view, Montesquieu (and Condorcet) did not go far enough: "They limited themselves to offering ingenious or novel views on social facts rather than seeking to create an entirely new discipline" (1900/1973:6). In sum, according to W. Watts Miller, Durkheim saw "Montesquieu as a pioneer of social science, freeing himself from earlier conceptions, but in some ways still their captive" (1993:694). Durkheim (1928/1962:142) gave Saint-Simon credit for first formulating the notion of a science of the social world, but Saint-Simon's ideas were seen as scattered and imperfect. Those ideas were, in Durkheim's view, perfected by Comte, "the first to make a coherent and methodical effort to establish the positive science of societies" (1900/1973:10).

Although the term *sociology* had been coined some years earlier by Comte, there was no field of sociology per se in late nineteenth-century France. There were no schools, departments, or even professors of sociology. There were a few thinkers who were dealing with ideas that were in one way or another sociological, but there was as yet no disciplinary "home" for sociology. Indeed, there was strong opposition from existing disciplines to the founding of such a field. The most significant opposition came from psychology and philosophy, two fields that claimed already to cover the domain sought by sociology. The dilemma for Durkheim, given his aspirations for sociology, was how to create for it a separate and identifiable niche.

To separate it from philosophy, Durkheim argued that sociology should be oriented toward empirical research. This seems simple enough, but the situation was complicated by Durkheim's belief that sociology was also threatened by a philosophical school *within* sociology itself. In his view, the two other major figures of the epoch who thought of themselves as sociologists, Comte and Spencer, were far more interested in philosophizing, in abstract theorizing, than they were in studying the social world empirically. If the field were to continue in the direction set by Comte and Spencer, Durkheim felt, it would become nothing more than a branch of philosophy. As a result, he found it necessary to attack both Comte and Spencer (Durkheim, 1895/1964:19–20). He accused both of substituting preconceived ideas of social phenomena for the actual study of the phenomena in the real world. Thus Comte was said to be guilty of assuming theoretically that the social world was evolving in the direction of an increasingly perfect society, rather than engaging in the hard, rigorous, and basic work of actually studying the changing nature of various societies. Similarly, Spencer was accused of assuming harmony in society rather than studying whether harmony actually existed.

SOCIAL FACTS

In order to help sociology move away from philosophy and to give it a clear and separate identity (Cormack, 1996), Durkheim (1895/1964) argued in *The Rules of Sociological Method* that the distinctive subject matter of sociology should be the study of social facts (see Gane, 1988, for a discussion of the major criticisms of this work as well as a defense of it; for a different, "constructionist" view, see S. Turner, 1995). The concept of social fact has several components, but crucial in separating sociology from philosophy is the idea that *social facts are to be treated as things* (S. Jones, 1996). In that they are to be treated as *things,* social facts are to be studied empirically, *not* philosophically.[1] Durkheim believed that ideas can be known introspectively (philosophically), but *things* "cannot be conceived by purely mental activity"; they require for their conception "data from outside the mind" (1895/1964:xliii). This empirical study of social facts as things sets Durkheimian sociology apart from the largely introspective theorizing of Comte and Spencer (for a critique of Durkheim's positivism, see Boudon, 1995).

External and Coercive

Although treating social facts as things countered the threat from philosophy (at least as far as Durkheim was concerned), it was only part of the answer to the problem of dealing with the threat coming from psychology. Like Durkheimian sociology, psychology was already highly empirical. To differentiate sociology from psychology, Durkheim argued that social facts were *external to,* and *coercive of,* the actor (for a different view, see Rawls, 1996). Sociology was to be the study of social facts, whereas the study of psychological facts was relegated to psychology. To Durkheim, psychological facts were basically inherited phenomena. Although this certainly does not describe psychology today (and was not a very accurate description of the subject matter of psychology even then), it did allow Durkheim to draw a clear differentiation between the two fields. Psychological facts are clearly internal (inherited), and social facts are external and coercive. As we will soon see, this differentiation is not so neat as Durkheim would have liked us to believe. Nevertheless, by defining a social fact as a *thing* that is *external to, and coercive of, the actor,* Durkheim seems to have done a reasonably good job (at least for that historical era) of attaining his objective of separating sociology from both philosophy and psychology. However, it should be noted that to do this, Durkheim took an "extremist" position (Karady, 1983:79–80), especially in limiting sociology to the study of social facts. This position was to limit at least some branches of sociology to the present day. Furthermore, Durkheim seemed to artificially sever sociology from neighboring fields. As Lemert puts it, "Because he defined sociology so exclusively in relation to its own facts, Durkheim cut it off from the other sciences of man" (1994a:91).

---

[1] It is worth noting, however, that Durkheim did a lot of what may be described as philosophizing.

Material and Nonmaterial

We know that a social fact is a thing and that it is external and coercive, but what else is a social fact? Actually, Durkheim differentiated between two broad types of social facts—material and nonmaterial. *Material social facts* are the clearer of the two because they are real, material entities, but they are also of lesser significance in Durkheim's work. As Durkheim put it, "The social fact is sometimes materialized so far as to become an element of the external world" (1897/1951:313). Architecture and the law would be two examples of what he meant by material social facts. We will encounter other examples in this chapter.

The bulk of Durkheim's work, and the heart of his sociology, lies in the study of nonmaterial social facts. Durkheim said: "Not all social consciousness achieves . . . externalization and materialization" (1897/1951:315). What sociologists now call *norms* and *values,* or more generally culture (see Alexander, 1988a), are good examples of what Durkheim meant by *nonmaterial social facts.* But this idea creates a problem: How can nonmaterial social facts like norms and values be external to the actor? Where could they be found except in the minds of actors? And if they are in the minds of actors, then are they not internal rather than external?

To clarify this issue, we must refine Durkheim's argument by contending that while material social facts are clearly external and coercive, nonmaterial social facts are not so clear-cut. (For a similar distinction, see Takla and Pope [1985:82].) To at least some extent, they are found in the minds of actors. The best way to conceptualize nonmaterial social facts is to think of them as external to, and coercive of, psychological facts. In this way we can see that both psychological facts and *some* social facts exist within and between consciousness. Durkheim made this clear in a number of places. At one point he said of social facts, "Individual minds, forming groups by mingling and fusing, give birth to a being, *psychological if you will,* but constituting a psychic individuality of a new sort" (Durkheim, 1895/1964:103; italics added). At another point, Durkheim said, "This does not mean that they [nonmaterial social facts] are not also mental after a fashion, since they all consist of ways of thinking or behaving" (1895/1964:xlix). Thus it is best to think of nonmaterial social facts, at least in part, as mental phenomena, but mental phenomena that are external to, and coercive of, another aspect of the mental process—psychological facts. This confounds Durkheim's differentiation between sociology and psychology somewhat, but it does serve to make the differentiation more realistic and as a result more defensible. Sociology *is* concerned with mental phenomena, but they are usually of a different order from the mental concerns of psychology. Durkheim thus was arguing that sociologists are interested in norms and values, whereas psychologists are concerned with such things as human instincts.

Levels of Social Reality

Social facts, then, play a central role in the sociology of Emile Durkheim. A useful way of extracting the most important social facts from his work, and for analyzing his thoughts on the relationships among these phenomena, is to begin with Durkheim's efforts to organize them into *levels* of social reality. He began at the level of material social facts, not because it was the most important level to him, but because its elements often take causal priority in his theorizing. They affect nonmaterial social facts, which are the real focus of his work. (Although we will focus here on both types of social facts, we will have some things to say later about Durkheim's thoughts on the more microscopic aspects of social reality.)

The major levels of social reality (Lukes, 1972:9–10) in Durkheim's work can be depicted as follows:

A. Material Social Facts
  1. Society
  2. Structural components of society (for example, church and state)
  3. Morphological components of society (for example, population distribution, channels of communication, and housing arrangements) (Andrews, 1993)
B. Nonmaterial Social Facts
  1. Morality
  2. Collective conscience
  3. Collective representations
  4. Social currents

The levels within the two categories are listed in terms of descending order of generality.

It is his focus on macro-level social facts that is one of the reasons why Durkheim's work played a central role in the development of structural functionalism, which has a similar, macro-level orientation (see Chapter 14, on Parsons). More specifically, drawing on biology and using an organismic analogy (Lehmann, 1993a:15), Durkheim saw society as composed of "organs" (social facts), or social structures, that had a variety of functions for society. Durkheim urged that we distinguish functions, or the ends served by various structures, from the factors that caused them to come into existence. Durkheim was interested in studying both the causes of social structures and the functions they perform, although he wanted to carefully differentiate between these two topics of study.

We can trace the logic of Durkheim's theory in his analysis of the development of the modern world. This is most clearly shown in one of his most important works, *The Division of Labor in Society* (Durkheim, 1893/1964), a work that has been called sociology's first classic (Tiryakian, 1994).

THE DIVISION OF LABOR IN SOCIETY

Durkheim based his analysis in *The Division of Labor in Society* on his conception of two ideal types of society (for a comparison with Spencer's evolutionary theory, see Perrin, 1995). The more primitive type, characterized by *mechanical solidarity,* has a relatively undifferentiated social structure, with little or no division of labor. The more modern type, characterized by *organic solidarity,* has a much greater and more refined division of labor. To Durkheim the *division of labor in society* is a material social fact that involves the degree to which tasks or responsibilities are specialized. People in primitive societies tend to occupy very general positions in which they perform a wide variety of tasks and handle a large number of responsibilities. In other words, a primitive person tended to be a jack-of-all-trades. In contrast, those who live in more modern societies occupy more specialized positions and have a much narrower range of tasks and responsibilities. For example, being a mother-housewife in primitive societies is a much less specialized position than it is in a modern society. Laundry services, diaper services, home delivery, and labor-saving devices (dishwashers, microwave ovens, Cuisinarts, and so forth) perform a number of tasks that were formerly the responsibility of the mother-housewife.

The changes in the division of labor have had enormous implications for the structure of society, and some of the more important implications are reflected in the differences between the two types of solidarity—mechanical and organic. In addressing the issue of solidarity, Durkheim was interested in what holds society together. A society characterized by mechanical solidarity is unified because all people are generalists. The bond among people is that they are all engaged in similar activities and have similar responsibilities. In contrast, a society characterized by organic solidarity is held together by the differences among people, by the fact that they have different tasks and responsibilities. Because people in modern society perform a relatively narrow range of tasks, they need many other people in order to survive. The primitive family headed by father-hunter and mother–food gatherer is practically self-sufficient, but the modern family, in order to make it through the week, needs the grocer, baker, butcher, auto mechanic, teacher, police officer, and so forth. These people, in turn, need the kinds of services that others provide in order to live in the modern world. Modern society, in Durkheim's view, is thus held together by the specialization of people and their need for the services of many others. Furthermore, Durkheim was concerned with the specialization not only of individuals but also of groups, structures, and institutions. One final difference between mechanical and organic solidarity is worth mentioning: Because people in societies characterized by mechanical solidarity are more likely to be similar to one another in terms of what they do, there is a greater likelihood of competition among them. In contrast, in societies with organic solidarity, differentiation allows people to cooperate more and to all be supported by the same resource base.

Thus a society characterized by organic solidarity leads to both more solidarity *and* more individuality than one characterized by mechanical solidarity (Rueschemeyer, 1994). In other words, Durkheim held the view that the social order and individual autonomy are compatible (Muller, 1994).

Dynamic Density

The division of labor was a material social fact to Durkheim because it is the pattern of interaction in the social world. Another, and closely related, material social fact is the major causal factor in Durkheim's theory of the transition from mechanical to organic solidarity—*dynamic density*. This concept refers to the number of people in a society and the amount of interaction that occurs among them. Neither population increase nor an increase in interaction, when taken separately, is a significant factor in societal change. An increase in numbers of people *and* an increase in the interaction among them (which is dynamic density) lead to the change from mechanical to organic solidarity because together they bring about more competition for scarce resources and a more intense struggle for survival among the various parallel and similar components of primitive society. Because individuals, groups, families, tribes, and so forth perform virtually identical functions, they are likely to clash over these functions, especially if resources are scarce. The rise of the division of labor allows people and the social structures they create to complement, rather than conflict with, one another, and this, in turn, makes peaceful coexistence more likely. Furthermore, the increasing division of labor makes for greater efficiency, with the result that resources increase, and more and more people can survive peacefully.

Although Durkheim was interested in explaining how the division of labor and dynamic density lead to different types of social solidarity, he was interested primarily in the impact of these material changes on, and the nature of, nonmaterial social facts in both mechanically and organically solidified societies. However, because of his image of what a *science* of sociology should be, Durkheim felt that it was impossible to study nonmaterial social facts directly. Direct consideration of nonmaterial social facts was, for him, more philosophical than sociological. In order to study nonmaterial social facts scientifically, the sociologist would have to seek and examine material social facts that reflect the nature of, and changes in, nonmaterial social facts. In *The Division of Labor in Society* it is law, and the differences between law in societies with mechanical solidarity and law in societies with organic solidarity, that plays this role.

Law

Durkheim argued that a society with mechanical solidarity is characterized by *repressive law*. Because people are very similar in this type of society, and because they tend to believe very strongly in a common morality, any offense against their shared value system is likely to be of significance to most individuals. Because most people feel the offense and believe deeply in the common morality, an offender is likely to be severely punished for any action that is considered an offense against the collective moral system. The theft of a pig must lead to the cutting off of the offender's hands; blaspheming against God or gods might well result in the removal of one's tongue. Because people are so involved in the moral system, an offense against it is likely to be met with swift, severe punishment.

In contrast, a society with organic solidarity is characterized by *restitutive law*. Instead of being severely punished for even seemingly minor offenses against the collective morality, individuals in this more modern type of society are likely simply to be asked to comply with the law or to repay—make restitution to—those who have been harmed by their actions. Although some repressive law continues to exist in a society with organic solidarity (for example, the death penalty), restitutive law is more characteristic. There is little or no powerful and coercive common morality; the vast majority of people do not react emotionally to a breach of the law. The monitoring of repressive law is largely in the hands of the masses in a society with mechanical solidarity, but the maintenance of restitutive law is primarily the responsibility of specialized agencies (for example, the police and the courts). This is consistent with the increased division of labor in a society with organic solidarity.

Changes in a material social fact like the law are, in Durkheim's theoretical system, merely reflections of changes in the more crucial elements of his sociology—nonmaterial social facts such as morality, collective conscience, collective representations, social

EMILE DURKHEIM: A Biographical Sketch

Emile Durkheim was born on April 15, 1858, in Epinal, France. He was descended from a long line of rabbis and himself studied to be a rabbi, but by the time he was in his teens, he had largely disavowed his heritage (Strenski, 1997:4). From that time on, his lifelong interest in religion was more academic than theological (Mestrovic, 1988). He was dissatisfied not only with his religious training but also with his general education and its emphasis on literary and esthetic matters. He longed for schooling in scientific methods and in the moral principles needed to guide social life. He rejected a traditional academic career in philosophy and sought instead to acquire the scientific training needed to contribute to the moral guidance of society. Although he was interested in scientific sociology, there was no field of sociology at that time, so between 1882 and 1887 he taught philosophy in a number of provincial schools in the Paris area.

His appetite for science was whetted further by a trip to Germany, where he was exposed to the scientific psychology being pioneered by Wilhelm Wundt (Durkheim, 1887/1993). In the years immediately after his visit to Germany, Durkheim published a good deal, basing his work, in part, on his experiences there (R. Jones, 1994). These publications helped him gain a position in the department of philosophy at the University of Bordeaux in 1887. There Durkheim offered the first course in social science in a French university. This was a particularly impressive accomplishment, because only a decade earlier, a furor had erupted in a French university by the mention of Auguste Comte in a student dissertation. Durkheim's main responsibility, however, was teaching courses in education to schoolteachers, and his most important course was in the area of moral education. His goal was to communicate a moral system to the educators, who he hoped would then pass the system on to young people in an effort to help reverse the moral degeneration he saw around him in French society.

The years that followed were characterized by a series of personal successes for Durkheim. In 1893 he published his French doctoral thesis, *The Division of Labor in Society,* as well as his Latin thesis on Montesquieu (Durkheim, 1892/1997; W. Miller, 1993). His major methodological statement, *The Rules of Sociological Method,* appeared in 1895, followed (in 1897) by his empirical application of those methods in the study *Suicide.* By 1896 he had become a full professor at Bordeaux. In 1902 he was summoned to the famous French university the Sorbonne, and in 1906 he was named professor of the science of education, a title that was changed in 1913 to professor of the science of education *and sociology.* The other of his most famous works, *The Elementary Forms of Religious Life,* was published in 1912.

Durkheim is most often thought of today as a political conservative, and his influence within sociology certainly has been a conservative one. But in his time, he was considered a liberal, and this was exemplified by the active public role he played in the defense of Alfred Dreyfus, the Jewish army captain whose court-martial for treason was felt by many to be anti-Semitic (Farrell, 1997).

currents, and, most questionably from a modern sociological perspective, the group mind. (All these concepts will be discussed in this chapter.)

At the most general and all-inclusive level, Durkheim (1887/1993) was a sociologist of morality (Mestrovic, 1988; Turner, 1993). Indeed, Ernest Wallwork (1972:182)

Durkheim was deeply offended by the Dreyfus affair, particularly its anti-Semitism. But Durkheim did not attribute this anti-Semitism to racism among the French people. Characteristically, he saw it as a symptom of the moral sickness confronting French society as a whole (Birnbaum and Todd, 1995). He said:

> When society undergoes suffering, it feels the need to find someone whom it can hold responsible for its sickness, on whom it can avenge its misfortunes: and those against whom public opinion already discriminates are naturally designated for this role. These are the pariahs who serve as expiatory victims. What confirms me in this interpretation is the way in which the result of Dreyfus's trial was greeted in 1894. There was a surge of joy in the boulevards. People celebrated as a triumph what should have been a cause for public mourning. At least they knew whom to blame for the economic troubles and moral distress in which they lived. The trouble came from the Jews. The charge had been officially proved. By this very fact alone, things already seemed to be getting better and people felt consoled.
>
> (Lukes, 1972:345)

Thus, Durkheim's interest in the Dreyfus affair stemmed from his deep and lifelong interest in morality and the moral crisis confronting modern society.

To Durkheim, the answer to the Dreyfus affair and crises like it lay in ending the moral disorder in society. Because that could not be done quickly or easily, Durkheim suggested more specific actions such as severe repression of those who incite hatred of others and government efforts to show the public how it is being misled. He urged people to "have the courage to proclaim aloud what they think, and to unite together in order to achieve victory in the struggle against public madness" (Lukes, 1972:347).

Durkheim's (1928/1962) interest in socialism is also taken as evidence against the idea that he was a conservative, but his kind of socialism was very different from the kind that interested Marx and his followers. In fact, Durkheim labeled Marxism as a set of "disputable and out-of-date hypotheses" (Lukes, 1972:323). To Durkheim, socialism represented a movement aimed at the moral regeneration of society through scientific morality, and he was not interested in short-term political methods or the economic aspects of socialism. He did not see the proletariat as the salvation of society, and he was greatly opposed to agitation or violence. Socialism for Durkheim was very different from what we usually think of as socialism; it simply represented a system in which the moral principles discovered by scientific sociology were to be applied.

Durkheim, as we will see throughout this book, had a profound influence on the development of sociology, but his influence was not restricted to it (Halls, 1996). Much of his impact on other fields came through the journal L'année sociologique, which he founded in 1898. An intellectual circle arose around the journal with Durkheim at its center. Through it, he and his ideas influenced such fields as anthropology, history, linguistics, and—somewhat ironically, considering his early attacks on the field—psychology.

Durkheim died on November 15, 1917, a celebrated figure in French intellectual circles, but it was not until over twenty years later, with the publication of Talcott Parsons's The Structure of Social Action (1937), that his work became a significant influence on American sociology.

argued that Durkheim's sociology is merely a by-product of his concern with moral issues. That is, Durkheim's interest in the moral problems of his day led him as a sociologist to devote most of his attention to the moral elements of social life. At its most basic level, Durkheim's great concern was with the declining strength of the common morality in the modern world. In Durkheim's view, people were in danger of a "pathological" loosening of moral bonds. These moral bonds were important to Durkheim, for without them the individual would be enslaved by ever-expanding and insatiable passions. People would be impelled by their passions into a mad search for gratification, but each new gratification would lead only to more and more needs. Durkheim held the seemingly paradoxical view that the individual needs morality and external control in order to be free. This is a curious definition of freedom.

Anomie

Many of the problems that occupied Durkheim stem from his concern with the decline of the common morality. In the concept of *anomie,* Durkheim best manifested his concern with the problems of a weakened common morality (Hilbert, 1986; Bar-Haim, 1997). Individuals are said to be confronted with anomie when they are not faced with sufficient moral constraint, that is, when they do not have a clear concept of what is and what is not proper and acceptable behavior.

The central "pathology" in modern society was, in Durkheim's view, the *anomic* division of labor. By thinking of anomie as a pathology, Durkheim manifested his belief that the problems of the modern world can be "cured." Durkheim believed that the structural division of labor in modern society is a source of cohesion that compensates for the declining strength of the collective morality. However, the thrust of his argument is that the division of labor cannot entirely make up for the loosening of the common morality, with the result that anomie is a pathology associated with the rise of organic solidarity. Individuals can become isolated and be cut adrift in their highly specialized activities. They can more easily cease to feel a common bond with those who work and live around them. But it is important to remember that this is viewed by Durkheim as an abnormal situation, because only in unusual circumstances does the modern division of labor reduce people to isolated and meaningless tasks and positions. The concept of anomie can be found not only in *The Division of Labor* but also in *Suicide* (Durkheim, 1897/1951) as one of the major types of suicide. Anomic suicide occurs because of the decline in collective morality and the lack of sufficient external regulation of the individual to restrain his or her passions.

Collective Conscience

Durkheim attempted to deal with his interest in common morality in various ways and with different concepts. In his early efforts to deal with this issue, Durkheim developed the idea of the *collective conscience,* which he characterized in *The Division of Labor in Society* in the following way:

> The totality of beliefs and sentiments common to average citizens of the same society forms a determinate system which has its own life; one may call it the *collective* or *common conscience.* . . . It is, thus, an entirely different thing from particular consciences, although it can be realized only through them.
>
> (Durkheim, 1893/1964:79–80)

Several points are worth underscoring in this definition, given our interest in the collective conscience as an example of a nonmaterial social fact. First, it is clear that Durkheim thought of the collective conscience as occurring throughout a given society when he wrote of the "totality" of people's beliefs and sentiments. Second, Durkheim clearly conceived of the collective conscience as being an independent, determinate cultural system. Although he held such views of the collective conscience, Durkheim also wrote of its being "realized" through individual consciousness. (That Durkheim did *not* conceive of the collective conscience as totally independent of individual consciousness will be important when we examine the charge that Durkheim holds a group-mind concept.)

The concept of the collective conscience allows us to return to Durkheim's analysis, in *The Division of Labor,* of material social facts and their relationship to changes in the common morality. The logic of his argument is that the increasing division of labor (brought on by the increasing dynamic density) is causing a transformation (a diminution but not a disappearance) of the collective conscience. The collective conscience is of much less significance in a society with organic solidarity than it is in a society with mechanical solidarity. People in modern society are more likely to be held together by the division of labor and the resulting need for the functions performed by others than they are by a shared and powerful collective conscience. Anthony Giddens (1972; see also Pope and Johnson, 1983) performed a useful service by pointing out that the collective conscience in the two types of society can be differentiated on four dimensions—volume, intensity, rigidity, and content. *Volume* refers to the number of people enveloped by the collective conscience; *intensity* to how deeply the individuals feel about it; *rigidity* to how clearly it is defined; and *content* to the form that the collective conscience takes in the two polar types of society. In a society characterized by mechanical solidarity, the collective conscience covers virtually the entire society and all its members; it is believed in with great intensity (as reflected, for one thing, by the use of repressive sanctions when it is violated); it is extremely rigid; and its content is highly religious in character. In a society with organic solidarity, the collective conscience is much more limited in its domain and in the number of people enveloped by it; it is adhered to with much less intensity (as reflected in the substitution of restitutive for repressive laws); it is not very rigid; and its content is best described by the phrase "moral individualism," or the elevation of the importance of the individual to a moral precept.

Collective Representations

The idea of the collective conscience, while useful to Durkheim, clearly is very broad and amorphous. Durkheim's dissatisfaction with the character of the concept of the collective conscience led him to abandon it (at least explicitly) progressively in his later work in favor of the much more specific concept of collective representations (Nemedi, 1995; Schmaus, 1994). *Collective representations* may be seen as specific states, or substrata, of the collective conscience (Lukes, 1972). In contemporary terms, we may think of collective representations as the norms and values of specific collectivities such as the family, occupation, state, and educational and religious institutions. The concept of collective representations can be used both broadly and specifically, but the critical point is that it allowed Durkheim to conceptualize nonmaterial social facts in a narrower way than the all-encompassing notion of the collective conscience. Despite their greater specificity, collective representations are *not* reducible to the level of individual consciousness: *"Representations collectives* result from the substratum of associated individuals . . . but they have *sui generis* characteristics" (Durkheim, cited in Lukes, 1972:7). The Latin term *sui generis* means "unique." When Durkheim used this term to refer to the structure of collective representations, he was saying that their unique character is not reducible to individual consciousness. This places them squarely within the realm of nonmaterial social facts. They transcend the individual because they do not depend on any particular individual for their existence. They are also independent of individuals in the sense that their temporal span is greater than the lifetime of any individual. Collective representations are a central component of Durkheim's system of nonmaterial social facts.

SUICIDE AND SOCIAL CURRENTS

Durkheim offered an even more specific (and more dynamic) and less crystallized concept that is also a nonmaterial social fact—*social currents.* These were defined by Durkheim as nonmaterial social facts "which have the same objectivity and the same ascendancy over the individual" as the social facts discussed above, but "without such crystallized form" (1895/1964:4). He gave as examples "the great movements of enthusiasm, indignation, and pity in a crowd" (Durkheim, 1895/1964:4). Although social currents are less concrete than other social facts, they are nevertheless social facts, as Durkheim made clear when he said, "They come to each one of us from without and can carry us away in spite of ourselves" (1895/1964:4).

Durkheim explicated the idea of social currents in *The Rules of Sociological Method* (1895/1964), but he used it as his major explanatory variable in an empirical study that became a model for the development of American empirical research (Selvin, 1958). In fact, the research reported in *Suicide* (1897/1951) can be seen as an effort to use the ideas developed in *The Rules* in an empirical study of a specific social phenomenon— suicide (for a series of appraisals of *Suicide* nearly 100 years after its publication, see Lester, 1994). In *Suicide* he demonstrated that social facts, in particular social currents, are external to, and coercive of, the individual. Durkheim chose to study suicide because it is a relatively concrete and specific phenomenon. There were relatively good data available on suicide, and above all it is generally considered to be one of the most private and personal of acts. Durkheim believed that if he could show that sociology had a role to play in explaining such a seemingly individualistic act as suicide, it would be relatively easy to extend sociology's domain to phenomena that are much more readily seen as open to sociological analysis. Finally, Durkheim chose to study suicide because if the intellectual community could be convinced of his case in the study of this phenomenon, then sociology would have a reasonable chance of gaining recognition in the academic world.

As a sociologist, Durkheim was not concerned with studying why any specific individual committed suicide. That was to be left to the psychologist. Instead, Durkheim was interested in explaining differences in suicide *rates,* that is, he was interested in why one group had a higher rate of suicide than another. Durkheim tended to assume that biological, psychological, and social-psychological factors remain essentially constant from one group to another or from one time period to another. If there is variation in suicide rates from one group to another or from one time period to another, Durkheim assumed that the difference would be the consequence of variations in sociological factors, in particular, social currents.

Committed as he was to empirical research, Durkheim was not content simply to dismiss other possible causes of differences in suicide rates; instead he tested them empirically. He began *Suicide* with a series of alternative ideas about the causes of suicide. Among these are individual psychopathology, alcoholism (Skog, 1991), race, heredity, and climate. Although Durkheim marshaled a wide range of facts to reject each of these as crucial to differences in suicide rates, his clearest argument, and the one that was most consistent with his overall perspective, was on the relevance of racial factors to the differences. One of the reasons that race was rejected is that suicide rates varied among groups *within* the same race. If race were a significant cause of differences in suicide rates, then we would assume that it would have a similar impact on the various subgroups. Another piece of evidence against race as a significant cause of variations in rates is the change in rates for a given race when it moves from one society to another. If race were a relevant social fact, it should have the same effect in different societies. Although Durkheim's argument is not powerful here, and is even weaker on the other factors that he rejected, this does give us a feel for the nature of Durkheim's approach to the problem of empirically dismissing what he considered extraneous factors so that he could get to what he thought of as the most important causal variables.

In addition to rejecting the factors discussed above, Durkheim examined and rejected the imitation theory associated with the early French social psychologist Gabriel Tarde (1843–1904). The theory of imitation argues that people commit suicide (and engage in a wide range of other actions) because they are imitating the actions of others who have committed suicide. This social-psychological approach to sociological thinking is foreign to Durkheim's focus on social facts. As a result, Durkheim took pains to reject it. For example, Durkheim reasoned that if imitation were truly important, we should find that the nations that border on a country with a high suicide rate would themselves have high rates. He looked at the data on the significance of this geographical factor and concluded that no such relationship existed. Durkheim admitted that some individual suicides may be the result of imitation, but it is such a minor factor that it has no significant effect on the overall suicide rate. In the end, Durkheim rejected imitation as a significant factor because of his view that only one social fact could be the cause of another social fact. Because imitation is a social-psychological variable, it cannot, in his system, serve as a significant cause of differences in social suicide rates. As Durkheim put it, "The social suicide-rate can be explained only sociologically" (1897/1951:299).

To Durkheim, the critical factors in changes in suicide rates were to be found in differences at the level of social facts. Of course, there are two types of social facts—material and nonmaterial. As usual, material social facts occupy the position of causal priority but not of causal primacy. For example, Durkheim looked at the significance of dynamic density for differences in suicide rates but found that its effect is only indirect. But differences in dynamic density (and other material social facts) do have an effect on differences in nonmaterial social facts, and these differences have a direct effect on suicide rates. Durkheim was making two related arguments. On the one hand, he was arguing that different collectivities have different collective consciences and collective representations. These, in turn, produce different social currents, which have differential effects on suicide rates. One way to study suicide is to compare different societies or other types of collectivities. On the other hand, Durkheim was arguing that changes in the collective conscience lead to changes in social currents, which, in turn, lead to changes in suicide rates. This leads to the historical study of changes in suicide rates within a given collectivity. In either case, cross-culturally or historically, the logic of the argument is essentially the same: differences or changes in the collective conscience lead to differences or changes in social currents, and these, in turn, lead to differences or changes in suicide rates. In other words, changes in suicide rates are caused by changes in social facts, primarily social currents. Durkheim was quite clear on the crucial role played by social currents in the etiology of suicide:

> Each social group has a collective inclination for the act, quite its own, and the source of all individual inclination rather than their result. It is made up of *currents of egoism, altruism or anomy* running through . . . society. . . . These tendencies of the whole social body, by affecting individuals, cause them to commit suicide.
>
> (Durkheim, 1897/1951:299–300; italics added)

The Four Types of Suicide

Durkheim's theory of suicide, and the structure of his sociological reasoning, can be seen more clearly if we examine each of his four types of suicide—egoistic, altruistic, anomic, and fatalistic (Bearman, 1991). Durkheim linked each of the types of suicide to the degree of integration into, or regulation by, society (Thorlindsson and Bjarnason, 1998). *Integration* refers to the degree to which collective sentiments are shared. Altruistic suicide is associated with a high degree of integration and egoistic suicide with a low degree of integration. *Regulation* refers to the degree of external constraint on people. Fatalistic suicide is associated with high regulation, anomic suicide with low regulation. Whitney Pope (1976:12–13) offered a very useful summary of the four types of suicide discussed by Durkheim. He did this by interrelating high and low degrees of integration and regulation in the following way:

$$
\begin{array}{llll}
 & \text{Low} & \rightarrow & \text{Egoistic suicide} \\
\text{Integration} & \text{High} & \rightarrow & \text{Altruistic suicide} \\
 & \text{Low} & \rightarrow & \text{Anomic suicide} \\
\text{Regulation} & \text{High} & \rightarrow & \text{Fatalistic suicide}
\end{array}
$$

Egoistic Suicide   High rates of *egoistic suicide* are likely to be found in those societies, collectivities, or groups in which the individual is not well integrated into the larger social unit. This lack of integration leads to a sense of meaninglessness among individuals. Societies with a strong collective conscience and the protective, enveloping social currents that flow from it are likely to prevent the widespread occurrence of egoistic suicide by, among other things, providing people with a sense of the broader meaning of their lives. When these social currents are weak, individuals are able rather easily to surmount the collective conscience and do as they wish. In large-scale social units with a weak collective conscience, individuals are left to pursue their private interests in whatever way they wish. Such unrestrained egoism is likely to lead to considerable personal dissatisfaction, because all needs cannot be fulfilled, and those that are fulfilled simply lead to the generation of more and more needs and, ultimately, to dissatisfaction—and, for some, to suicide (Breault, 1986). However, strongly integrated families, religious groups, and polities act as agents of a strong collective conscience and discourage suicide. Here is the way Durkheim puts it in terms of religious groups:

> Religion protects man against the desire for self-destruction. . . . What constitutes religion is the existence of a certain number of beliefs and practices common to all the faithful, traditional and thus obligatory. The more numerous and strong these collective states of mind are, the stronger the integration of the religious community, also the *greater its preservative* value.

> (Durkheim, 1897/1951:170; italics added)

The disintegration of society produces distinctive social currents, and these are the principal causes of differences in suicide rates. For example, Durkheim talked of societal disintegration leading to "currents of depression and disillusionment" (1897/1951:214). The moral disintegration of society predisposes the individual to commit suicide, but the currents of depression must also be there to produce differences in rates of egoistic suicide. Interestingly, Durkheim was here reaffirming the importance of social forces, even in the case of egoistic suicide, where the individual might be thought to be free of social constraints. Actors are *never* free of the force of the collectivity: "However individualized a man may be, there is always something collective remaining—the very depression and melancholy resulting from this same exaggerated individualism. He effects communion through sadness when he no longer has anything else with which to achieve it" (Durkheim, 1897/1951:214). The case of egoistic suicide indicates that in even the most individualistic, most private of acts, social facts are the key determinant.

Altruistic Suicide   The second type of suicide discussed by Durkheim is altruistic suicide. Whereas egoistic suicide is more likely to occur when social integration is too weak, *altruistic suicide* is more likely when "social integration is too strong" (Durkheim, 1897/1951:217). The individual is literally forced into committing suicide.

One notorious example of altruistic suicide was the mass suicide of the followers of the Reverend Jim Jones in Jonestown, Guyana. They knowingly took a poisoned drink and in some cases had their children drink it as well. They were clearly committing suicide because they were pushed, either forcefully or gently, into giving their lives for the tightly integrated society of Jones's fanatical followers. More generally, those who commit altruistic suicide do so because they feel that it is their duty to do so.

As was the case with egoistic suicide, the degree of integration (in this case, a high degree) is not the direct cause of altruistic suicide. Rather, different degrees of integration produce different social currents, and these different currents affect suicide rates. As with egoistic suicide, Durkheim saw melancholy social currents as the cause of high rates of altruistic suicide. Whereas higher rates of egoistic suicide stem from "incurable weariness and sad depression," the increased likelihood of altruistic suicide "springs

from hope, for it depends on the belief in beautiful perspectives beyond this life"
(Durkheim, 1897/1951:225).

Anomic Suicide   The final major form of suicide discussed by Durkheim is *anomic
suicide,* which is more likely to occur when the regulative powers of society are
disrupted. Such disruptions are likely to leave individuals dissatisfied because there is
little control over their passions, which are free to run wild in an insatiable race for gratification. Rates of anomic suicide are likely to rise whether the nature of the disruption
is positive (for example, an economic boom) or negative (an economic depression).
Either type of disruption renders the collectivity temporarily incapable of exercising its
authority over individuals. Such changes put people in new situations in which the old
norms no longer apply but new ones have yet to develop. Periods of disruption unleash
currents of anomie—moods of rootlessness and normlessness—and these currents lead
to an increase in rates of anomic suicide. This is relatively easy to envisage in the case
of a depression. The closing of a factory because of an economic depression may lead
to the loss of a job, with the result that the individual is cut adrift from the regulative
effect that both the company and the job may have had. Being cut off from these structures or others (for example, family, religion, and state) can leave the individual highly
vulnerable to the effects of currents of anomie. Somewhat more difficult to imagine is
the effect of an economic boom. In this case, it might be argued that sudden success
leads individuals away from the traditional structures in which they are embedded. Economic success may lead individuals to quit their jobs, move to a new community, perhaps even find a new spouse. All these changes disrupt the regulative effect of extant
structures and leave the individual in boom periods vulnerable to anomic social currents.
    The increases in rates of anomic suicide during periods of deregulation of social life
are consistent with Durkheim's views on the pernicious effect of individual passions
when freed of external constraint. People thus freed will become slaves to their passions
and as a result, in Durkheim's view, commit a wide range of destructive acts, including
killing themselves in greater numbers than they ordinarily would.

Fatalistic Suicide   There is a little-mentioned fourth type of suicide—fatalistic—
that Durkheim discussed only in a footnote in *Suicide* (Besnard, 1993). Whereas
anomic suicide is more likely to occur in situations in which regulation is too weak,
fatalistic suicide is more likely to occur when regulation is excessive. Durkheim described those who are more likely to commit fatalistic suicide as "persons with futures
pitilessly blocked and passions violently choked by oppressive discipline"
(1897/1951:276). The classic example is the slave who takes his own life because of the
hopelessness associated with the oppressive regulation of his every action. Too much
regulation—oppression—unleashes currents of melancholy that, in turn, cause a rise in
the rate of fatalistic suicide.

A Group Mind?

Given the emphasis on norms, values, and culture in contemporary sociology, we have
little difficulty accepting Durkheim's interest in nonmaterial social facts. It is true that

the concept of social currents does cause us a few problems. Particularly troublesome is the idea of a set of independent social currents "coursing" through the social world as if they are somehow suspended in a social void. This problem has led many to criticize Durkheim for having a group-mind orientation (Catlin, 1964:xxii–xxiii; see also Pope, 1976:192–194). Those who accuse Durkheim of having such a perspective argue that he accorded nonmaterial social facts an autonomous existence, separate from actors. But cultural phenomena cannot float by themselves in a social void, and Durkheim was well aware of this.[2]

As a specific component of the supposed group mind, the notion of social currents can be defended as an unfortunately named, but otherwise now widely accepted, part of the cultural world. In more contemporary terms, social currents can be viewed as sets of meanings that are shared intersubjectively by members of a collectivity. As such, they cannot be found in the mind of any given individual, but they are mentally shared by the set of actors in the collectivity. To take one of Durkheim's examples, a social current of "languorous melancholy" cannot be deduced from any one individual, but it can be derived from the mood of a significant segment of the total population. These collective "moods," or social currents, vary from one collectivity to another, with the result that there is variation in the rate of certain behaviors, including suicide. Similarly, as these collective "moods" change, the rates of suicide also may change (Douglas, 1967:42).

In defense of Durkheim at a more general level, it must be argued that Durkheim had a very modern conception of nonmaterial social facts that encompasses what we now call norms, values, culture, and a variety of shared social-psychological phenomena (Emirbayer, 1996). Such a conception is not susceptible to the group-mind charge, but its defense is complicated, because in order to lay out a separate domain for sociology, Durkheim often made some highly exaggerated claims about social facts. As we saw earlier in this chapter, Durkheim often talked as if social facts were rigidly separated from psychological facts, and such a separation would be supportive of the group-mind argument. However, in other places Durkheim admitted that this was an artificial dichotomy; in other words, nonmaterial social facts are firmly anchored in the mental processes of individuals (1893/1964:350; see also Lukes, 1972:16).

Durkheim put to rest once and for all the group-mind thesis:

> Either the *collective conscience* floats like a void, a kind of indescribable absolute, or else it is connected to the rest of the world by a substratum upon which, consequently, it is dependent. Moreover, what can this substratum be made up of, if it is not the members of society as they are combined socially?
>
> (Durkheim, cited in Giddens, 1972:159)

It seems that Durkheim, outside of some outrageous arguments made to justify a niche for the fledgling sociology, offered an eminently reasonable position on nonmaterial social facts. Durkheim began with an interest in this level, retained it throughout his career,

---

[2]Some Durkheimians would argue that Durkheim did offer, in many places, ideas that reflect a belief in something like a group mind.

and, if anything, grew even more interested in it in his later years. This increasing concern can best be seen in *The Elementary Forms of Religious Life,* published in 1912.

RELIGION

As we have seen, Durkheim felt the need to focus on material manifestations of nonmaterial social facts (for example, law in *The Division of Labor* and suicide rates in *Suicide*). But in *The Elementary Forms of Religious Life,* Durkheim felt comfortable enough to address nonmaterial social facts, in particular religion, more directly.[3] Religion is, in fact, the ultimate nonmaterial social fact, and an examination of it allowed him to shed new light on this entire aspect of his theoretical system. Religion has what Durkheim calls a "dynamogenic" quality; that is, it has the capacity not only to dominate individuals but also to elevate them above their ordinary abilities and capacities (R. Jones, 1986).

Although the research reported in *The Elementary Forms* is not Durkheim's own, he felt it necessary, given his commitment to empirical science, to embed his thinking on religion in published data. The major sources of his data were studies of a primitive Australian tribe, the Arunta. Durkheim felt it important to study religion within such a primitive setting for several reasons. First, he believed that it is much easier to gain insight into the essential nature of religion in a primitive setting than in more modern society. Religious forms in primitive society could be "shown in all their nudity," and it would require "only the slightest effort to lay them open" (Durkheim, 1912/1965:18). Second, the ideological systems of primitive religions are less well developed than those of modern religions, with the result that there is less obfuscation. As Durkheim put it, "That which is accessory or secondary . . . has not yet come to hide the principal elements. All is reduced to that which is indispensable, to that without which there could be no religion" (1912/1965:18). Third, whereas religion in modern society takes diverse forms, in primitive society there is "intellectual and moral conformity" (Durkheim, 1912/1965:18). As a result, religion can be studied in primitive society in its most pristine form. Finally, although Durkheim studied primitive religion, it was not because of his interest in that religious form per se. Rather, he studied it in order "to lead to an understanding of the religious nature of man, that is to say, to show us an essential and permanent aspect of humanity" (Durkheim, 1912/1965:13). More specifically, Durkheim examined primitive religion to shed light on religion in modern society.

Given the uniform and ubiquitous character of religion in primitive societies, we may equate that religion with the collective conscience. That is, religion in primitive society is an all-encompassing collective morality. But as society develops and grows more specialized, religion comes to occupy an increasingly narrow domain. Instead of being the collective conscience in modern society, religion becomes simply one of a number of collective representations. Although it expresses some collective sentiments, other institutions (for example, law and science) come to express other aspects of the collective morality. Although Durkheim recognized that religion per se comes to occupy an

---

[3]Alexander (1988a:11) argues that it is this work that forms the basis of renewed contemporary interest in cultural studies. R. Collins (1988b:108) sees it as his "most important book."

ever narrower domain, he also contended that most, if not all, of the various collective representations of modern society have their origin in the all-encompassing religion of primitive society.

Sacred and Profane

The ultimate question for Durkheim was the source of modern religion. Because specialization and the ideological smoke screen make it impossible to study directly the roots of religion in modern society, Durkheim addressed the issue in the context of primitive society. The question is: Where does primitive (and modern) religion come from? Operating from his basic methodological position that only one social fact can cause another social fact, Durkheim concluded that society is the source of all religion (Ossio, 1997). Society (through individuals) creates religion by defining certain phenomena as sacred and others as profane. Those aspects of social reality that are defined as *sacred*— that is, that are set apart and deemed forbidden—form the essence of religion. The rest are defined as *profane*—the everyday, the commonplace, the utilitarian, the mundane aspects of life. The sacred brings out an attitude of reverence, respect, mystery, awe, and honor. The respect accorded to certain phenomena transforms them from the profane to the sacred.

The differentiation between the sacred and the profane, and the elevation of some aspects of social life to the sacred level, are necessary but not sufficient conditions for the development of religion. Three other conditions are needed. First, there must be the development of a set of religious beliefs. These *beliefs* are "the representations which express the nature of sacred things and the relations which they sustain, either with each other or with profane things" (Durkheim, 1912/1965:56). Second, a set of religious *rites* is necessary. These are "the rules of conduct which prescribe how a man should comport himself in the presence of these sacred objects" (Durkheim, 1912/1965:56). Finally, a religion requires a *church,* or a single overarching moral community. The interrelationships among the sacred, beliefs, rites, and church led Durkheim to the following definition of a religion: *"A religion is a unified system of beliefs and practices which unite into one single moral community called a Church, all those who adhere to them"* (1912/1965:62).

Totemism

Durkheim's view that society is the source of religion shaped his examination of totemism among the Australian Arunta. *Totemism* is a religious system in which certain things, particularly animals and plants, come to be regarded as sacred and as emblems of the clan. Durkheim viewed totemism as the simplest, most primitive form of religion. It is paralleled by a similarly primitive form of social organization, the *clan.* If Durkheim could have shown that the clan is the source of totemism, he could have demonstrated his argument that society is at the root of religion. Here is the way that Durkheim made this argument:

> A religion so closely connected to a social system surpassing all others in simplicity may well be regarded as the most elementary religion we can possibly know. If we succeed in

discovering the origins of the beliefs which we have just analyzed, we shall very probably discover at the same time the causes leading to the rise of the religious sentiment in
humanity.

(Durkheim, 1912/1965:195)

Although a clan may have a large number of totems, Durkheim was not inclined to
view these as a series of separate, fragmentary beliefs about specific animals or plants.
Instead, he tended to view them as an interrelated set of ideas that give the clan a more
or less complete representation of the world. The plant or animal is not the source of
totemism; it merely represents that source. The totems are the material representations
of the immaterial force that is at their base. And that immaterial force is none other than
the now-familiar collective conscience of society:

> Totemism is the religion, not of such and such animals or men or images, but of an anony-
> mous and impersonal force, found in each of these beings but not to be confounded with
> any of them. . . . Individuals die, generations pass and are replaced by others; but this
> force always remains actual, living and the same. It animates the generations of today as
> it animated those of yesterday and as it will those of tomorrow.
>
> (Durkheim, 1912/1965:217)

Totemism, and more generally religion, is derived from the collective morality and becomes itself an impersonal force. It is not simply a series of mythical animals, plants,
personalities, spirits, or gods.

Collective Effervescence

The collective conscience is the source of religion, but where does the collective conscience itself come from? In Durkheim's view, it comes from only one source—society.
In the primitive case examined by Durkheim, this meant that the clan is the ultimate
source of religion: "Religious force is nothing other than the collective and anonymous
force of the clan" (1912/1965:253). How does the clan create totemism? The answer
lies in a central but little discussed component of Durkheim's conceptual arsenal—
collective effervescence (Ono, 1996; Tiryakian, 1995).

The notion of collective effervescence is not well spelled out in any of Durkheim's
works. He seemed to have in mind, in a general sense, the great moments in history
when a collectivity is able to achieve a new and heightened level of collective exaltation
that in turn can lead to great changes in the structure of society. The Reformation and
the Renaissance would be examples of historical periods when collective effervescence
had a marked effect on the structure of society. Durkheim also argued that it is out of
collective effervescence that religion arises: "It is in the midst of these effervescent social environments and out of this effervescence itself that the religious idea seems to be
born" (1912/1965:250). During periods of collective effervescence, the clan members
create totemism.

In sum, totemism is the symbolic representation of the collective conscience, and the
collective conscience, in turn, is derived from society. Therefore, society is the source
of the collective conscience, religion, the concept of God, and ultimately everything that
is sacred (as opposed to profane). In a very real sense, then, we can argue that the sacred

(and ultimately God, as something sacred) and society are one and the same. This is fairly clear-cut in primitive society. It remains true today, even though the relationship is greatly obscured by the complexities of modern society.

SOCIAL REFORMISM

Durkheim was a social reformer who saw problems in modern society as temporary aberrations and not as inherent difficulties (Fenton, 1984:45; Hearn, 1997). In taking this position, he stood in opposition to both the conservatives and the radicals of his day. Conservatives like Louis de Bonald and Joseph de Maistre saw no hope in modern society and sought instead a return to a more primitive type of existence. Radicals like the Marxists of Durkheim's time agreed that the world could not be reformed, but they hoped that a revolution would bring into existence socialism and communism. In contrast, Durkheim, following up on his analogy between social and biological processes, argued that the problems of the day were "pathologies" that could be "cured" by the "social physician" who recognized the moral nature of the modern world's problems and undertook structural reforms to alleviate them. For example, in *The Division of Labor*, Durkheim talked of three abnormal, or pathological, forms of the division of labor. These are caused by temporary or transient forces and are not inherent in modern society. The pathologies Durkheim described are anomie, inequality in the structure of the work world (the wrong people in the wrong positions), and inadequate organization (incoherence) in the work world.

Durkheim was a reformist, not a radical or a revolutionary. Thus, when he devoted a book to socialism, it was to study it as a social fact, not to outline a revolutionary doctrine (Durkheim, 1928/1962):

> Our reasoning is not at all revolutionary. We are even, in a sense, essentially conservative, since we deal with social facts as such, recognize their flexibility, but conceive them as deterministic rather than arbitrary. How much more dangerous is the doctrine which sees in social phenomena only the results of unrestrained manipulation, which can in an instant, by a simple dialectical artifice, be completely upset.
> (Durkheim, 1895/1964:xxxviii–xxxix)[4]

More specific to a communist revolution, Durkheim said:

> Let us suppose that by a miracle the whole system of property is entirely transformed overnight and that on the collectivist formula the means of production are taken out of the hands of the individual and made over absolutely to collective ownership. All the problems around us that we are debating today will still persist in their entirety.
> (Durkheim, 1957:30)

Occupational Associations

The major reform that Durkheim proposed for social pathologies was the development of occupational associations. In looking at the organizations of his time, Durkheim did

---

[4]Not only was Durkheim treating us to his own conservative politics, but he also was attacking the revolutionary theories of Marx and Marx's followers.

not believe that there was a basic conflict of interest among the various types of people found within them—owners, managers, and workers. In this, of course, he was taking a position diametrically opposed to that of Marx, who saw an essential conflict of interest between the owners and the workers. Durkheim believed that such a clash was occurring at that time because the various people involved lacked a common morality and that the lack of morality was traceable to the lack of an integrative structure. He suggested that the structure that was needed to provide this integrative morality was the occupational association, which would encompass "all the agents of the same industry united and organized into a single group" (Durkheim, 1893/1964:5). Such an organization was deemed to be different from, and superior to, such organizations as labor unions and employer associations, which in Durkheim's view served only to intensify the differences between owners, managers, and workers. Involved in a common organization, people in these categories would recognize their common interests as well as their common need for an integrative moral system. That moral system, with its derived rules and laws, would serve to counteract the tendency toward atomization in modern society as well as help stop the decline in significance of collective morality.

Cult of the Individual

In the end, structural reform was subordinated in Durkheim's mind to changes in the collective morality. He believed that the essential problems of modern society were moral in nature and that the only real solution lay in reinforcing the strength of the collective morality. Although Durkheim recognized that there was no returning to the powerful collective conscience of societies characterized by mechanical solidarity, he felt that a modern, although weakened, version of it was emerging. He labeled the modern form of the collective conscience the *cult of the individual* (Chriss, 1993a; Tole, 1993). This was a curious concept for Durkheim, because it seems to fuse the seemingly antagonistic forces of morality and individualism. Embedded in this concept is the idea that individualism is becoming the moral system of modern society:

> For Durkheim, this was an ethic of individualism that grounded human freedom in communal solidarity, an ethic which affirmed the rights of the individual in relation to the well-being of all citizens rather than to individual achievement in the pursuit of self-interest. It was an ethic that represented the true expression of the ideals of individualism, and for Durkheim was the only solution to the problem of how the individual could remain "more solidary while becoming more autonomous."
>
> (Tole, 1993:26)

Elevated to the status of a moral system, individualism was acceptable to Durkheim. What he continued to oppose was egoism, because this is individualism without a collective base; it is rampant hedonism. Presumably, by following a morality of individualism, the actor would be able to keep his or her passions in check. Ironically, paradoxically, and ultimately a bit unsatisfactorily, Durkheim proposed the cult of the individual as the solution to modern egoism. It appears that Durkheim came to recognize that there was no stemming the tide of individualism in modern society, so rather than continue to fight it, he made the best of a bad situation (judged by his moral principles) by elevating at least some forms of individualism to the level of a moral system. One of the many problems with this view is the virtual impossibility of differentiating in real life between actions based on moral individualism and those based on egoism. However, Durkheim might argue that it is possible to distinguish between people guided by a morality which requires them to give due recognition to the inherent dignity, rights, and freedom of the individual and people who are simply acting to promote their own egotistically defined self-interest.

THE ACTOR IN DURKHEIM'S THOUGHT

Durkheim's often overly zealous arguments for sociology and against psychology have led many to argue that he had little to offer on the human actor and the nature of action (Lukes, 1972:228). Many contend that Durkheim had little to say about individual consciousness (Nisbet, 1974:32; Pope, 1975:368, 374), because he did not feel that it was amenable to scientific analysis. As Robert Nisbet put it:

> We cannot go to internal states of mind. . . . Consciousness, though real enough, will not serve the austere tests of scientific method. If we are to study mere phenomena in an objective fashion, we must substitute for the internal fact of consciousness an external index which symbolizes it and study the former in light of the latter.
>
> (Nisbet, 1974:52; see also Pope, 1976:10–11)

Although there is some truth to this claim, it grossly exaggerates the reality to be found in Durkheim's work. Although Durkheim may have made statements against the study of consciousness, he did deal with it in a variety of places and ways. Nevertheless, it is true that he treated the actor, and the actor's mental processes, as secondary factors, or more commonly as dependent variables to be explained by the independent and focal factors—social facts.

Durkheim was critical of dealing with consciousness, but he demonstrated his awareness of the significance of mental processes and even integrated them directly into his work. Although he made a similar point in several places (for example, Durkheim, 1897/1951:315), the following is Durkheim's clearest statement of his interest in mental processes:

> In general, we hold that sociology has not completely achieved its task so long as it has not penetrated into the mind . . . of the individual in order to relate the institutions it seeks to explain to their psychological conditions. . . . Man is for us less a point of departure than a point of arrival.
>
> (Durkheim, cited in Lukes, 1972:498–499)

Durkheim focused on "external" facts—suicide rates, laws, and so forth—because they are open to scientific analysis, but he did not deem such a macroscopic focus sufficient in itself. The ultimate goal was to integrate an understanding of mental processes into his theoretical system. This is manifest, for example, in his work on suicide, in which social causes are linked to subjective states. Even though he never quite achieved an adequate integration, he did address the issue of consciousness in several different ways.

Assumptions about Human Nature

We may gain insight into Durkheim's views on consciousness by examining his assumptions about human nature. Despite having made a number of crucial assumptions about human nature, Durkheim denied that he had done so. He argued that he did *not* begin by postulating a certain conception of human nature in order to deduce a sociology from it. Instead, he said that it was from sociology that he sought an increasing understanding of human nature. However, Durkheim may have been less than honest with us, and perhaps even with himself.

Durkheim did in fact identify a number of components of human nature. At a basic level, he accepted the existence of biological drives. But of greater significance to sociology, he acknowledged the importance of social feelings, including "love, affection, sympathetic concern, and associated phenomena" (Wallwork, 1972:28). Durkheim viewed people as naturally social, for "if men were not naturally inclined toward their fellows, the whole fabric of society, its customs and institutions, would never arise" (Wallwork, 1972:29–30). However, these sentiments did not play an active role in his sociology, and he therefore relegated them to psychology. Another of Durkheim's basic assumptions, which received only scant attention from him, is the idea that people are able to think: "Men differ from animals, Durkheim contends, precisely because images and ideas intervene between innate inclinations and behavior" (Wallwork, 1972:30).

Passions   Whereas the preceding are of marginal significance to his work, another of Durkheim's assumptions about human nature—one that we have already encountered—may be viewed as the basis of his entire sociology. That assumption is that people are endowed with a variety of egoistic drives that, if unbridled, constitute a threat to themselves as well as to society. To Durkheim, people possess an array of passions. If these passions are unrestrained, they multiply to the point where the individual is enslaved by them. This led Durkheim to his curious (on the surface) definition of *freedom* as external control over passions. People are free when their passions are constrained by external forces, and the most general and most important of these forces is the common morality. It can be argued that Durkheim's entire theoretical edifice, especially his emphasis on collective morality, was erected on this basic assumption about people's passions. As Durkheim put it, "Passion individualizes, yet it also enslaves. Our sensations are essentially individual; yet we are more personal the more we are freed from our senses and able to think and act with concepts" (1912/1965:307–308). This same issue is manifest in the differentiation Durkheim made between body and soul and the eternal conflict between them (1914/1973). The body represents the passions; the soul stands for civilization's common morality. "They mutually contradict and deny each other" (Durkheim, 1914/1973:152). Clearly, Durkheim wished this conflict to be resolved in the direction of the soul rather than of the body: "It is civilization that has made man what he is; it is what distinguishes him from the animal: man is man only because he is civilized" (1914/1973:149).

For Durkheim, freedom came from without rather than from within. This requires a collective conscience to constrain the passions. "Morality begins with disinterest, with attachment to something other than ourselves" (Durkheim, 1914/1973:151). But freedom, or autonomy, has another sense in Durkheim's work. That is, freedom is also derived from the internalization of a common morality that emphasizes the significance and independence of the individual (Lukes, 1972:115, 131). However, in both senses freedom is a characteristic of society, not of individuals. Here, as elsewhere, we see the degree to which Durkheim emphasized nonmaterial social facts (in this case "moral individualism") over mental processes.

Individual Representations   We can also include *individual representations* within Durkheim's assumptions about human nature. Whereas collective representations are created by the interaction of people, individual representations are formed by the interaction of brain cells. Individual representations were relegated to psychology, as were many other aspects of Durkheim's thoughts on consciousness. This is the portion of the mental process that Durkheim was unwilling to explore, and it is on this that he is most vulnerable to attack. George Homans (1969), for example, argued that Durkheim exhibited a very limited conception of psychology by confining it to the study of instincts. The psychology of today goes far beyond the study of instincts and encompasses a number of social phenomena that Durkheim would have seen as part of sociology. Homans concluded that "sociology is surely not a corollary of the kind of psychology Durkheim had in mind" (1969:18). However, it is much harder, if not impossible, in Homans's view, to clearly separate sociology from the psychology of today.

Homo Duplex   Running through much of this discussion (body and soul; individual and collective representations) is a sense of the duality of human nature, of *homo duplex* (Shilling, 1997b). As Durkheim put it, "our inner life has something that is like a double center of gravity. On the one hand is our individuality—and, more particularly, our body in which it is based; on the other is everything in us that expresses something other than ourselves" (1914/1973:152). Not only do these dual states of consciousness exist within us, but they are mutually contradictory:

> It is not without reason, therefore, that man feels himself to be double: he actually is double. There are in him two classes of states of consciousness that differ from each other in origin and nature, and in the ends toward which they aim. One class merely expresses our organisms and the objects to which they are most directly related. Strictly individual, the states of consciousness of this class connect us only with ourselves, and we can no more detach them from us than we can detach ourselves from our bodies. The states of consciousness of the other class, on the contrary, come to us from society; they transfer society into us and connect us with something that surpasses us. Being collective, they are impersonal; they turn us toward ends that we hold in common with other men; it is through them and them alone that we can communicate with others. It is, therefore, quite true that we are made up of two parts, and are like two beings, which, although they are closely associated, are composed of very different elements and orient us in opposite directions.
>
> (Durkheim, 1914/1973:161–162)

Thus, we are led to live a double existence with the perpetual tension that this creates. Durkheim was most concerned with the need to strengthen the collective aspects of ourselves in order to better control the excesses of our individual passions.

Socialization and Moral Education

Given his views on innate human passions and the need to constrain them by common morality, it should come as no surprise that Durkheim was very much interested in the *internalization* of social morals through education and, more generally, through socialization. Social morality exists primarily at the cultural level, but it is also internalized by the individual. In Durkheim's words, common morality "penetrates us" and "forms part of us" (Lukes, 1972:131).

Durkheim was not concerned primarily with the issue of internalization but rather with how it bore upon the cultural and structural problems of his day (Pope, 1976:195). He did not specify how the common morality was internalized. He was much more concerned with what seemed to be a lessening of the power of this internalization of morality in contemporary society. The essence of the matter for Durkheim was the decline in the degree to which social facts exercise constraint upon consciousness. As Robert Nisbet put it, "Durkheim would never really abandon the idea that the Western society he knew was undergoing a major crisis and that the crisis consisted at bottom in a pathological loosening of moral authority upon the lives of individuals" (1974:192). Durkheim put it this way: "History records no crisis as serious as that in which European societies have been involved for more than a century. Collective discipline in its traditional form has lost its authority" (1973:101). Durkheim's interest in anomie in both *Suicide* and *The Division of Labor in Society* can be seen as a manifestation of this concern.

Much of Durkheim's work on education, and socialization in general, can be seen in light of this concern for moral decay and possible reforms to halt the spread of it. *Education* and *socialization* were defined by Durkheim as the processes by which the individual learns the ways of a given group or society—acquires the physical, intellectual, and, most important to Durkheim, moral tools needed to function in society (Durkheim, 1922/1956:71). Moral education has three important aspects (Wallwork, 1972).

First, its goal is to provide individuals with the *discipline* they need to restrain the passions that threaten to engulf them:

> The totality of moral regulations really forms about each person an imaginary wall, at the foot of which a multitude of human passions simply die without being able to go further. For the same reason—that they are contained—it becomes possible to satisfy them. But if at any point this barrier weakens, human forces—until now restrained—pour tumultuously through the open breach; once loosed, they find no limits where they can or must stop.
>
> (Durkheim, 1973:42)

More specifically, on the education of children, Durkheim says that only through discipline "and by means of it alone are we able to teach the child to rein in his desires, to set limits to his appetites of all kinds, to limit, and through limitation, to define the goals of his activity. This limitation is the condition of happiness and of moral health" (1973:43–44).

Second, individuals are provided with a sense of autonomy, but it is a characteristically atypical kind of autonomy in which "the child understands the reasons why the rules prescribing certain forms of behavior should be 'freely desired,' that is to say, 'willingly accepted' by virtue of 'enlightened assent' " (Wallwork, 1972:127).

Finally, the process of socialization aims at developing a sense of devotion to society and to its moral system. These aspects of moral education are efforts to combat the pathological loosening of the grip of collective morality on the individual in modern society.

At the most general level, Durkheim was concerned with the way in which collective morality constrains people both externally and internally. In one sense, nonmaterial social facts stand outside people and shape their thoughts (and actions). Of course, social facts cannot act on their own but only through their agents. Of greater importance, however, is the degree to which individuals constrain themselves by internalizing social morality. As Durkheim put it, "The collective force is not entirely outside of us; it does not act upon us wholly from without; but rather, since society cannot exist except in and through individual consciousness, this force must also penetrate us and organize itself within us" (1912/1965:240). In addition to making clear the process of internalization, the preceding quotation also shows once again that Durkheim rejected the idea of a group mind, for he stated that collective forces can exist only in individual consciousness. Ernest Wallwork did an excellent job of clarifying the importance of the internalization of morality in Durkheim's system:

> A normal mind, Durkheim observes, cannot consider moral maxims without considering them as obligatory. Moral rules have an "imperative character"; they "exercise a sort of ascendancy over the will which feels constrained to conform to them." This constraint is not to be confused with physical force or compulsion; the will is not forced to conform to the norms it entertains even if these norms are enforced by public opinion. Moral "constraint does not consist in an exterior and mechanical pressure; it has a more intimate and psychological character." But this intimate, psychological sense of obligation is, nevertheless, none other than the authority of public opinion which penetrates, like the air we breathe, into the deepest recesses of our being.
>
> (Wallwork, 1972:38)

Durkheim offered a specific example of internal constraint in his study on religion:

> If [an individual] acts in a certain way towards the totemic beings, it is not only because the forces resident in them are physically redoubtable, but because he feels himself morally obliged to act thus; he has the feeling that he is obeying an imperative, that he is fulfilling a duty.
>
> (Durkheim, 1912/1965:218)

All these concerns can be seen in the context of the constraining effect of collective morality on the actor. Whether the constraint is external or internal, it still comes down to collective morality controlling the thoughts and actions of individuals.

Durkheim's limited thoughts on consciousness led many people to assume that his ideal actor is one who is almost wholly controlled from without—a total conformist. Although there is much to recommend this view—and some modern sociologists in following Durkheim seem to have adopted this position—Durkheim himself did not subscribe to such an extreme view of the actor: "Conformity must not be pushed to the point where it completely subjugates the intellect. Thus it does not follow from a belief in the need for discipline that it must be blind and slavish" (cited in Giddens, 1972:113). Durkheim does see a role for individuals: they are all not simply mirror images of collective ideas; there is individuality. Each of us has unique temperaments, habits, and so

forth. "Each of us puts his own mark on them [collective ideas]; and this accounts for the fact that each person has his own particular way of thinking . . . about
the rules of common morality" (Durkheim, 1914/1973:161; see also Durkheim
1913–14/1983:91–92). Although Durkheim left open the possibility of individuality, the thrust of his work is in the direction of outlining external constraints on actors
and, furthermore, the desirability of such constraint.

Dependent Variables

In Durkheim's works, consciousness most often occupies the position of a dependent
variable, determined by various material and especially nonmaterial social facts.

> Durkheim viewed sociologically relevant subjective states as the product of social causes.
> They "are like prolongations . . . inside individuals" . . . of the social causes on which they
> depend. They may enter sociological explanations as effects, but never as causes. Appeal
> to subjective states as causal agents, according to Durkheim, threatened the legitimacy of
> sociology's claim to scientific status by reducing it to psychology.
>
> (Pope, Cohen, and Hazelrigg, 1975:419)

Although we will discuss several such dependent variables, it should be made clear that
Durkheim usually dealt with them in only a vague and cursory way. In *Suicide,* for example, Durkheim was quite uncertain about how social currents affect individual consciousness and how changed consciousness, in turn, leads to a heightened likelihood of
suicide (Pope, 1976:191). The same criticism applies to every other treatment by
Durkheim of consciousness.

   In *The Division of Labor,* consciousness was dealt with indirectly, but it is clear that
it is a dependent variable. That is, the sense of the argument is that changes at the cultural and societal levels lead to changes in the processes of individual consciousness. In
a society with mechanical solidarity, individual consciousness is limited and highly constrained by a powerful collective conscience. In a society with organic solidarity, individual potentials expand, as does individual freedom. But again, although this sense of
consciousness as a dependent variable is there, it was left largely implicit by Durkheim.
In *Suicide,* however, the status of consciousness as a dependent variable is much clearer.
Schematically, the main independent variable is collective morality, and the ultimate dependent variable is suicide rate, but intervening is another set of dependent variables
that can only be mental states. Steven Lukes, in the following statement about "weak
points" in the individual, implied the mental level: "The currents impinge from the outside on suicide-prone individuals at their 'weak points' " (1972:214).

   Lukes (1972:216–217) went further on this issue and argued that there is a social-
psychological theory beneath the "aggressively sociologistic language" found in *Suicide.* One part of that theory is the belief that individuals need to be attached to social
goals. Another aspect is that individuals cannot become so committed to such goals that
they lose all personal autonomy. Finally, as we have discussed before, there was
Durkheim's belief that individuals possess passions and that they can be contented and
free only if these passions are restrained from without.

   We find in *Suicide* specific conscious states associated with each of the three main
types of suicide:

> These subjective states, themselves effects of given social conditions, impel the individual to suicide. . . . The egoistic suicide is characterized by a general depression in the form either of melancholic languor or Epicurean indifference. . . . Anomic suicide is accompanied by anger, disappointment, irritation, and exasperated weariness . . . while the altruistic suicide may experience a calm feeling of duty, the mystic's enthusiasm, or peaceful courage.
>
> (Pope, 1976:197)

Durkheim perceived well-defined states of consciousness accompanying each form of suicide. It is clear that these were peripheral interests for him, as he maintained a consistently large-scale focus. Even such an ardent supporter as Nisbet wished that Durkheim had given more attention to individual consciousness: "Admittedly, one might wish that Durkheim had given more attention to the specific mechanisms by which collective representations in society are translated, in distinctly human, often creative ways, into the individual representations that reflect man's relationship to society" (1974:115). Lukes makes the same point: "[Durkheim's] exclusive concentration on the society end of the schema, on the impact of social conditions on individuals rather than the way individuals perceive, interpret, and respond to social conditions, led him to leave inexplicit and unexamined the social-psychological assumptions on which his theories rested" (1972:35).

Mental Categories   We can find a specific example of this tendency to accord priority to the level of society in Durkheim and Marcel Mauss's[5] work on the impact of the structure of society on the form of individual thought. Basically, Durkheim (and Mauss) argued that the form society takes affects the form that thought patterns take. Contesting those who believe that mental categories shape the social world, they believed that the social world shapes mental categories: "Far from it being the case . . . that the social relations of men are based on logical relations between things, in reality it is the former which have provided the prototype for the latter" (Durkheim and Mauss, 1903/1963:82). Although specific large-scale structures (for example, family structure and economic and political systems) play a role in shaping logical categories, Durkheim and Mauss devoted most of their attention to the effect of society as a whole:

> Society was not simply a model which classificatory thought followed; it was its own divisions which served as divisions for the system of classification. The first logical categories were social categories; the first classes of things were classes of men. . . . It was because men were grouped, and thought of themselves in the form of groups, that in their ideas they grouped other things, and in the beginning the two modes of grouping were merged to the point of being indistinct.
>
> (Durkheim and Mauss, 1903/1963:82–83)

Durkheim's emphasis on large-scale phenomena is well illustrated by this discussion of the impact of society on logical categories. However, Durkheim did not analyze the corresponding process—the way in which the operation of mental categories, in turn, shapes the structures of society.

---

[5]Marcel Mauss, Durkheim's nephew and a scholar of some note, coauthored the material on mental categories with Durkheim.

Weaknesses in Durkheim's Microsociology

To create a more adequate sociology, Durkheim had to do more with consciousness than treat it as an unexplored dependent variable. An almost total focus on large-scale phenomena leaves out important elements of an adequate sociological model. Lukes made some telling points in his discussion of *Suicide*. He argued, quite rightly, that an adequate explanation of suicide cannot stop with an examination of social currents. In his view, "Explaining suicide—and explaining suicide rates—*must* involve explaining why people commit it" (Lukes, 1972:221; italics added). But Durkheim was wrong in assuming that consciousness is not open to scientific inquiry and explanation. Such inquiry can and must be undertaken if we are to go beyond partial theories of social life. Nothing is solved by simply acknowledging the existence of consciousness and refusing to examine it. Durkheim's commitment to a narrow view of science led him astray, as did his tendency toward making radically sociologistic statements that rule out recourse to consciousness:

> He need only have claimed that "social" facts cannot be wholly explained in terms of "individual" facts; instead he claimed that they can only be explained in terms of social facts. . . . It would have been enough to have claimed that no social phenomenon, indeed few human activities, can either be identified or satisfactorily explained without reference, explicit or implicit, to social factors.
>
> (Lukes, 1972:20)

Durkheim also failed to give consciousness an active role in the social process. People are in general controlled by social forces in his system; they do not actively control those systems. Thus, Wallwork contended that "the principal weakness . . . is Durkheim's failure to consider *active* moral judgment" (1972:65; italics added). Durkheim gave too little independence to actors (Pope and Cohen, 1978:1364). Actors can reject some, most, or perhaps even all of the moral principles to which they are exposed. When Durkheim did talk of autonomy, it was in terms of the acceptance of moral norms of autonomy. Individuals seem capable of accepting moral constraint and of controlling themselves only through the internalization of such norms. But as Wallwork pointed out, autonomy has a much more active component: "Autonomy also involves willful exploration, spontaneous initiative, competent mastery, and creative self-actualization. . . . The child must also be encouraged to exercise his own will, initiative, and creativity" (1972:148).

Indeed, research into cognitive processes, in part done by Jean Piaget, who was working in the Durkheimian tradition, indicates that individual creativity is an important component of social life. In summarizing the work of Piaget, Lawrence Kohlberg (who did research on the cognitive elements in moral development), and others, Wallwork said:

> In addition to cultural conditioning, the cognitive activity of the subject is necessary to constitute the experience. Piaget and Kohlberg conclude from their studies that the distinctive phenomenological character of moral experience is always as much a product of the cognitive construction of the subject as it is an accommodation to cultural conditioning by the subject.
>
> (Wallwork, 1972:67)

In other words, a more complete sociology requires a more creative actor and deeper insight into the creative processes.

Durkheim was weakest in his work on individual action and interaction. Implied in his system are various changes at this level resulting from changes at the level of large-scale social phenomena, but they are not detailed. For example, it seems clear that the nature of action and interaction is quite different in societies with mechanical rather than organic solidarity. The individual in a society with mechanical solidarity is likely to be enraged at a violation of the collective conscience and to act quickly and aggressively toward the violator. In contrast, an individual in a society with organic solidarity is more likely to take a more measured approach, such as calling the police or suing in the courts.[6] Similarly, in *Suicide* the assumption behind the study of changes in suicide rates is that the nature of individual action and interaction changes as a result of alterations in social currents. Suicide rates are used as cumulative measures of changes at the individual level, but the nature of these changes is not explored, at least not in any detail. Similar points could be made about Durkheim's other works, but the critical point is that individual action and interaction are largely unanalyzed in Durkheim's work.

EARLY AND LATE DURKHEIMIAN THEORY

There has been growing awareness in recent years of differences between Durkheim's early thinking (in, for example, *The Division of Labor*) and his later thinking as represented in the preceding discussion of his work on religion. Alexander describes the early work as having an "emphasis on external constraints and 'coercive social facts' on the one hand, and with positivistic, often quantitative methods on the other" (1988c:2). In other words, his early work tended to be highly structural and scientistic. In contrast, in his later work Durkheim tended to focus more on culture than on structure. His interest in religion in general—and more specifically in the distinction between the sacred and the profane, totemism, collective effervescence, symbols, and rituals—can be included under the heading of culture. It was the early Durkheimian perspective that tended to influence sociological theory (especially structural functionalism) first, but in recent years it is the later work that has grown in importance (Alexander, 1988a), especially with the rise of the sociology of culture and of cultural studies outside sociology.

Part of this later work is the previously discussed work by Durkheim and Mauss (1903/1963) on mental categories. It is interesting to note that this work was influential in the development of a line of French social theory that has run through structuralism to poststructuralism to postmodernism (see Chapter 2). These theories, especially poststructuralism and postmodernism, represent a critique of mainstream sociological theory and pose a profound threat to that theory. Thus, interestingly, while early Durkheimian theory helped spawn mainstream sociological theory, his later work helped create theoretical developments that threaten that mainstream. As Lemert says, Durkheim's early work "began an intellectual labor that, in addition to producing sociology itself, gave

---

[6]Although in some cases (for example, an assault on one's baby), people in both types of society are likely to react violently. Thus, to some degree, differences between the two societies are dependent on the nature of the crime.

rise in due course to another body of thought and moral concern that aims today, rightly or wrongly, to rethink the world Durkheim and his sociology helped invent" (1994a:92).

SUMMARY

Emile Durkheim offered a more coherent theory than any of the other classical socio-logical theorists. He articulated a rather clear theoretical orientation and used it in a va-riety of specific works. Supporters would say that the clarity of Durkheim's thinking stems from this coherence, whereas detractors might contend that the clarity is the result of the comparative simplicity of his theory. Whatever the case, it is certainly easier to convey the essence of Durkheim's thinking than that of the other classical theorists.

The heart of Durkheim's theory lies in his concept of social fact. Durkheim differ-entiated between two basic types of social facts—material and nonmaterial. Although they often occupied a place of causal priority in his theorizing, material social facts (for example, division of labor, dynamic density, and law) were not the most important large-scale forces in Durkheim's theoretical system. The most important focus for Durkheim was on nonmaterial social facts. He dealt with a number of them, including collective conscience, collective representations, and social currents.

Durkheim's study of suicide is a good illustration of the significance of nonmaterial social facts in his work. In his basic causal model, changes in nonmaterial social facts ul-timately cause differences in suicide rates. Durkheim differentiated among four types of suicide—egoistic, altruistic, anomic, and fatalistic—and showed how each is affected by different changes in social currents. The study of suicide was taken by Durkheim and his supporters as evidence that sociology has a legitimate place in the social sciences. After all, it was argued, if sociology could explain so individualistic an act as suicide, then it certainly could be used to explain other, less individual aspects of social life.

Given his focus on nonmaterial social facts and some unfortunate statements made in an effort to define a distinctive domain for sociology, Durkheim is sometimes accused of having a metaphysical, "group-mind" orientation. Despite some seemingly indefen-sible statements, Durkheim did not believe in a group mind and, in fact, had a very mod-ern conception of culture.

In his later work, Durkheim focused on another aspect of culture, religion. In his analysis of primitive religion, Durkheim sought to show the roots of religion in the social structure of society. It is society that defines certain things as sacred and others as profane. Durkheim demonstrated the social sources of religion in his analysis of primitive totemism and its roots in the social structure of the clan. Furthermore, totemism was seen as a specific form of the collective conscience as manifested in a primitive society. Its source, as well as the source of all collective products, lies in the process of collective effervescence. In the end, Durkheim argued that religion and society are one and the same, two manifestations of the same general process.

Because he identified society with God, and because he deified society, Durkheim did not urge social revolution. Instead, he should be seen as a social reformer interested in improving the functioning of society. Whereas Marx saw irreconcilable differences between capitalists and workers, Durkheim believed that these groups could be united in occupational associations. He urged that these associations be set up to restore some collective morality to the modern world and to cope with some of the curable patholo-gies of the modern division of labor. But in the end, such narrow, structural reforms could not really cope with the broader cultural problems that plague the modern world. Here Durkheim invested some hope in the curious modern system of collective moral-ity that he labeled the "cult of the individual."

Durkheim had comparatively little to say about micro-level phenomena, but this is not to say he had nothing to offer here. He had useful insights into human nature ("homo duplex"), socialization, and moral education. But micro-level phenomena are most often treated in his work as dependent variables determined by large-scale changes. Although Durkheim dealt with all major levels of social reality, he focused on the large-scale forces and their causal impact on the individual level.

The chapter closes with some reflections on the growing realization that there are great differences between Durkheim's early, more structural work and his later cultural turn. While the early work played a key role in the rise of mainstream sociological theories like structural functionalism, the later work has been instrumental in the devel-opment of theoretical perspectives (especially poststructuralism and postmodernism) that pose a profound threat to that mainstream.

7

MAX WEBER

METHODOLOGY
    History and Sociology
    Verstehen
    Causality
    Ideal Types
    Values
SUBSTANTIVE SOCIOLOGY
    What Is Sociology?
    Social Action
    Class, Status, and Party
    Structures of Authority
    Rationalization
    Religion and the Rise of Capitalism

Max Weber (1864–1920) is probably the best-known and most influential figure in sociological theory (Collins, 1985; Goldman, 1988, 1992, 1993; Kalberg, 1994, forthcoming; see Burger, 1993, for a review essay on a number of recent works).[1] Weber's work is so varied and subject to so many interpretations that it has influenced a wide array of sociological theories. It certainly had an influence on structural functionalism, especially through the work of Talcott Parsons. It has also come to be seen as important to the conflict tradition (R. Collins, 1975, 1990) and to critical theory, which was shaped almost as much by Weber's ideas as it was by Marx's orientation, as well as to Jurgen Habermas, major inheritor of the critical-theory tradition (Outhwaite, 1994). Symbolic interactionists have been affected by Weber's ideas on *verstehen,* as well as by others of Weber's ideas. Alfred Schutz, whom we will consider in Chapter 13, was powerfully affected by Weber's work on meanings and motives, and he, in turn, played a crucial role in the development of both phenomenology and ethnomethodology. Weber was and is a widely influential theorist.

We begin this chapter with a discussion of Weber's (1903–17/1949) ideas on the methodology of the social sciences (which remain remarkably relevant and fruitful even today) (Ringer, 1997:171). A clear understanding of these ideas is necessary in dealing with Weber's substantive and theoretical ideas. Weber was opposed to pure abstract theorizing. Instead, his theoretical ideas are embedded in his empirical, usually historical, research. Weber's methodology shaped his research, and the combination of the two lies at the base of his theoretical orientation.

---

[1]For a time, his position was threatened by the increase in interest in the work of Karl Marx, who was already much better known to those in other fields and to the general public. But with the demise of world communism, Weber's position of preeminence seems secure once again.

METHODOLOGY

History and Sociology

Weber tended to de-emphasize methodological issues. As Lassman and Velody put it, "Clearly Weber has no concern with methodology in the sense of rulebooks for correct practice. . . . His methodological essays are more in the nature of philosophical reflections upon the nature and significance of claims to historical and social knowledge" (1989:192). A discussion of even these general matters was viewed by Weber as "mainly a precondition of fruitful intellectual work" (1903–17/1949:115; see also Marianne Weber, 1975:309). Weber focused on substantive work: "Only by laying bare and solving *substantive problems* can sciences be established and their methods developed. On the other hand, purely epistemological and methodological reflections have never played the crucial role in such developments" (1903–17/1949:116).

To deal with Weber's methodology, we first must clarify his thinking on the relationship between history and sociology. Even though Weber was a student of, and took his first academic job in, law, his early career was dominated by an interest in history. In fact, his doctoral dissertations were historical studies of the Middle Ages and of Rome. In his later years, however, he identified more and more with sociology. It has been argued that it was in 1909, the year Weber started writing his massive *Economy and Society,* that he began to devote himself fully to sociology (R. Frank, 1976:13).

As Weber moved more in the direction of the relatively new field of sociology, he sought to clarify its relationship to the established field of history. Although Weber felt that each field needed the other, his view was that the task of sociology was to provide a needed "service" to history (Roth, 1976:307). In Weber's words, sociology performed only a "preliminary, quite modest task" (cited in R. Frank, 1976:21). Weber explained the difference between sociology and history: "Sociology seeks to formulate type concepts and generalized uniformities of empirical processes. This distinguishes it from history, which is oriented to the causal analysis and explanation of individual actions, structures, and personalities possessing cultural significance" (1921/1968:19). Despite this seemingly clear-cut differentiation, in his own work Weber was able to combine the two. His sociology was oriented to the development of clear concepts so that he could perform a causal analysis of historical phenomena. Weber defined his ideal procedure as "the sure imputation of individual concrete events occurring in historical reality *to concrete, historically* given causes through the study of precise empirical data which have been selected from specific points of view" (1903–17/1949:69). We can think of Weber as a historical sociologist.

Weber's thinking on sociology was profoundly shaped by a series of intellectual debates (*Methodenstreit*) raging in Germany during his time. The most important of these was over the issue of the relationship between history and science. At the poles in this debate were those (the positivists) who thought that history was composed of general (*nomothetic*) laws and those (the subjectivists) who reduced history to idiosyncratic (*idiographic*) actions and events. (The positivists thought that history could be like a natural science; the subjectivists saw the two as radically different.) For example, a nomothetic thinker would generalize about social revolutions, whereas an idiographic analyst would focus on the specific events leading up to the American Revolution.

Weber rejected both extremes and in the process developed a distinctive way of dealing with historical sociology.   In Weber's view, history is composed of unique empirical events; there can be no generalizations at the empirical level.   Sociologists must, therefore, separate the empirical world from the conceptual universe that they construct.   The concepts never completely capture the empirical world, but they can be used as heuristic tools for gaining a better understanding of reality.   With these concepts, sociologists can develop generalizations, but these generalizations are not history and must not be confused with empirical reality.

Although Weber was clearly in favor of generalizing, he also rejected those historians who sought to reduce history to a simple set of laws: "For the knowledge of historical phenomena in their concreteness, the most general laws, because they are devoid of content, are also the least valuable" (1903–17/1949:80).   For example, Weber rejected one historian (Wilhelm Roscher) who took as his task the search for the laws of the historical evolution of a people and who believed that all peoples went through a typical sequence of stages (1903–06/1975).   As Weber put it, "The reduction of empirical reality . . . to 'laws' is meaningless" (1903–17/1949:80).   In other terms: "A systematic science of culture . . . would be senseless in itself" (Weber, 1903–17/1949:84).   This view is reflected in various specific historical studies.   For example, in his study of ancient civilizations, Weber admitted that, although in some respects earlier times were precursors of things to come, "the long and continuous history of Mediterranean-European civilization does not show either closed cycles or linear progress.   Sometimes phenomena of ancient civilizations have disappeared entirely and then come to light again in an entirely new context" (1896–1906/1976:366).

In rejecting these opposing views of German historical scholarship, Weber fashioned his own perspective, which constituted a fusion of the two orientations.   Weber felt that history (that is, historical sociology) was appropriately concerned with both individuality *and* generality.   The unification was accomplished through the development and utilization of general concepts (what we later will call "ideal types") in the study of particular individuals, events, or societies.   These general concepts are to be used "to identify and define the individuality of each development, the characteristics which made the one conclude in a manner so different from that of the other.   Thus done, one can then determine the causes which led to the differences" (Weber, 1896–1906/1976:385).   In doing this kind of causal analysis, Weber rejected, at least at a conscious level, the idea of searching for a single causal agent throughout history.[2]   He instead used his conceptual arsenal to rank the various factors involved in a given historical case in terms of their causal significance (Roth, 1971).

Weber's views on historical sociology were shaped in part by the availability of, and his commitment to the study of, empirical historical data.   His was the first generation of scholars to have available reliable data on historical phenomena from many parts of the world (MacRae, 1974).   Weber was more inclined to immerse himself in these historical data than he was to dream up abstract generalizations about the basic thrust of

---

[2]Ironically, Weber did seem (as we will see later in this chapter) to argue in his substantive work that there was such a causal agent in society—rationalization.

MAX WEBER: A Biographical Sketch

Max Weber was born in Erfurt, Germany, on April 21, 1864, into a decidedly middle-class family. Important differences between his parents had a profound effect upon both his intellectual orientation and his psychological development. His father was a bureaucrat who rose to a relatively important political position. He was clearly a part of the political establishment and as a result eschewed any activity or idealism that would require personal sacrifice or threaten his position within the system. In addition, the senior Weber was a man who enjoyed earthly pleasures, and in this and many other ways he stood in sharp contrast to his wife. Max Weber's mother was a devout Calvinist, a woman who sought to lead an ascetic life largely devoid of the pleasures craved by her husband. Her concerns were more otherworldly; she was disturbed by the imperfections that were signs that she was not destined for salvation. These deep differences between the parents led to marital tension, and both the differences and the tension had an immense impact on Weber.

Because it was impossible to emulate both parents, Weber was presented with a clear choice as a child (Marianne Weber, 1975:62). He first seemed to opt for his father's orientation to life, but later he drew closer to his mother's approach. Whatever the choice, the tension produced by the need to choose between such polar opposites negatively affected Max Weber's psyche.

At age eighteen, Max Weber left home for a short time to attend the University of Heidelberg. Weber had already demonstrated intellectual precocity, but on a social level he entered Heidelberg shy and underdeveloped. However, that quickly changed after he gravitated toward his father's way of life and joined his father's old dueling fraternity. There he developed socially, at least in part because of the huge quantities of beer he consumed with his peers. In addition, he proudly displayed the dueling scars that were the trademarks of such fraternities. Weber not only manifested his identity with his father's way of life in these ways but also chose, at least for the time being, his father's career—the law.

After three terms, Weber left Heidelberg for military service, and in 1884 he returned to Berlin and to his parents' home to take courses at the University of Berlin. He remained there for most of the next eight years as he completed his studies, earned his Ph.D., became a lawyer (see Turner and Factor, 1994, for a discussion of the impact of legal thinking on Weber's theorizing) and started teaching at the University of Berlin. In the process, his in-

history. Although this led him to some important insights, it also created serious problems in understanding his work; he often got so involved in historical detail that he lost sight of the basic reasons for the historical study. In addition, the sweep of his historical studies encompassed so many epochs and so many societies that he could do little more than make rough generalizations (Roth, 1971). Despite these problems, Weber's commitment to the scientific study of empirical phenomena made him attractive to the developing discipline of sociology in the United States.

In sum, Weber believed that history was composed of an inexhaustible array of specific phenomena. To study these phenomena, it was necessary to develop a variety of concepts designed to be useful for research on the real world. As a general rule, al-

terests shifted more toward his lifelong concerns—economics, history, and sociology. During his eight years in Berlin, Weber was financially dependent on his father, a circumstance he progressively grew to dislike. At the same time, he moved closer to his mother's values, and his antipathy to his father increased. He adopted an ascetic life and plunged deeply into his work. For example, during one semester as a student, his work habits were described as follows: "He continues the rigid work discipline, regulates his life by the clock, divides the daily routine into exact sections for the various subjects, saves in his way, by feeding himself evenings in his room with a pound of raw chopped beef and four fried eggs" (Mitzman, 1969/1971:48; Marianne Weber, 1975:105). Thus Weber, following his mother, had become ascetic and diligent, a compulsive worker—in contemporary terms a "workaholic."

This compulsion for work led in 1896 to a position as professor of economics at Heidelberg. But in 1897, when Weber's academic career was blossoming, his father died following a violent argument between them. Shortly thereafter Weber began to manifest symptoms that were to culminate in a nervous breakdown. Often unable to sleep or to work, Weber spent the next six or seven years in near-total collapse. After a long hiatus, some of his powers began to return in 1903, but it was not until 1904, when he delivered (in the United States) his first lecture in six and a half years, that Weber was able to begin to return to active academic life. In 1904 and 1905, he published one of his best-known works, *The Protestant Ethic and the Spirit of Capitalism*. In this work, Weber announced the ascendance of his mother's religion on an academic level. Weber devoted much of his time to the study of religion, though he was not personally religious.

Although he continued to be plagued by psychological problems, after 1904 Weber was able to function, indeed to produce some of his most important work. In these years, Weber published his studies of the world's religions in world-historical perspective (for example, China, India, and ancient Judaism). At the time of his death (June 14, 1920), he was working on his most important work, *Economy and Society*. Although this book was published, and subsequently translated into many languages, it was unfinished.

In addition to producing voluminous writings in this period, Weber undertook a number of other activities. He helped found the German Sociological Society in 1910. His home became a center for a wide range of intellectuals, including sociologists such as Georg Simmel, Robert Michels and his brother Alfred, as well as the philosopher and literary critic Georg Lukács (Scaff, 1989:186–222). In addition, Weber was active politically and wrote essays on the issues of the day.

There was a tension in Weber's life and, more important, in his work, between the bureaucratic mind, as represented by his father, and his mother's religiosity. This unresolved tension permeates Weber's work as it permeated his personal life.

though Weber (as we will see) did not adhere to it strictly and neither do most sociologists and historians, the task of sociology was to develop these concepts, which history was to use in causal analyses of specific historical phenomena. In this way, Weber sought to combine the specific and the general in an effort to develop a science that did justice to the complex nature of social life.

Verstehen

Weber felt that sociologists had an advantage over natural scientists. That advantage resided in the sociologist's ability to *understand* social phenomena, whereas the natural scientist could not gain a similar understanding of the behavior of an atom or a chemical compound. The German word for understanding is *verstehen*. Weber's special use of the term *verstehen* in his historical research is one of his best-known, and most controversial, contributions to the methodology of contemporary sociology. As we clarify what Weber meant by *verstehen*, we will also underscore some of the problems involved in his conceptualization of it. The controversy surrounding the concept of *verstehen*, and some of the problems involved in interpreting what Weber meant, grows out of a general problem with Weber's methodological thoughts. As Thomas Burger argued, Weber was neither very sophisticated nor very consistent in his methodological pronouncements (1976; see also Hekman, 1983:26). He tended to be careless and imprecise because he felt that he was simply repeating ideas that were well known in his day among German historians. Furthermore, as pointed out above, Weber did not think too highly of methodological reflections.

Weber's thoughts on *verstehen* were relatively common among German historians of his day and were derived from a field known as *hermeneutics* (Mueller-Vollmer, 1985; Pressler and Dasilva, 1996). Hermeneutics was a special approach to the understanding and interpretation of published writings. Its goal was to understand the thinking of the author as well as the basic structure of the text. Weber and others (for example, Wilhelm Dilthey) sought to extend this idea from the understanding of texts to the understanding of social life:

> Once we have realized that the historical method is nothing more or less than the classical method of interpretation applied to overt action instead of to texts, a method aiming at identifying a human design, a "meaning" behind observable events, we shall have no difficulty in accepting that it can be just as well applied to human interaction as to individual actors. From this point of view all history is interaction, which has to be interpreted in terms of the rival plans of various actors.
>
> (Lachman, 1971:20)

In other words, Weber sought to use the tools of hermeneutics to understand actors, interaction, and indeed all of human history.[3]

One common misconception about *verstehen* is that it is simply the use of "intuition" by the researcher. Thus many critics see it as a "soft," irrational, subjective research methodology. However, Weber categorically rejected the idea that *verstehen* involved simply intuition, sympathetic participation, or empathy (1903–17/1949). To him, *verstehen* involved doing systematic and rigorous research rather than simply getting a "feeling" for a text or social phenomenon. In other words, for Weber (1921/1968) *verstehen* was a rational procedure of study.

The key question in interpreting Weber's concept of *verstehen* is whether he thought that it was most appropriately applied to the subjective states of individual actors or to the subjective aspects of large-scale units of analysis (for example, culture). If we look only at Weber's bare position statements, there seems to be overwhelming evidence on the side of the individual-level interpretation of *verstehen* (for example, Weber,

---

[3]Hermeneutics has become a major intellectual concern in recent years, especially in the work of Martin Heidegger, Hans-Georg Gadamer, and Jurgen Habermas (Bleicher, 1980). For a strong argument in favor of using hermeneutics today, see Sica (1986), and for an appreciation of Weber's hermeneutics, see Oliver (1983).

1903–06/1975:125). This interpretation is supported by a number of observers (Burger, 1976; Schutz, 1932/1967; Warriner, 1969). But a number of people have interpreted *verstehen*, and Weber's statements about it, as a technique aimed at understanding culture. Susan Hekman sees this as the newer interpretation of what Weber meant by focusing on such cultural elements as "intersubjective meanings or socially constituted rules which define the meaning of action within a given society" (1983:46). L. M. Lachman was particularly clear on this: "The plan elements which interest us are not the millions of individual purposes pursued, but the common elements of norms, institutions, and of the general environment in which all these plans have to be carried out" (1971:21). Along the same lines, W. G. Runciman (1972) and Murray Wax (1967) saw *verstehen* as a tool for learning the culture and the language of a given society.

Finally, some have argued that *verstehen* involves both approaches. P. A. Münch (1975), for example, said that to understand action fully we must (1) identify the sense of the action as intended by the actor and (2) recognize the context in which the action belongs and makes sense.

The multiple interpretations of *verstehen* help us to see why Weber occupies such a central role in sociological theory. The cultural-level interpretation of *verstehen* would be consistent with large-scale theories (for example, structural functionalism), whereas an individual-level view is appropriate for small-scale theories (for example, symbolic interactionism). Münch's compromise position would be acceptable to both sets of theories. Which of these three interpretations is correct? At one level, we can say that it does not really matter. What is important is that there are different interpretations and that they have influenced different theoretical perspectives. On another level, we must come to some conclusion about *verstehen* on the basis of Weber's work. It is in his substantive work, rather than in his programmatic statements about methodology, that we will find the most reliable information on what Weber really meant by *verstehen* and by the other methodological tools that we encounter. As we will see, Weber's focus on the cultural and social-structural contexts of action leads us to the view that *verstehen* is a tool for macro-level analysis.

Causality

Another aspect of Weber's methodology was his commitment to the study of causality (Ringer, 1997:75). Weber was inclined to see the study of the causes of social phenomena as being within the domain of history, not sociology. Yet to the degree that history and sociology cannot be clearly separated—and they certainly are not clearly separated in Weber's substantive work—the issue of causality is relevant to sociology. Causality is also important because it is, as we will see, another place in which Weber sought to combine nomothetic and idiographic approaches.

By *causality* Weber (1921/1968) simply meant the probability that an event will be followed or accompanied by another event. It was not, in his view, enough to look for historical constants, repetitions, analogies, and parallels, as many historians are content to do. Instead, the researcher has to look at the reasons for, as well as the meanings of, historical changes (Roth, 1971). Although Weber can be seen as having a one-way causal model—in contrast to Marx's dialectical mode of reasoning—in his substantive sociology he was always attuned to the interrelationships among the economy, society, polity, organization, social stratification, religion, and so forth (Roth, 1968). Thus, Weber operates with a multicausal approach in which "*hosts* of interactive influences are very often effective causal factors" (Kalberg, 1994:13).

Weber was quite clear on the issue of multiple causality in his study of the relationship between Protestantism and the spirit of capitalism. Although he is sometimes interpreted differently, Weber (1904–05/1958) simply argued that the Protestant ethic was *one* of the causal factors in the rise of the modern spirit of capitalism. He labeled as "foolish" the idea that Protestantism was the sole cause. Similarly foolish, in Weber's view, was the idea that capitalism could have arisen "only" as a result of the Protestant Reformation; other factors could have led to the same result. Here is the way Weber made his point:

> We shall as far as possible clarify the manner and the general *direction* in which . . . the religious movements have influenced the development of material culture. Only when this has been determined with reasonable accuracy can the attempt be made to estimate to what extent the historical development of modern culture can be attributed to those *religious forces and to what extent to others.*
>
> (Weber, 1904–05/1958:91–92; italics added)

In *The Protestant Ethic and the Spirit of Capitalism,* as well as in most of the rest of his historical work, Weber was interested in the question of causality, but he did not operate with a simple one-way model; he was always attuned to the interrelationships among a number of social factors.

The critical thing to remember about Weber's thinking on causality is his belief that because we can have a special understanding of social life (*verstehen*), the causal knowledge of the social sciences is different from the causal knowledge of the natural sciences. As Weber put it: " 'Meaningfully' interpretable human conduct ('action') is identifiable by reference to 'valuations' and meanings. For this reason, our criteria for *causal* explanation have a unique kind of satisfaction in the 'historical' explanation of such an 'entity'" (1903–06/1975:185). Thus the causal knowledge of the social scientist is different from the causal knowledge of the natural scientist.

Weber's thoughts on causality were intimately related to his efforts to come to grips with the conflict between nomothetic and idiographic knowledge. Those who subscribe to a nomothetic point of view would argue that there is a necessary relationship among social phenomena, whereas the supporters of an idiographic perspective would be inclined to see only random relationships among these entities. As usual, Weber took a middle position, epitomized in his concept of "adequate causality." The notion of *adequate causality* adopts the view that the best we can do in sociology is make probabilistic statements about the relationship between social phenomena; that is, if *x* occurs, then it is *probable* that *y* will occur. The goal is to "estimate the *degree* to which a certain effect is 'favored' by certain 'conditions'" (Weber, 1903–17/1949:183).

Ideal Types

The ideal type is one of Weber's best-known contributions to contemporary sociology (Drysdale, 1996; Hekman, 1983; Lindbekk, 1992; McKinney, 1966). As we have seen,

Weber believed it was the responsibility of sociologists to develop conceptual tools, which could be used later by historians and sociologists. The most important such conceptual tool was the ideal type:

> An ideal type is formed by the one-sided *accentuation* of one or more points of view and by the synthesis of a great many diffuse, discrete, more or less present and occasionally absent *concrete individual* phenomena, which are arranged according to those one-sidedly emphasized viewpoints into a unified *analytical* construct. . . . In its conceptual purity, this mental construct . . . cannot be found empirically anywhere in reality.
>
> (Weber, 1903–17/1949:90)

In spite of this definition, Weber was not totally consistent in the way he used the ideal type. To grasp what the concept means initially, we will have to overlook some of the inconsistencies. At its most basic level, an *ideal type* is a concept constructed by a social scientist, on the basis of his or her interests and theoretical orientation, to capture the essential features of some social phenomenon.

The most important thing about ideal types is that they are heuristic devices; they are to be useful and helpful in doing empirical research and in understanding a specific aspect of the social world (or, a "historical individual"). As Lachman said, an ideal type is "essentially a measuring rod" (1971:26), or in Kalberg's terms, a "yardstick" (1994:87). Here is the way Weber put it: "Its function is the comparison with empirical reality in order to establish its divergences or similarities, to describe them with the *most unambiguously intelligible concepts,* and to understand and explain them causally" (1903–17/1949:43). Ideal types are heuristic devices to be used in the study of slices of historical reality. For example, social scientists would construct an ideal-typical bureaucracy on the basis of their immersion in historical data. This ideal type can then be compared to actual bureaucracies. The researcher looks for divergences in the real case from the exaggerated ideal type. Next, the social scientist must look for the causes of the deviations. Some typical reasons for these divergences are:

1 Actions of bureaucrats that are motivated by *misinformation.*
2 *Strategic errors,* primarily by the bureaucratic leaders.
3 *Logical fallacies* undergirding the actions of leaders and followers.
4 Decisions made in the bureaucracy on the basis of *emotion.*
5 Any *irrationality* in the action of bureaucratic leaders and followers.

To take another example, an ideal-typical military battle delineates the principal components of such a battle—opposing armies, opposing strategies, materiel at the disposal of each, disputed land ("no-man's" land), supply and support forces, command centers, and leadership qualities. Actual battles may not have all these elements, and that is one thing a researcher wants to know. The basic point is that the elements of any particular military battle may be compared with the elements identified in the ideal type.

The elements of an ideal type (such as the components of the ideal-typical military battle) are not to be thrown together arbitrarily; they are combined on the basis of their compatibility. As Hekman puts it, "Ideal types are not the product of the whim or fancy of a social scientist, but are logically constructed concepts" (1983:32). (However, they can and should reflect the interests of the social scientist.)

In Weber's view, the ideal type was to be derived inductively from the real world of social history. Weber did not believe that it was enough to offer a carefully defined set of concepts, especially if they were deductively derived from an abstract theory. The concepts had to be empirically adequate (Roth, 1971). Thus, in order to produce ideal types, researchers had first to immerse themselves in historical reality and then derive the types from that reality.

In line with Weber's efforts to find a middle ground between nomothetic and idiographic knowledge, he argued that ideal types should be neither too general nor too specific. For example, in the case of religion he would reject ideal types of the history of religion in general, but he would also be critical of ideal types of very specific phenomena, such as an individual's religious experience. Rather, ideal types are developed of intermediate phenomena such as Calvinism, Pietism, Methodism, and Baptism (Weber, 1904–05/1958).

Although ideal types are to be derived from the real world, they are not to be mirror images of that world. Rather, they are to be one-sided exaggerations (based on the researcher's interests) of the essence of what goes on in the real world. In Weber's view, the more exaggerated the ideal type, the more useful it will be for historical research.

The use of the word *ideal* or *utopia* should not be construed to mean that the concept being described is in any sense the best of all possible worlds. As used by Weber, the term meant that the form described in the concept was rarely, if ever, found in the real world. In fact, Weber argued that the ideal type need not be positive or correct; it can just as easily be negative or even morally repugnant (1903–17/1949).

Ideal types should make sense in themselves, the meaning of their components should be compatible, and they should aid us in making sense out of the real world. Although we have come to think of ideal types as describing static entities, Weber believed that they could describe either static or dynamic entities. Thus we can have an ideal type of structure, such as a bureaucracy, or of a social development, such as bureaucratization.

Ideal types also are not developed once and for all. Because society is constantly changing, and the interests of social scientists are as well, it is necessary to develop new typologies to fit the changing reality. This is in line with Weber's view that there can be no timeless concepts in the social sciences (Roth, 1968).

Although we have presented a relatively unambiguous image of the ideal type, there are contradictions in the way Weber defined the concept. In addition, in his own substantive work, Weber used the ideal type in ways that differed from the ways he said it was to be used. As Burger noted, "The ideal types presented in *Economy and Society* are a mixture of definitions, classification, and specific hypotheses seemingly too divergent to be reconcilable with Weber's statements" (1976:118). Although she disagrees with Burger on Weber's inconsistency in defining ideal types, Hekman (1983:38–59) also recognizes that Weber offers several varieties of ideal types:

   1 *Historical ideal types.* These relate to phenomena found in some particular historical epoch (for example, the modern capitalistic marketplace).
   2 *General sociological ideal types.* These relate to phenomena that cut across a number of historical periods and societies (for example, bureaucracy).

3 *Action ideal types.* These are pure types of action based on the motivations of the actor (for example, affectual action).

4 *Structural ideal types.* These are forms taken by the causes and consequences of social action (for example, traditional domination).

Clearly Weber developed an array of varieties of ideal types, and some of the richness in his work stems from their diversity, although common to them all is their mode of construction.

Kalberg (1994) argues that while the heuristic use of ideal types in empirical research is important, it should not be forgotten that they also play a key *theoretical* role in Weber's work. Although Weber rejects the idea of theoretical laws, he does use ideal types in various ways to create theoretical models. Thus, ideal types constitute the theoretical building blocks for the construction of a variety of theoretical models (for example, the routinization of charisma, the rationalization of society—both of which are discussed later in this chapter), and these models are then used to analyze specific historical developments.

Values

Modern sociological thinking in America on the role of values in the social sciences has been shaped to a large degree by an interpretation, often simplistic and erroneous, of Weber's notion of *value-free* sociology (Hennis, 1994). A common perception of Weber's view is that social scientists should *not* let their personal values influence their scientific research in any way. As we will see, Weber's work on values is far more complicated and should not be reduced to the simplistic notion that values should be kept out of sociology (Tribe, 1989:3).

Values and Teaching Weber (1903–17/1949) was most clear about the need for teachers to control their personal values in the classroom. From his point of view, academicians have a perfect right to express their personal values freely in speeches, in the press, and so forth, but the academic lecture hall is different. Weber was opposed to those teachers who preached "their evaluations on ultimate questions 'in the name of science' in governmentally privileged lecture halls in which they are neither controlled, checked by discussion, nor subject to contradiction . . . the lecture hall should be held separate from the arena of public discussion" (1903–17/1949:4). The most important difference between a public speech and an academic lecture lies in the nature of the audience. A crowd watching a public speaker has chosen to be there and can leave at any time. But students, if they want to succeed, have little choice but to listen attentively to their professor's value-laden positions. There is little ambiguity in this aspect of Weber's position on value-freedom. The academician is to express "facts," not personal values, in the classroom. Although teachers may be tempted to insert values because they make a course more interesting, teachers should be wary of employing values, because such values will "weaken the students' taste for sober empirical analysis" (Weber, 1903–17/1949:9). The only question is whether it is realistic to think that professors could eliminate most values from their presentations. Weber could adopt this position because he believed it possible to separate fact and value. However, Marx would disagree, because in his view fact and value are intertwined, dialectically interrelated.

Values and Research   Weber's position on the place of values in social research is far more ambiguous. Weber did believe in the ability to separate fact from value, and this view could be extended to the research world: "Investigator and teacher should keep unconditionally separate the establishment of empirical facts . . . and *his* own personal evaluations, i.e., his evaluation of these facts as satisfactory or unsatisfactory" (1903–17/1949:11). He often differentiated between existential knowledge of what is and normative knowledge of what ought to be (Weber, 1903–17/1949). For example, on the founding of the German Sociological Society, he said: "The Association rejects, in principle and definitely, all propaganda for action-oriented ideas from its midst." Instead, the association was pointed in the direction of the study of "what is, why something is the way it is, for what historical and social reasons" (Roth, 1968:5).

However, several facts point in a different direction and show that despite the evidence I have described, Weber did not operate with the simplistic view that values should be totally eliminated from social research. While, as we will see, Weber perceived a role for values in a specific aspect of the research process, he thought that they should be kept out of the actual collection of research data. By this Weber meant that we should employ the regular procedures of scientific investigation, such as accurate observation and systematic comparison.

Values are to be restricted to the time before social research begins. They should shape the selection of what we choose to study. Weber's (1903–17/1949:21) ideas on the role of values prior to social research are captured in his concept of *value-relevance*. As with many others of Weber's methodological concepts, value-relevance is derived from the work of the German historicist Heinrich Rickert, for whom it involved "a selection of those parts of empirical reality which for human beings embody one or several of those general cultural values which are held by people in the society in which the scientific observers live" (Burger, 1976:36). In historical research, this would mean that the choice of objects to study would be made on the basis of what is considered important in the particular society in which the researchers live. That is, they choose what to study of the past on the basis of the contemporary value system. In his specific case, Weber wrote of value-relevance from the "standpoint of the interests of the modern European" (1903–17/1949:30). For example, bureaucracy was a very important part of the German society of Weber's time, and he chose, as a result, to study that phenomenon (or the lack of it) in various historical settings.

Thus, to Weber, value judgments are not to be completely withdrawn from scientific discourse. Although Weber was opposed to confusing fact and value, he did not believe that values should be excised from the social sciences: "An *attitude of moral indifference* has no connection with *scientific* 'objectivity'" (1903–17/1949:60). He was prepared to admit that values have a certain place, though he warned researchers to be careful about the role of values: "It should be constantly made clear . . . exactly at which point the scientific investigator becomes silent and the evaluating and acting person begins to speak" (Weber, 1903–17/1949:60). When expressing value positions, sociological researchers must always keep themselves and their audiences aware of those positions.

There is a gap between what Weber said and what he actually did. Weber was not afraid to express a value judgment, even in the midst of the analysis of historical data. For example, he said that the Roman state suffered from a convulsive sickness of its social body. It can be argued that in Weber's actual work values were not only a basic device for selecting subjects to study but also were involved in the acquisition of meaningful knowledge of the social world. Gary Abraham (1992) has made the point that Weber's work, especially his views on Judaism as a world religion, was distorted by his values. In his sociology of religion (discussed later in this chapter), Weber termed the Jews "pariah people." Weber traced this position of outsider more to the desire of Jews to segregate themselves than to exclusion by the rest of society. Thus Weber, accepting the general view of the day, argued that Jews would need to surrender Judaism in order to be assimilated into German society. Abraham argues that this sort of bias affected not only Weber's ideas on Judaism, but his work in general. This casts further doubt on Weber as a "value-free" sociologist, as well as on the conventional view of Weber as a liberal thinker. As Abraham says, "Max Weber was probably as close to tolerant liberalism as majority Germany could offer at the time" (1992:22). Weber was more of a nationalist supporting the assimilation of minority groups than he was a classical liberal favoring pluralism, and those values had a profound effect on his work.

Most American sociologists regard Weber as an exponent of value-free sociology. The truth is that most American sociologists themselves subscribe to the idea of value-freedom, and they find it useful to invoke Weber's name in support of their position. As we have seen, however, Weber's work is studded with values.

One other aspect of Weber's work on values worth noting is his ideas on the role of the social sciences in helping people make choices among various ultimate value positions. Basically, Weber's view is that there is *no* way of scientifically choosing among alternative value positions. Thus, social scientists cannot presume to make such choices for people. "The social sciences, which are strictly empirical sciences, are the least fitted to presume to save the individual the difficulty of making a choice" (Weber, 1903–17/1949:19). The social scientist can derive certain factual conclusions from social research, but this research cannot tell people what they "ought" to do. Empirical research can help people choose an adequate means to an end, but it cannot help them choose that end as opposed to other ends. Weber says, "It can never be the task of an empirical science to provide binding norms and ideals from which directions for immediate practical activity can be derived" (1903–17/1949:52).

SUBSTANTIVE SOCIOLOGY

We turn now to Weber's substantive sociology. We will begin, as did Weber in his monumental *Economy and Society,* at the levels of action and interaction, but we will soon encounter the basic paradox in Weber's work: despite his seeming commitment to a sociology of small-scale processes, his work is primarily at the large-scale levels of the social world. (Many Weberians would disagree with this portrayal of paradox in Weber's work. Kalberg [1994], for example, argues that Weber offers a more fully integrated micro-macro, or agency-structure, theory.)

What Is Sociology?

In articulating his view on sociology, Weber often took a stance against the large-scale evolutionary sociology, the organicism, that was preeminent in the field at the time. For example, Weber said: "I became one [a sociologist] in order to put an end to collectivist notions. In other words, sociology, too, can only be practiced by proceeding from the action of one or more, few or many, individuals, that means, by employing a strictly 'individualist' method" (Roth, 1976:306). Despite his stated adherence to an "individualist" method, Weber was forced to admit that it is impossible to eliminate totally collective ideas from sociology.[4] But even when he admitted the significance of collective concepts, Weber ultimately reduced them to patterns and regularities of individual action: "For the subjective interpretation of action in sociological work these collectivities must be treated as *solely* the resultants and modes of organization of the particular acts of individual persons, since these alone can be treated as agents in a course of subjectively understandable action" (1921/1968:13).

At the individual level, Weber was deeply concerned with meaning, and the way in which it was formed. There seems little doubt that Weber believed in, and intended to undertake, a microsociology. But is that, in fact, what he did? Guenther Roth, one of Weber's foremost interpreters, provides us with an unequivocal answer in his description of the overall thrust of *Economy and Society:* "the first strictly *empirical comparison of social structure* and normative order in *world-historical* depth" (1968:xxvii). Mary Fulbrook directly addresses the discontinuity in Weber's work:

> Weber's overt emphasis on the importance of [individual] meanings and motives in causal explanation of social action does not correspond adequately with the true mode of explanation involved in his comparative-historical studies of the world religions. Rather, the ultimate level of causal explanation in Weber's substantive writings is that of the social-structural conditions under which certain forms of meaning and motivation can achieve historical efficacy.
>
> (Fulbrook, 1978:71)

Lars Udehn (1981) has cast light on this problem in interpreting Weber's work by distinguishing between Weber's methodology and his substantive concerns and recognizing that there is a conflict or tension between them. In Udehn's view, Weber uses an "individualist and subjectivist methodology" (1981:131). In terms of the latter, Weber is interested in what individuals do and why they do it (their subjective motives). In the former, Weber is interested in reducing collectivities to the actions of individuals. However, in most of his substantive sociology (as we will see), Weber focuses on large-scale structure (such as bureaucracy or capitalism) and is not focally concerned with what individuals do or why they do it.[5] Such structures are not reduced by Weber to the actions of individuals, and the actions of those in them are determined by the structures, not by their motives. There is little doubt that there is an enormous contradiction in Weber's work, and it will concern us through much of this chapter.

---

[4]In fact, Weber's ideal types *are* collective concepts.
[5]Udehn argues that one exception is Weber's analysis of the behavior of leaders.

With this as background, we are now ready for Weber's definition of *sociology:* "Sociology . . . is a *science* concerning itself with the *interpretive understanding* of *social action* and thereby with a *causal* explanation of its course and consequences" (1921/1968:4). Among the themes discussed earlier that are mentioned or implied in this definition are:

Sociology should be a science.

Sociology should be concerned with causality. (Here, apparently, Weber was combining sociology and history.)

Sociology should utilize interpretive understanding *(verstehen).*

We are now ready for what Weber meant by social action.

Social Action

Weber's entire sociology, if we accept his words at face value, was based on his conception of social action (S. Turner, 1983). He differentiated between action and purely reactive behavior. The concept of behavior is reserved, then as now, for automatic behavior that involves no thought processes. A stimulus is presented and behavior occurs, with little intervening between stimulus and response. Such behavior was not of interest in Weber's sociology. He was concerned with action that clearly involved the intervention of thought processes (and the resulting meaningful action) between the occurrence of a stimulus and the ultimate response. To put it slightly differently, action was said to occur when individuals attached subjective meanings to their action. To Weber, the task of sociological analysis involved "the interpretation of action in terms of its subjective meaning" (1921/1968:8). A good, and more specific, example of Weber's thinking on action is found in his discussion of *economic action,* which he defined as "a *conscious, primary* orientation to economic consideration . . . for what matters is not the objective necessity of making economic provision, but the belief that it is necessary" (1921/1968:64).

In embedding his analysis in mental processes and the resulting meaningful action, Weber (1921/1968) was careful to point out that it is erroneous to regard psychology as the foundation of the sociological interpretation of action. Weber seemed to be making essentially the same point made by Durkheim in discussing at least some nonmaterial social facts. That is, sociologists are interested in mental processes, but this is not the same as psychologists' interest in the mind, personality, and so forth.

Although Weber implied that he had a great concern with mental processes, he actually spent little time on them. Hans Gerth and C. Wright Mills called attention to Weber's lack of concern with mental processes: "Weber sees in the concept of personality a much abused notion referring to a profoundly irrational center of creativity, a center before which analytical inquiry comes to a halt" (1958:55). Schutz (1932/1967) was quite correct when he pointed out that although Weber's work on mental processes is suggestive, it is hardly the basis for a systematic microsociology. But it was the suggestiveness of Weber's work that made him relevant to those who developed the theories of individuals and their behavior—symbolic interactionism, phenomenology, and so forth.

In his action theory, Weber's clear intent was to focus on individuals and patterns and regularities of action and not on the collectivity. "Action in the sense of subjectively understandable orientation of behavior exists only as the behavior of one or more *individual* human beings" (Weber, 1921/1968:13). Weber was prepared to admit that for some purposes we may have to treat collectivities as individuals, "but for the subjective interpretation of action in sociological work these collectivities must be treated as *solely* the resultants and modes of organization of the particular acts of individual persons, since these alone can be treated as agents in a course of subjectively understandable action" (1921/1968:13). It would seem that Weber could hardly be more explicit: the sociology of action is ultimately concerned with individuals, *not* collectivities.

Weber utilized his ideal-type methodology to clarify the meaning of *action* by identifying four basic types of action. Not only is this typology significant for understanding what Weber meant by action, but it is also, in part, the basis for Weber's concern with larger social structures and institutions. Of greatest importance is Weber's differentiation between the two basic types of rational action. The first is *means–ends rationality,* or action that is "determined by expectations as to the behavior of objects in the environment and of other human beings; these expectations are used as 'conditions' or 'means' for the attainment of the actor's own rationally pursued and calculated ends" (Weber, 1921/1968:24). The second is *value rationality,* or action that is "determined by a conscious belief in the value for its own sake of some ethical, aesthetic, religious, or other form of behavior, independently of its prospects for success" (Weber, 1921/1968:24–25). *Affectual* action (which was of little concern to Weber) is determined by the emotional state of the actor. *Traditional* action (which was of far greater concern to Weber) is determined by the actor's habitual and customary ways of behaving.

It should be noted that although Weber differentiated four ideal-typical forms of action, he was well aware that any given action usually involves some combination of all four ideal types of action. In addition, Weber argued that sociologists have a much better chance of understanding action of the more rational variety than they do of understanding action dominated by affect or tradition.

We turn now to Weber's thoughts on social stratification, or his famous ideas on class, status, and party (or power). His analysis of stratification is one area in which Weber does operate, at least at first, as an action theorist.

Class, Status, and Party

One important aspect of this analysis is that Weber refused to reduce stratification to economic factors (or class, in Weber's terms) but saw it as multidimensional. Thus, society is stratified on the bases of economics, status, and power. One resulting implication is that people can rank high on one or two of these dimensions of stratification and low on the other (or others), permitting a far more sophisticated analysis of social stratification than is possible when stratification is simply reduced (as it was by some Marxists) to variations in one's economic situation.

Starting with class, Weber adhered to his action orientation by arguing that a class is not a community. Rather, a class is a group of people whose shared situation is a possible, and sometimes frequent, basis for action by the group. Weber contends that a "class situation" exists when three conditions are met:

> (1) A number of people have in common a specific causal component of their life chances, insofar as (2) this component is represented exclusively by economic interests in the possession of goods and opportunities for income, and (3) is represented under the conditions of the commodity or labor markets. This is "class situation."
>
> (Weber, 1921/1968:927)

The concept of "class" refers to any group of people found in the same class situation. Thus a class is *not* a community but merely a group of people in the same economic, or market, situation.

In contrast to class, status does normally refer to communities; status groups are ordinarily communities, albeit rather amorphous ones. "Status situation" is defined by Weber as "every typical component of the life of men that is determined by a specific, positive or negative, social estimation of *honor*" (1921/1968:932). As a general rule, status is associated with a style of life. (Status relates to consumption of goods produced, while class relates to economic production.) Those at the top of the status hierarchy have a different lifestyle than do those at the bottom. In this case, lifestyle, or status, is related to class situation. But class and status are not necessarily linked to one another: "Money and an entrepreneurial position are not in themselves status qualifications, although they may lead to them; and the lack of property is not in itself a status disqualification, although this may be a reason for it" (Weber, 1921/1968:306). There is a complex set of relationships between class and status, and it is made even more complicated when we add the dimension of party.

While classes exist in the economic order and status groups in the social order, parties can be found in the political order. To Weber, parties "are always *structures* struggling for domination" (cited in Gerth and Mills, 1958:195; italics added). Thus parties are the most organized elements of Weber's stratification system. Weber thinks of parties very broadly as including not only those that exist in the state but also those that may exist in a social club. Parties usually, but not always, represent class and/or status groups. Whatever they represent, parties are oriented to the attainment of power.

While Weber remained close to his action approach in his ideas on social stratification, these ideas already indicate a movement in the direction of macro-level communities and structures. In most of his other work, Weber focused on such large-scale units of analysis. Not that Weber lost sight of the action; the actor simply moved from being the focus of his concern to being largely a dependent variable determined by a variety of large-scale forces. For example, as we will see, Weber believed that individual Calvinists are impelled to act in various ways by the norms, values, and beliefs of their religion, but his focus was not on the individual but on the collective forces that impel the actor.

Structures of Authority

Weber's sociological interest in the structures of authority was motivated, at least in part, by his political interests. Weber was no political radical; in fact, he was often called the "bourgeois Marx" to reflect the similarities in the intellectual interests of Marx and Weber as well as their very different political orientations. Although Weber was almost as critical of modern capitalism as Marx was, he did not advocate revolution. He wanted to change society gradually, not overthrow it. He had little faith in the ability of the masses to create a "better" society. But Weber also saw little hope in the middle classes, which he felt were dominated by shortsighted, petty bureaucrats. Weber was critical of authoritarian political leaders like Bismarck. Nevertheless, for Weber the hope—if indeed he had any hope—lay with the great political leaders rather than with the masses or the bureaucrats. Along with his faith in political leaders went his unswerving nationalism. He placed the nation above all else: "The vital interests of the nation stand, of course, above democracy and parliamentarianism" (Weber, 1921/1968:1383). Weber preferred democracy as a political form not because he believed in the masses but because it offered maximum dynamism and the best milieu to generate political leaders (Mommsen, 1974). Weber noted that authority structures exist in every social institution, and his political views were related to his analysis of these structures in all settings. Of course, they were most relevant to his views on the polity.

Weber began his analysis of authority structures in a way that was consistent with his assumptions about the nature of action. He defined *domination* as the "probability that certain specific commands (or all commands) will be obeyed by a given group of persons" (Weber, 1921/1968:212). Domination can have a variety of bases, legitimate as well as illegitimate, but what mainly interested Weber were the legitimate forms of domination, or what he called *authority*. What concerned Weber, and what played a central role in much of his sociology, were the three bases on which authority is made legitimate to followers—rational, traditional, and charismatic. In defining these three bases, Weber remained fairly close to his ideas on individual action, but he rapidly moved to the large-scale structures of authority. Authority legitimized on *rational* grounds rests "on a belief in the legality of enacted rules and the right of those elevated to authority under such rules to issue commands" (Weber, 1921/1968:215). Authority legitimized on *traditional* grounds is based on "an established belief in the sanctity of immemorial traditions and the legitimacy of those exercising authority under them" (Weber, 1921/1968:215). Finally, authority legitimized by *charisma*[6] rests on the devotion of followers to the exceptional sanctity, exemplary character, heroism, or special powers (for example, the ability to work miracles) of leaders, as well as on the normative order sanctioned by them. All these modes of legitimizing authority clearly imply individual actors, thought processes (beliefs), and actions. But from this point, Weber, in his thinking about authority, did move quite far from an individual action base, as we will see when we discuss the authority structures erected on the basis of these types of legitimacy.

Legal Authority Legal authority can take a variety of structural forms, but the one that interested Weber most was the *bureaucracy,* which he considered "the purest type of exercise of legal authority" (1921/1968:220).

---

[6]The term *charisma* is used in Weber's work in a variety of other ways and contexts as well; see Miyahara (1983).

Ideal-Typical Bureaucracy   Weber depicted bureaucracies in ideal-typical terms:

> From a purely technical point of view, a bureaucracy is capable of attaining the highest degree of efficiency, and is in this sense formally the most rational known means of exercising authority over human beings. It is superior to any other form in precision, in stability, in the stringency of its discipline, and in its reliability. It thus makes possible a particularly high degree of calculability of results for the heads of the organization and for those acting in relation to it. It is finally superior both in intensive efficiency and in the scope of its operations and is formally capable of application to all kinds of administrative tasks.
>
> (Weber, 1921/1968:223)

Despite his discussion of the positive characteristics of bureaucracies, here and elsewhere in his work, there is a fundamental ambivalence in his attitude toward them. Although he detailed their advantages, he was well aware of their problems. Weber expressed various reservations about bureaucratic organizations. For example, he was cognizant of the "red tape" that often makes dealing with bureaucracies so trying and so difficult. His major fear, however, was that the rationalization that dominates all aspects of bureaucratic life was a threat to individual liberty. As Weber put it:

> No machinery in the world functions so precisely as this apparatus of men and, moreover, so cheaply. . . . Rational calculation . . . reduces every worker to a cog in this bureaucratic machine and, seeing himself in this light, he will merely ask how to transform himself into a somewhat bigger cog. . . . The passion for bureaucratization drives us to despair.
>
> (Weber, 1921/1968:liii)

Weber was appalled by the effects of bureaucratization and, more generally, of the rationalization of the world of which bureaucratization is but one component, but he saw no way out. He described bureaucracies as "escape proof," "practically unshatterable," and among the hardest institutions to destroy once they are established. Along the same lines, he felt that individual bureaucrats could not "squirm out" of the bureaucracy once they were "harnessed" in it (for a less ominous view of bureaucratization, see Klagge, 1997). Weber concluded that "the future belongs to bureaucratization" (1921/1968:1401), and time has borne out his prediction.

Weber would say that his depiction of the advantages of bureaucracy is part of his ideal-typical image of the way it operates. The ideal-typical bureaucracy is a purposeful exaggeration of the rational characteristics of bureaucracies. Such an exaggerated model is useful for heuristic purposes and for studies of organizations in the real world, but it is not to be mistaken for a realistic depiction of the way bureaucracies actually operate.

Weber distinguished the ideal-typical bureaucracy from the ideal-typical bureaucrat. He conceived of bureaucracies as structures and of bureaucrats as positions within those structures. He did *not,* as his action orientation might lead us to expect, offer a social psychology of organizations or of the individuals who inhabit those bureaucracies (as modern symbolic interactionists might).

The ideal-typical bureaucracy is a type of organization. Its basic units are offices organized in a hierarchical manner with rules, functions, written documents, and means of compulsion. All these are, to varying degrees, large-scale structures that represent the thrust of Weber's thinking. He could, after all, have constructed an ideal-typical bureaucracy that focused on the thoughts and actions of individuals within the bureaucracy. There is a whole school of thought in the study of organizations that focuses precisely on this level rather than on the structures of bureaucracies (see, for example, Blankenship, 1977).

The following are the major characteristics of the ideal-typical bureaucracy:

1 It consists of a continuous organization of official functions (offices) bound by rules.

2 Each office has a specified sphere of competence. The office carries with it a set of obligations to perform various functions, the authority to carry out these functions, and the means of compulsion required to do the job.

3 The offices are organized into a hierarchical system.

4 The offices may carry with them technical qualifications that require that the participants obtain suitable training.

5 The staff that fills these offices does not own the means of production associated with them;[7] staff members are provided with the use of those things that they need to do the job.

6 The incumbent is not allowed to appropriate the position; it always remains part of the organization.

7 Administrative acts, decisions, and rules are formulated and recorded in writing.

Any Alternatives? A bureaucracy is one of the rational structures that is playing an ever-increasing role in modern society, but one may wonder whether there is any alternative to the bureaucratic structure. Weber's clear and unequivocal answer was that there is no possible alternative: "The needs of mass administration make it today completely indispensable. The choice is only between bureaucracy and dilettantism in the field of administration" (1921/1968:223).

Although we might admit that bureaucracy is an intrinsic part of modern capitalism, we might ask whether a socialist society might be different. Is it possible to create a socialist society without bureaucracies and bureaucrats? Once again, Weber was unequivocal: "When those subject to bureaucratic control seek to escape the influence of existing bureaucratic apparatus, this is normally possible only by creating an organization of their own which is equally subject to the process of bureaucratization" (1921/1968:224). In fact, Weber believed that in the case of socialism we would see an increase, not a decrease, in bureaucratization. If socialism were to achieve a level of efficiency comparable to capitalism, "it would mean a tremendous increase in the importance of professional bureaucrats" (Weber, 1921/1968:224). In capitalism, at least the owners are not bureaucrats and therefore would be able to restrain the bureaucrats, but in socialism even the top-level leaders would be bureaucrats. Weber thus believed that even with its problems "capitalism presented the best chances for the preservation of individual freedom and creative leadership in a bureaucratic world" (Mommsen, 1974:xv). We are once again at a key theme in Weber's work: his view that there is

---

[7]Here and elsewhere in his work Weber adopts a Marxian interest in the means of production. This is paralleled by his concern with alienation, not only in the economic sector but throughout social life (science, politics, and so forth).

really no hope for a better world. Socialists can, in Weber's view, only make things worse by expanding the degree of bureaucratization in society. Weber noted: "Not summer's bloom lies ahead of us, but rather a polar night of icy darkness and hardness, no matter which group may triumph externally now" (cited in Gerth and Mills, 1958:128).

Any Hope?   A ray of hope in Weber's work—and it is a small one—is that professionals who stand outside the bureaucratic system can control it to some degree. In this category, Weber included professional politicians, scientists, intellectuals (Sadri, 1992), and even capitalists, as well as the supreme heads of the bureaucracies. For example, Weber said that politicians "must be the countervailing force against bureaucratic domination" (1921/1968:1417). His famous essay "Politics as a Vocation" is basically a plea for the development of political leaders with a calling to oppose the rule of bureaucracies and of bureaucrats. But in the end these appear to be rather feeble hopes. In fact, a good case can be made that these professionals are simply another aspect of the rationalization process and that their development serves only to accelerate that process (Nass, 1986; Ritzer, 1975c; Ritzer and Walczak, 1988).

In Weber's " 'Churches' and 'Sects' in North America: An Ecclesiastical Socio-Political Sketch" (1906/1985), Colin Loader and Jeffrey Alexander (1985) see a forerunner of Weber's thoughts on the hope provided by an ethic of responsibility in the face of the expansion of bureaucratization. American sects such as the Quakers practice an ethic of responsibility by combining rationality and larger values. Rogers Brubaker defines the *ethic of responsibility* as "the passionate commitment to ultimate values with the dispassionate analysis of alternative means of pursuing them" (1984:108). He contrasts this to the *ethic of conviction,* in which a rational choice of means is foregone and the actor orients "his action to the realization of some absolute value or unconditional demand" (1984:106; for a somewhat different view, see Gane, 1997). The ethic of conviction often involves a withdrawal from the rational world, whereas the ethic of responsibility involves a struggle within that world for greater humanness. The ethic of responsibility provides at least a modicum of hope in the face of the onslaught of rationalization and bureaucratization.

Traditional Authority   Whereas legal authority stems from the legitimacy of a rational-legal system, traditional authority is based on a claim by the leaders, and a belief on the part of the followers, that there is virtue in the sanctity of age-old rules and powers. The leader in such a system is not a superior but a personal master. The administrative staff, if any, consists not of officials but mainly of personal retainers. In Weber's words, "Personal loyalty, not the official's impersonal duty, determines the relations of the administrative staff to the master" (1921/1968:227). Although the bureaucratic staff owes its allegiance and obedience to enacted rules and to the leader, who acts in their name, the staff of the traditional leader obeys because the leader carries the weight of tradition—he or she has been chosen for that position in the traditional manner.

Weber was interested in the staff of the traditional leader and how it measured up to the ideal-typical bureaucratic staff. He concluded that it was lacking on a number of counts. The traditional staff lacks offices with clearly defined spheres of competence that are subject to impersonal rules. It also does not have a rational ordering of relations of superiority and inferiority; it lacks a clear hierarchy. There is no regular system of appointment and promotion on the basis of free contracts. Technical training is not a regular requirement for obtaining a position or an appointment. Appointments do not carry with them fixed salaries paid in money.

Weber used his ideal-type methodology not only to compare traditional to rational-legal authority and to underscore the most salient characteristics of traditional authority but also to analyze historically the different forms of traditional authority. He differentiated between two very early forms of traditional authority. A *gerontocracy* involves rule by elders, whereas *primary patriarchalism* involves leaders who inherit their positions. Both of these forms have a supreme chief but lack an administrative staff. A more modern form is *patrimonialism* which is traditional domination with an administration and a military force that are purely personal instruments of the master (Eisenberg, 1998). Still more modern is *feudalism,* which limits the discretion of the master through the development of more routinized, even contractual, relationships between leader and subordinate. This restraint, in turn, leads to more stabilized power positions than exist in patrimonialism. All four of these forms may be seen as structural variations of traditional authority, and all of them differ significantly from rational-legal authority.

Weber saw structures of traditional authority, in any form, as barriers to the development of rationality. This is our first encounter with an overriding theme in Weber's work—factors that facilitate or impede the development of (formal) rationality (see the next section). Over and over we find Weber concerned, as he was here, with the structural factors conducive to rationality in the Western world and the structural and cultural impediments to the development of a similar rationality throughout the rest of the world. In this specific case, Weber argued that the structures and practices of traditional authority constitute a barrier to the rise of rational economic structures—in particular, capitalism—as well as to various other components of a rational society. Even patrimonialism—a more modern form of traditionalism—while permitting the development of certain forms of "primitive" capitalism, does not allow for the rise of the highly rational type of capitalism characteristic of the modern West.

Charismatic Authority   Charisma is a concept that has come to be used very broadly (Oakes, 1997; Werbner and Basu, 1998). The news media and the general public are quick to point to a politician, a movie star, or a rock musician as a charismatic individual. By this they most often mean that the person in question is endowed with extraordinary qualities. The concept of charisma plays an important role in the work of Max Weber, but his conception of it was very different from that held by most laypeople today. Although Weber did not deny that a charismatic leader may have outstanding characteristics, his sense of charisma was more dependent on the group of disciples and the way that they *define* the charismatic leader (D. Smith, 1998). To put Weber's position bluntly, if the disciples define a leader as charismatic, then he or she is likely to be a charismatic leader irrespective of whether he or she actually possesses any outstanding traits. A charismatic leader, then, can be someone who is quite ordinary. What is crucial is the process by which such a leader is set apart from ordinary people and treated as if endowed with supernatural, superhuman, or at least exceptional powers or qualities that are not accessible to the ordinary person (Miyahara, 1983).

Charisma and Revolution   To Weber, charisma was a revolutionary force, one of the most important revolutionary forces in the social world. Whereas traditional authority clearly is inherently conservative, the rise of a charismatic leader may well pose a threat to that system (as well as to a rational-legal system) and lead to a dramatic change in that system. What distinguishes charisma as a revolutionary force is that it leads to changes in the minds of actors; it causes a "subjective or internal reorientation." Such changes may lead to "a radical alteration of the central attitudes and direction of action with a completely new orientation of all attitudes toward different problems of the world" (Weber, 1921/1968:245). Although Weber was here addressing changes in the thoughts and actions of individuals, such changes are clearly reduced to the status of dependent variables. Weber focused on changes in the structure of authority, that is, the rise of charismatic authority. When such a new authority structure emerges, it is likely to change people's thoughts and actions dramatically.

The other major revolutionary force in Weber's theoretical system, and the one with which he was much more concerned, is (formal) rationality. Whereas charisma is an internal revolutionary force that changes the minds of actors, Weber saw (formal) rationality as an external revolutionary force changing the structures of society first and then ultimately the thoughts and actions of individuals. We will have more to say about rationality as a revolutionary force later, but this closes our discussion of charisma as a revolutionary factor, because Weber had very little to say about it. Weber was interested in the revolutionary character of charisma as well as its structure and the necessity that its basic character be transformed and routinized in order for it to survive as a system of authority.

Charismatic Organizations and the Routinization of Charisma   In his analysis of charisma, Weber began, as he did with traditional authority, with the ideal-typical bureaucracy. He sought to determine to what degree the structure of charismatic authority, with its disciples and staff, differs from the bureaucratic system. Compared to that of the ideal-typical bureaucracy, the staff of the charismatic leader is lacking on virtually all counts. The staff members are not technically trained but are chosen instead for their possession of charismatic qualities or, at least, of qualities similar to those possessed by the charismatic leader. The offices they occupy form no clear hierarchy. Their work does not constitute a career, and there are no promotions, clear appointments, or dismissals. The charismatic leader is free to intervene whenever he or she feels that the staff cannot handle a situation. The organization has no formal rules, no established administrative organs, and no precedents to guide new judgments. In these and other ways, Weber found the staff of the charismatic leader to be "greatly inferior" to the staff in a bureaucratic form of organization.

Weber's interest in the organization behind the charismatic leader and the staff that inhabits it led him to the question of what happens to charismatic authority when the leader dies. After all, a charismatic system is inherently fragile; it would seem to be able to survive only as long as the charismatic leader lives. But is it possible for such an organization to live after the leader dies? The answer to this question is of greatest consequence to the staff members of the charismatic leader, for they are likely to live on after the leader dies. They are also likely to have a vested interest in the continued existence of the organization: if the organization ceases to exist, they are out of work.

Thus the challenge for the staff is to create a situation in which charisma in some adulterated form persists even after the leader's death. It is a difficult struggle because, for Weber, charisma is by its nature unstable; it exists in its pure form only as long as the charismatic leader lives.

In order to cope with the departure of the charismatic leader, the staff (as well as the followers) may adopt a variety of strategies to create a more lasting organization. The staff may search out a new charismatic leader, but even if the search is successful, the new leader is unlikely to achieve the same aura as his or her predecessor. A set of rules also may be developed that allows the group to identify future charismatic leaders. But such rules rapidly become tradition, and what was charismatic leadership is on the way toward becoming traditional authority. In any case, the nature of leadership is radically changed as the purely personal character of charisma is eliminated. Still another technique is to allow the charismatic leader to designate his or her successor and thereby to transfer charisma symbolically to the next in line. Again it is questionable whether this is ever very successful or whether it can be successful in the long run. Another strategy is having the staff designate a successor and having its choice accepted by the larger community. The staff could also create ritual tests, with the new charismatic leader being the one who successfully undergoes the tests. However, all these efforts are doomed to failure. In the long run, charisma cannot be routinized and still be charisma; it must be transformed into either traditional or rational-legal authority (or into some sort of institutionalized charisma like the Catholic Church).

Indeed, we find a basic theory of history in Weber's work. If successful, charisma almost immediately moves in the direction of routinization. But once routinized, charisma is en route to becoming either traditional or rational-legal authority. Once it achieves one of those states, the stage is set for the cycle to begin all over again. However, despite a general adherence to a cyclical theory, Weber believed that a basic change has occurred in the modern world and that we are more and more likely to see charisma routinized in the direction of rational-legal authority. Furthermore, he saw rational systems of authority as stronger and as increasingly impervious to charismatic movements. The modern, rationalized world may well mean the death of charisma as a significant revolutionary force (Seligman, 1993a). Weber contended that rationality—not charisma—is the most irresistible and important revolutionary force in the modern world.

Types of Authority and the "Real World"   In this section, we have discussed the three types of authority as ideal types, but Weber was well aware that in the real world, any specific form of authority involves a combination of all three. Thus we can think of Franklin D. Roosevelt as a president of the United States who ruled on all three bases. He was elected president in accord with a series of rational-legal principles. By the time he was elected president for the fourth time, a good part of this rule had traditional elements. Finally, many disciples and followers regarded him as a charismatic leader (McCann, 1997).

Although we have presented the three forms of authority as parallel structures, in the real world there is constant tension and, sometimes, conflict among them. The charismatic leader is a constant threat to the other forms of authority. Once in power, the charismatic leader must address the threat posed to it by the other two forms. Even if charismatic authority is successfully routinized, there then arises the problem of maintaining its dynamism and its original revolutionary qualities. Then there is the conflict produced by the constant development of rational-legal authority and the threat it poses to the continued existence of the other forms. If Weber was right, however, we might face a future in which the tension among the three forms of authority is eliminated, a world of the uncontested hegemony of the rational-legal system. This is the "iron cage" of a totally rationalized society that worried Weber so much. In such a society, the only hope lies with isolated charismatic individuals who manage somehow to avoid the coercive power of society. But a small number of isolated individuals hardly represent a significant hope in the face of an increasingly powerful bureaucratic machine.

Rationalization

There has been a growing realization in recent years that rationalization lies at the heart of Weber's substantive sociology (Antonio, 1979; Brubaker, 1984; R. Collins, 1980; Eisen, 1978; Kalberg, 1980, 1990; Levine, 1981a; Palomares and Laura, 1997; Ritzer, 1983, 1996; Scaff, 1989; Schluchter, 1981; Sica, 1988). As Kalberg recently put it, "It *is* the case that Weber's interest in a broad and overarching theme—the 'specific and peculiar "rationalism" of Western culture' and its unique origins and development—stands at the center of his sociology" (1994:18). However, it is difficult to extract a clear definition of *rationalization* from Weber's work.[8] In fact, he operated with a number of different definitions of the term, and he often failed to specify which definition he was using in a particular discussion (Brubaker, 1984:1). As we saw earlier, Weber did define *rationality;* indeed, he differentiated between two types—means–ends and value rationality. However, these concepts refer to types of *action.* They are the basis of, but not coterminous with, Weber's larger-scale sense of rationalization. Weber is interested in far more than fragmented action orientations; his main concern is with regularities and patterns of action within civilizations, institutions, organizations, strata, classes, and groups. Donald Levine (1981a) argues that Weber is interested in "objectified" rationality; that is, action that is in accord with some process of external systematization. Stephen Kalberg (1980) performs a useful service by identifying four basic types of ("objective") rationality in Weber's work. (Levine offers a very similar differentiation.) These types of rationality were "the basic heuristic tools [Weber] employed to scrutinize the historical fates of rationalization as sociocultural processes" (Kalberg, 1980:1172; for an application, see Takayama, 1998).

Types of Rationality   The first type is *practical rationality,* which is defined by Kalberg as "every way of life that views and judges worldly activity in relation to the individual's purely pragmatic and egoistic interests" (1980:1151). People who practice practical rationality accept given realities and merely calculate the most expedient ways of dealing with the difficulties that they present. This type of rationality arose with the

---

[8]It might be argued that there is no single definition because the various forms of rationality are so different from one another that they preclude such a definition. I would like to thank Jere Cohen for this point.

severing of the bonds of primitive magic, and it exists trans-civilizationally and trans-historically; that is, it is not restricted to the modern Occident. This type of rationality stands in opposition to anything that threatens to transcend everyday routine. It leads people to distrust all impractical values, either religious or secular-utopian, as well as the theoretical rationality of the intellectuals, the type of rationality to which we now turn.

Theoretical rationality involves a cognitive effort to master reality through increasingly abstract concepts rather than through action. It involves such abstract cognitive processes as logical deduction, induction, attribution of causality, and the like. This type of rationality was accomplished early in history by sorcerers and ritualistic priests and later by philosophers, judges, and scientists. Unlike practical rationality, theoretical rationality leads the actor to transcend daily realities in a quest to understand the world as a meaningful cosmos. Like practical rationality, it is trans-civilizational and trans-historical. The effect of intellectual rationality on action is limited. In that it involves cognitive processes, it need not affect action taken, and it has the potential to introduce new patterns of action only indirectly.

Substantive rationality (like practical rationality, but *not* theoretical rationality) directly orders action into patterns through clusters of values. Substantive rationality involves a choice of means to ends within the context of a system of values. One value system is no more (substantively) rational than another. Thus, this type of rationality also exists trans-civilizationally and trans-historically, wherever consistent value postulates exist.

Finally, and most important from the author's point of view, is *formal rationality,* which involves means–ends calculation (Cockerham, Abel, and Luschen, 1993). But whereas in practical rationality this calculation occurs in reference to pragmatic self-interests, in formal rationality it occurs with reference to "universally applied rules, laws, and regulations." As Brubaker puts it, "Common to the rationality of industrial capitalism, formalistic law and bureaucratic administration is its objectified, institutionalized, supra-individual form; in each sphere, rationality is embodied in the social structure and confronts individuals as something external to them" (1984:9). Weber makes this quite clear in the specific case of bureaucratic rationalization:

> Bureaucratic rationalization . . . revolutionizes with *technical means,* in principle, as does every economic reorganization, "from without": It *first* changes the material and social orders, and *through* them the people, by changing the conditions of adaptation, and perhaps the opportunities for adaptation, through a rational determination of means and ends.
> (Weber, 1921/1968:1116)

Although all the other types of rationality are trans-civilizational and epoch-transcending, formal rationality arose *only* in the West with the coming of industrialization. The universally applied rules, laws, and regulations that characterize formal rationality in the West are found particularly in the economic, legal, and scientific institutions, as well as in the bureaucratic form of domination. Thus, we have already encountered formal rationality in our discussion of rational-legal authority and the bureaucracy.

An Overarching Theory?   Although Weber had a complex, multifaceted sense of rationalization, he used it most powerfully and meaningfully in his image of the modern

Western world, especially in the capitalistic economy (R. Collins, 1980; Weber, 1927/1981) and bureaucratic organizations (I. Cohen, 1981:xxxi; Weber, 1921/ 1968:956–1005), as an iron cage (Mitzman, 1969/1971; Tiryakian, 1981) of formally rational structures.   Weber described capitalism and bureaucracies as "two great rationalizing forces" (1921/1968:698).[9] In fact, Weber saw capitalism and bureaucracies as being derived from the same basic sources (especially innerworldly asceticism), involving similarly rational and methodical action, reinforcing one another and in the process furthering the rationalization of the Occident.[10] In Weber's (1921/1968:227, 994) view, the only real rival to the bureaucrat in technical expertise and factual knowledge was the capitalist.

However, if we take Weber at his word, it is difficult to argue that he had an overarching theory of rationalization. He rejected the idea of "general evolutionary sequence" (Weber, 1927/1981:34). He was critical of thinkers like Hegel and Marx, who he felt offered general, teleological theories of society. In his own work, he tended to shy away from studies of, or proclamations about, whole societies. Instead, he tended to focus, in turn, on social structures and institutions such as bureaucracy, stratification, law, the city, religion, the polity, and the economy. Lacking a sense of the whole, he was unlikely to make global generalizations, especially about future directions. Furthermore, the rationalization process that Weber described in one social structure or institution was usually quite different from the rationalization of another structure or institution. As Weber put it, the process of rationalization assumes "unusually varied forms" (1922–23/1958:293; see also Weber, 1921/1958:30; 1904–05/1958:78), and "the history of rationalism shows a development which by no means follows parallel lines in the various departments of life" (1904–05/1958:77; see also Brubaker, 1984:9; Kalberg, 1980:1147). Weber also looked at many things other than rationalization in his various comparative-historical studies (Kalberg, 1994).

This being said, it is clear that Weber does have a deep concern for the overarching effect of the formal rationalization of the economy and bureaucracies on the Western world (Brubaker, 1984). For example, in *Economy and Society,* Weber says:

> This whole process of rationalization in the factory as elsewhere, and especially in the bureaucratic state machine, parallels the centralization of the material implements of organization in the hands of the master. Thus, discipline inexorably takes over ever larger areas as the satisfaction of political and economic needs is increasingly rationalized. This universal phenomenon more and more restricts the importance of charisma and of individually differentiated conduct.
>
> (Weber, 1921/1968:1156)

Formal rationalization will be our main, but certainly not only, concern in this section.

---

[9]In the 1920 introduction to *The Protestant Ethic and the Spirit of Capitalism,* Weber focused on "a specially trained organization of officials" (bureaucracy) in his discussion of rationalization, but he also mentioned capitalism in the same context as "the most fateful force in our modern life."

[10]Of course, these are not completely distinct because large capitalistic enterprises are one of the places in which we find bureaucracies (Weber, 1922–23/1958:299). On the other hand, Weber also sees the possibility that bureaucracies can stand in opposition to, can impede, capitalism.

Formal and Substantive Rationality   Various efforts have been made to delineate the basic characteristics of formal rationality. In our view, formal rationality may be defined in terms of six basic characteristics (Ritzer, 1983, 1996). First, formally rational structures and institutions emphasize *calculability,* or those things that can be counted or quantified. Second, there is a focus on *efficiency,* on finding the best means to a given end. Third, there is great concern with ensuring *predictability,* or that things operate in the same way from one time or place to another. Fourth, a formally rational system progressively reduces human technology and ultimately *replaces human technology with nonhuman technology.* Nonhuman technologies (such as computerized systems) are viewed as more calculable, more efficient, and more predictable than human technologies. Fifth, formally rational systems seek to gain *control* over an array of uncertainties, especially the uncertainties posed by human beings who work in, or are served by, them. Finally, rational systems tend to have a series of *irrational consequences* for people involved with them and for the systems themselves, as well as for the larger society (Sica, 1988). One of the irrationalities of rationality, from Weber's point of view, is that the world tends to become less enchanted, less magical and ultimately less meaningful to people (M. Schneider, 1993).[11]

Formal rationality stands in contrast to all the other types of rationality but is especially in conflict with substantive rationality (Brubaker, 1984:4). Kalberg argues that Weber believed that the conflict between these two types of rationality played "a particularly fateful role in the unfolding of rationalization processes in the West" (1980:1157).

In addition to differentiating among the four types of rationality, Kalberg also deals with their capacity to introduce methodical ways of life. Practical rationality lacks this ability because it involves reactions to situations rather than efforts to order them. Theoretical rationality is cognitive and therefore has a highly limited ability to suppress practical rationality and seems to be more of an end product than a producer. To Weber, substantive rationality is the *only* type with the "potential to introduce methodical ways of life" (Kalberg, 1980:1165). Thus, in the West, a particular substantive rationality with an emphasis on a methodical way of life—Calvinism—subjugated practical rationality and led to the development of formal rationality.

Weber's fear was that substantive rationality was becoming less significant than the other types of rationality, especially formal rationality, in the West. Thus practitioners of formal rationality, like the bureaucrat and the capitalist, were coming to dominate the West, and the type that "embodied Western civilization's highest ideals: the autonomous and free individual whose actions were given continuity by their reference to ultimate values" (Kalberg, 1980:1176) was fading away (for an alternative view on this, see Titunik, 1997).

---

[11]However, M. Schneider argues that Weber overstated the case and that in spite of rationalization, parts of the world continue to be enchanted: "Enchantment, we suggest, is part of our normal condition, and far from having fled with the rise of science [one of Weber's rationalized systems], it continues to exist (though often unrecognized) wherever our capacity to explain the world's behavior is slim, that is, where neither science nor practical knowledge seem of much utility" (1993:x). In an essay entitled "Risking Enchantment," Alexander, Smith, and Sherwood have articulated a similar view: "As we see it, society will never shed its mysteries . . . its demonic black magic . . . its fierce and incomprehensible emotionality" (1993:10).

Rationalization in Various Social Settings   Although we have emphasized the differences among Weber's four types of rationalization in this section, there are a number of commonalities among them. Thus as we move from institution to institution in the ensuing discussion, we, like Weber, focus sometimes on rationalization in general and at other times on the specific types of rationalization.

Economy   The most systematic presentation of Weber's thoughts on the rationalization of the economic institution is to be found in his *General Economic History*. Weber's concern is with the development of the rational capitalistic economy in the Occident, which is a specific example of a rational economy defined as a "functional organization oriented to money-prices which originate in the interest-struggles of men in the *market*" (Weber, 1915/1958:331). Although there is a general evolutionary trend, Weber, as always, is careful to point out that there are various sources of capitalism, alternative routes to it, and a range of results emanating from it (Swedberg, 1998). In fact, in the course of rejecting the socialistic theory of evolutionary change, Weber rejects the whole idea of a "general evolutionary sequence" (1927/1981:34).

Weber begins by depicting various irrational and traditional forms such as the household, clan, village, and manorial economies. For example, the lord of the manor in feudalism was described by Weber as being traditionalistic, "too lacking in initiative to build up a business enterprise in a large scale into which the peasants would have fitted as a labor force" (1927/1981:72). However, by the twelfth and thirteenth centuries in the Occident, feudalism began to break down as the peasants and the land were freed from control by the lord and a money economy was introduced. With this breakdown, the manorial system "showed a strong tendency to develop in a capitalistic direction" (Weber, 1927/1981:79).

At the same time, in the Middle Ages, cities were beginning to develop. Weber focuses on the largely urban development of industry involved in the transformation of raw materials. Especially important to Weber is the development of such industrial production beyond the immediate needs of the house community. Notable here is the rise of free craftsmen in the cities. They developed in the Middle Ages in the Occident because, for one thing, this society had developed consumptive needs greater than those of any other. In general, there were larger markets and more purchasers, and the peasantry had greater purchasing power. On the other side, forces operated against the major alternative to craftsmen—slaves. Slavery was found to be too unprofitable and too unstable, and it was made increasingly more unstable by the growth of the towns that offered freedom to the slaves.

In the Occident, along with free craftsmen came the development of the *guild,* defined by Weber as "an organization of craft workers specialized in accordance with the type of occupation . . . [with] internal regulation of work and monopolization against outsiders" (1927/1981:136). Freedom of association was also characteristic of the guilds. But although rational in many senses, guilds also had traditional, anticapitalistic aspects. For example, one master was not supposed to have more capital than another, and this requirement was a barrier to the development of large capitalistic organizations.

As the Middle Ages came to a close, the guilds began to disintegrate. This disintegration was crucial because the traditional guilds stood in the way of technological advance. With the dissolution of the guild system came the rise of the domestic system of production, especially the "putting out" system in the textile industry. In such a system, production was decentralized, with much of it taking place within the homes of the workers. Although domestic systems were found throughout the world, it was only in the Occident that the owners controlled the means of production (for example, tools, raw materials) and provided them to the workers in exchange for the right to dispose of the product. Whereas a fully developed domestic system developed in the West, it was impeded in other parts of the world by such barriers as the clan system (China), the caste system (India), traditionalism, and the lack of free workers.

Next, Weber details the development of the workshop (a central work setting without advanced machinery) and then the emergence of the factory in the fourteenth through sixteenth centuries. In Weber's view, the factory did not arise out of craft work or the domestic system, but alongside them. Similarly, the factory was not called into existence by advances in machinery; the two developments were correlated with each other. The factory was characterized by free labor that performed specialized and coordinated activities, ownership of the means of production by the entrepreneur, the fixed capital of the entrepreneur, and the system of accounting that is indispensable to such capitalization. Such a factory was, in Weber's view, a capitalistic organization. In addition to the development of the factory, Weber details the rise of other components of a modern capitalistic economy, such as advanced machinery, transportation systems, money, banking, interest, bookkeeping systems, and so on.

What most clearly defines modern rational capitalistic enterprises for Weber is their calculability, which is best represented in their reliance on modern bookkeeping. Isolated calculable enterprises existed in the past in the Occident as well as in other societies. However, an entire society is considered capitalistic only when the everyday requirements of the population are supplied by capitalistic methods and enterprises. Such a society is found only in the Occident and there only since the mid-nineteenth century.

The development of a capitalistic system hinged on a variety of developments within the economy as well as within the larger society. Within the economy, some of the prerequisites included a free market with large and steady demand, a money economy, inexpensive and rational technologies, a free labor force, a disciplined labor force, rational capital-accounting techniques, and the commercialization of economic life involving the use of shares, stocks, and the like. Many of the economic prerequisites were found only in the Occident. Outside the economy, Weber identified a variety of needed developments such as a modern state with "professional administration, specialized officialdom, and law based on the concept of citizenship" (1927/1981:313), rational law "made by jurists and rationally interpreted and applied" (1927/1981:313), cities, and modern science and technology. To these Weber adds a factor that will concern us in the next section, "a rational ethic for the conduct of life . . . a religious basis for the ordering of life which consistently followed out must lead to explicit rationalism" (1927/1981:313–314). Like the economic prerequisites, these noneconomic presuppositions occurred together only in the Occident. The basic point is that a rational economy is dependent upon a variety of noneconomic forces throughout the rest of society in order to develop.

Religion   Although we will focus on the rationalization of religion in this section, Weber spent much time analyzing the degree to which early, more primitive religions—and religions in much of the world—acted as impediments to the rise of rationality. Weber noted that "the sacred is the uniquely unalterable" (1921/1968:406). Despite this view, religion in the West did prove to be alterable; it was amenable to rationalization, and it did play a key role in the rationalization of other sectors of society (Kalberg, 1990).

Early religion was composed of a bewildering array of gods, but with rationalization, a clear and coherent set of gods (a pantheon) emerged. Early religions had household gods, kin-group gods, local political gods, and occupational and vocational gods. We get the clear feeling that Weber did believe that a cultural force of (theoretical) rationality impelled the emergence of this set of gods: "*Reason* favored the primacy of universal gods; and every consistent crystallization of a pantheon followed systematic *rational* principles" (1921/1968:417). A pantheon of gods was not the only aspect of the rationalization of religion discussed by Weber. He also considered the delimitation of the jurisdiction of gods, monotheism, and the anthropomorphization of gods as part of this development. Although the pressure for rationalization exists in many of the world's religions, in areas outside the Western world, the barriers to rationalization more than counterbalance the pressures for rationalization.

Although Weber had a cultural conception of rationalization, he did not view it simply as a force "out there" that impels people to act. He did not have a group-mind concept. In religion, rationalization is tied to concrete groups of people, in particular to priests. Specifically, the professionally trained priesthood is the carrier[12] and the expediter of rationalization. In this, priests stand in contrast to magicians, who support a more irrational religious system. The greater rationality of the priesthood is traceable to several factors. Members go through a systematic training program, whereas the training of magicians is unsystematic. Also, priests are fairly highly specialized, whereas magicians tend to be unspecialized. Finally, priests possess a systematic set of religious concepts, and this, too, sets them apart from magicians. We can say that priests are both the products and the expediters of the process of rationalization.

The priesthood is not the only group that plays a key role in rationalization. Prophets and a laity are also important in the process. Prophets can be distinguished from priests by their personal calling, their emotional preaching, their proclamation of a doctrine, and the fact that they tend to be unpopular and to work alone. The key role of the prophet is the mobilization of the laity, because there would be no religion without a group of followers. Unlike priests, prophets do not tend to the needs of a congregation. Weber differentiated between two types of prophets, ethical and exemplary. *Ethical prophets* (Mohammad, Jesus Christ, and the Old Testament prophets) believe that they have received a commission directly from God and demand obedience from followers as an ethical duty. *Exemplary prophets* (Buddha is a model) demonstrate to others by personal example the way to religious salvation. In either case, successful prophets are able to attract large numbers of followers, and it is this mass, along with the priests, that forms the heart of religion. Prophets are likely at first to attract a personal following, but it is necessary that that group be transformed into a permanent congregation. Once such a laity has been formed, major strides have been made in the direction of the rationalization of religion.

---

[12]For a general discussion of the role of carriers in Weber's work, see Kalberg (1994:58–62).

Prophets play a key initial role, but once a congregation is formed, they are no longer needed. In fact, because they are largely irrational, they represent a barrier to that rationalization of religion. A conflict develops between priests and prophets, but it is a conflict that must be won in the long run by the more rational priesthood. In their conflict, the priests are aided by the rationalization proceeding in the rest of society. As the secular world becomes more and more literate and bureaucratized, the task of educating the masses falls increasingly to the priests, whose literacy gives them a tremendous advantage over the prophets. In addition, while the prophets tend to do the preaching, the priests take over the task of day-to-day pastoral care. Although preaching is important during extraordinary times, pastoral care, or the daily religious cultivation of the laity, is an important instrument in the growing power of the priesthood. It was the church in the Western world that combined a rationalized pastoral character with an ethical religion to form a peculiarly influential and rational form of religion. This rationalized religion proved particularly well suited to winning converts among the urban middle class, and it was there that it played a key role in the rationalization of economic life as well as all other sectors of life.

Law   *Law* is defined by Weber not in terms of people's definitions, attitudes, and beliefs but rather as a body of norms (Kronman, 1983:12). Additionally, this body of norms is seen as being external to, and coercive of, individuals and their thoughts and actions. The emphasis is not on how people create law, interpret it, and daily re-create it but on its coercive effect on the individual.

As with his analysis of religion, Weber began his treatment of law with the primitive, which he saw as highly irrational. Primitive law was a rather undifferentiated system of norms. For example, no distinction was made between a civil wrong (a tort) and a crime. Thus cases involving differences over a piece of land and homicide were likely to be handled, and offenders punished, in much the same way. In addition, primitive law tended to lack any official machinery. Vengeance dominated reactions to a crime, and law was generally free from procedural formality or rules. Leaders, especially, were virtually unrestrained in what they could do to followers. From this early irrational period, Weber traced a direct line of development to a formalized legal procedure. And as was usual in Weber's thinking, it is only in the West that a rational, systematic theory of law is held to have developed.

Weber traced several stages in the development of a more rational legal system (Shamir, 1993). An early stage involves charismatic legal revelation through law prophets. Then there is the empirical creation and founding of law by honorary legal officials. Later there is the imposition of law by secular or theocratic powers. Finally, in the most modern case, we have the systematic elaboration of law and professionalized administration of justice by persons who have received their legal training formally and systematically.

In law, as in religion, Weber placed great weight on the process of professionalization: the legal profession is crucial to the rationalization of Western law. There are certainly other factors (for example, the influence of Roman law), but the legal profession was central to his thinking: "Formally elaborated law constituting a complex of maxims consciously applied in decisions has never come into existence without the decisive cooperation of trained specialists" (Weber, 1921/1968:775). Although Weber was aware that there was a series of external pressures—especially from the rationalizing economy—impelling law toward rationalization, his view was that the most important force was the internal factor of the professionalization of the legal profession (1921/1968:776).

Weber differentiated between two types of legal training but saw only one as contributing to the development of rational law. The first is *craft training,* in which apprentices learn from masters, primarily during the actual practice of law. This kind of training produces a formalistic type of law dominated by precedents. The goal is not the creation of a comprehensive, rational system of law but, instead, the production of practically useful precedents for dealing with recurring situations. Because these precedents are tied to specific issues in the real world, a general, rational, and systematic body of law cannot emerge.

In contrast, *academic legal training* laid the groundwork for the rational law of the West. In this system, law is taught in special schools, where the emphasis is placed on legal theory and science—in other words, where legal phenomena are given rational and systematic treatment. The legal concepts produced have the character of abstract norms. Interpretation of these laws occurs in a rigorously formal and logical manner. They are general, in contrast to the specific, precedent-bound laws produced in the case of craft training.

Academic legal training leads to the development of a rational legal system with a number of characteristics, including the following:

1 Every concrete legal decision involves the application of abstract legal propositions to concrete situations.

2 It must be possible in every concrete case to derive the decision logically from abstract legal propositions.

3 Law must tend to be a gapless system of legal propositions or at least be treated as one.

4 The gapless legal system should be applicable to all social actions.

Weber seemed to adopt the view that history has seen law evolve from a cultural system of norms to a more structured system of formal laws. In general, actors are increasingly constrained by a more and more rational legal system. Although this is true, Weber was too good a sociologist to lose sight completely of the independent significance of the actor. For one thing, Weber (1921/1968:754–755) saw actors as crucial in the emergence of, and change in, law. However, the most important aspect of Weber's work in this area—for the purposes of this discussion—is the degree to which law is regarded as part of the general process of rationalization throughout the West.

Polity The rationalization of the political system is intimately linked to the rationalization of law and, ultimately, to the rationalization of all elements of the social system. For example, Weber argued that the more rational the political structure becomes, the more likely it is to eliminate systematically the irrational elements within the law. A rational polity cannot function with an irrational legal system, and vice versa. Weber did not believe that political leaders follow a conscious policy of rationalizing the law; rather, they are impelled in that direction by the demands of their own increasingly rational means of administration. Once again, Weber took the position that actors are being impelled by structural (the state) and cultural (rationalization) forces.

Weber defined the *polity* as "a community whose social action is aimed at subordinating to orderly domination by the participants a territory and the conduct of the persons within it, through readiness to resort to physical force, including normally force of arms" (1921/1968:901). This type of polity has existed neither everywhere nor always. It does not exist as a separate entity where the task of armed defense against enemies is assigned to the household, the neighborhood association, an economic group, and so forth. Although Weber clearly viewed the polity as a social structure, he was more careful to link his thinking here to his individual action orientations. In his view, modern political associations rest on the prestige bestowed upon them by their members.

As was his usual strategy, Weber went back to the primitive case in order to trace the development of the polity. He made it clear that violent social action is primordial. However, the monopolization and rational ordering of legitimate violence did not exist in early societies but evolved over the centuries. Not only is rational control over violence lacking in primitive society, but other basic functions of the modern state either are totally absent or are not ordered in a rational manner. Included here would be functions like legislation, police, justice, administration, and the military. The development of the polity in the West involves the progressive differentiation and elaboration of these functions. But the most important step is their subordination under a single, dominant, rationally ordered state.

The City   Weber was also interested in the rise of the city in the West. The city provided an alternative to the feudal order and a setting in which modern capitalism, and more generally, rationality, could develop. He defined a *city* as having the following characteristics:

1 It is a relatively closed settlement.
2 It is relatively large.
3 It possesses a marketplace.
4 It has partial political autonomy.

Although many cities in many societies had these characteristics, Western cities developed a peculiarly rational character with, among other things, a rationally organized marketplace and political structure.

Weber looked at various other societies in order to determine why they did not develop the rational form of the city. He concluded that barriers like the traditional community in China and the caste system in India impeded the rise of such a city. But in the West, a number of rationalizing forces coalesced to create the modern city. For example, the development of a city requires a relatively rational economy. But of course the converse is also true: the development of a rational economy requires the modern city.

Art Forms   To give the reader a sense of the breadth of Weber's thinking, we need to say a few words about his work on the rationalization of various art forms. For example, Weber (1921/1958) viewed music in the West as having developed in a peculiarly rational direction. Musical creativity is reduced to routine procedures based on comprehensive principles. Music in the Western world has undergone a "transformation of the process of musical production into a calculable affair operating with known means, effective instruments, and understandable rules" (Weber, 1921/1958:li). Although the process of rationalization engenders tension in all the institutions in which it occurs, that tension is nowhere more noticeable than in music. After all, music is supposed to be an arena of expressive flexibility, but it is being progressively reduced to a rational, and ultimately mathematical, system.

Weber (1904–05/1958) sees a similar development in other art forms. For example, in painting, Weber emphasizes "the rational utilization of lines and spatial perspective—which the Renaissance created for us" (1904–05/1958:15). In architecture, "the rational use of the Gothic vault as a means of distributing pressure and of roofing spaces of all forms, and above all as the constructive principle of great monumental buildings and the foundation of a *style* extending to sculpture and painting, such as that created by our Middle Ages, does not occur elsewhere [in the world]" (Weber, 1904–05/1958:15).

We have now spent a number of pages examining Weber's ideas on rationalization in various aspects of social life. Although nowhere does he explicitly say so, we believe that Weber adopted the view that changes in the cultural level of rationality are leading to changes in the structures as well as in the individual thoughts and actions of the modern world. The rationalization process is not left to float alone above concrete phenomena but is embedded in various social structures and in the thoughts and actions of individuals. To put it slightly differently, the key point is that the cultural system of rationality occupies a position of causal priority in Weber's work. We can illustrate this in still another way by looking at Weber's work on the relationship between religion and economics—more specifically, the relationship between religion and the development, or lack of development, of a capitalist economy.

Religion and the Rise of Capitalism

Weber spent much of his life studying religion this in spite of, or perhaps because of, his being areligious, or, as he once described himself, "religiously unmusical" (Gerth and Mills, 1958:25). One of his overriding concerns was the relationship among a variety of the world's religions and the development only in the West of a capitalist economic system (Schlucter, 1996). It is clear that the vast bulk of this work is done at the social-structural and cultural levels; the thoughts and actions of Calvinists, Buddhists, Confucians, Jews, Muslims (B. Turner, 1974; Nafassi, 1998), and others are held to be affected by changes in social structures and social institutions. Weber was interested primarily in the systems of ideas of the world's religions, in the "spirit" of capitalism, and in rationalization as a modern system of norms and values. He was also very interested in the structures of the world's religions, the various structural components of the societies in which they exist that serve to facilitate or impede rationalization, and the structural aspects of capitalism and the rest of the modern world.

Weber's work on religion and capitalism involved an enormous body of cross-cultural historical research; here, as elsewhere, he did comparative-historical sociology (Kalberg, 1997). Freund summarized the complicated interrelationships involved in this research:

1 Economic forces influenced Protestantism.

2 Economic forces influenced religions other than Protestantism (for example, Hinduism, Confucianism, and Taoism).

3 Religious idea systems influenced individual thoughts and actions—in particular, economic thoughts and actions.

4 Religious idea systems have been influential throughout the world.

5 Religious idea systems (particularly Protestantism) have had the unique effect in the West of helping to rationalize the economic sector and virtually every other institution.

(Freund, 1968:213)

To this we can add:

6 Religious idea systems in the non-Western world have created overwhelming structural barriers to rationalization.

By according the religious factor great importance, Weber appeared to be simultaneously building on and criticizing his image of Marx's work. Weber, like Marx, operated with a complicated model of the interrelationship of primarily large-scale systems: "Weber's sociology is related to Marx's thought in the common attempt to grasp the interrelations of institutional orders making up a social structure: In Weber's work, military and religious, political and juridical institutional systems are functionally related to the economic order in a variety of ways" (Gerth and Mills, 1958:49). In fact, Weber's affinities with Marx are even greater than is often recognized. Although Weber, especially early in his career, gave primacy to religious ideas, he later came to see that material forces, not idea systems, are of greater importance (Kalberg, 1985:61). As Weber said, "Not ideas, but material and ideal interests, directly govern men's conduct. Yet very frequently the 'world images' that have been created by 'ideas' have, like switchmen, determined the tracks along which action has been pushed by the dynamic of interest" (cited in Gerth and Mills, 1958:280).

Paths to Salvation   In analyzing the relationship between the world's religions and the economy, Weber (1921/1963) developed a typology of the paths of salvation. *Asceticism* is the first broad type of religiosity, and it combines an orientation toward action with the commitment of believers to denying themselves the pleasures of the world. Ascetic religions are divided into two subtypes. *Otherworldly asceticism* involves a set of norms and values that command the followers not to work within the secular world and to fight against its temptations. Of greater interest to Weber, because it encompasses Calvinism, was *innerworldly asceticism*. Such a religion does not reject the world; instead, it actively urges its members to work within the world so that they can find salvation, or at least signs of it. The distinctive goal here is the strict, methodical control of the members' patterns of life, thought, and action. Members are urged to reject everything unethical, esthetic, or dependent on their emotional reactions to the secular world. Innerworldly ascetics are motivated to systematize their own conduct.

Whereas both types of asceticism involve some type of action and self-denial, *mysticism* involves contemplation, emotion, and inaction. Weber subdivided mysticism in the same way as asceticism. *World-rejecting mysticism* involves total flight from the world. *Innerworldly mysticism* leads to contemplative efforts to understand the meaning of the world, but these efforts are doomed to failure, because the world is viewed as being beyond individual comprehension. In any case, both types of mysticism and world-rejecting asceticism can be seen as idea systems that inhibit the development of capitalism and rationality. In contrast, innerworldly asceticism is the system of norms and values that contributed to the development of these phenomena in the West.

The Protestant Ethic and the Spirit of Capitalism   In Max Weber's best-known work, *The Protestant Ethic and the Spirit of Capitalism* (1904–05/1958), he traced the impact of ascetic Protestantism—primarily Calvinism—on the rise of the spirit of capitalism (H. Jones, 1997). This work is but a small part of a larger body of scholarship that traces the relationship between religion and modern capitalism throughout much of the world.

Weber, especially later in his work, made it clear that his most general interest was in the rise of the distinctive rationality of the West. Capitalism, with its rational organization of free labor, its open market, and its rational bookkeeping system, is but one component of that developing system. He directly linked it to the parallel development of rationalized science, law, politics, art, architecture, literature, universities, and the polity.

Weber did not directly link the idea system of the Protestant ethic to the structures of the capitalist system; instead, he was content to link the Protestant ethic to another system of ideas, the "spirit of capitalism." In other words, two systems of ideas are directly linked in this work. Although links of the capitalist economic system to the material world are certainly implied and indicated, they were not Weber's primary concern. Thus, *The Protestant Ethic* is not about the rise of modern capitalism but is about the origin of a peculiar spirit that eventually made modern rational capitalism (some form of capitalism had existed since early times) expand and come to dominate the economy.

Weber began by examining and rejecting alternative explanations of why capitalism arose in the West in the sixteenth and seventeenth centuries (for an alternative view on this, see R. Collins, 1997a). To those who contended that capitalism arose because the material conditions were right at that time, Weber retorted that material conditions were also ripe at other times and capitalism did not arise. Weber also rejected the psychological theory that the development of capitalism was due simply to the acquisitive instinct. In his view, such an instinct always has existed, yet it did not produce capitalism in other situations.

Evidence for Weber's views on the significance of Protestantism was found in an examination of countries with mixed religious systems. In looking at these countries, he discovered that the leaders of the economic system—business leaders, owners of capital, high-grade skilled labor, and more advanced technically and commercially trained personnel—were all overwhelmingly Protestant. This suggested that Protestantism was a significant cause in the choice of these occupations and, conversely, that other religions (for example, Roman Catholicism) failed to produce idea systems that impelled individuals into these vocations.

In Weber's view, the spirit of capitalism is not defined simply by economic greed; it is in many ways the exact opposite. It is a moral and ethical system, an ethos, that among other things stresses economic success. In fact, it was the turning of profit making into an ethos that was critical in the West. In other societies, the pursuit of profit was seen as an individual act motivated at least in part by greed. Thus it was viewed by many as morally suspect. However, Protestantism succeeded in turning the pursuit of profit into a moral crusade. It was the backing of the moral system that led to the unprecedented expansion of profit seeking and, ultimately, to the capitalist system. On a theoretical level, by stressing that he was dealing with the relationship between one ethos (Protestantism) and another (the spirit of capitalism), Weber was able to keep his analysis primarily at the level of systems of ideas.

The spirit of capitalism can be seen as a normative system that involves a number of interrelated ideas. For example, its goal is to instill an "attitude which seeks profit rationally and systematically" (Weber, 1904–05/1958:64). In addition, it preaches an avoidance of life's pleasures: "Seest thou a man diligent in business? He shall stand before kings" (Weber, 1904–05/1958:53). Also included in the spirit of capitalism are ideas such as "time is money," "be industrious," "be frugal," "be punctual," "be fair," and "earning money is a legitimate end in itself." Above all, there is the idea that it is people's duty to ceaselessly increase their wealth. This takes the spirit of capitalism out of the realm of individual ambition and into the category of ethical imperative. Although Weber admitted that a type of capitalism (for example, adventurer capitalism) existed in China, India, Babylon, and the classical world and during the Middle Ages, it was different from Western capitalism, primarily because it lacked "this particular ethos" (1904–05/1958:52).

Weber was interested not simply in describing this ethical system but also in explaining its derivations. He thought that Protestantism, particularly Calvinism, was crucial to the rise of the spirit of capitalism. Calvinism is no longer necessary to the continuation of that economic system. In fact, in many senses modern capitalism, given its secularity, stands in opposition to Calvinism and to religion in general. Capitalism today has become a real entity that combines norms, values, market, money, and laws. It has become, in Durkheim's terms, a social fact that is external to, and coercive of, the individual. As Weber put it:

> Capitalism is today an immense cosmos into which the individual is born, and which presents itself to him, at least as an individual, as an unalterable order of things in which he must live. It forces the individual, in so far as he is involved in the system of market relationships, to conform to capitalist rules of action.
>
> (Weber, 1904–05/1958:54)

Another crucial point here is that Calvinists did not consciously seek to create a capitalist system. In Weber's view, capitalism was an *unanticipated consequence* of the Protestant ethic. The concept of unanticipated consequences has broad significance in Weber's work, for he believed that what individuals and groups intend by their actions often leads to a set of consequences that are at variance with their intentions. Although Weber did not explain this point, it seems that it is related to his theoretical view that people create social structures but that those structures soon take on a life of their own, over which the creators have little or no control. Because people lack control over them, structures are free to develop in a variety of totally unanticipated directions. Weber's line of thinking led Arthur Mitzman (1970) to argue that Weber created a sociology of reification. Reified social structures are free to move in unanticipated directions, as both Marx and Weber showed in their analyses of capitalism.

Calvinism and the Spirit of Capitalism   Calvinism was the version of Protestantism that interested Weber most. One feature of Calvinism was the idea that only a small number of people are chosen for salvation. In addition, Calvinism entailed the idea of predestination; people were predestined to be either among the saved or among the damned. There was nothing that the individual or the religion as a whole could do to affect that fate. Yet the idea of predestination left people uncertain about whether they were among the saved. To reduce this uncertainty, the Calvinists developed the idea that *signs* could be used as indicators of whether a person was saved. People were urged to work hard, because if they were diligent, they would uncover the signs of salvation, which were to be found in economic success. In sum, the Calvinist was urged to engage in intense, worldly activity and to become a "man of vocation."

However, isolated actions were not enough. Calvinism, as an ethic, required self-control and a systematized style of life that involved an integrated round of activities, particularly business activities. This stood in contrast to the Christian ideal of the Middle Ages, in which individuals simply engaged in isolated acts as the occasion arose in order to atone for particular sins and to increase their chances of salvation. "The God of Calvinism demanded of his believers not single good works, but a life of good works combined into a unified system" (Weber, 1904–05/1958:117). Calvinism produced an ethical system and ultimately a group of people who were nascent capitalists. Calvinism "has the highest ethical appreciation of the sober, middle-class, self-made man" (Weber, 1904–05/1958:163). Weber neatly summarized his own position on Calvinism and its relationship to capitalism as follows:

> The religious valuation of restless, continuous, systematic work in a worldly calling, as the highest means of asceticism, and at the same time the surest and most evident proof of rebirth and genuine faith, must have been the most powerful conceivable lever for the expansion of . . . the spirit of capitalism.
>
> (Weber, 1904–05/1958:172)

In addition to its general link to the spirit of capitalism, Calvinism also had some more specific links. First, as already mentioned, capitalists could ruthlessly pursue their economic interests and feel that such pursuit was not merely self-interest but was, in fact, their ethical duty. This not only permitted unprecedented mercilessness in business but also silenced potential critics, who could not simply reduce these actions to self-interest. Second, Calvinism provided the rising capitalist "with sober, conscientious and unusually industrious workmen who clung to their work as to a life purpose willed by god" (Weber, 1904–05/1958:117). With such a work force, the nascent capitalist could raise the level of exploitation to unprecedented heights. Third, Calvinism legitimized an unequal stratification system by giving the capitalist the "comforting assurances that the unequal distribution of the goods of this world was a special dispensation of Divine Providence" (Weber, 1904–05/1958:117).

Weber also had reservations about the capitalist system, as he did about all aspects of the rationalized world. For example, he pointed out that capitalism tends to produce "specialists without spirit, sensualists without heart; this nullity imagines that it has attained a level of civilization never before achieved" (Weber, 1904–05/1958:182).

Although in *The Protestant Ethic* Weber focused on the effect of Calvinism on the spirit of capitalism, he was well aware that social and economic conditions have a reciprocal impact on religion. He chose not to deal with such relationships in this book, but he made it clear that his goal was not to substitute a one-sided spiritualist interpretation for the one-sided materialist explanation that he attributed to Marxists. (The same is true of much of the rest of his work, including his essays on the Russian Revolution; see Wells and Baehr, 1995:22.) As Kalberg (1996) has pointed out, *The Protestant Ethic* raises a wide number of issues that go to the heart of contemporary sociological theory.

If Calvinism was one of the causal factors in the rise of capitalism in the West, then the question arises: Why didn't capitalism arise in other societies? In his effort to answer this question, Weber dealt with spiritual and material barriers to the rise of capitalism. Let us look briefly at Weber's analysis of those barriers in two societies— China and India.

Religion and Capitalism in China   One crucial assumption that allowed Weber to make legitimate the comparison between the West and China is that both had the pre-requisites for the development of capitalism. In China, there was a tradition of intense acquisitiveness and unscrupulous competition. There was great industry and an enormous capacity for work in the populace. Powerful guilds existed. The population was expanding. And there was a steady growth in precious metals. With these and other material prerequisites, why didn't capitalism arise in China? As has been pointed out before, Weber's general answer was that social, structural, and religious barriers in China prevented the development of capitalism. This is not to say that capitalism was entirely absent in China. There were moneylenders and purveyors who sought high rates of profit. But a market, as well as various other components of a rational capitalistic system, was absent. In Weber's view, the rudimentary capitalism of China "pointed in a direction opposite to the development of rational economic corporate enterprises" (1916/1964:86).

Structural Barriers   Weber listed several structural barriers to the rise of capitalism in China. First, there was the structure of the typical Chinese community. It was held together by rigid kinship bonds in the form of sibs. The sibs were ruled by elders, who made them bastions of traditionalism. The sibs were self-contained entities, and there was little dealing with other sibs. This encouraged small, encapsulated land holdings and a household-based, rather than a market, economy. The extensive partitioning of the land prevented major technological developments, because economies of scale were impossible. Agricultural production remained in the hands of peasants, industrial production in the hands of small-scale artisans. Modern cities, which were to become the centers of Western capitalism, were inhibited in their development because the people retained their allegiance to the sibs. Because of the sibs' autonomy, the central government was never able to govern these units effectively or to mold them into a unified whole.

The structure of the Chinese state was a second barrier to the rise of capitalism. The state was largely patrimonial and governed by tradition, prerogative, and favoritism. In Weber's view, a rational and calculable system of administration and law enforcement, which was necessary for industrial development, did not exist. There were very few formal laws covering commerce, there was no central court, and legal formalism was rejected. This irrational type of administrative structure was a barrier to the rise of capitalism, as Weber made clear: "Capital investment in industry is far too sensitive to such irrational rule and too dependent upon the possibility of calculating the steady and rational operation of the state machinery to emerge within an administration of this type" (1916/1964:103). In addition to its general structure, a number of more specific components of the state acted against the development of capitalism. For example, the officials of the bureaucratic administration had vested material interests that made them oppose capitalism. Officials often bought offices primarily to make a profit, and this kind of orientation did not necessarily make for a high degree of efficiency.

A third structural barrier to the rise of capitalism was the nature of the Chinese language. In Weber's view, it militated against rationality by making systematic thought difficult. It remained largely in the realm of the "pictorial" and the "descriptive." Logical thinking was also inhibited because intellectual thought remained largely in the form of parables, and this hardly was the basis for the development of a cumulative body of knowledge.

Although there were other structural barriers to the rise of capitalism (for example, a country without wars or overseas trade), a key factor was the lack of the required "mentality," the lack of the needed idea system. Weber looked at the two dominant systems of religious ideas in China—Confucianism and Taoism—and the characteristics of both that militated against the development of a spirit of capitalism.

Confucianism   A central characteristic of Confucian thinking was its emphasis on a literary education as a prerequisite for office and for social status. To acquire a position in the ruling strata, a person had to be a member of the literati. Movement up the hierarchy was based on a system of ideas that tested literary knowledge, not the technical knowledge needed to conduct the office in question. What was valued and tested was whether the individual's mind was steeped in culture and whether it was characterized by ways of thought suitable to a cultured man. In Weber's terms, Confucianism encouraged "a highly bookish literary education." The literati produced by this system came to see the actual work of administration as beneath them, mere tasks to be delegated to subordinates. Instead, the literati aspired to clever puns, euphemisms, and allusions to classical quotations—a purely literary kind of intellectuality. With this kind of orientation, it is easy to see why the literati were unconcerned with the state of the economy or with economic activities. The world view of the Confucians ultimately grew to be the policy of the state. As a result, the Chinese state came to be only minimally involved in rationally influencing the economy and the rest of society. The Confucians maintained their influence by having the constitution decree that only they could serve as officials, and competitors to Confucians (for example, the bourgeoisie, prophets, and priests) were blocked from serving in the government. In fact, if the emperor dared to deviate from this rule, he was thought to be toying with disaster and his potential downfall.

Many other components of Confucianism militated against capitalism. It was basically an ethic of adjustment to the world and to its order and its conventions. Rather than viewing material success and wealth as a sign of salvation as the Calvinist did, the Confucian simply was led to accept things as they were. In fact, there was no idea of salvation in Confucianism, and this lack of tension between religion and the world also acted to inhibit the rise of capitalism. The snobbish Confucian was urged to reject thrift, because it was something that commoners practiced. In contrast to the Puritan work ethic, it was not regarded as proper for a Confucian gentleman to work, although wealth was prized. Active engagement in a profitable enterprise was regarded as morally dubious and unbecoming to a Confucian's station. The acceptable goal for such a gentleman was a good position, not high profits. The ethic emphasized the abilities of a gentleman rather than the highly specialized skills that could have proved useful to a developing capitalist system. In sum, Weber contended that Confucianism became a relentless canonization of tradition.

Taoism   Weber perceived Taoism as a mystical Chinese religion in which the supreme good was deemed to be a psychic state, a state of mind, and not a state of grace to be obtained by conduct in the real world. As a result, Taoists did not operate in a rational way to affect the external world. Taoism was essentially traditional, and one of its basic tenets was "Do not introduce innovations" (Weber, 1916/1964:203). Such an idea system was unlikely to produce any major changes, let alone one as far-reaching as capitalism.

One trait common to Taoism and Confucianism is that neither produced enough tension, or conflict, among the members to motivate them to much innovative action in this world:

> Neither in its official state cult nor in its Taoist aspect could Chinese religiosity produce sufficiently strong motives for a religiously oriented life for the individual such as the Puritan method represents. Both forms of religion lacked even the traces of the Satanic force or evil against which [the] pious Chinese might have struggled for his salvation.
>
> (Weber, 1916/1964:206)

As was true of Confucianism, there was no inherent force in Taoism to impel actors to change the world or, more specifically, to build a capitalist system.

Religion and Capitalism in India   For our purposes, a very brief discussion of Weber's (1916–17/1958) thinking on the relationship between religion and capitalism in India will suffice. The argument, though not its details, parallels the Chinese case. For example, Weber discussed the structural barriers of the caste system (Gellner, 1982:534). Among other things, the caste system erected overwhelming barriers to social mobility, and it tended to regulate even the most minute aspects of people's lives. The idea system of the Brahmans had a number of components. For example, Brahmans were expected to avoid vulgar occupations and to observe elegance in manners and proprieties in conduct. Indifference to the world's mundane affairs was the crowning idea of Brahman religiosity. The Brahmans also emphasized a highly literary kind of education. Although there certainly were important differences between Brahmans and Confucians, the ethos of each presented overwhelming barriers to the rise of capitalism.

The Hindu religion posed similar ideational barriers. Its key idea was reincarnation. To the Hindu, a person is born into the caste that he or she deserves by virtue of behavior in a past life. Through faithful adherence to the ritual of caste, the Hindu gains merit for the next life. Hinduism, unlike Calvinism, was traditional in the sense that salvation was to be achieved by faithfully following the rules; innovation, particularly in the economic sphere, could not lead to a higher caste in the next life. Activity in this world was not important, because the world was seen as a transient abode and an impediment to the spiritual quest. In these and other ways, the idea system associated with Hinduism failed to produce the kind of people who could create a capitalist economic system and, more generally, a rationally ordered society.

SUMMARY

Max Weber has had a more powerful positive impact on a wide range of sociological theories than any other sociological theorist. This influence is traceable to the sophistication, complexity, and sometimes even confusion of Weberian theory. Despite its problems, Weber's work represents a remarkable fusion of historical research and sociological theorizing.

We open this chapter with a discussion of the theoretical roots and methodological orientations of Weberian theory. We see that Weber, over the course of his career, moved progressively toward a fusion of history and sociology, that is, toward the development of a historical sociology. One of his most critical methodological concepts is *verstehen*. Although this is often interpreted as a tool to be used to analyze individual consciousness, in Weber's hands it was more often a scientific tool to analyze structural and institutional constraints on actors. We also discuss other aspects of Weber's methodology, including his propensity to think in terms of causality and to employ ideal types. In addition, we examine his analysis of the relationship between values and sociology.

The heart of Weberian sociology lies in substantive sociology, not in methodological statements. Although Weber based his theories on his thoughts about social action and social relationships, his main interest was the large-scale structures and institutions of society. We deal especially with his analysis of the three structures of authority—legal, traditional, and charismatic. In the context of legal authority, we deal with his famous ideal-typical bureaucracy and show how he used that tool to analyze traditional and charismatic authority. Of particular interest is Weber's work on charisma. Not only did he have a clear sense of it as a structure of authority, but he was also interested in the processes by which such a structure is produced.

Although his work on social structures—such as authority—is important, it is at the cultural level, in his work on the rationalization of the world, that Weber's most important insights lie. Weber articulated the idea that the world is becoming increasingly dominated by norms and values of rationalization. In this context, we discuss Weber's work on the economy, religion, law, the polity, the city, and art forms. Weber argued that rationalization was sweeping across all these institutions in the West, whereas there were major barriers to this process in the rest of the world.

Weber's thoughts on rationalization and various other issues are illustrated in his work on the relationship between religion and capitalism. At one level, this is a series of studies of the relationship between ideas (religious ideas) and the development of the spirit of capitalism and, ultimately, capitalism itself. At another level, it is a study of how the West developed a distinctively rational religious system (Calvinism) that played a key role in the rise of a rational economic system (capitalism). Weber also studied other societies, in which he found religious systems (for example, Confucianism, Taoism, and Hinduism) that inhibit the growth of a rational economic system. It is this kind of majestic sweep over the history of many sectors of the world that helps give Weberian theory its enduring significance.

8

GEORG SIMMEL

PRIMARY CONCERNS
    Levels and Areas of Concern
    Dialectical Thinking
INDIVIDUAL CONSCIOUSNESS
SOCIAL INTERACTION ("ASSOCIATION")
    Interaction: Forms and Types
SOCIAL STRUCTURES
OBJECTIVE CULTURE
THE PHILOSOPHY OF MONEY
    Money and Value
    Money, Reification, and Rationalization
    Negative Effects
    Tragedy of Culture
SECRECY: A CASE STUDY IN SIMMEL'S SOCIOLOGY
    Secrecy and Social Relationships
    Other Thoughts on Secrecy

The impact of the ideas of Georg Simmel (1858–1918) on American sociological theory, as well as sociological theory in general, differs markedly from that of the three theorists discussed in the preceding three chapters of this book (see Dahme, 1990; Featherstone, 1991; Kaern, Phillips, and Cohen, 1990; for a good overview of the secondary literature on Simmel, see Frisby, 1994). Marx, Durkheim, and Weber, despite their later significance, had relatively little influence on American theory in the early twentieth century. Simmel was much better known to the early American sociologists. Simmel was eclipsed by Marx, Durkheim, and Weber, although he is far more influential today than classical thinkers such as Comte or Spencer. In recent years we have seen an increase in Simmel's impact on sociological theory (Aronowitz, 1994; D. Levine, 1985; 1989; 1997; Scaff, forthcoming) as a result of the growing influence of one of his most important works, *The Philosophy of Money* (for an analysis of this work, see Poggi, 1993), as well as the linking of his ideas to one of the most important developments in social thought—postmodern social theory (Weinstein and Weinstein, 1993; 1998).

PRIMARY CONCERNS

Although we will focus on Simmel's contributions to sociological theory, we should point out that he was primarily a philosopher and that most of his publications dealt with philosophical issues (for example, ethics) and other philosophers (for example, Kant).

GEORG SIMMEL: A Biographical Sketch

Georg Simmel was born in the heart of Berlin on March 1, 1858. He studied a wide range of subjects at the University of Berlin. However, his first effort to produce a dissertation was rejected, and one of his professors remarked, "We would do him a great service if we do not encourage him further in this direction" (Frisby, 1984:23). Despite this, Simmel persevered and received his doctorate in philosophy in 1881. He remained at the university in a teaching capacity until 1914, although he occupied a relatively unimportant position as *Privatdozent* from 1885 to 1900. In the latter position, Simmel served as an unpaid lecturer whose livelihood was dependent on student fees. Despite his marginality, Simmel did rather well in this position, largely because he was an excellent lecturer and attracted large numbers of (paying) students (Frisby, 1981:17; Salomon, 1963/1997). His style was so popular that even cultured members of Berlin society were drawn to his lectures, which became public events.

Simmel's marginality is paralleled by the fact that he was a somewhat contradictory and therefore bewildering person:

> If we put together the testimonials left by relatives, friends, students, contemporaries, we find a number of sometimes contradictory indications concerning Georg Simmel. He is depicted by some as being tall and slender, by others as being short and as bearing a forlorn expression. His appearance is reported to be unattractive, typically Jewish, but also intensely intellectual and noble. He is reported to be hard-working, but also humorous and overarticulate as a lecturer. Finally we hear that he was intellectually brilliant [Lukács, 1991:145], friendly, well-disposed—but also that *inside* he was irrational, opaque, and wild.
> (Schnabel, cited in Poggi, 1993:55)

Simmel wrote innumerable articles ("The Metropolis and Mental Life") and books (*The Philosophy of Money*). He was well known in German academic circles and even had an international following, especially in the United States, where his work was of great significance in the birth of sociology. Finally, in 1900, Simmel received official recognition, a purely

With the exception of his contribution to the primarily macroscopic conflict theory (Coser, 1956; Simmel, 1908/1955), Georg Simmel is best known as a microsociologist who played a significant role in the development of small-group research (Caplow, 1968), symbolic interactionism, and exchange theory. All of Simmel's contributions in these areas reflect his belief that sociologists should study primarily forms and types of social interaction. Robert Nisbet presents this view of Simmel's contribution to sociology:

> It is the *microsociological* character of Simmel's work that may always give him an edge in timeliness over the other pioneers. He did not disdain the small and the intimate elements of human association, nor did he ever lose sight of the primacy of human beings, of concrete individuals, in his analysis of institutions.
> (Nisbet, 1959:480)

honorary title at the University of Berlin, which did not give him full academic status. Simmel tried to obtain many academic positions, but he failed in spite of the support of such scholars as Max Weber.

One of the reasons for Simmel's failure was that he was a Jew in a nineteenth-century Germany rife with anti-Semitism (Kasler, 1985). Thus, in a report on Simmel written to a minister of education, Simmel was described as "an Israelite through and through, in his external appearance, in his bearing and in his mode of thought" (Frisby, 1981:25). Another reason was the kind of work that he did. Many of his articles appeared in newspapers and magazines; they were written for an audience more general than simply academic sociologists (Rammstedt, 1991). In addition, because he did not hold a regular academic appointment, he was forced to earn his living through public lectures. Simmel's audience, both for his writings and his lectures, was more the intellectual public than professional sociologists, and this tended to lead to derisive judgments from fellow professionals. For example, one of his contemporaries damned him because "his influence remained . . . upon the general atmosphere and affected, above all, the higher levels of journalism" (Troeltsch, cited in Frisby, 1981:13). Simmel's personal failures can also be linked to the low esteem that German academicians of the day had for sociology.

In 1914 Simmel finally obtained a regular academic appointment at a minor university (Strasbourg), but he once again felt estranged. On the one hand, he regretted leaving his audience of Berlin intellectuals. Thus his wife wrote to Max Weber's wife: "Georg has taken leave of the auditorium very badly. . . . The students were very affectionate and sympathetic. . . . It was a departure at the full height of life" (Frisby, 1981:29). On the other hand, Simmel did not feel a part of the life of his new university. Thus, he wrote to Mrs. Weber: "There is hardly anything to report from us. We live . . . a cloistered, closed-off, indifferent, desolate external existence. Academic activity is = 0, the people . . . alien and inwardly hostile" (Frisby, 1981:32).

World War I started soon after Simmel's appointment at Strasbourg; lecture halls were turned into military hospitals, and students went off to war. Thus, Simmel remained a marginal figure in German academia until his death in 1918. He never did have a normal academic career. Nevertheless, Simmel attracted a large academic following in his day, and his fame as a scholar has, if anything, grown over the years.

David Frisby makes a similar point: "The grounding of sociology in some psychological categories may be one reason why Simmel's sociology has proved attractive not merely to the interactionist but also to social psychology" (1984:57; see also Frisby, 1992:20–41). However, it is often forgotten that Simmel's microsociological work on the forms of interaction is embedded in a broader theory of the relations between individuals and the larger society.

Levels and Areas of Concern

Simmel had a much more complicated and sophisticated theory of social reality than he is commonly given credit for in contemporary American sociology. Tom Bottomore and David Frisby (1978) argue that there are four basic levels of concern in Simmel's work.

First are his microscopic assumptions about the psychological components of social life. Second, on a slightly larger scale, is his interest in the sociological components of interpersonal relationships. Third, and most macroscopic, is his work on the structure of, and changes in, the social and cultural "spirit" of his times. Not only did Simmel operate with this image of a three-tiered social reality, but he adopted the principle of *emergence,* the idea that the higher levels emerge out of the lower levels: "Further development replaces the immediacy of interacting forces with the creation of higher supra-individual formations, which appear as independent representatives of these forces and absorb and mediate the relations between individuals" (1907/1978:174). He also said, "If society is to be an autonomous object of an independent science, then it can only be so through the fact that, out of the sum of the individual elements that constitute it, a new entity emerges; otherwise all problems of social science would only be those of individual psychology" (Frisby, 1984:56–57). Overarching these three tiers is a fourth that involves ultimate metaphysical principles of life. These eternal truths affect all of Simmel's work and, as we will see, lead to his image of the future direction of the world.

This concern with multiple levels of social reality is reflected in Simmel's (1950; originally published in 1918) definition of three separable problem "areas" in sociology. The first he described as "pure" sociology. In this area, psychological variables are combined with forms of interactions. Although Simmel clearly assumed that actors have creative mental abilities, he gave little explicit attention to this aspect of social reality. His most microscopic work is with the *forms* that interaction takes as well as with the *types* of people who engage in interaction (Korllos, 1994). The forms include subordination, superordination, exchange, conflict, and sociability. In his work on types, he differentiated between positions in the interactional structure, such as "competitor" and "coquette," and orientations to the world, such as "miser," "spendthrift," "stranger," and "adventurer." At the intermediate level is Simmel's "general" sociology, dealing with the social and cultural products of human history. Here Simmel manifested his larger-scale interests in the group, the structure and history of societies and cultures. Finally, in Simmel's "philosophical" sociology, he dealt with his views on the basic nature, and inevitable fate, of humankind. Throughout this chapter, we will touch on all these levels and sociologies. We will find that although Simmel sometimes separated the different levels and sociologies, he more often integrated them into a broader totality.

Dialectical Thinking

Simmel's way of dealing with the interrelationships among three basic levels of social reality (leaving out his fourth, metaphysical level) gave his sociology a dialectical character reminiscent of Marx's sociology (Levine, 1991b:109). A dialectical approach, as we saw earlier, is multicausal and multidirectional, integrates fact and value, rejects the idea that there are hard-and-fast dividing lines between social phenomena, focuses on social relations (B. Turner, 1986), looks not only at the present but also at the past and the future, and is deeply concerned with both conflicts and contradictions.

In spite of the similarities between Marx and Simmel in their use of a dialectical approach, there are important differences between them. Of greatest importance is the fact that they focused on very different aspects of the social world and offered very different images of the future of the world. Instead of Marx's revolutionary optimism, Simmel had a view of the future closer to Weber's image of an "iron cage" from which there is no escape (for more on the intellectual relationship between Simmel and Weber, see Scaff, 1989:121–151).

Simmel manifested his commitment to the dialectic in various ways (Featherstone, 1991:7). For one thing, Simmel's sociology was always concerned with relationships (Lichtblau and Ritter, 1991), especially interaction (*association*). More generally, Simmel was a "methodological relationist" (Ritzer and Gindoff, 1992) operating with the "principle that everything interacts in some way with everything else" (Simmel, cited in Frisby, 1992:9). Overall he was ever attuned to dualisms, conflicts, and contradictions in whatever realm of the social world he happened to be working on (Sellerberg, 1994). Donald Levine states that this perspective reflects Simmel's belief that *"the world can best be understood in terms of conflicts and contrasts between opposed categories"* (1971:xxxv). Rather than try to deal with this mode of thinking throughout Simmel's work, let us illustrate it from his work on one of his forms of interaction—*fashion*. Simmel used a similar mode of dialectical thinking in most of his essays on social forms and social types, but this discussion of fashion amply illustrates his method of dealing with these phenomena. We will also deal with the dialectic in Simmel's thoughts on subjective-objective culture and the concepts of "more-life" and "more-than-life."

Fashion   In one of his typically fascinating and dualistic essays, Simmel (1904/1971; Gronow, 1997, Nedelmann, 1990) illustrated the contradictions in fashion in a variety of ways. On the one hand, fashion is a form of social relationship that allows those who wish to conform to the demands of the group to do so. On the other hand, fashion also provides the norm from which those who wish to be individualistic can deviate. Fashion involves a historical process as well: at the initial stage, everyone accepts what is fashionable; inevitably individuals deviate from this; and finally, in the process of deviation, they may adopt a whole new view of what is in fashion. Fashion is also dialectical in the sense that the success and spread of any given fashion leads to its eventual failure. That is, the distinctiveness of something leads to its being considered fashionable; however, as large numbers of people come to accept it, it ceases to be distinctive and hence it loses its attractiveness. Still another duality involves the role of the leader of a fashion movement. Such a person leads the group, paradoxically, by *following* the fashion better than anyone else, that is, by adopting it more determinedly. Finally, Simmel argued that not only does following what is in fashion involve dualities but so does the effort on the part of some people to be out of fashion. Unfashionable people view those who follow a fashion as being imitators and themselves as mavericks, but Simmel argued that the latter are simply engaging in an inverse form of imitation. Individuals may avoid what is in fashion because they are afraid that they, like their peers, will lose their individuality, but in Simmel's view, such a fear is hardly a sign of great personal strength and independence. In sum, Simmel noted that in fashion "all . . . lead ing antithetical tendencies . . . are represented in one way or another" (1904/1971:317).

Simmel's dialectical thinking can be seen at a more general level as well. As we will see throughout this chapter, he was most interested in the conflicts and contradictions that exist between the individual and the larger social and cultural structures that individuals construct. These structures ultimately come to have a life of their own, over which the individual can exert little or no control.

Individual (Subjective) Culture and Objective Culture   People are influenced, and in Simmel's view threatened, by social structures and, more important, for Simmel, by their cultural products. Simmel distinguished between individual culture and objective culture. *Objective culture* refers to those things that people produce (art, science, philosophy, and so on). *Individual (subjective) culture* is the capacity of the actor to produce, absorb, and control the elements of objective culture. In an ideal sense, individual culture shapes, and is shaped by, objective culture. The problem is that objective culture comes to have a life of its own. As Simmel put it, "They [the elements of culture] acquire fixed identities, a logic and lawfulness of their own; this new rigidity inevitably places them at a distance from the spiritual dynamic which created them and which makes them independent" (1921/1968:11). The existence of these cultural products creates a contradiction with the actors who created them because it is an example of

> the deep estrangement or animosity which exists between organic and creative processes of the soul and its contents and products: the vibrating, restless life of the creative soul; which develops toward the infinite contrasts with its fixed and ideally unchanging product and its uncanny feedback effect, which arrests and indeed rigidifies this liveliness. Frequently it appears as if creative movement of the soul was dying from its own product.
> (Simmel, 1921/1968:42)

As K. Peter Etzkorn said, "In Simmel's dialectic, man is always in danger of being slain by those objects of his own creation which have lost their organic human coefficient" (1968:2).

More-Life and More-Than-Life   Another area of Simmel's thinking, his philosophical sociology, is an even more general manifestation of his dialectical thinking. In discussing the emergence of social and cultural structures, Simmel took a position very similar to some of Marx's ideas. Marx used the concept of the fetishism of commodities to illustrate the separation between people and their products. For Marx, this separation reached its apex in capitalism, could be overcome only in the future socialist society, and thus was a specific historical phenomenon. But for Simmel this separation is inherent in the nature of human life. In philosophical terms, there is an inherent and inevitable contradiction between "more-life" and "more-than-life" (Oakes, 1984b:6; Weingartner, 1959).

The issue of more-life and more-than-life is central in Simmel's essay "The Transcendent Character of Life" (1918/1971). As the title suggests, and Simmel makes clear, *"Transcendence is immanent in life"* (1918/1971:361). People possess a doubly transcendent capability. First, because of their restless, creative capacities (more-life), people are able to transcend themselves. Second, this transcendent, creative ability makes it possible for people to constantly produce sets of objects that transcend them. The objective existence of these phenomena (more-than-life) comes to stand in irreconcilable opposition to the creative forces (more-life) that produced the objects in the first place. In other words, social life "creates and sets free from itself something that is not life but 'which has its own significance and follows its own law'" (Weingartner, citing Simmel, 1959:53). Life is found in the unity, and the conflict, between the two. As Simmel concludes, "Life finds its essence, its process, in being more-life and more-than-life" (1918/1971:374).

Thus, because of his metaphysical conceptions, Simmel came to an image of the world far closer to Weber's than to Marx's. Simmel, like Weber, saw the world as becoming an iron cage of objective culture from which people have progressively less chance of escape. We will have more to say about a number of these issues in the following sections, which deal with Simmel's thoughts on the major components of social reality.

INDIVIDUAL CONSCIOUSNESS

At the individual level, Simmel focused on forms of association and paid relatively little attention to the issue of individual consciousness (for at least one exception, a discussion of memory, see Jedlowski, 1990), which was rarely dealt with directly in his work. Still, Simmel clearly operated with a sense that human beings possess creative consciousness. As Frisby put it, the bases of social life to Simmel were "conscious individuals or groups of individuals who interact with one another for a variety of motives, purposes, and interests" (1984:61). This interest in creativity is manifest in Simmel's discussion of the diverse forms of interaction, the ability of actors to create social structures, as well as the disastrous effects those structures have on the creativity of individuals.

All of Simmel's discussions of the forms of interaction imply that actors must be consciously oriented to one another. Thus, for example, interaction in a stratified system requires that superordinates and subordinates orient themselves to each other. The interaction would cease and the stratification system collapse if a process of mutual orientation did not exist. The same is true of all other forms of interaction.

Consciousness plays other roles in Simmel's work. For example, although Simmel believed that social (and cultural) structures come to have a life of their own, he realized that people must conceptualize such structures in order for them to have an effect on the people. Simmel stated that society is not simply "out there" but is also " 'my representation'—something dependent on the activity of consciousness" (1908/1959a:339).

Simmel also had a sense of individual conscience and of the fact that the norms and values of society become internalized in individual consciousness. The existence of norms and values both internally and externally

> explains the dual character of the moral command: that on the one hand, it confronts us as an impersonal order to which we simply have to submit, but that, on the other, no external power, but only our most private and internal impulses, imposes it upon us. At any rate, here is one of the cases where the individual, within his own consciousness, repeats the relationships which exist between him, as a total personality, and the group.
>
> (Simmel, 1908/1950a:254)

This very modern conception of internalization is a relatively undeveloped assumption in Simmel's work.

In addition, Simmel had a conception of people's ability to confront themselves mentally, to set themselves apart from their own actions, that is very similar to the views of George Herbert Mead (see Chapter 12) and symbolic interactionists (Simmel, 1918/1971:364; see also Simmel, 1907/1978:64). The actor can take in external stimuli, assess them, try out different courses of action, and then decide what to do. Because of these mental capacities, the actor is not simply enslaved by external forces. But there is a paradox in Simmel's conception of the actor's mental capacities. The mind can keep people from being enslaved by external stimuli, but it also has the capacity to reify social reality, to create the very objects that come to enslave it. As Simmel said, "Our mind has a remarkable ability to think of contents as being independent of the act of thinking" (1907/1978:65). Thus, although their intelligence enables people to avoid being enslaved by the same external stimuli that constrain lower animals, it also creates the structures and institutions that constrain their thoughts and actions.

Although we can find manifestations of Simmel's concern with consciousness in various places in his work, he did very little other than assume its existence. Raymond Aron clearly makes this point: "He [Simmel] must know the laws of behavior . . . of human reaction. But he does not try to discover or to explain what goes on in the mind itself" (1965:5–6).

SOCIAL INTERACTION ("ASSOCIATION")

Georg Simmel is best known in contemporary sociology for his contributions to our understanding of the patterns, or forms, of social interaction. He expressed his interest in this level of social reality in this way:

> We are dealing here with microscopic-molecular processes within human material, so to speak. These processes are the actual occurrences that are concatenated or hypostatized into those macrocosmic, solid units and systems. That people look at one another and are jealous of one another; that they exchange letters or have dinner together; that apart from all tangible interests they strike one another as pleasant or unpleasant; that gratitude for altruistic acts makes for inseparable union; that one asks another to point out a certain street; that people dress and adorn themselves for each other—these are a few casually chosen illustrations from the whole range of relations that play between one person and another. They may be momentary or permanent, conscious or unconscious, ephemeral or of grave consequence, but they incessantly tie men together. At each moment such threads are spun, dropped, taken up again, displaced by others, interwoven with others. These interactions among the atoms of society are accessible only to psychological microscopy.
>
> (Simmel, 1908/1959b:327–328)

Simmel made clear here that one of his primary interests was interaction (association) among conscious actors and that his intent was to look at a wide range of interactions that may seem trivial at some times but crucially important at others. His was not a Durkheimian expression of interest in social facts but a declaration of a smaller-scale focus for sociology.

Because Simmel sometimes took an exaggerated position on the importance of interaction in his sociology, many have lost sight of his insights into the larger-scale aspects of social reality. At times, for example, he equated society with interaction: "Society . . . is only the synthesis or the general term for the totality of these specific interactions. . . . 'Society' is identical with the sum total of these relations" (Simmel, 1907/1978:175). Such statements may be taken as a reaffirmation of his interest in interaction, but, as we will see, in his general and philosophical sociologies, Simmel held a much larger scale conception of society as well as culture.

Interaction: Forms and Types

One of Simmel's dominant concerns was the *form* rather than the *content* of social interaction. This concern stemmed from Simmel's identification with the Kantian tradition in philosophy, in which much is made of the difference between form and content. Simmel's position here, however, was quite simple. From Simmel's point of view, the real world is composed of innumerable events, actions, interactions, and so forth. To cope with this maze of reality (the "contents"), people order it by imposing patterns, or forms, on it. Thus, instead of a bewildering array of specific events, the actor is confronted with a limited number of forms. In Simmel's view, the sociologist's task is to do precisely what the layperson does, that is, impose a limited number of forms on social reality, on interaction in particular, so that it may be better analyzed. This methodology generally involves extracting commonalities that are found in a wide array of specific interactions. For example, the superordination and subordination forms of interaction are found in a wide range of settings, "in the state as well as in a religious community, in a band of conspirators as in an economic association, in art school as in a family" (Simmel, 1908/1959b:317). Donald Levine, one of Simmel's foremost contemporary analysts, describes Simmel's method of doing formal interactional sociology in this way: "His method is to select some bounded, finite phenomenon from the world of flux; to examine the multiplicity of elements which compose it; and to ascertain the cause of their coherence by disclosing its form. Secondarily, he investigates the origins of this form and its structural implications" (1971:xxxi). More specifically, Levine points out that "forms are the patterns exhibited by the associations" of people (1981b:65).[1]

Simmel's interest in the forms of social interaction has been subjected to various criticisms. For example, he has been accused of imposing order where there is none and of producing a series of unrelated studies that in the end really impose no better order on the complexities of social reality than does the layperson. Some of these criticisms are valid only if we focus on Simmel's concern with forms of interaction, his formal sociology, and ignore the other types of sociology he practiced.

However, there are a number of ways to defend Simmel's approach to formal sociology. First, it is close to reality, as reflected by the innumerable real-life examples employed by Simmel. Second, it does not impose arbitrary and rigid categories on social reality but tries instead to allow the forms to flow from social reality. Third, Simmel's approach does not employ a general theoretical schema into which all aspects of the social world are forced. He thus avoided the reification of a theoretical schema

---

[1] In the specific case of interaction, contents are the "*drives, purposes and ideas which lead people to associate* with one another" (Levine, 1981b:65).

that plagues a theorist like Talcott Parsons. Finally, formal sociology militates against the poorly conceptualized empiricism that is characteristic of much of sociology. Simmel certainly used empirical "data," but they are subordinated to his effort to impose some order on the bewildering world of social reality.

Social Geometry In Simmel's formal sociology, one sees most clearly his effort to develop a "geometry" of social relations. Two of the geometric coefficients that interested him are numbers and distance (others are position, valence, self-involvement, and symmetry [Levine, 1981b]).

Numbers Simmel's interest in the impact of numbers of people on the quality of interaction can be seen in his discussion of the difference between a dyad and a triad.

Dyad and triad. For Simmel (1950) there was a crucial difference between the *dyad* (two-person group) and the *triad* (three-person group). The addition of a third person causes a radical and fundamental change. Increasing the membership beyond three has nowhere near the same impact as adding a third member. Unlike all other groups, the dyad does not achieve a meaning beyond the two individuals involved. There is no independent group structure in a dyad; there is nothing more to the group than the two separable individuals. Thus, each member of a dyad retains a high level of individuality. The individual is not lowered to the level of the group. This is not the case in the triad. A triad does have the possibility of obtaining a meaning beyond the individuals involved. There is likely to be more to a triad than the individuals involved. It is likely to develop an independent group structure. As a result, there is a greater threat to the individuality of the members. A triad can have a general leveling effect on the members.

With the addition of a third party to the group, a number of new social roles become possible. For example, the third party can take the role of arbitrator or mediator in disputes within the group. Then the third party can use disputes between the other two for his or her own gain or become an object of competition between the other two parties. The third member also can intentionally foster conflict between the other two parties in order to gain superiority (divide and rule). A stratification system and an authority structure then can emerge. The movement from dyad to triad is essential to the development of social structures that can become separate from, and dominant over, individuals. Such a possibility does not exist in a dyad.

The process that is begun in the transition from a dyad to a triad continues as larger and larger groups and, ultimately, societies emerge. In these large social structures, the individual, increasingly separated from the structure of society, grows more and more alone, isolated, and segmented. This results finally in a dialectical relationship between individuals and social structures: "According to Simmel, the socialized individual always remains in a dual relation toward society: he is incorporated within it and yet stands against it. . . . The individual is determined, yet determining; acted upon, yet self-actuating" (Coser, 1965:11). The contradiction here is that "society allows the emergence of individuality and autonomy, but it also impedes it" (Coser, 1965:11).

Group size. At a more general level, there is Simmel's (1908/1971a) ambivalent attitude toward the impact of group *size*. On the one hand, he took the position that the increase in the size of a group or society increases individual freedom. A small group or society is likely to control the individual completely. However, in a larger society, the individual is likely to be involved in a number of groups, each of which controls only a small portion of his or her total personality. In other words, *"Individuality in being and action generally increases to the degree that the social circle encompassing the individual expands"* (Simmel, 1908/1971a:252). However, Simmel took the view that large societies create a set of problems that ultimately threaten individual freedom. For example, he saw the masses as likely to be dominated by one idea, the simplest idea. The physical proximity of a mass makes people suggestible and more likely to follow simplistic ideas, to engage in mindless, emotional actions.

Perhaps most important, in terms of Simmel's interest in forms of interaction, is that increasing size and differentiation tend to loosen the bonds between individuals and leave in their place much more distant, impersonal, and segmental relationships. Paradoxically, the large group that frees the individual simultaneously threatens that individuality. Also paradoxical is Simmel's belief that one way for individuals to cope with the threat of the mass society is to immerse themselves in small groups such as the family.

Distance   Another of Simmel's concerns in social geometry was *distance.* Levine offers a good summation of Simmel's views on the role of distance in social relationships: *"The properties of forms and the meanings of things are a function of the relative distances between individuals and other individuals or things"* (1971:xxxiv). This concern with distance is manifest in various places in Simmel's work. We will discuss it in two different contexts—in Simmel's massive *The Philosophy of Money* and in one of his cleverest essays, "The Stranger."

In *The Philosophy of Money* (1907/1978), Simmel enunciated some general principles about value—and about what makes things valuable—that served as the basis for his analysis of money. Because we deal with this work in detail later in this chapter, we discuss this issue only briefly here. The essential point is that the value of something is determined by its distance from the actor. It is not valuable if it is either too close and too easy to obtain or too distant and too difficult to obtain. Objects that are attainable, but only with great effort, are the most valuable.

Distance also plays a central role in Simmel's "The Stranger" (1908/1971b; Tabboni, 1995), an essay on a type of actor who is neither too close nor too far. If he (or she) were too close, he would no longer be a stranger, but if he were too far, he would cease to have any contact with the group. The interaction that the stranger engages in with the group members involves a combination of closeness and distance. The peculiar distance of the stranger from the group allows him to have a series of unusual interaction patterns with the members. For example, the stranger can be more objective in his relationships with the group members. Because he is a stranger, other group members feel more comfortable expressing confidences to him. In these and other ways, a pattern of coordination and consistent interaction emerges between the stranger and the other group members. The stranger becomes an organic member of the group. But Simmel not only considered the stranger a social type; he considered strangeness a form of social interaction. A degree of strangeness, involving a combination of nearness and remoteness, enters into all social relationships, even the most intimate. Thus we can examine a wide range of specific interactions in order to discover the degree of strangeness found in each.

Although geometric dimensions enter a number of Simmel's types and forms, there is much more to them than simply geometry. The types and forms are constructs that Simmel used to gain a greater understanding of a wide range of interaction patterns.

Social Types   We have already encountered one of Simmel's types, the stranger; others include the miser, the spendthrift, the adventurer, and the nobleman. To illustrate his mode of thinking in this area, we will focus on one of his types, the poor.

The Poor   As is typical of types in Simmel's work, the *poor* were defined in terms of social relationships, as being aided by other people or at least having the right to that aid. Here Simmel quite clearly did not hold the view that *poverty* is defined by a quantity, or rather a lack of quantity, of money.

Although Simmel focused on the poor in terms of characteristic relationships and interaction patterns, he also used the occasion of his essay "The Poor" (1908/1971c) to develop a wide range of interesting insights into the poor and poverty. It was characteristic of Simmel to offer a profusion of insights in every essay. Indeed, this is one of his great claims to fame. For example, Simmel argued that a reciprocal set of rights and obligations defines the relationship between the needy and the givers. The needy have the right to receive aid, and this right makes receiving aid less painful. Conversely, the giver has the obligation to give to the needy. Simmel also took the functionalist position that aid to the poor by society helps to support the system. Society requires aid to the poor "so that the poor will not become active and dangerous enemies of society, so as to make their reduced energies more productive, and so as to prevent the degeneration of their progeny" (Simmel, 1908/1971c:154). Thus aid to the poor is for the sake of society, not so much for the poor per se. The state plays a key role here, and, as Simmel saw it, the treatment of the poor grows increasingly impersonal as the mechanism for giving aid becomes more bureaucratized.

Simmel also had a relativistic view of poverty; that is, the poor are not simply those who stand at the bottom of society. From his point of view, poverty is found in *all* social strata. This concept foreshadowed the later sociological concept of *relative deprivation*. If people who are members of the upper classes have less than their peers, then they are likely to feel poor in comparison to them. Therefore, government programs aimed at eradicating poverty can never succeed. Even if those at the bottom are elevated, many people throughout the stratification system will still feel poor in comparison to their peers.

Social Forms   As with social types, Simmel looked at a wide range of social forms, including exchange, conflict, prostitution, and sociability. We can illustrate Simmel's (1908/1971d) work on social forms through his discussion of domination, that is, superordination and subordination.

Superordination and Subordination   Superordination and subordination have a reciprocal relationship. The leader does not want to determine completely the thoughts and actions of others. Rather, the leader expects the subordinate to react either positively or negatively. Neither this nor any other form of interaction can exist without mutual relationships. Even in the most oppressive form of domination, subordinates have at least some degree of personal freedom.

To most people, superordination involves an effort to eliminate completely the independence of subordinates, but Simmel argued that a social relationship would cease to exist if this were the case.

Simmel asserted that one can be subordinated to an individual, a group, or an objective force. Leadership by a single individual generally leads to a tightly knit group either in support of or in opposition to the leader. Even when opposition arises in such a group, discord can be resolved more easily when the parties stand under the same higher power. Subordination under a plurality can have very uneven effects. On the one hand, the objectivity of rule by a plurality may make for greater unity in the group than the more arbitrary rule of an individual. On the other hand, hostility is likely to be engendered among subordinates if they do not get the personal attention of a leader.

Simmel found subordination under an objective principle to be most offensive, perhaps because human relationships and social interactions are eliminated. People feel they are determined by an impersonal law that they have no ability to affect. Simmel saw subordination to an individual as freer and more spontaneous: "Subordination under a person has an element of freedom and dignity in comparison with which all obedience to laws has something mechanical and passive" (1908/1971d:115). Even worse is subordination to objects (for example, icons), which Simmel found a "humiliatingly harsh and unconditional kind of subordination" (1908/1971d:115). Because the individual is dominated by a thing, "he himself psychologically sinks to the category of mere thing" (Simmel, 1908/1971d:117).

Social Forms and Simmel's Larger Problematic   Guy Oakes (1984b) linked Simmel's discussion of forms to his basic problematic, the growing gap between objective and subjective culture. He begins with the position that in "Simmel's view, the discovery of objectivity—the independence of things from the condition of their subjective or psychological genesis—was the greatest achievement in the cultural history of the West" (Oakes, 1984b:3). One of the ways that Simmel addresses this objectivity is in his discussion of forms, but although such formalization and objectification are necessary and desirable, they can come to be quite undesirable:

> On the one hand, forms are necessary conditions for the expression and the realization of the energies and interests of life. On the other hand, these forms become increasingly detached and remote from life. When this happens, a conflict develops between the process of life and the configurations in which it is expressed. Ultimately, this conflict threatens to nullify the relationship between life and form, and thus to destroy the conditions under which the process of life can be realized in autonomous structures.
>
> (Oakes, 1984b:4)

SOCIAL STRUCTURES

Simmel said relatively little directly about the large-scale structures of society. In fact, at times, given his focus on patterns of interaction, he denied the existence of that level of social reality. A good example of this is found in his effort to define *society*, where he rejected the realist position exemplified by Emile Durkheim that society is a real, material entity. Lewis Coser notes, "He did not see society as a thing or an organism" (1965:5). Simmel was also uncomfortable with the nominalist conception that society is nothing more than a collection of isolated individuals. He adopted an intermediate position, conceiving of society as a set of interactions (Spykman, 1925/1966:88). "*Society* is merely the name for a number of individuals connected by 'interaction'" (Simmel, cited in Coser, 1965:5).

Although Simmel enunciated this interactionist position, in much of his work he operated as a realist, as if society were a real material structure. There is, then, a basic contradiction in Simmel's work on the social-structural level. Simmel noted, "Society transcends the individual and lives its own life which follows its own laws. It, too, confronts the individual with a historical, imperative firmness" (1908/1950a:258). Coser catches the essence of this aspect of Simmel's thought: "The larger superindividual structures—the state, the clan, the family, the city, or the trade union—turn out to be but crystallizations of this interaction, even though they may attain autonomy and permanency and confront the individual as if they were alien powers" (1965:5). Rudolph Heberle makes essentially the same point: "One can scarcely escape the impression that Simmel views society as an interplay of structural factors, in which the human beings appear as passive objects rather than as live and willing actors" (1965:117).

The resolution of this paradox lies in the difference between Simmel's formal sociology, in which he tended to adhere to an interactionist view of society, and his historical and philosophical sociologies, in which he was much more inclined to see society as an independent, coercive social structure. In the latter sociologies, he saw society as part of the broader process of the development of objective culture, which worried him. Although objective culture is best seen as part of the cultural realm, Simmel included the growth of large-scale social structures as part of this process. That Simmel related the growth of social structures to the spread of objective culture is clear in this statement: "The increasing objectification of our culture, whose phenomena consist more and more of impersonal elements and less and less absorb the subjective totality of the individual . . . also involves sociological structures" (1908/1950b:318). In addition to clarifying the relationship between society and objective culture, this statement leads to Simmel's thoughts on the cultural level of social reality.

OBJECTIVE CULTURE

One of the main focuses of Simmel's historical and philosophical sociology is the cultural level of social reality, or what he called the "objective culture." In Simmel's view, people produce culture, but because of their ability to reify social reality, the cultural world and the social world come to have lives of their own, lives that come increasingly to dominate the actors who created, and daily re-create, them. "The cultural objects become more and more linked to each other in a self-contained world which has increasingly fewer contacts with the [individual] subjective psyche and its desires and sensibilities" (Coser, 1965:22). Although people always retain the capacity to create and re-create culture, the long-term trend of history is for culture to exert a more and more coercive force on the actor.

> The preponderance of objective over [individual] subjective culture that developed during the nineteenth century . . . this discrepancy seems to widen steadily. Every day and

from all sides, the wealth of objective culture increases, but the individual mind can enrich the forms and content of its own development only by distancing itself still further from that culture and developing its own at a much slower pace.

(Simmel, 1907/1978:449)

In various places in his work, Simmel identified a number of components of the objective culture, for example, tools, means of transport, products of science, technology, arts, language, intellectual sphere, conventional wisdom, religious dogma, philosophical systems, legal systems, moral codes, and ideals (for example, the "fatherland"). The objective culture grows and expands in various ways. First, its absolute size grows with increasing modernization. This can be seen most obviously in the case of scientific knowledge, which is expanding exponentially, although this is just as true of most other aspects of the cultural realm. Second, the number of different components of the cultural realm also grows. Finally, and perhaps most important, the various elements of the cultural world become more and more intertwined in an ever more powerful, self-contained world that is increasingly beyond the control of the actors (Oakes, 1984b:12). Simmel was not only interested in describing the growth of objective culture but also greatly disturbed by it: "Simmel was impressed—if not depressed—by the bewildering number and variety of human products which in the contemporary world surround and unceasingly impinge upon the individual" (Weingartner, 1959:33).

What worried Simmel most was the threat to individual culture posed by the growth of objective culture. Simmel's personal sympathies were with a world dominated by individual culture, but he saw the possibility of such a world as more and more unlikely. It is this that Simmel described as the "tragedy of culture." (We will comment on this in detail in the discussion of *The Philosophy of Money*.) Simmel's specific analysis of the growth of objective culture over individual subjective culture is simply one example of a general principle that dominates all of life: "The total value of something increases to the same extent as the value of its individual parts declines" (1907/1978:199).

We can relate Simmel's general argument about objective culture to his more basic analysis of forms of interaction. In one of his best-known essays, "The Metropolis and Mental Life" (1903/1971), Simmel analyzed the forms of interaction that take place in the modern city (Vidler, 1991). He saw the modern metropolis as the "genuine arena" of the growth of objective culture and the decline of individual culture. It is the scene of the predominance of the money economy, and money, as Simmel often made clear, has a profound effect on the nature of human relationships. The widespread use of money leads to an emphasis on calculability and rationality in all spheres of life. Thus genuine human relationships decline, and social relationships tend to be dominated by a blasé and reserved attitude. Whereas the small town was characterized by greater feeling and emotionality, the modern city is characterized by a shallow intellectuality that matches the calculability needed by a money economy. The city is also the center of the division of labor, and as we have seen, specialization plays a central role in the production of an ever-expanding objective culture, with a corresponding decline in individual culture. The city is a "frightful leveler," in which virtually everyone is reduced to emphasizing unfeeling calculability. It is more and more difficult to maintain individuality in the face of the expansion of objective culture (Lohmann and Wilkes, 1996).

It should be pointed out that in his essay on the city (as well as in many other places in his work) Simmel also discussed the liberating effect of this modern development. For example, he emphasized the fact that people are freer in the modern city than in the tight social confines of the small town. We will have more to say about Simmel's thoughts on the liberating impact of modernity at the close of the following section, devoted to Simmel's book *The Philosophy of Money.*

Before we get to that work, it is necessary to indicate that one of the many ironies of Simmel's influence on the development of sociology is that his micro-analytic work is used, but its broader implications are almost totally ignored. Take the example of Simmel's work on exchange relationships. He saw exchange as the "purest and most developed kind" of interaction (Simmel, 1907/1978:82). Although all forms of interaction involve some sacrifice, it occurs most clearly in exchange relationships. Simmel thought of all social exchanges as involving "profit and loss." Such an orientation was crucial to Simmel's microsociological work and specifically to the development of his largely micro-oriented exchange theory. However, his thoughts on exchange are also expressed in his broader work on money. To Simmel, money is the purest form of exchange. In contrast to a barter economy, where the cycle ends when one object has been exchanged for another, an economy based on money allows for an endless series of exchanges. This possibility is crucial for Simmel because it provides the basis for the widespread development of social structures and objective culture. Consequently, money as a form of exchange represented for Simmel one of the root causes of the alienation of people in a modern reified social structure.

In his treatment of the city and exchange, one can see the elegance of Simmel's thinking as he related small-scale sociological forms of exchange to the development of modern society in its totality. Although this link can be found in his specific essays (especially Simmel, 1991), it is clearest in *The Philosophy of Money.*

THE PHILOSOPHY OF MONEY

The Philosophy of Money (1907/1978) illustrates well the breadth and sophistication of Simmel's thinking. It demonstrates conclusively that Simmel deserves at least as much recognition for his general theory as for his essays on microsociology, many of which can be seen as specific manifestations of his general theory.

Although the title makes it clear that Simmel's focus is money, his interest in that phenomenon is embedded in a set of his broader theoretical and philosophical concerns. For example, as we have already seen, Simmel was interested in the broad issue of value, and money can be seen as simply a specific form of value. At another level, Simmel was interested not in money per se but in its impact on such a wide range of phenomena as the "inner world" of actors and the objective culture as a whole. At still another level, he treated money as a specific phenomenon linked with a variety of other components of life, including "exchange, ownership, greed, extravagance, cynicism, individual freedom, the style of life, culture, the value of the personality, etc." (Siegfried Kracauer, cited in Bottomore and Frisby, 1978:7). Finally, and most generally, Simmel saw money as a specific component of life capable of helping us to understand the totality of life. As Tom Bottomore and David Frisby put it, Simmel sought no less than to extract "the totality of the spirit of the age from his analysis of money" (1978:7).

The Philosophy of Money has much in common with the work of Karl Marx. Like Marx, Simmel focused on capitalism and the problems created by a money economy. Despite this common ground, however, the differences are overwhelming. For example, Simmel saw the economic problems of his time as simply a specific manifestation of a more general cultural problem, the alienation of objective from subjective culture (Poggi, 1993). To Marx these problems are specific to capitalism, but to Simmel they are part of a universal tragedy—the increasing powerlessness of the individual in the face of the growth of objective culture. Whereas Marx's analysis is historically specific, Simmel's analysis seeks to extract timeless truths from the flux of human history. As Frisby says, "In his *The Philosophy of Money* . . . [w]hat is missing . . . is a historical sociology of money relationships" (1984:58). This difference in their analyses is related to a crucial political difference between Simmel and Marx. Because Marx saw economic problems as time-bound, the product of capitalist society, he believed that eventually they could be solved. Simmel, however, saw the basic problems as inherent in human life and held out no hope for future improvement. In fact, Simmel believed that socialism, instead of improving the situation, would heighten the kinds of problems discussed in *The Philosophy of Money*. Despite some substantive similarities to Marxian theory, Simmel's thought is far closer to that of Weber and his "iron cage" in terms of his image of both the modern world and its future.

The Philosophy of Money begins with a discussion of the general forms of money and value. Later the discussion moves to the impact of money on the "inner world" of actors and on culture in general. Because the argument is so complex, we can merely highlight it here.

Money and Value

One of Simmel's initial concerns in the work, as we discussed briefly earlier, is the relationship between money and value. In general, he argued that people create value by making objects, separating themselves from those objects, and then seeking to overcome the "distance, obstacles, difficulties" (Simmel, 1907/1978:66). The greater the difficulty of obtaining an object, the greater its value. However, difficulty of attainment has a "lower and an upper limit" (Simmel, 1907/1978:72). The general principle is that the value of things comes from the ability of people to distance themselves properly from objects. Things that are too close, too easily obtained, are not very valuable. Some exertion is needed for something to be considered valuable. Conversely, things that are too far, too difficult, or nearly impossible to obtain are also not very valuable. Things that defy most, if not all, of our efforts to obtain them cease to be valuable to us. Those things that are most valuable are neither too distant nor too close. Among the factors involved in the distance of an object from an actor are the time it takes to obtain it, its scarcity, the difficulties involved in acquiring it, and the need to give up other things in order to acquire it. People try to place themselves at a proper distance from objects, which must be attainable, but not too easily.

In this general context of value, Simmel discussed money. In the economic realm, money serves both to create distance from objects and to provide the means to overcome it. The money value attached to objects in a modern economy places them at a distance from us; we cannot obtain them without money of our own. The difficulty in obtaining the money and therefore the objects makes them valuable to us. At the same time, once we obtain enough money, we are able to overcome the distance between ourselves and the objects. Money thus performs the interesting function of creating distance between people and objects and then providing the means to overcome that distance.

Money, Reification, and Rationalization

In the process of creating value, money also provides the basis for the development of the market, the modern economy, and ultimately modern (capitalistic) society (Poggi, 1996). Money provides the means whereby these entities acquire a life of their own that is external to, and coercive of, the actor. This stands in contrast to earlier societies in which barter or trade could not lead to the reified world that is the distinctive product of a money economy. Money permits this development in various ways. For example, Simmel argued that money allows for "long-range calculations, large-scale enterprises and long-term credits" (1907/1978:125). Later, Simmel said that "money has . . . developed . . . the most objective practices, the most logical, purely mathematical norms, the absolute freedom from everything personal" (1907/1978:128). He saw this process of reification as but part of the more general process whereby the mind embodies and symbolizes itself in objects. These embodiments, these symbolic structures, become reified and come to exert a controlling force on actors.

Not only does money help to create a reified social world, but it also contributes to the increasing rationalization of that social world (Deutschmann, 1996; B. Turner, 1986). This is another of the concerns that Simmel shared with Weber. A money economy fosters an emphasis on quantitative rather than qualitative factors. Simmel stated:

> It would be easy to multiply the examples that illustrate the growing preponderance of the category of quantity over that of quality, or more precisely the tendency to dissolve quality into quantity, to remove the elements more and more from quality, to grant them only specific forms of motion and to interpret everything that is specifically, individually, and qualitatively determined as the more or less, the bigger or smaller, the wider or narrower, the more or less frequent of those colourless elements and awarenesses that are only accessible to numerical determination—even though this tendency may never absolutely attain its goal by mortal means. . . .
>
> Thus, one of the major tendencies of life—the reduction of quality to quantity— achieves its highest and uniquely perfect representation in money. Here, too, money is the pinnacle of a cultural historical series of developments which unambiguously determines its direction.
>
> (Simmel, 1907/1978:278–280)

Less obviously, money contributes to rationalization by increasing the importance of intellectuality in the modern world (B. Turner, 1986; Deutschmann, 1996). On the one hand, the development of a money economy presupposes a significant expansion of mental processes. As an example, Simmel pointed to the complicated mental processes that are required by such money transactions as covering bank notes with cash reserves. On the other hand, a money economy contributes to a considerable change in the norms and values of society; it aids in the "fundamental reorientation of culture towards intellectuality" (Simmel, 1907/1978:152). In part because of a money economy, intellect has come to be considered the most valuable of our mental energies.

Simmel saw the significance of the individual declining as money transactions become an increasingly important part of society and as reified structures expand. This is part of his general argument on the decline of individual subjective culture in the face of the expansion of objective culture (the "tragedy of culture"):

> The rapid circulation of money induces habits of spending and acquisition; it makes a specific quantity of money psychologically less significant and valuable, while money in general becomes increasingly important because money matters now affect the individual more vitally than they do in a less agitated style of life. We are confronted here with a very common phenomenon; namely, that the total value of something increases to the same extent as the value of its individual parts declines. For example, the size and significance of a social group often becomes greater the less highly the lives and interests of its individual members are valued; the objective culture, the diversity and liveliness of its content attain their highest point through a division of labour that often condemns the individual representative and participant in this culture to a monotonous specialization, narrowness, and stunted growth. The whole becomes more perfect and harmonious, the less the individual is a harmonious being.
>
> (Simmel, 1907/1978:199)

Jorge Arditi (1996) has recently put this issue in slightly different terms. Arditi recognizes the theme of increasing rationalization in Simmel's work, but argues that it must be seen in the context of Simmel's thinking on the nonrational. "According to Simmel, the nonrational is a primary, essential element of 'life,' an integral aspect of our humanity. Its gradual eclipse in the expanses of a modern, highly rationalized world implies, then, an unquestionable impoverishment of being" (Arditi, 1996:95). One example of the nonrational is love (others are emotions and faith), and it is nonrational because, among other things, it is impractical, is the opposite of intellectual experience, does not necessarily have real value, is impulsive, nothing social or cultural intervenes between lover and beloved, and it springs " 'from the completely *nonrational* depths of life' " (Simmel, in Arditi, 1996:96). With increasing rationalization, we begin to lose the nonrational and with it "we lose . . . the most meaningful of our human attributes: our authenticity" (Arditi, 1996:103). This loss of authenticity, of the nonrational, is a real human tragedy.

In some senses, it may be difficult to see how money can take on the central role that it does in modern society. On the surface, it appears that money is simply a means to a variety of ends or, in Simmel's worlds, "the purest form of the tool" (1907/1978:210). However, money has come to be the most extreme example of a means that has become an end in itself:

> Never has an object that owes its value exclusively to its quality as a means, to its convertibility into more definite values, so thoroughly and unreservedly developed into a psychological value absolute, into a completely engrossing final purpose governing our practical consciousness. This ultimate craving for money must increase to the extent that

money takes on the quality of a pure means. For this implies that the range of objects made available to money grows continuously, that things submit more and more defencelessly to the power of money, that money itself becomes more and more lacking in quality yet thereby at the same time becomes powerful in relation to the quality of things.

(Simmel, 1907/1978:232)

Negative Effects

A society in which money becomes an end in itself, indeed the ultimate end, has a number of negative effects on individuals (Beilharz, 1996), two of the most interesting of which are the increase in cynicism and in a blasé attitude. Cynicism is induced when both the highest and lowest aspects of social life are for sale, reduced to a common denominator—money. Thus we can "buy" beauty or truth or intelligence almost as easily as we can buy cornflakes or underarm deodorant. This leveling of everything to a common denominator leads to the cynical attitude that everything has its price, that anything can be bought or sold on the market. A money economy also induces a blasé attitude, "all things as being of an equally dull and grey hue, as not worth getting excited about" (Simmel, 1907/1978:256). The blasé person has lost completely the ability to make value differentiations among the ultimate objects of purchase. Put slightly differently, money is the absolute enemy of esthetics, reducing everything to formlessness, to purely quantitative phenomena.

Another negative effect of a money economy is the increasingly impersonal relations among people. Instead of dealing with individuals with their own personalities, we are increasingly likely to deal solely with positions—the delivery person, the baker, and so forth—regardless of who occupies those positions. In the modern division of labor characteristic of a money economy, we have the paradoxical situation that while we grow more dependent on other positions for our survival, we know less about the people who occupy those positions. The specific individual who fills a given position becomes progressively insignificant. Personalities tend to disappear behind positions that demand only a small part of them. Because so little is demanded of them, many individuals can fill the same position equally well. People thus become interchangeable parts.

A related issue is the impact of the money economy on individual freedom. A money economy leads to an increase in individual enslavement. The individual in the modern world becomes atomized and isolated. No longer embedded within a group, the individual stands alone in the face of an ever-expanding and increasingly coercive objective culture. The individual in the modern world is thus enslaved by a massive objective culture.

Another impact of the money economy is the reduction of all human values to dollar terms, "the tendency to reduce the value of man to a monetary expression" (Simmel, 1907/1978:356). For example, Simmel offers the case in primitive society of atonement for a murder by a money payment. But his best example is the exchange of sex for money. The expansion of prostitution is traceable in part to the growth of the money economy.

Some of Simmel's most interesting insights lie in his thoughts on the impact of money on people's styles of life. For example, a society dominated by a money economy tends to reduce everything to a string of causal connections that can be comprehended intellectually, not emotionally. Related to this is what Simmel called the "calculating character" of life in the modern world. The specific form of intellectuality that is peculiarly suited to a money economy is a mathematical mode of thinking. This, in turn, is related to the tendency to emphasize quantitative rather than qualitative factors in the social world. Simmel concluded that "the lives of many people are absorbed by such evaluating, weighing, calculating, and reducing of qualitative values to quantitative ones"(1907/1978:444).

The key to Simmel's discussion of money's impact on style of life is in the growth of objective culture at the expense of individual culture. The gap between the two grows larger at an accelerating rate:

> This discrepancy seems to widen steadily. Every day and from all sides, the wealth of objective culture increases, but the individual mind can enrich the forms and contents of its own development only by distancing itself still further from that culture and developing its own at a much slower pace.
>
> (Simmel, 1907/1978:449)

Tragedy of Culture

The major cause of this increasing disparity is the increasing division of labor in modern society (Oakes, 1984b:19). Increased specialization leads to an improved ability to create the various components of the cultural world. But at the same time, the highly specialized individual loses a sense of the total culture and loses the ability to control it. As objective culture grows, individual culture atrophies. One of the examples of this is that language in its totality has clearly expanded enormously, yet the linguistic abilities of given individuals seem to be declining. Similarly, with the growth of technology and machinery, the abilities of the individual worker and the skills required have declined dramatically. Finally, although there has been an enormous expansion of the intellectual sphere, fewer and fewer individuals seem to deserve the label "intellectual." Highly specialized individuals are confronted with an increasingly closed and interconnected world of products over which they have little or no control. A mechanical world devoid of spirituality comes to dominate individuals, and their lifestyles are affected in various ways. Acts of production come to be meaningless exercises in which individuals do not see their roles in the overall process or in the production of the final product. Relationships among people are highly specialized and impersonal. Consumption becomes little more than a devouring of one meaningless product after another.

The massive expansion of objective culture has had a dramatic effect upon the rhythm of life. In general, the unevenness that was characteristic of earlier epochs has been leveled and replaced in modern society by a much more consistent pattern of living. Examples of this leveling of modern culture abound.

In times past, food consumption was cyclical and often very uncertain. What foods were consumed and when they were available depended on the harvest. Today, with improved methods of preservation and transportation, we can consume virtually any food at any time. Furthermore, the ability to preserve and store huge quantities of food has helped to offset disruptions caused by bad harvests, natural catastrophes, and so forth.

In communication the infrequent and unpredictable mail coach has been replaced by the telegraph, telephone, daily mail service, fax machines and e-mail, which make communication available at all times.

In an earlier time, night and day gave life a natural rhythm. Now, with artificial lighting, the natural rhythm has been greatly altered. Many activities formerly restricted to daylight hours can now be performed at night as well.

Intellectual stimulation, which was formerly restricted to an occasional conversation or a rare book, is now available at all times because of the ready availability of books and magazines. In this realm, as in all the others, the situation has grown even more pronounced since Simmel's time. With radio, television, videotape recorders, and home computers, the availability and possibilities of intellectual stimulation have grown far beyond anything Simmel could have imagined.

There are positive elements to all this, of course. For example, people have much more freedom because they are less restricted by the natural rhythm of life. In spite of the human gains, problems arise because all these developments are at the level of objective culture and are integral parts of the process by which objective culture grows and further impoverishes individual culture.

In the end, money has come to be the symbol of, and a major factor in, the development of a relativistic mode of existence. Money allows us to reduce the most disparate phenomena to numbers of dollars, and this allows them to be compared to each other. In other words, money allows us to relativize *everything*. Our relativistic way of life stands in contrast to earlier methods of living in which people believed in a number of eternal verities. A money economy destroys such eternal truths. The gains to people in terms of increased freedom from absolute ideas are far outweighed by the costs. The alienation endemic to the expanding objective culture of a modern money economy is a far greater threat to people, in Simmel's eyes, than the evils of absolutism. Perhaps Simmel would not wish us to return to an earlier, simpler time, but he certainly would warn us to be wary of the seductive dangers associated with the growth of a money economy and objective culture in the modern world.

While we have focused most of our attention on the negative effects of the modern money economy, such an economy also has its liberating aspects (Beilharz, 1996; Levine, 1981b, 1991b; Poggi, 1993). First, it allows us to deal with many more people in a much-expanded marketplace. Second, our obligations to one another are highly limited (to specific services or products) rather than all-encompassing. Third, the money economy allows people to find gratifications that were unavailable in earlier economic systems. Fourth, people have greater freedom in such an environment to develop their individuality to a fuller extent. Fifth, people are better able to maintain and protect their subjective center, since they are involved only in very limited relationships. Sixth, the separation of the worker from the means of production, as Simmel points out, allows the individual some freedom from those productive forces. Finally, money helps people grow increasingly free of the constraints of their social groups. For example, in a barter economy people are largely controlled by their groups, but in the modern economic world such constraints are loosened, with the result that people are freer to make their own economic deals. However, while Simmel is careful to point out a variety of liberating effects of the money economy, and modernity in general, in our view the heart of his work lies in his discussion of the problems associated with modernity, especially the "tragedy of culture."

The Tragedy of Culture in Its Broader Context Birgitta Nedelmann (1991) has offered an interesting interpretation of the tragedy of culture in the context of what she regards as Simmel's three problems of culture. Let us briefly examine the first two problems, before turning to Nedelmann's thoughts on the tragedy of culture.

The first problem is one of *cultural malaise.* This is a result of the conflict between individuals as the creators of culture and the fixed and timeless cultural forms that confront them. While individuals should fulfill themselves in the creation of cultural forms, such fulfillment increasingly is not the case, at least in part because the "cultural system . . . lags behind the development of human creativity" (Nedelmann, 1991:175). One response by individuals to this dilemma is to turn inward, to retreat. This leads to what Nedelmann (1991:177) calls the *individualization of cultural creativity.* However, malaise sets in because creativity for oneself can never be as satisfying as the creation of larger cultural forms. Furthermore, those cultural forms themselves cease to be renewed by individual creations. The result is the "gradual self-destruction of both" the cultural system and the system of individual creativity (Nedelmann, 1991:178).

The second problem is *cultural ambivalence.* Here Simmel differentiates between style and art. Style relates to generality, to "those elements of the artistic object which it has in common with other objects belonging to the same category" (Nedelmann, 1991:180). Style involves objects created by craftspeople, such as a chair or a glass. Art, in contrast, relates to its singularity, to its "uniqueness and individuality" (Nedelmann, 1991:181). Modern man, however, "creates disorder in the aesthetic sphere" by seeing "objects of craft as if they were works of art and perceiving works of art as if they were objects of craft" (Nedelmann, 1991:183). People need both craft (generality) and art (uniqueness), but in hopelessly confusing the two the possibility "of attaining a balanced individuality has finally been transformed into an unrealizable ideal" (Nedelmann, 1991:184).

Finally, and most important, is the problem of the *tragedy of culture.* Nedelmann offers an interesting interpretation of this idea. She points out that this is a tragedy, rather than merely sad, because the "social destruction is the *necessary* result from the immanent logic" of culture (Nedelmann, 1991:189):

> The very idea of culture consists in creating material objects which are meant to be integrated into the subjective sphere of their creators and to be submitted to subsequent generations of individuals. But the very act of cultural creation itself generates a self-destructive potential. In his or her role as cultural receiver the subject becomes the addressee of the destructive effects of cultural objects he has created himself in his role as cultural creator.
>
> (Nedelmann, 1991:189)

Yet, paradoxically and tragically, the individual has no alternative but to go on creating cultural products. Furthermore, locked into a life of meaningless productivity, the individual "has neither the energy for revolting or protesting against the cultural system as system, nor for reacting in a deviant, exaggerated way" (Nedelmann, 1991:189). The inability to rebel against, or deviate from, this reality is yet another sense in which the modern world is tragic.

SECRECY: A CASE STUDY IN SIMMEL'S SOCIOLOGY

While *The Philosophy of Money* demonstrates that Simmel has a theoretical scope that rivals that of Marx, Weber, and Durkheim, it remains an atypical example of his work. Thus, in this closing section we return to a more characteristic type of Simmelian scholarship, his work on a specific form of interaction—secrecy. *Secrecy* is defined as the condition in which one person has the intention of hiding something while the other is seeking to reveal that which is being hidden. In this discussion, we are interested not only in outlining Simmel's many insightful ideas on secrecy but also in bringing together under one heading many of the sociological ideas raised through this chapter.

Simmel begins with the basic fact that people must know some things about other people in order to interact with them. For instance, we must know with whom we are dealing (for example, a friend, a relative, a shopkeeper). We may come to know a great deal about other people, but we can never know them absolutely. That is, we can never know all the thoughts, moods, and so on of other people. However, we do form some sort of unitary conception of other people out of the bits and pieces that we know about them; we form a fairly coherent mental picture of the people with whom we interact. Simmel sees a dialectical relationship between interaction (being) and the mental picture we have of others (conceiving): "Our relationships thus develop upon the basis of reciprocal knowledge, and this knowledge upon the basis of actual relations. Both are inextricably interwoven" (1906/1950:309).

In all aspects of our lives we acquire not only truth but also ignorance and error. However, it is in the interaction with other people that ignorance and error acquire a distinctive character. This relates to the inner lives of the people with whom we interact. People, in contrast to any other object of knowledge, have the capacity to *intentionally* reveal the truth about themselves *or* to lie and conceal such information.

The fact is that even if people wanted to reveal all (and they almost always do not), they could not do so because so much information "would drive everybody into the insane asylum" (Simmel, 1906/1950:312). Thus, people must select the things that they report to others. From the point of view of Simmel's concern with quantitative issues, we report only "fragments" of our inner lives to others. Furthermore, we choose which fragments to reveal and which to conceal. Thus, in all interaction, we reveal only a part of ourselves, and which part we opt to show depends on how we select and arrange the fragments we choose to reveal.

This brings us to the *lie,* a form of interaction in which the liar *intentionally* hides the truth from others. In the lie, it is not just that others are left with an erroneous conception but also that the error is traceable to the fact that the liar intended that the others be deceived.

Simmel discusses the lie in terms of social geometry, specifically his ideas on distance. For example, in Simmel's view, we can better accept and come to terms with the lies of those who are distant from us. Thus, we have little difficulty learning that the politicians who habituate Washington, D.C., frequently lie to us. In contrast, "If the persons closest to us lie, life becomes unbearable" (Simmel, 1906/1950:313). The lie of a spouse, lover, or child has a far more devastating impact on us than the lie of a government official whom we know only through the television screen.

More generally, in terms of distance, all everyday communication combines elements known to both parties with facts known to only one or the other. It is the existence of the latter that leads to "distanceness" in all social relationships. Indeed, Simmel argues that social relationships require both elements that are known to the interactants *and* those that are unknown to one party or the other. In other words, even the most intimate relationships require both nearness and distance, reciprocal knowledge and mutual concealment. Thus, secrecy is an integral part of all social relationships, although a relationship may be destroyed if the secret becomes known to the person from whom it was being kept.

Secrecy is linked to the size of society. In small groups, it is difficult to develop secrets; "Everybody is too close to everybody else and his circumstances, and frequency and intimacy of contact involve too many temptations to revelation" (Simmel, 1906/1950:335). Furthermore, in small groups, secrets are not even needed because everyone is much like everyone else. In large groups, in contrast, secrets can more easily develop and are much more needed because there are important differences among people.

On the issue of size, at the most macroscopic level, we should note that secrecy not only is a form of interaction (which, as we have seen, affects many other forms) but also can come to characterize a group in its entirety. Unlike the secret possessed by a single individual, the secret in a *secret society* is shared by all members and determines the reciprocal relations among them. As with the individual case, however, the secret of the secret society cannot be hidden forever. In such a society there is a constant tension caused by the fact that the secret can be uncovered, or revealed, and thus the entire basis for the existence of the secret society can be eliminated.

Secrecy and Social Relationships

Simmel examines various forms of social relationships from the point of view of reciprocal knowledge and secrecy. For example, we all are involved in a range of interest groups in which we interact with other people on a very limited basis, and the total personalities of these people are irrelevant to our specific concerns. Thus, in the university the student is concerned with what the professor says and does in the classroom and not in all aspects of the professor's life and personality. Linking this to his ideas on the larger society, Simmel argues that the increasing objectification of culture brings with it more and more limited-interest groups and the kinds of relationships associated with them. Such relationships require less and less of the subjective totality of the individual (individual culture) than do associations in premodern societies.

In the impersonal relationships characteristic of modern objectified society, *confidence,* as a form of interaction, becomes increasingly important. To Simmel "confidence is intermediate between knowledge and ignorance about a man" (1906/1950:318). In premodern societies people are much more likely to know a great deal about the people they deal with. But in the modern world we do not, and cannot, have a great deal of knowledge about most of the people with whom we have associations. Thus, students do not know a great deal about their professors (and vice versa), but they must have the confidence that their professors will show up at the appointed times and talk about what they are supposed to discuss.

Another form of social relationship is *acquaintanceship*. We know our acquaintances, but we do not have intimate knowledge of them: "One knows of the other only what he is toward the outside, either in the purely social-representative sense, or in the sense of that which he shows us" (Simmel, 1906/1950:320). Thus, there is far more secretiveness among acquaintances than there is among intimates.

Under the heading of "acquaintanceship," Simmel discusses another form of association—*discretion*. We are discrete with our acquaintances, staying "away from the knowledge of all the other does not expressly reveal to us. It does not refer to anything particular which we are not permitted to know, but to a quite general reserve in regard to the total personality" (Simmel, 1906/1950:321). In spite of being discrete, we often come to know more about other people than they reveal to us voluntarily. More specifically, we often come to learn things that others would prefer we do not know. Simmel offers a very Freudian example of how we learn such things: "To the man with the psychologically fine ear, people innumerable times betray their most secret thoughts and qualities, not only *although*, but often *because*, they anxiously try to guard them" (1906/1950:323–324). In fact, Simmel argues that human interaction is dependent on both discretion *and* the fact that we often come to know more than we are supposed to know.

Turning to another form of association, *friendship*, Simmel contradicts the assumption that friendship is based on total intimacy, full reciprocal knowledge. This lack of full intimacy is especially true of friendships in modern, differentiated society: "Modern man, possibly, has too much to hide to sustain a friendship in the ancient sense" (Simmel, 1906/1950:326). Thus, we have a series of differentiated friendships based on such things as common intellectual pursuits, religion, and shared experiences. There is a very limited kind of intimacy in such friendships and thus a good deal of secrecy. However, in spite of these limitations, friendship still involves some intimacy:

> But the relation which is thus restricted and surrounded by discretions, may yet stem from the center of the total personality. It may yet be reached by the sap of the ultimate roots of the personality, even though it feeds only part of the person's periphery. In its idea, it involves the same affective depth and the same readiness for sacrifice, which less differentiated epochs and persons connect only with a common *total* sphere of life, for which reservations and discretion constitute no problem.
>
> (Simmel, 1906/1950:326)

Then there is what is usually thought of as the most intimate, least secret form of association—*marriage*. Simmel argues that there is a temptation in marriage to reveal all to the partner, to have no secrets. However, in his view, this would be a mistake. For one thing, all social relationships require "a certain proportion of truth and error," and thus it would be impossible to remove all error from a social relationship (Simmel, 1906/1950:329). More specifically, complete self-revelation (assuming such a thing is even possible) would make a marriage matter-of-fact and remove all possibility of the unexpected. Finally, most of us have limited internal resources, and every revelation reduces the (secret) treasures that we have to offer to others. Only those few with a great storehouse of personal accomplishments can afford numerous revelations to a marriage partner. All others are left denuded (and uninteresting) by excessive self-revelation.

Other Thoughts on Secrecy

Next, Simmel turns to an analysis of the functions, the positive consequences, of secrecy. Simmel sees the secret as "one of man's greatest achievements . . . the secret produces an immense enlargement of life: numerous contents of life cannot even emerge in the presence of full publicity. The secret offers, so to speak, the possibility of a second world alongside the manifest world" (1906/1950:330). More specifically in terms of its functionality, the secret, especially if it is shared by a number of people, makes for a strong "we feeling" among those who know the secret. High status is also associated with the secret; there is something mysterious about superordinate positions and superior achievements.

Human interaction in general is shaped by secrecy and its logical opposite, *betrayal*. The secret is always accompanied dialectically by the possibility that it can be discovered. Betrayal can come from two sources. Externally, another person can discover our secret, while internally there is always the possibility that we will reveal our secret to others. "The secret puts a barrier between men but, at the same time, it creates the tempting challenge to break through it, by gossip or confession. . . . Out of the counterplay of these two interests, in concealing and revealing, spring nuances and fates of human interaction that permeate it in its entirety" (Simmel, 1906/1950:334).

Simmel links his ideas on the lie to his views on the larger society of the modern world. To Simmel, the modern world is much more dependent on honesty than earlier societies were. For one thing, the modern economy is increasingly a credit economy, and credit is dependent on the fact that people will repay what they promise. For another, in modern science, researchers are dependent on the results of many other studies that they cannot examine in minute detail. Those studies are produced by innumerable other scientists whom the researchers are unlikely to know personally. Thus, the modern scientist is dependent on the honesty of all other scientists. Simmel concludes: "Under modern conditions, the lie, therefore, becomes something much more devastating than it was earlier, something which questions the very foundations of our life" (1906/1950:313).

More generally, Simmel connects secrecy to his thoughts on the social structure of modern society. On the one hand, a highly differentiated society permits and requires a high degree of secrecy. On the other hand, and dialectically, the secret serves to intensify such differentiation.

Simmel associates the secret with the modern money economy; money makes possible a level of secrecy that was unattainable previously. First, money's "compressibility" makes it possible to make others rich by simply slipping them checks without anyone else noticing the act. Second, the abstractness and qualityless character of money makes it possible to hide "transactions, acquisitions, and changes in ownership" that could not be hidden if more tangible objects were exchanged (Simmel, 1906/1950:335). Third, money can be invested in very distant things, thereby making the transaction invisible to those in the immediate environment.

Simmel also sees that in the modern world, public matters, such as those relating to politics, have tended to lose their secrecy and inaccessibility. In contrast, private affairs are much more secret than they are in premodern societies. Here Simmel ties his thoughts on secrecy to those on the modern city by arguing that "modern life has developed, in the midst of metropolitan crowdedness, a technique for making and keeping private matters secret" (Simmel, 1906/1950:337). Overall, "what is public becomes even more public, and what is private becomes even more private" (Simmel, 1906/1950:337).

Thus, Simmel's work on secrecy illustrates many aspects of his theoretical orientation.

SUMMARY

The work of Georg Simmel has been influential in American sociological theory for many years. The focus of this influence seems to be shifting from microsociology to a general sociological theory. Simmel's microsociology is embedded in a broad dialectical theory that interrelates the cultural and individual levels. We identify four basic levels of concern in Simmel's work: psychological, interactional, structural and institutional, and the ultimate metaphysics of life.

Simmel operated with a dialectical orientation, although it is not as well articulated as that of Karl Marx. We illustrate Simmel's dialectical concerns in various ways. We deal with the way they are manifested in forms of interaction—specifically, fashion. Simmel was also interested in the conflicts between the individual and social structures, but his greatest concern was those conflicts that develop between individual culture and objective culture. He perceived a general process whereby objective culture expands and individual culture becomes increasingly impoverished in the face of this development. Simmel saw this conflict, in turn, as part of a broader philosophical conflict between more-life and more-than-life.

The bulk of this chapter is devoted to Simmel's thoughts on each of the four levels of social reality. Although he has many useful assumptions about consciousness, he did comparatively little with them. He had much more to offer on forms of interaction and types of interactants. In this formal sociology, we see Simmel's great interest in social geometry, for example, numbers of people. In this context, we examine Simmel's work on the crucial transition from a dyad to a triad. With the addition of one person, we move from a dyad to a triad and with it the possibility of the development of large-scale structures that can become separate from, and dominant over, individuals. This creates the possibility of conflict and contradiction between the individual and the larger society. In his social geometry, Simmel was also concerned with the issue of distance, as in, for example, his essay on the "stranger," including "strangeness" in social life. Simmel's interest in social types is illustrated in a discussion of the poor, and his thoughts on social forms are illustrated in a discussion of domination, that is, superordination and subordination.

At the macro level, Simmel had comparatively little to say about social structures. In fact, at times he seemed to manifest a disturbing tendency to reduce social structures to little more than interaction patterns. Simmel's real interest at the macro level was objective culture. He was interested in both the expansion of this culture and its destructive effects on individuals (the "tragedy of culture"). This general concern is manifest in a variety of his specific essays, for example, those on the city and exchange.

In *The Philosophy of Money* Simmel's discussion progressed from money to value to the problems of modern society and, ultimately, to the problems of life in general. Of particular concern is Simmel's interest in the tragedy of culture as part of a broader set of apprehensions about culture. Finally, we discussed Simmel's work on secrecy in order to illustrate the full range of his theoretical ideas. The discussion of Simmel's work on money, as well as his ideas on secrecy, demonstrates that he has a far more elegant and sophisticated theoretical orientation than he is usually given credit for by those who are familiar with only his thoughts on micro-level phenomena.

9

EARLY WOMEN SOCIOLOGISTS AND CLASSICAL SOCIOLOGICAL THEORY: 1830–1930

Patricia Madoo Lengermann
The George Washington University

Jill Niebrugge-Brantley
Gettysburg College

HARRIET MARTINEAU (1802–1876)

CHARLOTTE PERKINS GILMAN (1860–1935)

JANE ADDAMS AND THE WOMEN OF CHICAGO
Jane Addams (1860–1935)
The Women of Chicago

ANNA JULIA COOPER (1859–1964) AND
IDA WELLS-BARNETT (1862–1931)

MARIANNE SCHNITGER WEBER (1870–1954)

BEATRICE POTTER WEBB (1858–1943)

The history of sociology is typically linked to the development of sociological theory, understood as the systematic body of general ideas which informs and thus defines the profession of sociology as a distinctive discipline. In turn, the development of sociological theory is usually understood as the work of successive generations of theorists, each viewed as a loose cohort influenced by the particular social and intellectual circumstances of their historic period. Chapters 1 and 2 give an overview of these "stages" or generations of theorists who have created sociological theory and of the social and intellectual influences surrounding them.

As the story is conventionally told, sociological theory was first formulated in ambitious but rather imprecise terms by an early generation of men acting as public educators outside any formal university base. Comte, Spencer, and Marx are held to be the key representatives of this first, mid-nineteenth-century, generation. They were followed by a larger, more focused cohort of university-based thinkers, who set out to establish a profession and a discipline as well as to systematically build on the theories of the first generation. The work of this second generation of men, of whom Durkheim, Weber, Simmel, Mead, and Park are the most noteworthy, spans the period from about 1890 to 1930. Together with the work of the first (mid-nineteenth-century) generation, their work is what is usually treated as classical sociological theory.

Presented this way, the writing of the history of sociological theory is interesting as a possible exercise of gender politics in the profession, and calls for the characteristic critical inquiry of mobilized feminism—"*And what about the women?*" The response of sociology to the demands that women be included in disciplinary thinking and practice has been described as "an add-women-and-stir approach" (Bunch, 1987; Ward, 1993). But adding women creates a result akin to a chemical reaction that makes the whole base dissolve and recrystallize in a new form. Adding the contributions of women to the history of sociological theory problematizes history, sociology, and theory. The reconstruction of the history of sociology, as with any discipline, is a matter of constituting the discipline in the very act of reconstituting it. A discipline may be understood as the canon of its classic works, but that canon changes over time, depending in part on whether the discipline is engaged in the practice of "normal" or "revolutionary" science (Kuhn, 1970). In moments of revolutionary science, the discipline of sociology has frequently reached out to incorporate new or forgotten figures (for example, Parsons's reintroduction of Weber in the 1930s and the collective effort to incorporate Marx in the 1960s). A part of the only (at best) half-completed feminist revolution in sociology (see Alway, 1995; Stacey and Thorne, 1985) must be the reclamation of the founding mothers of sociological theory. This reclamation is currently under way in the burgeoning of feminist-inspired research of the last decade (Broschart, 1991a, b; Collins, 1990; Costin, 1983; Deegan, 1988, 1991; Fish, 1981, 1985; Fitzpatrick, 1990; Hill, 1989; Hoecker-Drysdale, 1992; Keith, 1991; Lemert, 1995; Lemert and Bhan, 1998; Lengermann and Niebrugge-Brantley, 1998; McDonald, 1994; Reinharz, 1992, 1993; Rosenberg, 1982; Ryndbrandt, 1999; Sklar, 1995).

It is our intention in this chapter to modify the conventional history of classical sociological theory in the following ways. First, we add one woman, Harriet Martineau (1802–1876), to the first, mid-nineteenth century, generation of sociology's founders, affirming that Martineau is not only a key theorist of this generation but that she is perhaps sociology's original founder. Second, we describe a larger, interconnected community of women on both sides of the Atlantic who in the period 1890–1930—that is, the period of the second generation of "classical" sociological theorists—worked with extraordinary energy to create both a sociology and a sociological theory which reflected their sense of the appropriate form for the emerging discipline. We review the ideas of just a few of these women—Charlotte Perkins Gilman, Jane Addams, Florence Kelley, Anna Julia Cooper, Ida Wells-Barnett, Marianne Weber, and Beatrice Potter Webb. The company is so numerous and the records so incomplete that we have had to be very selective in our presentation.

In making our selection, we have been guided by Dorothy E. Smith's conception that "a sociology is a systematically developed consciousness of society and of social relations" (1987:2). By "systematically developed consciousness," we mean that the person doing the thinking is doing so with a view to understanding society and that that understanding finds expression in an ability to identify and relate the parts that constitute society and social relations. The parts that seem essential to any social theory are some sense of (1) the fundamental unit to be used in social analysis, (2) the nature of the human being, (3) the relation between ideas and materiality, and (4) the purpose and methods appropriate to social-science study. The women whose theories we describe developed such an understanding, and that understanding is essentially feminist.

By describing these theories as feminist, we mean that from the vantage point of contemporary feminist sociological theory, we recognize certain themes and concerns central to the theories of these women. These include: (1) the theorist's awareness of her gender and her stance in that gender identity as she develops her sociological theory, (2) an awareness of the situatedness of her analysis and of the situatedness of the vantage points of others, (3) a consistent focus on the lives and work of women, (4) a critical concern with the practices of social inequality, and (5) a commitment to the practice of sociology in pursuit of social amelioration.

HARRIET MARTINEAU (1802–1876)

Harriet Martineau belongs to the generation of social thinkers of the middle decades of the nineteenth century who undertook the ambitious task of delineating the boundaries, characteristics, and significance of an intellectual undertaking which would systematically and scientifically study human societies—a field they came to call "sociology." Although any such intellectual endeavor can be linked back to earlier anticipations of it, this group of nineteenth-century thinkers is typically viewed as sociology's "founding generation"; that role in sociology's history is typically represented in contemporary thinking through descriptions of the ideas of three male theorists—Comte (1797–1857; see Chapter 3), Spencer (1820–1903; see Chapter 4), and Marx (1818–1884; see Chapter 5). As recent feminist research shows, Harriet Martineau's place in this founding generation is indisputable (Deegan, 1991; Hill, 1989; Hill and Hoecker-Drysdale, 2000; Hoecker-Drysdale, 1994; Rossi, 1973; Yates, 1985). As early as 1831, a decade before Comte published *The Positive Philosophy,* Martineau wrote about the need for general public education in a science of society, a science she called, as did her British contemporaries, "political economy," a science which is, as both Comte and Spencer later also portray it, about material *and* moral existence:

> The people then must become practically acquainted with the principles of political economy. . . . Viewing this science as we do,—as involving the laws of social duty and social happiness,—we hold it as a positive obligation on every member of society . . . to inform himself of its leading principles. . . . We think this study partakes much more of the nature of a moral than a mathematical science, and are quite certain that it modifies, or ought to modify, our moral philosophy.
>
> (Martineau, 1836:275–277)

Beginning the next year, 1832, Martineau deliberately undertook the task of so educating the public. Between 1832 and 1834 she published twenty-five didactic novels in a series called *Illustrations of Political Economy,* intended to teach the principles of the new science of society to a general middle class and working class readership through the medium of a story (often set in some distant or exotic place); Martineau concluded each volume with a summary of the principles of the new science that shaped her plot. In 1834, Martineau followed this enormously successful venture into public education with more theoretical work: she drafted the first text on sociological research techniques, *How to Observe Morals and Manners* (which was published in 1838). Between 1834 and 1836 she applied and expanded these research strategies in an extensive field study of American society, published in 1836 in three volumes as *Society in America*—though she had wanted it titled "Theory and Practice of Society in America" to better capture the intent of her social-science project. By 1837, her reputation as Britain's pre-eminent social analyst led to a request from her publishers that she "become editor of a proposed new periodical 'to treat of philosophical principles, abstract and applied, of sociology'" (cited in Hoecker-Drysdale, 1992:70–71).[1] Personal uncertainty and family pressure led Martineau to refuse the offer, but she continued her projects of social research and of popularizing sociology. In 1853 she published an extensively edited English translation of Comte's *Positive Philosophy,* a version he so approved that he substituted it, translated back into French, for his original edition. It is only in this relationship to Comte that, until the present decade, Martineau's name survived in the record of sociology's history. But the claim may indeed be made that she is the first sociologist—sociology's "founding mother."

In her self-established role as public educator in the principles and insights of sociology, Martineau defined her audience democratically and inclusively—the educated intelligentsia like herself, the political class of Britain, the ordinary working people of both the middle and working class, women, children (by means of a popular series of children's stories), her public in America (where since 1837 her popularity had been enormous), feminists and abolitionists on both sides of the Atlantic, even—in what must be a sociological first—the disabled—in this case, those who, like her, were deaf (1830/1836).

Despite this project of making sociology popular, Martineau held that the formulation of sociology, its subject matter and its method, should be developed in a disciplined and systematic way:

> In an attempt to develop any science, whether deductive or inductive, the very first step . . . is to define your subject methodically, to lay down the definition of your terms and instruments, and to ascertain what are the principles upon which the science essentially turns.
>
> (Martineau, cited in Hoecker-Drysdale, 1992:112)

Sociology's subject matter, in Martineau's sociology, is *social life in society*—its patterns, causes, consequences, and problems. In this focus she is both like and unlike Comte and Spencer. She is like them in choosing society, understood as roughly

---

[1]The phrase "to treat of philosophical principles, abstract and applied, of *sociology*" (italics added) is from two letters from Harriet to her brother James, December 12 and 21, 1837 (as cited in Hoecker-Drysdale, 1992:77). While Comte is conventionally seen as inventing the word "sociology," Martineau's use here shows that the term had general currency in the 1830s and that her usage, together with Comte's, may reflect some emerging consensus about the name for the new field.

HARRIET MARTINEAU: A Biographical Sketch

Harriet Martineau was born on June 12, 1802, in Norwich, England. The sixth of eight children in a business family of comfortable means and of the liberal Unitarian faith, Harriet, as a child, was given as good an education as her brothers. An able student, she turned eagerly to scholarship, not only because of its intrinsic appeal, but also as a respite from her childhood shyness and from the deafness that overcame her in early adolescence. She had an extraordinary facility for writing and began publishing in 1820, writing on women's unequal treatment in education and religion for the Unitarian journal *The Repository.*

The failure of the family business left her penniless in 1829. Faced with the choice of earning her—and her mother's—living as a seamstress or a writer, she chose the latter, settling on a plan for writing in which she would educate the public, in a pleasing and acceptable form, in the principles of the emerging discipline of sociology. Between 1832 and 1834, she wrote didactic novels in the series, *Illustrations of Political Economy.* The series was enormously successful, averaging 10,000 copies a month at its height and outselling even Dickens. The success of this venture won her financial independence, fame, and political influence.

Martineau would build on this propitious beginning, writing for the rest of her life for her living, for social reputation, and for political influence. She published over seventy volumes in many genres, including adult fiction, children's stories, poetry, history, religious tracts, autobiography, literary criticism, and social and political analysis. She also wrote over 1500 newspaper columns.

Despite this grueling writing schedule, Martineau was not a recluse. She traveled extensively in Britain, the United States, and the Middle East. She spoke and traveled on behalf of innumerable public causes, including women's rights and the abolition of slavery. A prominent feminist thinker, she led a busy social life and was connected to the significant British intellectuals of her day.

The quality that comes through most strongly as we study her life and writings is her valor in the face of deafness, poor health, financial vulnerability, and the disadvantages of being a woman making her way from modest beginnings on her own in nineteenth-century England. Harriet Martineau was determined to make the best of what life had dealt her, and she did so with enormous discipline, considerable talent, and a capacity for joy in the details of her daily experiences. She died on June 27, 1876, at the home she had earned for herself—The Knoll, Ambleside, in England's Lake District.

equivalent to a nation state or politico-cultural entity, as the framing structure for sociological investigation, and in her belief that the life of any society is influenced by some very general social laws, including the principle of progress, the emergence of science as the most advanced product of human intellectual endeavor, and the significance of population dynamics and the natural physical environment.

Martineau's sociology is unlike Comte's and Spencer's in some significant and feminist ways. First, for her, the most important law of social life is that "the great ends of human association" aim above all "to the grand one,—the only general one,— . . .

human happiness" (1838b:12). From this, she argues that a system of social arrangements is conducive to human happiness to the extent that it allows individuals to act as
autonomous moral and practical agents. The opposite of autonomy is domination, the
enforced "submission of one's will to another" (1838a:411). Sociology's project is,
thus, to assess the extent to which a people develop "morals and manners" which produce or subvert this great end of all social life, human happiness. By "morals"
Martineau means a society's collective ideas of prescribed and proscribed behavior; by
"manners," its patterns of action and association. The principle that the aim of human
association is human happiness—for Martineau as much a "law of nature" as any of the
others, that is, one to which societies should conform if they are to progress—distinguishes her sociology from that of Comte and Spencer, giving her theory of society a
critical tone essentially absent from their theories. She shares that critical posture with
Marx, although his theory would focus on class injustice and be militant, while hers
would be woman-centered and reformist.

Martineau's sociology, thus, also differs from that of Comte and Spencer in that her
interest is much less in building a model of an ideal-typical, ahistorical, generalized
"social system" or in creating an abstract typology of societies in terms of their "stages"
of development. Rather, she chooses to study the social life, the actual patterns of human relationships and activities, in historically developed societies—England, Ireland,
the United States, and those of the Middle East. In conceptualizing the social system,
Martineau focuses on these patterns of social life as profoundly interesting and significant in and of themselves. In the truest sense of the term she is a qualitative, comparative
sociologist. In her analysis, the actions and interactions of a society can be classified as
relating to various institutional zones—government, economy, law, education, marriage
and family, religion, communication, popular culture, and so on. But social activities
can also be constructed less formally, as the fluid relational tissue or texture of social
life. Thus, Martineau studies hospitality, travel, colloquialisms, attitudes toward money
and toward nature, decorum and entertainment, children's comportment, norms of housing, relations around sexuality, and so on. The life of each society in its uniqueness
from, as well as its similarities to, other societies is her immediate subject of attention.

Together with this descriptive task, Martineau wishes to analyze each society in
terms of its general economic and moral well-being. She does this in two ways. First,
she sets out to discover the moral principles which the society's members have collectively set up for themselves, their cultural aspirations or "Morals." Their well-being is
in part to be assessed in terms of the gap or the closeness between moral codes and actual behaviors or manners. Second, she tries to ascertain a society's progress or malaise
in terms of the degree to which it promotes autonomy or allows domination; she develops three measures of this progress: (1) the condition of the less powerful—women,
racial minorities, prisoners, servants, those in need of charity; (2) cultural attitudes toward authority and autonomy; (3) the extent to which all people are provided with the
necessities for autonomous moral and practical action.

This concern with issues of measurement is part of Martineau's deep interest in
methods for research and for sound scientific thinking. The latter she spells out as tools
for right thinking for the ordinary person in daily life in "Essays on the Art of Thinking,"
written around 1830 and published in *Miscellanies* (Martineau, 1836). Here she outlines
strategies for disciplined observation, classification of data, definition of vocabulary,

investigation of cause and effect, experimentation, comparison, control of personal bias, use of secondary data sources, and reflection on or analysis of one's data:

> The principal object which is attained by the exercise of reflection is the deduction of general principles from the facts which observation furnishes; and . . . the application of these general principles to the elucidation of new facts.
>
> (Martineau, 1836:Vol. 2, 103)

In the final portion of these essays, she links the individual's scientific quest for truth to the quest for a sound moral system. It is a remarkable document not only for its methodological clear-sightedness but also in its assumption that she is communicating with "Everyperson" in whose capacities for positivistic thinking she absolutely believes.

In *How to Observe Morals and Manners* (1838) she focuses more sharply on the research work of the social scientist and develops the first methods text in the history of sociology. Again she believes everyone capable of instruction in social scientific procedures of observation and she takes as her audience the person in everyday life who in the role of "traveler" wishes to make informed observations about society. In *How to Observe,* Martineau gives instruction in the appropriate attitude of the sociologist toward the research experience, in problems of sampling, and in the identification of social indicators. The sociologist must try to develop a sympathetic understanding as a strategy for discovering the meanings of an activity for the actors—for "actions and habits do not always carry their moral impress visibly to all eyes" (1838b:17). To overcome problems of sampling the sociologist must look for "things" which represent the collectivity. In a passage which anticipates Durkheim's much later statement (*Rules of Sociological Method,* 1895/1964), she says that one must begin the "'inquiry into morals and manners with the study of THINGS' . . . facts to be collected from architectural remains, epitaphs, civic registers, national music or any other of the thousand manifestations of the common mind which may be found among every people" (1838b:63). She goes on to elaborate strategies for field work, including a diary of one's views, a journal of one's observations, a notebook for recording events. This concern with disciplined research is sustained after the American investigation in all her other sociological investigations. In the detail of her directives and her application of these directives in social research, Martineau is much more advanced sociologically than Comte or Spencer, and she anticipates the work of the next generation of academically based or trained sociologists, both male and female. If Martineau is the founder of a feminist sociology, then that sociology is to be both theoretical and firmly grounded in empirical research.

Martineau's feminist approach to social analysis is evident in *Society in America* (1836/1837) in her pervasive interest in and investigation of the conditions of women's lives. She makes the relational facts of marriage in the United States a key index of the moral condition of that society (her conclusions are pessimistic). The enslavement of the African-American population is her second key index, and she does not miss the significance of the interplay of gender and race. For Martineau the domination of women closely parallels the domination of slaves. Like the slave, the woman is described—even to herself—as being indulged, but "indulgence is given her as a substitute for justice. Her case differs from that of the slave, as the principle, just so far as this; that the indulgence is large and universal, instead of petty and capricious. In both cases, justice is denied on no better plea than the right of the strongest" (1836/1837:II:227).

In her writing and research after the study of U.S. society, Martineau continued this woman-centered sociology with investigations of women's education, family, marriage and the law, violence against women, the tyranny of fashion, the inhumanity of the Arab harem, the inhumanity of the British treatment of prostitution, and in study after study, the nature of women's paid work, in terms of its brutally heavy physical demands and wretchedly low wages. Her particular focus was on the wage labor of working-class women—in factories, in agriculture, in domestic service. In these studies, she brings together the double oppressions of class and gender.

Martineau did not restrict the sociology she was developing to women's issues. She expanded her analytic efforts to an enormous number of other topics. She continued her comparative case studies with field research in Ireland and in the Middle East; the latter research was published in the three-volume work *Eastern Life: Present and Past,* in 1848. Later Martineau wrote about the origins and functions of religion, crime and its punishment, the lives of the poor, labor conflicts, colonialism and war, illness, both physical and mental, and health care practices related to illness. Her sociological perspective, though anchored in her gendered life experience and permeated by a woman-centered sensibility, did not produce only a sociology of gender. It is a general sociology with theoretical relevance for all aspects of social life.

To some extent the most basic connection of Martineau's sociology and her feminism was her understanding of herself as a gendered being in a world in which gender mattered and in which the fact that she was a woman would always frame others' response to her and her work. Her consciousness of this gender framing and, consequently, of a particular duty to women is visible from her very first publications—"Female Writers on Practical Divinity" (1822) and "On Female Education" (1823)—to her great achievements, *Society in America* (1836/1837) and *How to Observe Morals and Manners* (1838b). She opens *Society in America* by answering the charge that her being a woman has made her research difficult—"In this I do not agree. I am sure, I have seen much more of domestic life than could possibly have been exhibited to any gentleman traveling through the country. The nursery, the boudoir, the kitchen are all excellent schools in which to learn the morals and manners of a people" (1836/1837:I:xiii).

In the end Harriet Martineau was defeated by the very issue she knew to be inseparable from others' reactions to her work—her gender. Although she worked with modesty, discipline, and prodigious productivity to prove her worth as a human being and a woman, and although she maintained a public reputation as a social scientist, political advocate, and intellectual in her lifetime, at her death the patriarchal currents in both general intellectual life and in sociology would flood in to defeat her. The record of her achievement would be washed away almost without trace in the century in which the field in which she had been so creative and dedicated—sociology—would emerge as a distinct scholarly discipline.

CHARLOTTE PERKINS GILMAN (1860–1935)

In her analytic writings, Charlotte Perkins Gilman, more than any other female sociologist of the classic period, approximates in tone and intention the work of her male contemporaries in sociology—Durkheim (see Chapter 6), Weber (see Chapter 7), Simmel (see Chapter 8), Mead (see Chapter 12), and Park (see Chapter 2). Gilman's project was to present, in the impersonal, objective, imperious voice which we have come to associate with authoritative theorizing, a formal, theoretical analysis of society, understood both as a general or typical phenomenon and in its particular industrialized patternings in turn-of-the-century North Atlantic societies. In a passage which presents us with the central thesis of her feminist sociological theory of society, Gilman writes:

> Since we learned to study the development of human life as we study . . . species through the animal kingdom. . . . [W]e begin to see that . . . our lives are but the natural results of natural causes. . . . [T]he general course of life shows the inexorable effect of conditions upon humanity. Of these conditions we share with other living things . . . the material universe. . . . With animals we farther [*sic*] share the effect of our own activity. . . . What we do, as well as what is done to us, makes us what we are. But beyond these forces, we come under the effect of a third set of conditions peculiar to our human status; namely, social conditions. In the organic interchanges which constitute social life, we are affected to a degree beyond what is found even among the most gregarious of animals. This third factor, the social environment, is of enormous force as a modifier of human life. Throughout all these environing conditions, . . . economic necessities are most marked in their influence. . . . Under all the influence of his later and wider life, all the reactive effect of social institutions, the individual is still inexorably modified by his means of livelihood . . . the daily processes of supplying economic needs. . . .
>
> In view of these facts, attention is now called to certain marked and peculiar economic conditions affecting the human race, and unparalleled in organic life. We are the only animal species in which the female depends on the male for food, the only animal species in which the sex-relation is also an economic relation. With us an entire sex lives in a relation of economic dependence upon the other sex, and the economic relation is combined with the sex-relation.

(Gilman, 1898/1966:1–5)

Gilman argues that in the foundational social institution, the economy, we find a basic stratificational practice which explains most of the ills observable in societies, in individual experience, and in history: that practice is gender inequality. Gilman, who like all the writers of this period lacked the term and concept "gender," uses "sex" to name the stratificational practice she identifies and theorizes. "Sex" in her usage conflates physiological sex traits with sociocultural gender processes and sociocultural emotional patternings of sexuality. Thus conceptualized, gender stratification is the primary tension in the economies of all known societies, producing in effect, two sex classes—men as a "master class" and women as a class of subordinated and disempowered social beings. Gilman calls this pattern the "sexuo-economic arrangement."

Gilman's explication of the consequences of this sexuo-economic arrangement parallels Marx's exploration of the implications of economic class conflict for history and society. (That Marx is more familiar to us reflects not only his position in world history but a massive politics of knowledge in both society and sociology which has periodically advanced the Marxian thesis and systematically erased Gilman's feminist thesis.) For Gilman, as for Marx, the economy is the basic social institution, the area of physical human work which produces individual and social life, moves society progressively forward, and lets individuals potentially realize their species-nature as agentic producers. Our personalities are formed by our actual experiences of work. In her best-known

CHARLOTTE PERKINS GILMAN: A Biographical Sketch

Charlotte Perkins Gilman was a woman of extraordinary energy. She was most fulfilled when she was most active, a personal experience which she would generalize to her sociological views about human nature. She published over 2000 works in her lifetime—novels, poetry, journalistic accounts, autobiography, and above all, sociological commentary on society, politics, and women's lives. She was an activist and organizer on women's issues, a public speaker in constant demand, the editor and sole author of her own journal, *The Forerunner,* from 1909 to 1916, and a constant traveler who crisscrossed the United States and visited Europe on several occasions.

Born in Hartford, Connecticut, on July 3, 1860, she was related on her father's side to the eminent and established Beecher family (her aunt was Harriet Beecher Stowe, author of *Uncle Tom's Cabin*), but her own life was marked by instability and unconventionality. After her parents divorced in 1869, she was raised in genteel poverty by her mother, moving from one relative's home to another and erratically receiving education. Her first marriage, in 1884, pushed her to the edge of madness, vividly portrayed in *The Yellow Wall-Paper* (1892/1973), and ended in divorce a decade later. Determined to have an independent lifestyle, Gilman helped effect the marriage of her best friend to her former husband and turned her daughter over to them while she pursued her public and professional career. In 1900, after several passionate attachments with other women, she married a cousin, Houghton Gilman, who was considerably younger than she and who supported her need for independence and public visibility in what was to be a very satisfactory marriage for them both.

In her own life, Gilman achieved enormous visibility. Her book *Women and Economics* (1898/1966) went through nine editions in her lifetime, was translated into seven languages, and was reviewed by the male establishment and by almost all the women sociologists discussed in this chapter—Addams, Kelley, Taft, Weber, and Webb. All of her other sociological books received significant attention. She was an active member of both the sociological and economic scholarly communities, an occasional resident at Hull House, and a cofounder, with Jane Addams, of the Women's Peace Party.

Ill with inoperable breast cancer, she died by her own hand on August 17, 1935.

---

work, the novella *The Yellow Wall-Paper,* written in 1892, six years before her first sociological book, *Women and Economics,* Gilman horrifyingly dramatizes this theme as the female first-person narrator descends into madness because of the inactivity enforced on her by her doctor-husband and relatives, that is, by the sexuo-economic arrangements in society. This understanding of human nature is developed in all of Gilman's sociological writings: meaningful work is the essence of human self-realization; restricting or denying the individual access to meaningful work reduces the individual to a condition of nonhumanity.

The sexuo-economic arrangement presents just this barrier to self-actualizing work, for both women and men, though for women much more than men. This systemic pollution of the human essence leads not merely to individual unhappiness but to an enormous catalogue of social pathologies: class conflict, political corruption, distorted sexuality, greed, poverty, waste and environmental exploitation, inhuman conditions in both wage labor and unpaid household labor, harmful educational practices, child neglect and abuse, ideological excess, war, and above all, a systemic structural condition of human alienation. Gilman presented programmatic strategies for ameliorating the situation—another hallmark of critical and feminist social theory. Working systematically through this comprehensive and critical theory of society and gender is the project of Gilman's feminist sociology.

Like many feminist writers today, Gilman experimented with the forms in which her views of the individual in society might be presented. But the overwhelming majority of her 2173 publications (Scharnhorst, 1985) were social commentary and analysis. She published hundreds of articles of this type, not only in her own journal, *The Forerunner,* which she founded in 1909 and both edited and wrote until 1916, but also in mainstream publications like *The Independent* and sociological journals like *The American Journal of Sociology, Annals of the American Academy of Political and Social Science,* and *Publications of the American Sociological Society,* which later became the *American Sociological Review* (Keith, 1991). Gilman also published six books of sociological theory which developed, in the coherent, authoritative, systematic, and accessible style already noted, her theory of society and gender. *Women and Economics* (1898/1966) lays out her basic thesis; *Concerning Children* (1900) presents her critical theory of child development, socialization, education, gender education, and the essential reforms needed in all these areas; *The Home* (1903) is a critical exploration of the contemporary household and of the organization of domestic work, with radical, concrete suggestions for the reorganization of this institution, and consequently for both family relations and society; *Human Work* (1904) offers an ambitious and critical assessment of both paid and unpaid human labor, and of human alienation and class struggle in contemporary society; *The Man-Made World or Our Androcentric Culture* (1911) traces the ramifications of cultural themes of masculinity and femininity on "family, health and beauty, art, literature, games and sports, ethics and religion, education, society and fashion, law and government, crime and punishment, politics and warfare, and industry and economics" (Ceplair, 1991:189); and *His Religion and Hers* (1923) explores religion as an institution from a consciously feminist sociological viewpoint. In combination, these books give us as comprehensive an analysis of society as any offered by Gilman's male contemporaries—an analysis anchored in her critical, indeed radical, feminist sociological theory.

Three themes from her sociology are particularly relevant to the concerns of contemporary feminist sociology: the production and reproduction of gender stratification; the impact of gender stratification on societal organization in general and on economic and class relations in particular, and her strategies for social change.

Central to much of Gilman's work is an exploration of the processes that produce gender stratification. Here she uses evolutionary imagery in much the same way as Engels, for example, in *The Origins of the Family* (1884/1970), develops a mythic prehistory for humankind. But stripped of this imagery, Gilman in fact makes a remarkable claim: *man's domination of woman springs from his need for sociability with or recognition by an Other.* This is an argument with much currency in modern feminism (Chodorow, 1978; Benjamin, 1988; Lengermann and Niebrugge, 1995). Gilman writes in *Women and Economics:*

[T]he human individual [has] the imperative demand for the establishment of a common consciousness between . . . hitherto irreconcilable individuals. The first step in nature towards this end is found in the relation between mother and child . . . [when] we have the overlapping of personality, the mutual need . . . that holds together these interacting personalities. . . . Therefore between the mother and child [is] born . . . the common consciousness . . . mutual attraction. . . . As the male . . . steadily encroaches upon the freedom of the female until she is reduced to the state of . . . dependence . . . [h]e fulfils . . . in his own person the thwarted uses of maternity . . . [the] common interest, existing now not only between mother and child, but between father, mother and child.

(Gilman, 1898/1966:124–125)

Out of this primary though distorted need for sociability or recognition arises male domination and female subordination. "So he instituted the custom of enslaving the female" (Gilman, 1898/1966:60), psychologically bonding with her while increasingly appropriating all economic agency in the relationship and thus all relational control. She, thus, becomes increasingly dependent, increasingly disempowered economically, increasingly maimed in terms of personal growth. Gender will be her only instrument of countervailing power, the wiles of femininity, a focus on sexuality, the fact as well as the ploy of her economic helplessness. Out of this class arrangement arises masculinity and femininity as pervasive cultural themes—the aggressive, assertive man, the yielding, compliant woman. These structures become deeply embedded in the dailiness of habit and go sociologically unscrutinized because they are assumed to be attributes of the individual person. From birth on, socialization and education inculcate these relational, structural, and stratificational modes, and all of culture conspires to reinforce them through life. Thus the sexuo-economic relation is continuously reproduced.

The ramifications of this system are not only psychological and cultural; they profoundly penetrate and distort economic and community life. The sexuo-economic arrangement gives rise to the individual family, the individual mating or married couple, the individual household. Unlike economic class relations, dominants and subordinates in the sexuo-economic system are intimately linked in pairs, each pair isolated in its own "little household." Society can be understood as dividing between the public economy of the marketplace and the private economy of the household. The first is the sphere of manly action, and women are marginal to it. The second is the sphere of women's labor, labor dependent on the economic power of the man. The household is an area of untrained, unprofessional demanding labor, wasteful of the woman, wasteful of society's economic resources in its replication of need from house to house—an area often of unregulated consumption. The market is a place where man's gender power becomes an oppressive economic responsibility for the provision of his household. From this pressure arises a social system encouraging individualism, competition, conflict, class divisions, excessive greed, and wealth hand in hand with crippling exploitation and deprivation. In this pathological system, people wander unguided into whatever occupation comes to hand, and there, trapped by the burden of the household, they remain if they can, "square pegs in round holes," hanging on to security, but in their deep unfulfillment doing second-rate work, and thus reproducing the incompetence, waste, inefficiency, and alienation of the contemporary economy (Gilman, 1904:157–226).

The solution to this wasteful sexuo-economic arrangement is to break up the arrangement of the sex classes. The first step to achieving this is the economic emancipation of women—one goal of the women's movement of Gilman's own day, as it is in ours. This goal is not a simple one for Gilman. It requires fundamental changes in gender socialization and in education. It requires the physical development of women to their full size and strength, a rethinking and renegotiation of the personal, relational, and sexual expectations between women and men. But most basically, it requires the rational dismantling and reconstruction of the institution of the household, so that women can have freedom to do the work they choose and so that society may thus be enriched by their labor. In this last strategy, we have Gilman's most novel and problematic approach to a revolution in gender relations. In extraordinary detail she sets herself the project of redesigning domestic space and domestic activity. In Gilman's transformed world of the home, each person will have "a room of their own" and space for association with the family of their choice and construction. Child care, food service, laundry, and household cleaning will be handled professionally by enlightened, well-paid workers, in humane work spaces—and by people who find their calling and their dignity in such work. Surrounding them all—those working in the newly designed domestic spaces, those being reared there, and those coming "home" there from work elsewhere—will be cultural, intellectual, recreational, and health facilities for the new communal lifestyle, paid for by the saving from earlier wasteful domestic drudgery and earlier wasteful marketplace drudgery. This scenario is Gilman's utopia, as communism was Marx's utopia. In its closest real-world realization, perhaps, and on a scale much smaller than Gilman envisioned, this was the organizational form of Jane Addams's Hull House, which we will discuss shortly.

Although she did everything that one might expect of a significant sociological theorist in a language, English, that means she has always been accessible to American sociologists, Charlotte Perkins Gilman has been systematically written out of American sociology's construction of its own sociological and theoretical past. Let us first restate the case that she performed as a sociological theorist. She is a member of the American Sociological Society from its foundation in 1895 to her death in 1935. She presents before its annual convention in 1908 and 1909. Her writing is replete with the awareness that she is bringing a sociological consciousness to her work. Her tone is recognizably that of the sociological theorist, and her theory is not implicit in writings with another purpose; it is her project. In her framing, we find ideas which are now familiar to us as "markers" of classical sociological theory—comparison with other species (Darwin, Spencer, Park, Mead); an assumption of human societal development (Spencer, Durkheim, Weber, Mead, Park); conditioning social facts (Marx, Durkheim) and interactions (Simmel, Mead, Park); the centrality of economic life (Marx, Weber). The arrangement of these arguments is both sufficiently familiar and sufficiently innovative to distinguish Gilman's work as a distinctive body of theory. It is true that social evolutionary vocabulary permeates many of her statements, and that these referents have fallen out of favor, but Spencer, Durkheim, Mead, and Park—even, to a degree, Marx— also weave this vocabulary through their presentations, and contemporary historians of sociological theory have learned to screen these referents out, as they reach for what is perceived as valuable in the theories of these men. Together with the explications of her theoretical effort, and its embedded sociological referents, we also have the massive production of her writings, their enormous visibility in her own time, and her explicit engagement with and acknowledgment by the professional sociological communities—both male and female—of her day.

Only a complex process of antiwoman and antifeminist bias explains Gilman's disappearance from the record of sociology and sociological theory. As with all the other women discovered in this chapter, Gilman's gender diminished her authority as a sociological spokesperson in an increasingly male-dominated profession. So too did her development of a general theory out of her own lived experience as a woman and out of her women-centered concerns—home, children, sexuality, housework, gender identity, femininity and masculinity. Moreover, her activist and feminist stance, for radical reform of both gender and class relations, for the systematic restructuring of home life, education, work, culture, and religion, would make her seem too political and valuational to a field moving rapidly toward a value-neutral stance, a field that by the 1930s would make Weber's "Politics as a Vocation" and "Science as a Vocation" guiding documents. Without a large population of women in the profession or a strong feminist movement in society after 1920, Gilman could be first marginalized and then allowed to disappear. Only now, with the reversal of both these trends is the moment right for her rediscovery.

JANE ADDAMS AND THE WOMEN OF CHICAGO

At the same time that men at the University of Chicago were building what was to become "the Chicago school" (see Chapter 2), the group of women we shall call "the women of Chicago" were also creating a sociology and a sociological theory. The focal energy in this group was Jane Addams (1860–1935). The women worked out of two bases, the University of Chicago and Hull House, the settlement founded by Jane Addams and Ellen Gates Starr in 1889.

Although connected to the men of the University of Chicago (Deegan, 1988), these women formed their real professional and personal networks with each other (Gordon, 1994; Fitzpatrick, 1990; Rosenberg, 1982). It is hard to overstate the significance of this network for the women personally, for U.S. history in the Progressive Era (1880–1916) and beyond, and for a feminist reconstruction of the history of sociology. This network included women who studied or taught at the University of Chicago and/or who lived as residents or did research instituted by Hull House. Besides Addams, this network included: Edith and Grace Abbott, Sophonisba Breckinridge, Florence Kelley, Frances Kellor, Julia Lathrop, Annie Marion MacLean, Virginia Robinson, Anna Garlin Spencer, Jessie Taft, and Marion Talbot, among others. They were part of a larger women's network described by Gordon (1994), a remarkable set of "social innovators" (Scott, 1964) who devised an astounding range of policies and associations to protect subordinate groups as the United States confronted the effects of the Industrial Revolution and its own intense individualistic, classist, racist, and sexist politics. Further, this network touched the lives and work of other women discussed in this chapter: Charlotte Perkins Gilman was a resident at Hull House from 1895 to 1896; Marianne Weber visited there, as did Beatrice Potter Webb; Ida B. Wells-Barnett and Jane Addams were partners in the

JANE ADDAMS: A Biographical Sketch

Jane Addams, though often trivialized in popular school-ing as an ever-beloved "Lady Bountiful," was a deeply thoughtful, ethically committed person, of only modest personal wealth, who genuinely tried to love her neigh-bors, and who in her lifetime both was on the FBI's list of "most dangerous radicals" (during the 1920s "Red Scare") and won the Nobel Peace Prize (in 1931).

Born in Freeport, Illinois, on September 6, 1860, into a family involved in both business and politics, she at-tended Rockford Seminary, where she began some seri-ous spiritual thinking and excelled academically, graduating as valedictorian in 1881.

The years from 1881 to 1888, when she at last settled on the plan that would become Hull House, were difficult ones—marked by her father's death, her own illness, and illness in her family which demanded her attention. Worse though, she found that she did not know what to do with her life; she had leisure but not purpose. In her travels in Europe, she gradually formed the conviction that she should try to imitate the settlement experiment she had seen in London.

In 1889 she and Ellen Gates Starr arranged to rent Hull House on Halsted Street in Chicago's nineteenth ward, an area of working-class immigrants. Their plan, which Addams recounts in *Twenty Years at Hull-House* (1910/1990), was to try to learn and help by living simply as neighbors among the poor. Addams showed a remarkable ability to do just that. Hull House attracted other "residents," mainly educated young women who wished to put their education to use. Collectively they embarked upon a range of social experiments in-cluding social clubs, garbage collection, apartments for working women, consumer cooper-atives, evening classes, trade unions, industrial reform legislation, investigations of working conditions, debating societies, and intervening in strikes, unemployment, and hysteria about anarchists (many of whom took part in Hull House debates). Hull House became identified in the public mind of Addams's own day not simply with good works but with radical thought and change. This identification was all but sealed when Addams held to her commitment to pacifism during the patriotic fervor of World War I.

Following the pragmatic creed of testing the truth of ideas by experience, Addams drew on her Hull House work to develop a sociological theory based on the conviction that people had now to begin to work collectively and cooperatively—which meant learning to tolerate dif-ferences. She traces the need for cooperation and growth in understanding in a series of books and articles, among the most important of which are *Twenty Years at Hull-House* (1910), *Democracy and Social Ethics* (1902), *Newer Ideals of Peace* (1907), *The Long Road of Women's Memory* (1916), *Peace and Bread in Times of War* (1922), and *The Second Twenty Years at Hull-House* (1930).

Her most noted personal quality—her ability to understand another person's position with-out necessarily agreeing with it and to communicate that understanding—may also be the quality that most emerges for the feminist reader of her sociology. Her long-time friend Emily Greene Balch remembers Addams's special concern with vantage point: "Significant of her relation to her Halsted Street neighbors is the habit that she had when she made a speech about Hull House of taking one of them with her so that they all knew that when Hull House was described to important people downtown it sounded exactly like Hull House as they knew it" (1941/1972:206). Jane Addams died on May 21, 1935.

struggle for African-American and women's rights. (To close the circle, we note that Edith Abbott [1906] wrote an article on Harriet Martineau in *The Journal of Political Economy,* and Martineau herself had written a lively description of Chicago as a frontier settlement in 1836.)

The women of Chicago, like many of the men, defined the purpose of sociology and their role as sociologists as the reform and improvement of society. The years from 1890 to 1914 were a golden era for the reform movement of "Progressivism." Inspired by the theories of "reform Social Darwinism," the teaching of the "social gospel" and the philosophy of pragmatism, Progressives sought to take control of the chaotic and exploitative conditions of life created by the interconnected events of the Industrial Revolution, the influx of immigrants and the rise of the cities.

Although battling intense sexism in university and professional life (Deegan, 1988; Fitzpatrick, 1990; Rosenberg, 1982), the women used sociological theory, analysis, and research to win numerous victories for the rights of women and for the Progressive movement. The Chicago women helped lead the fight for women's suffrage, factory legislation, child labor laws, protection of working women, aid for dependent mothers and children, better sanitation in the cities, trade unions, arbitration of labor disputes, minimum wages, and minimum-wage boards. Much of what the women fought for became the stuff of New Deal legislation in the 1930s.

Jane Addams and the women of Chicago were both products and creators of this extraordinary period. What they may have created above all was a tremendous energy born of the faith that something could indeed be done.

Jane Addams (1860–1935)

As much as any theorist in the history of sociology, Jane Addams directly put her theory on the line in the everyday world of personal interactions and political struggle. She is a critical sociological theorist in action. The work of reclaiming Addams as a sociologist and locating her career in the gender politics of sociology has been done in Mary Jo Deegan's landmark study, *Jane Addams and the Men of the Chicago School* (1988). Here we focus on Addams's sociological theory.

In tone and purpose, Addams presents a feminist sociological theory created around the pursuit of a distinctively cultural feminist goal for society. In common with Martineau and Comte, and also with some of the Chicago men—most notably Mead and Small—Addams sees the goal of social theory as social amelioration. She defines the particular amelioration of her age as the need to "socialize democracy," to create a society in which relations are based in what contemporary feminists describe as *inclusivity, empowerment, and vantage point.* Addams comes to this goal by reflecting on her personal life experience in the light of an amalgam of the thought of her day: reform social Darwinism's emphasis on human responsibility in the evolutionary process; philosophical pragmatism's demand that one test the truth of a proposition by the experiential difference between its being true or false; a developing cultural feminism that valued female virtues as equal or superior to male attitudes; and a reinterpretation of Christianity in the terms of the Social Gospel which preached that the meaning of faith could be found only in action.

Addams chose her life's work as an activist and social theorist after a series of experiences that contemporary sociological theorist Dorothy E. Smith (1987:6–8) might label "bifurcated consciousness" (the awareness of a division between formal textual descriptions of life and one's own lived experience). For Addams, this bifurcation was in the division between the world seen through literature and a series of glimpses of "real life." In *Twenty Years at Hull House* (1910/1990), Addams tells of a time in London, when from an omnibus she sees poor people desperately bidding for rotten food and eating it raw; what horrifies Addams is not only the experience, but her response to it. She responds by remembering, instantaneously as she sees these people, a short story by Thomas DeQuincey, "The Vision of Sudden Death," and she realizes that she is, like DeQuincey, in that story, retreating from life into literature—*distancing from the immediate world into the safety of text.* Addams condemns herself for doing what she felt many women of her class were doing, substituting sentiment and book learning for action. Her sociological theory reflects her attempt to turn herself to life and action: "While I may receive valuable suggestions from classic literature, when I really want to learn about life, I must depend upon my neighbors, for, as William James insists, the most instructive human documents live along the beaten pathway" (Addams, 1916:xi). As a pragmatist, Addams values her own experience over textual authority. She begins her theoretical work as a theorist who distrusts theory.

Because she "privileges" personal experience over theory, Addams has a distinctive way of writing theory. Her analysis is developed not so much through the crafting of theoretical generalizations as through the presentation of paradigmatic case studies from participant observation and key informants at Hull House and in the city of Chicago. She makes fewer generalizations than do most male theorists, she rarely speaks in their tone of detached imperious objectivity, and her illustrations are strikingly concrete and particular. She illustrates a point not with hypothetical, ahistorical figures—such as Max Weber uses—but with detailed accounts of the lives of men and women she has known. Addams seeks something more than *verstehen;* she seeks to establish what contemporary feminist theorists call for in research: an authentic, caring relation between the researcher and the subject of the research. In all her research Addams pursues the issue of vantage point—both as a question for the people about whom she writes and as a question governing her relationship to them. She tries to be true in her own analyses to her subjects' accounts of their lives; always her analyses bear the imprint of someone who not only saw but cared what was happening to the person about whom she writes.

Addams develops the central tenet of her sociological theory, the need to socialize democracy, on the basis of a series of implicit propositions about society, human nature, and social change. Addams envisions society as a vast network of individual human beings coming together in a variety of diverse and not necessarily analytically parallel structures—family, household, neighborhood, industry, education, war and peace, philanthropy, recreation, art. Her interest is not in establishing the appropriate analytic categories to name these structures—"institutions," "organizations," "processes"—but in seeing how to make them all possess certain common qualities—qualities of social democracy—which she assumes that evolution now demands. Her conception of society is not in terms of social structures, as it is with Comte, Spencer, Marx, Durkheim, or Park, but in the relationships of human beings in interaction, as with Simmel and Mead.

She is distinctive among interactionists, although representative of cultural feminists, in focusing on human beings not only as subjectivities but as bodies, and upon subjectivity not only as reason but also as emotion. Drawing on her Hull House experiences, Addams repeatedly describes the *embodied* subject:

> A man who works by night sleeps regularly by day, but a woman finds it impossible to put aside the household duties which crowd upon her, and a conscientious girl finds it hard to sleep with her mother washing and scrubbing within a few feet of her bed. One of the most painful impressions of those first years is that of pale, listless girls, who worked regularly in the factory of the vicinity which was then running full night time. . . . Thus confronted by that old conundrum of the interdependence of matter and spirit, the conviction was forced upon us . . . that the power to overcome temptation reaches its limit almost automatically with that of physical resistance.
>
> (Addams, 1910/1990:120)

The democratic social ideal rests in the recognition of the independent agentic subjectivity of the human being: "We are not content to include all men in our hopes, *but have become conscious that all men are hoping* and are part of the same movement of which we are a part" (1902/1907:179; italics added). This capacity of the individual subjectivity to hold to her or his own will or sense of the world has been, Addams argues, too little realized in social thought. She criticizes the eighteenth-century drafters of the Constitution as representing "the first type of humanitarian who loves the people without really knowing them . . . and expects the people whom he does not know to forswear altogether the right of going their own way, and to be convinced of the beauty and value of his way" (Addams, 1905:425–426). Drawing on her experience, Addams argues that a democracy cannot be built by people who expect other people to "see the light," that such demands for change are grounded in a lack of respect for the vantage point of the other.

Further, she conceives of human subjectivity as a complex of reason and emotion, especially the emotion of kindness. She sees reason and emotion working together, manifesting themselves in the coexistence in the individual of rational judgment and sympathy. All people, no matter how materially hard-pressed, desire "an outlet for more kindliness," seek "to do a favor for a friend," to find expression for that "kindheartedness [that] lies in ambush to incorporate itself in our larger relations," hoping that "it shall be given some form of governmental expression" (Addams, 1907:2–3). Addams describes this desire as what the French mean in the "phrase *l'imperieuse bonté* by which they designate those impulses towards compassionate conduct which will not be denied" (1907:21). The idea of human beings desiring sociality is well developed in sociology in the theories of Simmel, Mead, W. I. Thomas, and Park. But the extension of this desire into a description of an embodied person who actively seeks an outlet for kindness is Addams's distinctive contribution.

The human being is located in a society that is always evolving or changing, but this process of change is one that humans must now control through the collective exercise of mind. Change, or evolution, does not necessarily proceed at the same pace in all parts of society; many social problems are the result of a disjunction between the rate and type of change in one part and those of another—a disjunction that Addams and other women of Chicago speak of as "belatedness." Although Addams sees that industrial change is currently forcing adjustments in other areas of social life, she does not accept that the material base always determines the pace and direction of change but believes that at certain moments, social organization or human mind and emotion may determine change. She explains social tensions much less in terms of class conflict than of people caught in processes of change that they have not yet brought into alignment.

Addams finds herself at a moment in history when humans must, by the invention of new means of association, realize the democratic social ethic.

> [W]e are . . . brought to a conception of Democracy not merely as a sentiment which desires the well-being of all men, nor yet as a creed which believes in the essential dignity and equality of all men, but as that which affords a rule of living as well as a test of faith. . . . To attain individual morality in an age demanding social morality, to pride oneself on the results of personal effort when the time demands social adjustment, is utterly to fail to apprehend the situation.
>
> (Addams, 1902/1907:2–3, 6)

A democratic social ethic would be based on the facts, revealed in one's own experience, that (1) no "one set of people are of so much less importance than another, that a valuable side of life pertaining to them should be sacrificed for the other" (Addams, 1902/1907:124); (2) that all people may be active agents, not simply included in the hopes of some elite but themselves actively hoping, planning, participating, thinking; (3) that as active agents all people seek opportunities to enact the imperative to kindliness which has evolved in humanity, and (4) that the personal safety of all members of the democratic social unit is tied to the personal safety of each.

Much of Addams's sociological theory is devoted to analyzing how to transform democracy from a political creed, enacted occasionally in elections, into a social creed enacted in all human interactions, and to why this transformation should be so difficult. She points to two major problems. One is the tension in society between the old ways (or "claim" of individualism) and the new ways (or "claim" of the social or collective ethic). The second is the difficulty in all collective enterprises of people recognizing each other's vantage point.

The tension between individual and collective ethics permeates society. In the organization of industry, it shows itself in the insistence of owners on keeping absolute control of production processes, enforcing specialization on the workers and refusing to share organizational control with them. "The division of labor" instituted by the factory owner "robs" the workers of a common and shared interest in their work and leaves only "the mere mechanical fact of interdependence" (Addams, 1902/1907:211). This alienation can be overcome only by an industrial democracy that allows workers to participate in the organization of production.

Within the household and in women's lives, in particular, "democracy is making inroads upon the family, the oldest of human institutions" in advancing "a claim . . . which is in a certain sense larger than the family claim" (Addams, 1902/1907:73, 77). The person most feeling the tension between the old family claim and the new social claim may be the college-educated woman, "educated to recognize a stress of social obligation which her family did not in the least anticipate when they sent her to college" (Addams,

1902/1907:84–85). Addams argues that "parents, as well as daughters, [must] feel the democratic impulse and recognize" the daughter's desire to fulfill the social claim as a legitimate and conscientious action (1902/1907:77–78).

All of Addams's considerable arguments for women's suffrage turn not upon any assertion of natural rights, which she felt assumed a fixed rather than an evolving human nature, but on the duty and need of every citizen to answer the social claim; to antisuffrage women, she argued that they had no right to reject the social claim and attempt to live within the narrow confines of the family claim.

Fulfilling the social claim depends upon an ability to take the vantage point of the other. Addams's second chapter in *Democracy and Social Ethics* (1902/1907), "Charitable Effort," focuses on a now extinct social status, "the charitable visitor," to explore the problems of vantage point and class division. (This interest in the social activity of the giving and receiving of charity is a way that Addams and other early women sociologists—including Gilman, Florence Kelley, Marianne Weber, and Beatrice Webb—focus on their own class position and the crisis facing the middle-class woman at the end of the nineteenth century.) At the time Addams was writing *Democracy and Social Ethics,* charity was still largely a private activity. In her exploration of the role of the charitable visitor, Addams analyzes the problems of the persistence of old habits which do not fit new conditions, the difficulties for the new college-educated woman in this world, the failure of an elite class to understand the real and valuable ethics of the poor, the need for a general ethic that understands the world of multiple viewpoints, the problems of "organized" charity as it affects human nature, and the general tendency of society to overvalue the "industrial" element of social productivity. She turns her attention to the difference in ethical standards between the neighborhood and the charity visitor, making a compelling case for the importance of taking into account the standpoints of the actors.

> Let us take a neighborhood of poor people, and test their ethical standards by those of the charity visitor. . . . A most striking incongruity, at once apparent, is the difference between the emotional kindness with which relief is given by one poor neighbor, and the guarded care with which relief is given by the charity visitor to the charity recipient. The neighborhood mind is at once confronted not only by the difference of method, but by an absolute clashing of two ethical standards.
>
> (Addams, 1902/1907:20–21)

Addams here explores the concrete taking-the-role-of-the-other dynamics missed in more abstract conceptions, including those that Mead was beginning to develop around this time. In the conception of "the neighborhood mind," Addams recognizes that there is not a single "generalized other," but many generalized others which can clash when the subjectivities that embody them meet.

Addams's central principle for change is that people must commit to learning and inventing ways to form democratic social relations and associations in all areas of life. She offers three strategies. In part, people can be taught the legitimacy of the social claim through formal education if the educational system is reformed, along lines suggested by Dewey (a frequent Hull House visitor), to "give the child's own social experience a value" (Addams, 1902/1907:180). But the schools often fail to teach this principle of "connectedness" because "the same tendency to division of labor has also produced over-specialization in scholarship, with the sad result that . . . the scholar . . . cannot bring healing and solace because he himself is suffering from the same disease" (Addams, 1902/1907:206).

The second, and most important, way for people to learn democracy as a way of relating is through constant and varied experiences of social interaction; people learn to work together by working together. People can change old habits and develop new norms and sensibilities through social interaction "not so much by the teaching of moral theorems [but] by the direct expression of social sentiments and by the cultivation of practical habits" (Addams, 1907:8). Hull House, trade unions, labor arbitration, social clubs, debating societies, elections, government committees, and neighborhood organizations are for Addams all avenues for the direct expression of social sentiments and the cultivation of practical habits of social interaction.

A third way Addams sees change occurring is in individuals' "memory"—or reflection shared and retold with others. In *The Long Road of Women's Memory* (1916), Addams links women's memory, or individual subjectivity, and social change, arguing that memory is used in two different but often complementary ways: for "interpreting and appeasing life for the individual" and as "a selective agency in social reorganization" (Addams, 1916:xi). People often remember events of their lives in ways that lead them to react against conventions or to reinterpret their part in historic changes so as to experience their own connectedness. *The Long Road of Women's Memory* contains some of Addams's most persuasive case histories. Through these histories, Addams argues that memory may be a kind of consciousness raising in which people realign themselves with the larger impersonal forces that have shaped their lives and in that realignment prepare the way for social change.

The Women of Chicago

Addams's core belief—that society needs not individual but collective action realized in democratic association— is clearly visible in the relationships, work, and sociology of the circle we have called "the Chicago women": Edith and Grace Abbott, Sophonisba Breckinridge, Florence Kelley, Frances Kellor, Julia Lathrop, Annie Marion MacLean, Virginia Robinson, Anna Garlin Spencer, Jessie Taft, and Marion Talbot, among others. It is possible, as Gordon (1994) has documented, to see these women as clannish and in-bred, but it is also possible to see this network of women possessing, as both Gordon (1994:70) and Costin (1983:100) quote, what Supreme Court Justice Felix Frankfurter described as "'a rare degree of disinterestedness and indifference to the share of [their] own ego in the cosmos.'"

Four major propositions frame their sociological theory. First, the governing principle of modern society is the interdependence of human beings and of the structures in which they come together. One cannot separately analyze industry, family, neighborhood, education, recreation, municipal government, and so on. Every person and activity potentially relates to every other. Everything that happens potentially affects women's lives, and women must find ways to exercise greater power. Second, people must now act in association or collectively to shape the environment and direct future human development. The world is evolving not by the action of some invisible law but

through the efforts of men and women. These efforts, heretofore uncoordinated, now require that people become inventive in forms of association and in the formulation of
state policies as one means for the enactment of the collective will. Third, the groups
most affected by change and the failures to control change are the socially disenfran-
chised: women, children, the elderly poor, immigrants, African-Americans, and
working-class and poor people in general. Fourth, the role of the social scientist is to
give people the tools for understanding and action by presenting facts about social conditions, plans for associations, and proposals for state policies. Besides conducting research, the Chicago women helped found the Urban League, the National Consumers
League, the National Association for the Advancement of Colored People, the National
Federation of Women's Clubs, the Association of College Alumnae (later to be the
American Association of University Women), and other associations for "social
amelioration."

Perhaps because they reinforced each other in this view of society, certainly because
they were philosophic pragmatists, their sociological theory came to focus on those
epistemological issues typically denoted as "methodology." One of their great sociological innovations is the methods they designed for studying and publicizing a problem—indeed, they were inventors of "social problems," in the sense that they took
situations which most people took for granted as unavoidable and redefined them as
subject to social control, social improvement, and social elimination. In presenting the
taken-for-granted as a social problem, these women invented an array of techniques for
discovering and reporting their evidence using both primary and secondary quantitative
and qualitative data sources—personal and historic documents, statistical tables, maps
of demographic traits, interviews, key informants, participant observations, and pho-
tographs. Good examples of the use of multiple research strategies are Edith Abbott's
Women in Industry (1910) and *The Tenements of Chicago* (1936/1970), Sophonisba
Breckinridge's *New Homes for Old* (1921/1971), Frances Kellor's *Out of Work*
(1905/1915), and *Hull-House Maps and Papers* (1895), compiled under the general direction of Florence Kelley. Probably the first published report of sociological participant observation is Annie Marion MacLean's "Two Weeks in Department Stores," in
The American Journal of Sociology, May 1899, which illustrates the Chicago women's
attention to methodology, their emphasis on empirical data, their commitment to fostering social change, and their interconnectedness as thinkers and researchers. MacLean
undertook this research as part of the work of the new Consumers' League of Illinois,
"organized by the collegiate alumnae" of Chicago as an early attempt to get consumers
to use their power to improve working conditions for women and children. MacLean
introduces her purpose:

> The necessity for a thorough investigation of the work of women and children in the
> large department stores in the city was apparent and the difficulties manifold. With a
> view to ascertaining some things which could be learned only from the inside, . . . [i]t
> seemed evident that valuable information could be obtained if someone were willing to
> endure the hardships of the saleswoman's life, and from personal experience be able to
> pass judgment upon observed conditions. [This] led me to join the ranks of the retail
> clerks for two weeks during the rush of the holiday trade.
>
> (MacLean, 1899:721–722)

The most daring explorations of collective action may have been done by Florence Kelley (1859–1932), who in 1887 published both the first English translation of Engels's *The Conditions of the Working Class in England in 1844* and a remarkable work of her own, "The Need for Theoretical Preparation for Philanthropic Work." The theoretical preparation Kelley proposes is the application of Marxist theory to philanthropy. In this essay, which she first presented at a meeting of the New York chapter of the Association of Collegiate Alumnae, Kelley argues that all bourgeois philanthropy, no matter how well intended, is really only a palliative, a restitution to the working class, the real creators of wealth, of what has been taken from them. It is an absolute statement of class conflict, describing a "division of society into two warring classes," producing two different kinds of philanthropy, bourgeois and proletarian.

> Our bourgeois philanthropy, whatever form it may take, is really only the effort to give back to the workers a little bit of that which our whole social system, systematically, robs them of, and so to prop up that system yet a little longer. . . . It is the workers who produce all values; but the lion's share of what they produce falls to the lion—the capitalist class. . . . [F]or the capitalist class as a whole, all philanthropic effort is a work of restitution for self-preservation.
>
> (Kelley, 1887/1986:94)

Settling into work at Hull House, Kelley became Chief Inspector of Factories under the reform Illinois Factory and Workshop Inspection Law of 1893. She fought its gutting by the Illinois Supreme Court until she was replaced by the next governor for a too vigorous enforcement. Her analysis of this and other attempts at reform legislation are offered in her still-used text, *Some Ethical Gains through Legislation* (1905/1969).

Momentarily defeated in terms of state policies, Kelley turned her attention to the possibility of voluntary associations bringing about changes in industrial organization. By the end of 1899, she published in *The American Journal of Sociology* "Aims and Principles of the Consumers' League." Here Kelley attempts to give consciousness to a new social category, "consumers." She will call consumers into being as a conscious social aggregate to redress the balance between capital and labor which the state seems impotent or unwilling to do.

> [T]hroughout our lives we are choosing, or choice is made for us, as to the disposal of money. . . . As we [make these choices], we help to decide, however unconsciously, how our fellow-men shall spend their time in making what we buy. . . . Those of us who enjoy the privilege of voting may help, once or twice in a year. . . . But all of us, all the time, are deciding by our expenditures what industries shall survive at all, and under what conditions. Broadly stated, it is the aim of the National Consumers' League to moralize this decision, to gather and make available information which may enable us all to decide in the light of knowledge, and to appeal to the consciences, so that the decision when made shall be a righteous one.
>
> (Kelley, 1899:289–290)

The essential principles of the sociology of the Chicago women are all in this statement: that social science must act for change; that all citizens, including women still denied suffrage, are nevertheless morally responsible for the welfare of the country; that every action ties a person to other people; that effective personal virtue today must be done through associations because it is only in associations that people can gain the knowledge and the power to make their individual action truly "righteous"—that is, both democratic and effective.

ANNA JULIA COOPER (1859–1964) AND IDA WELLS-BARNETT (1862–1931)

Anna Julia Cooper and Ida Wells-Barnett were both African-American women of the same generation as Gilman, Addams, and many of the Chicago women sociologists discussed in the previous section. Their ideas are currently being incorporated into classical sociological theory by contemporary feminist sociologists (Broschart, 1991b; P. Collins, 1990; Deegan, 1991) and by sociologists influenced by feminism (Lemert, 1995, 1999; Lemert and Bhan, 1998). Though probably neither Cooper nor Wells-Barnett would have identified herself as a sociologist, that fact reflects more the enormous barriers to their active participation in the sociological community posed by the combination of racism and sexism than any intellectual alienation on their parts from a project like sociology. Wells-Barnett opens her famous empirical study of lynching with a claim to a sociological perspective:

> The student of American sociology will find the year 1894 marked by a pronounced awakening of the public conscience to a system of anarchy and outlawry which had grown up during [the past] ten years.
>
> (Wells-Barnett, 1894/1969:7)

Cooper, in her best-known book, *A Voice From the South* (1892), discusses Comte and Spencer and presents her most general principle of societal organization as a sociological one:

> This . . . law holds good in sociology as in the world of matter, *that equilibrium, not repression among conflicting forces is the condition of natural harmony, of permanent progress, and of universal freedom.*
>
> (Cooper, 1892/1969:160)

Cooper and Wells-Barnett both consciously drew on their lived experiences as African-American women to develop a "systematic consciousness of society and social relations." As such, these women foreshadow the current development of a feminist sociological theory based in the interests of women of color.

Ida Wells-Barnett was primarily a researcher whose theory of society is implicit in her research. This research is sociological and inventive. It uses statistics, interviews, and secondary accounts to describe the lynching of African-Americans that became epidemic in the southern United States during the 1890s (and continued into the 1930s) and to analyze the causes of this development. Wells-Barnett deliberately adopts the unusual strategy of letting the oppressor give us our data. She builds her analysis on white newspaper reports of lynchings in an effort to protect herself from the charge of distorting her research. She then "deconstructs" those reports to find their underlying themes of domination and oppression.

Cooper, in contrast, is explicitly engaged in theoretical work. She seeks, self-consciously, to describe the patterns of social life and to situate herself in that work of

ANNA JULIA COOPER AND IDA WELLS-BARNETT: Biographical Sketches

Anna Julia Hayward Cooper was born a slave in Raleigh, North Carolina, in 1859, to a slave mother and to a master whom, she presumed, was also her father. Freed by the Emancipation Proclamation of 1863, and apparently of extraordinary intellectual ability, she battled racism, sexism, and limited finances all her life in pursuit of an education. By age nine she was working as a "pupil-teacher" at St. Augustine's Normal and Collegiate Institute, an Episcopal school for African-Americans, where she was one of a very few female students. She worked her way, as a student-tutor, through Oberlin College in the 1880s—Oberlin being one of the very few white colleges to admit blacks—earning her bachelor's degree in 1884 and an honorary master's in 1887. Supporting herself all her life as a teacher, she taught for forty years in the Washington, D.C., school system, where from 1901 to 1906 she served as principal of the M Street High School (now Dunbar High School), the second black woman principal in the school's history. From that base, she actively fought racism on behalf of both her students and herself, lectured widely, and in 1892 published *A Voice From the South by a Black Woman from the South,* the primary statement of her sociological views. Studying at Columbia University and at the Sorbonne, in Paris, during summer breaks and various leaves of absence, she completed the work for her doctoral degree from the Sorbonne in 1925, defending her dissertation and accepting her degree at age sixty-five. Her dissertation, *Slavery and the French Revolutionists 1788–1805,* was written in French (she was a gifted linguist) and has only since 1988 been available in English. These two works, which show Cooper to be a significant sociological theorist of race and society both in the United States and globally, form the basis of our discussion here.

Ida Wells-Barnett was born to slave parents in Holly Springs, Mississippi, in 1862. After supporting her orphaned siblings as a teacher from 1878 to 1883, she moved to Memphis in 1883, where she studied at both Fiske and LeMoyne Institute. A lifelong activist on behalf of African-American and women's rights, she worked primarily as a journalist, initiating a one-woman campaign against lynching in 1883 with a series of publications which present a detailed empirical study of that horrific practice of racial terrorism. That campaign would build into a national and international protest. Living in Chicago for most of her adult life, Wells-Barnett was well acquainted with Jane Addams, Hull House, and the activist social-science work of that institution (Wells-Barnett, 1970). A prominent figure in the women's club movement of this period, Wells-Barnett helped found the National Association of Colored Women, the National Afro-American Council, and the National Association for the Advancement of Colored People. Her writings on lynching were compiled in 1969 into a single volume, *On Lynching* (1894/1969).

theoretical creation. The development of her views on society is also far more extensive than that of Wells-Barnett. In support of those views, Cooper uses statistical data, a virtuoso display of literary references, and historical documentation.

In the social theory of both Cooper and Wells-Barnett, power is the fundamental relation of social life. They understand that power can include the most unqualified type of oppression, both physical and economic. If unfettered by law, power is the corrupting process that gives the lie to Western society's claim to progress, civilization, and development. Cooper and Wells-Barnett base this theory of domination on their understanding of race relations. Cooper writes:

> Black slavery was an institution founded solely on the abuse of power. In all aspects created by a barbarous and shortsighted politics, and maintained by violence. . . . [I]t was done without pretext and without excuse. And only in the name of the right of the strongest.
>
> (Cooper, 1925/1988:131)

And in a more concrete and journalistic style, Wells-Barnett would say of lynching, "The more I studied the situation the more I was convinced that the Southerner had never gotten over his resentment that the Negro was no longer his plaything, his servant, and his source of income" (Wells-Barnett, 1970:10).

Race, then, is at the center of both women's social theories; the relations between whites and blacks in Western history and contemporary American society give them their paradigm of domination and of stratification. In this insistence that domination, inequality, and injustice are structurally pervasive in modern society, Cooper and Wells-Barnett differ from the white women sociologists of their day, all of whom, even the radical feminist Gilman, would blur the issue of domination in themes about evolution and progress.

Using race relations as a lens on oppression and stratification, both Cooper and Wells-Barnett explore other stratificational practices in society. Cooper analyzes gender inequality as a general stratificational practice, between white women and men, and between African-American women and men (1892/1969:9–149). And she explores the complex interplay of race and gender through her own embodied experience in society. She recalls a time when, traveling by train, she arrived at a shabby railway station and looked for a bathroom: "I see two dingy little rooms with 'For Ladies' swinging over one and 'For Colored People' over the other, while wondering under which head I come" (1892/1969:96). More generally, she writes, "The colored woman today occupies . . . a unique position. . . . She is confronted by both a woman question and a race problem, and is as yet an unknown or unacknowledged factor in both" (1892/1969:134).

Wells-Barnett looks at an even more explosive interaction of race and gender, exploring the interplay of those issues around sexuality. She dissolves the rationale for the lynching of black men offered by white society, the myth that the victim has raped a white woman. She provides case studies of the emotional/sexual attraction between white women and black men as a normal part of social relations in the South and of the attraction of white men to black women. The former is so taboo a possibility that it results in mob rumors of rape and in lynching. The latter is so condoned and unreprimanded, no matter how resisted by black women, that it has resulted in "the many shades of the race." Wells-Barnett's Memphis newspaper was burned to the ground and her life threatened for opening up this topic in the 1890s.

Both women further expand the theme of social inequality to class relations. Cooper describes the relation between capitalists and labor (her terms) in modern society, the interpolation of class and race in both urban and rural America, the internal economic and status divisions in the African-American population, the interaction of class and race in educated women's circles, shade stratification in the societies of the Caribbean, and status differences among African-American women. Wells-Barnett traces social class tensions in the women's club movement of her day and in Great Britain, to which she traveled as part of her antilynching campaign. She also locates some of the problems of lynching in the class/race nexus: "Lynching was an excuse to get rid of Negroes who were acquiring wealth and property and thus 'keep the nigger down'" (Wells-Barnett, 1970:64). Finally, both women understand that domination, inequality, and race conflict are not only issues in the various nation-states of the West, but a process in the "global order" of capitalism. Wells-Barnett discusses the situation of Indians in Britain in the heyday of the British Empire. Cooper's dissertation (1925/1988) focuses on the contradiction between black enslavement as an economic "resource" for eighteenth-century capitalist economies and the democratic aspiration of their white, bourgeois revolutions. Slavery gave the lie to the democratic revolutionary claims of the French (and supposedly the American) revolution, and resulted in the defeat of white lower- and working-class aspirations in those revolutions.

From this systematic grasp of domination and inequality, Cooper develops both a theory of social organization and an epistemology for her project of social critique. Society she sees as a system—of institutions like economy, family, education and religion; of stratificational groupings resulting from class, race, and gender distinctions and from their parallel as well as overlapping dynamics; of cultural aspirations and themes. She gives serious attention to the cultural themes of masculinity and femininity and to the outcome of those themes for personality and for societal functioning. Order in this system may take two forms. It may result from domination and oppression, the situation in much of the contemporary world, or it may result from a dynamic and competitive interdependence between all sectors of a society. This latter condition is Cooper's hope for the United States and for black-white relations in the United States.

Epistemologically Cooper presents us with an argument that resonates with that of contemporary African-American feminism. She will insert herself into sociological analysis by speaking from her distinctive vantage point as a black woman. This is the claim for which she is best known (Alexander, 1995; Giddings, 1984; Harley, 1978). She can make this claim most clearly for herself and so we end with Cooper's words:

> One muffled strain from the silent South . . . has been and still is the Negro and of that muffled chord, the one mute and voiceless note has been the Black Woman. . . . It is because I feel it essential to perfect understanding that this . . . voice is added. . . . The "other side" has not been represented by one who "lives there." And not many can more sensibly . . . tell the weight and the fret of the "long dull pain" than the open-eyed but still voiceless Black woman. . . . Only the BLACK WOMAN can say "when and where I enter."

(Cooper, 1892/1969:i, ii, 31)

MARIANNE SCHNITGER WEBER (1870–1954)

Marianne Weber is known in American sociology solely through her biography of her husband, *Max Weber: A Biography* (1926/1975; see Chapter 7). Her self-portrait there is of the dutiful, uncritical, self-effacing Victorian wife, hovering on the edge of the grand life and figure of Max Weber. Perhaps this depiction amused her, for it hides much of the truth of her life. She was among the first generation of German women formally admitted for university study (Roth, 1990:67). Her studies were in the general area of social science. After Max's nervous breakdown in 1897 and his retreat to a semireclusive life, Marianne became the public figure in the marriage, building her reputation as a feminist scholar and public speaker. She published her first book on the relationship of Fichte and Marx in 1900, her first journal article "Politics and the Woman's Movement" in 1901, and over the next thirty-five years eight books and dozens of articles in sociology and on feminist issues. In 1918 German women won the vote, and in 1919 Marianne became the first female member of parliament for Baden. In 1920, the year of Max's death, she was president of the Federation of German Women's Organizations, Germany's most powerful feminist organization. In 1924 she was granted an honorary doctorate in law by Heidelberg University "in recognition of her legal study and editorial work" (Roth, 1990:66).

It is part of the gender politics of sociology that until recently none of Marianne Weber's writings had been translated into English except her biography of Max, and we can glean only a few details of her sociological work from brief English discussions of her, which frequently lack an appropriate framing in feminist sociology (Britton, 1979; Hackett, 1976; Kandal, 1988; Roth, 1990; Scaff, 1988; J. Thomas, 1985; Tijssen, 1991). In 1998 the first essays from her 1919 collection *Reflections on Women and Women's Issues* became available in English (see translation by Elizabeth Kirchen in Lengermann and Niebrugge-Brantley, 1998). From these materials, we can see that she wrote as a feminist social theorist who drew on and responded critically to the theories of Simmel, Max Weber, Marx and Engels, and feminist writers like Charlotte Perkins Gilman, whom we discussed earlier in this chapter.

The overriding concern of Marianne Weber's theory is with the creation of a sociology from the standpoint of women. She claims that there is a distinctive women's standpoint: "The goals of the women's movement" must only be "those demands which are raised from woman's standpoint as such and for women as such" (Hackett, 1976:126). She partly defines this standpoint by contrasting women's experiences and understandings with men's—of marriage, public and household life, the importance of housework, power and other relational arrangements, ethics, and war. She develops three major themes around this central concern: the need for an autonomy for women equal to that of men (a debate with Max); the significance of women's work in the production of culture (a debate with Simmel); the situated differences of standpoint among women (a debate partially with Gilman). Marianne Weber uses legal research, historical data, and statistical data as empirical bases for her theoretical arguments.

In the work that established her as a leading feminist scholar, *Ehefrau und Mutter in der Rechtsentwicklung* ("Marriage and Motherhood in the Development of Law") (1907) and her 1912 essay restating some of its major arguments, "Authority and Autonomy in Marriage," she brings a woman-centered perspective to bear on Max

Weber's famous typology of power. For women, she argues, in their experiences of masculine domination within marriage, the key distinction is not between legitimate power (authority) and illegitimate power (coercion). Since all societies have framed marriage relations with law, all legal power relations between husband and wife are culturally legitimate. But over the long course of Western history, which she chronicles in detail, men have transformed law and culture in the direction of greater individual autonomy for themselves, greater possibilities for freedom in self-definition. The tension then may be construed not as one between coercion and authority but as one between autonomy and domination, between a free exercise of one's will in action and subordinating one's will to another. While men have changed law and culture to gain such autonomy, they have skillfully contrived to keep the family patriarchal, their "authority" perhaps softened a little but essentially intact; women continue to experience this relationship of male "authority" as one which denies them autonomous action and will. Weber explores legal, normative, and cultural changes that might lead to a transformation of marriage into one of a bond between independent actors, something she regards as a difficult, indeed a near-miraculous achievement (Marianne Weber 1912a/1919/1998). In her later book, *Women and Love* (1935) she explores conventional and unconventional ways in which women may find the love they typically seek through marriage—the latter include relationships between younger men and older women, between women, and the sublimated ideal of public service. All these are alternatives to the structure of conventional marriage.[2]

Continuing her exploration of structural conditions for autonomy, Marianne rebuts Georg Simmel's (Chapter 8) sociology of gender in which he idealizes women's distinct and spiritual nature and suggests the existence of two distinctive spheres of culture, the "objective" or male world of public achievement and the "personal" or female world of inner self development (Oakes, 1984; Tijssen, 1991). Weber begins very practically by pointing out that there is much about women's work in the household that is not spiritual but intensely practical, instrumental, and objective. She then moves to suggest that women's work in the home constitutes a third realm of culture production, which she calls "the middle ground of immediate daily life," in which the individual person is constructed and reproduced as a social being capable of sympathetic and intelligent responses to others. She questions Simmel's assumption of distinctively male and female natures, arguing that while one can discern some typical differences between the two genders, individuals within each gender vary too much to support the assumption of separate natures. She concludes that it is more useful to think of a common nature and of typical maleness and femaleness as circles intersecting within the common space. This idea allows one to think of women developing their autonomy more fully, men their capacities for caring, and individuals of each gender moving as freely between public and private culture as they individually choose (Marianne Weber, 1918/1919/1998).

But she also sees that there are differences among women in standpoint because of social class stratification. This theme is developed in "Jobs and Marriage" (1905/1919)

---

[2]Our discussion also draws on initial aid in translation by C. Joanna Sheldon of Ithaca, New York, to whom we express our deepest appreciation for her help.

and "The Valuation of Housework" (1912b/1919/1998), in which she grounds her theory of women's standpoint in her sociological understanding of societal organization, social class stratification, and the data of the German census. She contrasts the life experiences of women in agricultural work, paid domestic employment, factory work, and professional employment. She points out that much of women's "professional" work is relatively low status (61 percent of this category are midwives). Only a small fraction (2 percent) of professional women in Germany hold the high-status, self-actualizing jobs that she sees the women's movement depicting as the ideal for women's workplace participation. Yet the standpoint of the spokespersons of this movement is in this tiny privileged group. Weber argues that it is absurd to speak from this standpoint about the reforms needed in all women's home and work lives. She chides her "American sister in struggle" Gilman for succumbing to this totalizing error.

The interaction of capitalism and patriarchy creates barriers to the attempts of women, especially nonelite women to seek greater liberty and autonomy. Capitalistic work arrangements doom women to wage-sector work that is typically exhausting, onerous, and grossly underpaid—and an experience of meaninglessness and alienation. Indeed, most working women have not chosen to work outside the home but have been forced by capitalistic and class pressures to seek wages, however small. Working women bear the double burden of wage-work demands and unaltered expectations that they are fully responsible for child care and housework. Under these conditions, working-class women's lives are little improved by wage-sector involvement. Nor does Weber romanticize the home situations of women as an alternative to wage work. She sees that housework for most women is an area of incessant drudgery, that women who stay at home, whatever their class, are oppressed by economic dependency and by patriarchal male authority. Only fundamental reform holds any hope for women's escape from these two sites of oppression. Weber discusses legal reforms such as spousal rights, job training for women as a route to better employment and more meaningful lives, and, most radical of all, various formulae that would provide monetary independence for the housewife, including wages for housework.

Her position is that to improve women's situation one should begin by reforming the patriarchal household rather than the capitalistic workplace. She sees that capitalism may offer some emancipation for women in its acceleration of individualism and its erosion of ancient relational patterns like patriarchy (J. Thomas, 1985). A reformed, that is, nonpatriarchal household, is one setting in which women can find vocation and self-actualization. Weber's acute consciousness of women's varied vantage points, however, leads her also to recommend the pursuit of a public career, either paid or voluntary, as another avenue to self-actualization for some women.

The exploration of Marianne Weber's theory is currently under way. What is apparent is that she is a significant contributor to an international effort by women sociologists to create a feminist sociological theory in the classic period of sociology's history.

BEATRICE POTTER WEBB (1858–1943)

Beatrice Potter Webb was an amalgam of contradictions—a woman born to extreme wealth, she was nevertheless "self-made"; a member of the British upper class, she devoted herself as a sociologist and theorist to the problems of "poverty amidst riches" (1926:209); a student and lifelong friend of Herbert Spencer, she became a leading British socialist; a solid empiricist, she is nevertheless moved to her descriptive and analytic studies by what she calls "a consciousness of sin" (1926:167). Webb's father, Richard Potter, was a wealthy industrialist who made his living in railroad speculation; her mother, Laurencina, was a close friend of Spencer, a frequent visitor to the Potter household. Webb grew to maturity just before women began to be admitted to British universities and was largely self-educated, by reading, by travels with her father, by conversation with Spencer, and by reflection in her voluminous personal diaries. Two paths were primarily open to her as member of her class, generation, and gender—a "suitable" marriage or good works; she chose neither. She chose instead to become what she describes as "a female brain worker" (in contrast to a manual worker), a social investigator; the problems she focused on were economic inequality, the causes of poverty, and ways to reform the capitalist economy. The marriage she eventually made, to Sidney Webb, a British Fabian socialist, considered "unsuitable" by her family, became an intellectual and political partnership which left a policy-oriented body of empirical research that laid the foundation for the twentieth-century British welfare state.

In her autobiography, *My Apprenticeship* (1926), Webb explores the motivations that led her to social research: "Why did I select the chronic destitution of whole sections of the people, whether illustrated by overcrowded homes, by demoralized casual labor at the docks, or by the low wages, long hours, and insanitary conditions of the sweated industries, as the first subject for enquiry?" (1926:167). She admits that she was not moved by charity but by an unease affecting much of the class of wealthy British capitalists to which her family belonged as they confronted the fact that four-fifths of the population of Britain had not benefited from the Industrial Revolution and were indeed the worse off for it. Her intellectual curiosity was a response to debates about whether the misery of the many must be a necessary condition for the wealth and advancement of the few and whether the poor are responsible for their poverty or are the victims of larger social forces.

Seeking to understand the causes of poverty, Webb first worked as "a charity visitor" but her interest was not in good works but in understanding. She moved from this charity work to assisting Charles Booth in his seventeen-volume study, *The Life and Labour of the People of London* (1892–1902). Her experiences working with the poor and with Booth led her to the insight that the best way to understand how to reform the capitalist economic system was not to study the desperately poor but to find examples of working-class people successfully organizing to create alternative economic systems. She came to argue that in real social life "experiments" of this type were taking place all the time in businesses, collectives, and local government. This line of thought culminated in her most important single-authored monograph, *The Co-operative Movement in Great Britain* (1891). In this study, which she did as participant observation research in Lancastershire, Webb outlines how economic equity can be arrived at through democratic decision-making by showing how a British working-class buyers' co-operative functioned, that is, how working people could combine their purchasing power to control the price and quality—and potentially, the conditions of production—of material goods and services.

This research led Webb to an interest in Fabian Socialism and her acquaintance with Sidney Webb. The Fabian Socialists, a relatively small party, sought to influence the course of reform in Britain by a process of "permeation," that is, by supplying information and platform planks to any political party that would champion any aspect of the reform of inequality. The Webbs as Fabians were guided by three main principles: (1) that Marx is wrong in his prediction of the "withering away of the state"; rather the state must intervene in order to control—or socialize—basic elements of the economy; (2) inequality has advanced to such a point of social crisis that such intervention is inevitable; and (3) therefore, it is possible for socialists to advocate gradual rather than revolutionary reforms because gradualism is inevitable.

Webb's vision of society is, above all, of *the working out of processes between structures in which people are contained*—structures like state, class, trade unions, sweatshops. The key structures she concentrates on are the state and social classes. The key process she believes she is witnessing in her lifetime is the growth of state intervention in the conduct of the economy and the society. She accounts for this growth in intervention by the fact that in her lifetime conditions of inequality in Great Britain and the world are reaching a point where there is no choice but for state intervention. What Webb sees as the great social change of her day is that "our actions whether legislative or voluntary, individual or collective, are becoming more and more inspired and guided by *descriptions* of our social state" ([1887] 1926:403), that is, that actions increasingly are taken on the basis of information about society. She points to the vast increase in the interventions of government in the conduct of the economy as her prime proof. She sees that if reforms are to work, it is of critical importance that information be accurate, and she devotes much of her sociology to detailed explanations of how to do both quantitative and qualitative empirical research. She sees the primary function of sociology as being to provide the information on which a reformist state can be established and make policy. With Sidney, she writes some eight major books encompassing some 4,000 pages; the direction of this work is what we may term "a critical empiricism," that is, it is quantitative and qualitative research done with a view to social change.

One reason for Webb's relative neglect as a sociologist may lie in feminist sociologists' reaction to her antisuffrage stance in the 1880s and 1890s. While Webb later claimed that she was sorry almost immediately after signing an antisuffrage petition, she did not publicly recant for twenty years; she gave her essential reason for her stance as "I had never myself suffered the disabilities assumed to arise from my sex" (1926:343). Yet this assertion is shown as decidedly untrue in various incidents in *My Apprenticeship*. What is more likely the case is that Webb could not see herself as a *member* of a subordinate class, in this case, women, though she would work all her life to help the subordinated.

SUMMARY

The history of the development of sociological theory in the classic period 1830–1930 is typically a description of the work of male theorists. A complex gender politics in academic life, in sociology, in intellectual productivity, and in historiography explains the absence of women from these histories. As part of the contemporary feminist project of deconstructing this politics and of affirming women's contribution to the world of intellectual achievement, this chapter introduces the ideas of several women to the record, and hopefully the canon, of sociology's theoretical development. Harriet Martineau is restored to her rightful place in sociology's founding generation, and a selection of theorists including Charlotte Perkins Gilman, Jane Addams and her network of women sociologists, Anna Julia Cooper, Ida Wells-Barnett, Marianne Schnitger Weber, and Beatrice Potter Webb are discussed as contributors to sociology's classic period of theoretical development, from 1890 to 1930.

Each of these women had that "systematic consciousness of society and social relations" which is the hallmark of a sociological theorist. And although each woman's theory is distinctively framed by the intellectual and social influences of her biography and by her theoretical and ethical preferences, all these theories are also patterned by some common themes: awareness of the fact that they spoke from the particular vantage point of women, an analysis and ethical concern with society's power arrangements, a commitment to sound research as a necessary means to social amelioration and change. Each woman's theory can thus be understood and evaluated as a distinctive individual contribution to sociology. But taken together, these women can also be rediscovered as the collectivity who introduced a feminist theoretical tradition into the history of the discipline.

10

THORSTEIN VEBLEN

INTELLECTUAL INFLUENCES
  Marxian Theory
  Evolutionary Theory
  Economic Theory
BASIC PREMISES
  Human Nature
  The Industrial Arts
  Cultural Lag
  Cultural Borrowing
SUBSTANTIVE ISSUES
  Theory of the Leisure Class
  Business versus Industry
  Higher Learning
  Politics

In Thorstein Veblen we encounter a unique figure in the pantheon of classical social theorists. Veblen has always had a small, but significant, following in the social sciences. However, his influence has increased recently because his famous work on "conspicuous consumption" is in line with both the growing importance of consumption (both absolutely and in comparison to production) in American society and much of the rest of the world, as well as the increasing interest in sociology (and other fields) in consumption.[1] Yet, the irony is that Veblen was very much a product of his times (late eighteenth- and early nineteenth-century America) and, as a result, he shares with the other classical theorists of the day a focal interest in issues relating to production. The increasing interest in his work on consumption has led to a reexamination of Veblen's work on production and while it is not without its problems (for example, the repetition of a single theme in a series of books and articles covering a span of many decades), there is much more to Veblen's theorizing than his valuable work on consumption (Rosenberg, 1956).

INTELLECTUAL INFLUENCES

Thorstein Veblen was influenced by the ideas of a wide range of social thinkers, but he synthesized inputs from those bodies of thought and, in the process, created a perspective that is quite distinctive. Among those who influenced Veblen were Karl Marx, a

---

[1]It is also seen as a contribution to at least one other contemporary field, leisure studies (Rojek, 1995).

variety of evolutionary thinkers (Charles Darwin, Herbert Spencer, William Graham Sumner), and a number of economists (Adam Smith, Alfred Marshall) and even some "anonymous authors of the Icelandic sagas" (Rosenberg, 1963:2).[2] It would be useful at the beginning of this chapter to introduce the complex relationship between the thinking of Veblen and Marxian theory, as well as the impact of evolutionary and economic theory on Veblen.

Marxian Theory

Although he recognizes many subdivisions within each social class, Veblen, like Marx, operates with essentially a two-class model of social stratification (the business and industrial classes, with the former controlling the latter), but in contrast to Marx, Veblen's model is *not* based on ownership of the means of production, but rather on amount of wealth and whether or not control is exercised over others. The *business class* "own[s] wealth invested in large holdings and . . . thereby control[s] the conditions of life for the rest"; the *industrial class* does "not own wealth in sufficiently large holdings, and [its] conditions of life are therefore controlled by others" (Veblen, 1919/1964:161). Other ways of putting the distinction between the two classes is that there is a division between those "who live on free income [essentially, unearned income; see below] and those who live by work"; "between those who control the conditions of work and the rate and volume of output and to whom the net output of industry goes as free income, on the one hand, and those others who have the work to do and to whom a livelihood is allowed by these persons in control, on the other hand"; "between the kept classes and the underlying community from which their keep is drawn" (Veblen, 1919/1964:162). Later, Veblen (1923:9) puts the issue in an explicitly non-Marxist way: "this . . . cleavage, in material interest and in sentiment, runs not between those who own something and those who own nothing, as has habitually been set out in the formulas of the doctrinaires, but between those who own more than they personally can use and those who have urgent use for more than they own."

Another key difference between Marx and Veblen is that for Marx the creative force is labor, while Veblen sees the "industrial arts" (defined by Veblen [1923:63] as "the accumulated knowledge of ways and means"), especially technology, as creative forces (we will have more to say about the industrial arts later in this chapter).[3] For example, Veblen (1923:63) argues, "The state of the industrial arts . . . must in the nature of things always be the prime factor in human industry." One consequence of this is that labor and its emancipation does not occupy the central role in Veblen's work that it does in Marx's. In fact, Veblen has a rather low regard for the working class. It is those who create and maintain the industrial arts, the technologists and engineers, who are central and who would lead a revolution against the business class, were it to occur. Workers, at best, would follow their lead.

---

[2]There were other inputs, as well, including philosophy (e.g., John Dewey).

[3]However, it is the case that the "instinct of workmanship" (see below) plays a role in Veblen's work that has some resemblance to the role played by "species being" in Marx's work.

One of the basic principles that Veblen does share with Marx is a materialistic orientation. Veblen (1923:205) defines material conditions as "the ways and means of living and of procuring a livelihood." The industrial arts are part of the material conditions, as is the population base. Veblen argues: "in the long run, of course, the pressure of changing material circumstances will have to shape the lines of human conduct, on pain of extinction" (Veblen, 1923:17). Thus, for example, changes in norms, values, and ways of thinking follow changes in the material bases (and are therefore always out of date; see below for a discussion of Veblen's contribution to our understanding of "cultural lag").

In spite of a number of similarities, Veblen (1906/1963) was *not* a Marxist.[4] Veblen criticizes Marx for a number of things including buying into the doctrine of natural rights (e.g., the laborer's right to the entire product of labor); being in the thrall of Hegelian philosophy; adopting the latter's theory of change rather than a Darwinian evolutionary perspective of a cumulative sequence of change without a teleology, or final perfect end (to Veblen [1906/1963:72], "Darwinism has largely supplanted Hegelianism"); operating with other ideas (conscious class struggle) that do not fit well with a Hegelian approach; using outmoded psychological assumptions (hedonistic calculus based on self-interest); using the ideas of the political economists in ways that were not consistent with their intended use; having nothing to say about the future society that is supposed to replace capitalism; and making a series of predictions that have not been borne out by later events. Overall, while Veblen was not a Marxist, at least some of his ideas show the impact of Marxian theory.

Evolutionary Theory

Influenced by Darwin and the Social Darwinists (especially Herbert Spencer and William Graham Sumner), Veblen operated with an evolutionary perspective. He views human society as being dominated by a struggle for existence with the fittest social institutions and habits of thought surviving. He sees progress in human history with not only the fit social institutions and individuals surviving, but the unfit perishing. Furthermore, he sees a process of institutions and habits of thought adapting to changing circumstances. Above all, and most generally, an evolutionary perspective is useful to Veblen in allowing him to emphasize the fact that social institutions change and develop.

The selective adaptation that lies at the core of evolutionary theory is never totally successful. Institutions are received from the past and exist in the present because they have survived the process of selective adaptation. However, they are still derived from the past and as such are never fully in tune with present circumstances; institutions adapted from the past can never catch up with changing social circumstances. Thus, Veblen (1899/1994:191) concludes, "institutions of to-day—the present accepted scheme of life—do not entirely fit the situation of to-day." However, as a result of inherent inertia or conservatism there is a tendency for social institutions to persist even

---

[4]Paul Sweezy (1958:180), among others, disagrees, arguing that "the Veblenian framework is fundamentally Marxian."

when they are not fully adapted to changing circumstances. This means that people are, at least to some degree, rendered ill-equipped to handle present-day demands. However, they are likely to become aware of the discontinuity between the demands of their current life and the social institutions which are holdovers from the past. This awareness is one of the things that leads to changes in social institutions designed to bring them more into line with present realities. However, some groups (such as the leisure class to be discussed later) are sheltered from everyday realities, especially everyday economic exigencies, with the result that their way of life is able to remain more attuned to past realities. Such groups, especially if they are of high status and are emulated by other groups, are likely to be conservative forces that retard social progress and the efforts of others to bring social institutions up to date. In spite of such opposition, social institutions do change and develop; they selectively adapt to changing circumstances.

Veblen distinguishes between the evolution of the community and the evolution of the individual. He argues that the difference between them has led to an important discontinuity in evolution. Communities have, in Veblen's view, evolved to the point where they no longer need to compete with one another but rather need to cooperate in industrial matters. However, individuals have retained the need to compete in order to succeed and further their own interests and careers. Thus, individuals "lag" behind changes at the collective level.

Overall, Veblen operated with a basic, two-stage model of evolution. The earlier stage is termed "savage society" and Veblen tends to have a positive view of it describing it as a good society being characterized by peace and cooperation. In contrast to Hobbes, Veblen saw the primitive, savage state as pointing rather to "peace than to war as the habitual situation" (Veblen, 1922/1964:100). The later stage of predatory "barbarism" is viewed much more negatively as being characterized by a warlike and competitive character. The focus here is on the achievement of the individual than the well-being of the collectivity. In the early, savage culture, the industrial arts were employed for the common good. However, in the predatory, barbarian culture, the focus shifts to self-interest and to using the industrial arts to gain advantages at the expense of others. While the world had moved beyond the early stages of barbarism through handicrafts and the machine age, Veblen believed that the society he analyzed and lived in was only a later stage of barbarism. Thus, even the machine age is characterized by individual competitiveness and is, as we will see, conducive to warlike relations among nations.

A key aspect of this evolutionary process is a shift from free workmanship in savage society, a situation in which workmanship is the basis of industry, to the predatory, barbarian society in which property relations, or pecuniary interests, control industry. The basis for pecuniary control arises when production yields income above and beyond that which is needed by the workers to subsist. In addition, material factors such as raw material and technology tie industry to a particular place with the result that the surveillance, control, and economic exploitation of workers becomes more possible. It becomes profitable to own the material means of industry and along with that comes control over the more immaterial aspects of the industrial arts. Ownership of the means of production often comes about as a result of warfare and, as a result, is clearly part of a predatory, barbarian culture. All of this finds its most perfect expression in the great pecuniary cultures of the Occident.

While not devoid of utility, Veblen's evolutionary theory now seems like an unfortunate product of his intellectual times, which were dominated by Darwinian theory, Social Darwinism, and Spencerian evolutionism. It leads, to put it mildly, to a questionable and simplistic model of human history. It also gives his work a very dated feel and it leads Veblen into some very unfortunate positions. For example, he adopts a racist view of evolution when he discusses the evolution of "lower ethnic elements" (Veblen, 1899/1994:217), viewing "the negro population of the South" as "low in economic efficiency, or in intelligence, or both" (Veblen, 1899/1994:322).

Economic Theory

If Veblen was identified with any field during his lifetime, it was economics (he was offered the presidency of the American Economic Association, but refused the position). However, Veblen was highly critical of mainstream economics (he was associated with institutional economics [Seckler, 1975], which has been pushed to the margins of the discipline by the kind of economics of which he was so critical). Among other things, he was critical of economic theory for adopting the idea of natural laws that led to the orderly unfolding of human conduct to reach the ordained end of human happiness (Veblen, 1899/1900/1964). Adam Smith, among others, is accused of operating with such a perspective and for making the facts fit with his preconceptions about natural law and the teleology of the theory. Later economists replaced the achievement of such an end with a hedonistic, utilitarian view, which sees conduct as "the pursuit of the greatest gain or least sacrifice" (Veblen, 1899/1900/1964:97). Still later economists (e.g. Alfred Marshall) offer a sense of a "consummately [sic] conceived and self-balanced mechanism" (Veblen, 1899/1900:143). All of these are rejected for Veblen's preferred Darwinian evolutionary view of a "cumulatively unfolding process of an institutional adaptation to cumulatively unfolding exigencies" (Veblen, 1899/1900/1964:143).

Veblen (1909/1964) sees more recent marginal utility economics as a variant of, and sharing some of the same problems with, classical economic theory. It is a static, hedonistic, rationalistic, teleological (current events are governed by their future consequences), deductive theory which accepts natural rights, especially that of ownership. Marginal utility theory is seen as solely concerned with distribution and having little to offer on such issues as consumption. More importantly, it is dominated by an interest in "the method of inference by which an individual is presumed invariably to balance pleasure and pain under given conditions that are presumed to be normal and invariable" (Veblen, 1909/1964:162). Given its teleological and deductive character, it has little to say on cause and effect in general, and more specifically on that which is of greatest importance to Veblen (1909/1964:152), "the causes of change or the unfolding sequence of the phenomena of economic life." Thus, on what, as we will see, is the most important issue in economic life to Veblen, the growth of the industrial arts (as well as the pecuniary interests of business) in the preceding two centuries, marginal utility theory had, in Veblen's view, been silent.

Marginal utility theory is also accused of ignoring larger cultural and institutional issues and concentrating, instead, on making theoretical deductions. The focus is on hedonistic actors making rational choices in order to maximize their pleasure (and minimize their pain), and larger cultural factors are, in the main, ignored by marginal utility theorists. Also ignored is "discriminating forethought," habit, and convention since marginal utility economists focus solely on rational calculation based on future conse-quences. Finally, in Veblen's view, marginal utility theory reflects the current business and pecuniary situation, but it mistakes that for the only way in which economic behav-ior can occur.

BASIC PREMISES

In this section we deal with some of the basic premises of Veblen's theory, including his ideas on human nature, the industrial arts, cultural lag, and cultural borrowing.

Human Nature

Veblen operates with a very strong sense of human nature and of its importance in social life. *Instincts* are at the core of his thinking about human nature (Ayres, 1958) and they are defined as "the innate and persistent propensities of human nature" (Veblen, 1922/1964:2). There are a number of such inherited human instincts. They all relate to the objective ends of human endeavors; in other words, instincts are teleological. In fact, instincts differ from one another on the basis of their ends or purposes. Another component of Veblen's thinking on human nature is "tropismatic action." Tropismatic action is seen as "automatic" behavior involving no conscious thought processes, as mere "physiological reflexes" (F. Hill, 1958:134). In contrast, instinctive action in-volves intelligence, or "consciousness and adaptation to an end aimed at" (Veblen, 1922/1964:4). With the ends of life defined instinctively, the ways and means to those ends are defined intelligently, socially and culturally. The latter is especially important to Veblen. Over time, intelligently chosen means become traditional and part of the larger culture; they become habitual. Ultimately, they become institutionalized; they be-come conventional, consistent, and sanctioned by the larger culture. Thus, while Veblen bases his thinking on instincts, they are inherently intertwined with larger social factors.

There are, in Veblen's view, individual and racial differences in instincts. Here, he accords an advantage to groups like Europeans (and their colonies), which are com-posed of racially mixed, or "hybrid," stocks. Because of racial homogeneity, "lower cultures" are at a disadvantage relative to Europeans. In terms of instincts, there is greater evolutionary adaptation on the part of the European "races" than is found in the lower cultures. This is because "the hybrid populations afford a greater scope and range of variation in their human nature than could be had within the limits of any pure-bred race" (Veblen, 1922/1964:23). While Veblen sees only slight genetic differences be-tween the races, those differences may come to represent decisive differences as they work themselves out over time. Thus, Veblen (1922/1964:24) does accord much im-portance to race, and "in the last resort any race is at the mercy of its instincts."

While race and attendant instincts are generally stable (although mutations are pos-sible), the associated habitual elements of life, the social institutions, change continu-ally. While such changes are necessary, it is possible that social institutions will arise that are, as we have already seen, at variance with the demands of various instincts. In-stitutions that are at such variance are what Veblen often calls "imbecile institutions."

Instinct of Workmanship   The primary human instinct, and one that has a crucial place in Veblen's thinking, is the instinct of workmanship. It involves the efficient use of available means and adequate management of available resources. It is concerned with "practical expedients, ways and means, devices and contrivances of efficiency and economy, proficiency, creative work, and technological mastery of facts . . . a proclivity for taking pains" (Veblen, 1922/1964:33). While it sounds as if it deals with means, the instinct of workmanship, as well as those things involved in it, is an end in its own right. This instinct is manifest at the micro level in terms of the technical efficiency of the individual worker and at the macro level in the technological proficiency and accomplishments of the community as a whole (the "industrial arts"). Although it is primary, the instinct of workmanship, like all instincts, must work itself out in a give-and-take with all other instincts. The instinct of workmanship is manifest throughout the social world in domains as diverse as the arts, religion, and law. In a way, this instinct relates to all ends since it is concerned with achieving ends in the best possible way.

As important as it is, the instinct of workmanship has certain weaknesses. For example, it does not have the tenacity of other instincts and is likely to yield to them. It is also relatively easy to bend this instinct to institutional developments of one kind or another. In lower cultures, there was little institutional development to adversely affect the instinct of workmanship, but in later cultures a more developed institutional system has a far more negative impact on that instinct. However, the most important obstruction to the instinct of workmanship comes, at least theoretically, from within the instinct itself in the form of *animism.* By this, Veblen means the belief that inanimate objects are invested with souls and the ability to do things. More specifically, within the instinct of workmanship this involves "the sentimental propensity to impute workmanlike qualities and conduct to external facts" (Veblen, 1922/1964:80). One example might be the view that it is the "market" or the organization that accomplishes work rather than workers endowed with the instinct of workmanship. Such mystical views stand in contrast to the matter-of-factness that lies at the heart of the instinct of workmanship.

Parental Bent   The only instinct close to the instinct of workmanship in importance is the "parental bent" and the two have much in common. The parental bent is defined as "an unselfish solicitude for the well-being of the incoming generation—a bias for the highest efficiency and fullest volume of life in the group" (Veblen, 1922/1964:46).

Idle Curiosity   Veblen (1922/1964:85) sees people as endowed with an instinctive curiosity, "an 'idle' curiosity by force of which men, more or less insistently, want to know things, when graver interests do not engage their attention." While it may be pushed to the background in the short run by more immediate needs such as food, in the long run, it has led to our most important achievements in systematic knowledge. This instinct plays a central role in Veblen's discussion of "higher learning" (Kaplan, 1958; see below).

Veblen does not emphasize the fact that this curiosity is "hard-wired" in people, but rather focuses on how it has developed into ancient habits of thought that have persisted through centuries of existence and use. Especially important are the "habitual canons of knowledge and belief" through which people "construct those canons of conduct which serve as guide and standards in practical life" (Veblen, 1919/1964:6). As important as these habits of thinking are, they are constantly subject to revision as a result of changes in the material environment. This makes it clear, once again, that Veblen was ultimately a materialist, believing that what shapes everything else is "the exigencies that beset men in their everyday dealings with the material means of life; inasmuch as these material facts are insistent and uncompromising" (Veblen, 1919/1964:9). The economy is one of the key elements of material existence. As it changes, people's habits of thought (also defined as social institutions) change, but social and cultural change is limited by "changeless native proclivities" (Veblen, 1919/1964:11). In fact, if habits of thought grow too far out of line with human nature, those ways of thinking will be modified so that they are in better alignment with human nature.

Emulation Veblen relates the instinct of workmanship to yet another of his instincts—emulation: "Men are moved by many impulses and driven by many instinctive dispositions. Among these abiding dispositions are a strong bent to admire and defer to persons of achievement and distinction, as well as a workmanlike disposition to find merit in any work that serves the common good" (Veblen, 1923:115). We will have more to say about this instinct in our later discussion of conspicuous consumption and waste.

The Industrial Arts

The industrial arts, or technological knowledge, is "a common stock, held and carried forward collectively by the community, which is in this relation to be conceived as a going concern" (Veblen, 1922/1964:103). It is a historical product and it is continually changing. However, the new additions are slight in comparison to the total body handed down from the past. While he sees the industrial arts as a collective possession, Veblen offers a very contemporary sounding micro-macro model of its genesis:

> Each successive move in advance, every new wrinkle of novelty, improvement, invention, adaptation, every further detail of workmanlike innovation, is of course made by individuals and comes out of individual experience and initiative, since the generations of mankind live only in individuals. But each move so made is necessarily made by individuals immersed in the community and exposed to the discipline of group life as it runs in the community, since all life is necessarily group life . . . Any new technological departure necessarily takes its rise in the workmanlike endeavours of given individuals, but it can do so only by force of their familiarity with the body of knowledge which the group already has in hand.
>
> (Veblen, 1922/1964:104)

Just as the industrial arts of the collectivity could not exist without the contributions of individuals, individual workers would be helpless without access to that collective body of knowledge and skill.

The industrial efficiency of individual workers, as well as the community as a whole, is a function of the state of the industrial arts. Efficiency is apt to be high when the arts are well-developed and it is likely to be low when they are underdeveloped.

As in many places in his work, race plays a role here. The state of industrial arts depends on the individual abilities of the worker, but the kind and the degree of the abilities of individuals in this regard vary among the races.

Cultural Lag

As we have already seen several times, Veblen operates with a theory of cultural lag, an idea that is usually more associated with William Fielding Ogburn (1922/1964). This concept is most notable in his discussion of the advances in science and technology in the modern world and the resulting centrality of a matter-of-fact, mechanistic way of thinking. In fact, he sees this way of thinking, and its scientific and practical application, as the "main line of march for civilisation" (Veblen, 1919/1964:12). The "lag" occurs because "the system of law and custom, which governs the relations of men to one another and defines their mutual rights, obligations, advantages and disabilities" has tended to be "somewhat in arrears" (Veblen, 1919/1964:11–12). More specifically, Veblen (1923:206) argues, "The principles (habits of thought) which govern knowledge and belief, law and morals, have accordingly lagged behind, as contrasted with the forward drive in industry and in the resulting workday conditions of living." However, it was in his view only a matter of time until those systems of thought would be brought more into line with the matter-of-fact way of thinking predominant in science and technology.

Among the system of laws and customs, Veblen focuses on the vested right of owner-ship, and the time-honored principles that lie at its base. From his point of view, these vested rights have "become the focus of vexation and misery in the life of civilised peo-ples" (Veblen, 1919/1964:22). They have done so because they have lagged behind and put limits on the development of the industrial arts with its factories, mechanical equip-ment, standardized procedures and possession of the "accumulated technological wis-dom of the community" (Veblen, 1919/1964:37). The expansion of the industrial arts has been accompanied by a change in ownership, with the personal employer-owner be-ing progressively replaced by impersonal corporate capital. The problem is that those who possess such capital have come to gain control over the industrial arts at the same time that they have grown increasingly distant from, and less knowledgeable about, them. Thus, capital has come to be a barrier to the industrial arts and their further development. To put it another way, ownership and the ideas that lie at its base, have tended to lag behind changes in the industrial arts and, given their position, they have had the ability to impede the operation and progress of the industrial arts. In sum, "Twentieth-century technology has outgrown the eighteenth-century system of vested rights" (Veblen 1921:100).

Cultural Borrowing

Veblen offers a very interesting theory of borrowing by cultures. Elements borrowed from other cultures, especially in early historical epochs, are easily and quickly assimi-lated by a new culture. Furthermore, they come to the new culture without much of the excess baggage (e.g. mystical ideas) that may have come to inhibit their use in the orig-inating culture. Stripped of these spiritual attributes, the borrowed item is employed be-cause of its practical utility and characteristics. As Veblen (1922/1964:136) puts it, "The borrowing being (relatively) unencumbered with ritual restrictions and magical exac-tions attached to their employment, they would fall into the scheme of things as mere matter-of-fact, to be handled with the same freedom and unhindered sagacity with which a workman makes use of his own hands, and could, without reservation, be turned to any use for which they were mechanically suited."

Furthermore, innovations age over time, but the originating culture tends to stay with aging innovations given the high cost of their creation and the even higher cost involved in their replacement. The borrowing culture does not have this excess cultural baggage (although it may have cultural impediments of its own) and it is able to create brand-new versions of the innovation much more rapidly than the innovating culture. Furthermore, in creating new versions, the borrowing culture is able to learn from the mistakes of the originating culture. Overall, Veblen (1915/1942:38) contends:

> The borrowed elements of industrial efficiency would be stripped of their fringe of conventional inhibitions and waste, and the borrowing community would be in a position to use them with a freer hand and with a better chance of utilising them to their full capacity, and also with a better chance of improving on their use, turning them to new uses, and carrying the principles (habits of thought) involved in the borrowed items out, with unhampered insight, into farther ramifications of technological proficiency. The borrowers are in a position of advantage, intellectually, in that the new expedient comes into their hands more nearly in the shape of a concrete expedient applicable under given physical conditions, rather than in the shape of a concrete expedient applicable within the limits of traditional use, personal, magical, conventional. It is, in other words, taken over in a measure without the defects of its qualities.
>
> (Veblen, 1915/1942:38)

Thus, the borrowing culture is generally at an advantage over the culture involved in the creation of some culture object: "technological innovations and creations of an institutional nature have in many cases reached their fullest serviceability only at the hands of other communities and other peoples than those to whom these cultural elements owed their origin and initial success" (Veblen, 1915/1942:24).

However, Veblen recognizes that the borrowing culture also faces problems. For example, the knowledge and belief systems of that culture may be threatened and in any case they may not be well suited to the utilization of the innovations. In some cases, the innovation may be so enormous, and the adaptation so difficult, that the borrowing culture collapses as a result.

Germany in the mid-nineteenth century is a good example of a society that was backward technologically and advanced dramatically by drawing on innovations created elsewhere, particularly in Great Britain. Of course, the latter had also borrowed at an earlier point in history (for example, ship-building and navigation from the Dutch), but it had also engaged in a great deal of creative innovation. Like all innovating cultures, Great Britain gained from being innovative, but it also suffered for its leadership position, "paying the penalty for having been thrown into the lead and so having shown the way" (Veblen, 1915/1942:132). In comparison, it is relatively easy for the acquiring culture since it requires "no profound or occult insight, no reach of shrewd wisdom and cunning, no exploit of faith or of poetic vision, no stretch of imagination or of ascetic contemplation" (Veblen, 1915/1942:189). Germany and the German people were well suited to adapt and expand upon these innovations and, in any case, adaptation is easier than innovation.

SUBSTANTIVE ISSUES

A number of substantive issues lie at the core of Veblen's thinking, including his theories of the leisure class, the inherent conflict between business and industry, higher learning, and politics.

Theory of the Leisure Class

Veblen's first and best-known book, *The Theory of the Leisure Class,* was also his most important work. He begins by making an early variant of a distinction that, as we alluded to above (although in other terms) and will discuss more extensively below (under the heading "Business versus Industry"), informs his life work. He argues that activities fall into two classes in primitive society.   First, there is *industry* (or "drudgery"), the "effort that goes to create a new thing, with a new purpose given it by the fashioning hand of its maker out of passive ('brute') material" (Veblen, 1899/ 1994:12). Then there is *exploit,* which involves "so far as it results in an outcome useful to the agent . . . the conversion to his own ends of energies previously directed to some other end by another agent" (Veblen, 1899/1994:12–13). An "invidious distinction"[5] (a key phrase in Veblen's work) is made between the two with employment involving exploit coming to be seen as "worthy, honourable, noble," while that involving industry (or drudgery) is viewed as "unworthy, debasing, ignoble" (Veblen, 1899/ 1994:13). It is this distinction that lies at the root of the development of social classes.

Veblen explores the "psychological ground" of this invidious distinction, which he sees as rooted in a concept that, as we have seen, is fundamental to his work—the instinct of workmanship. He describes this aptitude (or propensity) as follows: "man is an agent . . . seeking in every act the accomplishment of some concrete, objective, impersonal end. By force of his being such an agent he is possessed of a taste for effective work, and a distaste for futile effort. He has a sense of the merit of serviceability or efficiency and of the demerit of futility, waste, or incapacity" (Veblen, 1899/1994:13). Invidious comparisons tend to be made between people on the basis of their efficiency in doing work. As a result, people seek to make their efficiency visible to others so that they may gain esteem and be emulated by others. In peaceful barbarian societies this most often takes the form of gaining esteem on the basis of one's industrial efficiency. Later, in more predatory societies, the focus shifts to exploit and to the demonstration of tangible evidence of prowess and aggression such as booty and trophies. Obtaining these by force comes to be valued with the result that obtaining them by other methods, including industry, comes to be disesteemed. An invidious distinction is made between exploit and industry and the latter comes to be seen as lacking in dignity and even irksome to perform.

---

[5]Veblen claims, somewhat disingenuously, that he is not using this term in a negative sense. Rather, he contends that he is using it "in a technical sense as describing a comparison of persons with a view to rating and grading them in respect of relative worth or value—in an aesthetic or moral sense—and so awarding and defining the relative degrees of complacency with which they may legitimately be contemplated by themselves and by others. An invidious comparison is a process of valuation of persons in respect of worth" (Veblen, 1899/1994:34).

Operating with an evolutionary model that, as we saw above, pervades all his work, Veblen argues that with the beginning of ownership there dawns a leisure class. The roots of ownership lie in the seizure of women as trophies, as demonstrations of male prowess. From there ownership extends to the products of industry. Most often ownership of private property is traced to the need for subsistence, but while this may be true in earlier societies, in more contemporary societies the motive that lies at the base of owning and accumulating things is emulation. That is, private property is the basis of esteem and everyone else in society seeks to emulate, or even outdo, those who have a great deal of it. This is true of manual workers, but it is even more true in the higher reaches of the stratification system.

In an earlier era, wealth was seen as evidence of efficiency, of the instinct of workmanship. However, more recently, the possession of wealth itself has come to be seen as meritorious. The importance of how one acquired the wealth, whether or not one gained it on the basis of efficient industry, tends to fade from view. In fact, at a later stage, greater prestige is awarded to wealth obtained by inheritance than to that obtained by dint of a person's own efforts. Self-esteem comes to be based on material possessions and whether one has as many, or better more, possessions than do those one considers one's peers. Thus, emulation lies at the base of this desire for material goods. As a result, the desire for wealth can never be satisfied as it might be if it were driven by the need to subsist: "since the struggle is substantially a race for reputability on the basis of invidious comparison, no approach to a definitive attainment is possible" (Veblen, 1899/1994:32). Thus, the instinct of workmanship is transformed into an effort to outdo others in terms of the possession of the symbols of economic achievement.

Conspicuous Leisure   In the working class there persists, at least to some degree, a focus on work and an emulation of those who are good at what they do. However this is not the case in the leisure, or superior pecuniary, class. Until the early industrial stage of development, the leisure class tends to demonstrate its wealth, and thereby gain esteem, by leading a life of leisure; by ostentatiously *not* working. This Veblen calls *conspicuous leisure*. It is not that the leisure class is necessarily indolent or quiescent, but rather that it consumes time nonproductively because of a sense that productive work is unworthy. Such activity is also evidence of its ability to be able to afford to devote its life to idleness. The leisure class seeks to develop and present "evidence" that it has not been engaged in productive labor and such evidence includes "the knowledge of dead languages and the occult sciences; of correct spelling; of syntax and prosody; of the various forms of domestic music and other household art; of the latest properties of dress, furniture, and equipage; of games, sports, and fancy-bred animals, such as dogs and race-horses" (Veblen, 1899/1974:45). Similar evidence comes from demonstrations of "manners and breeding, polite usage, decorum, and formal and ceremonial observances generally" (Veblen, 1899/1974:45–46). The leisure class is apt to employ servants who, because they produce nothing, also serve to demonstrate that time is being wasted in the care and maintenance of the master and his household and that the master has the ability to pay for such a waste of time. In addition, wives do the consumption for the master, further demonstrating his leisure and his ability to pay for it.

Conspicuous Consumption   As society evolves further, *conspicuous consumption* tends to replace conspicuous leisure among the leisure class. In modern societies the only practicable way of impressing large numbers of transient others is with abundantly obvious indicators of one's ability to waste money, and consumer goods are more obvious than leisure activities. Both conspicuous consumption and conspicuous leisure involve waste.[6] The latter involves the waste of time and the former the waste of money. The leisure class is expected to consume not only a great deal, but also the best "in food, drink, narcotics, shelter, services, ornaments, apparel, weapons and accoutrements, amusements, amulets, and idols or divinities" (Veblen, 1899/1994:73). The members of the leisure class not only must consume these things, but must consume them in the "proper" manner, and they must become connoisseurs of them. Further, it is not enough to consume for oneself, but one must give expensive presents and throw lavish parties.

Those in other social classes seek to emulate the conspicuous consumption (and leisure) of the leisure class. However, in the lower classes the head of the household cannot afford not to work. The obligation then falls upon the wife to demonstrate conspicuous leisure by performing household tasks that indicate that it is not necessary for her to be gainfully employed. The housewife also tends to obtain those things that are signs of conspicuous consumption in this social class. She consumes such things in order to enhance the reputation of her spouse.

More generally, the leisure classes stand on the pinnacle of the stratification system and it is incumbent on all classes that rank below them, including even the very lowest classes, to emulate the way they live. However, the influence of the leisure class is not direct, except on the class immediately below it in the hierarchy. In Veblen's view, each class tends to emulate the one in the stratum immediately above. It is rare to compare oneself to those in strata that are far above or those that rank below. The ways that the leisure class lives and thinks ultimately determine the ways of life and modes of thought of the entire community. However, this effect takes place gradually over time as the process of emulation works its way through the stratification system. Thus, the leisure class cannot bring about an abrupt revolution that dramatically alters the way the community thinks and consumes.

To the degree that they can, all social classes engage in conspicuous consumption and conspicuous leisure. Thus, Veblen (1899/1994:85) contends: "no class of society, not even the abjectly poor, foregos all customary conspicuous consumption. The last items of this category of consumption are not given up except under stress of the direst necessity. Very much of squalor and discomfort will be endured before the last trinket or the last pretense of pecuniary decency is put away."

Waste   Veblen makes it clear that, while all social classes engage in waste, most people do not intentionally seek to waste money or time. Rather, they do so as a result of "a wish to conform to established usage, to avoid unfavourable notice and comment, to live up to the accepted canons of decency in the kind, amount, and grade of goods consumed, as well as in the decorous employment of . . . time and effort" (Veblen, 1899/1994:115).

---

[6]In another disingenuous aside, Veblen (1899/1994:97–98) claims that he is not using the term *waste* in a negative sense as illegitimate or to deprecate the ends or motives of the consumer. Rather, *waste* is used "technically" as expenditures that do "not serve human life or human well-being on the whole." However, he quickly adds that from the everyday perspective of the instinct of workmanship such waste is deprecated.

It is not just that this principle of waste affects consumption; it affects habits of thought more generally, including "the sense of duty, the sense of beauty, the sense of utility, the sense of devotional or ritualistic fitness, and the scientific sense of truth" (Veblen, 1899/1994:116). Thus, for example, churches are constructed with an eye to demonstrating at least some degree of wasteful expenditure. Clerical clothing is often costly, ornate, and quite uncomfortable. Clerics are not expected to engage in work that is productive from an industrial point of view. Things that we consider to be beautiful tend also to be expensive; if they are not expensive, they are not likely to be deemed beautiful. We consider useless household pets like dogs beautiful, while the barnyard animals like hogs and cattle are useful and, as result, not considered beautiful. The dog comes under particular merciless (and humorous) attack: "He is the filthiest of the domestic animals in his person and the nastiest in his habits. For this he makes up in servile, fawning attitude towards his master, and a readiness to inflict damage and discomfort on all else . . . he is also an item of expense, and commonly serves no industrial purpose" (Veblen, 1899/1994:141). Thus, it can easily be argued that we conspicuously consume in the domestic animals we choose to purchase and maintain (to say nothing of the way in which we maintain them). Veblen makes a similar argument about fast horses, which are also expensive to maintain, wasteful and useless, except in that they can be used to win races and thereby satisfy the owner's need for aggression and dominance.

Veblen looks at female beauty in much the same way. For example, such beauty is associated with small hands and a narrow waist. However, from the point of view of doing most types of productive work, these are structural faults that "show that the person so affected is incapable of useful effort and must therefore be supported in idleness by her owner. She is useless and expensive, and she is consequently valuable as evidence of pecuniary strength" (Veblen, 1899/1994:149). He makes the same point about the propensity of the Chinese to bind and mutilate women's feet. Similarly, clothing, especially women's clothing, is considered desirable and beautiful if it demonstrates that the wearer is unable to work. The high heel is one example, as is the skirt, which women persist in wearing even though "it is expensive and hampers the wearer at every turn and incapacitates her for all useful exertion" (Veblen, 1899/1994:171). The corset is a "mutilation" that is "undergone for the purpose of lowering the subject's vitality and rendering her permanently and obviously unfit for work" (Veblen, 1899/1994:172).

Veblen offers a hilarious discussion of our preference for handmade over industrially produced products. It is clear that the industrial product is the more perfect product. Handmade products tend to be full of imperfections and irregularities. The process of handmaking things is far more wasteful than making them industrially. Nonetheless, we prefer the handmade product because it demonstrates more honorific waste.

Strikingly, Veblen goes further to argue that we engage in conspicuous consumption not only in those things that are seen publicly, but even in those things that are consumed in total privacy. Thus the habit of mind associated with conspicuous consumption has pervaded virtually every domain.

Other Characteristics of the Leisure Class   Veblen associates a number of other characteristics with the leisure class that are modern survivals of demonstrations of prowess in an earlier stage of barbarian society associated with a predatory instinct and an animistic habit of mind. All of these have tended to outlive their usefulness.

1 A propensity to fight, duel, to have a martial spirit, to be patriotic. Here, as else-where, Veblen sees a similarity between the frames of mind of the leisure class and lower-class delinquents. He sees this as a case of "arrested spiritual development" that the industrial classes have, to a large degree, been able to overcome.

2 Sport, which is related to aggression, and is ultimately futile, or purposeless. In contrast, "the instinct of workmanship demands purposeful action" (Veblen, 1899/1994:259) with the result that sporting activity is much more occasional among the industrial classes.

3 Gambling is enjoyed by the leisure class because it involves a belief in luck and it offers the opportunity of gaining at the advantage of the loser. However, like everything else about the leisure class, it "is recognised to be a hindrance to the highest industrial efficiency" (Veblen, 1899/1994:276). The notion of luck stands in contradiction to the industrial concern with causal sequences.

4 Religiosity is another characteristic of the leisure class and Veblen (1899/1994: 295) sees the religious temperament as related to sporting and gambling temperaments in that all involve "the belief in an inscrutable propensity or a preternatural interposition in the sequence of events."

Overall, the leisure class, and its pecuniary orientation, are associated with "waste, futility, and ferocity" (Veblen, 1899/1994:351). In encouraging such things, the leisure class tends to stand in opposition to the needs of modern, industrial society: "In this as in other relations, the institution of a leisure class acts to conserve, and even to rehabil-itate, that archaic type of human nature and those elements of the archaic culture which the industrial evolution of society in its later stages acts to eliminate" (Veblen, 1899/1994:331).

Business versus Industry

In the course of his discussion of the leisure class Veblen introduces the distinction be-tween "business" and "industry" (see above discussion of his model of social change) that informs virtually all of his life's work. While to our way of thinking these terms seem closely related, to Veblen there is a stark contrast, in fact an inherent conflict, be-tween them: "The material interest of the underlying population [largely those associ-ated with industry] is best served by maximum output at a low cost, while the business interests of the industry's owners ["business"] may best be served by a moderate output at an enhanced price." Veblen (1923:249) takes the United States as the "exemplar" of the conflict between business and industry, as well as of the predominance of business.

Business Veblen details a historic change in the nature of business and business leaders. The early leaders tended to be entrepreneurs who were designers, builders, shop managers, and financial managers. They were more likely to have earned their in-come because, at least in part, it was derived from their direct contribution to production (industry). Today's business leaders are almost exclusively concerned with financial matters, and therefore, at least in Veblen's view, they are not earning their income since finance makes no direct contribution to industry. (In fact, if anything, as we will see,

THORSTEIN VEBLEN: A Biographical Sketch

Thorstein Veblen was born in rural Wisconsin on July 30, 1857. His parents were poor farmers of Norwegian origin (Dorfman, 1966). Thorstein was the sixth of twelve children. He was able to escape the farm and at the age of 17 began studying at Carleton College in Northfield, Minnesota. Early in his schooling he demonstrated both the bitterness and the sense of humor that were to characterize his later work. He met his future first wife, the niece of the president of Carleton College, at the school (they eventually married in 1888). Veblen graduated in 1880 and obtained a teaching position, but the school soon closed and he went East to study philosophy at Johns Hopkins University. However, he failed to obtain a scholarship and moved on to Yale in the hopes of finding economic support for his studies. He managed to get by economically and obtained his Ph.D. from Yale in 1884 (one of his teachers was an early giant of sociology, William Graham Sumner). However, in spite of strong letters of recommendation, he was unable to obtain a university position because, at least in part, of his agnosticism, his lack (at the time) of a professional reputation, and the fact that he was perceived as an immigrant lacking the polish needed to hold a university post. He was idle for the next few years (he attributed this idleness to ill health), but by 1891 he returned to his studies, this time focusing more on the social sciences at Cornell University. With the help of one of his professors of economics (A. Laurence Laughlin) who was moving to the University of Chicago, Veblen was able to become a fellow at that university in 1892. He did much of the editorial work associated with *The Journal of Political Economy,* one of the many new academic journals created during this period at Chicago. Veblen was a marginal figure at Chicago, but he did teach some courses and, more importantly, used the *Journal of Political Economy* as an outlet for his writings. His work also began to appear in other outlets, including *The American Journal of Sociology,* another of the University of Chicago's new journals.

In 1899 he published his first and what became his best-known book, *The Theory of the Leisure Class,* but his position at Chicago remained tenuous. In fact, when he asked for a customary raise of a few hundred dollars, the university president made it clear that he would not be displeased if Veblen left the university. But the book received a great deal of attention and Veblen was eventually promoted to the position of assistant professor. While some students found his teaching inspiring, most found it abysmal. One of his Chicago students said that he was " 'an exceedingly queer fish . . . Very commonly with his cheek in hand, or in some such position, he talked in a low, placid monotone, in itself a most uninteresting delivery and manner of conducting the class' " (Dorfman, 1966:248–249). It was not unusual for him to begin a course with a large number of students who had heard of his growing fame, but for the class to dwindle to a few diehards by the end of the semester.

Veblen's days at Chicago were numbered for various reasons including the fact that his marriage was crumbling and he offended Victorian sentiments with affairs with other women. In 1906 Veblen took an associate professorship at Stanford University. Unlike the situation at Chicago, he taught mainly undergraduates at Stanford and many of them were put off by

finance inhibits industry rather than enhancing it.) A further development involved the routinization of financial matters and the resulting handling of them by large financial organizations (e.g., investment bankers). As a result, the business leader is left as an intermediary between industry and finance with little concrete knowledge of either one.

his appearance (one said he looked like a "tramp") and his boring teaching style. But what did Veblen in once again was his womanizing which forced him to resign from Stanford in 1909 under circumstances that made it difficult for him to find another academic position. But with help of a colleague and friend who was the head of the department of economics at the University of Missouri, Veblen was able to obtain a position there in 1911. He also obtained a divorce in that year and in 1914 married a divorcee and former student.

Veblen's appointment at Missouri was at a lower rank (lecturer) and paid less than the position at Stanford. In addition, he hated the then-small town, Columbia, Missouri, that was the home of the university (he reportedly called it a "woodpecker hole of a town" and the state a " 'rotten stump' " [Dorfman, 1966:306]). However, it was during his stay at Missouri that another of his best-known books, *The Instinct of Workmanship and the State of the Industrial Arts* appeared (1914). Veblen's stormy academic career took another turn in 1917 when he moved to Washington, D.C., to work with a group commissioned by President Wilson to analyze possible peace settlements for World War I. After working for the U.S. Food Administration for a short time, Veblen moved to New York City as one of the editors of a magazine, *The Dial*. The magazine shifted its orientation and within a year Veblen lost his editorial position. However, in the interim he had become connected with the New School for Social Research. His pay there was comparatively high (a good portion of it contributed by one of his former students at Chicago) and since he lived frugally, the great critic of American business began investing his money, at first in raisin vineyards in California and later in the stock market.

Veblen returned to California in 1926 and by the next year was living in a town shack in northern California. His economic situation became a disaster as he lost the money he had invested in the raisin industry and his stocks became worthless. He continued to earn $500 to $600 a year from royalties and his former Chicago student continued to send him $500 a year.

Veblen was, to put it mildly, an unusual man. For example, he could often sit for hours and contribute little or nothing to a conversation going on around him. His friends and admirers made it possible for him to become president of the American Economic Association, but he declined the offer. The following vignette offered by a bookseller gives a bit more sense of this complex man:

> a man used to appear every six or eight weeks quite regularly, an ascetic, mysterious person . . . with a gentle air. He wore his hair long . . . I used to try to interest him in economics . . . I even once tried to get him to begin with *The Theory of the Leisure Class*. I explained to him what a brilliant port of entry it is to social consciousness . . . He listened attentively to all I said and melted like a snow drop through the door. One day he ordered a volume of Latin hymns. "I shall have to take your name because we will order this expressly for you," I told him. "We shall not have an audience for such a book as this again in a long time, I am afraid." "My name is Thorstein Veblen," he breathed rather than said.
> (cited in Tilman, 1992:9–10)

Thorstein Veblen died on August 3, 1929, just before the Depression that many felt his work anticipated.

Business tends to define the world of Veblen's day, especially the interests of the upper classes. A business orientation is defined by a pecuniary approach to economic processes; that is, the dominant interest is money. The focus is not on the interest of the larger community but rather on the profitability of the organization. Relatedly, it is oriented to acquisition, not production and it serves the interest of invidious rather than noninvidious interests. The occupations of those with a business interest tend to relate to ownership and acquisition. It is the leisure class that tends to occupy these positions. Thus, the "captains of industry"[7] as well as the "captains of solvency" (the investment bankers, financiers who come eventually to control the captains of industry) have a business orientation. Since it is nonproductive, Veblen sees a business orientation as parasitic and exploitative: "the chances are that the owner has contributed less than his per-capita quota, if anything, to that common fund of knowledge on the product of which he draws by virtue of his ownership, because he is likely to be fully occupied with other things,—such things as lucrative business transaction, e.g., or the decent consumption of superfluities" (Veblen, 1919/1964:69). Instead of production, business leaders focus on "sharp practice," " 'cornering the market,' " and " 'sitting tight' " (Veblen, 1923:34). He sees such a system as a holdover from earlier, predatory societies and one that is not well adapted to the new realities.

Veblen gives the business leader credit for increasing productive capacity, but as we will see, Veblen's (1904) most distinctive contribution here is to see such leaders as being at least as much involved in "disturbing" production and in restricting capacity as they are in increasing it. Veblen associates business leaders not only with the waste of material resources, equipment, and manpower as a result of the restriction of capacity, but with other ills as well. Businesspeople are responsible for the unproductive and wasteful expansion of "salesmanship" and the attendant sales costs that are passed on to the consumer. Veblen (1923:78) sees salesmanship as meaning "little else than prevarication." In addition, Veblen attributes to businesspeople the production of unnecessary and useless products and the dislocation of industrial processes through sabotage.

Veblen sees the modern corporation as a type of business. As such, its interests are in financial matters like profit and in sales and not in production and workmanship. As he puts it, "the corporation is always a business concern, not an industrial appliance. It is a means of making money, not of making goods" (Veblen, 1923: 85).

Industry   Industry has to do with "the apprehension and coordination of mechanical facts and sequences, and to their appreciation and utilisation for the purposes of human life" (Veblen, 1899/1994:232). An industrial orientation is associated with those involved in workmanship and production. It is the working classes that are most likely to be involved in these activities and to have such an orientation. Unlike business's pecuniary orientation which leads to a personal standpoint, the industrial orientation leads to an "impersonal standpoint, of sequence, quantitative relations, mechanical efficiency, or use" (Veblen, 1899/1994:239).

Unfortunately, industry is controlled by the captains of industry who have little or no understanding of it and only understand the "higgling of the market" and "financial intrigue" (Veblen, 1919/1964:89). In fact, the main interest of those leaders is to restrict production, restrict the free operation of the industrial system, in order to keep prices (and therefore profits) high. The result is that the main task of the business leader to

---

[7]Another term favored by Veblen (1923), especially in his later writings, is *absentee ownership*.

Veblen is to obstruct, retard, and sabotage[8] the operation of the industrial system. Without such obstructions, the extraordinary productivity of the industrial system would drive prices and profits progressively lower.

Veblen also calls those associated with a business orientation "vested interests," or those with the "marketable right to get something for nothing" (Veblen, 1919/1964: 100). While they may be getting something for nothing, they cost the larger society a great deal. These costs stem from three business activities aimed at increasing profit— limitation of the supply of products, obstruction of their traffic, and publicity. All these are aimed at salesmanship, not workmanship. They add nothing to production and, as a result, are viewed by Veblen as waste.[9] He argues that although it may benefit the pecuniary interests of the captains of industry, the work that salesmen and accountants perform "is, on the whole, useless or detrimental to the community at large" (Veblen, 1904:63). To the costs associated with these activities, Veblen adds illegal business activities such as fraud. Not only are the captains of industry parasites, but Veblen (1904:64) describes entire industries—advertising, military equipment, and those involved in "turning out goods for conspicuously wasteful consumption"—as parasitic.

The increasingly tightly interlocking industrial system lends itself to cooperative undertakings, but this characteristic makes it increasingly vulnerable to the efforts of business and national leaders to sabotage it. This may be done consciously or as a result of the business leader's increasing ignorance of industrial operations (Veblen [1921:64] writes of the "one-eyed captains of industry"). In either case, it results in hardship to the community in the form of unemployment, idle factories, and wasted resources. Veblen (1904:213–214) even goes so far as to imply that business leaders are consciously responsible for depressions; they reduce production because under certain market conditions they feel they cannot derive what they emotionally consider to be a "reasonable" profit from their goods.[10]

> Industrial depression means that the business men engaged do not see their way to derive a satisfactory gain from letting the industrial process go forward on the lines and in the volume for which the material equipment of industry is designed. It is not worth their while, and it might even work them pecuniary harm. Commonly their apprehension of the discrepancy which forbids an aggressive pursuit of industrial business is expressed by the phrase "overproduction."
>
> (Veblen, 1904:213–214)

To Veblen, from the point of view of the larger community, there is no such thing as overproduction. However, even with the activities of the business leaders, including the creation of depressions, the industrial system is still so effective and efficient that it allows business leaders and their investors huge profits.

---

[8]Veblen also saw most labor unions, especially the American Federation of Labor, as engaged in such sabotage.

[9]Riesman (1953/1995) argues that one of the ways to look at the basic conflict in Veblen's work is the conflict between workmanship and wastemanship.

[10]It is this that leads Veblen (1904:241) to argue: "Depression is primarily a malady of the affections of the business men."

Free Income   The modern industrial system—"mechanical, specialised, standard-ised, drawn on a large scale"—is highly productive. In fact, it is so productive that it yields returns far beyond those required to cover costs and to give reasonable returns to owners and investors. These additional returns are the source of what Veblen calls "free income." Most generally, free income is that "income for which no equivalent in useful work is given" (Veblen, 1923:126). This free income is attributed by business leaders to intangible assets of the firm such as possession of a trade secret, a trademark, patent, and monopoly. The problem is that these intangibles produce nothing. Rather, the free income that goes to the captains of industry and their investors is the result of the con-straints that these intangible assets place on the free operation of the industrial system. In addition to harming industrial efficiency, these intangibles also adversely affect the entire community because far less is produced than could be. Veblen (1919/1964:76) sees an analogy between the operations of business leaders and "blackmail, ransom, and any similar enterprise that aims to get something for nothing." (Immediately following this assertion Veblen [1919/1964:76] offers one of his snide caveats contending that the analogy should "not be taken to cast any shadow of suspicion on the legitimacy of all the businesslike sabotage that underlies this immaterial corporate capital and its earning capacity.")

The free income earned by the captains of industry has been capitalized by the firm and this results in pressure on the firm to keep prices and profits high. The following is a good summary of Veblen's (1921:15) thinking on this issue:

> these large earnings (free income) have been capitalized; their capitalized value has been added to the corporate capital and covered with securities bearing a fixed income-charge; this income-charge, representing free income, has thereby become a liability on the earn-ings of the corporation; this liability cannot be met in case the concern's net aggregate earnings fall off in any degree; therefore prices must be kept up to such a figure as will bring the largest net aggregate return.
>
> (Veblen, 1921:15)

This, of course, leads the captain of industry in the direction of restriction of output and other means of sabotage.

Capitalization of the firm is no longer just the cost of the plant, but also the "good will" of the organization including "established customary business relations, reputation for upright dealing, franchises and privileges, trade-marks, brands, patent rights, copy-rights, exclusive use of special processes guarded by law or by secrecy, exclusive con-trol of particular sources of materials" (Veblen, 1904:139). The problem with all of these things is that they "give a differential advantage to their owners, but they are of no aggregate advantage to the community. They are wealth to the individuals concerned—differential wealth; but they make no part of the wealth of nations" (Veblen, 1904:139–140).

The Price System   Veblen traces many of the problems within the economy to the operation of the price system. For example, he argues that the nature of the price system and the need to maintain prices so that a reasonable profit may be earned and business recession prevented make it necessary for the captains of industry to sab-otage production through "peaceable or surreptitious restriction, delay, withdrawal, or obstruction" (Veblen, 1921:4). The "problem," again, is that the industrial system is so productive that business leaders must sabotage it to some degree or else prices and profits will plunge.

Veblen sees the relationship between the price system and business leaders in much the same way that Marx sees the relationship between the capitalist system and the capitalists. That is, both are seen as structures that are constraining on actors. Thus, in Veblen's case, even if a business leader wanted to ignore profits and concentrate on producing more goods so that the larger community might benefit, that business leader would quickly be pushed to the brink of bankruptcy. More generally, Veblen (1921:14) sees businesspeople as "creatures and agents" of the price system.

Who Should Be in Charge?   In Veblen's view, the industrial system should be run by "production engineers" (industrial experts, skilled technologists, etc.), but because business leaders do not understand them, they have been employed "only reluctantly, tardily, sparingly, and with shrewd circumspection" (Veblen, 1921:64). The industrial system forms an interlocking network that not only is vulnerable to the meddling of business leaders, but requires production engineers throughout the system to work together, or at least not to work at cross-purposes. In this sense, it is in the interest of companies, communities, and even nations to work together to enhance the operation of the industrial system to their mutual benefit. As Veblen (1921:52) puts it, "In point of material welfare, all the civilized peoples have been drawn together by the state of the industrial arts into a single going concern." Of course, such a view is anathema to the vested interests in specific companies and nations. Thus, Veblen believes that control should be wrested away from these vested interests and put in the hands of the engineers who are presumed to be interested solely in increasing the efficiency of industry. Here, Veblen is operating with the questionable view that engineers have no personal, professional, or commercial biases that will, themselves, have a negative effect on industry.

Employing Marxian terminology, Veblen (1921:71) argues that "these technologists have begun to become uneasily 'class-conscious.' " They are recognizing both their indispensability and the waste that exists under the regime of the captains of industry. It is these technologists who can become the solution to the problem created by the opposition between business and industry. Thus, Veblen, unlike Marx, sees no hope in the working class, especially in representatives such as the AFL (although workers might well follow the leadership of a revolution undertaken by the technologists). The technologists have a common purpose, the elimination of the pervasive confusion, obstructionism, and wastefulness that is so characteristic of a business orientation. And they have the possibility of coming together to accomplish this end: "So slight are their numbers, and so sharply defined and homogeneous is their class, that a sufficiently compact and inclusive organization of their forces should arrange itself almost as a matter of course, so soon as any appreciable proportion of them shall be moved by any common purpose" (Veblen, 1921:80). Veblen (1921:82) is optimistic about their chances of success: "a general strike of the technological specialists in industry need involve no more than a minute fraction of one percent of the population; yet it would swiftly bring a collapse of the old order and sweep the timeworn fabric of finance and absentee sabotage into the discard for good and all."

Veblen deemed the Russian Revolution reasonably successful, and taking it at least in part as a model, he discussed a "Soviet of technicians," although he felt that the opposition of business leaders made such a development highly unlikely (Veblen, 1921:134). Such a soviet would include technical people from productive industry, transportation, and distribution, as well as consulting "production economists," but there would no place in it for the current business leaders or even those trained in business. In spite of hopeful comments about a general strike of technologists, Veblen sees no immediate possibility of a revolution led by such soviets, especially since vested interests oppose it, there is no evidence that technologists want it, and in any case the mind-set of the American public is to prefer businesspeople as leaders and to distrust technicians.

The Impact of Industry and the Machine on Society   Veblen (1904:323) sees the machine and its ubiquity as the "unequivocal mark of the Western culture of to-day as contrasted with the culture of other times and places." As such, it has a powerful impact on other institutions in society such as the state, law, and "matter-of-fact" science, which come to operate in a machinelike manner. Machines affect all classes, although their most direct impact is on those who work most directly with them. Most generally, the machine affects the habits of thought, the ways of thinking, within society as a whole. And Veblen (1901:372–373) sees this as spreading:

> The machine discipline, however, touches wider and wider circles of the population, and touches them in an increasingly intimate and coercive manner. In the nature of the case, therefore, the resistance opposed to this cultural trend given by the machine discipline on grounds of received conventions weakens with the passage of time. The spread of materialistic, matter-of-fact preconceptions takes place at a cumulatively accelerating rate.
>
> (Veblen, 1904:372–373)

The only thing that can impede its spread is some other cultural factor such as business interests, which may, as we have seen, at times see the proliferation of industry and the machine as contrary to its pecuniary interests. However, in the long run Veblen (1904) is certain that the machine and industry will win out. One of the reasons that the machine process and industry will emerge victorious is that "it touches larger classes of the community and inculcates its characteristic habits of thought more unremittingly" (Veblen, 1904:381).

Trained Incapacity   The idea of "trained incapacity" plays a minor role in Veblen's work, but it has received an inordinate amount of attention from sociologists and other social scientists. One of the places that Veblen (1919/1964) raises it is in the context of a discussion of the role played by owners, bankers, and workers in modern industry. His basic point is that all of these focus, in their own way, on pecuniary matters with the result that the most important task—the efficient and effective operation of industry—suffers. As Veblen (1919/1964:347) puts it, the problems of modern industry are at least in part traceable to the "trained incapacity on the part of the several contestants to appreciate large and general requirements of the industrial situation." In being socialized to look after their own interests, the members of each of these groups is unable to understand the larger picture and especially what is of utmost importance in the modern world. The term "trained incapacity" is now often used more generally to describe any situation in which a particular type of training serves to incapacitate, at least in some way, those who have undergone such socialization.

Higher Learning

Veblen begins his work on higher education with the assumption that esoteric knowledge is considered to be of great intrinsic value in all societies since it is "taken to embody a systematization of fundamental and eternal truth" (Veblen, 1918/1965:2). This body of higher learning, of science and scholarship, has reached its most mature phase. However, such knowledge is always shaped by the life and circumstances in which it is found. Two constraining factors are the state of the industrial arts and what Veblen (1918/1965:3) calls "the received scheme of use and wont," which, at that time was the pursuit of business. Thus, we are back to Veblen's overriding interest in the relationship, especially the conflict, between industry and business.

The current industrial situation leads to habits of thought that govern the search for knowledge. However, the problem is that in Veblen's day the industrial situation itself was being shaped, even distorted, by business and its emphasis on ownership and money. Thus, business affects learning not only directly, but indirectly through its impact on industry.

In the past, knowledge was valued if it served some practical interest. Today, however, learning has become an end in itself. In fact, it has become "the most valued spiritual asset of civilized mankind" (Veblen, 1918/1965:11). This is a defining characteristic of modern, Occidental society and no other society at any point in history has produced anything like the body of matter-of-fact knowledge that characterizes the modern Western world. There is, however, a dark side to this. Knowledge is available to all, including the forces of evil in the world.

Undergraduate Education The value placed on knowledge is extended to the settings—universities—in which it is produced and enhanced. The main task of the university is higher learning and that can be broken down into "scientific and scholarly inquiry" and teaching. The latter, however, has a place in the university only insofar as it furthers the main task of the university—the advance of academic inquiry. In such a situation, students are to be more like apprentices to the master scholars and scientists. However, the university has taken on the task of educating vast numbers of undergraduates and Veblen feels that while the accomplishment of such a task is valuable to the community, it does not belong in the university. Such education is to be left to secondary, professional, and technical schools and not to the university.

However, undergraduate teaching has become a crucial component of every university. Not only has such teaching, in Veblen's view, no place in the university, but undergraduate education is serving to shape and corrupt graduate education. Undergraduate education has been rationalized and dominated by standardization, quantification, efficiency, surveillance, and control.[11] However, Veblen believes that higher learning

---

[11]A strong interest in Weberian rationalization runs through this as well as many other aspects of Veblen's work.

requires personal contact, is not measurable, and suffers when efforts are made to standardize, observe, and control it. Higher learning is not only at odds with undergraduate education, but also with professional and technical education, which is oriented to the practical, whereas higher knowledge is essentially impractical. In fact, the existence of such "lower" forms of education within the university tends to corrupt science and scholarship by leading the latter to operate with a more practical, utilitarian frame of mind. Furthermore, the technical school's appreciation of what works mechanically and the professional school's (e.g., law school) interest in pecuniary gain mesh well with the orientation of the business man and all are opposed to anything that is not utilitarian. Thus, they pose a powerful alliance in opposition to the scholar and scientist. As a result, Veblen proposes that universities be separated from professional and technical schools (as well as the task of undergraduate education) and that they be freed from pressures from the business world.

Undergraduate students also come under Veblen's scrutiny. There had been an increase in student enrollment in Veblen's day, but many of these students are a "contingent from the leisure class" not interested in the pursuit of knowledge (Veblen, 1918/1965:102). Aware of this, the university offers them sports, fraternities, clubs and the like to keep them content and enrolled. These extracurricular activities are "designed to cultivate expensive habits of life" and lead students in the direction of business careers (Veblen, 1918/1965:133). Furthermore, "the mental discipline exercised by these sports and polite events greatly favours the growth of tactful equivocation and a guarded habit of mind, such as makes for worldly wisdom and success in business, but which is worse than useless in the scholar or scientist" (Veblen, 1918/1965:134).

In order to control the mass of largely uninterested students, systems of surveillance, standardization, accountancy, and uniformity are put in place. While these may help to control the students, they are principles that are at odds with those that govern higher learning. Sarcastically, Veblen argues that academic demands must be constructed so that "its demands on the student's time and energy [not] be allowed seriously to interfere with these sports and 'student activities' that make up the chief attraction of college life for a large proportion of the university's young men" (Veblen, 1918/1965:104). That academic work that is performed by students tends to be perfunctory and mediocre.

University Administration   Much of Veblen's attention is devoted to the governing boards (many of their members are businessmen) and leaders of the universities. Both are strongly influenced by business and a business mentality and these, of course, stand in opposition to science and scholarship. Of governing boards, Veblen contends that they have little understanding of higher learning, yet they interfere with the work of science and scholarship primarily through the budget which they control. The success of their members in business has nothing to do with the essential work of a university. Further, since higher learning is of no use to business, board members tend to consider science and scholarship of little or no use. Veblen would obviously like to see other types of people on these boards, but he sees little possibility of change because of the dominance of the system of private ownership; the nature of the boards will not change until there is a fundamental change in that economic system.

Veblen is also critical of the academic heads of universities. In part, they are constrained by the governing boards and especially the control over the budget exercised by such boards. In addition, the boards select the academic heads and that selection is made on the basis of business qualifications. The result is that those who are selected for such posts are likely to be quite mediocre scholar/scientists. Instead of talented scholar/scientists, Veblen snidely remarks that "a plausible speaker with a large gift of assurance, a businesslike 'educator' or clergyman, some urbane pillar of society, some astute veteran of the scientific *demi-monde,* will meet all reasonable requirements" for the position of academic head (Veblen, 1918/1965:83).

The academic head is confronted with role conflict. On the one side, there is the governing board, which wants the university run with businesslike efficiency. On the other side are the academic personnel, who want and need to be left alone to pursue knowledge. However, the academic head is hired by, and responsible to, the governing board and is, as a result, far more responsive to its demands. The faculty has little or no influence over the decisions of the academic head. In fact, Veblen (1918/1965:117) argues that "the body of academic employes are as defenceless and unorganized as any class of the wage-earning population."

Competition   Veblen also criticizes the university for its interest in competition and therefore in appearances that will help one university outdo its competitors. Under the influence of business, the university turns in the direction of "salesmanship" in order to create the illusion, if not the delusion, of superiority. While competition and salesmanship may be useful to the university in giving it differential gains, it is of no use to the larger community; indeed Veblen (1918/1965:137) deems it a "bootless waste." Furthermore, the emphasis on salesmanship diverts attention from scholarship and has an adverse effect on it. In the quest for competitive advantage, it is difficult to sell a university on the basis of something so obscure as scholarship. Thus, the focus shifts to the "conspicuous extensions" of material equipment such as "laboratory and library buildings, assembly halls, curious museum exhibits, grounds for athletic contests, and the like" (Veblen, 1918/1965:139). Far more money and attention is devoted to the university's buildings and grounds than to the needs of the faculties and their salaries. As a result, the needs of higher learning languish while the rest of the university engages in an orgy of conspicuous consumption. The university "wastes" large sums of money that could be better spent on advancing science and scholarship. Veblen (1918/1965:146) raises the issue of "the fitness of housing a quest for truth in an edifice of false pretences."

Faculty   The faculty, too, is affected by this emphasis on business. We have already touched on the negative effect of spending on appearances on the work of the scholar. In addition, the university prefers (at least it did in Veblen's day) to hire faculty members with money either from inheritance or marriage. The reason is that they will be better "able to live on such a scale of conspicuous expensiveness as to make a favourable impression on those men of pecuniary refinement and expensive tastes with whom they are designed to come in contact" (Veblen, 1918/1965:154). Such well-to-do faculty members also serve as models to be emulated by their less-well-off colleagues in terms of the need for conspicuous consumption. The latter may well even be forced to take outside work in order to afford such displays. To assure tenure, faculty members are well advised to spend as much as they can on conspicuous consumption and on administrative duties rather than on the advance of scholarship. Veblen (1918/1965:163) seems to have himself in mind when he argues that a professor

> may make his chance of preferment less assured, and may even jeopardize his tenure, by a conspicuously parsimonious manner of life, or by too pronounced an addiction to scientific or scholarly pursuits, to the neglect of those polite exhibitions of decorum that conduce to the maintenance of the university's prestige in the eyes of the (pecuniarily) cultured laity.
>
> (Veblen, 1918/1965:163)

In order to please the potential donors to the university (aging captains of industry), academicians, especially in the moral and social sciences that touch on the concerns of such people, are led to do work that does not offend them. This means that they do not follow matters to their logical conclusions and, as a result, produce mediocre work. They do "quasi science" designed to support the status quo rather than "real" science.

Relatedly, Veblen castigates the university for involving faculty in an array of pageants and ceremonies that help to sell the university to the public. Thus, he sarcastically comments that "no requirement of the academic routine should be allowed to stand in the way of an available occasion for a scholastic pageant" (Veblen, 1918/1965:158).

Professional Schools   Vocational training, especially in the university's schools of business and commerce, comes under particularly merciless attack. This, of course, is related to Veblen's (1918/1965:208) more general critique of business for being "occupied with the competitive acquisition of wealth, not with its production." As a result, there is no gain to society in producing more businesspeople; indeed in his view there are already far too many people in business. Business schools (along with law schools and athletic programs) drain resources from scholarly pursuits and adversely affect the scholarly way of thinking.

Does Veblen offer any hope? While academicians are profoundly influenced by all of this, the impact never quite reaches the extremes found in the business world: "This perfect scheme of low-cost perfunctory instruction, high-cost stage properties and press-agents, public song and dance, expensive banquets, speech-making and processions, is never fully rounded out" (Veblen, 1918/1965:171). The reason is that no matter how much it is compromised, the faculty never completely loses its sense of science (derived from the instinct of "idle curiosity") and scholarship.

While Veblen holds out little hope of the academic world changing until the larger economic system is overhauled, he does suggest the abolition of the governing boards and academic heads of universities. This is not difficult to do from his point of view since they make no useful contribution to the main business of the university—scholarly pursuit. With the elimination of these leaders, the huge university bureaucracy would crumble. As a result, the running of the university would be left in the hands of the various faculties. These faculties can be counted on to run the university a bit clumsily and ineffectively, but that would be fine since great efficiency has been used in the past to undermine scholarly activities.

Politics

Veblen tends to approach politics in much the same way he does the economy. The reason for this, at least in part, is that political leaders are seen as being the tools of the "vested interests" and the "captains of industry." He sees the national government as being "charged with the general care of the country's business interests" (Veblen, 1921:19). He views the nation with its legal and military powers negatively as something that is needed by business "to enforce the claims of its business men abroad" (Veblen, 1919/1964:155). The warlike nature of relationships between businesses is reflected in warlike relationships between nations. According to Veblen (1904:398): "The quest of profits leads to a predatory national policy."

While the nation may be operated in the interest of business, it retards industry which is inherently international in scope. National boundaries serve only to retard international industrial exchanges and the international development of industrial processes. Tariffs are a specific example of a national act that operates against the interests of industry, which require free passage in order to operate most effectively. Thus, tariffs are an example of "sabotage," this time being practiced at the level of the nation rather than the business enterprise. Nations are oriented to self-aggrandizement and stand in opposition to the principle of "live and let live" that Veblen thinks should govern international (and all other) relationships. Like businesses, nations operate with what they perceive to be the right "to seek their own advantage at the cost of the rest" (Veblen, 1919/1964:120). Thus, the nation is "a predatory organism, in practical effect an association of persons moved by a community interest in getting something for nothing by force and fraud" (Veblen, 1923:442). Wars are fought and nations engage in imperialism in order to strengthen their own position and fortify the economic positions of their business interests.

The Case of Imperial Germany   Veblen's analysis of the state and the economy comes together in one of his most satisfying works, *Imperial Germany and the Industrial Revolution* (Veblen, 1915/1942). Written in the midst of World War I, it can be seen as anticipating World War II and Germany's role in it. One of many places where Veblen (1915/1942:216) seems to anticipate future developments is in a discussion of the need for "a place in the sun" for the German people. This can be taken to mean that, for example, an increasing German population needs more land, or it can mean that German culture needs to be conserved and propagated. On the latter, Veblen characteristically argues that there is no such thing as German culture. Much of it was borrowed from other cultures and is shared with them.

In examining the character of Germany, and especially its belligerent position in World War I, Veblen rejects race as the factor (Germans were a "hybrid" not much different from those in neighboring countries).[12] Nor is the explanation to be found in leaders like Bismarck. Rather, Veblen argues that it is its culture and habits that serves to distinguish Germany from other nations. While it had a longer history, Veblen traces

---

[12]This, of course, contradicts the later Nazi belief in the distinctiveness of the Aryans.

the emergence of the modern German state to 1870 and its advances include "a gain in population, in industrial efficiency, and in military force" (Veblen, 1915/1942:61). However, the prime mover in Germany's ascendancy, in Veblen's view, has been the increase in industrial efficiency. With the arrival of advanced industrial arts, local principalities could no longer remain self-sufficient and powerful, but had to give way to a centralized state. As Veblen (1915/1942:176) puts it, "modern technology does not tolerate a minuscular State after the fashion of the German principalities." In the case of Germany and its culture, it was a "dynastic state . . . of a competitive, or rapacious, character, and free to use any expedient that comes to hand" that came to power (Veblen, 1915/1942:79). Better than any other European nation, Germany was able to use the increase in industry to the advantage of the state and its warlike character. The subservience of the population to the state was guaranteed by "a policy of warlike aggression, and . . . by a system of bureaucratic surveillance and unremitting interference in the private life of subjects" (Veblen, 1915/1942:80). Not only did war serve to discipline the population, but the "experience of war induces a warlike frame of mind; and the pursuit of war, being an exercise in the following of one's leader and execution of arbitrary orders, induces an animus of enthusiastic subservience and unquestioning obedience to authority" (Veblen, 1915/1942:81). (The latter personality traits were to play a central role in the coming to power and ascendancy of the Nazis as well as in the carrying out of the gruesome acts associated with the Holocaust.) More generally, liberty in Germany came to mean "flunkeyism," or the "freedom to give orders and freely to follow orders" (Veblen, 1915/1942:172).

In contrast to England (and other nations), the state was central in Germany. While in England and other advanced European societies, subservience to the state had been on the wane, in Germany it was sustained. Thus, in contrast to the "flunkeyism" of Germans, liberty to the British meant more an anarchism, an exemption from taking orders. Furthermore, while for England military power was to be kept at the minimum level needed to maintain peace, in Germany all available resources were to be lavished on the military. However, Veblen holds out hope for Germany since its dynastic system had not been in place nearly as long as the British system. The passage of time might bring the German system more into line with that found in England.

Also hopeful is the fact that German Imperial state is in an unstable relationship with the development of the industrial system. In fact, in the long run the industrial system "undermines the foundations of the State" (Veblen, 1915/1942:271). Thus, in the long run, it is the industrial system and not the German state that is likely to win out.

Consistent with his views on the industrial arts, Veblen criticizes the German state for creating restrictions (such as tariffs) that interrupted the free, international flow of industry. Without these restrictions, Germany would have been more deeply implicated in the world economy and this "would have made a breach of the peace by Germany or with Germany nearly impossible, since the dependence of the German people on foreign markets in such a case would involve as its counterfoil the like dependence of the other parties to the traffic" (Veblen, 1915/1942:183).

SUMMARY

Thorstein Veblen's ideas were shaped, both positively and negatively, by a variety of theoretical inputs, especially those from evolutionary theory, Marxian theory, and economics. Much of his theory is based on a series of assumptions about human nature, especially the instinct of workmanship, the parental bent, idle curiosity, and emulation. While such instincts are important, they are shaped and affected by larger social and cultural factors. Also basic to his theory is the notion of industrial arts, or the stock of knowledge, especially technology, that is common to the community. He operates with the view that there is a tendency for cultural lag, with changes in law and custom particularly likely to lag behind changes in the industrial arts. Veblen accords great importance to cultural borrowing and he offers a distinctive perspective on the advantages that a borrowing culture has over an innovating culture.

The theory of the leisure class is undoubtedly Veblen's first and most lasting contribution to contemporary social theory. Particularly notable is his thinking on invidious distinctions, emulation, and conspicuous leisure and conspicuous consumption. While best known today for that theory, Veblen was most concerned throughout much of his career with the conflict between business and industry. Industry was capable of almost unlimited production in the modern world and this high level of productivity would greatly benefit the entire community. However, the resulting flood of goods would serve to lower prices and profits. As a result, it is in the interest of business, indeed it is necessary for business, given the price system, to sabotage industry so that it is not nearly as productive as it could be. Much else that business does relates to salesmanship rather than workmanship and in that sense not only contributes nothing to the common welfare, but is a drag on it. Because it contributes nothing to industry, business obtains "free income" and that income is attributed to, and is capitalized in the firm as, such nonmaterial assets as "good will." Once capitalized, things like good will become a liability against the firm which can be met only by keeping the income and profits high, and that is done by sabotaging industry. Veblen argues for a system run not by business leaders, but by engineers who understand the way industry really works. In any case, because they would not be dominated by the profit motive, engineers would have no interest in undermining industry. Industry and the machine technology have a wide range of effects on society, including the matter-of-fact way in which people in general, and scientists in particular, think.

The conflict between business and industry shapes Veblen's thinking on higher education and the university. Basically, he argues that business has perverted and sabotaged the university in much the same way it did industry. As members of the boards of universities, business leaders have selected college presidents sympathetic to their perspective. In any case, their control over the budget ensures that the university will be run in accord with business principles. Yet, the principles of academics and scientists (especially the free creation and flow of ideas) are different from, and adversely affected by, business principles. Also interfering with academic work is the placement of undergraduate colleges and professional schools in the university. All these influences, as well as other distractions relating to the selling of the university, should be removed so that the "idle curiosity" of academicians can be allowed to flourish without restraint.

Similarly, Veblen's thinking about politics is affected by the business–industry conflict. Business seeks to control the state and to use the state to sabotage (by tariffs, for example) the free trade between nations. This adversely affects industry around the world as well as the lives of people in the affected nations. Nations themselves, as well as the politicians that lead them, develop a similar interest in self-aggrandizement (e.g., nationalism) that adversely affects international industrial processes. Veblen singles out Germany for analysis and shows how its interference with free trade made it easier for it to engage in war. Although the state was able to gain control over industry in Germany, Veblen holds out hope that in the long term industry will win out and that will serve to integrate Germany into the world community.

Thorstein Veblen has been the subject of more than his share of criticisms. Tilman (1992) has demonstrated that his work has been attacked from a wide range of positions on the political spectrum—conservative (e.g., business is more important than Veblen indicates), liberal (he is too radical a critic of modern society), and radical (Veblen underestimated the importance of the working class). More generally, he has been criticized for his pessimism and for his tendency to criticize contemporary society without offering a blueprint for an alternative society (Dowd, 1966). Among other major criticisms are his adoption of an outmoded evolutionary perspective, a lack of clarity, a tendency to conceal his true views and motivations (often behind irony), a need to be humorous, which served to alienate the serious audience for his work, his technological determinism (given the centrality of the industrial arts dominated by technology), and his technical elitism (as reflected in his thinking on a soviet of engineers). In spite of these and many other criticisms, Veblen's legacy continues and is even growing with the increasing relevance of his work to the emerging consumer society.

KARL MANNHEIM

THE SOCIOLOGY OF KNOWLEDGE
  The Sociology of Knowledge and the Theory of Ideology
  A Sociological Approach
IDEOLOGY AND UTOPIA
  Ideology
  Utopia
CONSERVATISM
RATIONALITY AND THE IRRATIONALITY OF THE TIMES
  Types of Rationality and Irrationality
PLANNING AND SOCIAL RECONSTRUCTION IN THE
MODERN WORLD
A CRITICAL ANALYSIS OF MANNHEIM'S WORK

In some ways, Karl Mannheim is an unusual figure to deal with in a book on classical sociological theory. For example, unlike many others, Mannheim is not viewed by most observers as having created a "grand theory" that has stood the test of time.[1] As Longhurst put it, "Mannheim did not attempt to produce a completely closed and unified theory or system" (1988:24). Furthermore, while all of the other classical theorists discussed in this book have created many memorable theoretical ideas, it is hard to associate more than a few such ideas with Mannheim. Mannheim was an essayist who wrote no great tomes like Marx's *Capital* or Weber's *Economy and Society*. Finally, unlike the other classic theorists discussed here, Mannheim's critics have far outnumbered his adherents. Even Robert Merton, an early and sympathetic analyst of Mannheim's work, ends his famous essay on that work on a highly critical note: It "is by no means definitive—a term which strikes a harsh discord when applied to any work of science" (1941/1957:508).

Because, in part, his work is spread across many essays written over several decades, it tends to be repetitious and disjointed. Many ideas are raised but never completely and fully developed. At innumerable points in Mannheim's work one encounters phrases like "but I do not have time to deal with this issue now." There are also many inconsistencies in the body of Mannheim's work, and while he was well aware of them, he never undertook a comprehensive and systematic effort to reconcile them.[2] Said Mannheim:

---

[1] At the close of this chapter we will argue that perhaps one can see the outlines of a grand theory in Mannheim's work.

[2] Although a posthumous book misleadingly entitled *Systematic Sociology: An Introduction to the Study of Society* (Mannheim, 1957) was published. This book was based on Mannheim's lectures and did not offer an overarching theoretical perspective.

> I use this method [essays] because I think that in a marginal field of human knowledge we should not conceal inconsistencies, so to speak covering up our wounds, but our duty is to show the sore spots in human thinking at its present stage. . . . these inconsistencies are the thorn in the flesh from which we have to start.
>
> (Mannheim, cited in Kettler, Meja, and Stehr, 1982:26–27)

Further complicating matters is the fact that in 1933, Mannheim was forced to move from Germany to England as a result of the Nazis' ascent to power. His work in Germany (and prior to that in Hungary) was very different from the essays he wrote in England, and this difference contributed to the impression that his work is disjointed.

Given all of this, the obvious question is: Why bother writing (to say nothing of reading) a chapter devoted to the work of Karl Mannheim? The answer is that Mannheim was *the* major figure in the invention of a field, the *sociology of knowledge (Wissenssoziologie),* that has been, and is, of great interest to sociologists in general and sociological theorists in particular (McCarthy, 1996; Pels, 1996). Furthermore, it was Mannheim's intellectual efforts over a period of many years that played *the* key role in institutionalizing the field. Few individual thinkers can be credited with the central role in the "invention" of a field, as well as with successfully nurturing it into becoming an established subfield within sociology. Today the sociology of knowledge is such a field, and those who work within it owe a great debt to the ideas of Karl Mannheim. In spite of his critical orientation toward Mannheim's work, Merton makes this clear:

> Mannheim has sketched the broad contours of the sociology of knowledge with remarkable skill and insight. . . . Mannheim's procedures and substantive findings clarify relations between knowledge and social structure which have hitherto remained obscure. . . . we may await considerable enlightenment from further explorations of the territory in which he pioneered.
>
> (Merton, 1941/1957:508)

Given this introduction, we turn immediately to the heart of Mannheim's legacy to sociological theory (and sociology more generally)—the sociology of knowledge.

THE SOCIOLOGY OF KNOWLEDGE

While there are many other forerunners, Mannheim makes it quite explicit that "the sociology of knowledge emerged from Marx" (1931/1936:309).

The Sociology of Knowledge and the Theory of Ideology

Mannheim argues that Marx created the prototype of the sociology of knowledge, the "theory of ideology." As we saw in Chapter 5, Marx sees ideologies as distortions of reality that reflect the interests of the ruling class (the capitalists). Mannheim argues that such ideologies are seen by Marxists as "more or less conscious deceptions and disguises" (1931/1936:265). To the followers of Marx, the goal of the study of ideologies is to unmask these conscious distortions.

While Mannheim acknowledges the importance of the theory of ideology as a starting point, he also believes that it has great limitations. For one thing, ideologies need *not,* in his view, involve the *conscious* intention to distort reality. Rather, distortions are more likely to occur simply because ideas emerge from specific sectors of the social world and are therefore *inherently* limited, one-sided, and *distorted.* Thus, while Marx uses the term ideology in a negative sense, to Mannheim ideology "has no moral or denunciatory intent" (Mannheim, 1931/1936:266). Ideologies are almost inevitable because ideas emerge from specific and circumscribed areas of the social world.

For another thing, ideologies are not, as the Marxists suggested, simply the product of social classes, especially the ruling class, but can emerge from any and all sectors of the social world, including "generations, status groups, sects, occupational groups, schools, etc." (Mannheim, 1931/1936:276). In spite of these multiple sources, Mannheim concludes that *"class stratification is the most significant,* since in the final analysis all the other social groups arise from and are transformed as parts of the more basic conditions of production and domination"[3] (1931/1936:276; italics added). Nonetheless, Mannheim defines the sociology of knowledge, far more broadly than would a Marxist, as the study of "the relationship between human thought and the conditions of existence in general" (1931/1936:277).

In differentiating between ideological and sociological analyses of knowledge, Mannheim distinguishes between intrinsic and extrinsic perspectives. If one peers out from within one's own group, one tends to believe that it produces "ideas," while all other groups produce "ideologies." However, adopting the extrinsic perspective of the sociologist, one is able to see that *all* systems of ideas, including those emanating from one's own group, are ideologies. "The sociological consideration of intellectual phenomena is a special class of extrinsic interpretation of ideas" (Mannheim, 1926/1971:119).

Generations   Mannheim's (1928–29/1952) discussion of the relationship between generations and knowledge illustrates well the difference between his orientation and that of Marx. The position of a person's generation vis-à-vis other generations is clearly not economic in nature, but it nonetheless has a profound effect on the thinking of those associated with it. The members of a generation are not a "concrete group" in the sense that they do not interact with one another in a patterned and repetitive manner. However, they can be considered as a kind of a group by virtue of the fact that they share a particular social *location.* A generation has this characteristic in common with a social class. However, the nature of their social locations is different. Social classes are defined by their location in the political-economic system, while generations "share the same year of birth, are endowed, to that extent, with a common location in the historical dimension of the social process" (Mannheim, 1928–29/1952:290). (Another group of people that Mannheim [1932/1993] describes as sharing a social location is women [Kettler and Meja, 1993].) The key to a generation is not the biological fact of the common year of birth, but the sociological implications of that biological fact (Pilcher, 1994). For example, what is crucial is the fact that the members of each generation share in a distinctive phase of the collective historical process. They experience a common set of events, a set that is different from that experienced by all generations that have come before or will come after (Cherrington, 1997).

---

[3]Here Mannheim is anticipating the view of the structural Marxists that the economy is, in the end, the most important social institution.

While they occupy different locations, classes and generations "both endow the individuals sharing in them with a common location in the social and historical process, and thereby limit them to a specific range of potential experience, predisposing them for a certain characteristic mode of thought and experience, and a characteristic type of historically relevant action" (Mannheim, 1928–29/1952:290).

Mannheim refines his notion of generation by arguing that a *generation as actuality* emerges when members of a generation begin to orient themselves to one another, both positively and negatively, on the basis of larger ideas and their interpretation of them. Then there are *generation units,* or members of a generation who share common ideas and develop a much more concrete bond with one another. Any generation may be made up of a number of different generation units.

Thus, Mannheim's use of the concept of generations is useful in allowing us to begin to get a better sociological understanding of intra- and intergenerational differences in thought and action. That is, a given generation can be made up of a number of generation units that may differ, and even conflict, with one another. It is even more likely that different generations will have conflicting viewpoints.

Politics   In contrast to the Marxian perspective, the major goal of the sociology of knowledge to Mannheim is not the unmasking of distortions, but rather the careful *study* of the social sources of distorted thinking. Thus, while for Marx the theory of ideology is primarily political in orientation, Mannheim's sociology of knowledge is more academic and scientific in its approach. As Simonds puts it, "Throughout his work, the sociology of knowledge is recommended not as a means for discrediting, undermining, or devaluing knowledge, but as a tool of *understanding*" (1978:30).

This is not to say, however, that Mannheim's sociology of knowledge is apolitical. We will deal with the political implications of Mannheim's thinking toward the close of this chapter. Anticipating that discussion, Mannheim believed that the problems of his day, especially the rise of fascism, were a result of the fact that thought had grown out of control. The sociology of knowledge promised to regain control over knowledge by uncovering its unconscious motivations, presuppositions, and roots. Once these were uncovered, they could be controlled. Conversely, they could not be controlled as long as we are unaware of them. Thus, in Mannheim's view, the sociology of knowledge can lead to the "scientific guidance of political life" (1929/1936:5). In other words, it can help the political system prevent knowledge systems from spiraling out of control.

Thus, Mannheim wants his approach to be *both* political *and* scientific. As a result, Pels writes of the "obvious tensions between involvement and detachment which seem to ravage Mannheim's work from beginning to end" (1993:49).

A Sociological Approach

Although his work is divided on the issue of politics and science, there is no ambiguity over the fact that it is sociological in orientation. For example, Mannheim describes the sociology of knowledge as "one of the youngest branches of sociology" (1931/1936: 264). Mannheim took as his goal the institutionalization of the sociology of knowledge as a subfield within sociology: "The sociological analysis of thought, undertaken thus far only in a fragmentary and casual fashion, now becomes the object of a comprehensive scientific programme" (1925/1971:105).

While Mannheim sometimes describes the sociology of knowledge as a theory, at other times as a method, it is certainly *empirical,* since it is oriented to the study, description, and (theoretical) analysis of the ways in which social relationships influence thought. One of the most common ways in which Mannheim describes the sociology of knowledge is in terms of its concern with "existential determination of knowledge." In other words, knowledge is determined by social existence (with the individual actor standing between, or mediating, the relationship between the social world and knowledge). However, even though he uses the word "determines," unlike some Marxists (but not Marx himself), Mannheim is *not* a determinist: "this does not mean to say that mind and thought are nothing but the expression and reflex of various 'locations' in the social fabric, and that there exist[s] . . . no potentiality or 'freedom' granted in mind" (Mannheim, 1952/1971b:260–261). He means, rather, that there is always some sort of relationship between existence and knowledge, but the precise nature of that relationship varies and can only be determined by empirical study.

While knowledge is amenable to a variety of types of empirical research, Mannheim is most interested in historical-sociological research tracing the forms taken by the relationship between knowledge and existence over time:

> The most important task of the sociology of knowledge at present is to demonstrate its capacity in actual research in the historical-sociological realm. In this realm it must work out criteria for exactness for establishing empirical truths and for assuring their control. It must emerge from the stage where it engages in casual intuitions and gross generalizations.
>
> (Mannheim, 1931/1936:306)

Positivism   Mannheim's interest in "exact" empirical research might lead one to believe that he was a positivist. While Mannheim (1953b:195) clearly wanted the sociology of knowledge to be scientific (as opposed to philosophical), and more generally a "science of society," he regarded positivism as a "deluded school" because it emphasizes only one type of empiricism (the collection of data in the manner that it is done in the natural sciences) and because it sees no role for philosophical and theoretical orientations. Thus, Mannheim (1953b) criticized the American sociology of his day on these grounds by, for example, attacking its "exactitude complex" and its lack of concern for the great theoretical problems of the day. The natural science approach was not deemed useful for analyzing the most important factors in social life.

Mannheim, like Weber,[4] sees many advantages in the human sciences over the positivistic natural sciences, especially their ability to "understand" and interpret the phenomena (knowledge, the human mind, and its products) they are studying. For example, Mannheim argues that "by the use of the technique of understanding, the functional interpenetration of psychic experiences and social situations . . . can . . . be much

---

[4]More generally, both Weber and Mannheim were part of the German hermeneutic tradition known as *Geisteswissenschaften.*

more intensively penetrated in their essential character than if coefficients of correlation were established between the various factors" (1929/1936:44–45). Furthermore, while Mannheim wanted the sociology of knowledge to be empirical, he also wanted it to involve the theoretical (even philosophical) interpretation of its results.

However, the greatest weakness of positivism in Mannheim's view is its focus on reality that is experienced as real and material. As a result, "its methods are entirely inadequate especially in treating intellectual-spiritualistic reality" (Mannheim, 1925/ 1971:76). The natural science model is well suited to the study of material realities (Durkheim's material social facts), but not to immaterial realities such as ideas (Durkheim's nonmaterial social facts) that are the concern of the sociology of knowledge. Similarly, positivism is inadequate from a phenomenological perspective (see Chapter 13, on Alfred Schutz) because it is "blind to the fact that perception and knowledge of meaningful objects as such involves interpretation and understanding" (Mannheim, 1925/1971:76).

In spite of the fact that he was not a positivist and was highly critical of positivism, this viewpoint was important to Mannheim for three reasons. First, Mannheim (controversially) saw Marx as a positivist and it was Marx who, as we have seen, was considered by Mannheim to be the founder of the modern study of the sociology of knowledge. Second, positivism shifted the center of experience to the economic-social sphere, and it is in this existential realm that Mannheim embeds knowledge. Finally, positivism led to the granting of primacy to empirical reality and to empirical research. As such, it helped to end the predominance of pure speculation in the study of ideas. As a result, one could no longer merely philosophize and theorize about knowledge, but had to go out and collect empirical data on knowledge. Theory was possible, but only on the basis of empirical results. Mannheim did not want to do natural science, but he did want to do a kind of "science" that was suitable to the study of knowledge: "Mannheim's sociology of knowledge represented an attempt to do justice to the meaningful nature of social thought without thereby surrendering the aspiration to establish 'objective' (in the sense of intersubjectively communicable) knowledge about social phenomena" (Simonds, 1978:20).

Phenomenology   Another important input into Mannheim's sociology of knowledge was phenomenology, especially the work of Max Scheler. The phenomenologist points to the importance of the mental, something which the (Marxian) materialist either overlooks or subordinates in importance and sees as an epiphenomenon. However, the phenomenologist operates purely within the realm of the mental, accepting the idea that the mental world has an immanent logic of its own. While accepting the phenomenologist's emphasis on mental phenomena, Mannheim seeks the integration of "the real and the mental," arguing that "there is something true in the materialist conception of history" (1925/1971:85, 86). In other words, Mannheim seeks to integrate Marxian theory and phenomenology.

In addition to criticizing phenomenology for ignoring the real, material world, Mannheim is dissatisfied with its belief in "supratemporally valid truths," such as the "transcendental ego" (1925/1971:80). In contrast, Mannheim is a *historicist.* Historicism leads to the view that there are no supratemporal truths, but rather "various essential meanings come into being together with the epochs to which they belong" (Mannheim, 1925/1971:96). This historicism means that Mannheim is committed to the study of the social roots of knowledge in specific historical settings, as well as to the study of the changing relationship over time between ideas and their social sources.

Other Approaches   A similar contrast is drawn with another field, the history of ideas. As its name suggests, the history of ideas is concerned with the relationships among ideas over time. In this sense, it focuses on ideas themselves and ignores the social roots of those ideas. In contrast, according to Mannheim, we need to look at "how the various intellectual standpoints and 'styles of thought' are rooted in an underlying historico-social reality" (1925/1971:107).

By focusing on the empirical study of the effect of the social world on knowledge, or more generally the relationship between being and thought, Mannheim is distinguishing the sociology of knowledge from other, more philosophical fields that are interested in the way in which the development of knowledge is affected by factors internal to knowledge itself.

A Sociology of the Sociology of Knowledge   Mannheim even does a sociology-of-knowledge analysis of the rise of the sociology of knowledge. For example, he argues that the sociology of knowledge could not have arisen during a historical period (say, the Middle Ages) when there was social stability and substantial agreement, even unity, over world views. However, in more recent years this belief in unity has been destroyed, largely by the increase in social mobility. What increased mobility has done is "to reveal the multiplicity of styles of thought" (Mannheim, 1929/1936:7). Mannheim distinguishes between horizontal and vertical mobility. Horizontal mobility leads people to see that other people think differently, but it does not lead them to question their own group's knowledge system. Because people are moving horizontally, no group is "better" than any other. As a result, no thought system is seen as preferable to any other. However, vertical mobility leads people not only to see that others think differently, but also to be uncertain, even skeptical of their own group's mode of thought. This uncertainty is especially likely to occur when one encounters different thought systems in groups that stand higher in the stratification system than one's own. Vertical mobility also tends to lead to a "democratization" of thought whereby the ideas of the lower strata can come to confront those of the upper strata on more equal footing. More generally, all of this leads to the following questions:

> How is it possible that identical human thought-processes concerned with the same world produce different conceptions of that world? And from this point it is only a step further to ask: Is it not possible that the thought processes which are involved here are not at all identical? May it not be found . . . that there are numerous alternative paths which can be followed?
>
> (Mannheim, 1929/1936:9)

These questions lead to a crisis in society in which there seems to be nothing to believe in, all ideas appear equal, and everything seems to be up for grabs. But in Mannheim's view, this crisis, and the questions that led to it, also lead dialectically to the development of the field—the sociology of knowledge—that offers potential solutions to the crisis. However, Mannheim believes that there is some urgency for those interested in doing a sociology of knowledge in order to help cope with the crisis because "the opportunity may be lost, and the world will once again present a static, uniform, and inflexible countenance" (Mannheim, 1929/1936:85).

Relativism and Relationism   Mannheim contrasts the "relationism" that he prefers to see as characteristic of the sociology of knowledge with the "relativism" that he fears because it leads people to feel that there is nothing to believe in, that truth is *"socially and historically conditioned"* (Remmling, 1967:45; Goldman, 1994). *Relativism* leads to the viewpoint that there are no absolute standards by which one can judge right or wrong, good or bad, and so on. *Relationism,* on the other hand, is simply the idea that there is a relationship among specific ideas, the larger system of ideas of which they are part, and the social system in which they are found. To the relationist, the effort to discover truth independent of historical and social meanings is a "vain hope" (Mannheim, 1929/1936:80). Instead of searching for fixed, immutable ideas, Mannheim urges that we "learn to think dynamically and relationally rather than statically" (1929/1936:87). However, there *are* criteria of right and wrong, good and bad, but they cannot be formulated absolutely, once and for all. Such criteria can be defined for a given social situation and must be redefined anew with each change in social reality; "there *is* a moral obligation, but . . . this obligation *is derived from the concrete situation to which it is related*" (Mannheim, 1953b:212). Says Mannheim, "The dynamic relationism for which I stand has nothing to do with nihilism. . . . It . . . does not despair of the solubility of the crisis of our existence and thought" (1929/1971:267).

The sociology of knowledge can be used nonevaluatively or evaluatively. It can be used nonevaluatively simply to analyze the relationship between a social situation and ideas, or it can be used evaluatively: "A theory . . . is wrong if in a given practical situation it uses concepts and categories which, if taken seriously, would prevent man from adjusting himself at that historical stage" (Mannheim, 1929/1936:95). Mannheim enumerates three examples of idea systems that could cause such maladjustment. The first is the continued existence of antiquated norms. The second is living by absolutes that may have applied to one social setting but which no longer apply to the changed social setting. Finally, there is the use of forms of knowledge that are no longer capable of comprehending present realities. This leads Mannheim to a new definition of the Marxian concept of false consciousness: "Knowledge is distorted and ideological when it fails to take account of the new realities applying to a situation, and when it attempts to conceal them by thinking of them in categories which are inappropriate" (Mannheim, 1929/1936:96).

Relatedly, Mannheim asks how knowledge and objectivity are possible once it is recognized that any "given finding should contain the traces of the position of the knower" (1931/1936:296). Mannheim responds that this reality should not be denied, but rather we should ask, "How, granted these perspectives, knowledge and objectivity are still possible" (Mannheim, 1931/1936:296). He responds with the argument that we need to juxtapose a series of partial perspectives in order to achieve a new level of objectivity. In so doing, we need to reject the positivistic idea that there is some detached, impersonal, ideal realm of truth, some "sphere of perfection" (Mannheim, 1931/1936:297). Rather, we must strive to constantly enlarge our knowledge of what we are studying through the juxtaposition of a number of all-too-human partial perspectives. Furthermore, we can compare points of view and determine which one "gives evidence of the greatest comprehensiveness and the greatest fruitfulness in dealing with empirical material" (Mannheim, 1931/1936:301).

The Intelligentsia The changing nature of society produces a dramatic change in what Mannheim calls the "intelligentsia,"[5] or the "social groups whose special task it is to provide an interpretation of the world for that society" (Mannheim, 1929/1936:10; 1932/1993). In previous, static societies, the intelligentsia tended to be not only well defined, but also "static and lifeless." The members of the intelligentsia are oriented more by their own need to systematize ideas than by the need to use those ideas to deal with life's concrete problems. In the modern world this closed intelligentsia has been replaced by what Mannheim calls *socially unattached (or free) intelligentsia* (Loader, 1997). Today's intelligentsia is derived from a number of different social strata, and its members are no longer rigidly organized or constrained by such an organization. As a result, "the intellectual's illusion that there is only one way of thinking disappears" (Mannheim, 1929/1936:12). Thus, various groups of the intelligentsia, buying into different sets of ideas, openly compete with one another for the attention of the larger world.

The appearance and spread of a socially unattached intelligentsia has mixed implications. On the one hand, the intelligentsia has helped to produce the "profound disquietude" of Mannheim's (1929/1936:13) day. That is, intellectuals, and people in general, no longer accept one system of ideas; society is a buzzing confusion of competing idea systems. On the other hand, it is the intelligentsia that is able to rise above the limitations of a restricted vision to find truth.[6] It is from this new intelligentsia that the sociologist of knowledge emerged, and it is this sociologist who is in a distinctive position to offer a solution to the world's intellectual chaos. According to Simonds:

> Mannheim's faith in the intellectuals is, then, a faith in the powers of the intellect to overcome the limitations of this or that personal experience as a ground of knowledge, to expand the self by engaging in authentic communication with others, to aspire to a more comprehensive view of our shared human condition by virtue of the communicative ability to gain access to contexts of thought other than the one into which we are born.
>
> (Simonds, 1978:131)

Before it created the sociology of knowledge, this new intelligentsia created two other methods of thought and investigation. One was *epistemology,* an immanent theory of knowledge which emerged out of a process of pure contemplation. The other was *psychology,* which focused on such things as the genesis of meaning within the individual. In different ways, both of these approaches were, from Mannheim's point of view, guilty of separating the individual mind from the larger community. It is this error that

---

[5]Mannheim took this idea from the work of Max Weber's brother, Alfred, himself a noted scholar of his day.

[6]Remmling finds the creation of the intelligentsia as a solution to the problem of truth to be a "dubious construction" (1967:45).

KARL MANNHEIM: A Biographical Sketch

Two major facts defined a good portion of the life of Karl Mannheim: ill health and refugee status.

Mannheim was born in Budapest, Hungary, on March 27, 1893. A heart defect made him sickly from birth; he had a slight heart attack when he was only twenty and he died prematurely from a heart attack on January 9, 1947, at the age of fifty-three (Woldring, 1986). Although he accomplished much during his life, one wonders what he might have accomplished had he been blessed with better health and a longer life.

Mannheim was born into a middle-class Jewish family. He attended the University of Budapest (as well as the University of Berlin, where he frequented lectures by Georg Simmel), from which he received a doctorate in philosophy in 1918. He encountered the leading Hungarian scholar of the time, Georg Lukács, and participated in the circle that surrounded him. In fact, Lukács became his early mentor, and Mannheim declared himself a "respectful follower" of Lukács (Loader, 1985:13).

In 1918 Hungary experienced a revolution in which a bourgeois-socialist regime under Mihály Károlyi came to power. However, it was short-lived and was replaced in early 1919 by Béla Kun's communist regime. Lukács had become a communist in late 1918 and became a government official under Kun. Although Mannheim had remained largely apolitical, Lukács appointed him lecturer in philosophy in the College of Education at the University of Budapest. By mid-1919, however, Kun had been replaced by a counterrevolutionary, fascist, anti-Semitic regime headed by Admiral Miklós Horthy. (Interestingly, much of Mannheim's later thinking was to be affected by the relationship among the three ideologies—bourgeois, communist, fascist—he encountered in his intellectually formative years in Hungary.) Given his linkages to Lukács, and thereby indirectly to communism, and the fact that he was Jewish, Mannheim was forced to flee Hungary by the end of 1919 and became a refugee for the first time.

After several intermediate stops, Mannheim ended up in Heidelberg, Germany, in March, 1921. In that same month he married Juliska Lang, the daughter of a very prosperous Budapest family. The latter disapproved of their daughter's marriage to a relatively impoverished academic. Juliska Lang was an intellectual herself, with a Ph.D. in psychology, and she later held a professorship at the University of Amsterdam. The marriage was childless. Juliska was to play a key role in Mannheim's work, especially in the posthumous publication of many of his essays.

In Heidelberg, Mannheim became a member of the "Weber group." Although Max Weber had died the preceding year, the group continued on headed by his wife, Marianne, and his brother, Alfred, himself a noted scholar. It was Alfred Weber who succeeded Georg Lukács as Mannheim's mentor.

Over the next several years Mannheim lived as a private scholar in Heidelberg. Finally, in mid-1926 Mannheim became a privatdocent (the same marginal position occupied by

the sociology of knowledge serves to correct. As Mannheim put it, "Knowledge is from the beginning a cooperative process of group life, in which everyone unfolds his knowledge within the framework of a common fate, a common activity, and the overcoming of common difficulties" (1929/1936:29).

Simmel for much of his academic life) at Heidelberg. After his appointment, Mannheim applied for German citizenship and was naturalized. It appeared as if his days as a refugee were over. In 1930 Mannheim stepped up to the position of professor and director of the College of Sociology at Goethe University in Frankfurt.

However, Mannheim now found himself deeply affected by two ideologies of which he disapproved—communism and Nazism. His disapproval of communism served to distance him from the famous Institute of Social Research in Frankfurt (the so-called Frankfurt school), even though the Institute was housed in the same building as the sociology department (Pels, 1993). This school produced a number of famous sociologists (Max Horkheimer, Theodor Adorno, and others) as well as a theoretical orientation, "critical theory," that was to play an important role in the future of sociology. While he was put off by its communist orientation, Mannheim did share with the Frankfurt school an opposition to Nazism. For their part, the critical theorists were angered by Mannheim's lack of interest in practical and political matters (Wiggershaus, 1994).

In January 1933, Adolf Hitler came to power, and as a Jew, Mannheim was almost immediately given a "leave of absence" from the university. Sensing imminent grave danger, Mannheim left Germany within a few months and eventually arrived in London in May, 1933, as a result of an invitation from the London School of Economics. He was once again a refugee, a position he was to occupy until 1940, when he became a naturalized British citizen.

For many years Mannheim held temporary lectureships in England, and it was not until 1945 that he was awarded a full-time professorship (in sociology *and* education) at the University of London. After the war, Mannheim was invited to return to the University of Budapest as professor of sociology, but he refused.

Mannheim's work went through a variety of stages that reflected changes in his personal life and in the society and world in which he lived (Remmling, 1975). His earliest work, 1918 to 1924, was highly philosophical. In Germany between 1925 and 1932, his work became largely sociological, with his most notable, albeit controversial contribution (Kettler and Meja, 1994, 1995; Shils, 1995) in this period being *Ideology and Utopia* (1929/1936). After 1933 and his move to England, Mannheim grew more interested in applying sociological ideas to a variety of issues, especially the planning of society. His most important book during this period was *Man and Society in an Age of Reconstruction* (1935/1940).

Mannheim lived much of his life as a refugee from Hungary, first in Germany and then in England. This marginality, and others (for example, his position vis-à-vis Marxist revolutionaries), led him to become a member of what became a central idea in his work, the "socially unattached intelligentsia." Living in a variety of social and cultural settings, the intelligentsia is in a unique position to have a diverse set of experiences. But Mannheim went beyond simply relishing this diversity; he used it to synthesize a variety of antithetical ideas and social forces (Kettler, Meja, and Stehr, 1984). It was Mannheim's unique, "unattached" position, as well as his desire to use that position to synthesize a wide variety of ideas, that helped to give his work its unique qualities.

The modern world has led not only to the realization that there is a multitude of views, but also to the desire, linked to Marx's theory of ideology, to "unmask" the unconscious motivations that lie behind systems of ideas. This desire to see what lies behind idea systems has led to the sense that there is a "collective unconscious" that is the irrational foundation of systems of ideas. Intellectuals are not the only ones involved in the unmasking of these irrational foundations; members of all groups are involved in the unmasking of the ideas of those in other, often competing, groups. The result of all of this questioning is, once again, the undermining of "man's confidence in human thought in general" (Mannheim, 1929/1936:41). As a result of this inability to believe in anything, "more and more people took flight into scepticism and irrationalism" (Mannheim, 1929/1936:41). This is one of the ways that Mannheim links the intellectual and social crises of his day, especially the irrationalism associated with the rise of fascism. Hungry for something to believe in, people were vulnerable to the irrational idea systems put forth by the fascists.

Yet, dialectically, this process of unmasking not only creates a crisis, but once again provides the basis for the resolution of that crisis. As Mannheim puts it, "What seems so unbearable in life itself, namely, to continue to live with the unconscious uncovered, is the historical prerequisite of scientific critical self-awareness" (1929/1936:47). That is, it allows for greater insight into the social determination of knowledge, and such knowledge can provide the basis for emancipation from such social determination.

Weltanschauung   In his sociology of knowledge, Mannheim (1952/1971a) is generally not interested in isolated ideas and beliefs, but rather in getting at the *Weltanschauung,* or systematic totality of ideas of an epoch or group which, in turn, is composed of a series of mutually interdependent parts. The *Weltanschauung* is more than the sum of its parts, but each of the parts can be studied in order to give us a sense of the *Weltanschauung*. But there is a dialectical relationship between the *Weltanschauung* and its parts: "We understand the whole from the part, and the part from the whole. We derive the 'spirit of the epoch' from its individual *documentary* manifestations on the basis of what we know about the spirit of the epoch" (Mannheim, 1952/1971a:49; italics added).

Mannheim sees three levels of meaning in cultural products such as knowledge. The objective level of meaning is that which is inherent in the product itself. The expressive level of meaning is what the actor intended in producing the product. Finally, and most important to Mannheim, the documentary meaning is that the product serves as a "document," or allows us to get a sense, of the *Weltanschauung*. Mannheim is generally not interested in specific cultural products, but what they allow him to deduce about the *Weltanschauung* in which they exist. And he is not so much interested in unmasking individual ideas as he is in "determining the functional role of any thought whatever" within the *Weltanschauung* (Mannheim, 1925/1971:69).

Functional analysis is key to Mannheim. He is interested not only in the functional relationship between specific ideas and the *Weltanschauung,* but also in the functional relationship between ideas and the larger social setting. One of Mannheim's more important definitions of the sociology of knowledge is "a discipline which explores the functional dependence of each intellectual standpoint on the differentiated social group reality standing behind it, and which sets itself the task of retracing the evolution of the various standpoints" (Mannheim, 1925/1971:115). In doing a sociology of knowledge, Mannheim is doing a *functional* analysis; that is, he is viewing knowledge as a function of the social world from which it emanates and of the *Weltanschauung* of which it is part.

Steps in Practicing the Sociology of Knowledge   This definition leads Mannheim to identify a series of steps involved in the practice of the sociology of knowledge. First, it is necessary to specify, for each historical period under study, "the various systematic intellectual standpoints on which the thinking of creative individuals and groups was based" (Mannheim, 1925/1971:114).   Second, the sociologist is to explore the "non-theoretical, vital roots" of these standpoints by uncovering "the hidden metaphysical premises of the various systematic positions; then we must ask further which of the 'world postulates' coexisting in a given epoch are the correlates of a given style of thought" (Mannheim, 1925/1971:114).   Third, in uncovering the latter we will, in the process, have identified the various intellectual strata at work at a given point in time.   It is Mannheim's view that these intellectual strata will be in conflict with one another in an effort to gain preeminence for a particular *Weltanschauung*.   Finally, there is what Mannheim considers the sociological task proper:

> finding the social strata making up the intellectual strata in question.   It is only in terms of these latter strata within the overall process, in terms of their attitudes toward the emerging new reality, that we can define the fundamental aspirations and world postulates existing at a given time which can absorb already existing ideas and methods and subject them to a change of function—not to speak of new created forms.
>
> (Mannheim, 1925/1971:114)

In other words, the basic task of the sociology of knowledge is getting at the nature of the social group that lies at the base of the intelligentsia as well as the idea systems under consideration.

As we have seen, for a variety of reasons Mannheim sees his era as being in the midst of an intellectual crisis.   It is in the context of this crisis that Mannheim deals with two of his most important ideas—ideology and utopia.   Mannheim sees them as characterizing the "final intensification of the intellectual crisis" (1929/1936:39–40).   Let us look now in some detail at what Mannheim has to say about these two idea systems.

IDEOLOGY AND UTOPIA

Mannheim's most systematic thoughts on the concepts of ideology and utopia are to be found, not surprisingly, in his best-known work, *Ideology and Utopia* (Mannheim, 1929/1936; Kettler and Meja, 1994; B. Turner, 1995).

Ideology

We have already encountered a few of Mannheim's thoughts on ideology in our discussion of the roots of the sociology of knowledge in Marx's theory of ideology.   An ideology, as well as a utopia, is a system of ideas, a *Weltanschauung*.   An *ideology* is a set of ideas which "conceals the present by attempting to comprehend it in terms of the past" (Mannheim, 1929/1936:97).   A *utopia*, in contrast, is a set of ideas which "transcends the present and is oriented to the future" (Mannheim, 1929/1936:97).   Those who use ideologies are attempting to defend the status quo by obscuring certain things about it, while those who use utopias are endeavoring to overthrow the status quo by emphasizing the advantages of an alternative social form.   Those who adopt a utopia are seeking a goal "which seems to be unrealizable only from the point of view of a given social order which is already in existence" (Mannheim, 1929/1936:196). Thus, there is always a fundamental conflict of interest between those accepting a utopia and those buying into an ideology.

In fact, it is usually the opposing group that labels a set of ideas as either an ideology or a utopia: "It is always the dominant group which is in full accord with the existing order that determines what is to be regarded as utopian, while the ascendant group which is in conflict with things as they are is the one that determines what is regarded as ideological" (Mannheim, 1929/1936:203). In this sense, "ideology" and "utopia" are labels that one group places on the ideas of an opposing group.

In order for him to be able to judge whether ideas are ideological or utopian Mannheim needs a more objective base point, and that is provided by his concept of *adequate* ideas: "Ideas which correspond to the concretely existing and *de facto* order are designated as 'adequate' and situationally congruous. These are relatively rare and only a state of mind that has been sociologically fully clarified operates with situationally congruous ideas and motives" (Mannheim, 1929/1936:194). In contrast to those ideas that are "properly" rooted in the present, there are ideas that are anchored in the past (ideologies) and in the future (utopias). It can be very difficult to judge what category a specific complex of ideas fits into, but Mannheim feels that it can be done by an external observer. But Mannheim is forced to admit, "To determine concretely, however, what in a given case is ideological and what utopian [as well as 'adequate'] is extremely difficult" (1929/1936:196).

One of the complicating factors in making this judgment is the fact that in historical reality, the two are not clearly separated from one another. For example, "The utopias of ascendant classes are often, to a large extent, permeated with ideological elements" (Mannheim, 1929/1936:203). Another is that the noise of partisan conflict serves to make it unclear which ideas are utopian and which ideological. As a result, Mannheim is forced to conclude that the only way one can really tell whether one is dealing with an ideology or with a utopia is with the hindsight of history: "Ideas which later turned out to have been only distorted representations of a past or potential social order were ideological, while those which were adequately realized in the succeeding social order were relative utopias" (Mannheim, 1929/1936:204).

Judged from the point of view of adequate ideas, *both* ideologies and utopias are distorted mental structures. One task of the sociologist of knowledge is to unmask the distortions in the two idea systems. More important, the objective is the uncovering of their social sources. Most generally, the goal of the sociologist of knowledge is to "attempt to escape ideological and utopian distortions . . . a quest for reality" (Mannheim, 1929/1936:98). Only the external observer, the socially unattached intellectual, the sociologist of knowledge, is able to discover this undistorted social reality.

Mannheim distinguishes between the particular and the total conception of ideology. *Particular* ideologies refer to the ideas of our opponents and are typically seen as conscious distortions. *Total* ideologies are the ideas of a concrete sociohistorical group, or even of an entire age or epoch, and are not typically viewed as involving conscious distortions. Mannheim draws three other distinctions between particular and total ideologies. First, in the case of a particular ideology, only a portion of an opponent's idea system is considered ideological, while in a total ideology an opponent's entire *Weltan-schauung* is thought to be ideological. Second, in the case of a particular ideology, opposing groups continue to share some ideas, such as the basic standards of validity. In contrast, the total ideologies of opposing groups differ on everything; they are "fundamentally divergent thought-systems" (Mannheim, 1929/1936:57). Third, the study of particular ideologies involves a psychological analysis of the interests of those involved with the idea system. The study of total ideologies involves a functional (or sociological) analysis in which there is a study of the "correspondence between a given social situation and a given perspective" (Mannheim, 1929/1936:58). Thus, a particular ideology is in line with the way Marxists use the term ideology, whereas total ideology reflects the orientation of the sociology of knowledge.[7]

The Marxists, of course, used the idea of ideology to critique and discredit the views of the capitalists. However, as Weber pointed out, those same tools can be used to analyze Marxian thinking: " 'The materialist conception of history is not to be compared to a cab that one can enter or alight from at will, for once they enter it, even revolutionaries themselves are not free to leave it' " (Weber, cited in Mannheim, 1929/1936:74). Or, in Mannheim's terms, "Nothing was to prevent the opponents of Marxism from availing themselves of the weapon and applying it to Marxism itself" (Mannheim, 1929/1936:75). Ultimately, of course, everyone could use the total conception of ideology and apply it to any and all idea systems. Crucial in Mannheim's eyes is the willingness and the ability to apply the total conception of ideology not only to other idea systems, but to one's own idea system as well.

Utopia

While Mannheim's thinking on ideology is deeply tied to its Marxian roots, he is more original in his thinking on utopia, as well as on its relationship to ideology. A utopia, like an ideology, is incongruous with reality. However, what distinguishes a utopia is the fact that it not only "transcends reality," but also "breaks the bond of the existing reality" (Mannheim, 1929/1936:192). Although utopias are revolutionary *ideas,* they can affect action which will "tend to shatter either partially or wholly, the order of things prevailing at the time" (Mannheim, 1929/1936:192).

Mannheim has a dialectical view of utopias (and most other things). An existing order tends to give birth to a series of "unrealized and unfulfilled tendencies which represent the needs of each age" (Mannheim, 1929/1936:199). That is, dialectically, a given social order has within it the seeds of its own destruction. Mannheim sees these ideas as "explosive material" capable of overturning the extant order. When these revolutionary ideas are transformed into action, they are capable of breaking "the bonds of the existing order, leaving it free to develop in the direction of the next order of existence" (Mannheim, 1929/1936:199). When that "next" order of existence comes into being, the stage is presumably set for the process to begin again with the rise of the next set of utopian ideas.

---

[7]However, Mannheim (1929/1936:74) does give Marxian theory credit for discovering the total conception of ideology and fusing it with the psychological (particular) approach.

Of course, all utopian ideas must overcome the opposition of countervailing ideologies. Ideologies serve to protect the existing social order, while utopias perform "the function of bursting the bonds of the existing order" (Mannheim, 1929/1936:206). The group espousing a utopia may, in fact, achieve power and come to be the dominant group within society. In that case, the utopian mentality can reach its end point; that is, it becomes "completely infused into every aspect of the dominating mentality of the time" (Mannheim, 1929/1936:209). However, since the group carrying the idea has come into power, the utopia is gradually transformed into an ideology which sooner or later gives birth to one or more counter-utopias.

Where does a utopia come from? Mannheim makes it clear that a utopia can emerge from a single individual: "It happens very often that the dominant utopia first arises as the wish-fantasy of a single individual and does not until later become imported into the political aims of a more inclusive group" (Mannheim, 1929/1936:209). Following Weber, Mannheim sees such an individual as "charismatic." However, the utopian ideas of the charismatic individual must, in order to survive and succeed, be in touch with the collective problems of the day and be linked in various ways with some group. For one thing, the ideas of the individual must be in accord with the collective impulse of a larger group. In other words, the individual must be giving expression to sentiments that are already present as currents within a collectivity. For another, more important thing, in order for the utopia to be effective in tearing asunder the existing order, the ideas must be taken up by some group and translated by it into action. In other words, individuals are not capable of social revolution; only a group can bring about such a revolution. While, as we saw above, many groups can espouse utopias and bring about social revolutions, in the last resort social classes are the most important of these groups. In spite of the centrality of social classes, we should not lose sight of the fact that utopias can be produced by other social groups. As Mannheim puts it, "the key to the intelligibility of utopias is the structural situation of the social stratum which at any given time espouses them" (1929/1936:208).

Mannheim identifies four historical ideal types of utopias. The first is *orgiastic chiliasm*.[8] Chiliasts tend to be irrational, unreflective, ecstatic-orgiastic, and like all utopians, oriented to transcending the existing world. The carriers of this utopia were members of the lowest strata within society. The second type is the *liberal-humanitarian* utopia carried by the middle strata of bourgeoisie and intellectuals. The utopian image here is of a more rational future toward which we are gradually moving. Third is the *conservative* utopia (discussed later in this chapter) that develops in reaction to the liberal-humanistic and chiliastic utopias. The utopian goal here is a world in which everything that does exist continues to exist. Great value is placed on things that are derived from the past and that continue to exist in the present. Conservative utopian ideas tend to be carried by those groups that have made it in society and are interested in protecting their position. Finally, there is the *socialist-communist* utopia. The goal of this type is the overthrow of the present society and the creation of a classless society. The carrier is the proletariat, or other ascendant social groups.

When he looks at the contemporary world, Mannheim tends to see the demise of utopias, and he seems to regret their disappearance greatly. Why do utopias tend to

---

[8]This type of utopia is usually associated with the Anabaptists, a religious sect.

disappear? For one thing, as we have seen, when a group espousing a utopia moves into established positions, it tends to adapt its ideas to the existing reality. A second factor is the warfare among utopias and the fact that "different coexistent forms of utopian mentality are destroying one another in reciprocal conflict" (Mannheim, 1929/1936:250). Finally, out of this conflict of utopias, and the propensity toward critical examination of one another's idea systems, is the more general tendency toward critical analysis of the historical and social roots of all ideas, including utopian ideas.

The result of all this is that our earlier utopias have come to be nothing more than a number of different points of view. We are left with a series of atomistic viewpoints; we are left without a comprehensive view of the world. To put it another way, with the demise of utopias comes the disappearance of total points of view.

Disenchantment   Mannheim goes further and, in another viewpoint that resembles Weberian theory, tends to see a progressive disenchantment of the world. In this case, we are seeing the disappearance of *both* utopias *and* ideologies; we are moving toward a world in which "all ideas have been discredited and all utopias have been destroyed" (Mannheim, 1929/1936:256). In an excellent description of the disenchantment of the world, Mannheim describes the movement toward the "complete destruction of all spiritual elements, the utopian as well as the ideological . . . emergence of a 'matter of factness' . . . in sexual life, art, and architecture, and the expression of the natural impulses in sports" (Mannheim, 1929/1936:256).

In spite of this progressive disenchantment of the world, Mannheim argues that this disenchantment is to be regretted because people need utopias (and ideologies). As Mannheim puts it,

> It is possible, therefore, that in the future, in a world in which there is never anything new, in which all is finished and each moment is a repetition of the past, there can exist a condition in which thought will be utterly devoid of all ideological and utopian elements. But the complete elimination of reality-transcending elements from our world would lead us to a "matter-of-factness" which ultimately would mean the decay of the human will.
>
> (Mannheim, 1929/1936:262)

Yet, while Mannheim regrets the progressive disappearance of both ideologies and utopias, it is the demise of the latter which is the far greater problem. The reason is that while the death of an ideology would pose a crisis for the social strata espousing it, the disappearance of utopias would have a profoundly negative effect on human nature and human development as a whole:

> The disappearance of utopia brings about a static state of affairs in which man himself becomes no more than a thing. We would be faced then with the greatest paradox imaginable, namely that man, who has achieved the highest degree of rational mastery of existence, left without any ideals, becomes a mere creature of impulses. Thus, after a long tortuous, but heroic development, just at the highest stage of awareness, when history is ceasing to be blind fate, and is becoming more and more man's own creation, with the relinquishment of utopias, man would lose his will to shape history and therewith his ability to understand it.
>
> (Mannheim, 1929/1936:262–263)

Hope for the Future   The hope for the future lies in the fact that there are still two groups that are capable of instilling the world with tension. First, there are the "strata whose aspirations are not yet fulfilled" and the fact that they "will always cause the counter-utopias to rekindle and flare up again" (Mannheim, 1929/1936:257). Mannheim associates the strata whose aspirations are unfulfilled with the proletariat and its communist utopia, and the major counter-utopia with conservatism. However, when looked at from the vantage point of the world of the twenty-first century, while there are certainly still strata whose aspirations remain unfulfilled, there is little or no faith in communism or socialism as viable alternatives to the extant system. It seems clear that the strata are still there, but at the moment they are lacking a utopian vision.

The other group that offers some hope as far as Mannheim is concerned is his favored "socially unattached intellectuals." This group of intellectuals, which has always existed to some degree, is seen by Mannheim as expanding. They are being drawn from all strata of society, not just the privileged classes; are increasingly separated from the rest of society; and are increasingly dependent on their own resources. Four alternatives are open to such intellectuals. First, they can affiliate themselves with radical socialists and communists. Second, they can become skeptics dedicated to the elimination of all ideology. Third, they can orient themselves romantically to the past and attempt to "revive religious feeling, idealism, symbols, and myths" (Mannheim, 1929/1936:259). Finally, they can renounce the world, as well as any interest in radical politics. However, in choosing the latter alternative, intellectuals become part of the problem rather than a potential solution, since they then come to "take part in the great historical process of disillusionment" (Mannheim, 1929/1936:259–260). It seems clear that Mannheim prefers the second alternative as the course to be taken by the intelligentsia.

CONSERVATISM

Another set of ideas studied by Mannheim (1953/1971) is conservative thought. In fact, he describes his essay on conservatism as an experiment utilizing the "recently developed sociology of knowledge" (Mannheim, 1953/1971:132). This long and complex essay offers much more than can be dealt with here, but we will endeavor to cover a few highlights that offer further insight into the ways in which Mannheim utilized his sociology of knowledge.

Mannheim is specifically interested in the development of conservative thinking in Germany in the first half of the nineteenth century. Conservatism arose in Germany in response to the French Revolution. However, whereas in France the revolution led primarily to action, in Germany the counterreaction led mainly to changes in thought, especially the rise of conservative thought. To Mannheim, Germany was too socially backward at the time to react politically to the French Revolution. However, at the same time Germany was a "culturally mature society" (Mannheim, 1953/1971:132). As a result, the revolution induced a cultural, specifically an intellectual, response among the Germans. Thus, Mannheim links the nature of a nation's action to its larger social structure. The socially advanced French undertook a social revolution, while the culturally advanced Germans responded with an intellectual revolution.

In addition to demonstrating the relationship between knowledge and social structure, German conservatism was a useful test case of Mannheim's sociology of knowledge for two reasons: it remained purely intellectual, and it was taken to its logical extreme. Here is the way Mannheim puts it:

> Under the ideological pressure of the French Revolution there developed in Germany an intellectual counter-movement which retained its purely intellectual character over a long period and was thus able to develop its logical premises to the fullest possible extent. It was "thought through" to the end.
>
> (Mannheim, 1953/1971:140)

One of the key themes in Mannheim's sociology of knowledge is that ideas emerge out of confrontation with other idea systems. This theme is certainly explicit in the preceding discussion of the relationship between ideology and utopia. In this case, Mannheim argues that "conservative thought emerged as an independent current when it was forced into conscious opposition to bourgeois-revolutionary thought" (Mannheim, 1953/1971:140). Neither thought system, indeed no thought system, emerges "ready-made." Rather, these thought systems are involved in a continuous and reciprocal process of development. Changes in one lead to adaptations in the other and so they go round and round in a continual process of mutual adaptation and refinement.

Furthermore, the competition among idea systems is rooted in the competition between various social groups for social power. Among the things that each group wants is to have its interpretation of the world be accepted as the universal interpretation of that world (Mannheim, 1952/1971b). Mannheim, therefore, emphasizes competition between ideas as well as between the groups that stand behind those ideas. In fact, even more generally, to Mannheim "competition lies at the heart of human associative life" (Longhurst, 1988:33).

Let us look at a few aspects of the bourgeois-rational thought that stood behind the French Revolution, as well as the oppositional idea developed by the German conservatives. First, the bourgeois rationalists emphasized thinking and the role of reason in social life, while the conservatives emphasized the importance of being over thinking. Second, in contrast to the bourgeois rationalist idea that the social world operated in a rational manner, the conservatives emphasized the essentially irrational character of the social world. Third, against the claims of the bourgeois rationalists that certain ideas and principles were of universal validity, the conservatives emphasized the individuality and distinctiveness of each case. Relatedly, while the liberal-bourgeois thinker saw all political and social innovations as universally applicable, the conservative thinker emphasized the idea that each society was a distinctive social organism and that innovations developed in one society could not simply be transplanted into another society. There are other differences between the two modes of thinking, but the ones mentioned here illustrate the differences between, and the oppositional and relational character of, these two idea systems.

Another central issue in Mannheim's sociology of knowledge is the carrier of conservatism within German society in the early nineteenth century. Mannheim concluded that it was mainly the nobility that became the carrier of conservatism in that time and place. The nobility wished to rule the state from below, but it was opposed by the monarchy and the bureaucrats who sought to control the state from above. The nobility adopted the conservative view of society as an organic entity and, in a typically conservative approach, sought a return to the corporate structure of medieval society, in which the nobility had wielded far more power. The nobility also adopted a romantic point of view, meaning that, among other things, they approved the irrational. Interestingly, in spite of its conservative ideas, the nobility was the revolutionary force in the nineteenth-century German context, and it was opposed by the bureaucracy and monarchy operating with at least some of the ideas of the bourgeois-rational orientation. This example serves to illustrate quite well the basic position of the sociology of knowledge on the importance of examining ideas (and their carriers) in particular sociohistorical contexts.

RATIONALITY AND THE IRRATIONALITY OF THE TIMES

Mannheim, very much influenced by the work of Weber (and Simmel), developed a theory of rationality which, among other things, allowed him to deal with many of the problems of his day under the heading of irrationality. In *Ideology and Utopia* (1929/1936), Mannheim offered a gross differentiation between rationality and irrationality which he refined later in his work. In that early work, the *rational* sphere of society was defined as "consisting of settled and routinized procedures in dealing with situations that recur in an orderly fashion" (Mannheim, 1929/1936:113). The *irrational* sphere was defined residually, although Mannheim made it clear that it continued to be more prevalent than the rational sectors of society: "Rationalized as our life may seem to have become, all the rationalizations that have taken place so far are merely partial since the most important realms of our social life are even now anchored in the irrational" (1929/1936:115). The economy, for example, was still dominated by irrational free competition rather than having become a more rational planned economy. Similarly, in the stratification system, one's place was still determined by competition and struggle, not by objective tests that decided one's position within that system. And in politics, planning had not yet been able to eliminate the struggle for dominance at the national and international levels.

While the irrational continues to predominate, Mannheim seems to imply that rationalization is a process that has invaded various sectors of society and that others are likely to come under its sway in the future. In other words, the irrational is likely to retreat in the face of the forward march of the rational. As Mannheim puts it, "The chief characteristic of modern culture is the tendency to include as much as possible in the realm of the rational and to bring it under administrative control—and, on the other hand, to reduce the 'irrational' element to the vanishing point" (1929/1936:114).

Mannheim was forced to back away from this optimistic view in his later work in the face of the increasing prevalence of such irrationalities as economic depression, war, fascism, and so on. It became increasingly hard in Mannheim's day to argue that irrationalities were in the process of disappearing. If anything, the opposite seemed to be the case. As we will see, Mannheim came to feel that rationality could not be left to advance on its own but had to be helped along through planning. Furthermore, as he came to refine his sense of rationality, he came to see that the forward march of at least one type of rationality may in fact be a major *cause* of at least some of these irrationalities (more on this shortly).

Rationalization, for Mannheim, involves behavior that is in accord with some rational structure or framework. Rational actors follow definite prescriptions "entailing no personal decision whatsoever" (Mannheim, 1929/1936:115). The image is of the actor following the dictates of some larger bureaucratically organized structure, and this image is supported by the examples offered by Mannheim—petty officials, judges, factory workers, and so on. Rational action is contrasted to *conduct,* which begins "where rationalization has not yet penetrated, and where we are forced to make decisions in situations which have *as yet* not been subjected to regulation" (Mannheim, 1929/1936: 115; italics added). In this early work, conduct is clearly associated with the irrational realm. It is also clear that Mannheim holds the view that conduct, like irrationality more generally, will sooner or later come to be limited or even eliminated by the process of rationalization.

Mannheim is ambivalent on this process of rationalization. On the one hand, he clearly favors the progressive rationalization of sectors that have heretofore been dominated by the irrational. Since they will come to be controlled by administrative dictates, irrational decisions and actions will be reduced or eliminated. On the other hand, Mannheim cannot really want a world in which all decisions are controlled—in which there is no personal decision making, no personal freedom, whatsoever. We will return to this issue when we discuss Mannheim's view on planning, but before we do we need to discuss his later and more sophisticated delineation of the difference between the rational and the irrational.

Types of Rationality and Irrationality

Mannheim had much more to say about rationality and irrationality in one of the essays included in *Man and Society in an Age of Reconstruction* (1935/1940). Here he argues that both rationality and irrationality can be subdivided into the substantial and the functional. Substantial rationality and irrationality deal with *thinking,* while functional rationality and irrationality are concerned with *action. Substantial rationality,* then, is defined as "an act of thought which reveals intelligent insight into the inter-relations of events in a given situation" (Mannheim, 1935/1940:53). Adopting once again a residual notion of irrationality, Mannheim defines *substantial irrationality* as "everything else which either is false or not an act of thought at all (as for example drives, impulses, wishes and feelings, both conscious and unconscious)" (Mannheim, 1935/1940:53). This clearly is a very different sense of the distinction between rational and irrational, since previously Mannheim had associated rationality with the lack of thought, while here substantial irrationality involves a lack of thought. However, previously the lack of thought had been associated with administrative control, while in the case of substantial irrationality it is linked to drives, impulses, wishes, and feelings.

Mannheim comes closer to his earlier sense of rationality in his definition of *functional rationality* as "a series of actions . . . organized in such a way that it leads to a previously defined goal, every element in this series of actions receiving a functional position and role" (Mannheim, 1935/1940:53). The series of actions is functionally rational in that each has a role to play in the achievement of the ultimate goal, although the goal itself can be either rational or irrational. Thus, for example, salvation is defined as an irrational goal, but it can be sought through a series of functionally rational actions.

Mannheim's concept of functional rationality has much in common with Weber's sense of formal rationality. For example, efficiency is a central characteristic of rationality from Weber's point of view, and Mannheim argues that a "functional organization of a series of actions will, moreover, be at its best when, in order to attain the given goal, it coordinates the means most efficiently" (1935/1940:53).

Interestingly, to Mannheim functional and substantive rationality may be substitutes for, or even in conflict with, one another. For example, a soldier may act in accord with the functional organization of the military without thinking through his or her action. In fact, a functional organization like the military often wants its members to act in accord with its dictates and *not* to think things through on their own.

Finally, *functional irrationality* is defined, once again residually, as "everything which breaks through and disrupts functional ordering" (Mannheim, 1935/1940:54). Violence committed by unruly individuals is an example of functional irrationality. The functionally rational actions of those in one organization can also be functionally irrational from the point of view of those in another organization. For example, when state officials raise taxes on corporations, those taxes may be seen as functionally irrational from the perspective of those in such businesses. Thus, " 'functional irrationality' never characterizes an act itself but only with reference to its position in the entire complex of conduct of which it is part" (Mannheim, 1935/1940:55).

Weber was most interested in the spread of formal rationality in the West, and Mannheim has a similar level of concern for, and offers a similar hypothesis about, the spread of functional rationality:

> The more industrialized a society is and the more advanced its division of labour and organization, the greater will be the number of spheres of human activity which will be functionally rational and hence also calculable in advance. Whereas the individual in earlier societies acted only occasionally and in limited spheres in a functionally rational manner, in contemporary society he is *compelled* to act in this way in more and more spheres of life.
>
> (Mannheim, 1935/1940:55; italics added)

Mannheim goes beyond functional rationalization to posit the intimately related phenomenon of *self-rationalization,* or "the individual's systematic control of his impulses" (Mannheim, 1935/1940:55). In fact, self-rationalization is sometimes described as a type of functional rationalization, and in any case the two are closely linked—"the functional rationalization of objective activities ultimately evokes self-rationalization" (Mannheim, 1935/1940:56). There is a high level of rationalization when functional rationalization and self-rationalization occur together. This situation is most likely to arise in the administrative staff of large organizations. Here the external control of the organization's rules and regulations is supplemented by self-rationalization, especially in the case of staff members and their careers. In Mannheim's words, the career prescribes "not only the actual processes of work but also the prescriptive regulation both of the ideas and feelings one is permitted to have and of one's leisure time" (1935/1940:56). Thus, self-regulation exerts control over matters (ideas, feelings, leisure time) that functional rationalization cannot reach.

However, self-rationalization is *not* the highest and most extreme form of rational-ization. That honor goes to what Mannheim calls *self-observation.* Self-rationalization involves a

> process of mental training, subordinating my inner motives to an external aim. Self-observation, on the other hand, is more than such form of mental training. Self-observation aims primarily at inner *self-transformation.* Man reflects about himself and his actions mostly for the sake of remoulding or transforming himself more radically.
>
> (Mannheim, 1935/1940:57)

Mannheim thus seems to envision a hierarchy running from substantial rationaliza-tion to functional rationalization, self-rationalization, and ultimately self-observation. Although in the earlier stages of modernity society may have been able to rely on func-tional rationalization, more complex and rapidly changing modern societies require self-rationalization and especially self-observation, which control people better and more efficiently and enable them to adapt more readily to complex new situations.

Returning to his central concepts, Mannheim argues that industrialization has led to an increase in functional rationalization, but not necessarily substantial rationalization. In fact, Mannheim goes further by arguing that functional rationalization has tended to "paralyze" substantial rationalization by leaving people less and less room to utilize their independent judgment. This idea seems to be Mannheim's version of Weber's ir-rationality of rationality. That is, the irrational consequence of the spread of functional rationality is the decline of substantial rationality. Here Mannheim differentiates be-tween those at the top of the organization and those below them. Those at the top tend to retain substantial rationality, while the substantial rationality of those below them de-clines as the responsibility for decision making is turned over to those at the top. This process has disastrous consequences for a person who does not occupy a high-level, decision-making position:

> He becomes increasingly accustomed to being led by others and gradually gives up his own interpretation of events for those others give him. When the rationalized mechanism of social life collapses in terms of crisis, the individual cannot repair it by his own insight. Instead his own impotence reduces him to a state of terrified helplessness.
>
> (Mannheim, 1935/1940:59)

Another irrationality of rationality stems from the fact that because of industrializa-tion, great masses of people are crowded together in large cities. In other words, indus-trialization brings with it the creation of what has come to be called "mass society." Thus, paradoxically, as large-scale industrial society produces increases in functional rationality, self-rationalization, and self-observation, it also creates the conditions in mass society for irrational threats to that rational system:

> It produces all the irrationalities and emotional outbreaks which are characteristic of amorphous human agglomerations. As an industrial society, it so refines the social mech-anism that the slightest irrational disturbance can have the most far-reaching effects, and as a mass society it favors a great number of irrational impulses and suggestions and pro-duces an accumulation of unsublimated psychic energies which, at every moment, threat-ens to smash the whole subtle machinery of social life.
>
> (Mannheim, 1935/1940:61)

While Mannheim retains the view that irrationality is not always a problem, in the modern world irrationalities are finding their way into places where rational planning and control are indispensable.

Thus, in Mannheim's view the basic sources of the irrational in modern life are the *same* as the sources of the formally rational. In other words, Mannheim has offered a *sociological,* not a psychological, theory of the origins of both rationality and irrationality. He sees the sources of *both* as being built into the structure of modern society:

> They are driven, now in one direction, now in another by the dual nature of the social structure that certain human beings are now calculating creatures who work out their actions to the very last detail, and now volcanic ones who think it right that at a given time they should reveal the worst depths of human brutality and sadism.
>
> (Mannheim, 1935/1940:66)

There is another dialectical aspect to Mannheim's thinking. That is, increasing formal rationality leads not only to an increase in certain irrationalities, but also to the beginning of a rational sense that *planning* is needed to deal with these problems; not just piecemeal planning, but rather planning at the level of the whole of society. The rationalization of society, as well as its growing irrationality, has made planning inevitable, but the issue is: Who will do that planning? Those who represent narrow interest groups? Or those who have the interests of society as a whole in mind? Clearly, Mannheim prefers that the latter do the planning, and they are either sociologists, or they have the kind of totalistic perspective that only sociology can offer.

PLANNING AND SOCIAL RECONSTRUCTION IN THE MODERN WORLD

Mannheim has used his theory of rationality to describe the modern world, the source of its major problems, and the hope for solving those problems. Mannheim grew increasingly interested in *applying* his theory of rationality, and more generally his sociology of knowledge, to the modern world: "The theory that thought is socially conditioned and changes at different periods in history is only instructive, if its implications are fully realized and applied to our age" (Mannheim, 1935/1940:366). Specifically, Mannheim wants to use his sociology of knowledge to produce an "intelligently planned society" (1935/1940:349; Jenkins, 1996). His view is that planning does not necessarily pose a threat to democracy; democracy and planning are compatible. In fact, one way of articulating his goal is as the "control of control" (Mannheim, 1935/1940:326). In other words, Mannheim wants to develop a planned society in which the control exercised over people is controlled.

Thus we arrive at one of the central problems (to Mannheim) in the modern world—the unrestrained control over people exercised in his time by totalitarian regimes such as the Nazis. In fact, Mannheim takes the Nazis and other totalitarian developments of his day as evidence of the failure of the general theory of increasing rationality articulated in his earlier work:

Philosophers and sociologists once thought that there was a tendency towards rational and moral progress inherent in the human mind. That this is untrue is clear to everyone who knows what is happening in the contemporary world, for it can be asserted with confidence that in the last decades we have receded rather than advanced as far as moral and rational progress is concerned.

(Mannheim, 1935/1940:51)

Mannheim viewed the rise of Nazism with alarm and was concerned, at least before the start of World War II, with how the development of such a totalitarian system could be prevented in England. In order to prevent such an occurrence, planning was inevitable, but it had to be democratic, not dictatorial, planning.

While Mannheim wanted to avoid the possibility of totalitarianism, he also felt that a totally laissez-faire system did not represent a viable alternative in the modern world. A laissez-faire system could lead only to chaos in modern, large-scale society. In fact, the other major social problem of Mannheim's day, the economic depression that was ravaging much of the world at that time, was due, at least in part, to the fact that there had been little or no economic planning—that laissez-faire economics had been allowed to run rampant. Thus, Mannheim argues that there is "no longer any choice between planning and laisser-faire, but only between good planning and bad" (1935/1940:6). Thus, Mannheim offered a society based on "democratic planning" as a "third way," as an alternative to totalitarianism and laissez-faire systems. It was clear that the planning offered by totalitarianism was bad planning. What, then, represented "good planning"?

To Mannheim, sound planning "means a conscious attack on the sources of maladjustment in the social order on the basis of a thorough knowledge of the whole mechanism of society and the way in which it works" (1935/1940:114). Thus, planning would require a thorough sociological analysis of the workings of society. Such analysis requires totalistic, interdependent thinking, but most fields, including sociology, are dominated by partial thinking, as is reflected by things like the specialization of subject matter and methodology. Sociologists need to lead the way in the direction of a more interdependent mode of thinking. Mannheim concludes, "Planned thinking rests primarily on the new capacity for perceiving interdependent connections in a social structure" (1935/1940:228).

While society cannot be left to its own devices, it cannot be completely controlled either. For example, it should not suppress criticism: "A complete suppression of criticism can have only negative results" (Mannheim, 1935/1940:109). Society must also be wary of exercising so much control that it becomes static—that it loses its dynamism. Similarly, planning needs to create an institutional sphere which permits free creative activity. As Mannheim puts it, "Planning in this sense means planning for freedom" (1935/1940:264). Thus we return to Mannheim's thoughts on the "charms" of the irrational (such as creativity). While Mannheim wants to develop rational control over the irrational, he does not want to "rob it of its peculiar charm" (1935/1940:267).

The fascists sought to control society, but they did it in far too heavy-handed a way. Furthermore, they fiddled with one part of society without having the slightest sense of how such changes would affect other parts of society. Thus, Mannheim feels that democratic planning based on sociological insight into the interdependent nature of society would have many advantages over fascistic planning. In Mannheim's words, democratic planning would exhibit a "finer mastery of the social keyboard" (1935/1940:267). It would be a far more subtle means of planning social life. While Mannheim believes that planning and democracy are compatible, he recognizes that we would have to surrender some freedom in a planned society. However, "it seems to be greater slavery to be able to do as we like in an unjust or badly organized society, than to accept the claims of planning in a healthy society, which we ourselves have chosen" (Mannheim, 1935/1940:377).

Planning is made more necessary by various social changes which have made society more vulnerable to irrational outbursts. One such change is the increasing democratization of society and culture which, among other things, has stirred groups that were formerly passive. Democratization has not only served to bring irrationality to a broader area of society, but it has also made for more sudden and abrupt social disruptions. For example, Mannheim argues that democratization has brought with it "uninhibited expression of momentary emotional impulses" and "national self-assertion and aggressiveness" (1956/1971:273). Another relevant social change is the growing interpenetration of individual actions. The result is that irrationalities that start in a limited sector of society quickly reverberate throughout society.

The result is that Mannheim grew very concerned about the plight of the society of his day and where it was headed. On the one hand, he was worried about the rise of Nazism, the threat of war, and the depression—the "earthquakes which we are all experiencing today" (Mannheim, 1935/1940:79). On the other, he was worried about the broader "disintegration of culture" (Mannheim, 1935/1940:79).

Later, Mannheim (1943, 1950:305) began to argue more explicitly that the crisis of his day was a crisis of values resulting, at least in part, from the clash of a wide array of value systems in the modern world. Without a clear and widely shared set of values, society was suffering from a spiritual crisis, and it needed a spiritual regeneration to deal with it. According to Gerth and Bramstedt, "Mannheim assigns to religion, freed from authoritarian and superstitious admixtures, the task of an ultimate integration of all human activities" (1950:xiv). He began to explore the role that Christian spirituality could play in resolving that crisis. Historically, the Catholic Church had provided the best example of dealing with such a crisis through a type of planning that allowed for individuality. Mannheim was not espousing, as Comte had, that society should be organized along the lines of the Catholic Church. But he was arguing that in dealing with the crisis of the day people could learn from the successes and failures of the church.

Mannheim did not create a grandiose plan for the restructuring and control of society as a whole. Rather, his thoughts on planning are far more humble and limited. Nor did Mannheim offer a complete blueprint of the society that was to emerge from all of this planning. As he put it, he was not offering "a detailed program for the administrator"; rather, his goal was to "convey the general vision of the kind of society we want to build" (Mannheim, 1950:xvii). Most generally, "real planning consists in co-ordination of institutions, education, valuations and psychology" (Mannheim, 1950:xviii). Somewhat more specific is Mannheim's (1950:29) description of his special kind of planning, which must involve:

1 *"planning for freedom,* subjected to democratic control"

2 *"planning, but not restrictionist* so as to favor group monopolies either of entrepreneurs or workers' associations, but 'planning for plenty,' i.e., full employment and
full exploitation of resources"

3 *"planning for social justice* rather than absolute equality, with differentiation of rewards and status on the basis of genuine equality rather than privilege"

4 *"planning not for a classless society* but for one that abolishes the extremes of
wealth and poverty"

5 *"planning for cultural standards* without 'leveling down'—a planned transition
making for progress without discarding what is valuable in tradition"

6 *"planning that counteracts the dangers of a mass society* by co-ordination of the
means of social control but interfering only in cases of institutional or moral deteriora-
tion defined by collective criteria"

7 *"planning for balance* between centralization and dispersion of power"

8 *"planning* for gradual transformation of a society *in order to encourage the growth
of personality"*

9 "in short, *planning but not regimentation"*

Mannheim placed great importance on education as a way of coping with the cultural
crisis. However, the education of his day suffered from the problem of specialization
and compartmentalization that plagued intellectual life in general. Thus, as with knowledge in general, Mannheim (1944/1971) made the case for more integrated education.
For one thing, he wanted to see an end to the separation between education and the rest
of life. For another, he wanted to end the overspecialization of educational subjects.
Mannheim also felt that education should not be restricted to childhood, but should go
on throughout life.

Mannheim felt that both teachers and students must become knowledgeable about
sociology, because only sociology offers the comprehensive perspective needed to overcome narrow specialization (Mannheim and Stewart, 1962). Mannheim argues that to
be effective, teachers must know the social world from which pupils come and for
which they are to be prepared. In order to prepare students better, schools and universities are urged to "introduce sociology as a basic science" (Mannheim, 1953b:208). For
both students and teachers, a fundamental problem was a lack of "social awareness," an
awareness which is necessary if democracy is to survive. That "lack of awareness on
social affairs . . . is nothing but the lack of a comprehensive sociological orientation"
(Mannheim, 1944/1971:374).

An integrative educational system would lead to more integrative behavior, which
Mannheim saw as "the archetype of democratic behavior" (1950:200). Integrative
behavior involves an unwillingness to impose one's views on others, but tolerance and
willingness to absorb the views of others into one's own world view. Integrative
behavior involves being amenable to change, to compromise, and to cooperation in a
common way of life. In other words, it is a prerequisite to the kind of democratic society Mannheim was intent on seeing constructed.

A CRITICAL ANALYSIS OF MANNHEIM'S WORK

Mannheim's reputation is based on the fact that he is credited with inventing a subfield of sociology that remains viable to this day. However, much of the work that he did under that heading has come under severe attack (Meja and Stehr, 1990). While, as we will see, there is much of merit in those critiques, the critiques also have often been too harsh and have ignored a number of Mannheim's more specific contributions. For example, although it is derived from the work of Simmel and Weber, Mannheim's theory of rationality is in many ways clearer than those of Simmel and Weber, and it is more clearly linked to his diagnosis of the problems—the irrationalities—of his day. This being said, there are a number of important criticisms of Mannheim's approach that must be dealt with here.

Merton (1941/1957) got to the heart of the matter with two devastating criticisms of Mannheim's work. The first is that in a body of work designed to create and legitimize the sociology of *knowledge,* Mannheim never offered a clear-cut definition of what he meant by knowledge. As Merton put it, "Knowledge is at times regarded so broadly as to include every type of assertion and every mode of thought from folkloristic maxims to rigorous positive science" (1941/1957:497). Among those things dealt with as knowledge in Mannheim's work are "ethical convictions, epistemological postulates, material predications, synthetic judgments, political beliefs, the categories of thought, eschatological doxies, moral norms, ontological assumptions and observations of empirical fact" (Merton, 1941/1957:497).

Along the same lines, Mannheim sometimes uses other terms to describe his field of concern. For example, he sometimes writes about the "sociology of the mind," defined as the "study of mental functions in the context of action" (Mannheim, 1953). The mind and knowledge are hardly coterminous. We can conceive of the mind in a micro sense as belonging to an individual actor or in a macro sense as a collective mind. In either case, the mind is a process, and one of the results of that process is the creation of knowledge. Further complicating matters, at other times Mannheim writes about the sociology of thought and the sociology of cognition as if they were coterminous with the sociology of knowledge (and mind).

Unclear about knowledge, Mannheim was also obscure on the *relationship* between knowledge and society. According to Merton, Mannheim is guilty of a "failure to specify the *type* or *mode* of relations between social structure and knowledge" (1941/1957: 498). Merton reviews Mannheim's work on this relationship and finds in it arguments that knowledge is *in accord with* industrial society or with the time, that social structures are the *causal determinants* of ideological errors, that ideas are *bound up with* a given social setting, that ideas *grow out of* such a setting, that ideas change *in harmony with* social changes, that changes in ideas are *closely connected* to structural realities, that ideas change *in close conjunction with* social forces, and so on. The point is that a wide range of relationships between knowledge and society are discussed in Mannheim's work. He does not clearly differentiate one from the others, nor does he show how all of these diverse relationships might be combined under a single broad heading.

Because of its vagueness about what knowledge is and its ambiguity about the relationship between knowledge and society, Mannheim's sociology of knowledge is, not surprisingly, riddled with gaping holes. Given these holes, one wonders why the sociology of knowledge caught on as it did, why it has had staying power, and why Mannheim occupies such a dominant place in the history of that subfield. Part of the answer lies, perhaps, in Thomas Kuhn's (1962, 1970) notion of a paradigm (see the Appendix). To Kuhn, a successful new paradigm must *both* offer a new way of looking at the world *and* leave open many questions to be answered by those who were later to become attracted to working on the paradigm. Mannheim's sociology of knowledge fits the paradigm concept very well, at least in these senses of the term. It *did* offer an attractive new way of looking at a part of the social world (knowledge), and it certainly left open many issues for those who were to follow in Mannheim's footsteps.

Merton offers another criticism, one that most analysts of Mannheim's work make. This criticism is that, in spite of a number of different efforts, Mannheim never did solve the problem of relativism (Goldman, 1994). It does appear that a consequence of Mannheim's approach is that it is impossible to believe in anything fully, including Mannheim's own views, since all ideas emanate from inherently limited positions in society.

Mannheim's later, more political work, is even easier to criticize. In that work, Mannheim was writing for a more general audience, not other academics, as had been the case in his earlier writings in Hungary and Germany. The result is a considerable discontinuity in the two bodies of work.[9] Much of the earlier work is dense, at times impenetrable, while the later work is much easier to read. The problem is that after reading it, one is left feeling that there is not much of substance there. The later work contains relatively little sociology, and the sociology that is there yields relatively few striking insights.

The later work also suffers from being timely. This seems like a strange problem, since sociologists, especially sociological theorists, are generally criticized for doing work that is irrelevant to the concerns of the day. (Indeed, much of Mannheim's early work has this character.) In his later work, Mannheim was struggling with the problems of his day and was trying to offer timely solutions to those problems. Thus, for example, Mannheim was struggling with the threat posed by fascism, especially Nazism. While certainly a problem for England in the late 1930s and early 1940s, fascism in general and Nazism in particular inspire little fear these days. More generally, Mannheim often described cataclysmic threats to society, threats that would destroy society unless there was a dramatic response of the type he described. However, from today's vantage point, the threats described by Mannheim did not pose anywhere near the danger he forecast. Furthermore, society did not implement his suggestions, and it does not seem to have suffered for it. Read from today's vantage point, Mannheim's fears seem overdrawn and his reforms Pollyannish.

---

[9]Longhurst disagrees: "*Ideology and Utopia* represents the high point of Mannheim's development of a detailed sociology of knowledge and after this he increasingly concerned himself with more general problems of sociology and society, though these had, of course, always been present in the sociology of knowledge" (1988:16). Of *Man and Society in an Age of Reconstruction* (Mannheim, 1935/1940), Longhurst says, "The basic tenets of a sociology of knowledge are accepted as given."

There is an interesting parallel between the work of Mannheim and that of Comte. In both cases, the early work was serious and scholarly and constitutes their lasting contribution to sociology. In addition, later in life both men turned to more practical, political writings that seem unfortunate when examined from today's vantage point. In fact, Mannheim came close to elevating sociology to a Comtian vision of the "queen of the sciences," by defining "*sociology* as the basic discipline of the social sciences" (1953b:203). More specifically, "it is only structural sociology which is capable of a comprehensive synthesis of all these facts which are the outcome of the separate social sciences" (Mannheim, 1953b:208). Both Comte and Mannheim also came to a kind of religious orientation late in their careers, although Mannheim, unlike Comte, never envisioned himself as the "pope" of a new religion. More specifically, both came to see Catholicism as offering a model for the new world.

There is a troublesome elitism and conservatism about Mannheim's ideas. He seemed to have little regard for the masses and saw them as a potential threat to modern society. He saw the need for elites to run society. For example, he argued that "democracy is characterized, not by the absence of elite strata, but rather by a new mode of elite selection and a new self-interpretation of the elite" (Mannheim, 1956/1971:300). Later, he saw the need for elite planners to come up with designs for society so that it could avoid the looming disasters. However, all of this requires trust in the elites and the planners. How is society to control them? What is to prevent them from forming the kind of fascistic regime that Mannheim so feared and detested?

We might close this chapter with some thoughts on the point with which we began— that Mannheim was not a grand theorist in the tradition of Weber or Marx. That is, Mannheim's contributions have been restricted largely to the sociology of knowledge and did not involve a grand theory of society. While there is much truth in this position, it can be argued that the sociology of knowledge is about more than just knowledge, but is relevant to all sociocultural phenomena. That is, all cultural products can, indeed must, be analyzed in the same way that knowledge is analyzed by Mannheim. In fact, Mannheim defines cultural sociology as the "science of the embeddedness of cultural formations within social life" (1982:55). In other words, as Simonds puts it, "the sciences of men are themselves hermeneutical" (1978:136). The fact is that there is increasing support these days in many quarters of sociological theory for the idea that some sort of hermeneutic approach is preferable to one inspired by positivism. In this sense, Mannheim can be seen as a pioneer of the hermeneutic approach in sociology. More specifically, his work on knowledge can be seen as an exemplar for similar work on the full panoply of cultural phenomena.

There is another sense in which it can be argued that Mannheim had a more general, if not a "grand," theory—that is, his effort to develop a theory of the relationship between the individual and society, which in today's terms is called micro-macro or agency-structure integration. For example, Mannheim concerns himself with the "unceasing interplay between our primary impulses which seek for satisfaction" and social institutions, or the "network of already established relationships," which remakes and remolds those impulses (1953b:240).

More generally, Mannheim sought to develop a synthetic theory, a "sociological psychology," which synthesized insights from the disciplines of psychology and sociology, as well as other social sciences. Both disciplines look at the same material, but the sociologist looks at attitudes and behaviors with reference to the social context, while the psychologist tends to concentrate on the individual. What is needed is a sociological psychology that fuses the insights provided by these two disciplines and in the process provides the kind of integrative perspective so valued by Mannheim. The effort to synthesize various theories is another characteristic of modern sociological theory, one that was clearly anticipated by Mannheim in his ideas on sociological psychology.

Thus, while Mannheim's work certainly has its weaknesses, it *did* lead to the development of the sociology of knowledge and it *may* have embedded in it the kind of integrative and synthetic theory that is very much in line with the latest developments in sociological theory. Although many have followed up on Mannheim's ideas on the sociology of knowledge, at least until recently few have explored the possibilities inherent in his broader theoretical perspective.

SUMMARY

Karl Mannheim's theoretical work does not have the broad sweep of most of the other theorists covered in this book. However, his work did lead to the creation and development of an important field in contemporary sociology—the sociology of knowledge, or the study of the "existential determination of knowledge."

In creating the sociology of knowledge, Mannheim drew on a number of sources, most important Karl Marx's ideas on ideologies. However, unlike Marx, Mannheim did not see ideologies as necessarily involving conscious distortions or emanating from social classes. Mannheim demonstrated that ideologies could emanate from generations (and other social sources) just as they could from social classes.

Mannheim focused on knowledge, approaching it from a sociological point of view. He was interested in studying knowledge empirically, especially using historical methods. Although he was interested in empirical research, Mannheim rejected the excesses of positivism. Among other things, he did not think that positivism was well suited to the study of ideas. Mannheim accepted much of the phenomenological approach, although he criticized phenomenology for ignoring material reality and for its search for ahistorical truths.

Mannheim sees a crisis in his time—relativism—in which all ideas seem to be equal and there appears to be nothing to believe in. However, he sees the sociology of knowledge arising out of this milieu and offering solutions to the problems associated with relativism. In contrast to the lack of absolute standards to make judgments associated with relativism, Mannheim sees the sociology of knowledge as characterized by relationism, or the idea that there is a relationship among specific ideas, larger idea systems, and the social system. While this idea leads to the view that there are no eternal standards, there are standards specific to a given context that allow one to judge right and wrong. The intelligentsia, which plays a key role in Mannheim's thinking, is the group best able to make these kinds of judgments because it is the most capable of rising above a specific, limited viewpoint.

In his sociology of knowledge, Mannheim is generally not interested in specific ideas, but rather in the *Weltanschauung*—the systematic totality of ideas of an epoch or group. Much of this chapter focuses on three examples of a *Weltanschauung* that are of central importance to Mannheim—ideology, utopia, and conservatism. An ideology is a set of ideas that conceals the present by attempting to understand it in terms of the past, while a utopia is an idea system that endeavors to transcend the present and is oriented to the future. Mannheim emphasizes the fundamental conflict of interest among these two idea systems. While ideology and utopia are treated more generically, conservatism is dealt with mainly in terms of its development in the first half of the nineteenth century. The confrontation of ideas is as important in Mannheim's thinking about conservatism as it is in the relationship between ideology and utopia.

Mannheim offered a number of important insights into the idea of rationality. Most important is his distinction between substantive and functional rationality and irrationality. He places great importance on the increase in functional rationalization, and its extension in the form of self-rationalization, and ultimately self-observation. The chief irrationality of the increase in functional rationality is the fact that it tends to paralyze substantive rationality. Mannheim also worries about the irrationalities associated with mass society.

Later in his career Mannheim turned to the issue of social planning and the reconstruction of society in light of the major events of his time, especially the Depression, the rise of fascism, and World War II. The problem was to plan society so that its worst problems were ameliorated without threatening individual freedom in the process.

GEORGE HERBERT MEAD

INTELLECTUAL ROOTS
  Behaviorism
  Pragmatism
  Dialectics
THE PRIORITY OF THE SOCIAL
THE ACT
  Stages
  Gestures
  Significant Symbols
MENTAL PROCESSES AND THE MIND
  Intelligence
  Consciousness
  Mind
SELF
  Child Development
  Generalized Other
  "I" and "Me"
SOCIETY
EVOLUTION
DIALECTICAL THINKING

As we will see throughout this chapter, the social-psychological theories of George Herbert Mead were shaped by a variety of intellectual sources (Joas, 1985), but of great importance was the influence of psychological behaviorism.[1]

INTELLECTUAL ROOTS

Behaviorism

Mead defines *behaviorism* in its broadest sense as "simply an approach to the study of the experience of the individual from the point of view of his *conduct*" (1934/1962:2; italics added). (*Conduct* is used here as another word for behavior.) Mead has no trouble with this approach to behaviorism, but he does have difficulty with the way in which behaviorism came to be defined and practiced by the most prominent behaviorist of Mead's day, John B. Watson (Buckley, 1989).

[1]For a critique of this position, see Natanson (1973b).

The behaviorism of Mead's time, as practiced by Watson and most others and then applied to humans, had been imported from animal psychology, where it worked quite well. There it was based on the premise that it is impossible through introspection to get at the private, mental experiences (assuming they exist) of lower animals and therefore all that can and should be done is to focus on animal behavior. Rather than seek to adapt behaviorism to the fact that there are obvious mental differences between animals and humans, Watson simply applied the principles of animal behavior to humans. To Watson, people are little more than "organic machines" (Buckley, 1989:x). Given this view of people, and the analogy between humans and animals, Watson rejected the idea of the study of human consciousness by introspection or any other method. As Mead puts it, in colorful fashion, "John B. Watson's attitude was that of the Queen in *Alice in Wonderland*—'Off with their heads!' " (1934/1962:2–3).

In Mead's view, Watson seeks to use behavior (conduct) to explain individual experience, without a concern for inner experience, consciousness, and mental imagery. In contrast, Mead believes that even inner experience can be studied from the point of view of the behaviorist, as long as this viewpoint is *not* narrowly conceived. Thus, Mead *is* a behaviorist, albeit what he calls a "social" behaviorist. However, this seemingly slight extension makes an enormous theoretical difference. The symbolic-interactionist theory that emerged, in significant part from Mead's theory, is very different from behaviorist theories (like early exchange theory), and indeed they exist in different sociological paradigms (Ritzer, 1975a; see also the Appendix).[2]

While Mead wants to include what goes on within the mind as part of social behaviorism, he is as opposed as is Watson to the use of introspection to study mental processes. Mead wants to study the mind behavioristically, rather than introspectively:

> The opposition of the behaviorist to *introspection* is justified. It is *not* a *fruitful* undertaking from the point of view of psychological study. . . . What the behaviorist is occupied with, and what we have to come back to, is the actual reaction itself, and it is only in so far as we can translate the content of introspection over into response that we can get any satisfactory psychological doctrine.
>
> (Mead, 1934/1962:105; italics added)

Instead of studying the mind introspectively, Mead focuses on the *act* or, if other people are involved, the *social* act. Acts are behaviors defined in part in terms of the behaviorists' notions of stimulus and response. That is, some external stimulus causes the person to respond with an act. Mead's extension here is to argue that "part of the act lies within the organism and only comes to expression later; it is that side of behavior which I think Watson has passed over" (1934/1962:6). Mead does not ignore the inner experience of the individual, because that inner experience is *part,* indeed a crucial part, of the act (we will have much more to say about the act shortly). It is in this sense that Mead contends that "the existence as such of mind or consciousness, in some sense or other, must be admitted" (1934/1962:10). Mead is aware that the mind cannot be reduced solely to behaviors, but he argues that it is possible to explain it in behavioral terms without denying its existence.

---

[2]However, there are those (for example, Lewis and Smith, 1980) who argue that this difference has more to do with the way Mead's work was interpreted by his successors, especially Herbert Blumer, than with Mead's theories themselves (see also McPhail and Rexroat, 1979).

Mead defines the mind in *functional* rather than idealist terms. That is, the mind is viewed in terms of what it does, the role it plays in the act, rather than as some transcendental, subjective phenomenon. The mind is a part, the key part, of the central nervous system, and Mead seeks to extend the analysis of the act, especially the social act, to what transpires in the central nervous system: "What I am insisting upon is that the patterns which one finds in the central nervous system are patterns of action—not of contemplation" (1934/1962:26). Furthermore, what goes on in the central nervous system is not really separable from the act; it is an integral part of the act. Thus, Mead does not want to think of the mind in subjective terms but rather as something which is part of an objective process.

Pragmatism

Another important intellectual input into Mead's thinking was *pragmatism;* indeed, Mead was one of the key figures in the development of pragmatic philosophy (others were John Dewey and Charles Peirce) (Lewis and Smith, 1980). Mead (1938/1972) regarded pragmatism as a "natural American outgrowth." Pragmatism reflected the triumph of science and the scientific method within American society and their extension into the study of the social world (Baldwin, 1986). Instead of being contemplative and otherworldly, as were previous philosophical systems, pragmatism adopted a focus on this world, on empirical reality. Pragmatists believe in the superiority of scientific data over philosophical dogma and all other types of knowledge. As John Baldwin summarizes, "Science is superior to trial-and-error learning, introspection, a priori logic, religious dogma, idealism, speculative philosophy, and all other nonempirical sources of knowledge" (1986:16). Science is seen as the optimum means not only for obtaining knowledge but also for analyzing and solving social problems. Scientific theories, as well as ideas in general, are to be tested using the full array of scientific procedures. The ideas that survive are those that are likely to provide knowledge that is useful and solves problems. Pragmatists reject the idea that there are such things as absolute truths. Rather, following the scientific model, they regard all ideas as provisional and subject to change in light of future research.

Pragmatism also involves a series of ideas that relate more directly to Mead's sociological theory (Charon, 1995). First, to pragmatists, truth and reality do not exist "out there" in the real world; they are "actively created as we act in and toward the world" (Hewitt, 1984:8; see also Shalin, 1986). Second, people remember the past and base their knowledge of the world on what has proved useful to them. They are likely to alter what no longer "works." Third, people define the social and physical "objects" that they encounter in the world according to their use for them. Finally, if we want to understand actors, we must base our understanding on what they actually do in the world. Given these viewpoints, we can understand John Baldwin's contention that pragmatism is "rooted in a 'rough and ready' American ethic developed by the settlers who had faced the challenges of new frontiers and dealt with the practical problems of taming a new land" (1986:22). In sum, pragmatism is a "pragmatic" philosophy in several senses, including the fact that it adopts the scientists' focus on the here and now as well as scientific methods, it is concerned with what people actually do, and it is interested in generating practical ideas that can help us cope with society's problems.

Lewis and Smith (1980) differentiate between two strands of pragmatism—*nominalist pragmatism* (associated with John Dewey and William James) and *philosophical realism* (associated with Mead). The nominalist position is that although societal phenomena exist, they do not exist independently of people and do not have a determining effect upon individual consciousness and behavior (in contrast to Durkheim's social facts and the reified worlds of Marx, Weber, and Simmel). More positively, this view "conceives of the individuals themselves as existentially free agents who accept, reject, modify, or otherwise 'define' the community's norms, roles, beliefs, and so forth, according to their own personal interests and plans of the moment" (Lewis and Smith, 1980:24). In contrast, to social realists the emphasis is on society and how it constitutes and controls individual mental processes. Rather than being free agents, actors and their cognitions and behaviors are controlled by the larger community.[3]

Given this distinction, Lewis and Smith conclude that Mead's work fits better into the realist camp. There is much of merit in this position, and it will inform some of the ensuing discussion (especially on the priority Mead accords to the social). However, to classify Mead as a realist would be to include him in the same category as Durkheim, and this is unacceptable, because there are clearly important differences between their theories. In fact, Mead's theory cannot be forced into either of these categories. There are elements of *both* nominalism and realism in Mead's thinking. To put it more concretely, in most of Mead's work, social processes and consciousness mutually inform one another and cannot be clearly distinguished. In other words, there is a dialectic between realism and nominalism in Mead's work.

Dialectics

This brings us to another important source of Mead's thinking—the philosophy of Hegel, especially his dialectical approach. We have already encountered the dialectic, especially in Chapter 5, on Marx, and many of the ideas expressed there apply to Mead's thinking. We will return to this issue later in the chapter because, as we will see, dialectical thinking makes it almost impossible to separate Mead's many theoretical ideas; they are dialectically related to one another. However, adopting the strategy followed by Mead himself, we will differentiate among various concepts for the sake of clarity of discussion. Bear in mind (and occasionally the reader will be reminded) through each of the specific discussions that there is a dialectical interrelationship among the various concepts.

THE PRIORITY OF THE SOCIAL

In his review of Mead's best-known work, *Mind, Self and Society,* Ellsworth Faris argued that "not mind and then society; but society first and then minds arising with that society . . . would probably have been [Mead's] preference" (cited in Miller, 1982a:2). Faris's inversion of the title of this book reflects the widely acknowledged fact, recognized by Mead himself, that society, or more broadly the social, is accorded priority in Mead's analysis.

[3]For a criticism of this distinction, see D. Miller (1982b, 1985).

In Mead's view, traditional social psychology began with the psychology of the individual in an effort to explain social experience; in contrast, Mead always gives priority to the social world in understanding social experience. Mead explains his focus in this way:

> We are not, in social psychology, building up the behavior of the social group in terms of the behavior of separate individuals composing it; rather, we are *starting out with a given social whole* of complex group activity, into which we analyze (as elements) the behavior of each of the separate individuals composing it. . . . We attempt, that is, to explain the conduct of the social group, rather than to account for the organized conduct of the social group in terms of the conduct of the separate individuals belonging to it. For social psychology, the *whole (society) is prior to the part (the individual),* not the part to the whole; and the part is explained in terms of the whole, not the whole in terms of the part or parts.
> (Mead, 1934/1962:7; italics added)

To Mead, the social whole precedes the individual mind both logically and temporally. A thinking, self-conscious individual is, as we will see later, logically impossible in Mead's theory without a prior social group. The social group comes first, and it leads to the development of self-conscious mental states.

THE ACT

Mead considers the act to be the most "primitive unit" in his theory (1982:27). In analyzing the act, Mead comes closest to the behaviorist's approach and focuses on stimulus and response. However, even here the stimulus does not elicit an automatic, unthinking response from the human actor. As Mead says, "We conceive of the stimulus as an occasion or opportunity for the act, not as a compulsion or a mandate" (1982:28).

Stages

Mead (1938/1972) identified four basic and interrelated stages in the act (Schmitt and Schmitt, 1996); the four stages represent an organic whole (in other words, they are dialectically interrelated). Both lower animals and humans act, and Mead is interested in the similarities, and especially the differences, between the two.

Impulse   The first stage is that of the *impulse,* which involves an "immediate sensuous stimulation" and the actor's reaction to the stimulation, the need to do something about it. Hunger is a good example of an impulse. The actor (both nonhuman and human) may respond immediately and unthinkingly to the impulse, but more likely the human actor will think about the appropriate response (for example, eat now or later). In thinking about a response, the person will consider not only the immediate situation but also past experiences and anticipated future results of the act.

Hunger may come from an inner state of the actor or may be elicited by the presence of food in the environment, or, most likely, it may arise from some combination of the two. Furthermore, the hungry person must find a way of satisfying the impulse in an environment in which food may not be immediately available or plentiful. This impulse, like all others, may be related to a problem in the environment (that is, the lack of

GEORGE HERBERT MEAD: A Biographical Sketch

Most of the important theorists discussed throughout this book achieved their greatest recognition in their lifetimes for their published work. George Herbert Mead, however, was at least as important, at least during his lifetime, for his teaching as for his writing. His words had a powerful impact on many people who were to become important sociologists in the twentieth century. As one of his students said, "Conversation was his best medium; writing was a poor second" (T. V. Smith, 1931:369). Let us have another of his students, himself a well-known sociologist—Leonard Cottrell—describe what Mead was like as a teacher:

For me, the course with Professor Mead was a unique and unforgettable experience. . . . Professor Mead was a large, amiable-looking man who wore a magnificent mustache and a Vandyke beard. He characteristically had a benign, rather shy smile matched with a twinkle in his eyes as if he were enjoying a secret joke he was playing on the audience. . . .

As he lectured—always without notes—Professor Mead would manipulate the piece of chalk and watch it intently. . . . When he made a particularly subtle point in his lecture he would glance up and throw a shy, almost apologetic smile over our heads—never looking directly at anyone. His lecture flowed and we soon learned that questions or comments from the class were not welcome. Indeed, when someone was bold enough to raise a question there was a murmur of disapproval from the students. They objected to any interruption of the golden flow. . . .

His expectations of students were modest. He never gave exams. The main task for each of us students was to write as learned a paper as one could. These Professor Mead read with great care, and what he thought of your paper was your grade in the course. One might suppose that students would read materials for the paper rather than attend his lectures but that was not the case. Students always came. They couldn't get enough of Mead.

(Cottrell, 1980:49–50)

Mead had enormous difficulty writing and this troubled him a great deal. " 'I am vastly depressed by my inability to write what I want to' " (cited in G. Cook, 1993:xiii). However, over the years many of Mead's ideas came to be published, especially in *Mind, Self and Society*

immediately available food), a problem that must be overcome by the actor. Indeed, while an impulse like hunger may come largely from the individual (although even here hunger can be induced by an external stimulus, and there are also social definitions of when it is appropriate to be hungry), it is usually related to the existence of a problem in the environment (for example, the lack of food). Overall, the impulse, like all other elements of Mead's theory, involves both the actor and the environment.

Perception   The second stage of the act is *perception,* in which the actor searches for, and reacts to, stimuli that relate to the impulse, in this case hunger as well as the various means available to satisfy it. People have the capacity to sense or perceive stimuli

(a book based on students' notes from a course taught by Mead). This book and others of Mead's works had a powerful influence on the development of contemporary sociology, especially symbolic interactionism.

Born in South Hadley, Massachusetts, on February 27, 1863, Mead was trained mainly in philosophy and its application to social psychology. He received a bachelor's degree from Oberlin College (where his father was a professor) in 1883, and after a few years as a secondary-school teacher, surveyor for railroad companies, and private tutor, Mead began graduate study at Harvard in 1887. After a few years of study at Harvard, as well as at the Universities of Leipzig and Berlin, Mead was offered an instructorship at the University of Michigan in 1891. It is interesting to note that Mead *never* received any graduate degrees. In 1894, at the invitation of John Dewey, he moved to the University of Chicago and remained there for the rest of his life.

As Mead makes clear in the following excerpt from a letter, he was heavily influenced by Dewey: " 'Mr. Dewey is a man of not only great originality and profound thought but the most appreciative thinker I have ever met. I have gained more from him than from any one man I ever met'" (cited in Cook, 1993:32). This was especially true of Mead's early work at Chicago and he even followed Dewey into educational theory (Dewey left Chicago in 1904). However, Mead's thinking quickly diverged from Dewey's and led him in the direction of his famous social psychological theories of mind, self, and society. He began teaching a course on social psychology in 1900. In 1916–1917 it was transformed into an advanced course (the stenographic student notes from the 1928 course became the basis of *Mind, Self and Society*) that followed a course in elementary social psychology that was taught after 1919 by Ellsworth Faris of the sociology department. It was through this course that Mead had such a powerful influence on students in sociology (as well as psychology and education).

In addition to his scholarly pursuits, Mead became involved in social reform. He believed that science could be used to deal with social problems. For example, he was heavily involved as a fund raiser and policy maker at the University of Chicago Settlement House which had been inspired by Jane Addams's Hull House. Perhaps most importantly, he played a key role in social research conducted by the settlement house.

Although eligible for retirement in 1928, he continued to teach at the invitation of the university and in the summer of 1930 became chair of the philosophy department. Unfortunately, he became embroiled in a bitter conflict between the department and the president of the university. This led in early 1931 to a letter of resignation from Mead written from his hospital bed. He was released from the hospital in late April, but died from heart failure the following day. Of him, John Dewey said he was "'the most original mind in philosophy in the America of the last generations'" (Cook, 1993:194).

through hearing, smell, taste, and so on. Perception involves incoming stimuli, as well as the mental images they create. People do not simply respond immediately to external stimuli but rather think about, and assess, them through mental imagery. People are not simply subject to external stimulation; they also actively select characteristics of a stimulus and choose among sets of stimuli. That is, a stimulus may have several dimensions, and the actor is able to select among them. Furthermore, people are usually confronted with many different stimuli, and they have the capacity to choose which to attend to and which to ignore. Mead refuses to separate people from the objects that they perceive. It is the act of perceiving an object that makes it an object to a person; perception and object cannot be separated from (are dialectically related to) one another.

Manipulation   The third stage is *manipulation*. Once the impulse has manifested itself and the object has been perceived, the next step is manipulating the object or, more generally, taking action with regard to it. In addition to their mental advantages, people have another advantage over lower animals. People have hands (with opposable thumbs) that allow them to manipulate objects far more subtly than can lower animals. The manipulation phase constitutes, for Mead, an important temporary pause in the process so that a response is not manifested immediately. A hungry human being sees a mushroom, but before eating it, he or she is likely to pick it up first, examine it, and perhaps check in a guidebook to see whether that particular variety is edible. The lower animal, on the other hand, is likely to eat the mushroom without handling and examining it (and certainly without reading about it). The pause afforded by handling the object allows humans to contemplate various responses. In thinking about whether to eat the mushroom, both the past and the future are involved. People may think about past experiences in which they ate certain mushrooms that made them ill, and they may think about the future sickness, or even death, that might accompany eating a poisonous mushroom. The manipulation of the mushroom becomes a kind of experimental method in which the actor mentally tries out various hypotheses about what would happen if the mushroom were consumed.

Consummation   On the basis of these deliberations, the actor may decide to eat the mushroom (or not), and this constitutes the last phase of the act, *consummation,* or more generally the taking of action which satisfies the original impulse. Both humans and lower animals may consume the mushroom, but the human is less likely to eat a bad mushroom because of his or her ability to manipulate the mushroom and to think (and read) about the implications of eating it. The lower animal must rely on a trial-and-error method, and this is a less-efficient technique than the capacity of humans to think through their actions.[4] Trial-and-error in this situation is quite dangerous; as a result, it seems likely that lower animals are more prone to die from consuming poisonous mushrooms than are humans.

While, for ease of discussion, the four stages of the act have been separated from one another in sequential order, the fact is that Mead sees a dialectical relationship among the four stages. John Baldwin expresses this idea in the following way: "Although the four parts of the act sometimes *appear* to be linked in linear order, they actually interpenetrate to form one organic process: Facets of each part are present at all times from the beginning of the act to the end, such that each part affects the other" (1986:55–56). Thus, the later stages of the act may lead to the emergence of earlier stages. For example, manipulating food may lead the individual to the impulse of hunger and the perception that one is hungry and that food is available to satisfy the need.

Gestures

While the act involves only one person, the *social act* involves two or more persons. The *gesture* is in Mead's view the basic mechanism in the social act and in the social

---

[4]For a critique of Mead's thinking on the differences between humans and lower animals, see Alger and Alger, 1997.

process more generally. As he defines them, "gestures are movements of the first organism which act as specific stimuli calling forth the (socially) appropriate responses of the second organism" (Mead, 1934/1962:14; see also Mead, 1959:187). Both lower animals and humans are capable of gestures in the sense that the action of one individual mindlessly and automatically elicits a reaction by another individual. The following is Mead's famous example of a dog fight in terms of gestures:

> The act of each dog becomes the stimulus to the other dog for his response. . . . The very fact that the dog is ready to attack another becomes a stimulus to the other dog to change his own position or his own attitude. He has no sooner done this than the change of attitude in the second dog in turn causes the first dog to change his attitude.
>
> (Mead, 1934/1962:42–43)

Mead labels what is taking place in this situation a "conversation of gestures." One dog's gesture automatically elicits a gesture from the second; there are no thought processes taking place on the part of the dogs.

Humans sometimes engage in mindless conversations of gestures. Mead gives as examples many of the actions and reactions that take place in boxing and fencing matches, when one combatant adjusts "instinctively" to the actions of the second. Mead labels such unconscious actions "nonsignificant" gestures; what distinguishes humans is their ability to employ "significant" gestures, or those that require thought on the part of the actor before a reaction.

The vocal gesture is particularly important in the development of significant gestures. However, not all vocal gestures are significant. The bark of one dog to another is not significant; even some human vocal gestures (for example, a mindless grunt) may not be significant. However, it is the development of vocal gestures, especially in the form of language, which is the most important factor in making possible the distinctive development of human life: "The specialization of the human animal within this field of the gesture has been responsible, ultimately, for the origin and growth of present human society and knowledge, with all the control over nature and over the human environment which science makes possible" (Mead, 1934/1962:14).

This development is related to a distinctive characteristic of the vocal gesture. When we make a physical gesture, such as a facial grimace, we cannot see what we are doing (unless we happen to be looking in the mirror). On the other hand, when we utter a vocal gesture, we hear ourselves just as others do. One result is that the vocal gesture can affect the speaker in much the same way that it affects the listeners. Another is that we are far better able to stop ourselves in vocal gestures than we are able to do in physical gestures. In other words, we have far better control over vocal gestures than physical ones. This ability to control oneself and one's reactions is critical, as we will see, to the other distinctive capabilities of humans. More generally, "it has been the vocal gesture that has preeminently provided the medium of social organization in human society" (Mead, 1959:188).

Significant Symbols

A significant symbol is a kind of gesture, one which only humans can make. Gestures become *significant symbols* when they arouse in the individual who is making them the same kind of response (it need not be identical) as they are supposed to elicit from those to whom the gestures are addressed. Only when we have significant symbols can we truly have communication; communication in the full sense of the term is not possible among ants, bees, and so on. Physical gestures can be significant symbols, but as we have seen, they are not ideally suited to be significant symbols because people cannot easily see or hear their own physical gestures. Thus, it is vocal utterances that are most likely to become significant symbols, although not all vocalizations are such symbols. The set of vocal gestures most likely to become significant symbols is *language:* "a symbol which answers to a meaning in that experience of the first individual and which also calls out the meaning in the second individual. Where the gesture reaches that situation it has become what we call 'language.' It is now a significant symbol and it signifies a certain meaning" (Mead, 1934/1962:46). In a conversation of gestures, only the gestures themselves are communicated. However, with language the gestures and their meanings are communicated.

One of the things that language, or significant symbols more generally, does is call out the same response in the individual who is speaking as it does in others. The word *dog* or *cat* elicits the same mental image in the person uttering the word as it does in those to whom it is addressed. Another effect of language is that it stimulates the person speaking as it does others. The person yelling "fire" in a crowded theater is at least as motivated to leave the theater as are those to whom the shout is addressed. Thus, significant symbols allow people to be the stimulators of their own actions.

Adopting his pragmatist orientation, Mead also looks at the "functions" of gestures in general and of significant symbols in particular. The function of the gesture "is to make adjustment possible among the individuals implicated in any given social act with reference to the object or objects with which that act is concerned" (Mead, 1934/ 1962:46). Thus, an involuntary facial grimace may be made in order to prevent a child from going too close to the edge of a precipice and thereby prevent him or her from being in a potentially dangerous situation. While the nonsignificant gesture works, the "significant symbol affords far greater facilities for such adjustment and readjustment than does the nonsignificant gesture, because it calls out in the individual making it the same attitude toward it . . . and enables him to adjust his subsequent behavior to theirs in the light of that attitude" (Mead, 1934/1962:46). From a pragmatic point of view, a significant symbol works better in the social world than does a nonsignificant gesture. In other words, in communicating our displeasure to others, an angry verbal rebuke works far better than contorted body language. The individual who is manifesting displeasure is not usually conscious of body language and therefore is unlikely to be able to consciously adjust later actions in light of how the other person reacts to the body language. On the other hand, a speaker is conscious of uttering an angry rebuke and reacts to it in much the same way (and at about the same time) as the person to whom it is aimed reacts. Thus, the speaker can think about how the other person might react and can prepare his or her reaction to that reaction.

Of crucial importance in Mead's theory is another function of significant symbols— that they make the mind, mental processes, and so on, possible. It is only through significant symbols, especially language, that human *thinking* is possible (lower animals cannot think, in Mead's terms). Mead defines *thinking* as "simply an internalized or implicit conversation of the individual with himself by means of such gestures"

(1934/1962:47). Even more strongly, Mead argues: "Thinking is the same as talking to other people" (1982:155). In other words, thinking involves talking to oneself. Thus, we can see clearly here how Mead defines thinking in behaviorist terms. Conversations involve behavior (talking), and that behavior also occurs within the individual; when it does, thinking is taking place. This is not a mentalistic definition of thinking; it is decidedly behavioristic.

Significant symbols also make possible *symbolic interaction*.[5] That is, people can interact with one another not just through gestures but also through significant symbols. This ability, of course, makes a world of difference and makes possible much more complex interaction patterns and forms of social organization than would be possible through gestures alone.

The significant symbol obviously plays a central role in Mead's thinking. In fact, David Miller (1982a:10–11) accords the significant symbol *the* central role in Mead's theory.

MENTAL PROCESSES AND THE MIND

Mead uses a number of similar-sounding concepts when discussing mental *processes,* and it is important to sort them out. Before we do, the point should be made that Mead is always inclined to think in terms of processes rather than structures or contents. In fact, Mead is often labeled a "process philosopher" (Cronk, 1987; D. Miller, 1982a).

Intelligence

One term that sounds as though it belongs under the heading of "mental processes" but actually does not in Mead's thinking is *intelligence*.[6] Mead defines *intelligence* most broadly as the mutual adjustment of the acts of organisms. By this definition, lower animals clearly have "intelligence," because in a conversation of gestures they adapt to one another. Similarly, humans can adapt to one another through the use of nonsignificant symbols (for example, involuntary grimaces). However, what distinguishes humans is that they can also exhibit intelligence, or mutual adaptation, through the use of significant symbols. Thus, a bloodhound has intelligence, but the intelligence of the detective is distinguished from that of the bloodhound by the capacity to use significant symbols.

Mead argues that animals have "unreasoning intelligence." In contrast, humans have "reason," which Mead defines in a characteristically behavioristic manner: "When you are reasoning you are indicating to yourself the characters that call out certain responses—and that is all you are doing" (1934/1962:93). In other words, individuals are carrying on conversations with themselves.

What is crucial to the reflective intelligence of humans is their ability to inhibit action temporarily, to delay their reactions to a stimulus (Mead, 1959:84). In the case of

---

[5]This is the label that was ultimately affixed (by Herbert Blumer) to the sociological theory derived, in significant part, from Mead's ideas.

[6]Although, as we will see later, Mead uses this term inconsistently; sometimes it includes mental processes.

lower animals, a stimulus leads immediately and inevitably to a reaction; lower animals lack the capacity to inhibit their reactions temporarily. As Mead puts it, "Delayed reaction is necessary to intelligent[7] conduct. The organization, implicit testing, and final selection . . . would be impossible if his overt responses or reactions could not in such situations be delayed" (1934/1962:99). There are three components here. First, humans, because of their ability to delay reactions, are able to organize in their own minds the array of possible responses to a situation. Humans possess in their minds the alternative ways of completing a social act in which they are involved. Second, people are able to test out mentally, again through an internal conversation with themselves, the various courses of action. In contrast, lower animals lack this capacity and therefore must try out reactions in the real world in trial-and-error fashion. The ability to try out responses mentally, as we saw in the case of the poison mushroom, is much more effective than the trial-and-error method. There is no social cost involved in mentally trying out a poorly adapted response. However, when a lower animal actually uses such a response in the real world (for example, when a dog approaches a poisonous snake), the results can be costly, even disastrous. Finally, humans are able to pick out one stimulus among a set of stimuli rather than simply reacting to the first or strongest stimulus. In addition, humans can select among a range of alternative actions, whereas lower animals simply act. As Mead says:

> It is the entrance of the alternative possibilities of future response into the determination of present conduct in any given environmental situation, and their operation, through the mechanism of the central nervous system, as part of the factors or conditions determining present behavior, which *decisively* contrasts intelligent conduct or behavior with reflex, instinctive, and habitual conduct or behavior-delayed reaction with immediate reaction.
> (Mead, 1934/1962:98; italics added)

The ability to choose among a range of actions means that the choices of humans are likely to be better adapted to the situation than are the immediate and mindless reactions of lower animals. As Mead contends, "Intelligence is largely a matter of selectivity" (1934/1962:99).

Consciousness

Mead also discusses *consciousness,* which he sees as having two distinguishable meanings (1938/1972:75). The first is that to which the actor alone has access, that which is entirely subjective. Mead is less interested in this sense of consciousness than the second, which basically involves reflective intelligence. Thus, Mead is less interested in the way in which we experience immediate pain or pleasure than he is in the way in which we think about the social world.

Consciousness is to be explained or accounted for within the social process. That is, in contrast to most analysts, Mead believes that consciousness is *not* lodged in the brain: "Consciousness is functional not substantive; and in either of the main senses of the

---

[7]Here is one place where Mead is using *intelligence* in a different sense from that employed in the previous discussion.

term it must be located in the objective world rather than in the brain—it belongs to, or is a characteristic of, the environment in which we find ourselves. What is located, what does take place, in the brain, however, is the physiological process whereby we lose and regain consciousness" (1934/1962:112).

In a similar manner, Mead (1934/1962:332) refuses to position *mental images* in the brain but sees them as social phenomena: "What we term 'mental images' . . . can exist in their relation to the organism without being lodged in a substantial consciousness. The mental image is a memory image. Such images which, as symbols, play so large a part in thinking, belong to the environment."

Meaning is yet another related concept that Mead addresses behavioristically. Characteristically, Mead rejects the idea that meaning lies in consciousness: "Awareness or consciousness is not necessary to the presence of meaning in the process of social experience" (1934/1962:77). Similarly, Mead rejects the idea that meaning is a "psychical" phenomenon or an "idea." Rather, *meaning* lies squarely within the social act: "Meaning arises and lies within the field of the relation between the gesture of a given human organism and the subsequent behavior of this organism as indicated to another human organism by that gesture. If that gesture does so indicate to another organism the subsequent (or resultant) behavior of the given organism, then it has meaning" (Mead, 1934/1962:75–76). It is the adjustive response of the second organism that gives meaning to the gesture of the first organism. The meaning of a gesture can be seen as the "ability to predict the behavior that is likely to occur next" (Baldwin, 1986:72).

While meaning is to be found in behavior, it becomes conscious when meaning is associated with symbols. However, although meaning can become conscious among humans, it is present in the social act *prior* to the emergence of consciousness and the awareness of meaning. Thus, in these terms, lower animals (and humans) can engage in meaningful behavior even though they are not aware of the meaning.

Mind

Like consciousness, the *mind,* which is defined by Mead as a process and not a thing, as an inner conversation with one's self, is not found within the individual; it is not intracranial but is a social phenomenon. It arises and develops within the social process and is an integral part of that process. The social process precedes the mind; it is not, as many believe, a product of the mind. Thus, the mind, too, is defined functionally rather than substantively. Given these similarities to ideas like consciousness, is there anything distinctive about the mind? We have already seen that humans have the peculiar capacity to call out in themselves the response they are seeking to elicit from others. A distinctive characteristic of the mind is the ability of the individual "to call out in himself not simply a single response of the other but the response, so to speak, of the community as a whole. That is what gives to an individual what we term 'mind.' To do anything now means a certain organized response; and if one has in himself that response, he has what we term 'mind' " (Mead, 1934/1962:267). Thus, the mind can be distinguished from other like-sounding concepts in Mead's work by its ability to respond to the overall community and put forth an organized response.

Mead also looks at the mind in another, pragmatic way. That is, the mind involves thought processes oriented toward problem solving. The real world is rife with problems, and it is the function of the mind to try to solve those problems and permit people to operate more effectively in the world.

SELF

Much of Mead's thinking in general, and especially on the mind, involves his ideas on the critically important concept of the *self,* basically the ability to take oneself as an object; the self is the peculiar ability to be both subject and object. As is true of all Mead's major concepts, the self presupposes a social process: communication among humans. Lower animals do not have selves, nor do human infants at birth. The self arises with development and through social activity and social relationships. To Mead, it is impossible to imagine a self arising in the absence of social experiences. However, once a self has developed, it is possible for it to continue to exist without social contact. Thus, Robinson Crusoe developed a self while he was in civilization, and he continued to have it when he was living alone on what he thought for a while was a deserted island. In other words, he continued to have the ability to take himself as an object. Once a self is developed, people usually, but not always, manifest it. For example, the self is not involved in habitual actions or in immediate physiological experiences of pleasure or pain.

The self is dialectically related to the mind (we will have more to say shortly about the dialectic in Mead's thought). That is, on the one hand, Mead argues that the body is not a self and becomes a self only when a mind has developed. On the other hand, the self, and its reflexiveness, is essential to the development of the mind. Of course, it is impossible to separate mind and self, because the self is a mental process. However, even though we may think of it as a mental process, the self is a social process. In his discussion of the self, as we have seen in regard to all other mental phenomena, Mead resists the idea of lodging it in consciousness and instead embeds it in social experience and social processes. In this way, Mead seeks to give a behavioristic sense of the self: "But it is where one does respond to that which he addresses to another and where that response of his own becomes a part of his conduct, where he not only hears himself but responds to himself, talks and replies to himself as truly as the other person replies to him, that we have *behavior* in which the individuals become objects to themselves" (1934/1962:139; italics added). The self, then, is simply another aspect of the overall social process of which the individual is a part.

The general mechanism for the development of the self is reflexivity, or the ability to put ourselves unconsciously into others' places and to act as they act. As a result, people are able to examine themselves as others would examine them. As Mead says:

> It is by means of reflexiveness—the turning-back of the experience of the individual upon himself—that the whole social process is thus brought into the experience of the individuals involved in it; it is by such means, which enable the individual to take the attitude of the other toward himself, that the individual is able consciously to adjust himself to that process, and to modify the resultant process in any given social act in terms of his adjustment to it.

(Mead, 1934/1962:134)

The self also allows people to take part in their conversations with others. That is, one is aware of what one is saying and as a result is able to monitor what is being said and to determine what is going to be said next.

In order to have selves, individuals must be able to get "outside themselves" so that they can evaluate themselves, so that they can become objects to themselves. To do this, people basically put themselves in the same experiential field as they put everyone else. Everyone is an important part of that experiential situation, and people must take themselves into account if they are to be able to act rationally in a given situation. Having done this, they seek to examine themselves impersonally, objectively, and without emotion.

However, people cannot experience themselves directly. They can do so only indirectly by putting themselves in the position of others and viewing themselves from that standpoint. The standpoint from which one views one's self can be that of a particular individual or that of the social group as a whole. As Mead puts it, most generally, "It is only by taking the roles of others that we have been able to come back to ourselves" (1959:184–185).

Child Development

Mead is very interested in the genesis of the self. He sees the conversation of gestures as the background for the self, but it does not involve a self, since in such a conversation the people are not taking themselves as objects. Mead traces the genesis of the self through two stages in childhood development.

Play Stage   The first stage is the *play stage;* it is during this stage that children learn to take the attitude of particular others to themselves. While lower animals also play, only human beings "play at being someone else" (Aboulafia, 1986:9). Mead gives the example of a child playing (American) "Indian": "This means that the child has a certain set of stimuli which call out in itself the responses they would call out in others, and which answer to an Indian" (Mead, 1934/1962:150). As a result of such play, the child learns to become both subject and object and begins to become able to build a self. However, it is a limited self because the child can take only the role of distinct and separate others. Children may play at being "mommy" and "daddy" and in the process develop the ability to evaluate themselves as their parents, and other specific individuals, do. However, they lack a more general and organized sense of themselves.

Game Stage   It is the next stage, the *game stage,* that is required if the person is to develop a self in the full sense of the term. Whereas in the play stage the child takes the role of discrete others, in the game stage the child must take the role of everyone else involved in the game. Furthermore, these different roles must have a definite relationship to one another. In illustrating the game stage, Mead gives his famous example of a baseball (or, as he calls it, "ball nine") game:

> But in a game where a number of individuals are involved, then the child taking one role must be ready to take the role of everyone else. If he gets in a ball nine he must have the responses of each position involved in his own position. He must know what everyone

else is going to do in order to carry out his own play. He has to take all of these roles. They do not all have to be present in consciousness at the same time, but at some moments he has to have three or four individuals present in his own attitude, such as the one who is going to throw the ball, the one who is going to catch it, and so on. These responses must be, in some degree, present in his own make-up. In the game, then, there is a set of responses of such others so organized that the attitude of one calls out the appropriate attitudes of the other.

(Mead, 1934/1962:151)

In the play stage, children are not organized wholes because they play at a series of discrete roles. As a result, in Mead's view they lack definite personalities. However, in the game stage,[8] such organization begins and a definite personality starts to emerge. Children begin to become able to function in organized groups and, most important, to determine what they will do within a specific group.

Generalized Other

The game stage yields one of Mead's (1959:87) best-known concepts, the *generalized other.* The generalized other is the attitude of the entire community or, in the example of the baseball game, the attitude of the entire team. The ability to take the role of the generalized other is essential to the self: "Only in so far as he takes the attitudes of the organized social group to which he belongs toward the organized, co-operative social activity or set of such activities in which that group is engaged, does he develop a complete self" (Mead, 1934/1962:155). It is also crucial that people be able to evaluate themselves from the point of view of the generalized other and not merely from the viewpoint of discrete others. Taking the role of the generalized other, rather than that of discrete others, allows for the possibility of abstract thinking and objectivity (Mead, 1959:190). Here is the way Mead describes the full development of the self:

So the self reaches its full development by organizing these individual attitudes of others into the organized social or group attitudes, and by thus becoming an individual reflection of the general systematic pattern of social or group behavior in which it and others are involved—a pattern which enters as a whole into the individual's experience in terms of these organized group attitudes which, through the mechanism of the central nervous system, he takes toward himself, just as he takes the individual attitudes of others.

(Mead, 1934/1962:158)

In other words, to have a self, one must be a member of a community and be directed by the attitudes common to the community. While play requires only pieces of selves, the game requires a coherent self.

Not only is taking the role of the generalized other essential to the self, but it is also crucial for the development of organized group activities. A group requires that individuals direct their activities in accord with the attitudes of the generalized other. The generalized other also represents Mead's familiar propensity to give priority to the social, since it is through the generalized other that the group influences the behavior of individuals.

---

[8]Although Mead uses the term "games," it is clear, as Aboulafia (1986:198) points out, that he means any system of organized responses (for example, the family).

Mead also looks at the self from a pragmatic point of view. At the individual level, the self allows the individual to be a more efficient member of the larger society. Because of the self, people are more likely to do what is expected of them in a given situation. Since people often try to live up to group expectations, they are more likely to avoid the inefficiencies that come from failing to do what the group expects. Furthermore, the self allows for greater coordination in society as a whole. Because individuals can be counted on to do what is expected of them, the group can operate more effectively.

The preceding, as well as the overall discussion of the self, might lead us to believe that Mead's actors are little more than conformists and that there is little individuality, since everyone is busy conforming to the expectations of the generalized other. But Mead is clear that each self is different from all others. Selves share a common structure, but each self receives unique biographical articulation. In addition, it is clear that there is not simply one grand generalized other but that there are many generalized others in society, because there are many groups in society. People, therefore, have multiple generalized others and, as a result, multiple selves. Each person's unique set of selves makes him or her different from everyone else. Furthermore, people need not accept the community as it is; they can reform things and seek to make them better. We are able to change the community because of our capacity to think. But Mead is forced to put this issue of individual creativity in familiar, behavioristic terms: "The only way in which we can react against the disapproval of the entire community is by setting up a higher sort of community which in a certain sense out-votes the one we find . . . he may stand out by himself over against it. But to do that he has to comprehend the voices of the past and of the future. That is the only way the self can get a voice which is more than the voice of the community" (1934/1962:167–168). In other words, to stand up to the generalized other, the individual must construct a still larger generalized other, composed not only from the present but also from the past and the future, and then respond to it.

Mead identifies two aspects, or phases, of the self, which he labels the "I" and the "me" (for a critique of this distinction, see Athens, 1995). As Mead puts it, "The self is essentially a social process going on with these two distinguishable phases" (1934/1962:178). It is important to bear in mind that the "I" and "me" are processes within the larger process of the self; they are not "things."

"I" and "Me"

The "I" is the immediate response of an individual to others. It is the incalculable, unpredictable, and creative aspect of the self. People do not know in advance what the action of the "I" will be: "But what that response will be he does not know and nobody else knows. Perhaps he will make a brilliant play or an error. The response to that situation as it appears in his immediate experience is uncertain" (Mead, 1934/1962:175). We are never totally aware of the "I," and through it we surprise ourselves with our actions. We know the "I" only after the act has been carried out. Thus, we know the "I" only in our memories. Mead lays great stress on the "I" for four reasons. First, it is a key source of novelty in the social process. Second, Mead believes that it is in the "I" that our most important values are located. Third, the "I" constitutes something that we all seek—the realization of the self. It is the "I" that permits us to develop a "definite personality." Finally, Mead sees an evolutionary process in history in which people in primitive societies are dominated more by "me" while in modern societies there is a greater component of "I."

The "I" gives Mead's theoretical system some much-needed dynamism and creativity. Without it, Mead's actors would be totally dominated by external and internal controls. With it, Mead is able to deal with the changes brought about not only by the great figures in history (for example, Einstein) but also by individuals on a day-to-day basis. It is the "I" that makes these changes possible. Since every personality is a mix of "I" and "me," the great historical figures are seen as having a larger proportion of "I" than most others have. But in day-to-day situations, anyone's "I" may assert itself and lead to change in the social situation. Uniqueness is also brought into Mead's system through the biographical articulation of each individual's "I" and "me." That is, the specific exigencies of each person's life give him or her a unique mix of "I" and "me."

The "I" reacts against the "me," which is the "organized set of attitudes of others which one himself assumes" (Mead, 1934/1962:175). In other words, the "me" is the adoption of the generalized other. In contrast to the "I," people are conscious of the "me"; the "me" involves conscious responsibility. As Mead says, "The 'me' is a conventional, habitual individual" (1934/1962:197). Conformists are dominated by "me," although everyone—whatever his or her degree of conformity—has, and must have, substantial "me." It is through the "me" that society dominates the individual. Indeed, Mead defines the idea of *social control* as the dominance of the expression of the "me" over the expression of the "I." Later in *Mind, Self and Society,* Mead elaborates on his ideas on social control:

> Social control, as operating in terms of self-criticism, exerts itself so intimately and extensively over individual behavior or conduct, serving to integrate the individual and his actions with reference to the organized social process of experience and behavior in which he is implicated. . . . Social control over individual behavior or conduct operates by virtue of the social origin and basis of such [self-] criticism. That is to say, self-criticism is essentially social criticism, and behavior controlled socially. Hence social control, so far from tending to crush out the human individual or to obliterate his self-conscious individuality, is, on the contrary, actually constitutive of and inextricably associated with that individuality.
>
> (Mead, 1934/1962:255)

Mead also looks at the "I" and "me" in pragmatic terms. The "me" allows the individual to live comfortably in the social world, while the "I" makes the change of society possible. Society gets enough conformity to allow it to function, and it gets a steady infusion of new developments to prevent it from stagnating. The "I" and the "me" are thus part of the whole social process and allow both individuals and society to function more effectively.

SOCIETY

At the most general level, Mead uses the term *society* to mean the ongoing social process that precedes both the mind and the self. Given its importance in shaping the mind and self, society is clearly of central importance to Mead. At another level, society to Mead represents the organized set of responses that are taken over by the individual in the form of the "me." Thus, in this sense individuals carry society around with them, giving them the ability through self-criticism, to control themselves. Mead also, as we will see, deals with the evolution of society. But Mead has relatively little to say explicitly about society, in spite of its centrality in his theoretical system. His most important contributions lie in his thoughts on mind and self. Even John Baldwin, who sees a much more societal (macro) component in Mead's thinking, is forced to admit: "The macro components of Mead's theoretical system are not as well developed as the micro" (1986:123).

At a more specific societal level Mead does have a number of things to say about social *institutions*. Mead broadly defines an *institution* as the "common response in the community" or "the life habits of the community" (1934/1962:261, 264; see also Mead, 1936:376). More specifically, he says that "the whole community acts toward the individual under certain circumstances in an identical way . . . there is an identical response on the part of the whole community under these conditions. We call that the formation of the institution" (Mead, 1934/1962:167). We carry this organized set of attitudes around with us, and they serve to control our actions, largely through the "me."

Education is the process by which the common habits of the community (the institution) are "internalized" in the actor. This is an essential process, since, in Mead's view, people neither have selves nor are genuine members of the community until they can respond to themselves as the larger community does. To do so, people must have internalized the common attitudes of the community.

But again Mead is careful to point out that institutions need not destroy individuality or stifle creativity. Mead recognizes that there are "oppressive, stereotyped, and ultra-conservative social institutions—like the church—which by their more or less rigid and inflexible unprogressiveness crush or blot out individuality" (1934/1962:262). However, he is quick to add: "There is no necessary or inevitable reason why social institutions should be oppressive or rigidly conservative, or why they should not rather be, as many are, flexible and progressive, fostering individuality rather than discouraging it" (Mead, 1934/1962:262). To Mead, institutions should define what people ought to do only in a very broad and general sense and should allow plenty of room for individuality and creativity. Mead here demonstrates a very modern conception of social institutions as both constraining individuals *and* enabling them to be creative individuals (see Giddens, 1984).

What Mead lacks in his analysis of society in general, and institutions in particular,[9] is a true macro sense of them in the way that theorists like Comte, Spencer, Marx, Weber, and Durkheim dealt with this level of analysis. This is true in spite of the fact that Mead does have a notion of *emergence* in the sense that the whole is seen as more than the sum of its parts. More specifically, "Emergence involves a reorganization, but the reorganization brings in something that was not there before. The first time oxygen

---

[9]There are at least two places where Mead offers a more macro sense of society. At one point he defines *social institutions* as "organized forms of group or social activity" (Mead, 1934/1962:261). Earlier, in an argument reminiscent of Comte, he offers a view of the family as the fundamental unit within society and as the base of such larger units as the clan and state.

and hydrogen come together, water appears. Now water is a combination of hydrogen and oxygen, but water was not there before in the separate elements" (Mead, 1934/1962:198). However, Mead is much more prone to apply the idea of emergence to consciousness than to apply it to the larger society. That is, mind and self are seen as emergent from the social process. Moreover, Mead is inclined to use the term *emergence* merely to mean the coming into existence of something new or novel (D. Miller, 1973:41).

EVOLUTION

We have already encountered a bit of Mead's thinking on the evolutionary process in the movement from primitive societies dominated by "me" to modern societies dominated by "I." Influenced by bioevolutionists Charles Darwin and Jean Baptiste Lamarck, as well as by Hegel, Mead sees humans, like all other organisms, as evolving in the direction of greater adaptation to their environment as well as increased ability to exercise control over the environment. Mead looks at the evolutionary process in pragmatic terms: "Evolution is the process of meeting and solving problems" (1936:143). As a result, Mead does not see evolution as a single, uniform process but as a diverse set of ways of solving problems. Evolution will take different forms depending on local conditions, but all these forms *are* shaped by their adaptation to those conditions.

The evolution of human society has progressed far beyond that of other organisms and has still greater potential in the future. Humans, unlike lower animals, have the ability to alter their inorganic environment. Humans, of course, have this capacity because of their self-consciousness. Self-consciousness allows people to alter their environment, make progressive social changes in the social world, and develop their personalities so that they can keep pace with the changes they are making in society. In Mead's view, "The realization of the self in the intelligent performance of a social function remains the higher stage [in evolution] in the case of nations as of individuals" (1934/1962:317). While Mead sees considerable evolution among humans, he also makes it clear that there is a long way to go before the evolutionary process is anywhere near complete.

Mead sees science as a crucial product of the evolutionary process. To Mead, science is the surest kind of knowledge that we possess (Moore, 1936). In pragmatic terms, science simply involves problem-solving activity. But the problem-solving activity is distinctive in that it formally adopts a research attitude involving, among other things, the development of hypotheses to be tested (and a rejection of all dogma), the use of observational methods to find something novel or unanticipated, and the search for uniformities, rules, and laws. However, even if new laws are discovered, they never become dogma, and the scientist is always prepared to revise or drop a law when new, contradictory data become available. Scientists continue to use given hypotheses as long as these hypotheses work, and they are willing to drop them when they no longer fit the facts. Scientists also do not look toward some vague, distant goal and then plot a course to it. Rather, scientists focus on problems in the current system and on what can be done to solve those problems. The test of a scientific solution is whether it enables the system to work better than it did in the past.

To Mead, science simply does more quickly and efficiently what people in general have done throughout the evolutionary process. That is, while in normal evolution solutions to problems emerge gradually over very long periods of time, in the modern world "we solve the problem directly by what we call the 'scientific method' " (Mead, 1936:365). Mead details several steps in the experimental method of science—the presence of a problem, the statement of a problem in terms of how it can be solved, the formation of hypotheses, the mental testing of hypotheses, and finally the experimental or observational testing of hypotheses. But Mead then goes on to say that these are "merely the elaboration of the simple processes of everyday inference by which we meet our constantly recurring difficulties" (1938/1972:83).

The evolution of science is related to the overall evolution of the human mind. Here is the way Mead relates to evolution many of the ideas outlined earlier on mental processes:

> When we reach the human form with its capacity for indicating what is important in a situation, through the process of analysis; when we get to the position in which a mind can arise in the individual form, that is, where the individual can come back upon himself and stimulate himself just as he stimulates others; where the individual can call out in himself the attitudes of the whole group; where he can acquire the knowledge that belongs to the whole community; where he can respond as the whole community responds under certain conditions when they direct this organized intelligence toward particular ends; then we have this process which provides solutions for problems working in a self-conscious way. In it we have the *evolution* of the human mind which makes use directly of the sort of intelligence which has been developed in the whole process of *evolution*.
>
> (Mead, 1936:366; italics added)

Clearly, a mind with these characteristics is capable of science, and science, in turn, is a formal expression of those distinctive human capabilities. Mead leaves no doubt about his position: "After all, the scientist is simply making a technique out of human intelligence" (1936:373).

Mead also relates his ideas on the evolution of science to the need for society to maintain order but still be able to change and progress. In his view, science offers a method by which society can change, but in an orderly fashion. This idea is also linked to Mead's social reformism, in which ideas derived from scientific study can be used to expedite the evolutionary process and ameliorate problems in society.

DIALECTICAL THINKING

As we indicated at the outset of this chapter, while Mead's concepts are discussed separately, it is clear that they are dialectically related to one another (Cronk, 1987:3). Mead's dialectical approach may be traced to a number of philosophical sources, especially the work of Hegel, and it is similar in at least some respects to Marx's dialectic.

At the most general level, one cannot clearly separate the concepts, especially mind, self, and society, that have been discussed throughout this chapter. They are intimately related to each other, and all are aspects or phases of the social process, most broadly defined. Ferguson also makes this point: "These concepts are related dialectically, for intrinsic to each factor is its relationship to the other factors. The act of defining any one of them demands an examination of its relationship to others" (1980:26). Let us look at the major elements of the dialectic and the way in which they are manifest in Mead's work.

First, the dialectician refuses to look at the world in one-way, causal terms. There are many places in Mead's work where he looks at the reciprocal relationships among social phenomena. For example, the self is seen as arising out of society, and selves then contribute to the development of a more elaborately organized society and to the increased differentiation, evolution, and organization of society (Mead, 1934/1962:164; see also 180, 196). For another example, as was already pointed out, the four stages of the act need not occur in sequence, and each later stage may act back on earlier stages.

Second, the dialectician refuses to separate fact and value, and although Mead's work is not nearly as value-laden as Marx's, Mead is not averse to making value judgments such as the one mentioned earlier involving his aversion to the church as a constraining social institution.

Third, the dialectician does not see hard-and-fast dividing lines among social phenomena, as Mead demonstrates with his unwillingness to clearly separate mind, self, and society. This view is quite explicit in a discussion of selves in which Mead argues: "Selves can only exist in definite relationships to other selves. No *hard-and-fast* line can be drawn between our own selves and the selves of others, since our own selves exist and enter as such into our experience only in so far as the selves of others exist and enter as such into our experience also. The individual possesses a self only in relation to the selves of the other members of his social group" (1934/1962:164; italics added; see also Mead, 1907/1964:81, 1982:73).

Fourth, dialectical thinkers take a relational view to the world. Ferguson discusses, most generally, "the relational character of Mead's analysis" (1980:66). Again this is clear throughout Mead's thinking on mind, self, and society, but it is manifest in his thinking on the relationship between the "I" and the "me," which require one another in order to exist: "There would not be an 'I' in the sense in which we use the term if there were not a 'me'; there would not be a 'me' without a response in the form of this 'I' " (1934/1962:182). Ferguson contends that the "I" and "me" "are dialectically related in such a way that each can only be defined in terms of the other" (1980:33). Similarly, Natanson discusses "the 'I'–'me' dialectic" (1973b:60). More generally, Berger and Luckmann argue that Mead offered a "theory of the dialectic between society and the individual" (1967:194).

Fifth, dialectical thinkers are interested not only in the present but also in its relationship to both the past and the future. This interest in past, present, and future is manifest most generally in Mead's thinking on social evolution. Mead takes the position that the past and the future are to be found in the present: "The functional boundaries of the present are those of its undertaking—of what we are doing. The pasts and the futures indicated by such activity belong to the present. They arise out of it and are criticized and tested by it" (1959:88). Again, to give a more specific example, Mead looks at intelligence[10] in this way: "Intelligence is essentially the ability to solve the problems of *present* behavior in terms of its possible *future* consequences as implicated on the

---

[10]Here is another instance in which Mead is using the term *intelligence* differently from the way it was defined initially in this chapter.

basis of *past* experience—the ability, that is, to solve the problems of *present* behavior in the light of, or by reference to, both the *past* and *future;* it involves both memory and foresight" (1934/1962:100; italics added).

Sixth, the dialectician does not have a deterministic view of the future. While Mead (like Marx) does have an ideal state toward which he sees society evolving (to Mead it is a world of free, open, and perfect communication), he does not see it as inevitable that we will reach that state. What people, either the great figures in history or people on a daily basis, do matters and will determine how far we will progress toward the evolutionary ideal.

The seventh element of the dialectic is a concern for conflict and contradiction. This concern, too, can be found in Mead's work, but it is not nearly as pronounced as in Marx's theories. There are important conflicts and contradictions in Mead's work, such as between the "I" and the "me," as well as between the need to conform to society and the need to be innovative and change society. Cronk (1987) sees a model of interaction between consensus and conflict in Mead's work, with the interaction leading to resolutions and new forms of consensus. There are even, in Mead's work, ideas of the negation of the present through revolutionary activities. However, these conflicts and contradictions do not seem to be as crucially important as they are in Marx's work. Furthermore, while Marx sees the resolution of conflicts in new syntheses, the logic of Mead's work leads us to assume that there must be a continuation of a healthy conflict between "I" and "me," self and society, conformity and change.

Thus, all the elements of the dialectic can be applied to Mead's work. Although not often recognized as such, Mead *was* a dialectical thinker, and an understanding of this fact greatly enhances our ability to comprehend his work.

SUMMARY

George Herbert Mead developed his sociological theory out of the confluence of a number of intellectual inputs, the most important of which was behaviorism. Basically, Mead accepted the behavioristic approach and its focus on conduct but sought to extend it to a concern for mental processes. He was also a creator of, and influenced by, pragmatism. Pragmatism gave Mead a powerful faith in science and, more generally, in conduct motivated by reflective intelligence. It, like behaviorism, led Mead to focus on what people actually "do" in the social world. He was also strongly influenced by Hegel, and this is manifest in a number of places (for example, his focus on evolution), especially in his dialectical approach to the social world.

Substantively, Mead's theory accorded primacy and priority to the social world. That is, it is out of the social world that consciousness, the mind, the self, and so on emerge. The most basic unit in his social theory is the act, which includes four dialectically related stages—impulse, perception, manipulation, and consummation. Even in his thoughts on the act Mead does not emphasize external stimuli (as a behaviorist would); rather, he holds that a stimulus is an opportunity, not a compulsion, to act. A *social* act involves two or more persons, and the basic mechanism of the social act is the gesture. While lower animals and humans are capable of having a conversation of gestures, only humans can communicate the conscious meaning of their gestures.

Humans are peculiarly able to create vocal gestures, and this capacity leads to the distinctive human ability to develop and use significant symbols. Significant symbols lead to the development of language and the distinctive capacity of humans to communicate, in the full sense of the term, with one another. Significant symbols also make possible thinking as well as symbolic interaction.

Mead looks at an array of mental processes as part of the larger social process; such mental processes include reflective intelligence, consciousness, mental images, meaning, and, most generally, the mind. Humans have the distinctive capacity to carry on an inner conversation with themselves. All the mental processes, in Mead's view, are lodged not in the brain but rather in the social process.

The self is the ability to take oneself as an object. Again, the self arises within the social process. The general mechanism of the self is the ability of people to put themselves in the place of others and to act as others act and to see themselves as others see them. Mead traces the genesis of the self through the play and game stages of childhood. Especially important in the latter stage is the emergence of the generalized other. The ability to see oneself from the viewpoint of the community is essential to the emergence of the self as well as of organized group activities. The self also has two phases—the "I," which is the unpredictable and creative aspect of the self, and the "me," which is the organized set of attitudes of others assumed by the actor. Social control is manifest through the "me," while the "I" is the source of innovation in society.

Mead has relatively little to say about society, which he sees most generally as the ongoing social processes that precede mind and self. Mead largely lacks a macro sense of society. Institutions are defined as little more than collective habits. Mead does have a strong sense of evolution, especially of reflective intelligence as well as of science, the latter being merely a concrete and formalized manifestation of that intelligence. Finally, Mead manifests dialectical thinking throughout his theoretical system.

Mead's theory is not as broad as those of most of the other theorists examined in this book. Nevertheless, it continues to be influential in contemporary symbolic interactionism, social psychology, and sociology more generally. Work continues to emerge in sociology (as well as in philosophy), building upon Mead's theories (for example, Collins, 1989b). Mead's work still attracts theorists both in the United States and in the rest of the world (for example, Habermas, 1984). This is the case in spite of a number of notable weaknesses in his theory. The greatest weakness, one that has been mentioned several times in this chapter, is that he has little to offer to our understanding of the macro-societal level. Other weaknesses include some vague and fuzzy concepts; an inconsistent definition of concepts (especially intelligence); the difficulty in clearly differentiating one of his concepts from the others; his lack of concern, in spite of his focus on the micro level, for emotional and unconscious aspects of human conduct; and the fact that about the only source of social change in his theoretical system appears to be the individual, especially through the "I." In spite of these and other weaknesses, Mead offers a powerful and important theory that is likely to be influential in sociology for many years to come.

13

ALFRED SCHUTZ

INTERPRETATIONS OF SCHUTZ'S WORK
THE IDEAS OF EDMUND HUSSERL
SCIENCE AND THE SOCIAL WORLD
   Life-World versus Science
   Constructing Ideal Types
TYPIFICATIONS AND RECIPES
THE LIFE-WORLD
INTERSUBJECTIVITY
   Knowledge
   Private Components of Knowledge
REALMS OF THE SOCIAL WORLD
   Folgewelt and *Vorwelt*
   Umwelt and We Relations
   Mitwelt and They Relations
CONSCIOUSNESS, MEANINGS, AND MOTIVES
INTERPRETING SCHUTZIAN THEORY

Of all the theorists discussed in this book, Alfred Schutz is the most controversial inclusion. Schutz is not often included in the pantheon of classical sociological theorists because his work has only recently come to be widely influential in sociology, especially in the contemporary theories of phenomenological sociology and ethnomethodology. However, because of its recently expanding influence, as well as the fact that it offers a profound, wide-ranging, and distinctive perspective (Rogers, forthcoming), Schutzian theory warrants full-chapter treatment in this text on classical sociological theory. It is thought of as *classical* theory because of its nature and scope, as well as the time of its development. Schutz's most important theoretical statement, *The Phenomenology of the Social World* (1932/1967), was published in the 1930s—the same decade that witnessed the publication of other now-classical theoretical works such as Mead's *Mind, Self and Society* and Parsons's *The Structure of Social Action*.

INTERPRETATIONS OF SCHUTZ'S WORK

We can divide traditional interpretations of Schutz's work into several camps. First, ethnomethodologists and phenomenologists saw in Schutz the source of their interest in the way actors create or construct social reality. Among the ethnomethodologists, for example, Hugh Mehan and Houston Wood argued that the focus of their approach was on the way actors "create situations and rules, and so at once create themselves and their

ALFRED SCHUTZ: A Biographical Sketch

Alfred Schutz was not widely known during his lifetime, and only in recent years has his work attracted the attention of large numbers of sociologists. Although his obscurity was in part a result of his intellectual orientation—his then highly unusual interest in phenomenology—a more important cause was his very unusual career as a sociologist.

Born in Vienna, Austria, in 1899, Schutz received his academic training at the University of Vienna (Wagner, 1983). Soon after completing his law examination, he embarked on a lifelong career in banking. Although rewarding economically, banking did not satisfy his need for deeper meaning in his life. Schutz found that meaning in his work on phenomenological sociology. He was not an academician in the 1920s, but many of his friends were, and he participated in a number of informal lecture and discussion circles (Prendergast, 1986). Schutz was drawn to Weberian theory, especially Weber's work on action and the ideal type. Although impressed with Weber's work, Schutz sought to overcome its weaknesses by integrating ideas from the philosophers Edmund Husserl and Henri Bergson. According to Christopher Prendergast (1986), Schutz was motivated to provide the Austrian School of Economics with a scientific, subjective theory of action. These influences led to the publication by Schutz in 1932 of what was to become a very important book in sociology, *The Phenomenology of the Social World.* It was not translated into English until 1967, so a wide appreciation of Schutz's work in the United States was delayed thirty-five years.

As World War II approached, Schutz emigrated, with an intervening period in Paris, to the United States, where for many years he divided his time between serving as legal counsel to a number of banks and writing about and teaching phenomenological sociology. Simultaneously with his work in banking, Schutz began teaching courses in 1943 at the New School for Social Research in New York City. As Richard Grathoff points out, the result was that "the

social realities" (1975:115). They went on to say that "ethnomethodologists adopted this research program from Schutz" (Mehan and Wood, 1975:115). Monica Morris, in her book on creative sociology, came to a similar conclusion: "For Schutz, the subject matter of sociology is the manner in which human beings constitute, or create, the world of everyday life" (1977:15). These commentators, as well as many others, generally have seen Schutz as focusing on the way actors create social reality, and they have lauded him for this micro orientation.

Other commentators have taken a similar view of the substance of his work but have come to very different conclusions about it. A good example is Robert Bierstedt, who criticized Schutz for his focus on the way actors construct social reality and his corresponding lack of concern with the reality of the larger structures of society:

> The phenomenological reduction . . . has consequences of a . . . rather serious kind for sociology. . . . Society itself, as an objective phenomenon, tends to disappear in the realm of the intersubjective. That is, society itself . . . comes to be a creation of the mind in intersubjectivity and something that is wholly exhausted in the common-place affairs of daily living.
>
> (Bierstedt, 1963:91)

social theorist for whom scientific thought and everyday life defined two rather distinct and separate realms of experience upheld a similar division in his personal life" (1978:112). Not until 1956 did Schutz give up his dual career and concentrate entirely on teaching and writing phenomenological sociology. Because of his interest in phenomenology, his dual career, and his teaching at the then avant-garde New School, Schutz remained on the periphery of sociology during his lifetime. Nevertheless, Schutz's work and his influence on students (for example, Peter Berger, Thomas Luckmann, Harold Garfinkel) moved him to the center of sociological theory.

Another factor in Schutz's marginal position in sociological theory was that his theory seemed highly abstract and irrelevant to the mundane social world. Although Schutz did separate theory from reality, he did not feel that his work was irrelevant to the world in which he lived. To put it in terms of his phenomenology, he saw a relationship between the everyday construction of reality and the pregiven historical and cultural world. To think otherwise is to think that the man who fled National Socialism (Nazism) regarded his academic work as irrelevant. The following quotation from one of his letters indicates that although Schutz was not optimistic, he was not prepared to accept the irrelevance of his theorizing and, more generally, the social construction of reality to the world as a whole:

> You are still optimist enough to believe that phenomenology may save itself among the ruins of this world—as the *philosophica aera perennis?* I do not believe so. More likely the African natives must prepare themselves for the ideas of national socialism. This shall not prevent us from dying the way we have lived; and we must try, therefore, to build . . . order into *our* world, which we must find lacking in—our *world.* The whole conflict is hidden in this shift of emphasis.
>
> (Schutz, cited in Grathoff, 1978:130)

In short, although the ability of people to affect the larger society is restricted by such phenomena as Nazism, they must continue to strive to build a social and cultural reality that is *not* beyond their reach and control.

Alfred Schutz died in 1959.

Thus Bierstedt criticized Schutz for precisely the same thing for which Mehan and Wood, Morris, and others praised him.

Although these two camps came to very different conclusions about Schutz's work, they did at least agree on its micro focus. A third school of thought, however, views Schutz in an almost diametrically opposite way, as a cultural determinist. For example, Robert Gorman (1975a, 1975b, 1977) suggested that, contrary to the interpretations of the ethnomethodological and sociological establishments, Schutz emphasized the constraints imposed on the actor by society. Actors do not freely choose beliefs or courses of action, nor do they freely construct a sense of social reality. Rather, as members of society, they are free only to obey.

> Socially determined action patterns are adhered to by free actors. Each actor bases his action on his stock of knowledge at hand, and this knowledge consists of these socially determined action patterns. Each of us chooses, for himself, to act as these patterns prescribe, even though they have been imposed from outside.
>
> (Gorman, 1975a:11)

Gorman concluded that for Schutz "social behavior is apparently caused by factors independent of the subject [actor]" (1977:71).

As we review Schutz's theory, we will see that the most legitimate perspective involves a combination of the first and third views of his work. That is, Schutz's actors do create social reality, but that creation takes place in, and is constrained by, socially determined action patterns (Thomason, 1982). We will also see that the second position, articulated by Bierstedt, is erroneous and ignores the constraining reality of culture and society in Schutz's theory.

THE IDEAS OF EDMUND HUSSERL

Before turning to the theories of Alfred Schutz, we need to deal with the ideas of his most important intellectual predecessor, the philosopher Edmund Husserl. While other thinkers (for example, Henri Bergson and Max Weber) had a strong impact on Schutz, the influence of Husserl stands above that of all the others.

Husserl's highly complicated philosophy is not easily translated into sociological concepts; indeed, a good portion of it is not directly relevant to sociology (Srubar, 1984). We discuss here a few of his ideas that proved useful to Alfred Schutz, as well as to other phenomenological sociologists.

In general, Husserl believed that people view the world as a highly ordered place; actors are always engaged in the active and highly complex process of ordering the world. However, people are unaware that they are patterning the world; hence they do not question the process by which this is accomplished. Actors see the social world as naturally ordered, not structured by them. Unlike people in the everyday world, phenomenologists are acutely aware that patterning is taking place, and that ordering process becomes for them an important subject of phenomenological investigation (Freeman, 1980).

Husserl's scientific phenomenology involves a commitment to penetrate the various layers constructed by actors in the social world in order to get to the essential structure of consciousness, the transcendental ego. Schutz defines the *transcendental ego* as "the universe of our conscious life, the stream of thought in its integrity, with all its activities and with all its cogitations and experiences" (1973:105).

The idea of the transcendental ego reflects Husserl's interest in the basic and invariant properties of human consciousness. As Schutz says, "According to Husserl, phenomenology aims to be an eidetical science, dealing not with existence but with essence" (1973:113), especially the essence of consciousness—the transcendental ego.

Although he is often misinterpreted on this point, Husserl did not have a mentalistic, metaphysical conception of consciousness. For him, consciousness is not a thing or a place but a process. Consciousness is found not in the head of the actor but in the relationship between the actor and objects in the world. Husserl expressed this in the idea of *intentionality.* For him, consciousness is always consciousness of something, some object. Consciousness is found in this relationship; consciousness is not interior to the actor. Heap and Roth argue simply that "consciousness *is* intentional" (1973:355). Furthermore, meaning inheres not in objects but in the relationship of actors to objects. This conception of consciousness as a process that gives meaning to objects is at the heart of Husserl's phenomenology and is the starting point for Schutzian theory.

Another key to Husserl's work was his orientation to the *scientific* study of the basic structures of consciousness. Husserl sought to develop "philosophy as a rigorous science" (Kockelmans, 1967b:26). However, to Husserl science did not mean empiricism and statistical analysis of empirical data. In fact, he feared that such a science would reject consciousness as an object of scientific scrutiny and that consciousness would be found either to be too metaphysical or to have been turned into something physical.

What Husserl did mean by science was a philosophy that was methodologically rigorous, systematic, and critical. In using science in this way, Husserl believed that phenomenologists ultimately could arrive at absolutely valid knowledge of the basic structures of actors' "lived experience" (especially that which is conscious). This orientation to science has had two effects on later phenomenologists, including Alfred Schutz. First, phenomenologists continue to eschew the tools of modern social-science research (although they do research; see Psathas, 1989)—standardized methods, high-powered statistics, and computerized results. They prefer, as did Husserl, attention to, and description of, all social phenomena—including social situations, events, activities, interaction, and social objects—as *experienced* by human beings. Second, phenomenologists continue to oppose vague, "soft" intuitionism. In other words, they are opposed to "subjectivism" that is not concerned with discovering the basic structures of phenomena as experienced by people. Philosophizing about consciousness is a rigorous and systematic enterprise.

Husserl conceived of actors' natural standpoint, or their "natural attitude," as the major obstacle to the scientific discovery of phenomenological processes. Because of actors' natural attitude, conscious ordering processes are hidden to them. These processes will remain hidden to phenomenologists unless they are able to overcome their own natural attitudes. Phenomenologists must be able to accomplish the very difficult task of "disconnecting," or "setting aside" ("bracketing"), the natural attitude so that they will be able to get at the most basic aspects of consciousness involved in the ordering of the world (Freeman, 1980). In Husserl's view, the natural attitude is a source of bias and distortion to the phenomenologist.

Once the natural attitude is set aside, or "bracketed," the phenomenologist can begin to examine the invariant properties of consciousness that govern all people. Here is the way Schutz describes Husserl's orientation on this issue:

> The phenomenologist does not deny the existence of the outer world, but for his analytical purpose he makes up his mind to suspend belief in its existence—that is, to refrain intentionally and systematically from all judgments related directly or indirectly to the existence of the outer world. . . . Husserl called this procedure "putting the world in brackets" or "performing the phenomenological reduction" . . . [to] go beyond the natural attitude of man living within the world he accepts, be it reality or mere appearance . . . to disclose the pure field of consciousness.
>
> (Schutz, 1973:104)

The phenomenologist also must set aside the incidental experiences of life that tend to dominate consciousness. Husserl's ultimate objective was to get at the pure form of consciousness, stripped of all empirical content.

Ilja Srubar (1984) argues that Husserl not only did a rigorous philosophy of consciousness but also laid the groundwork for a phenomenological sociology. That is, Husserl found it necessary to extend his work to the world of interpersonal relations, the "life-world."   Thus Husserl's work helps point to the position that "phenomenology must become a science of the life world" (Srubar, 1984:70).   However, Schutz concluded that "the least satisfactory part of [Husserl's] analysis is that dealing with sociality and social groups" (1975:38).   As a result, while Husserl's work largely turned inward to the transcendental ego, Schutz's work turned outward to intersubjectivity, the social world, and the life-world.   Here is the way Wagner explained the task confronting Schutz:

> The phenomenological method, by definition, serves the exploration of the solitary consciousness.   It can procure access to the social realm of human experience only if it offers a solution for what Husserl called the problem of intersubjectivity.   A viable theory of intersubjectivity, in turn, would be the strongest, albeit indirect, support for the sociology of understanding that phenomenology could supply. . . . Schutz placed the whole problem on the level of mundanity, that of everyday life.   Here, he was confident, a phenomenological-psychological bridge between ego and alter could be found.
>
> (Wagner, 1983:43)

We will have much more to say about intersubjectivity and the life-world later, but before we do, we need to discuss Schutz's ideas on science and typifications.

SCIENCE AND THE SOCIAL WORLD

As was true of Husserl, Schutz sees phenomenology as a rigorous science.   He explicitly counters many of the critics of phenomenology by arguing that it is *not* based on "a kind of uncontrollable intuition or metaphysical revelation" (Schutz, 1973:101).   Also in accord with Husserl, Schutz sees science as a theoretical and conceptual endeavor.   The science of sociology, from Schutz's point of view, is not merely about describing the social world but involves the construction of rigorous conceptual and theoretical models of that world.   As Schutz put it:

> We should certainly be surprised if we found a cartographer in mapping a town restricting himself to collecting information from natives.   Nevertheless, social scientists frequently choose this strange method.   They forget that their scientific work is done on a level of [theoretical] interpretation and understanding different from the naive attitudes of orientation and interpretation peculiar to people in daily life.
>
> (Schutz, 1976:67)

We gain considerable insight into Schutz's views on science when we understand that he considers science to be one of a multitude of "realities."   To Schutz there are a number of different realities, including the worlds of dreams, art, religion, and the insane. The *paramount reality,* however, is the intersubjective world of everyday life (the life-world) because it is "the archetype of our experience of reality.   All the other provinces of meaning may be considered as its modifications" (Schutz, 1973:xlii).   As we will see, Schutz is focally concerned in his phenomenological sociology with the life-world, but our interest here is with the relationship of the life-world to another reality, that of science.

Life-World versus Science

There are several key differences between the life-world and the world of science, especially social science.   First, the common-sense actor in the life-world is oriented toward dealing pragmatically with the mundane problems of everyday life. The social scientist, in contrast, is "aloof," a "disinterested observer" who is not pragmatically involved in the life-world of the actors being studied and their mundane problems. Second, the stock of knowledge of the common-sense actor is derived from the everyday world, whereas the scientist works with the stock of knowledge that belongs to the body of science. The social scientist exists in a world of problems stated, solutions suggested, methods worked out, and results obtained by other social scientists. Third, in their theorizing, as we have already discussed, social scientists must detach themselves from (must "bracket") their own biographical situations in the life-world and operate in that province of meaning labeled "the world of science." Common-sense actors, in contrast, are enmeshed in their biographical situations and operate in the life-world. These three differences not only help us define the world of science, but furthermore the social scientist who fulfills these criteria can be seen as having attained the scientific attitude needed to study the life-world. To have the proper scientific attitude, social scientists must be detached from (that is, have a nonpragmatic interest in) the life-world of those they are studying, enmeshed in the world of science, and must bracket their own biographical situation within the life-world.

While the world of everyday life is populated by people who act sensibly or reasonably, scientists must create a model of that world which is composed of people who act rationally. In the everyday world people act *sensibly,* that is, their actions are in accord with socially approved rules for dealing with typical problems using typical means to achieve typical ends. People may also act *reasonably* in making "judicious" choices of means to ends, even if they merely follow traditional or habitual patterns. While people may act sensibly or reasonably in the everyday world, it is only in the theoretical models created by social scientists that they act *rationally* in the full sense of the term, possessing "clear and distinct insight into the ends, the means, and the secondary results" (Schutz, 1973:28). (Here Schutz is using rationality in the same way that Weber used means-ends rationality.) Schutz makes it quite clear that rationality is a theoretical construct in his work: "Thus, the concept of rationality in the strict sense already defined does not refer to actions within the common-sense experience of everyday life in the social world; it is the expression for a *particular* type of construct of certain *specific* models of the social world made by the social scientist for certain methodological purposes" (1973:42). Action in everyday life is, at best, only partly rational. People who act sensibly or reasonably are rational only to some degree; they are far from fully rational. Thus, it is the task of the social scientist to construct rational theoretical models of the largely less-than-fully-rational everyday social world. This need to construct such models is premised on the belief that the social scientist can, indeed must, use rational models to analyze the less-than-rational behavior that is found in the life-world. (Again, this is similar to Weber and his development and use of ideal types.)

But the everyday social world is "meaningful" to the actors in it, and the social scientist is confronted with the problem of constructing fully rational systems of knowledge of the subjective-meaning structures of everyday life. Schutz found himself in the paradoxical position of attempting to develop a subjective sociology in the tradition of Max Weber while also meeting the demands of a rigorous conception of science. As Schutz put the question (the answer to which lies at the heart of his theoretical system): "How is it, then, possible to grasp by a system of objective knowledge subjective meaning structures?" (1973:35). Schutz's response is that "it is possible to construct a model of a sector of the social world consisting of typical human interaction and to analyze this typical interaction pattern as to the meaning it might have for the personal types of actors" (1973:36).

Constructing Ideal Types

The ability to accomplish this is based on the fact that both in the world of everyday life and in science we rely on constructs (ideal types) in order to interpret reality and grasp the part of reality that is relevant to us. The constructs that we use in the life-world are first-order constructs ("typifications"; see the next section), and the social scientist develops second-order constructs on the basis of these first-order constructs. It is this building of scientific constructs on everyday constructs that makes an objective, rational science of subjectivity possible. However, to meet the demands of science, the meaning of the world from the actor's perspective must be captured in abstraction from its unique and unpredictable expression within immediate reality. Schutz is not concerned with specific, unique actors but with typical actors and typical actions. All observers in the life-world develop constructs that allow them to understand what is going on there, but the ability to understand the life-world is increased in science because the (scientific) observer systematically creates much more abstract and standardized constructs with which to understand everyday life.

The key to Schutz's scientific approach is the construction of these second-order constructs or, in more conventional sociological terms, ideal types of social actors and social action. (Good examples are set forth in Schutz's essays on the "stranger" and the "homecomer.") Developing second-order constructs involves the theoretical replacement of human beings in the life-world with puppets (or as Schutz often calls them, "homunculi") created by the social scientist. The scientific model of the life-world is "not peopled with human beings in their full humanity, but with puppets, with *types;* they are constructed as though they could perform working actions and reactions" (Schutz, 1973:255). Schutz thinks in terms of types of people as well as types of courses of action that actors might take.

Social scientists restrict the puppets' consciousness to what is necessary to perform the typical course of action relevant to the scientific problem under consideration. The puppets are not able to selectively perceive objects in their environment that may be relevant for the solution of problems at hand. They exist in situations created not by them but by the social scientist. The puppets do not choose, nor do they have knowledge outside of the typical knowledge granted them by the social scientist. The following is one of Schutz's most complete articulations of the nature of the social scientist's puppets:

> A merely specious consciousness is imputed to them by the scientist, which is constructed in such a way that its presupposed stock of knowledge at hand (including the ascribed set of invariant motives) would make actions originating from it subjectively understandable, provided that these actions were performed by real actors within the social world. But the puppet and his artificial consciousness is not subjected to the ontological conditions of human beings. The homunculus was not born, he does not grow old, and he will not die. He has no hopes and fears; he does not know anxiety as the chief motive of all of his

deeds. He is not free in the sense that his acting could transgress the limits his creator, the social scientist, has predetermined. He cannot, therefore, have other conflicts of interest and motives than those the social scientist has imputed to him. He cannot err, if to err is not his typical destiny. He cannot choose, except among the alternatives the social scientist has put before him as standing to his choice . . . the homunculus, placed into a social relationship is involved therein in his totality. He is nothing else but the originator of his typical function because the artificial consciousness imputed to him contains merely those elements which are necessary to make such functions subjectively meaningful.

(Schutz, 1973:41)

Thus, through the construction of ideal-typical actors and actions, the social scientist develops the tools needed to analyze the social world.

The construction of these puppets (or ideal types, more generally) is not an arbitrary process. To adequately reflect the subjective reality of the life-world and the demands of a rigorous science, ideal types must meet the following criteria:

1 *Postulate of relevance:* Following Weber, Schutz asserted that the topic being investigated in the social world should determine what is to be studied and how it is to be approached. In other words, what the social scientist does must be relevant to the topic being investigated in the life-world.

2 *Postulate of adequacy:* According to this principle, ideal types should be constructed by the social scientist so that the typifications of the actors' behavior in the life-world would make sense to the actors themselves as well as to their contemporaries.

3 *Postulate of logical consistency:* Types must be constructed with a high degree of consistency, clarity, and distinctness and must be compatible with the principles of formal logic. Fulfillment of this postulate "warrants the objective validity of the thought objects constructed by the social scientist" (Schutz, 1973:43).

4 *Postulate of compatibility:* The types constructed by the social scientist must be compatible with the extant body of scientific knowledge or must demonstrate why at least part of this body of knowledge is inadequate.

5 *Postulate of subjective interpretation:* The scientific types, as well as the more general model of the social world, must be based on, and be compatible with, the subjective meaning that action has for real actors in the world of everyday life.

In Schutz's view, the social scientist who adheres to these five postulates will create types and models that meet the need to be true both to the subjective meaning of actors in the life-world and to the demands of a rigorous science.

TYPIFICATIONS AND RECIPES

In the preceding section we discussed Schutz's use of ideal types (second-order constructs)[1] to analyze the social world scientifically. However, as we have already mentioned, people also develop and use *typifications* (first-order constructs) in the

---

[1]While people use first-order constructs on a day-to-day basis, social scientists use second-order constructs (Schutz's "stranger," for example) in their work.

social world. In any given situation in the world of everyday life an action is determined "by means of a type constituted in earlier experiences" (Schutz and Luckmann,
1973:229). Typifications ignore individual, unique features and focus on only generic
and homogeneous characteristics.

While we routinely typify others, it is also possible for people to engage in self-
typification: "Man typifies to a certain extent his own situation within the social world
and the various relations he has to his fellow-men and cultural objects" (Schutz,
1976:233).

Typification takes many forms. When we label something (for example, a man, a
dog), we are engaging in typification. More generally, any time we are using language,
we are typifying, that is, we are applying linguistic types. Indeed, Schutz calls language
"the typifying medium *par excellence*" (1973:75). Language can be thought of as a
"treasure house" of types that we use to make sense of the social world. While we routinely typify others, it is also possible for people to engage in self-typification. "Man
typifies to a certain extent his own situation within the social world and the various
relations he has to his fellow-men and cultural objects" (Schutz, 1976:233).

The linking of typifications to language makes it clear that typifications exist in the
larger society and that people acquire and store typifications throughout the socialization process, indeed throughout their lives. The types that we use are largely socially
derived and socially approved. They have stood the test of time and have come to be
institutionalized as traditional and habitual tools for dealing with social life. While the
individual may create some typifications, most of them are preconstituted and derived
from the larger society.

Schutz sometimes talks of *recipes,* which, like typifications, "serve as techniques for
understanding or at least controlling aspects of . . . experience" (Natanson, 1973a:xxix).
People use recipes to handle the myriad routine situations that they encounter each day.
Thus, when someone greets us with the recipe "How are you?" we respond with the
recipe "Fine, and you?" Continuing the cooking analogy, Schutz argues that we function with "cook-book knowledge . . . recipes . . . to deal with the routine matters of daily
life. . . . Most of our daily activities from rising to going to bed are of this kind. They
are performed by following recipes reduced to cultural habits of unquestioned plati-
tudes" (1976:73–74). Even when we encounter unusual or problematic situations, we
first try to use our recipes. Only when it is abundantly clear that our recipes won't work
do we abandon them and seek to create, to work out mentally, new ways of dealing with
situations.

Schutz and Luckmann (1973:231) outline conditions under which situations become
problematic and people must create new ways of dealing with them (new recipes or typifications). If there is no recipe available to handle a novel situation, or if a recipe does
not allow one to handle the situation it is supposed to deal with, a new one must be
created. In other words, when the stock of knowledge currently available is inadequate,
the person must add to it by creating new recipes (or typifications).

Because of the recurrent existence of problematic situations, people cannot rely
totally on recipes and typifications. They must be adaptive enough to deal with unfore-
seen circumstances. People need "practical intelligence" in order to deal with unpredictable situations by assessing alternative courses of action and devising new ways of
handling situations.

THE LIFE-WORLD

The *life-world* (or *Lebenswelt*) is Schutz's term (derived from Husserl) for the world in which the taken-for-granted, the mundane, takes place. Schutz uses many terms to communicate his sense of this world, including "common-sense world," "world of everyday life," "everyday working world," "mundane reality," "the paramount reality of common-sense life," and so on (Natanson, 1973a:xxv). It is in this world that people operate in the "natural attitude"; that is, they take the world for granted and do not doubt its typifications and recipes until a problematic situation arises.

Schutz defines six basic characteristics of the life-world. First, there is a special tension of consciousness, which Schutz labels "wide-awakeness" (1973:213), in which the actor gives "full attention to life and its requirements." Second, the actor suspends doubt in the existence of this world. Third, it is in the life-world that people engage in working; that is, they engage in "action in the outer world, based upon a project and characterized by the intention to bring about the projected state of affairs by bodily movement" (Schutz, 1973:212). It is work that lies at the heart of the life-world:

> The core region of the life-world is the world of working. . . . Specifically, it is a sphere of activities directed upon objects, animals, and persons "within our actual reach." Typically, operations in it follow "tested recipes of action": it is "my world of routine activities." . . . Such working is planful physical acting upon tangible objects in order to shape and use them for tangible purposes.
>
> (Wagner, 1983:290)

Fourth, there is a specific form of experiencing one's self in which the working self is experienced as the total self. Fifth, the life-world is characterized by a specific form of sociality involving the "common intersubjective world of communication and social action" (Schutz, 1973:230). Obviously, the worlds of dreams and fantasies are not intersubjective worlds. Finally, in the life-world there is a specific time perspective that involves the intersection of the person's own flow of time and the flow of time in the larger society. By contrast, in dreams or fantasies the person's flow of time is usually out of touch with the flow of time in the larger society. That is, one may fantasize, for example, about life in the Middle Ages while one is living in the twentieth century.

While Schutz writes often as if there is only one life-world, the fact is that each of us has his or her own life-world, although there are many common elements in all of them. Thus, others belong to our life-world and we belong to the life-worlds of many others.

The life-world is an intersubjective world, but it is one which existed long before our birth; it was created by our predecessors. It (particularly typifications and recipes, but also social institutions and so on) is given to us to experience and to interpret. Thus in experiencing the life-world, we are experiencing an obdurate world that constrains what we do. However, we are not simply dominated by the preexisting structure of the life-world:

> We have to dominate it and we have to change it in order to realize the purposes which we pursue within it among our fellow-men . . . these objects offer resistance to our acts which we have either to overcome or to which we have to yield . . . a pragmatic motive governs our natural attitude toward the world of everyday life. World, in this sense, is something that we have to modify by our actions or that modifies our actions.
>
> (Schutz, 1973:209)

It is here that we begin to get a sense of Schutz's thinking as dialectical, with actors and structures mutually affecting one another. Wagner takes such a dialectical position when he argues that Schutz's ideas on the life-world blend individual experience "not only with those of social interaction and therefore with the life worlds of others but also with the socially pregiven interpretive schemes and prescriptions [typifications and recipes] for practical conduct" (1983:289).

This dialectic is even clearer in Schutz's thinking about the cultural world. On the one hand, it is clear that the cultural world was created by people in the past as well as in the present, since it "originates in and has been instituted by human actions, our own and our fellow-men's, contemporaries and predecessors. All cultural objects—tools, symbols, language systems, works of art, social institutions, etc.—point back by their very origin and meaning to the activities of human subjects" (Schutz, 1973:329). On the other hand, this cultural world is external and coercive of actors: "I find myself in my everyday life within a world not of my own making . . . I was born into a preorganized social world which will survive me, a world shared from the outset with fellow-men who are organized in groups" (Schutz, 1973:329).

In his analysis of the life-world, Schutz was concerned mainly with the shared social stock of knowledge that leads to more or less habitual action. We have already discussed *knowledge of typifications and recipes,* which is a major component of the stock of knowledge. Schutz views such knowledge as the most variable element in our stock of knowledge because in a problematic situation we are able to come up with innovative ways of handling the situation. Less likely to become problematic are the other two aspects of our stock of knowledge. *Knowledge of skills* (for example, how to walk) is the most basic form of knowledge in that it rarely becomes problematic (an exception in the case of walking would be temporary paralysis) and thus is accorded a high degree of certainty. *Useful knowledge* (for example, driving a car or playing the piano) is a definite solution to a situation that was once problematic. Useful knowledge is more problematic (for example, needing to think about one's driving in an emergency situation) than knowledge of skills, but it is not as likely to become problematic as recipes and typifications.

INTERSUBJECTIVITY

Most broadly, Schutz's phenomenological sociology focuses on intersubjectivity not only because intersubjectivity was largely ignored by Husserl but also because Schutz believed it to be taken for granted and unexplored by any other science. The study of intersubjectivity seeks to answer questions such as these: How do we know other motives, interests, and meanings? Other selves? How is a reciprocity of perspectives possible? How is mutual understanding and communication possible?

An intersubjective world is not a private world; it is common to all. It exists "because we live in it as men among other men, bound to them through common influence and work, understanding others and being understood by them" (Schutz, 1973:10). Intersubjectivity exists in the "vivid present" in which we speak and listen to each other. We share the same time and space with others. "This simultaneity is the essence of intersubjectivity, for it means that *I grasp the subjectivity of the alter ego at the same time as I live in my own stream of consciousness. . . .* And this grasp in simultaneity of the other as well as his reciprocal grasp of me makes possible *our* being in the world together" (Natanson, 1973a:xxxii–xxxiii; italics added).

The italicized portion of the last quotation gets to the essence of Schutz's thinking on intersubjectivity. Schutz was interested in interaction, but mainly as the vehicle whereby people grasp each other's consciousnesses, the manner in which they relate to one another intersubjectively.

Knowledge

Schutz also uses the idea of intersubjectivity in a broader sense to mean anything that is social. He argues that knowledge is intersubjective (or social) in three senses. First, there is a *reciprocity of perspectives* in which we assume that other people exist and objects are known or knowable by all. In spite of this reciprocity of perspectives, it is clear that the same object may mean somewhat different things to different people. This difficulty is overcome in the social world by the existence of two "idealizations." The idealization of the *interchangeability of standpoints* assumes that if we stood in the place of others, we would see things as they do. The idealization of the *congruency of the system of relevance* assumes that we can ignore our differences and that objects are defined sufficiently alike to allow us to proceed on a practical basis as if the definitions were identical. (Schutz calls these two idealizations the "general thesis of reciprocal perspectives.")

The second sense in which knowledge is intersubjective (or social) is in the *social origin of knowledge*. Individuals create a very small part of their own knowledge; most of it exists in shared stocks of knowledge and is acquired through social interaction with parents, teachers, and peers.

Third, knowledge is intersubjective in that there is a *social distribution of knowledge*. That is, the knowledge people possess varies according to their position in the social structure. In our common-sense thinking we take into account the fact that the stock of actual knowledge varies from individual to individual according to their social positions.

Thus, while Husserl identified the transcendental ego as his primary focus, Schutz turned phenomenology outward to a concern for the intersubjective, social world. (Although this is an important difference, we should not lose sight of the fact that both thinkers focused on subjectivity, Husserl within the realm of consciousness and Schutz in the social world.)

Private Components of Knowledge

Schutz also was aware that all the elements of the cultural realm can and often do vary from individual to individual[2] because personal experience differs. The stock of knowledge is "biographically articulated":

> That means that I "know" more or less adequately that it is the "result" of prior situations. And further, I "know" that this, my situation, is in that respect absolutely "unique." Indeed, the stock of knowledge, through which I determine the present situation, has its

---

[2]And from group to group because the social stock of knowledge is stratified.

"unique" biographical articulation. This refers not only to the content, the "meaning" of all the prior experiences sedimented in it, in situations. It refers also to the intensity, . . . duration, and sequence of these experiences. This circumstance is of singular importance, since it really constitutes the individual stock of knowledge.

(Schutz and Luckmann, 1973:111–112)

Thus, according to Schutz, the stock of knowledge always has a private component. However, even this unique and private component of the stock of knowledge is not solely of the actor's own making: "It must be stressed . . . that sequence, experiential depth and nearness, and even the duration of experiences and the acquisition of knowledge, are socially objectivated and determined. In other words, there are social categories of biographical articulation" (Schutz and Luckmann, 1973:113).

Because of their source in individual biography, private stocks of knowledge are not part of the life-world. Because they are biographical in nature, Schutz felt that the unique and private components of knowledge are not amenable to scientific study. They are, in Schutz's view, nonetheless important components of the everyday life of actual actors.

REALMS OF THE SOCIAL WORLD

Schutz identified four distinct realms of social reality. Each is an abstraction of the social world and is distinguished by its degree of immediacy (the degree to which situations are within reach of the actor) and determinability (the degree to which they can be controlled by the actor). The four realms are *umwelt,* the realm of directly experienced social reality; *mitwelt,* the realm of indirectly experienced social reality; *folgewelt,* the realm of successors; and *vorwelt,* the realm of predecessors. The realms of successors and predecessors (*folgewelt* and *vorwelt*) were of peripheral interest to Schutz. However, we shall deal with them briefly because the contrast between them illustrates some of the characteristics of Schutz's major focus—the *umwelt* and the *mitwelt.*

Folgewelt and Vorwelt

The future (*folgewelt*) is a purely residual category in Schutz's work (in contrast to Marx's, for example, where it plays a crucial role in his dialectic). It is a totally free and completely indeterminant world. It can be anticipated by the social scientist only in a very general way and cannot be depicted in any great detail. One could not place great stock in the ideal types and models of the future constructed by the social scientist. Thus, there is little that Schutz's phenomenological science has to offer to the conventional scientist seeking to understand or predict the future.[3]

The past (*vorwelt*), on the other hand, is somewhat more amenable to analysis by the social scientist. The action of those who lived in the past is totally determined; there is no element of freedom, because the causes of their actions, the actions themselves, and their outcomes have already occurred. Despite its determinacy, the study of predecessors presents difficulties for a subjective sociology. It is difficult to interpret the actions of people who lived in an earlier time because we would probably have to use contemporary categories of thought in the historical glance back rather than the categories that

---

[3]We can study what contemporaries *expect* of the future, but we cannot study the future itself.

prevailed at the time. The interpretation of contemporaries is likely to be more accurate because sociologists share interpretive categories with those whose action they seek to understand. Thus, although a subjective sociology of the past is possible, the probability of misinterpretation is great.

The essential point here is that the objective for Schutz was to develop a sociology based on the interpretations of the social world made by the actors being studied. It is difficult to know the interpretations of predecessors and impossible to understand those of successors. However, it is possible to understand contemporaries (*mitwelt*) and the interpretations of those with whom we are in immediate face-to-face contact (*umwelt*).

Umwelt and We Relations

The *umwelt* involves what Schutz calls "consociates," or people involved in face-to-face relationships with one another. Thus, the idea of the *umwelt* is "equally applicable to an intimate talk between friends and the co-presence of strangers in a railroad car" (Schutz, 1973:16). Being in face-to-face contact is all that is required to be considered part of the *umwelt*. There is a unique character and intensity in the *umwelt*:

> Each partner participates in the on-rolling life of the other, can grasp in a vivid present the other's thoughts as they are built up step by step. They may thus share one another's anticipations of the future as plans, or hopes or anxieties. In brief, consociates are mutually involved in one another's biography; they are growing older together; they live, as we may call it, in a pure we-relationship.
>
> (Schutz, 1973:16–17)

We relations are defined by a relatively high degree of intimacy, which is determined by the extent to which the actors are acquainted with one another's personal biographies. The pure we relation is a face-to-face relationship "in which the partners are aware of each other and sympathetically participate in each other's lives for however short a time" (Schutz, 1932/1967:164). The we relation encompasses the consciousness of the participants as well as the patterns of action and interaction that characterize face-to-face interaction. The we relation is characterized by a "thou orientation," which "is the universal form in which the other is experienced 'in person'" (Schutz and Luckmann, 1973:62). In other words, we relations are highly personal and immediate.

The immediacy of interaction has two implications for social relations. First, in a we relation, unlike in a they relation, there are abundant indicators of the other's subjective experience. Immediacy allows each actor to enter into the consciousness of the other. Second, when entering any social relation, an individual has only typical knowledge of the other. However, in the continuing process of a face-to-face interaction, typifications of the other are tested, revised, reenacted, and modified. That is, interaction with others necessarily modifies typologies.

Schutz not only offered a number of insights into we relations per se but also linked these relationships to cultural phenomena in the real world. For example, in we relations actors learn the typifications that allow them to survive socially. People not only learn recipes in we relations but use them there as well—trying them out, altering them when they prove ineffective or inappropriate.

Schutz was aware that there is considerable give-and-take among actors in we relations. People try out different courses of action on other people. They may quickly abandon those that elicit hostile reactions and continue to use those that are accepted. People also may find themselves in situations where recipes do not work at all, and they must create appropriate and workable sets of actions. In other words, in we relations people constantly adjust their actions with regard to those with whom they interact.

People also adjust their conceptions of others. They enter a given relationship with certain assumptions about what the other actors are thinking. In general, people assume that the thinking of others is of the same order as their own. Sometimes this is confirmed by what they find, but in other circumstances the facial expressions, the movements, the words, and the actions of others are inconsistent with people's sense of what others are thinking. People then must revise their view of others' thought processes and then adjust their responses on the basis of this new image of what others are thinking. This is an indirect process, because people cannot actually know what others are thinking. Thus they may tentatively change their actions in the hope that this will elicit responses consistent with what they now think is going on in others' minds. People may be forced to revise their conception of others' thought processes and their actions a number of times before they are able to understand why others are acting in a particular way. It is even conceivable that in some instances people cannot make an adequate number of adjustments, with the result that they are likely to flee the particular interaction, completely confused. In such a case, they may seek more comfortable situations where familiar recipes can be applied.

Even within we relations in everyday life, most action is guided by recipes. People do not *usually* reflect on what they do or on what others do. However, when they encounter problems, inappropriate thoughts and actions, they must abandon their recipes and reflect on what is going on to create an appropriate response. This departure from recipes is psychologically costly, because people prefer to act and interact in accord with recipes.

Because of the freedom of actors within it, the *umwelt* is clearly difficult to deal with from a scientific point of view. In the *umwelt* people and their actions are often not typified. However, people in the *umwelt* do employ typifications of other people and their courses of action. The result is that the social scientist can, albeit with some difficulty, construct typifications of the *umwelt*. In other words, rational models of this often nonrational world can be constructed, and these models can be used to understand life in the *umwelt* better. At the minimum, they can be used to assess differences between the rational models and the way people actually behave. In this approach, Schutz (1976:81) is using typifications in much the same way that Weber used his ideal types.

Before we turn to the *mitwelt,* it should be pointed out that it is in the *umwelt* that the typifications used in daily life (first-order constructs) are created. Thus, to Schutz the *umwelt* is the crucial source of first-order constructs (in contrast to the second-order constructs used in the social sciences), and it is an important, albeit difficult, arena of scientific study. While it is difficult to analyze the *umwelt* scientifically, it is far easier to study the *mitwelt* in this manner. However, although it may be easier to study the *mitwelt,* such study is not likely to be as rewarding as a study of the *umwelt* because of the latter's key role in the creation of typifications and its central role in the social lives of people in the life-world.

Mitwelt and They Relations

The *mitwelt* is that aspect of the social world in which people deal only with types of people or with larger social structures rather than with actual actors. People do fill these types and these structures, but in this world of "contemporaries," these people are not experienced directly. Because actors are dealing with types rather than with actual people, their knowledge of people is not subject to constant revision on the basis of face-to-face interaction. This relatively constant knowledge of general types of subjective experience can be studied scientifically and can shed light on the general process by which people deal with the social world. A number of specific examples of the *mitwelt* will be discussed below.

Whereas in the *umwelt* people coexist in the same time and space, in the *mitwelt* spatial distances make it impossible to interact on a face-to-face basis. If the spatial situation changes and the people draw closer to each other, then face-to-face interaction becomes possible, but if it occurs, we have returned to the *umwelt*. People who were once in my *umwelt* may draw away from me and ultimately, because of spatial distances, become part of the *mitwelt*. Thus, there is a gradual transition from *umwelt* to *mitwelt* as people grow apart from one another. Here is the way Schutz describes this gradual transition:

> Now we are face-to-face, saying good-bye, shaking hands; now he is walking away. Now he calls back to me; now I see him waving to me; now he has disappeared around the corner. It is impossible to say at which precise moment the face-to-face situation ended and my partner became a mere contemporary of whom I have knowledge (he has, probably, arrived home) but no direct experience.

> (Schutz, 1976:37)

Similarly, there are no clear dividing lines among the various levels of the *mitwelt* discussed below.

The *mitwelt* is a stratified world with levels arranged by degree of anonymity. The more anonymous the level, the more people's relationships are amenable to scientific study. Some of the major levels within the *mitwelt*, beginning with the least anonymous, are:

1 Those whom actors encountered face-to-face in the past and could meet again. Actors are likely to have fairly current knowledge of them because they have been met before and could be met again. Although there is a relatively low level of anonymity here, such a relationship does not involve ongoing face-to-face interaction. If these people were to be met personally at a later date, this relationship would become part of the *umwelt* and no longer be part of the *mitwelt*.

2 Those once encountered not by us but by people whom we deal with. Because this level is based on second-hand knowledge of others, it involves more anonymity than the level of relationships with people we have encountered in the past. If we were ever to meet people at this level, the relationship would become part of the *umwelt*.

3 Those whom we are on the way to meet. As long as we have not yet met them, we relate to them as types, but once we actually meet them, the situation again becomes part of the *umwelt*.

4 Those whom we know not as concrete individuals but simply as positions and roles. For example, we know that there are people who sort our mail or process our checks, but although we have attitudes about them as types, we never encounter them personally.

5 Collectivities whose function we may know without knowing any of the individuals who exist within them. For example, we know about the Senate, but few people actually know any of the individuals in it, although we do have the possibility of meeting those people.

6 Collectivities that are so anonymous that we have little chance of ever encountering people in them. For most people, the Mafia would be an example of such a collectivity.

7 Objective structures of meaning that have been created by contemporaries with whom actors do not have and have not had face-to-face interaction. The rules of English grammar would be an example of such a structure of meaning.

8 Physical artifacts that have been produced by a person we have not met and whom we are not likely to meet. For example, people would have a highly anonymous relationship with a museum painting.

As we move further into the *mitwelt* relationships, they become more impersonal and anonymous. People do not have face-to-face interaction with others and thus cannot know what goes on in others' minds. Their knowledge is therefore restricted to "general types of subjective experience" (Schutz, 1932/1967:181).

They relations, which are found in the *mitwelt,* are characterized by interaction with impersonal contemporaries (for example, the unseen postal employee who sorts our mail) rather than consociates (for example, a personal friend). In they relations, the thoughts and actions of people are dominated by anonymous typifications.

In the "pure" they relation, the typical schemes of knowledge used to define other actors are not available for modification. Because we do not interact with actual people but with impersonal contemporaries, information that varies from our typifications is not provided to us. In other words, new experiences are not constituted in they relations. Cultural typifications determine action, and they cannot be altered by the thoughts and actions of actors in a they relationship. Thus, whereas we relations are subject to negotiation, they relations are not.

In spite of the distinction between we and they relations, the typifications used in they relations have their historical roots in we relations: "The first and originally objective solution of a problem was still largely dependent on the subjective relevance awareness of the individual" (Schutz and Luckmann, 1973:225). However, these solutions ultimately become more typified and anonymous—in short, more and more a part of the cultural realm.

CONSCIOUSNESS, MEANINGS, AND MOTIVES

While Husserl had focused on consciousness, especially the universal structures of consciousness, Schutz turned away from consciousness and toward the direction of intersubjectivity, the life-world, and we and they relations. Thus consciousness is not of focal concern to Schutz; rather, it constitutes the point of departure for his science of intersubjectivity.

Schutz believed that in the everyday world, as long as things are running smoothly in accord with recipes, reflective consciousness is relatively unimportant, and actors pay little attention to what is going on in their minds or in the minds of others. Similarly, Schutz (1932/1967:190) believed that in the science of phenomenological sociology one

could ignore individual consciousness. In fact, because Schutz found the mind impervious to scientific study, and because he wanted to focus on intersubjectivity, he admitted in his own work that he was going to abandon the traditional phenomenological
focus on mental processes (1932/1967:97). We thus have the seemingly paradoxical situation of a sociologist who is the field's most famous phenomenologist abandoning the
approach for which phenomenology is best known. However, the paradox is resolved
when we realize that Schutz does carry on the traditional phenomenological concern
with subjectivity. Instead of focusing on individual subjectivity (as Husserl did), Schutz
focuses, as we have seen throughout this chapter, on intersubjectivity.

Despite Schutz's avowed focus on intersubjectivity, he offered many insights into
consciousness. In fact, Schutz argued that the base of all his sociological concerns lay
in the "processes of meaning establishment and understanding occurring within individuals, processes of interpretation of the behavior of other people and processes of self-
interpretation" (1932/1967:11).

The philosophical basis of Schutz's image of the social world, albeit a basis that is,
for him, not amenable to scientific study, is deep consciousness (*durée*), in which is
found the process of meaning establishment, understanding, interpretation, and self-
interpretation. A phenomenological sociology must be based on "the way meaning is
constituted in the individual experience of the solitary Ego. In so doing we shall track
meaning to its very point of origin in the inner time consciousness in the duration of the
ego as it lives through its experience" (Schutz, 1932/1967:13). This is the domain that
was of central concern to Schutz's philosophical predecessors, Henri Bergson and
Edmund Husserl. They were interested in philosophizing about what went on in the
mind, but a central question to Schutz was how to turn this interest into a scientific
sociological concern.

Schutz was drawn to the work of Max Weber, particularly that part of Weber's work
concerned with social action, because it reflected, he thought, both an interest in consciousness and a concern for a scientific sociology. As we saw in Chapter 7, the interest in individual action was only a minor and secondary concern for Weber, who was
more concerned with the impact of social structures on action than with the bases of
action in consciousness. According to Prendergast, Schutz had "no apparent interest in
Weber's theory of bureaucracy, sociology of religion, political sociology, or general
economic history" (1986:15). Schutz, therefore, was concerned with only a small
and peripheral portion of Weber's sociology. But even in that, Weber was a less-than-
satisfying model for Schutz but not for the reasons implied above. To Schutz, the
problem with Weber's work was that there were inadequacies in his conception of consciousness. Weber failed to distinguish among types of meanings, and he failed to distinguish meanings from motives. In clarifying what Weber failed to do, Schutz told us
much about his own conception of consciousness.

Schutz argued that we must distinguish meanings from motives. In the process, he
differentiated between two subtypes of both meanings and motives. Although he did not
always succeed in keeping them neatly separated, for Schutz *meanings* concern how actors determine what aspects of the social world are important to them, whereas *motives*
involve the reasons that actors do what they do. One type of meaning is the *subjective
meaning context*. That is, through our own independent mental construction of reality,

we define certain components of reality as meaningful. However, although this process is important in the everyday life-world, Schutz did not see it as amenable to scientific study, because it is too idiosyncratic.

Of concern to scientific sociology is the second type of meaning, the *objective* meaning context, the sets of meanings that exist in the culture as a whole and that are the shared possession of the collectivity of actors. In that these sets of meanings are shared rather than idiosyncratic, they are as accessible to sociologists as to anyone else. In that they have an objective existence, they can be studied scientifically by the sociologist, and they were one of Schutz's main concerns. Schutz was critical of Weber for failing to differentiate between subjective and objective meaning and for failing to make it clear that objective meaning contexts can be most easily scrutinized in scientific sociology.

Schutz also differentiated between two types of motives—"in-order-to" and "because" motives. Both involve reasons for an individual's actions, but only because motives are accessible to both the person acting and the sociologist. *In-order-to motives* are the reasons that an actor undertakes certain actions; actions are undertaken to bring about some future objective or occurrence. They exist only when action is taking place. In-order-to motives are "subjective." They are private and can be known by the actor but are inaccessible to others. In-order-to motives can be grasped only retrospectively by the actor, after the action is completed and the objective is (or is not) achieved. Sociology is little concerned with in-order-to motives because they are difficult to study scientifically. But sociology can study *because motives,* or retrospective glances at the past factors (for example, personal background, individual psyche, environment) that caused individuals to behave as they did. Since because motives are "objective," they can be studied retrospectively using scientific methods. Since the actions have already occurred, the reasons for them are accessible to both the actor and the social scientist. However, neither other actors nor social scientists can know others' motives, even because motives, fully. Both actors and scientists must be satisfied with being able to deal with typical motives.

In spite of their greater accessibility to the social scientist, because motives were of little more interest to Schutz than were in-order-to motives. They represented a Husserlian return to a concern for consciousness, but Schutz, as we have seen many times, was interested in moving on to the intersubjective world. However, Schutz believed that all social interaction is founded on a reciprocity of motives: "[T]he actor's in-order-to motives will become because-motives of his partner and vice versa" (1976:23).

Schutz embeds his most basic sociological concepts in consciousness. *Action,* for example, is "conduct self-consciously projected by the actor" (Natanson, 1973a:xxxiv), "conduct devised by the actor in advance" (Schutz, 1973:19). More explicitly, Natanson argues: "The crucial feature of action in every case is its purposive and projective character. Action has its source in the *consciousness* of the actor" (1973a:xxxiv; italics added). *Social action* is "action which involves the attitudes and actions of others and is oriented to them in its course" (Schutz, 1976:13).

One other point should be made about Schutz's thoughts on consciousness. Schutz sees within consciousness a fundamental human anxiety that lies at the base of his intersubjective world:

I know that I shall die and I fear to die. This basic experience we suggest calling the *fundamental anxiety.* It is the primordial anticipation from which all the others originate. From the fundamental anxiety spring the many interrelated systems of hopes and fears, of wants and satisfactions, of chances and risks which incite man within the natural attitude to attempt the mastery of the world; to overcome obstacles, to draft projects and to realize them.

(Schutz, 1973:228)

INTERPRETING SCHUTZIAN THEORY

In many ways, Schutzian theory is more difficult to interpret than the work of any other major theorist discussed thus far in this book. First, Schutz (along with, perhaps, Mead) is probably the most single-mindedly abstract theorist whom we have encountered. Others have been much more deeply involved in the empirical world. Weber, for example, offered us his theory embedded in a great deal of historical detail. Marx moved back and forth between theoretical abstraction and the real-world evils of capitalism. Even Parsons, whom we encounter in the next chapter and who was a highly abstract thinker, touched base now and again with the real world. As close as Schutz (1976) ever came to the real world were his abstract essays on social types such as the stranger and the homecomer.

Second, Schutz's theory is embedded in a philosophical tradition that is foreign to sociology and translates only with great difficulty into sociological terms. James Heap and Phillip Roth (1973) argue that it is highly questionable whether Husserl's phenomenology, which is one of the main roots of Schutzian theory, can be translated into sociology. We can characterize Schutz's work as an effort to do just that. The success of Schutz's efforts is illustrated by the popularity of theories derived from his work— particularly ethnomethodology. Nevertheless, his roots in phenomenological philosophy make it difficult for us to grasp his sociology adequately.

Thus, we return to the debate with which we began this chapter. First, some commentators praise Schutz for his micro focus on how actors create the social world. Others criticize him for this focus. Still others see Schutz as having a large-scale, cultural focus. The view developed in this chapter constitutes a rejection of the second position and an integration of the first and third positions. That is, Schutz was dialectically concerned with how actors create the social world and with the impact on actors of the large-scale social and cultural world that they create. While Schutz shares this dialectic with many classical theorists, what distinguishes his approach is that it is purely and exclusively subjective.

SUMMARY

Alfred Schutz took the phenomenological philosophy of Edmund Husserl, which was aimed inward toward an understanding of the transcendental ego, and turned it outward toward a concern for intersubjectivity, the life-world, and the social world.

The key to understanding Schutz's approach is a comprehension of his sense of science. Science was one of a number of worlds examined by Schutz—others included the worlds of dreams, fantasies, insanity, and especially the "paramount reality" of the everyday world. Scientists are not pragmatically involved in the everyday world of the subjects they study or, while they are doing science, their own everyday world. Instead, they are involved in the world of science and rely on its stock of knowledge rather than on the stock of knowledge associated with life in the everyday world.

While in the everyday world people may behave sensibly or reasonably, only in the theoretical models of the social scientist can they behave in a fully rational manner. The rational models and (second-order) constructs of the social scientists (that is, the "ideal types") are based upon the first-order constructs that people must use to function in their daily lives. The social scientists' analyses result in constructed ideal types of fully rational actors (puppets, or "homunculi") and their courses of action. The construction of these ideal types must meet the demands of a rigorous science. It is this type of theorizing, says Schutz, that makes an objective rational science of subjectivity possible.

Implied in much of the preceding discussion is the centrality of typifications to both social scientists and people in the everyday world. Typifications are usually socially derived and socially approved and allow people to function on a daily basis. It is only in problematic situations that people (reluctantly) abandon their typifications (and recipes) and create new ways of dealing with the social world.

As mentioned earlier, Schutz was focally concerned with intersubjectivity, or the way in which people grasp the consciousness of others while they live within their own streams of consciousness. Much of Schutz's work focuses on the life-world, or the world of everyday life. This is an intersubjective world in which people both create social reality and are constrained by the preexisting social and cultural structures created by their predecessors. While much of the life-world is shared, there are also private (biographically articulated) aspects of that world.

There are four realms of the social world—the future (*folgewelt*); the past (*vorwelt*); the present world of consociates, with whom we have face-to-face contact (*umwelt*); and the present world of contemporaries whom we know only as types (*mitwelt*). First-order constructs are created in the *umwelt;* the social scientists' second-order constructs can be applied most easily to the *mitwelt,* although they are most importantly applied to the *umwelt.* Intimate we relations are found in the *umwelt,* and typified they relations characterize the *mitwelt.*

While Schutz had turned away from consciousness, he did offer insights into it, especially in his thoughts on meaning and motives.

Although there is controversy over whether Schutz offers a micro or a macro theory, the view in this chapter is that his theory is concerned with the dialectical relationship between the way people construct social reality and the already present, obdurate cultural reality that others have constructed and are continuing to construct. People are influenced by these realities, but they are also capable of "making sense" of, interpreting, and even reconstructing the cultural world.

14

TALCOTT PARSONS

PARSONS'S INTEGRATIVE EFFORTS
GENERAL PRINCIPLES
    Philosophical and Theoretical Roots
    Action Theory
    The Turn Away from Action Theory
    Pattern Variables
    AGIL
    Consistency in Parsonsian Theory: Integration and Order
THE ACTION SYSTEM
    Social System
    Cultural System
    Personality System
    Behavioral Organism
CHANGE AND DYNAMISM IN PARSONSIAN THEORY
    Evolutionary Theory
    Generalized Media of Interchange

We come now to the last, and most contemporary, of the classical theorists to be discussed in this book, Talcott Parsons (1902–1979). Although Parsons died only a short time ago, it is appropriate to discuss his work in this book for two major reasons. For one thing, it was Parsons, in *The Structure of Social Action* (1937), who brought European classical theory, especially the work of Weber and Durkheim, to the attention of American sociology (Camic, 1989). For another, Parsons created his own distinctive "grand" (or classical) theory. Parsons's theory rivals in scope and grandeur the classical theories discussed in the preceding chapters of this book.

Parsons was undoubtedly the most important American sociological theorist. His written work was widely cited and used by sociologists. Even more important, he shaped the structure of a large portion of American sociological theory, as well as sociology in general, from his position as professor at Harvard University. Many of the most important American theorists were his students, and they went on to endow their own departments, and their own students, with Parsonsian-style theory. Among the many theorists who worked with Parsons at Harvard were Robert Merton, Kingsley Davis, Robin Williams, Wilbert Moore, Marion Levy, and Neil Smelser.

PARSONS'S INTEGRATIVE EFFORTS

Of all the sociological theorists discussed in this book, Parsons was the most explicit in his intention to develop an integrated approach to sociological theory (see the Appendix). There are a number of manifestations of this. First, Parsons founded the Department of Social Relations at Harvard University with the intention of unifying the various social sciences. Included in his integrative goal were such fields as clinical psychology, behavioral psychology, anthropology, and sociology. Second, in his own theorizing Parsons developed a clear sense of levels of social analysis, best exemplified in his notion of four action systems—behavioral organism, personality, social system, and cultural system. Finally, Parsons argued in one of his most important works, *The Social System,* that the integration of levels of social analysis is of central importance in the social world:

> This *integration* of a set of common value patterns with the internalized need-disposition structure of the constituent personalities is the core phenomenon of the dynamics of social systems. That the stability of any social system except the most evanescent interaction process is dependent on a degree of such integration may be said to be the *fundamental dynamic theorem of sociology.*
>
> (Parsons, 1951:42; italics added)

Parsons made a similar point when he argued that the key issue to him was "the problem of theoretical formulation of the relations between the *social system* and the *personality* of the individual" (1970a:1; italics added).

This integrative goal, which runs through a large portion of Parsons's work, is to be lauded and indeed has been applauded by some; however, others (for example, Alexander, 1978; Menzies, 1977) came to see it as "muddled" and "confused." These critics argued that Parsons began *The Structure of Social Action* as a micro-oriented action theorist but that even before he finished that work, and progressively as the years passed, he moved more and more in the direction of a macro-oriented structural-functional theory. Some of the confusion in Parsons's work resulted from his inability to give up older theoretical positions or to integrate them adequately with newer ones. As early as the preface to the second edition of *The Structure of Social Action,* Parsons spoke of his shift

> from the analysis of the structure of social action as such to the structural-functional analysis of social systems. They are, of course, in the last analysis, systems of social action. But the structure of such systems is, in the newer version, treated not directly in action terms, but as "institutionalized patterns."
>
> (Parsons, 1949:D)

One view (Menzies, 1977), shared by this author, is that a basic problem of Parsons's work stems from his never having completed the shift from action theory to structural functionalism, with the result that the two theories are interrelated in a muddled fashion throughout his work. It is not that the integration of action theory and structural functionalism is impossible or undesirable; rather, it is that Parsons never did reconcile them adequately. They often stand side by side in his work rather than being intertwined.

Parsons's frequent use of two different definitions of many key concepts reflects the continuing duality of his theoretical orientation. For example, Ken Menzies (1977) said that in defining *deviance,* Parsons used both a structural-functional approach, emphasizing the larger system's failure to socialize the actor adequately, and an action-theory approach, defining *deviance* as a "motivated tendency for an actor to behave in contravention of one or more institutionalized normative patterns" (Parsons, 1951:250).

In part, Parsons's integrative work is muddled because he never reconciled his Weberian action theory (as he interpreted Weber) with his Durkheimian structural functionalism. It is this duality, along with other factors we will discuss as we proceed, that mars, but does not destroy, Parsons's theoretical approach.[1]

GENERAL PRINCIPLES

A starting point for getting at the substance of Parsons's theoretical orientation is the general principles behind his theory building (Devereux, 1961). Parsons set as his goal the construction of an adequate general theory, a grand theory[2] that was to be analytical, systematic, complete, and elegant. First, such a theory must, from his point of view, be an action theory in which "the central mechanism must always be some notion of actors orienting themselves to situations, with various sorts of goals, values, and normative standards, and behaving accordingly" (Devereux, 1961:19). Second, such a theory must be based on the principle of *voluntarism,* that is, an actor's "choice among alternative values and courses of action must remain at least potentially free" (Devereux, 1961:20). Third, such cultural phenomena as ideas, ideals, goals, and norms must be considered causally relevant factors. Fourth, Parsons adopted the idea of *emergence*—the notion that higher-order systems emerge out of lower-order systems. Such higher-order systems, he felt, must not be able to be inferred from, or explained in terms of, component parts. Finally, the emergent systems must never become wholly detached from their component parts. We will have numerous occasions in this chapter to question how well Parsons actually carried through on these principles in the course of his theoretical work. Although Parsons moved away from this base as his career progressed, the principles are those upon which he built his entire theory.

Philosophical and Theoretical Roots

The source of these ideas on theory can be found in Parsons's 1937 analysis of the roots of modern sociology. Here, and in other works, Parsons always gave the impression that he felt the whole of recent intellectual history was converging in him and his work. He analyzed and criticized utilitarianism and classical economics for dealing with isolated individuals, for assuming individual rationality, and for holding the view that social order came either from the pursuit of individual self-interest or from externally imposed sanctions. Parsons believed that we need to analyze nonrational as well as rational

---

[1]As will be seen throughout this chapter, the author tends to adopt an admiring, but critical, stance toward Parsons's work. For an even more positive analysis, see Richard Münch (1981, 1982).

[2]Ironically, Parsons praised Durkheim for *not* doing grand theory, for doing what many critics felt Parsons never did, that is, integrating theory and reality: "Durkheim was a scientific theorist in the best sense of one who never theorized 'in the air,' never indulged in 'idle speculation' but was always seeking the solution of crucially important empirical problems" (1937:302).

TALCOTT PARSONS: A Biographical Sketch

Talcott Parsons was born in 1902 in Colorado Springs, Colorado. He came from a religious and intellectual background; his father was a Congregational minister, a professor, and ultimately president of a small college. Parsons got an undergraduate degree from Amherst College in 1924 and set out to do graduate work at the London School of Economics. In the next year, he moved on to Heidelberg, Germany. Max Weber had spent a large portion of his career at Heidelberg, and although he had died five years before Parsons arrived, Weber's influence survived and his widow continued to hold meetings in her home, meetings that Parsons attended. Parsons was greatly affected by Weber's work and ultimately wrote his doctoral thesis at Heidelberg, dealing, in part, with Weber's work.

Parsons became an instructor at Harvard in 1927, and although he switched departments several times, Parsons remained at Harvard until his death in 1979. His career progress was not rapid; he did not obtain a tenured position until 1939. Two years previously, he had published *The Structure of Social Action,* a book that not only introduced major sociological theorists like Weber to large numbers of sociologists but also laid the groundwork for Parsons's own developing theory.

After that, Parsons made rapid academic progress. He was made chairman of the Harvard sociology department in 1944 and two years later set up and chaired the innovative Department of Social Relations, which included not only sociologists but a variety of other social scientists. By 1949 he had been elected president of the American Sociological Association. In the 1950s and into the 1960s, with the publication of such books as *The Social System* (1951), Parsons became the dominant figure in American sociology.

However, by the late 1960s, Parsons came under attack from the emerging radical wing of American sociology. Parsons was seen as being a political conservative, and his theory was considered highly conservative and little more than an elaborate categorization scheme. But in the 1980s, there was a resurgence in interest in Parsonian theory not only in the United States but around the world (Alexander, 1982–83; Buxton, 1985; Camic, 1990; Holton and Turner, 1986; Sciulli and Gerstein, 1985). Holton and Turner have perhaps gone the farthest, arguing that "Parsons' work . . . represents a more powerful contribution to sociological theory than that of Marx, Weber, Durkheim or any of their contemporary followers" (1986:13). Furthermore, Parsons's ideas influenced not only conservative thinkers but neo-Marxian theorists as well, especially Jurgen Habermas.

action and that we need to look toward institutionalized common values for the source of social order. He attacked positivism for its view of the world as a closed, deterministic system leaving no room for such critical notions as mind, consciousness, values, ends, and norms. Finally, Parsons lauded idealism for accepting the very ideas rejected by positivism, but he rejected the view that all the social world could be explained by such cultural factors.

The bulk of *The Structure of Social Action* is devoted to a discussion of Alfred Marshall, Vilfredo Pareto, Emile Durkheim, and Max Weber, who developed ideas that were converging on what Parsons called the "voluntaristic theory of action." Parsons's work on these four thinkers is largely a summary of their work, and there is little that is new in it. However, it has been criticized severely for being highly biased and deceptive.

Upon Parsons's death, a number of his former students, themselves sociologists of considerable note, reflected on his theory, as well as on the man behind the theory (for a more recent, and highly personal, reminiscence, see Fox, 1997). In their musings, these sociologists offered some interesting insights into Parsons and his work. The few glimpses of Parsons reproduced here do not add up to a coherent picture, but they do offer some provocative glimpses of the man and his work.

Robert Merton was one of his students when Parsons was just beginning his teaching career at Harvard. Merton, who became a noted theorist in his own right, makes it clear that graduate students came to Harvard in those years to study not with Parsons but rather with Pitirim Sorokin, the senior member of the department, who was to become Parsons's archenemy:

> Of the very first generation of graduate students coming to Harvard . . . precisely none came to study with Talcott. They could scarcely have done so for the simplest of reasons: in 1931, he had no public identity whatever as a sociologist.
>
> Although we students came to study with the renowned Sorokin, a subset of us stayed to work with the unknown Parsons.
>
> (Merton, 1980:69)

Merton's reflections on Parsons's first course in theory are interesting too, especially because the material provided the basis for one of the most influential theory books in the history of sociology:

> Long before Talcott Parsons became one of the Grand Old Men of world sociology, he was for an early few of us its Grand Young Man. This began with his first course in theory. . . . [It] would provide him with the core of his masterwork, *The Structure of Social Action* which . . . did not appear in print until five years after its first oral publication.
>
> (Merton, 1980,69–70)

Although all would not share Merton's positive evaluation of Parsons, they would acknowledge the following:

> The death of Talcott Parsons marks the end of an era in sociology. When [a new era] does begin . . . it will surely be fortified by the great tradition of sociological thought which he has left to us.
>
> (Merton, 1980:71)

What is significant is that Parsons used their work to derive a number of ideas that proved crucial to him, including the nonrational, action, voluntarism, norms, and values. Basically Parsons was saying that these thinkers had freed themselves from their theoretical roots (such as utilitarianism, positivism) and by so doing provided *him* with the tools *he* needed to construct a voluntaristic theory of action.

Action Theory

As a result of these influences and interpretations, Parsons's early work is heavily oriented to action theory. Not too many years ago, a book on sociological theory would have devoted a great deal of attention to action theorists (MacIver, 1931, 1942; Parsons,

1937; Znaniecki, 1934). Today, however, interest in action theory has faded, although some more recent work (Coleman, 1986; Sciulli, 1986) has helped resuscitate it to some degree.

Action theory had its origin in Max Weber's work on social action (see Chapter 7). Although Weber embedded his work in assumptions on actors and action, his real interest was in the cultural and structural constraints on them. Instead of focusing on this aspect of Weber's work, action theory operated at the level of individual thought and action, as is clear from Roscoe Hinkle's summary of the tenets of action theory:

1 Men's social activities arise from their consciousnesses of themselves (as subjects) and of others and the external situations (as objects).
2 As subjects, men act to achieve their (subjective) intentions, purposes, aims, ends, objectives, or goals.
3 They use appropriate means, techniques, procedures, methods, and instruments.
4 Their courses of action are limited by unmodifiable conditions or circumstances.
5 Exercising will or judgment, they choose, assess, and evaluate what they will do, are doing, and have done.
6 Standards, rules, or moral principles are invoked in arriving at decisions.
7 Any study of social relationships requires the researcher to use subjective investigative techniques such as "*verstehen,*" imaginative or sympathetic reconstruction, or vicarious experience.

(Hinkle, 1963:706–707)

There is some evidence that such a micro-level action approach was anticipated by pre-World War I sociologists such as Lester Ward, E. A. Ross, Franklin Giddings, Albion Small, and Charles H. Cooley, although their link to modern action theory is tenuous. Most of these early sociologists were preoccupied with the large-scale question of societal evolution. They discussed an active, creative view of the individual but tended to give society coercive power over the individual.

The exception to this tendency was Cooley. Although he accepted some of the tenets of his contemporaries, and their interest in evolution, "what became ultimately significant in social life [were] subjective consciousness and personal feelings, sentiments, ideas, or ideals in terms of which men initiate and terminate their actions toward one another" (Hinkle, 1963:709).

Sociologists who worked between the end of World War I and the Depression exhibited far more connection with later action theory. Among the more important of these sociologists were Robert Park, Ellsworth Faris, W. I. Thomas, George Herbert Mead, and Talcott Parsons. Parsons was the major inheritor of the Weberian orientation, and his use of action theory in his early work gave that approach its widest audience.

Parsons's Action Theory Parsons was eager to differentiate action theory from behaviorism. In fact, he chose the term *action* because it had a different connotation from that of *behavior. Behavior* implies mechanical response to stimuli, whereas *action* implies an active, creative, "mental" process. As Parsons put it, "A theory which, like behaviorism, insists on treating human beings in terms which exclude his subjective aspect, is not a theory of action" (1937:77–78).

Three concepts lie at the heart of Parsons's action theory—the unit act, voluntarism, and *verstehen.* The most basic phenomenon in Parsons's action theory is what he called the *unit act,* which he defined in terms of four components. First, it implies the existence of an *actor.* Second, the unit act involves an *end,* or a future state toward which action is oriented. Third, the action takes place in a *situation* that involves two elements: things the actor cannot control *(conditions)* and those over which the actor can exert control *(means).* Finally, *norms* and *values* serve to shape the actor's choice of means to ends (Parsons, 1937). Parsons said that there is "no such thing as action except as effort to conform to norms" (1937:76–77). Already in the unit act we see the integrative concerns that were to dominate Parsons throughout his life. Although he began with an interest in actors and their actions, he implied an interest in consciousness in terms of the voluntary choice of means to ends. But that choice is not free, which implies an interest on Parsons's part in the social structures that constrain action. Cultural entities such as norms and values play a key role here, as they do throughout Parsons's work. Intimately related to the unit act is Parsons's concept of voluntarism. *Voluntarism* pertains to actors who are seen as making choices in social situations (Procter, 1978). This is not to say that the actors are totally free in those choices; voluntarism is not equivalent to "free will." Nevertheless, the concept of voluntarism clearly implies a mind, consciousness, and individuals making decisions. Finally, there is the concept of *verstehen,* or the need to analyze action from the subjective perspective.

The Turn Away from Action Theory

In our view, while Parsons never abandoned the idea of individual choice constrained by external forces, he did abandon the focus on consciousness and action implied strongly in *The Structure of Social Action.* This is reflected in the degree to which Parsons backed off from three central concepts in his early work—the unit act, voluntarism, and *verstehen* (which he interpreted as a method largely oriented to the study of consciousness and action).

The unit act lay at the very core of the theoretical contribution of *The Structure of Social Action,* but it progressively disappeared as Parsons's theories developed. In *The Social System* (1951) the unit act is cited only three times in a book that runs close to 600 pages. When it is cited, the impression is that Parsons simply used it to legitimize his earlier work and that it has no relevance to the project at hand. In *The Social System,* Parsons perfunctorily remarked that the unit act is still the basic unit, but

> for most purposes of the more macroscopic analysis of social systems . . . it is convenient to make use of a higher order unit than the act, namely the status-role . . . . It is the structure of the *relations* between the actors as involved in the interactive process which is essentially the structure of the social system . . . . It is the *participation* of an actor in a patterned interactive relationship which is for many purposes the most significant unit of the social system.

> (Parsons, 1951:25)

The unit act and the status-role are very different phenomena, as far as we are concerned. Whereas the unit act refers to actor and action, the *status-role* refers to position within a structure of interaction. In his later work Parsons developed the concept of need-disposition as the most significant unit at the personality level; value orientations occupy the same position in the cultural system. As we will see later, *need-dispositions* are biological needs shaped by external forces, and *value orientations* are internalized cultural standards. The issue here is whether these three new concepts have "emerged" from the unit act or whether they are entirely new concepts. Only the value orientation is traceable directly to the unit act and Parsons's thinking in 1937. Status-role and need-disposition are entirely new, arising out of Parsons's later thought. In his preface to the second edition of *The Structure of Social Action* (1949), Parsons admitted that in the 1937 edition he did not include two critical influences—those of Sigmund Freud on the psychological side and those of anthropologists such as Franz Boas. It is from these sources that Parsons's concepts of need-disposition and status-role undoubtedly came. Clearly, we do not need the unit act to understand the three later concepts. Furthermore, Parsons did not need (or use) the unit act to analyze the social, cultural, and personality systems. As he became, in turn, a structural functionalist, a functionalist, and an evolutionist, the unit act became increasingly extraneous. In his basic work on evolution, *Societies* (1966), the unit act disappears completely.

John F. Scott (1963) is the strongest proponent of the idea that Parsons abandoned voluntarism after 1937 as part of a general abandonment of small-scale sociology. Jonathan Turner and Leonard Beeghley (1974; see also R. Münch, 1982) argued for continuity in Parsons's thinking, contending that he never abandoned the voluntaristic thesis. Scott's error, they said, was equating voluntarism with free will. Parsons never argued for a free-will position; instead, he always believed that individual choice is circumscribed by norms, values, ideas, situations, and so forth. While Turner and Beeghley are correct in their interpretation of voluntarism, the fact is that Parsons turned away from individual choice and came to focus instead on norms, values, and the rest of the more macro-level phenomena.

Finally, there is the disappearance of *verstehen* from Parsons's theory. As Parsons put it: "Contrary to the point of view held by the author in *The Structure of Social Action,* it now appears that this postulate [the subjective point of view] is not essential to the frame of reference of action in its most elementary form" (1951:543). Thus *verstehen* followed the unit act and voluntarism into Parsonsian oblivion. In fact, the subjective perspective had to go when Parsons deserted the unit act and voluntarism. It was because he was looking at a voluntaristic unit act that Parsons needed a subjective methodology. According to Scott, it was the influence of behaviorism that helped to move Parsons away from *verstehen*. Finally, a sociologist need not use *verstehen* in order to study need-dispositions, status-roles, or value orientations, concepts that characterized the next phase of Parsons's work (see the next section).

Need-Dispositions   In work published in the early 1950s, Parsons's interest in the individual level took a new turn. Parsons moved from the unit act, voluntarism, and *verstehen* to need-dispositions and the orientations of actors to situations. There is a concern with consciousness here, albeit a constrained one, one devoid of virtually all creativity. Actors are depicted as being driven by need-dispositions to seek the optimization of gratification; that is, they are impelled by innate needs that are shaped and molded by external forces into dispositions. Within this context Parsons dealt with the motivational and value orientations of actors.

Motivational Orientations   Actors use the framework of motivational orientations to analyze social phenomena that are of interest to them. Of major concern is the degree to which the phenomena represent actual or potential satisfaction of their need-dispositions. This process involves three dimensions. First, actors must analyze the situation *cognitively*. That is, they must:

1 Locate social phenomena (individuals, collectivities, physical culture objects).
2 Differentiate them from other social phenomena.
3 Relate them to general classes of objects.
4 Determine the social phenomenon's properties.
5 Determine the social phenomenon's actual or potential functions.

Simultaneously, the actors must assess the *cathectic* significance of the social phenomenon: they must decide how much affect, or emotion, to invest in each phenomenon they perceive. That determination is influenced by the degree to which a phenomenon is likely to gratify or deprive actors in terms of their need-dispositions. Then actors go through an *evaluative* process in which they determine how to allocate their energies in order to optimize gratification and minimize deprivation.

This discussion of motivational orientation relates to consciousness to some extent. However, it is not the conscious process but the norms and values that shape this process that were of prime significance to Parsons.

Value Orientations   It is in the context of norms and values that Parsons dealt with value orientations, or the cultural standards for judging solutions to each of the three motivational issues discussed in the previous section. Through the socialization process, actors internalize these standards, which become aspects of the actors' orientations, and commit them to the observance of certain norms, standards, and criteria of selection whenever they must make *choices*. Parsons described three value orientations that parallel the three modes of motivational orientation.

First, the actors acquire a set of *cognitive* standards. Among other things, these standards help the actors decide whether the data they are receiving are important, whether their observations are useful, and the relative importance of various situations and problems. In other words, cognitive standards handle informational problems associated with a motivational decision. Then there are *appreciative* standards that allow actors to assess the appropriateness and the consistency of the amount of cathectic energy they have invested in various social phenomena. These are the social rules that help us determine whether a given social entity will satisfy our need-dispositions. Finally, there are *moral* standards that permit actors to assess the consequences of their actions for the integrity of and relationship between the personality and social systems. Overall, the existence of these three sets of standards in Parsons's work, and the sense that they guide (to a large extent even determine) actors' choices, leads us to doubt that Parsons retained very much of a sense of voluntarism.

Types of Action   Parsons used the three modes of motivational and value orientation to develop four basic types of action. *Intellectual action* involves cognitive motivational interests and cognitive value standards; *expressive action* combines cathectic interests and appreciative standards; and *moral action* involves evaluative interests and moral standards. *Instrumental action,* the fourth type, is more complex. It involves future goals determined by cathectic interests and appreciative standards and means to those goals determined by cognitive standards.[3]

Although Parsons was willing to offer us a static typology of action, there is in fact very little sense of dynamic individual action in his work. He based his model of a social system on the interaction of ego and alter ego, but he had very little to say about this, using it only as a base on which to build his large-scale sense of the social system. This lack of action in Parsons's model, even when he was supposedly an action theorist, led William F. Whyte to argue that "in the world of Talcott Parsons, actors are constantly orienting themselves to situations and very rarely, if ever, acting" (1961:255).

Pattern Variables

Returning to Parsons's work on action and consciousness, we encounter the famous, or infamous, pattern variables, which reflect Parsons's overwhelming penchant for parallelisms and conceptual neatness. At the most basic level, the *pattern variables* are a conceptual set of five dichotomous choices of action that actors must make in every situation. At this level they are tools for analyzing conscious processes. The pattern variables are universal choices an actor must make before a situation will have determinate meaning; they address the fundamental problem of orienting oneself to a situation (Parsons, 1951:60). The pattern variables are:

1 *Affectivity—affective neutrality:*   The attitudinal problem of how we feel toward a social phenomenon—how much emotion, affect, to invest in it. For example, should physicians develop emotional ties to patients or should physicians keep patients at a distance?

2 *Specificity—diffuseness:* The attitudinal problem of whether to orient ourselves to part or all of the social phenomenon. Should patients accept advice from physicians on all kinds of problems or only on those within the physicians' area of expertise?

3 *Universalism—particularism:* The problem of how to categorize social phenomena. Are we to judge them in terms of general standards that apply universally to all such entities, or are we to use more specific, more emotional standards in such judgments? For example, we are likely to judge potential physicians with universal standards, but we are likely to assess our own children with more particular standards.

4 *Ascription—achievement:* The problem of whether we characterize social phenomena by what they are endowed with or by what they acquire. Are people born with the ability to become physicians, or are such abilities learned?

5 *Self—collectivity:* The dilemma of whether we should pursue our own private interests or those shared with other members of the collectivity. Is the physicians' desire to earn a good living incompatible with their stated goal of helping humankind?

---

[3]As a matter of fact, this is a good definition of Weber's "value-rational action."

Parsons went on to use the pattern variables to analyze other aspects of his theoretical system. They can be used to differentiate habits of choice within the personality system, to examine the different role expectations within the social system, and to differentiate among the various normative patterns in the cultural system. This tendency to use the same conceptual scheme at different levels of social analysis gives Parsons's work an orderly feel, but it also created problems for him. There is no obvious reason why the same concepts should fit such diverse levels. As Alfred Baldwin said: "The problem of integrating motives within the person bears only a slight resemblance to that of integrating people in society" (1961:185). In general, there is no persuasive reason to believe that all systems, no matter what their level of complexity, have the same set of dilemmas.

AGIL

As has been pointed out previously in this chapter, over the course of his career Parsons moved from action theory to structural functionalism. We will encounter some of Parsons's thoughts on structures and systems shortly, but first we will discuss some of his ideas on functionalism. A *function* is "a complex of activities directed towards meeting a need or needs of the system" (Rocher, 1975:40). Using this definition, Parsons believed that there are four functional imperatives that are necessary for (characteristic of) all systems—adaptation (A), goal attainment (G), integration (I), and latency (L). Together, these four functional imperatives are known as the AGIL scheme. In order to survive, a system must perform these four functions:

1 *Adaptation:* A system must cope with external situational exigencies. It must adapt to its environment and adapt the environment to its needs.

2 *Goal attainment:* A system must define and achieve its primary goals.

3 *Integration:* A system must regulate the interrelationship of its component parts. It also must manage the relationship among the other three functional imperatives (A, G, L).

4 *Latency (pattern maintenance):* A system must furnish, maintain, and renew both the motivation of individuals and the cultural patterns that create and sustain the motivation.

As with the pattern variables, Parsons designed the AGIL scheme to be used at *all* levels in his theoretical system (for one example, see Paulsen and Feldman, 1995). As Chandler Morse noted:

> The four functional imperatives, or problems, operate at both a micro-analytic and a macro-analytic level in the Parsonsian model. At the micro-level they purport to specify the phases through which *individual actors* in a small action system and the action system as a whole must progress during an action cycle. At the macro-level the imperatives provide a means of (a) allocating roles analytically among four functional subsystems of any given system, and of (b) sorting out the input-output flows among those sub-systems.
> (Morse, 1961:116)

In the discussion below on the four action systems, we will illustrate how Parsons uses the AGIL system; later, we will show how he applies it to society.

At their most general level, the four functional imperatives are linked to the four action systems (discussed in detail shortly). The *behavioral organism* is the action

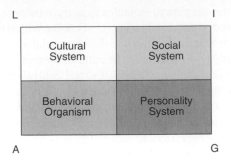

FIGURE 14.1
Structure of the General Action System

system that handles the adaptation function by adjusting to and transforming the external world. The *personality system* performs the goal-attainment function by defining system goals and mobilizing resources to attain them. The *social system* copes with the integration function by controlling its component parts. Finally, the *cultural system* performs the latency function by providing actors with the norms and values that motivate them for action. Figure 14.1 summarizes the structure of the action system in terms of the AGIL schema.

Consistency in Parsonsian Theory: Integration and Order

We have been stressing some of the changes in Parsonsian theory but have, if anything, understated them, since Parsonsian theory takes many other twists and turns. For example, in his later work Parsons came to think of his approach not so much as action, structural functional, or functional but as cybernetic. His concern was with communication among action systems as well as control of lower-order systems by higher-order ones. In spite of all these dramatic changes, there were consistent elements in Parsonsian theory. Parsons himself, while he came to admit certain shifts, emphasized his "essential continuity over the forty-year period since *The Structure of Social Action*" (1977a:2).

One of Parsons's most important concerns from the beginning was the question of order in society (Burger, 1977b). Given a modern, complex society, the question arises of how a "war of all against all," rampant social conflict, is avoided. Throughout his career, Parsons argued that power is not the force that prevents such social warfare. In his view, power is not a sound means of maintaining order in society. Although exercises of power may work in the short run, in the long run they are only likely to bring about more disorder. The use of power evokes negative reactions that lead to further disintegration in society. Furthermore, constant vigilance is required in order for the exercise of power to work. It is difficult, time-consuming, and expensive to maintain order in society on the basis of power. In short, power is an inadequate and inefficient method of maintaining order in society. This antipower position was a consistent theme of Parsons from his earliest works.

Another consistent idea of Parsons was his alternative solution to the problem of order. To Parsons, the ideal way for a society to maintain order is to develop a cultural

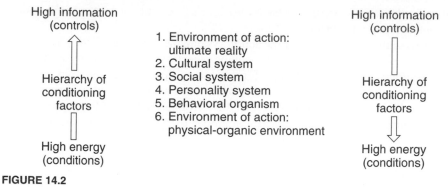

FIGURE 14.2
Parsons's Action Schema

system that emphasizes cooperation and then have that set of ideas internalized in the actors through socialization. This idea relates to Parsons's fundamental theorem, which involves the integration of "common value patterns" (culture) and "need-dispositions" (personality). Put somewhat crudely, order in society is best maintained when people are put in the position of constraining themselves. Because people carry common value patterns around in their heads, they are able to determine for themselves if they are out of line and are able to realign themselves with the cultural value system. Ideally, no external power source is needed to maintain order in society; the society that governs least governs best. Of course, in some instances power is necessary, but these should be few and far between. If the authorities are forced to use power too often, then a society is in deep trouble, perhaps even in danger of disintegration.

This issue of order, power, and integration was an essential theme of Parsons throughout his career. At the end of *The Structure of Social Action* (1937), Parsons considered the solution of the power question to be in value integration. The integration of values and need-dispositions lies at the heart of *The Social System* (1951) and is central to many of Parsons's books and essays after that time. For example, in a well-known essay on organizations, Parsons argued that his "main point of reference for analyzing the [organization] . . . is its value pattern" (1960:20). Although he did discuss power, his primary interest was in cultural dimensions that provide organizational integration. Thus, while most people conceive of organizations as arenas of power and power struggles, Parsons emphasized the values that held organizations together. This kind of thinking over the years earned Parsons the title of "consensus" theorist. We will have occasion to return to this theme in the next section.

THE ACTION SYSTEM

We are now ready to discuss the overall shape of Parsons's action system. Figure 14.2 is an outline of the major levels of Parsons's schema.

It is obvious that Parsons had a clear notion of "levels" of social analysis as well as their interrelationship. The hierarchical arrangement is clear, and the levels are integrated in Parsons's system in two ways. First, each of the lower levels provides the conditions, the energy, needed for the higher levels. Second, the higher levels control those below them in the hierarchy.

In terms of the environments of the action system, the lowest level, the physical and organic environment, involves the nonsymbolic aspects of the human body, its anatomy and physiology. The highest level, ultimate reality, has, as Jackson Toby suggests "a metaphysical flavor," but Toby also argues that Parsons "is not referring to the supernatural so much as to the universal tendency for societies to address symbolically the uncertainties, concerns, and tragedies of human existence that challenge the meaningfulness of social organization" (1977:3).

The heart of Parsons's work is found in his four action systems. In discussing these systems and their interrelationships, Parsons moved away from his earlier action theory and in the direction of structural functionalism (this move is also clear in the earlier discussion of AGIL). In the assumptions that Parsons made regarding his action systems, we encounter once again the problem of order that was his overwhelming concern and that has become a major source of criticism of his work (Schwanenberg, 1971). The Hobbesian problem of order—what prevents a social war of all against all—was not answered to Parsons's (1937) satisfaction by the earlier philosophers. Parsons found his answer to the problem of order in structural functionalism, which operates in his view with the following set of assumptions:

1 Systems have the property of order and interdependence of parts.

2 Systems tend toward self-maintaining order, or equilibrium.[4]

3 The system may be static or involved in an ordered process of change.

4 The nature of one part of the system has an impact on the form that the other parts can take.

5 Systems maintain boundaries with their environments.

6 Allocation and integration are two fundamental processes necessary for a given state of equilibrium of a system.

7 Systems tend toward self-maintenance involving the maintenance of boundaries and of the relationships of parts to the whole, control of environmental variations, and control of tendencies to change the system from within.

These assumptions led Parsons to make the analysis of the *ordered* structure of society his first priority. In so doing, he did little with the issue of social change, at least until later in his career:

> We feel that it is uneconomical to describe changes in systems of variables before the variables themselves have been isolated and described; therefore, we have chosen to begin by studying particular combinations of variables and to move toward description of how these combinations change only when a firm foundation for such has been laid.
>
> (Parsons and Shils, 1951:6)

Parsons was so heavily criticized for his static orientation that he devoted more and more attention to change; in fact, as we will see, he eventually focused on the evolution

---

[4]Most often, to Parsons, the problem of order related to the issue of why action was nonrandom or patterned. The issue of equilibrium was a more empirical question to Parsons. Nonetheless, Parsons himself often conflated the issues of order and equilibrium.

of societies. However, in the view of most observers, even his work on social change tended to be highly static and structured.

In reading about the four action systems, the reader should keep in mind that they do not exist in the real world but are, rather, analytical tools for analyzing the real world.

Social System

Parsons's conception of the social system begins at the micro level with interaction between ego and alter ego, defined as the most elementary form of the social system. He spent little time analyzing this level, although he did argue that features of this interaction system are present in the more complex forms taken by the social system. Parsons defined a *social system* thus:

> A social system consists in a plurality of individual actors *interacting* with each other in a situation which has at least a physical or environmental aspect, actors who are motivated in terms of a tendency to the "optimization of gratification" and whose relation to their situations, including each other, is defined and mediated in terms of a system of culturally structured and shared symbols.
>
> (Parsons, 1951:5–6)

This definition seeks to define a social system in terms of many of the key concepts in Parsons's work—actors, interaction, environment, optimization of gratification, and culture.

Despite his commitment to viewing the social system as a system of interaction, Parsons did not take interaction as his fundamental unit in the study of the social system. Rather, he used the *status role* complex as the basic unit of the system. As mentioned earlier, this is neither an aspect of actors nor an aspect of interaction, but rather a *structural* component of the social system. *Status* refers to a structural position within the social system, and *role* is what the actor does in such a position, seen in the context of its functional significance for the larger system. The actor is viewed not in terms of thoughts and actions but instead (at least in terms of position in the social system) as nothing more than a bundle of statuses and roles.

In his analysis of the social system, Parsons was interested primarily in its structural components. In addition to a concern with the status-role, Parsons (1966:11) was interested in such large-scale components of social systems as collectivities, norms, and values. In his analysis of the social system, however, Parsons was not simply a structuralist but also a functionalist. He thus delineated a number of the functional prerequisites of a social system. First, social systems must be structured so that they operate compatibly with other systems. Second, to survive, the social system must have the requisite support from other systems. Third, the system must meet a significant proportion of the needs of its actors. Fourth, the system must elicit adequate participation from its members. Fifth, it must have at least a minimum of control over potentially disruptive behavior. Sixth, if conflict becomes sufficiently disruptive, it must be controlled. Finally, a social system requires a language in order to survive.

It is clear in Parsons's discussion of the functional prerequisites of the social system that his focus was large-scale systems and their relationship to one another (societal functionalism). Even when he talked about actors, it was from the point of view of the system. Also, the discussion reflects Parsons's concern with the maintenance of order within the social system.

Actors and the Social System   However, Parsons did not completely ignore the issue of the relationship between actors and social structures in his discussion of the social system. In fact, as we saw earlier, he called the integration of value patterns and need-dispositions "the fundamental dynamic theorem of sociology" (Parsons, 1951:42). Given his central concern with the social system, of key importance in this integration are the processes of internalization and socialization. That is, Parsons was interested in the ways that the norms and values of a system are transferred to the actors within the system. In a successful socialization process these norms and values are internalized; that is, they become part of the actors' "consciences." As a result, in pursuing their own interests, the actors are in fact serving the interests of the system as a whole. As Parsons put it, "The combination of value-orientation patterns which is acquired [by the actor in socialization] *must in a very important degree be a function of the fundamental role structure and dominant values of the social system"* (1951:227).

In general, Parsons assumed that actors usually are passive recipients in the socialization process.[5] Children learn not only how to act but also the norms and values, the morality, of society. Socialization is conceptualized as a conservative process in which need-dispositions (which are themselves largely molded by society) bind children to the social system, and it provides the means by which the need-dispositions can be satisfied. There is little or no room for creativity; the need for gratification ties children to the system as it exists. Parsons sees socialization as a lifelong experience. Because the norms and values inculcated in childhood tend to be very general, they do not prepare children for the various specific situations that they encounter in adulthood. Thus socialization must be supplemented throughout the life cycle with a series of more specific socializing experiences. Despite this need later in life, the norms and values learned in childhood tend to be stable and, with a little gentle reinforcement, tend to remain in force throughout life.

Despite the conformity induced by lifelong socialization, there is a wide range of individual variation in the system. The question is: Why is this normally not a major problem for the social system, given its need for order? For one thing, a number of social control mechanisms can be employed to induce conformity. However, as far as Parsons was concerned, social control is strictly a second line of defense. A system runs best when social control is used only sparingly. For another thing, the system must be able to tolerate some variation, some deviance. A flexible social system is stronger than a brittle one that accepts no deviation. Finally, the social system should provide a wide range of role opportunities that allow different personalities to express themselves without threatening the integrity of the system.

---

[5]This is a controversial interpretation of Parsons's work with which many disagree. François Bourricaud, for example, talks of "the dialectics of socialization" (1981:108) in Parsons's work and not of passive recipients of socialization.

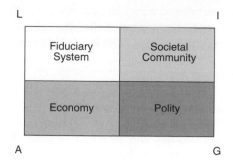

FIGURE 14.3
Society, Its Subsystems, and the Functional Imperatives

Socialization and social control are the main mechanisms that allow the social system to maintain its equilibrium. Modest amounts of individuality and deviance are accommodated, but more extreme forms must be met by reequilibrating mechanisms. Thus, social order is built into the structure of Parsons's social system:

> Without deliberate planning on anyone's part there have developed in our type of social system, and correspondingly in others, mechanisms which, within limits, are capable of forestalling and reversing the deep-lying tendencies for deviance to get into the vicious circle phase which puts it beyond the control of ordinary approval-disapproval and reward-punishment sanctions.

> (Parsons, 1951:319)

Again, Parsons's main interest was the system as a whole rather than the actor in the system—how the system controls the actor, not how the actor creates and maintains the system. This reflects Parsons's commitment on this issue to a structural-functional orientation.

Society Although the idea of a social system encompasses all types of collectivities, one specific and particularly important social system is *society*, "a relatively self-sufficient collectivity the members of which are able to satisfy all their individual and collective needs and to live entirely within its framework" (Rocher, 1975:60).[6] As a structural functionalist, Parsons distinguished among four structures, or subsystems, in society in terms of the functions (AGIL) they perform (see Figure 14.3). The *economy* is the subsystem that performs the function for society of adapting to the environment through labor, production, and allocation. Through such work, the economy adapts the environment to society's needs, and it helps society adapt to these external realities. The *polity* (or political system) performs the function of goal attainment by pursuing societal objectives and mobilizing actors and resources to that end. The *fiduciary system* (for example, in the schools, the family) handles the latency function by transmitting culture (norms and values) to actors and allowing it to be internalized by them. Finally, the integration function is performed by the *societal community* (for example, the law), which coordinates the various components of society (Parsons and Platt, 1973).

---

[6]Barber (1993, 1994) argues that while there is considerable terminological confusion in Parsons's work, the idea of a social system should be restricted to inclusive, total systems like societies.

As important as the structures of the social system were to Parsons, the cultural system was more important. In fact, as we saw earlier, the cultural system stood at the top of Parsons's action system, and Parsons (1966) labeled himself a "cultural determinist."

Cultural System

Parsons conceived of culture as the major force binding the various elements of the social world, or, in his terms, the action system. Culture mediates interaction among actors and integrates the personality and the social systems. Culture has the peculiar capacity to become, at least in part, a component of the other systems. Thus, in the social system culture is embodied in norms and values, and in the personality system it is internalized by the actor. But the cultural system is not simply a part of other systems; it also has a separate existence in the form of the social stock of knowledge, symbols, and ideas. These aspects of the cultural system are available to the social and personality systems, but they do not become part of them (Morse, 1961:105; Parsons and Shils, 1951:6).

Parsons defined the cultural system, as he did his other systems, in terms of its relationship to the other action systems. Thus *culture* is seen as a patterned, ordered system of symbols that are objects of orientation to actors, internalized aspects of the personality system, and institutionalized patterns (Parsons, 1990) in the social system. Because it is largely symbolic and subjective, culture is readily transmitted from one system to another. Culture can move from one social system to another through diffusion and from one personality system to another through learning and socialization. However, the symbolic (subjective) character of culture also gives it another characteristic, the ability to control Parsons's other action systems. This is one of the reasons that Parsons came to view himself as a cultural determinist.

Again establishing parallelism and orderliness in his thinking, Parsons argued that the cultural system has three components that parallel the three modes of motivational orientation discussed earlier. The *cognitive* motivational orientation is paralleled in culture by systems of beliefs and idea systems that represent guidelines to the solution of motivational problems. The *cathectic* motivational orientation has its parallel in culture in systems of expressive symbols, means of expressing a cathectic attachment to a social object. Finally, the *evaluative* motivational orientation is paralleled by similar cultural guidelines—systems of value orientations. (Each component can be subdivided in precisely the same way. Thus, for example, as discussed earlier, the system of value orientations can be broken down into cognitive, appreciative, and moral standards.) Parsons came to the conclusion that the moral standards are "the superordinate integrative techniques of a system of action" (Parsons and Shils, 1951:170). This conclusion reflects the crucial idea in Parsons's theory—that the cultural system is preeminent. But if culture is preeminent, Parsons's integrative work is questionable, for any kind of determinism is suspect from the point of view of an integrated sociology. (For a more integrated conception of Parsons's work, see Camic, 1990). This problem is exacerbated when we look at the personality system and see how weakly it is developed in Parsons's work.

Personality System

The personality system is controlled not only by the cultural system but also by the social system. Parsons's early conception of consciousness and action, in terms of his work on the unit act, voluntarism, and so forth, was reviewed earlier and found wanting. Parsons seemed to be aware of the charge that he had given up his earlier emphasis on voluntarism, and he sought to salvage his position by according some independence to the personality system:

> My view will be that, while the main content of the structure of the personality is derived from social systems and culture through socialization, the personality becomes an independent system through its relations to its own organism and through the uniqueness of its own life experience; it is not a mere epiphenomenon.
>
> (Parsons, 1970a:82)

We get the feeling here that Parsons is protesting too much. If the personality system is not an epiphenomenon, it is certainly reduced to secondary or dependent status in his theoretical system.

The *personality* is defined as the organized system of orientation and motivation of action of the individual actor. The basic component of the personality is the need-disposition, a concept we discussed earlier but which now needs further explication. Parsons and Shils defined *need-dispositions* as the "most significant units of motivation of action" (1951:113). They differentiated need-dispositions from drives, which are innate tendencies—"physiological energy that makes action possible" (Parsons and Shils, 1951:111). In other words, drives are better seen as part of the biological organism. Need-dispositions are then defined as "these same tendencies when they are not innate but acquired through the process of action itself" (Parsons and Shils, 1951:111). In other words, need-dispositions are drives that are shaped by the social setting.

Need-dispositions impel actors to accept or reject objects presented in the environment or to seek out new objects if the ones that are available do not adequately satisfy need-dispositions. Parsons differentiated among three basic types of need-dispositions. The first type impels actors to seek love, approval, and so forth from their social relationships. The second type includes internalized values that lead actors to observe various cultural standards. Finally, there are the role expectations that lead actors to give and get appropriate responses.

This gives a very passive image of actors. They seem to be either impelled by drives, dominated by the culture, or, more usually, shaped by a combination of drives and culture (that is, by need-dispositions). A passive personality system is clearly a weak link in an integrated theory, and Parsons seemed to be aware of it. On various occasions, he tried to endow the personality with some creativity. For example, he said: "We do not mean . . . to imply that a person's values are entirely 'internalized culture' or mere adherence to rules and laws. The person makes creative modifications as he internalizes culture; but the novel aspect is not the culture aspect" (Parsons and Shils, 1951:72). Despite claims such as these, the dominant impression that emerges from Parsons's work is one of a passive personality system.

Parsons's emphasis on need-dispositions creates other problems. Because it leaves out so many other important aspects of personality, his system becomes a largely impoverished one. Alfred Baldwin, a psychologist, makes precisely this point:

> It seems fair to say that Parsons fails in his theory to provide the personality with a reasonable set of properties or mechanisms aside from need-dispositions, and gets himself into trouble by not endowing the personality with enough characteristics and enough different kinds of mechanisms for it to be able to function.
>
> (A. Baldwin, 1961:186)

Baldwin makes another telling point about Parsons's personality system, arguing that even when Parsons analyzed the personality system, he was really not focally interested in it: "Even when he is writing chapters on personality structure, Parsons spends many more pages talking about social systems than he does about personality" (1961:180). This is reflected in the various ways that Parsons linked the personality to the social system. First, actors must learn to see themselves in a way that fits with the place they occupy in society (Parsons and Shils, 1951:147). Second, role expectations are attached to each of the roles occupied by individual actors. Then there is the learning of self-discipline, internalization of value orientations, identification, and so forth. All these forces point toward the integration of the personality system with the social system, which Parsons emphasized. However, he also pointed out the possible malintegration, which is a problem for the system that needs to be overcome.

Another aspect of Parsons's work—his interest in internalization as the personality system's side of the socialization process—reflects the passivity of the personality system. Parsons (1970a:2) derived this interest from Durkheim's work on internalization, as well as from Freud's work, primarily that on the superego. In emphasizing internalization and the superego, Parsons once again manifested his conception of the personality system as passive and externally controlled.

Although Parsons was willing to talk about the subjective aspects of personality in his early work, he progressively abandoned that perspective. In so doing, he limited his possible insights into the personality system. Parsons at one point stated clearly that he was shifting his attention away from the internal meanings that the actions of people may have: "The organization of observational data in terms of the theory of action is quite possible and fruitful in modified behavioristic terms, and such formulation avoids many of the difficult questions of introspection or empathy" (Parsons and Shils, 1951:64).

Behavioral Organism

Though he included the behavioral organism as one of the four action systems, Parsons had very little to say about it. It is included because it is the source of energy for the rest of the systems. Although it is based on genetic constitution, its organization is affected by the processes of conditioning and learning that occur during the individual's life.[7] The behavioral organism is clearly a residual system in Parsons's work, but at the

---

[7]Because of this social element, in his later work Parsons developed the word *organism* and labeled this the "behavioral system" (1975:104).

minimum Parsons is to be lauded for including it as a part of his sociology, if for no other reason than that he anticipated the interest in sociobiology and the sociology of the body (B. Turner, 1985) among at least a few sociologists.

CHANGE AND DYNAMISM IN PARSONSIAN THEORY

Evolutionary Theory

Parsons's work with conceptual tools such as the pattern variables, the functional imperatives, and the four action systems led to the accusation that he offered a structural theory that was unable to deal with social change. Parsons had long been sensitive to this charge, arguing that although a study of change was necessary, it must be preceded by a study of structure. But by the 1960s he could resist the charges no longer and made another major shift in his work, this time to the study of social change,[8] particularly the study of social evolution. By Parsons's (1977b:50) own testimony that interest was first stimulated by a seminar on social evolution held in 1963.

Parsons's (1966) general orientation to the study of social change was shaped by biology. To deal with this process, Parsons developed what he called "a paradigm of evolutionary change."

The first component of that paradigm is the process of *differentiation*. Parsons assumed that any society is composed of a series of subsystems that differ in terms of both their *structure* and their *functional* significance for the larger society. As society evolves, new subsystems are differentiated. This is not enough, however; they also must be more adaptive than earlier subsystems. Thus, the essential aspect of Parsons's evolutionary paradigm was the idea of *adaptive upgrading*. Parsons described this process:

> If differentiation is to yield a balanced, more evolved system, each newly differentiated substructure . . . must have increased adaptive capacity for performing its *primary* function, as compared to the performance of *that* function in the previous, more diffuse structure. . . . We may call this process the *adaptive upgrading* aspect of the evolutionary change cycle.
>
> (Parsons, 1966:22)

This is a highly positive model of social change (although Parsons certainly had a sense of its darker side). It assumes that as society evolves, it grows generally better able to cope with its problems. In contrast, in Marxian theory social change leads to the eventual destruction of capitalist society. For this reason, among others, Parsons is often thought of as a very conservative sociological theorist. In addition, while he did deal with change, he tended to focus on the positive aspects of social change in the modern world rather than on modernity's negative side.

Next, Parsons argued that the process of differentiation leads to a new set of problems of *integration* for society. As subsystems proliferate, the society is confronted with new problems in coordinating the operations of these units.

---

[8]To be fair, we must report that Parsons had done some earlier work on social change, but it did not become a paramount concern, and his contributions were minimal, until the 1960s (see Parsons, 1942, 1947; see also Alexander, 1981; Baum and Lechner, 1981).

A society undergoing evolution must move from a system of ascription to one of achievement. A wider array of skills and abilities is needed to handle the more diffuse subsystems. The generalized abilities of people must be freed from their ascriptive bonds so that they can be utilized by society. Most generally, this means that groups formerly excluded from contributing to the system must be freed for inclusion as full members of the society.

Finally, the *value* system of the society as a whole must undergo change as social structures and functions grow increasingly differentiated. However, since the new system is more diverse, it is harder for the value system to encompass it. Thus a more differentiated society requires a value system that is "couched at a higher level of generality in order to legitimize the wider variety of goals and functions of its subunits" (Parsons, 1966:23). However, this process of generalization of values often does not proceed smoothly as it meets resistance from groups committed to their own narrow value systems.

Evolution proceeds through a variety of cycles, but no general process affects all societies equally. Some societies may foster evolution, whereas others may "be so beset with internal conflicts or other handicaps" that they impede the process of evolution, or they may even "deteriorate" (Parsons, 1966:23). What most interested Parsons were those societies in which developmental "breakthroughs" occur, since he believed that once they occurred, the process of evolution would follow his general evolutionary model.

Although Parsons conceived of evolution as occurring in stages, he was careful to avoid a unilinear evolutionary theory: "We do not conceive societal evolution to be either a continuous or a simple linear process, but we can distinguish between broad levels of advancement without overlooking the considerable variability found in each" (1966:26). Making it clear that he was simplifying matters, Parsons distinguished three broad evolutionary stages—primitive, intermediate, and modern. Characteristically, he differentiated among these stages primarily on the basis of cultural dimensions. The crucial development in the transition from primitive to intermediate is the development of language, primarily written language. The key development in the shift from intermediate to modern is "the institutionalized codes of normative order," or law (Parsons, 1966:26).

Parsons next proceeded to analyze a series of specific societies in the context of the evolution from primitive to modern society. One particular point is worth underscoring here: Parsons turned to evolutionary theory, at least in part, because he was accused of being unable to deal with social change. However, his analysis of evolution is *not* in terms of process; rather, it is an attempt to "order structural types and relate them sequentially" (Parsons, 1966:111). This is comparative *structural* analysis, not really a study of the processes of social change. Thus, even when he was supposed to be looking at change, Parsons remained committed to the study of structures and functions.

Generalized Media of Interchange

One of the ways in which Parsons introduces some dynamism, some fluidity (Alexander, 1983:115) into his theoretical system is through his ideas on the generalized media of interchange within and among the four action systems (especially within the social system) discussed above. The model for the generalized media of interchange is money, which operates as such a medium within the economy. But instead of focusing on material phenomena such as money, Parsons focuses on *symbolic* media of exchange. Even when Parsons does discuss money as a medium of interchange within the social system, he focuses on its symbolic rather than its material qualities. In addition to money, and more clearly symbolic, are other generalized media of interchange—political power, influence, and value commitments. Parsons makes it quite clear why he is focusing on symbolic media of interchange: "The introduction of a theory of media into the kind of structural perspective I have in mind goes far, it seems to me, to refute the frequent allegations that this type of structural analysis is inherently plagued with a static bias, which makes it impossible to do justice to dynamic problems" (1975:98–99).

Symbolic media of interchange have the capacity, like money, to be created and to circulate in the larger society. Thus, within the social system, those in the political system are able to create political power. More importantly, they can expend that power, thereby allowing it to circulate freely in, and have influence over, the social system. Through such an expenditure of power, leaders presumably strengthen the political system as well as the society as a whole. More generally, it is the generalized media that circulate between the four action systems and within the structures of each of those systems. It is their existence and movement that gives dynamism to Parsons's largely structural analyses.

As Alexander (1983:115) points out, generalized media of interchange lend dynamism to Parsons's theory in another sense. They allow for the existence of "media entrepreneurs" (for example, politicians) who do not simply accept the system of exchange as it is. That is, they can be creative and resourceful and in this way alter not only the quantity of the generalized media but also the manner and direction in which the media flow.

SUMMARY

In a few short years Talcott Parsons went from being the dominant figure in sociological theory to being, in some quarters, nearly a theoretical outcast. Neither extreme status is deserved. Parsons's theoretical system always had serious weaknesses, but it is certainly not without major significance.

To his credit, Parsons articulated early in his work an interest in integrating the diverse levels of social analysis, and he maintained that interest, despite basic changes in his theoretical system, throughout his life. Most basically, Parsons was interested in integrating the social and personality systems. Despite such a laudable goal, his work has been marred by some basic confusions, specifically the uncomfortable mix of action theory and structural functionalism. On the basis of his analyses of the people whom he considered to be the major thinkers in the history of sociology, Parsons initially articulated what seemed to be a micro orientation in his action theory. This orientation is particularly clear in his emphasis on the unit act and voluntarism in his early work. However, over the years the unit act and voluntarism tended to disappear from Parsons's theory, as did action theory. In its place, there evolved a structural-functional theory in which actors were seen not as acting in a voluntaristic manner but as constrained primarily by social structures and culture. In the 1940s and 1950s Parsons developed new concepts such as need-dispositions, motivational orientations, and value orientations. They all reflected Parsons's increasing tendency to see actors as constrained by external structures rather than as voluntaristic actors. Other well-known Parsonsian concepts were developed in this period, including the pattern variables and later the AGIL system. Through these changes Parsons retained a lifelong interest in order and a preference for cultural rather than power solutions to the problem of order.

The heart of Parsons's theory lies in his sense of the major levels of social analysis, especially the four action systems. Although Parsons is probably best known for his work on the social system, the most important level in his theory is the cultural system. It stands at the pinnacle of the four action systems and exercises control over the other three (the social, personality, and behavioral organism systems). Although the other levels are not completely controlled by the cultural system, Parsons described himself as a "cultural determinist." Parsons retained an interest in the actor in his later work, but he talked of the personality system, not voluntaristic actors. The problem here is that Parsons tended to see the personality system as determined by the systems that stand above it, the social system and, particularly, the cultural system.

In his later work, Parsons sought to give his perspective more of a change orientation. This is reflected in his work on the evolution of societies. However, despite an apparent focus on change, Parsons's ideas on evolution remained more structural and functional than change-oriented. Also in his later work, Parsons sought to give his approach more dynamism through his ideas on the generalized media of interchange.

SOCIOLOGICAL METATHEORIZING AND A METATHEORETICAL SCHEMA FOR ANALYZING SOCIOLOGICAL THEORY

METATHEORIZING IN SOCIOLOGY
  Pierre Bourdieu's Reflexive Sociology
THE IDEAS OF THOMAS KUHN
SOCIOLOGY: A MULTIPLE-PARADIGM SCIENCE
TOWARD A MORE INTEGRATED SOCIOLOGICAL PARADIGM
  Levels of Social Analysis: An Overview
  Levels of Social Analysis: A Model

One of the most recent developments in sociological theory is the growth in interest in sociological metatheorizing. While theorists take the social world as their subject matter, metatheorists engage in *the systematic study of the underlying structure of sociological theory* (Ritzer, 1991; Zhao, forthcoming). Among our goals in this Appendix is a look at the increase in interest in metatheorizing in sociology and the basic parameters of this approach. Furthermore, the entire structure of this book rests on a specific set of metatheoretical perspectives developed by the author (Ritzer, 1975a, 1981a). Thus, another objective of this Appendix is to present the metatheoretical ideas that inform the text, but before we can do that, we need to present an overview of metatheorizing in sociology.

METATHEORIZING IN SOCIOLOGY

Sociologists are not the only ones to do meta-analysis, that is, to reflexively study their own discipline. Others who do such work include philosophers (Radnitzky, 1973), psychologists (Gergen, 1973, 1986; Schmidt et al., 1984), political scientists (Connolly, 1973), a number of other social scientists (various essays in Fiske and Shweder, 1986), and historians (White, 1973).

Beyond the fact that meta-analysis is found in other fields, various kinds of sociologists, not just metatheorists, do such analysis (Zhao, 1991). We can group the types of meta-analysis in sociology under the heading "metasociology," which we can define as *the reflexive study of the underlying structure of sociology in general, as well as of its various components*—substantive areas (for example, Hall's [1983] overview of occupational sociology), concepts (Rubinstein's [1986] analysis of the concept of "structure"), methods

455

(*metamethods;* for example, Brewer and Hunter's [1989] and Noblit and Hare's [1988] efforts to synthesize sociological methods), data (*meta-data-analysis;*[1] for example, Fendrich, 1984; Hunter, Schmidt, and Jackson, 1982; Polit and Falbo, 1987; Wolf, 1986), and theories. It is the latter, *metatheorizing,* that will concern us in this Appendix.

What distinguishes work in this area is not so much the process of metatheorizing (or systematically studying theories, which all metatheorists share) but rather the nature of the end products. There are three varieties of metatheorizing, largely defined by differences in end products (Ritzer, 1991a, 1991b, 1991c, 1992b, 1992c). The first type, *metatheorizing as a means of attaining a deeper understanding of theory* (M_U), involves the study of theory in order to produce a better, more profound understanding of extant theory (Ritzer, 1988). M_U is concerned, more specifically, with the study of theories, theorists, and communities of theorists, as well as the larger intellectual and social contexts of theories and theorists. The second type, *metatheorizing as a prelude to theory development* (M_P), entails the study of extant theory in order to produce new sociological theory. There is also a third type, *metatheorizing as a source of perspectives that overarch sociological theory* (M_O), in which the study of theory is oriented toward the goal of producing a perspective, one could say a metatheory, that overarches some part or all of sociological theory. (As we will see, it is this type of metatheorizing that provided the framework used in constructing this book.) Given these definitions, let us examine each type of metatheorizing in greater detail.

The first type of metatheorizing, M_U, is composed of four basic subtypes, all of which involve the formal or informal study of sociological theory to attain a deeper understanding of it. The first subtype (internal-intellectual) focuses on intellectual or cognitive issues that are internal to sociology. Included here are attempts to identify major cognitive paradigms (Ritzer, 1975a, 1975b; see also the discussion below) and "schools of thought" (Sorokin, 1928), more dynamic views of the underlying structure of sociological theory (Harvey, 1982, 1987; Wiley, 1979; Nash and Wardell, 1993; Holmwood and Stewart, 1994), and the development of general metatheoretical tools with which to analyze existing sociological theories and to develop new theories (Alexander et al., 1987; Edel, 1959; Gouldner, 1970; Ritzer, 1989b, 1990a; Wiley, 1988). The second subtype (internal-social) also looks within sociology, but it focuses on social rather than cognitive factors. The main approach here emphasizes the communal aspects of various sociological theories and includes efforts to identify the major "schools" in the history of sociology (Bulmer, 1984, 1985; Tiryakian, 1979, 1986; Cortese, 1995), the more formal, network approach to the study of the ties among groups of sociologists (Mullins, 1973, 1983), as well as studies of theorists themselves that examine their institutional affiliations, their career patterns, their positions within the field of sociology, and so on (Gouldner, 1970; Camic, 1992). The third variant (external-intellectual) turns to other academic disciplines for ideas, tools, concepts, and theories that can be used in the analysis of sociological theory (for example, Brown, 1987, 1990a). Baker (1993) has looked at the implications of chaos theory, with its roots in physics, for sociological theory. Bailey has argued that while explicit attention to metatheorizing may be relatively new in sociology, "general systems theory has long been marked by widespread metatheorizing" (1994:27). Such metatheorizing was made necessary by the multidisciplinary character of systems theory and the need to study and bring together ideas from different fields. He later continues, arguing that social-systems theory "embraces metatheorizing" (Bailey, 1994:82). In fact,

---

[1]I have labeled this (somewhat awkwardly) "meta-data-analysis" in order to differentiate it from the more generic meta-analysis. In meta-data-analysis the goal is to seek ways of cumulating research results across research studies. In his introduction to Wolf's *Meta-Analysis,* Niemi defines *meta-analysis* as "the application of statistical procedures to collections of empirical findings from individual studies for the purpose of integrating, synthesizing, and making sense of them" (Wolf, 1986:5).

Bailey uses a metatheoretical approach to analyze developments in systems theory and their relationship to developments in sociological theory.

Finally, the external-social approach shifts to a more macro level to look at the larger society (national setting, sociocultural setting, etc.) and the nature of its impact on sociological theorizing (for example, Vidich and Lyman, 1985).

Of course, specific metatheoretical efforts can combine two or more types of M_U. For example, Jaworski has shown how Lewis Coser's 1956 book, *Functions of Social Conflict*, "was a deeply personal book and a historically situated statement" (1991:116). Thus, Jaworski touches on the impact of his family (internal-social) and of the rise of Hitler in Germany (external-social) on Coser's life and work. Jaworski also deals with the effect of external-intellectual (American radical political thought) and internal-intellectual (industrial sociology) factors on Coser's thinking. Thus, Jaworski combines all four subtypes of M_U in his analysis of Coser's work on social conflict.

Most metatheorizing in sociology is not M_U; rather, it is the second type, metatheorizing as a prelude to the development of sociological theory (M_P). Most important classical and contemporary theorists developed their theories, at least in part, on the basis of a careful study of, and reaction to, the work of other theorists. Among the most important examples are Marx's theory of capitalism (see Chapter 5), developed out of a systematic engagement with Hegelian philosophy as well as other ideas, such as political economy and utopian socialism; Parsons's action theory (see Chapter 14), developed out of a systematic study of the work of Durkheim, Weber, Pareto, and Marshall; Alexander's (1982–83) multidimensional, neofunctional theory, based on a detailed study of the work of Marx, Weber, Durkheim, and Parsons; and Habermas's (1987a) communication theory, based on his examination of the work of various critical theorists, as well as that of Marx, Weber, Parsons, Mead, and Durkheim. Let us look in more detail at M_P as it was practiced by one of the theorists discussed in this book—Karl Marx.

In *Economic and Philosophic Manuscripts of 1844,* Marx (1932/1964) develops his theoretical perspective on the basis of a detailed and careful analysis and critique of the works of political economists like Adam Smith, Jean-Baptiste Say, David Ricardo, and James Mill; philosophers like G. W. F. Hegel, the Young Hegelians (for example, Bruno Bauer), and Ludwig Feuerbach; utopian socialists like Etienne Cabet, Robert Owen, Charles Fourier, and Pierre Proudhon; and a variety of other major and minor intellectual schools and figures. It seems safe to say that in almost its entirety the *Manuscripts of 1844* is a metatheoretical treatise in which Marx develops his own ideas out of an engagement with a variety of idea systems.

What of Marx's other works? Are they more empirical? Less metatheoretical? In his preface to *The German Ideology* (Marx and Engels, 1845–46/1970), C. J. Arthur describes that work as composed mainly of "detailed line by line polemics against the writings of some of their [Marx and Engels's] contemporaries" (1970:1). In fact, Marx himself describes *The German Ideology* as an effort "to set forth together our conception as opposed to the ideological one of German philosophy, in fact to settle accounts with our former philosophical conscience. The intention was carried out in the form of a critique of post-Hegelian philosophy" (1859/1970:22). *The Holy Family* (Marx and Engels, 1845/1956) is, above all, an extended critique of Bruno Bauer, the Young Hegelians, and their propensity toward speculative "critical criticism."[2] In their foreword, Marx and Engels make it clear that this kind of metatheoretical work is a prelude to their coming theorizing: "We therefore give this polemic as a preliminary to the independent works in which we . . . shall present our positive

---

[2]In fact, the book is subtitled *Against Bruno Bauer and Co.*

view" (1845/1956:16). In the *Grundrisse* Marx (1857–58/1974) chooses as his metatheoretical antagonists the political economist David Ricardo and the French socialist Pierre Proudhon (Nicolaus, 1974). Throughout the *Grundrisse* Marx is struggling to solve an array of theoretical problems, in part through a critique of the theories and theorists mentioned here and in part through an application of ideas derived from Hegel. In describing the introduction to the *Grundrisse,* Nicolaus says that it "reflects in its every line the struggle of Marx against Hegel, Ricardo and Proudhon. From it, Marx carried off the most important objective of all, namely the basic principles of writing history dialectically" (1974:42). *A Contribution to the Critique of Political Economy* (Marx, 1859/1970) is, as the title suggests, an effort to build a distinctive economic approach on the basis of a critique of the works of the political economists.

Even *Capital* (1867/1967)—which is admittedly one of Marx's most empirical works, since he deals more directly with the reality of the capitalist work world through the use of government statistics and reports—is informed by Marx's earlier metatheoretical work and contains some metatheorizing of its own. In fact, the subtitle, *A Critique of Political Economy,* makes the metatheoretical roots absolutely clear. However, Marx is freer in *Capital* to be much more "positive," that is, to construct his own distinctive theoretical orientation. This freedom is traceable, in part, to his having done much of the metatheoretical groundwork in earlier works. Furthermore, most of the new metatheoretical work is relegated to the so-called fourth volume of *Capital,* published under the title *Theories of Surplus Value* (Marx, 1862–63/1963, 1862–63/1968). *Theories* is composed of many extracts from the work of the major political economists (for example, Smith, Ricardo) as well as critical analysis of them by Marx. In sum, it is safe to say that Marx was, largely, a metatheorist, perhaps the *most* metatheoretical of all classical sociological theorists.

While we have singled out Marx for detailed discussion, virtually all classical and contemporary theorists were metatheorists, and, more specifically, they practiced M_P.

There are a number of examples of the third type of metatheorizing, M_O. They include Wallace's (1988) "disciplinary matrix," Ritzer's (1979, 1981a) "integrated sociological paradigm" (discussed later in this Appendix), Furfey's (1953/1965) positivistic metasociology, Gross's (1961) "neodialectical" metasociology, Alexander's (1982) "general theoretical logic for sociology," and Alexander's (1995) later effort to develop a postpositivist approach to universalism and rationality. A number of theorists (Bourdieu and Wacquant, 1992; Emirbayer, 1997; Ritzer and Gindoff, 1992, 1994) have been engaged in an effort to create what Ritzer and Gindoff have called "methodological relationism"[3] to complement the extant overarching perspectives of "methodological individualism" (Bhargava, 1992) and "methodological holism." Methodological relationism is derived from a study of works on micro-macro and agency-structure integration, as well as a variety of works in social psychology.

The three varieties of metatheory are ideal types. In actual cases there is often considerable overlap in the objectives of metatheoretical works. Nevertheless, those who do one type of metatheorizing tend to be less interested in achieving the objectives of the other two types. Of course, there are sociologists who at one time or another have done all three types of metatheorizing. For example, Alexander (1982–83) creates overarching perspectives (M_O) in the first volume of *Theoretical Logic in Sociology,* uses them in the next three volumes to achieve a better understanding (M_U) of the classic theorists, and later sought to help create neofunctionalism (M_P) as a theoretical successor to structural functionalism (Alexander and Colomy, 1990a).

---

[3]Swartz (1997) does a particularly good job of delineating this metatheory as well as the other metatheories that inform Bourdieu's theorizing.

Pierre Bourdieu's Reflexive Sociology

An important contemporary metatheorist (although he would resist that label, indeed any label) is Pierre Bourdieu. Bourdieu calls for a reflexive sociology: "For me, sociology ought to be meta but *always vis-à-vis itself.* It must use its own instruments to find out what it is and what it is doing, to try to know better where it stands" (Bourdieu and Wacquant, 1992:191; see also, Meisenhelder, 1997). Or, using an older and less well defined label ("sociology of sociology") for metasociology, Bourdieu says, "The sociology of sociology is a fundamental dimension of sociological epistemology" (Bourdieu and Wacquant, 1992:68). Sociologists, who spend their careers "objectivizing" the social world, ought to spend some time objectivizing their own practices. Thus, sociology "continually turns back onto itself the scientific weapons it produces" (Bourdieu and Wacquant, 1992:214). Bourdieu even rejects certain kinds of metatheorizing (for example, the internal-social and internal-intellectual forms of M_U) as "a complacent and intimist return upon the private *person* of the sociologist or with a search for the intellectual *Zeitgeist* that animates his or her work" (Bourdieu and Wacquant, 1992:72; for a discussion of Bourdieu's more positive view of even these kinds of metatheorizing, see Wacquant, 1992:38). However, a rejection of certain kinds of metatheorizing does not represent a rejection of the undertaking in its entirety. Clearly, following the logic of *Homo Academicus,* (1984b), Bourdieu would favor examining the habitus and practices of sociologists within the fields of sociology as a discipline and the academic world, as well as the relationship between those fields and the fields of stratification and politics. His work *Distinction* (1984a) would lead Bourdieu to concern himself with the strategies of individual sociologists, as well as of the discipline itself, to achieve distinction. For example, individual sociologists might use jargon to achieve high status in the field, and sociology might wrap itself in a cloak of science so that it could achieve distinction vis-à-vis the world of practice. In fact, Bourdieu has claimed that the scientific claims of sociology and other social sciences "are really euphemized assertions of power" (Robbins, 1991:139). Of course, this position has uncomfortable implications for Bourdieu's own work:

> Bourdieu's main problem during the 1980s has been to sustain his symbolic power whilst simultaneously undermining the scientificity on which it was originally founded. Some would say that he has tied the noose around his own neck and kicked away the stool from beneath his feet.
>
> (Robbins, 1991:150)

Given his commitment to theoretically informed empirical research, Bourdieu would also have little patience with most, if not all, forms of M_O which he has described as "universal metadiscourse on knowledge of the world" (Bourdieu and Wacquant, 1992:159). More generally, Bourdieu would reject metatheorizing as an autonomous practice, setting metatheorizing apart from theorizing about and empirically studying the social world (see Wacquant, 1992:31).

Bourdieu makes an interesting case for metatheorizing when he argues that sociologists need to *"avoid being the toy of social forces in [their] practice of sociology"* (Bourdieu and Wacquant, 1992:183). The only way to avoid such a fate is to understand the nature of the forces acting upon the sociologist at a given point in history. Such forces can be understood only via metatheoretical analysis, or what Bourdieu calls "socioanalysis" (Bourdieu and Wacquant, 1992:210). Once sociologists understand the nature of the forces (especially external-social and external-intellectual) operating on them, they will be in a better position to control the impact of those forces on their work. As Bourdieu puts it, in personal terms, "I continually use sociology to try to cleanse my work of . . . social determinants" (Bourdieu and Wacquant, 1992:211). Thus, the goal of metatheorizing from Bourdieu's point of view is not to undermine sociology, but to free it from those forces which determine it. Of course, what Bourdieu says of his own efforts is equally true of metatheoretical endeavors in general. While he strives to limit the effect of external factors on his work, Bourdieu is aware of the limitations of such efforts: "I do not for one minute believe or claim that I am fully liberated from them [social determinants]" (Bourdieu and Wacquant 1992:211).

Similarly, Bourdieu wishes to free sociologists from the symbolic violence committed against them by other, more powerful sociologists. This objective invites internal-intellectual and internal-social analyses of sociology in order to uncover the sources and nature of that symbolic violence. Once the latter are understood, sociologists are in a better position to free themselves of, or at least limit, their effects. More generally, sociologists are well positioned to practice "epistemological vigilance" in order to protect themselves from these distorting pressures (Bourdieu, 1984b:15).

What is most distinctive about Bourdieu's metatheoretical approach is his refusal to separate metatheorizing from the other facets of sociology.[4] That is, he believes that sociologists should be continually reflexive as they are doing their sociological analyses. They should reflect on what they are doing, and especially on how it might be distorting what they are examining, during their analyses. This reflection would limit the amount of "symbolic violence" against the subjects of study.

Although Bourdieu is doing a distinctive kind of metatheoretical work, it is clear that his work is, at least in part, metatheoretical. Given his growing significance in social theory, the association of Bourdieu's work with metatheorizing is likely to contribute further to the growth of interest in metatheorizing in sociology.

With this overview, we now turn to the specific metatheoretical approach that undergirds this book. As will become clear, it involves a combination of M_U and M_O. We begin with a brief review of the work of Thomas Kuhn, and then we examine my (M_U) analysis of sociology's multiple paradigms. Finally, we review the metatheoretical tool—the integrated sociological paradigm (M_O)—that is the source of the levels of analysis used to analyze sociological theories throughout this book.

THE IDEAS OF THOMAS KUHN

In 1962 the philosopher of science Thomas Kuhn published a rather slim volume entitled *The Structure of Scientific Revolutions* (Hoyningen-Huene, 1993). Because this work grew out of philosophy, it appeared fated to a marginal status within sociology, especially because it focused on the hard sciences (physics, for example) and had little directly to say about the social sciences. However, the theses of the book proved extremely interesting to people in a wide range of fields (for example, Hollinger, 1980, in history; Searle, 1972, in linguistics; Stanfield, 1974, in economics), and to none was it more important than to sociologists. In 1970 Robert Friedrichs published the first important work from a Kuhnian perspective, *A Sociology of Sociology.* Since then there has been a steady stream of work from this perspective (Eckberg and Hill, 1979; Effrat, 1972; Eisenstadt and Curelaru, 1976; Falk and Zhao, 1990a, 1990b; Friedrichs, 1972a; Greisman, 1986; Guba and Lincoln, 1994; Lodahl and Gordon, 1972; Phillips, 1973, 1975; Quadagno, 1979; Ritzer, 1975a, 1975b, 1981b;

[4]This leads Swartz (1997:11) to argue that "Bourdieu does not share Ritzer's (1988) vision of establishing sociological metatheory as a legitimate subfield within the discipline of sociology."

Rosenberg, 1989; Snizek, 1976; Snizek, Fuhrman, and Miller, 1979). There is little doubt that Kuhnian theory is an important variety of M_U, but what exactly is Kuhn's approach?

One of Kuhn's goals in *The Structure of Scientific Revolutions* was to challenge commonly held assumptions about the way in which science changes. In the view of most laypeople and many scientists, science advances in a cumulative manner, with each advance building inexorably on all that preceded it. Science has achieved its present state through slow and steady increments of knowledge. It will advance to even greater heights in the future. This conception of science was enunciated by the physicist Sir Isaac Newton, who said, "If I have seen further, it is because I stood on the shoulders of giants." But Kuhn regarded this conception of cumulative scientific development as a myth and sought to debunk it.

Kuhn acknowledged that accumulation plays some role in the advance of science, but the truly major changes come about as a result of revolutions. Kuhn offered a theory of how major changes in science occur. He saw a science at any given time as dominated by a specific *paradigm* (defined for the moment as a fundamental image of the science's subject matter). *Normal science* is a period of accumulation of knowledge in which scientists work to expand the reigning paradigm. Such scientific work inevitably spawns *anomalies,* or findings that cannot be explained by the reigning paradigm. A *crisis* stage occurs if these anomalies mount, and this crisis may ultimately end in a scientific revolution. The reigning paradigm is overthrown as a new one takes its place at the center of the science. A new dominant paradigm is born, and the stage is set for the cycle to repeat itself. Kuhn's theory can be depicted diagrammatically:

$$\text{Paradigm I} \rightarrow \text{Normal Science} \rightarrow \text{Anomalies} \rightarrow$$
$$\text{Crisis} \rightarrow \text{Revolution} \rightarrow \text{Paradigm II}$$

It is during periods of revolution that the truly great changes in science take place. This view places Kuhn clearly at odds with most conceptions of scientific development.

The key concept in Kuhn's approach, as well as in this section, is the paradigm. Unfortunately, Kuhn is vague on what he means by a paradigm (Alcala-Campos, 1997). According to Margaret Masterman (1970), he used it in at least twenty-one different ways. We will employ a definition of *paradigm* that we feel is true to the sense and spirit of Kuhn's early work.

A paradigm serves to differentiate one scientific community from another. It can be used to differentiate physics from chemistry or sociology from psychology. These fields have different paradigms. It can also be used to differentiate between different historical stages in the development of a science (Mann, Grimes, and Kemp, 1997). The paradigm that dominated physics in the nineteenth century is different from the one that dominated it in the early twentieth century. There is a third usage of the paradigm concept, and it is the one that is most useful to us here. Paradigms can differentiate among cognitive groupings *within* the same science. Contemporary psychoanalysis, for example, is differentiated into Freudian, Jungian, and Horneyian paradigms (among others)—that is, there are *multiple paradigms* in psychoanalysis—and the same is true of sociology and of most other fields.

We can now offer a definition of *paradigm* that we feel is true to the sense of Kuhn's original work:

A paradigm is a fundamental image of the subject matter within a science. It serves to define what should be studied, what questions should be asked, how they should be asked, and what rules should be followed in interpreting the answers obtained. The paradigm is the broadest unit of consensus within a science and serves to differentiate one scientific

GEORGE RITZER: Autobiography as a Metatheoretical Tool

Biographical and autobiographical work is useful in helping us understand the work of sociological theorists, and of sociologists generally. The historian of science, Thomas Hankin, explains it this way:

[A] fully integrated biography of a scientist which includes not only his personality, but also his scientific work and the intellectual and social context of his times, [is] . . . still the best way to get at many of the problems that beset the writing of history of science . . . science is created by individuals, and however much it may be driven by forces outside, these forces work through the scientist himself. Biography is the literary lens through which we can best view this process.

(Hankin, 1979:14)

What Hankin asserts about scientists generally informs my orientation to the biographies of sociological theorists, including myself. This autobiographical snippet is designed to suggest at least a few ways in which biography can be a useful tool for metatheoretical analysis.

While I have taught in sociology departments for more than thirty years, have written extensively about sociology, and have lectured all over the world on the topic, none of my degrees are in sociology. This lack of a formal background in the field has led to lifelong study of sociology in general and sociological theory in particular. It has also, at least in one sense, aided my attempt to understand sociological theory. Because I had not been trained in a particular "school," I came to sociological theory with few prior conceptions and biases. Rather, I was a student of all "schools of thought"; they were all equal grist for my theoretical mill.

My first metatheoretical work, *Sociology: A Multiple Paradigm Science* (1975a), sought not only to lay out sociology's separable, and often conflicting, paradigms but also to make the case for paradigm linking, leaping, bridging, and integrating. Uncomfortable with paradigmatic conflict, I wanted to see more harmony and integration in sociology. That desire led to the publication of *Toward an Integrated Sociological Paradigm* (1981a), in which I more fully developed my sense of an integrated paradigm. The interest in resolving theoretical conflict led to a focus on micro-macro (1990a) and agency-structure (Ritzer and Gindoff, 1994) integration as well as the larger issue of theoretical syntheses (1990b).

---

community (*or subcommunity*) from another. It subsumes, defines, and interrelates the exemplars, *theories* [italics added], and methods and instruments that exist within it.

(Ritzer, 1975a:7)

With this definition we can begin to see the relationship between paradigms and theories. *Theories are only part of larger paradigms.* To put it another way, a paradigm may encompass two or more *theories,* as well as different *images* of the subject matter, *methods* (and instruments), and *exemplars* (specific pieces of scientific work that stand as a model for all those who follow).

SOCIOLOGY: A MULTIPLE-PARADIGM SCIENCE

My work on the paradigmatic status of sociology (Ritzer, 1975a, 1975b, 1980) provides the basis for the metatheoretical perspective that has guided the analysis of sociological theory

My interest in metatheoretical work is explained by my desire to understand theory better and to resolve unnecessary conflict within sociological theory. In *Metatheorizing in Sociology* (1991b) and in an edited volume, *Metatheorizing* (1992b), I made a case for the need for the systematic study of sociological theory. I believe that we need to do more of this in order to understand theory better, produce new theory, and produce new overarching theoretical perspectives (or metatheories). Metatheoretical study is also oriented to clarifying contentious issues, resolving disputes, and allowing for greater integration and synthesis.

Having spent many years seeking to clarify the nature of sociological theory, in the early 1990s I grew weary of the abstractions of metatheoretical work. I sought to apply the various theories that I had learned to very concrete aspects of the social world. I had done a little with this in the 1980s applying Weber's theory of rationalization to fast food restaurants (1983) and the medical profession (Ritzer and Walczak, 1988). I revisited the 1983 essay and the result was a book, *The McDonaldization of Society* (1993, 1996), which argued that while in Weber's day the model of the rationalization process was the bureaucracy, today the fast food restaurant has become a better model of that process (additional essays on this topic are to be found in *The McDonaldization Thesis* [1998]). In *Expressing America: A Critique of the Global Credit Card Society,* I turned my attention to another everyday economic phenomenon which I analyzed not only from the perspective of rationalization theory, but from other perspectives including Georg Simmel's theoretical ideas on money.

This work on fast food restaurants and credit cards led to the realization that what I was really interested in was the sociology of consumption, a field little developed in the United States, at least in comparison to Great Britain and other European nations. That led to *Enchanting a Disenchanted World: Revolutionizing the Means of Consumption* (1999), in which I used Weberian, Marxian, and postmodern theory to analyze the revolutionary impact of a range of new means of consumption (superstores, megamalls, cybermalls, home shopping television, casinos, theme parks, cruise ships, as well as fast food restaurants and other franchises) on the way Americans and the rest of the world consume goods and services.

While I cannot rule out a return to more metatheoretical issues, my current plans are to continue to apply social theory to the realm of consumption. I also envision exploring the relationship between various social theories of rationalization and the McDonaldization thesis.

Source: Adapted (and updated) from George Ritzer, "I Never Metatheory I Didn't Like," *Mid-American Review of Sociology,* 15:21–32, 1991.

throughout this book. In my view, there are *three* paradigms that dominate sociology, with several others having the potential to achieve paradigmatic status. I label the three paradigms the *social-facts, social-definition,* and *social-behavior* paradigms. Each paradigm is analyzed in terms of the four components of a paradigm.

The Social-Facts Paradigm

1 *Exemplar:* The model for social factists is the work of Emile Durkheim, particularly *The Rules of Sociological Method* and *Suicide.*

2 *Image of the subject matter:* Social factists focus on what Durkheim termed social facts, or large-scale social structures and institutions. Those who subscribe to the social-facts paradigm focus not only on these phenomena but on their effect on individual thought and action.

3 *Methods:* Social factists are more likely than those who subscribe to the other paradigms to use the interview-questionnaire[5] and historical-comparative methods.

4 *Theories:* The social-facts paradigm encompasses a number of theoretical perspectives. *Structural-functional* theorists tend to see social facts as neatly interrelated and order as maintained by general consensus. *Conflict* theorists tend to emphasize disorder among social facts as well as the notion that order is maintained by coercive forces in society. Although structural functionalism and conflict theory are the dominant theories in this paradigm, there are others, including *systems* theory.

The Social-Definition Paradigm

1 *Exemplar:* To social definitionists, the unifying model is Max Weber's work on social action.

2 *Image of the subject matter:* Weber's work helped lead to an interest among social definitionists in the way actors define their social situations and the effect of these definitions on ensuing action and interaction.

3 *Methods:* Social definitionists, although they are most likely to use the interview-questionnaire method, are more likely to use the observation method than those in any other paradigm (Prus, 1996). In other words, observation is the distinctive methodology of social definitionists.

4 *Theories:* There are a wide number of theories that can be included within social definitionism: *action theory, symbolic interactionism, phenomenology, ethnomethodology,* and *existentialism.*

The Social-Behavior Paradigm

1 *Exemplar:* The model for social behaviorists is the work of the psychologist B. F. Skinner.

2 *Image of the subject matter:* The subject matter of sociology to social behaviorists is the unthinking *behavior* of individuals. Of particular interest are the rewards that elicit desirable behaviors and the punishments that inhibit undesirable behaviors.

3 *Methods:* The distinctive method of social behaviorism is the experiment.

4 *Theories:* Two theoretical approaches in sociology can be included under the heading "social behaviorism." The first is *behavioral sociology,* which is very close to pure psychological behaviorism. The second, which is much more important, is *exchange theory.*[6]

TOWARD A MORE INTEGRATED SOCIOLOGICAL PARADIGM

In addition to detailing the nature of sociology's multiple paradigms, I sought to make the case for more paradigmatic integration in sociology. Although there is reason for extant par-

---

[5]William Snizek (1976) has shown that the interview-questionnaire is dominant in *all* paradigms.

[6]Analyses of this paradigm schema include Eckberg and Hill (1979); Friedheim (1979); Harper, Sylvester, and Walczak (1980); Snizek (1976); and Staats (1976).

adigms to continue to exist, there is also a need for a more integrated paradigm.[7] Contrary to a claim by Nash and Wardell (1993), I am *not* arguing for a new hegemonic position in sociology; I am *not* arguing that "the current diversity represents an undesirable condition needing elimination" (Nash and Wardell, 1993:278). On the contrary, I am arguing for *more* diversity through the development of an integrated paradigm to supplement extant paradigms. Like Nash and Wardell, I *favor* theoretical diversity.

Extant paradigms tend to be one-sided, focusing on specific levels of social analysis while paying little or no attention to the others. This characteristic is reflected in the social factists' concern with macro structures; the social definitionists' concern with action, interaction, and the social construction of reality; and the social behaviorists' concern with behavior. It is this kind of one-sidedness that has led to a growing interest in a more integrated approach among a wide range of sociologists (Ritzer, 1991d). (This is but part of a growing interest in integration within and even among many social sciences; see especially Mitroff and Kilmann, 1978.) For example, Robert Merton, representing social factism, saw it and social definitionism as mutually enriching, as "opposed to one another in about the same sense as ham is opposed to eggs: they are perceptively different but mutually enriching" (1975:30).

The key to an integrated paradigm is the notion of *levels* of social analysis (Ritzer, 1979, 1981a). As the reader is well aware, *the social world is not really divided into levels.* In fact, social reality is best viewed as an enormous variety of social phenomena that are involved in continuing interaction and change. Individuals, groups, families, bureaucracies, the polity, and numerous other highly diverse social phenomena represent the bewildering array of phenomena that make up the social world. It is extremely difficult to get a handle on such a large number of wide-ranging and mutually interpenetrating social phenomena. Some sort of conceptual schema is clearly needed, and sociologists have developed a number of such schemas in an effort to deal with the social world. The idea of levels of social analysis employed here should be seen as but one of a large number of such schemas that can be, and have been, used for dealing with the complexities of the social world.

Levels of Social Analysis: An Overview

Although the idea of levels is implicit in much of sociology, it has received relatively little explicit attention. (However, there does seem to be some explicit interest in this issue, as reflected, for example, in the work of Hage [1994a], Whitmeyer [1994], and especially Jaffee [1998] and Smelser [1997].) In concentrating on levels here, we are making explicit what has been implicit in sociology.

The close of this Appendix will offer a conceptualization of the major levels of social analysis. An adequate understanding of that conceptualization requires some preliminary differentiations. As you will see, two continua of social reality are useful in developing the major levels of the social world. The first is the *microscopic-macroscopic* continuum. Thinking of the social world as being made up of a series of entities ranging from those large in scale to those small in scale is relatively easy, because it is so familiar. Most people in their day-to-day lives conceive of the social world in these terms. A number of thinkers have worked with a micro-macro continuum. For laypeople and academics alike, the continuum is based on the simple idea that social phenomena vary greatly in size. At the macro end of

---

[7]There are other possibilities, including a postmodern paradigm (Milovanovic, 1995) and more inter-paradigmatic dialogue (Chriss, 1996).

the continuum are such large-scale social phenomena as groups of societies (for example, the capitalist and socialist world-systems), societies, and cultures. At the micro end are individual actors and their thoughts and actions. In between are a wide range of meso-level phenomena—groups, collectivities, social classes, and organizations. We have little difficulty recognizing these distinctions and thinking of the world in micro-macro terms. There are no clear dividing lines between the micro social units and the macro units. Instead, there is a continuum ranging from the micro to the macro ends.

The second continuum is the *objective-subjective* dimension of social analysis. At each end of the micro-macro continuum (and everywhere in-between) we can differentiate between objective and subjective components. At the micro, or individual, level, there are the subjective mental processes of an actor and the objective patterns of action and interaction in which he or she engages. *Subjective* here refers to something that occurs solely in the realm of ideas; *objective* relates to real, material events. This same differentiation is found at the macro end of the continuum. A society is made up of objective structures, such as governments, bureaucracies, and laws, and subjective phenomena, such as norms and values.

Now let us turn to the work of several sociologists on the objective-subjective continuum. As we saw in Chapters 1 and 5, an important influence on Karl Marx was German idealism, particularly the work of G. W. F. Hegel. The Hegelian dialectic was a subjective process taking place within the realm of ideas. Although affected by this view, Marx and, before him, the Young Hegelians, were dissatisfied with the dialectic because it was not rooted in the objective, material world. Marx, building on the work of Ludwig Feuerbach and others, sought to extend the dialectic to the material world. On the one hand, he was concerned with real, sentient actors rather than idea systems. On the other hand, he came to focus on the objective structures of capitalist society, primarily the economic structure. Marx became increasingly interested in the real material structures of capitalism and the contradictions that exist among and within them. This is not to say that Marx lost sight of subjective ideas; in fact, notions of false and class consciousness play a key role in his work. It is the materialism-idealism split, as manifest in the work of Marx and others, that is one of the major philosophical roots of the objective-subjective continuum in modern sociology.

We can also find this continuum, although in a different form, in the work of Emile Durkheim (see Chapter 6). In his classic work on methodology, Durkheim differentiated between material (objective) and nonmaterial (subjective) social facts. In *Suicide,* Durkheim said, "The social fact is sometimes materialized as to become an element of the external world" (1897/1951:313). He discussed architecture and law as two examples of material (objective) social facts. However, most of Durkheim's work emphasizes nonmaterial (subjective) social facts:

> Of course it is true that not all social consciousness achieves such externalization and materialization. Not all aesthetic spirit of a nation is embodied in the works it inspires; not all morality is formulated in clear precepts. The greater part is diffused. There is a large collective life which is at liberty; all sorts of currents come, go, circulate everywhere, cross and mingle in a thousand different ways, and just because they are constantly mobile are never crystallized in an objective form. Today a breath of sadness and discouragement descends on society: tomorrow, one of joyous confidence will uplift all hearts.
>
> (Durkheim, 1897/1951:315)

These social currents do not have material existence; they can exist only within the consciousness of individuals and between them. In *Suicide,* Durkheim concentrated on examples of this kind of social fact. He related differences in suicide rates to differences in social currents. For example, where there are strong currents of anomie (normlessness), we find high rates of anomic suicide. Social currents such as anomie, egoism, and altruism clearly do not have a material existence, although they may have a material effect by causing differences in suicide rates. Instead, they are intersubjective phenomena that can exist only in the consciousness of people.

Peter Blau (1960) differentiated between institutions (subjective entities) and social structures (objective entities) is of this genre. He defined *subjective institutions* as "the common values and norms embodied in a culture or subculture" (Blau, 1960:178). Conversely, there are *social structures* that are "the networks of social relations in which processes of social interaction become organized and through which social positions of individuals and subgroups become differentiated" (Blau, 1960:178).

It can be argued that the objective-subjective continuum plays a crucial role in the thought of people like Marx, Durkheim, Blau, and many others. But there is a rather interesting problem in their use of the continuum: they employ it almost exclusively at the macroscopic level. However, it also can be applied at the microscopic level. Before giving an example, we need to underscore the point that we must deal not only with the microscopic-macroscopic and objective-subjective continua *but also with the interaction between them.*

One example of the use of the objective-subjective continuum at the microscopic level is an empirical study by Mary and Robert Jackman (1973) of what they called "objective and subjective social status." Their micro-subjective concern was "the individual's perception of his own position in the status hierarchy" (Jackman and Jackman, 1973:569). Micro subjectivity in this study involved the feelings, perceptions, and mental aspects of the actors' positions in the stratification system. These are related to various components of the micro-objective realm that include the actor's socioeconomic status, social contacts, amount of capital owned, ethnic group membership, or status as a breadwinner or a union member. Instead of dealing with actors' feelings, these dimensions involve the more objective characteristics of the individuals—the patterns of action and interaction in which they actually engage.

Interest in the microscopic aspect of the objective-subjective continuum is manifest in both the social-definition and social-behavior paradigms. Both tend to focus on micro-objective patterns of action and interaction, but they part company on the micro-subjective dimension. All the theoretical components of the social-definition paradigm (for example, symbolic interactionism, ethnomethodology, and phenomenology) share an interest in micro subjectivity—the feelings and thoughts of actors. However, the social behaviorists reject the idea that it is necessary to study the micro-subjective components of social life. This rejection is exemplified by B. F. Skinner's (1971) attack on what he called the idea of "autonomous man." To Skinner, we imply that people are autonomous when we attribute to them such ideas as feeling, minding, freedom, and dignity. To Skinner, the idea that people have such an inner, autonomous core is a mystical, metaphysical position of the kind that must be eliminated from the social sciences: "Autonomous man serves to explain only the things we are not yet able to explain in other ways. His existence depends on our ignorance, and he naturally loses status as we come to know more about behavior" (1971:12). Although we need to reject this kind of political diatribe, the key point is this: the microscopic level has *both* a subjective and an objective dimension.

Levels of Social Analysis: A Model

The most important thinker on the issue of levels of social reality was the French sociologist Georges Gurvitch. Although he did not use the same terms, Gurvitch (1964) had a sense of *both* micro-macro and objective-subjective continua. Even more important, he had a

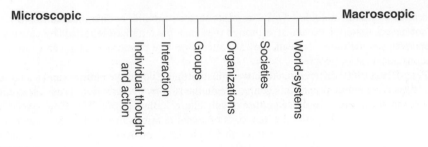

FIGURE A.1
The Microscopic-Macroscopic Continuum, with Identification of Some Key Points on the Continuum

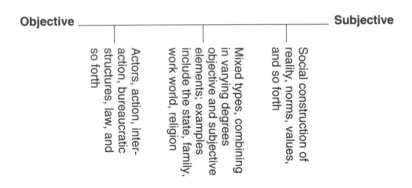

FIGURE A.2
The Objective-Subjective Continuum, with Identification of Some Mixed Types

profound sense of how these two continua are related. To his credit, he also steadfastly refused to treat the two continua and their interrelationships as static tools but used them to underscore the dynamic quality of social life. But Gurvitch has one major difficulty: his analytical schema is extremely complex and cumbersome.

The social world is very complicated, and in order to get a handle on it, we need relatively simple models. The simple model we are seeking is formed out of the intersection of the two continua of levels of social reality discussed in the last several pages. The first, the microscopic-macroscopic continuum, can be depicted as in Figure A.1.

The objective-subjective continuum presents greater problems, yet it is no less important than the micro-macro continuum. In general, an objective social phenomenon has a real, material existence. We can think of the following, among others, as objective social phenomena: actors, action, interaction, bureaucratic structures, law, and the state apparatus. It is possible to see, touch, or chart all these objective phenomena. However, there are social phenomena that exist *solely* in the realm of ideas; they have no material existence. These are sociological phenomena such as mental processes, the social construction of reality (Berger and Luckmann, 1967), norms, values, and many elements of culture. The problem with the objective-subjective continuum is that there are many phenomena in the middle that have *both* objective and subjective elements. The family, for example, has a real material existence as well as a series of subjective mutual understandings, norms, and values. Similarly, the polity is composed of objective laws and bureaucratic structures as well as subjective political norms and values. In fact, it is probably true that the vast majority of social phenomena are mixed types representing some combination of objective and subjective elements. Thus it is best to think of the objective-subjective continuum as two polar types with a series of variously mixed types in the middle. Figure A.2 shows the objective-subjective continuum.

Although these continua are interesting in themselves, the interrelationship of the two continua is what concerns us here. Figure A.3 is a schematic representation of the intersection of these two continua and the four major levels of social analysis derived from it.

The contention here is that an integrated sociological paradigm must deal with the four basic levels of social analysis identified in the figure and their interrelationships (for similar models, see Alexander, 1985a; Wiley, 1988). It must deal with macro-objective entities like bureaucracy, macro-subjective realities like values, micro-objective phenomena like patterns of interaction, and micro-subjective facts like the process of reality construction. We must remember that in the real world, all these gradually blend into the others as part of the larger social continuum, but we have made some artificial and rather arbitrary differentiations in order to be able to deal with social reality. These four levels of social analysis are posited for heuristic purposes and are not meant to be accurate depictions of the social world.

While there is much to be gained from the development of an integrated sociological paradigm, one can expect resistance from many quarters. Lewis has argued that opposition to an integrated paradigm comes from those theorists, "paradigm warriors" (Aldrich, 1988), who are intent on defending their theoretical turf, come what may:

> Much of the objection to an integrated paradigm is not on theoretical, but on political grounds; an integrated paradigm threatens the purity and independence—and perhaps even the existence—of theoretical approaches which derive their inspiration from *opposition* to existing theory. . . . An integrated paradigm, such as Ritzer proposes, allows and even encourages a broader perspective than some find comfortable. Adopting an integrated paradigm means relinquishing belief in the ultimate truth of one's favorite theory. . . . Acceptance of an integrated paradigm requires an understanding, and indeed an appreciation, of a broad range of theoretical perspectives—an intellectually challenging task. . . . Although Ritzer does not discuss the issue, this author maintains that overcoming massive *intellectual agoraphobia* presents the greatest challenge to acceptance of an integrated paradigm.
>
> (Lewis, 1991:228–229)

An obvious question is how the four levels of the integrated paradigm relate to the three paradigms discussed earlier, as well as to the integrated paradigm. Figure A.4 relates the four levels to the three paradigms.

The social-facts paradigm focuses primarily on the macro-objective and macro-subjective levels. The social-definition paradigm is concerned largely with the micro-subjective world and that part of the micro-objective world that depends on mental processes (action). The social-behavior paradigm deals with that part of the micro-objective world that does not involve the minding process (behavior). Whereas the three extant paradigms cut across the levels of social reality horizontally, an integrated paradigm cuts across vertically. This depiction makes it clear why the integrated paradigm does not supersede the others. Although each of the three existing paradigms deals with a given level or levels in great detail, the integrated paradigm deals with all levels but does not examine any given level in anything like the degree of intensity of the other paradigms. Thus the choice of a paradigm depends on the kind of question being asked. Not all sociological issues require an integrated approach, but at least some do.

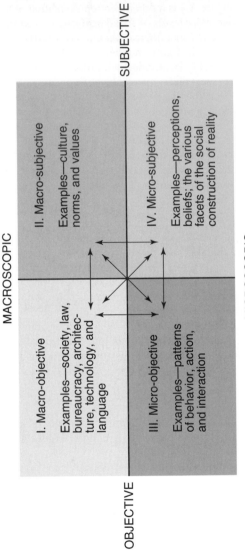

FIGURE A.3

Ritzer's Major Levels of Social Analysis*

*Note that this is a "snapshot" in time. It is embedded in an ongoing historical process.

LEVELS OF SOCIAL REALITY   SOCIOLOGICAL PARADIGMS

Macro-subjective
Macro-objective

Micro-subjective
Micro-objective

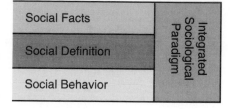

FIGURE A.4
Levels of Social Analysis and the Major Sociological Paradigms

What has been outlined in the preceding pages is a model for the image of the subject matter of an integrated sociological paradigm. This sketch needs to be detailed more sharply, but that is a task for another time (see Ritzer, 1981a). The goal of this discussion is not the development of a new sociological paradigm but the delineation of an overarching metatheoretical schema (M_O) that allows us to analyze sociological theory in a coherent fashion. The model developed in Figure A.3 forms the basis for this book.

Sociological theory is analyzed using the four levels of social analysis depicted in Figure A.3. This figure provides us with a metatheoretical tool that can be used in the comparative analysis of sociological theories. It enables us to analyze the concerns of a theory and how they relate to the concerns of all other sociological theories.

To be avoided at all costs is the simple identification of a theory or a theorist with specific levels of social analysis. Although it is true, given the preceding description of the current paradigmatic status of sociology, that sociological theorists who adhere to a given paradigm tend to focus on a given level or levels of social analysis, it often does them an injustice simply to equate the breadth of their work with one or more levels. For example, Karl Marx is often thought of as focusing on macro-objective structures—in particular, on the economic structures of capitalism. But the use of the schema in which there are multiple levels of social analysis allows us to see that Marx had rich insights regarding *all* levels of social reality and their interrelationships. Similarly, symbolic interactionism is generally considered a perspective that deals with micro subjectivity and micro objectivity, but it is not devoid of insights into the macroscopic levels of social analysis (Maines, 1977).

It is also important to remember that the use of levels of social analysis to analyze a theory tends to break up the wholeness, the integrity, and the internal consistency of the theory. Although the levels are useful for understanding a theory and comparing it to others, one must take pains to deal with the interrelationship among levels and with the totality of a theory.

In sum, the metatheoretical schema outlined in Figure A.3, the development of which was traced in this Appendix, provides the basis for the analysis of the sociological theories discussed in this book.

REFERENCES

Abbott, Andrew
1988   *The System of Professions: An Essay on the Division of Labor.* Chicago:
            University of Chicago Press.
Abbott, Edith
1906   "Harriet Martineau and the Employment of Women in 1836." *Journal of
            Political Economy* 14:611–626.
1910   *Women in Industry.* New York: Appleton.
1936/1970   *The Tenements of Chicago 1908–1935.* New York: Arno.
Aboulafia, Mitchell
1986   *The Mediating Self: Mead, Sartre, and Self-Determination.* New Haven:
            Yale University Press.
Abraham, Gary A.
1992   *Max Weber and the Jewish Question: A Study of the Social Outlook of
            His Sociology.* Urbana: University of Illinois Press.
Abrams, Philip
1968   *The Origins of British Sociology: 1834–1914.* Chicago: University of
            Chicago Press.
1982   *Historical Sociology.* Ithaca, N.Y.: Cornell University Press.
Abrams, Philip, Deem, Rosemary, Finch, Janet, and Rock, Paul
1981   *Practice and Progress: British Sociology 1950–1980.* London: Allen
            and Unwin.
Addams, Jane
1902/1907   *Democracy and Social Ethics.* New York: Macmillan.
1905   "Problems of Municipal Administration." *American Journal of Sociology*
            10:425–444.
1907   *Newer Ideals of Peace.* New York: Macmillan.
1910/1990   *Twenty Years at Hull-House.* James Hurt (ed.). Urbana: University of
            Illinois Press.
1916   *The Long Road of Women's Memory.* New York: Macmillan.
1922   *Peace and Bread in Times of War.* New York: Macmillan.
1930   *The Second Twenty Years at Hull-House.* New York: Macmillan.
Agger, Ben
1998   *Critical Social Theories: An Introduction.* Boulder, Colo.: Westview.
Alcala-Campos, Raul
1997   "Thomas S. Kuhn: Between Modernity and Postmodernity." *Acta
            Sociologica* 19:59–77.
Aldrich, Howard
1988   "Paradigm Warriors: Donaldson versus the Critics of Organization Theory."
            Organization Studies 9:19–25.

Alexander, Elizabeth
1995   "'We Must Be about Our Father's Business': Anna Julia Cooper and the
            Incorporation of the Nineteenth Century African-American Woman
            Intellectual." *Signs* 20:336–356.
Alexander, Jeffrey
1978   "Formal and Substantive Voluntarism in the Work of Talcott Parsons:
            A Theoretical and Ideological Reinterpretation." *American Sociological
            Review* 43:177–198.
1981   "Revolution, Reaction, and Reform: The Change Theory of Parsons's Middle
            Period." *Sociological Inquiry* 51:267–280.
1982   *Theoretical Logic in Sociology.* Vol. 1, *Positivism, Presuppositions, and
            Current Controversies.* Berkeley: University of California Press.
1982–1983   *Theoretical Logic in Sociology.* 4 vols. Berkeley: University of
            California Press.
1983   *Theoretical Logic in Sociology.* Vol. 4, *The Modern Reconstruction
            of Classical Thought: Talcott Parsons.* Berkeley: University of
            California Press.
1984   "The Parsons Revival in German Sociology." In R. Collins (ed.),
            Sociological Theory—1984. San Francisco: Jossey-Bass: 394–412.
1985a   "The 'Individualist Dilemma' in Phenomenology and Interactionism." In
            S. N. Eisenstadt and H. J. Helle (eds.), *Macro-Sociological Theory.* Vol. 1.
            London: Sage: 25–57.
1987   "Action and Its Environments." In J. Alexander et al. (eds.), *The Micro-
            Macro Link.* Berkeley: University of California Press: 289–318.
1988b   "Culture and Political Crisis: 'Watergate' and Durkheimian Sociology." In
            J. C. Alexander (ed.), *Durkheimian Sociology: Cultural Studies.* Cambridge:
            Cambridge University Press: 187–224.
1988c   "Introduction: Durkheimian Sociology and Cultural Studies Today." In
            J. C. Alexander (ed.), *Durkheimian Sociology: Cultural Studies.* Cambridge:
            Cambridge University Press: 1–21.
1995   *Fin de Siecle Social Theory: Relativism, Reduction, and the Problem of
            Reason.* London: Verso.
1998a   *Neofunctionalism and After.* Malden, Mass.: Blackwell.
Alexander, Jeffrey (ed.)
1985b   *Neofunctionalism.* Beverly Hills, Calif.: Sage.
1988a   *Durkheimian Sociology: Cultural Studies.* Cambridge: Cambridge
            University Press.
Alexander, Jeffrey, and Colomy, Paul
1985   "Toward Neo-Functionalism." *Sociological Theory* 3:11–23.
1990   "Neofunctionalism: Reconstructing a Theoretical Tradition." In G. Ritzer
            (ed.), *Frontiers of Social Theory: The New Syntheses.* New York: Columbia
            University Press: 33–67.
1992   "Traditions and Competition: Preface to a Postpositivist Approach to
            Knowledge Cumulation." In G. Ritzer (ed.), *Metatheorizing.* Newbury
            Park, Calif.: Sage: 27–52.
Alexander, Jeffrey, Giesen, Bernard, Münch, Richard, and Smelser, Neil J. (eds.)
1987   *The Micro-Macro Link.* Berkeley: University of California Press.

Alexander, Jeffrey C., Smith, Philip, and Sherwood, Steven Jay
1993   "Risking Enchantment: Theory and Method in Cultural Studies." *Newsletter of the Sociology of Culture Section of the American Sociological Association* 8:10–14.
Alford, Robert R., and Friedland, Roger
1985   *Powers of Theory: Capitalism, the State, and Democracy.* Cambridge: Cambridge University Press.
Alger, Janet M., and Alger, Steven F.
1997   "Beyond Mead: Symbolic Interaction between Humans and Felines." *Society and Animals* 5:65–81.
Alt, John
1985–1986   "Reclaiming C. Wright Mills." *Telos* 66:6–43.
Althusser, Louis
1969   *For Marx.* Harmondsworth, Eng.: Penguin.
Alway, Joan
1995   "The Trouble with Gender: Tales of the Still Missing Feminist Revolution in Sociological Theory." *Sociological Theory* 13:209–226.
Amsterdamska, Olga
1985   "Institutions and Schools of Thought." *American Journal of Sociology* 91:332–358.
Andreski, Stanislav
1971   *Herbert Spencer: Structure, Function and Evolution.* New York: Scribner's.
Andrews, Howard F.
1993   "Durkheim and Social Morphology." In S. P. Turner (ed.), *Emile Durkheim: Sociologist and Moralist.* London: Routledge: 111–135.
Antonio, Robert J.
1979   "Domination and Production in Bureaucracy." *American Sociological Review* 44:895–912.
1985   "Values, History and Science: The Metatheoretic Foundations of the Weber-Marx Dialogues." In R. J. Antonio and R. M. Glassman (eds.), *A Weber-Marx Dialogue.* Lawrence: University Press of Kansas: 20–43.
1990   "The Decline of the Grand Narrative of Emancipatory Modernity: Crisis or Renewal in Neo-Marxian Theory?" In G. Ritzer (ed.), *Frontiers of Social Theory: The New Syntheses.* New York: Columbia University Press: 88–116.
forthcoming "Karl Marx." In George Ritzer (ed.), *The Blackwell Companion to Major Social Theorists.* Oxford, England, and Cambridge, Mass.: Blackwell.
Antonio, Robert J., and Glassman, Ronald M. (eds.)
1985   *A Weber-Marx Dialogue.* Lawrence: University Press of Kansas.
Antonio, Robert, and Kellner, Douglas
1992   "Metatheorizing Historical Rupture: Classical Theory and Modernity." In G. Ritzer (ed.), *Metatheorizing.* Beverly Hills, Calif.: Sage: 88–106.
Archer, Margaret S.
1982   "Morphogenesis versus Structuration: On Combining Structure and Action." *British Journal of Sociology* 33:455–483.
1988   *Culture and Agency: The Place of Culture in Social Theory.* Cambridge: Cambridge University Press.
1995   *Realist Social Theory: The Morphogenetic Approach.* Cambridge: Cambridge University Press.

Arditi, Jorge
1996   "Simmel's Theory of Alienation and the Decline of the Nonrational."
            Sociological Theory 14:93–108.
Aron, Raymond
1965   *Main Currents in Sociological Thought,* Vol. 1. New York: Basic Books.
Aronowitz, Stanley
1994   "The Simmel Revival: A Challenge to American Social Science."
            Sociological Quarterly 35:397–414.
Aronson, Ronald
1995   *After Marxism.* New York: Guilford Press.
Arthur, C. J.
1970   "Editor's Introduction." In K. Marx and F. Engels, *The German Ideology.*
            Part 1. New York: International Publishers: 4–34.
Asante, Molefi Kete
1996   "The Afrocentric Metatheory and Disciplinary Implications." In Mary F.
            Rogers (ed.), *Multicultural Experiences, Multicultural Theories.* New York:
            McGraw-Hill: 61–73.
Athens, Lonnie
1995   "Mead's Vision of the Self: A Pair of 'Flawed Diamonds.' " *Studies in
            Symbolic Interaction* 18:245–261.
Avineri, Shlomo
1968   *The Social and Political Thought of Karl Marx.* London: Cambridge
            University Press.
Ayres, C. E.
1958   "Veblen's Theory of Instincts Reconsidered." In Douglas F. Dowd (ed.),
            Thorstein Veblen: A Critical Reappraisal. Ithaca, N.Y.: Cornell University:
            25–37.
Bailey, Cathryn
1997   "Making Waves and Drawing Lines: The Politics of Defining the
            Vicissitudes of Feminism." *Hypatia* 12:16–28.
Bailey, Kenneth
1994   *Sociology and the New Systems Theory: Toward a Theoretical Synthesis.*
            Albany: State University of New York Press.
Baker, Patrick L.
1993   "Chaos, Order, and Sociological Theory." *Sociological Inquiry* 63:123–149.
Balch, Emily Greene
1941/1972   *Beyond Nationalism: The Social Thought of Emily Balch Greene.*
            New York: Twayne.
Baldwin, Alfred
1961   "The Parsonian Theory of Personality." In M. Black (ed.), *The Social
            Theories of Talcott Parsons.* Englewood Cliffs, N.J.: Prentice-Hall:
            153–190.
Baldwin, John
1986   *George Herbert Mead: A Unifying Theory for Sociology.* Newbury Park,
            Calif.: Sage.
Ball, Richard A.
1979   "The Dialectical Method: Its Application to Social Theory." *Social Forces*
            57:785–798.

Ball, Terence
1991   "History: Critique and Irony." In T. Carver (ed.), *The Cambridge Companion to Marx*. Cambridge: Cambridge University Press: 124–142.

Banks, Alan, Billings, Dwight, and Tice, Karen
1996   "Appalachian Studies and Postmodernism." In Mary F. Rogers (ed.), *Multicultural Experiences, Multicultural Theories*. New York: McGraw-Hill: 81–90.

Banner, Lois
1984   *Women in Modern America: A Brief History*. New York: Harcourt Brace Jovanovich.

Baran, Paul, and Sweezy, Paul M.
1966   *Monopoly Capital: An Essay on the American Economic and Social Order*. New York: Monthly Review Press.

Barbalet, J. M.
1983   *Marx's Construction of Social Theory*. London: Routledge and Kegan Paul.

Barber, Bernard
1993   *Constructing the Social System*. New Brunswick, N.J.: Transaction.
1994   "Talcott Parsons on the Social System: An Essay in Clarification and Elaboration." *Sociological Theory* 12:101–105.

Bar-Haim, Gabriel
1997   "The Dispersed Sacred: Anomie and the Crisis of Ritual." In Stewart M. Hoover and Knut Lundby (eds.), *Rethinking Media, Religion, and Culture*. Thousand Oaks, Calif.: Sage: 133–145.

Baudrillard, Jean
1970/1998   *The Consumer Society*. London: Sage.
1972/1981   *For a Critique of the Political Economy of the Sign*. St. Louis: Telos Press.
1983   *Simulations*. New York: Semiotext(e).

Baum, Rainer C., and Lechner, Frank J.
1981   "National Socialism: Toward an Action-Theoretical Perspective." *Sociological Inquiry* 51:281–308.

Bauman, Zygmunt
1976   *Towards a Critical Sociology: An Essay on Commonsense and Emancipation*. London: Routledge and Kegan Paul.

Bearman, Peter S.
1991   "The Social Structure of Suicide." *Sociological Forum* 6:501–524.

Beck, Ulrich
1992   *Risk Society: Towards a New Modernity*. London: Sage.

Beilharz, Peter
1996   "Negation and Ambivalence: Marx, Simmel and Bolshevism on Money." *Thesis Eleven* 47:21–32.

Bell, Daniel
1992   "George C. Homans (11 August 1910–29 May 1989)." *Proceedings of the American Philosophical Society* 136:587–593.

Bender, Frederick (ed.)
1970   *Karl Marx: The Essential Writings*. New York: Harper.

Benjamin, Jessica
1988   *The Bonds of Love: Psychoanalysis, Feminism, and the Problem of Domination*. New York: Pantheon.

Berger, Joseph, Wagner, David G., and Zelditch, Morris
1989   "Theory Growth, Social Processes and Metatheory." In J. Turner (ed.),
            Theory Building in Sociology: Assessing Theoretical Cumulation.
            Newbury Park, Calif.: Sage: 19–42.
Berger, Peter, and Luckmann, Thomas
1967   *The Social Construction of Reality.* Garden City, N.Y.: Anchor.
Berki, R. N.
1983   *Insight and Vision: The Problem of Communism in Marx's Thought.*
            London: J. M. Dent and Sons.
Berlin, Isaiah
1954   *Historical Inevitability.* London: Oxford University Press.
Bernstein, Richard J.
1971   *Praxis and Action: Contemporary Philosophies of Human Activity.*
            Philadelphia: University of Pennsylvania Press.
Besnard, Philippe
1983b   "The 'Année Sociologique' Team." In P. Besnard (ed.), *The Sociological
            Domain.* Cambridge: Cambridge University Press: 11–39.
1993   "Anomie and Fatalism in Durkheim's Theory of Regulation." In S. P. Turner
            (ed.), *Emile Durkheim: Sociologist and Moralist.* London: Routledge:
            169–190.
Besnard, Philippe (ed.)
1983a   *The Sociological Domain.* Cambridge: Cambridge University Press.
Best, Steven, and Kellner, Douglas
1991   *Postmodern Theory: Critical Interrogations.* New York: Guilford Press.
Bhargava, Rajeev
1992   *Individualism in Social Science: Forms and Limits of a Methodology.*
            Oxford: Clarendon Press.
Bierstedt, Robert
1963   "The Common Sense World of Alfred Schutz." *Social Research*
            30:116–121.
1981   *American Sociological Theory: A Critical History.* New York:
            Academic Press.
Biggart, Nicole Woolsey
1991   "Explaining Asian Economic Organization: Toward a Weberian Institutional
            Perspective." *Theory and Society* 20:199–232.
Birnbaum, Pierre, and Todd, Jane Marie
1995   "French Jewish Sociologists between Reason and Faith: The Impact of the
            Dreyfus Affair." *Jewish Social Studies* 2:1–35.
Blalock, Hubert, and Wilken, Paul
1979   *Intergroup Processes: A Micro-Macro Perspective.* New York: Free Press.
Blankenship, Ralph L. (ed.)
1977   *Colleagues in Organization: The Social Construction of Professional Work.*
            New York: Wiley.
Blau, Peter
1960   "Structural Effects." *American Sociological Review* 25:178–193.
1964   *Exchange and Power in Social Life.* New York: Wiley.
Bleicher, Josef
1980   *Contemporary Hermeneutics: Hermeneutics as Method, Philosophy and
            Critique.* London: Routledge and Kegan Paul.

Blum, Nancy S.
1991   "The Management of Stigma by Alzheimer Family Caregivers." *Journal of Contemporary Ethnography* 20:263–284.

Blumberg, Dorothy
1966   *Florence Kelley: The Making of a Social Pioneer.* New York: Augustus M. Kelley.

Bolt, Christine
1993   *The Women's Movements in the United States from the 1740's to the 1920's.* Amherst: University of Massachusetts Press.

Bookman, Ann, and Morgen, Sandra (eds.)
1988   *Women and the Politics of Empowerment.* Philadelphia: Temple University Press.

Bosserman, Phillip
1968   *Dialectical Sociology: An Analysis of the Sociology of Georges Gurvitch.* Boston: Porter Sargent.

Boswell, Terry, and Dixon, William J.
1993   "Marx's Theory of Rebellion: A Cross-National Analysis of Class Exploitation, Economic Development, and Violent Revolt." *American Sociological Review* 58:681–702.

Bottomore, Tom
1984   *The Frankfurt School.* Chichester, Eng.: Ellis Horwood.

Bottomore, Tom, and Frisby, David (eds.)
1978   Introduction to the translation of Georg Simmel, *The Philosophy of Money* (orig. 1907). London: Routledge and Kegan Paul: 1–49.

Boudon, Raymond
1995   "Should One Still Read Durkheim's Rules after One Hundred Years?" (Interview with Massimo Borlandi), *Schweizerische Zeitschrift fur Soziologie* 21:559–573.

Bourdieu, Pierre
1977   *Outline of a Theory of Practice.* London: Cambridge University Press.
1984a   *Distinction: A Social Critique of the Judgment of Taste.* Cambridge, Mass.: Harvard University Press.
1984b   *Homo Academicus.* Stanford, Calif.: Stanford University Press.

Bourdieu, Pierre, and Wacquant, Loïc J. D.
1992   "The Purpose of Reflexive Sociology (The Chicago Workshop)." In P. Bourdieu and L. J. D. Wacquant (eds.), *An Invitation to Reflexive Sociology.* Chicago: University of Chicago Press: 61–215.

Bourricaud, François
1981   *The Sociology of Talcott Parsons.* Chicago: University of Chicago Press.

Bowles, Samuel, and Gintis, Herbert
1986   *Democracy and Capitalism: Property, Community, and the Contradictions of Modern Social Thought.* New York: Basic Books.

Bramson, Leon
1961   *The Political Context of Sociology.* Princeton: Princeton University Press.

Braverman, Harry
1974   *Labor and Monopoly Capital: The Degradation of Work in the Twentieth Century.* New York: Monthly Review Press.

Breault, K. D.
1986   "Suicide in America: A Test of Durkheim's Theory of Religion, 1933–1980."
            American Journal of Sociology 92:628–656.
Breckinridge, Sophonisba
1921/1971   *New Homes for Old.* Montclair, N.J.: Patterson Smith.
Brewer, John, and Hunter, Albert
1989   *Multimethod Research: A Synthesis of Styles.* Newbury Park, Calif.: Sage.
Britton, Anne Camden
1979   "The Life and Thought of Marianne Weber." Master's thesis.
            San Francisco, Calif.: San Francisco State University.

Broschart, Kay
1991a   "Beatrice Webb." In M. J. Deegan (ed.), *Women in Sociology: A Bio-*
            Bibliographical Sourcebook. Westport, Conn.: Greenwood Press: 425–431.
1991b   "Ida B. Wells-Barnett." In M. J. Deegan (ed.), *Women in Sociology:*
            A Bio-Bibliographical Sourcebook. Westport, Conn.: Greenwood Press:
            432–439.
Brown, Richard H.
1987   *Society as Text: Essays on Rhetoric, Reason and Reality.* Chicago:
            University of Chicago Press.
1990   "Social Science and the Poetics of Public Truth." *Sociological Forum*
            5:55–74.

Brubaker, Rogers
1984   *The Limits of Rationality: An Essay on the Social and Moral Thought of*
            Max Weber. London: George Allen and Unwin.

Brugger, Bill
1995   "Marxism, Asia, and the 1990s." *Positions* 3:630–641.
Bryant, Christopher G. A.
1985   *Positivism in Social Theory and Research.* New York: St. Martin's.
Buckley, Kerry W.
1989   *Mechanical Man: John Broadus Watson and the Beginnings of Behaviorism.*
            New York: Guilford Press.
Buffalohead, W. Roger
1996   "Reflections on Native American Cultural Rights and Resources." In
            Mary F. Rogers (ed.), *Multicultural Experiences, Multicultural Theories.*
            New York: McGraw-Hill: 154–156.

Bulmer, Martin
1984   *The Chicago School of Sociology: Institutionalization, Diversity, and the*
            Rise of Sociological Research. Chicago: University of Chicago Press.
1985   "The Chicago School of Sociology: What Made It a 'School'?" *The History*
            of Sociology: An International Review 5:62–77.
Burawoy, Michael
1979   *Manufacturing Consent: Changes in the Labor Process under Monopoly*
            Capitalism. Chicago: University of Chicago Press.
Burger, Thomas
1976   *Max Weber's Theory of Concept Formation: History, Laws and Ideal Types.*
            Durham, N.C.: Duke University Press.
1977a   "Max Weber's Interpretive Sociology, the Understanding of Actions and
            Motives, and a Weberian View of Man." *Sociological Inquiry* 47:127–132.

1977b   "Talcott Parsons, the Problem of Order in Society, and the Program of an
             Analytical Sociology." *American Journal of Sociology* 83:320–334.
1993   "Weber's Sociology and Weber's Personality." *Theory and Society*
             22:813–836.

Burke, Peter
1986   "Strengths and Weaknesses of the History of Mentalities." *History of
             European Ideas* 7:439–451.

Buttel, Frederick H. (ed.)
1990   "Symposium: Evolution and Social Change." *Sociological Forum*
             5:153–212.

Button, Graham
1991   "Introduction: Ethnomethodology and the Foundational Respecification of
             the Human Sciences." In G. Button (ed.), *Ethnomethodology and the
             Human Sciences.* Cambridge: Cambridge University Press: 1–19.

Buxton, William
1985   *Talcott Parsons and the Capitalist Nation-State: Political Sociology as a
             Strategic Vocation.* Toronto: University of Toronto Press.
1998   "From the 'Missing Fragment' to the 'Lost Manuscript': Reflections on
             Parsons's Engagement with Simmel." *American Sociologist* 29:57–76.

Camic, Charles
1987   "The Making of a Model: A Historical Reinterpretation of the Early
             Parsons." *American Sociological Review* 52:421–439.
1989   "Structure after 50 Years: The Anatomy of a Charter." *American Journal of
             Sociology* 95:38–107.
1990   "An Historical Prologue." *American Journal of Sociology* 55:313–319.
1992   "Reputation and Predecessor Selection: Parsons and the Institutionalists."
             American Sociological Review 57:421–445.

Camic, Charles (ed.)
1997   *Reclaiming the Sociological Classics: The State of Scholarship.* Oxford:
             Blackwell.

Caplan, Paula
1993   *Lifting a Ton of Feathers: A Woman's Guide to Surviving in the Academic
             World.* Toronto: University of Toronto Press.

Caplow, Theodore
1968   *Two against One: Coalition in Triads.* Englewood Cliffs, N.J.: Prentice Hall.

Carden, Maren Lockwood
1974   *The New Feminist Movement.* New York: Russell Sage Foundation.

Carver, Terrell
1983   *Marx and Engels: The Intellectual Relationship.* Bloomington: Indiana
             University Press.

Carveth, Donald
1982   "Sociology and Psychoanalysis: The Hobbesian Problem Revisited."
             Canadian Journal of Sociology 7:201–229.

Catlin, George E. G.
1964   "Introduction." In E. Durkheim, *The Rules of Sociological Method.*
             New York: Free Press: xi–xxxvi.

Ceplair, Larry (ed.)
1991   *Charlotte Perkins Gilman: A Non-Fiction Reader.* New York: Columbia
             University Press.

Cerullo, John J.
1994   "The Epistemic Turn: Critical Sociology and the 'Generation of 68.'"
            International Journal of Politics, Culture and Society. 8:169–181.
Chafetz, Janet Saltzman
1984   *Sex and Advantage.* Totowa, N.J.: Rowman and Allanheld.
Chafetz, Janet Saltzman, and Dworkin, Anthony Gary
1986   *Female Revolt: Women's Movements in World and Historical Perspectives.*
            Totowa, N.J.: Rowman and Allanheld.
Chapoulie, Jean-Michel
1996   "Everett Hughes and the Chicago Tradition." *Sociological Theory* 14:3–29.
Charon, Joel
1995   *Symbolic Interaction: An Introduction, an Interpretation, an Integration.*
            5th ed. Englewood Cliffs, N.J.: Prentice-Hall.
Cherrington, Ruth
1997   "Generational Issues in China: A Case Study of the 1980s Generation of
            Young Intellectuals," *British Journal of Sociology* 48: 302–320.
Chitnis, Anand C.
1976   *The Scottish Enlightenment: A Social History.* Totowa, N.J.: Rowman and
            Littlefield.
Chodorow, Nancy
1978   *The Reproduction of Mothering: Psychoanalysis and the Sociology of
            Gender.* Berkeley: University of California Press.
Chriss, James J.
1993   "Durkheim's Cult of the Individual as Civil Religion: Its Appropriation by
            Erving Goffman." *Sociological Spectrum* 13:251–275.
1996   "Toward an Interparadigmatic Dialogue on Goffman." *Sociological
            Perspectives* 39:333–339.
Clark, Priscilla P., and Clark, Terry Nichols
1982   "The Structural Sources of French Structuralism." In I. Rossi (ed.),
            Structural Sociology. New York: Columbia University Press: 22–46.
Clayman, Steven E.
1993   "Booing: The Anatomy of a Disaffiliative Response." *American
            Sociological Review* 58:110–130.
Cockerham, William C., Abel, Thomas and Luschen, Gunther
1993   "Max Weber, Formal Rationality, and Health Lifestyles." *Sociological
            Quarterly* 34:413–425.
Cockshott, Paul, Cottrell, Allin, and Michaelson, Greg
1995   "Testing Marx: Some New Results from UK Data." *Capital and Class*
            55:103–129.
Cohen, G. A.
1978   *Karl Marx's Theory of History: A Defence.* Princeton, N.J.: Princeton
            University Press.
Cohen, Ira
1981   "Introduction to the Transaction Edition." In M. Weber, *General Economic
            History.* New Brunswick, N.J.: Transaction: xv–lxxxiii.
Cohen, Jere, Hazelrigg, Lawrence, and Pope, Whitney
1975   "DeParsonizing Weber: A Critique of Parsons' Interpretation of Weber's
            Sociology." *American Sociological Review* 40:229–241.

Coleman, James
1968   Review of H. Garfinkel, *Studies in Ethnomethodology.* *American Sociological Review* 33:126–130.
1971   "Community Disorganization and Conflict." In R. Merton and R. Nisbet (eds.), *Contemporary Social Problems.* 3rd ed. New York: Harcourt Brace Jovanovich: 657–708.
1986   "Social Theory, Social Research, and a Theory of Action." *American Journal of Sociology* 91:1309–1335.
1990   *Foundations of Social Theory.* Cambridge: Belknap Press of Harvard University Press.

Colfax, J. David, and Roach, Jack L.
1971   *Radical Sociology.* New York: Basic Books.

Collins, F. Howard
1889   *An Epitome of the Synthetic Philosophy.* London and Edinburgh: Williams and Norgate.

Collins, Patricia Hill
1990   *Black Feminist Thought: Knowledge, Consciousness and the Politics of Empowerment.* Boston: Unwin Hyman.
1998   *Fighting Words: Black Women and the Search for Justice.* Minneapolis: University of Minnesota Press.

Collins, Randall
1975   *Conflict Sociology: Toward an Explanatory Science.* New York: Academic Press.
1980   "Weber's Last Theory of Capitalism: A Systematization." *American Sociological Review* 45:925–942.
1981a   "On the Microfoundations of Macrosociology." *American Journal of Sociology* 86:984–1014.
1981b   "Micro-Translation as Theory-Building Strategy." In K. Knorr-Cetina and A. Cicourel (eds.), *Advances in Social Theory and Methodology.* New York: Methuen: 81–108.
1981c   "Introduction." In R. Collins (ed.), *Sociology since Midcentury: Essays in Theory Cumulation.* New York: Academic Press: 1–9.
1985   *Weberian Sociological Theory.* Cambridge: Cambridge University Press.
1986a   "Is 1980s Sociology in the Doldrums?" *American Journal of Sociology* 91:1336–1355.
1986b   "The Passing of Intellectual Generations: Reflections on the Death of Erving Goffman." *Sociological Theory* 4:106–113.
1987a   "Interaction Ritual Chains, Power and Property: The Micro-Macro Connection as an Empirically Based Theoretical Problem." In J. Alexander et al. (eds.), *The Micro-Macro Link.* Berkeley: University of California Press: 193–206.
1987b   "A Micro-Macro Theory of Intellectual Creativity: The Case of German Idealistic Philosophy." *Sociological Theory* 5:47–69.
1988a   "The Micro Contribution to Macro Sociology." *Sociological Theory* 6:242–253.
1988b   "The Durkheimian Tradition in Conflict Sociology." In J. Alexander (ed.), *Durkheimian Sociology: Cultural Studies.* Cambridge: Cambridge University Press: 107–128.

1989a   "Sociology: Proscience or Antiscience?" *American Sociological Review*
             54:124–139.
1989b   "Toward a Neo-Meadian Sociology of Mind." *Symbolic Interaction* 12:1–32.
1990   "Conflict Theory and the Advance of Macro-Historical Sociology." In
             G. Ritzer (ed.), *Frontiers of Social Theory: The New Syntheses.* New York:
             Columbia University Press: 68–87.
1993a   "Heroizing and Deheroizing Weber." *Theory and Society* 36:289–313.
1993b   "What Does Conflict Theory Predict about America's Future?" *Sociological
             Perspectives* 22:861–870.
1997a   "An Asian Route to Capitalism: Religious Economy and the Origins of Self-
             Transforming Growth in Japan." *American Sociological Review* 62:843–865.
1997b   "A Sociological Guilt Trip: Comment on Connell." *American Journal of
             Sociology* 102:1558–1564.

Colomy, Paul
1986   "Recent Developments in the Functionalist Approach to Change."
             Sociological Focus 19:139–158.
1990   "Introduction: The Neofunctionalist Movement." In P. Colomy (ed.),
             Neofunctionalist Sociology. Brookfield, Vt.: Elgar Publishing: xi–xli.

Comte, Auguste
1830–1842/   *The Positive Philosophy of Auguste Comte.* New York:
1855   Calvin Blanchard.
1851/1957   *A General View of Positivism.* New York: R. Speller.
1851/1968   *System of Positive Polity,* Vol. 1. New York: Burt Franklin.
1852/1968   *System of Positive Polity,* Vol. 2. New York: Burt Franklin.
1853/1968   *System of Positive Polity,* Vol. 3. New York: Burt Franklin.
1854/1968   *System of Positive Polity,* Vol. 4. New York: Burt Franklin.
1891/1973   *The Catechism of Positive Religion.* Clifton, N.J.: A. M. Kelley.

Connell, R. W.
1996   "Men and the Women's Movement." In Mary F. Rogers (ed.), *Multicultural
             Experiences, Multicultural Theories.* New York: McGraw-Hill: 409–415.
1997   "How Is Classical Theory Classical?" *American Journal of Sociology*
             102:1511–1557.

Connolly, William E.
1973   "Theoretical Self-Consciousness." *Polity* 6:5–35.

Cook, Gary
1993   *George Herbert Mead: The Making of a Social Pragmatist.* Urbana:
             University of Illinois Press.

Cook, Judith, and Fonow, Mary Margaret
1986   "Knowledge and Women's Interests: Issues of Epistemology and
             Methodology in Feminist Sociological Research." *Sociological Inquiry*
             56:2–29.

Cook, Karen S. (ed.)
1987a   *Social Exchange Theory.* Beverly Hills, Calif.: Sage.
1987b   "Emerson's Contributions to Social Exchange Theory." In Karen S. Cook
             (ed.), *Social Exchange Theory.* Beverly Hills, Calif.: Sage: 209–222.

Cook, Karen, O'Brien, Jodi, and Kollock, Peter
1990   "Exchange Theory: A Blueprint for Structure and Process." In G. Ritzer
             (ed.), *Frontiers of Social Theory: The New Syntheses.* New York: Columbia
             University Press: 158–181.

Cooper, Anna Julia
1892/1969   *A Voice from the South by a Black Woman from the South.* New York:
              Negro University Press.
1925/1988   *Slavery and the French Revolutionists (1788–1805).* Frances Richardson
              Keller (trans.). Queenston, Ontario: Edwin-Mellen Press.
Cooper, Dereck
1991   "On the Concept of Alienation." *International Journal of Contemporary
              Sociology* 28:7–26.
Cormack, Patricia
1996   "The Paradox of Durkheim's Manifesto: Reconsidering *The Rules of
              Sociological Method." Theory and Society* 25:85–104.
Cortese, Anthony
1995   "The Rise, Hegemony, and Decline of the Chicago School of Sociology,
              1892–1945." *Social Science Journal* 32:235–254.
Coser, Lewis
1956   *The Functions of Social Conflict.* New York: Free Press.
1975a   Presidential Address: "Two Methods in Search of a Substance." *American
              Sociological Review* 40:691–700.
1975b   "Structure and Conflict." In P. Blau (ed.), *Approaches to the Study of Social
              Structure.* New York: Free Press: 210–219.
1977   *Masters of Sociological Thought.* 2nd ed. New York: Harcourt Brace
              Jovanovich.
Coser, Lewis (ed.)
1965   *Georg Simmel.* Englewood Cliffs, N.J.: Prentice-Hall.
Costin, Lela
1983   *Two Sisters for Social Justice: A Biography of Edith and Grace Abbott.*
              Urbana: University of Illinois Press.
Cottrell, Jr., Leonard S.
1980   "George Herbert Mead: The Legacy of Social Behaviorism." In R. K. Merton
              and M. W. Riley (eds.), *Sociological Traditions from Generation to Generation:
              Glimpses of the American Experience.* Norwood, N.J.: Ablex: 45–65.
Crippen, Timothy
1994   "Toward a Neo-Darwinian Sociology: Its Nomological Principles and Some
              Illustrative Applications." *Sociological Perspectives* 37:309–335.
Crombie, A. C.
1986   "What Is the History of Science?" *History of European Ideas* 7:21–31.
Cronk, George
1987   *The Philosophical Anthropology of George Herbert Mead.* New York:
              Peter Lang.
Curtis, Bruce
1981   *William Graham Sumner.* Boston: Twayne.
Dahme, Heinz-Jurgen
1990   "On the Current Rediscovery of Georg Simmel's Sociology—A European
              Point of View." In M. Kaern, B. S. Phillips, and R. S. Cohen (eds.), *Georg
              Simmel and Contemporary Sociology.* Dordrecht: Kluwer: 13–37.
Dahms, Harry
1997   "Theory in Weberian Marxism: Patterns of Critical Social Theory in Lukács
              and Habermas." *Sociological Theory* 15:181–214.

Dahrendorf, Ralf
1959   *Class and Class Conflict in Industrial Society.* Stanford, Calif.:
            Stanford University Press.
Daniels, Arlene Kaplan
1988   *Invisible Careers: Women Civic Leaders from the Volunteer World.* Chicago:
            University of Chicago Press.
Dant, Tim
1996   "Fetishism and the Social Value of Objects." *Sociological Review*
            44:495–516.
Davies, Christie
1992   "The Protestant Ethic and the Comic Spirit of Capitalism." *British Journal
            of Sociology* 43:421–442.
Davis, Kingsley, and Moore, Wilbert
1945   "Some Principles of Stratification." *American Sociological Review*
            10:242–249.
Dawe, Alan
1978   "Theories of Social Action." In T. Bottomore and R. Nisbet (eds.),
            A History of Sociological Analysis. New York: Basic Books:
            362–417.
Deckard, Barbara Sinclair
1979   *The Women's Movement: Political, Socioeconomic and Psychological Issues.*
            New York: Harper & Row.
Deegan, Mary Jo
1988   *Jane Addams and the Men of the Chicago School 1892–1913.*
            New Brunswick, N.J.: Transaction Books.
1991   *Women in Sociology: A Bio-Bibliographical Sourcebook.* Westport, Conn.:
            Greenwood Press.
Densimore, Dana
1973   "Independence from the Sexual Revolution." In A. Koedt et al. (eds.),
            Radical Feminism. New York: Quadrangle: 107–118.
Deutschmann, Christoph
1996   "Money as a Social Construction: On the Actuality of Marx and Simmel."
            Thesis Eleven 47:1–19.
DeVault, Marjorie L.
1991   *Feeding the Family: The Social Organization of Caring as Gendered Work.*
            Chicago: University of Chicago Press.
Devereux, Edward C.
1961   "Parsons's Sociological Theory." In M. Black (ed.), *The Social Theories of
            Talcott Parsons.* Englewood Cliffs, N.J.: Prentice-Hall: 1–63.
Dingwall, Robert, and King, Michael D.
1995   "Herbert Spencer and the Professions: Occupational Ecology Reconsidered."
            Sociological Theory 13:14–24.
Ditton, Jason (ed.)
1980   *The View from Goffman.* New York: St. Martin's.
Donovan, Josephine
1985   *Feminist Theory: The Intellectual Traditions of American Feminism.*
            New York: Ungar.
Dorfman, Joseph
1966   *Thorstein Veblen and His America: With New Appendices.* New York:
            Augustus M. Kelley.

Douglas, Jack
1967   *The Social Meanings of Suicide.* Princeton, N.J.: Princeton University Press.
1980   "Introduction to the Sociologies of Everyday Life." In J. Douglas et al.
            (eds.), *Introduction to the Sociologies of Everyday Life.* Boston: Allyn and
            Bacon: 1–19.
Douglas, Jack, and Johnson, John
1977   "Introduction." In J. Douglas et al. (eds.), *Existential Sociology.*
            Cambridge: Cambridge University Press: vii–xv.
Dowd, Douglas F.
1966   *Thorstein Veblen.* New York: Washington Square Press.
Drysdale, John
1996   "How Are Social-Scientific Concepts Formed? A Reconstruction of Max
            Weber's Theory of Concept Formation." *Sociological Theory* 14:71–88.
Durand, Jean-Pierre, and Hayter, Teresa
1997   "Can We Make Our Own History? The Significance of the Dialectic Today."
            Capital and Class 62:143–158.
Durkheim, Emile
1887/1993   *Ethics and the Sociology of Morals.* Buffalo: Prometheus Books.
1892/1997   *Montesquieu: Quid Secundatus Politicae Scientiae Instituendae Contulerit.*
            Oxford: Durkheim Press.
1893/1960   *Montesquieu and Rousseau: Forerunners of Sociology.* Ann Arbor:
            University of Michigan Press.
1893/1964   *The Division of Labor in Society.* New York: Free Press.
1895/1964   *The Rules of Sociological Method.* New York: Free Press.
1897/1951   *Suicide.* New York: Free Press.
1900/1973   "Sociology in France in the Nineteenth Century." In R. Bellah (ed.), *Emile
            Durkheim: On Morality and Society.* Chicago: University of Chicago Press:
            3–32.
1912/1965   *The Elementary Forms of Religious Life.* New York: Free Press.
1913–1914/ *Pragmatism and Sociology.* Cambridge: Cambridge
1983   University Press.
1914/1973   "The Dualism of Human Nature and Its Social Condition." In R. Bellah
            (ed.), *Emile Durkheim.* Chicago: University of Chicago Press: 149–163.
1922/1956   *Education and Sociology.* New York: Free Press.
1928/1962   *Socialism.* New York: Collier Books.
1957   *Professional Ethics and Civil Morals.* London: Routledge and Kegan Paul.
1973   *Moral Education: A Study in the Theory and Application of the Sociology of
            Education.* New York: Free Press.
Durkheim, Emile, and Mauss, Marcel
1903/1963   *Primitive Classification.* Chicago: University of Chicago Press.
Eckberg, Douglas Lee, and Hill, Lester
1979   "The Paradigm Concept and Sociology: A Critical Review." *American
            Sociological Review* 44:925–937.
Edel, Abraham
1959   "The Concept of Levels in Social Theory." In L. Gross (ed.), *Symposium on
            Sociological Theory.* Evanston, Ill.: Row Peterson: 167–195.
Effrat, Andrew
1972   "Power to the Paradigms: An Editorial Introduction." *Sociological Inquiry*
            42:3–33.

Eisen, Arnold
1978   "The Meanings and Confusions of Weberian 'Rationality.'" *British Journal of Sociology* 29:57–70.
Eisenberg, Andrew
1998   "Weberian Patrimonialism and Imperial Chinese History." *Theory and Society* 27:83–102.
Eisenstadt, S. N., with Curelaru, M.
1976   *The Form of Sociology: Paradigms and Crises.* New York: Wiley.
Elster, Jon
1982   "Marxism, Functionalism and Game Theory: The Case for Methodological Individualism." *Theory and Society* 11:453–482.
1985   *Making Sense of Marx.* Cambridge: Cambridge University Press.
Emerson, Richard M.
1972a   "Exchange Theory, Part I: A Psychological Basis for Social Exchange." In J. Berger, M. Zelditch, Jr., and B. Anderson (eds.), *Sociological Theories in Progress,* Vol. 2. Boston: Houghton-Mifflin: 38–57.
1972b   "Exchange Theory, Part II: Exchange Relations and Networks." In J. Berger, M. Zelditch, Jr., and B. Anderson (eds.), *Sociological Theories in Progress,* Vol. 2. Boston: Houghton-Mifflin: 58–87.
1981   "Social Exchange Theory." In M. Rosenberg and R. H. Turner (eds.), *Social Psychology: Sociological Perspectives.* New York: Basic Books: 30–65.
Emirbayer, Mustafa
1997   "Manifesto for a Relational Sociology." *American Journal of Sociology* 103:281–317.
Engels, Friedrich
1884/1970   *The Origins of the Family, Private Property and the State.* New York: International.
1890/1972   "Letter to Joseph Bloch." In R. C. Tucker (ed.), *The Marx-Engels Reader.* New York: Norton: 640–642.
Eriksson, Bjorn
1993   "The First Formulation of Sociology: A Discursive Innovation of the 18th Century." *Archives of European Sociology* 34:251–276.
Etzkorn, K. Peter (ed.)
1968   *Georg Simmel: The Conflict in Modern Culture and Other Essays.* New York: Teachers College Press, Columbia University.
Evans, Sara
1980   *Personal Politics: The Roots of the Women's Liberation Movement in the Civil Rights Movement and the New Left.* New York: Vintage.
Faghirzadeh, Saleh
1982   *Sociology of Sociology: In Search of . . . Ibn-Khaldum's Sociology Then and Now.* Teheran: Soroush Press.
Faia, Michael A.
1986   *Dynamic Functionalism: Strategy and Tactics.* Cambridge: Cambridge University Press.
Falk, William, and Zhao, Shanyang
1990a   "Paradigms, Theories and Methods in Contemporary Rural Sociology: A Partial Replication." *Rural Sociology* 54:587–600.
1990b   "Paradigms, Theories and Methods Revisited: We Respond to Our Critics." *Rural Sociology* 55:112–122.

Fararo, Thomas J.
1989   "The Spirit of Unification in Sociological Theory." *Sociological Theory*
            7:175–190.
Faris, R. E. L.
1970   *Chicago Sociology: 1920–1932.* Chicago: University of Chicago Press.
Farnham, C. (ed.)
1987   *The Impact of Feminist Research on the Academy.* Bloomington: Indiana
            University Press.
Farrell, Chad R.
1997   "Durkheim, Moral Individualism and the Dreyfus Affair." *Current
            Perspectives in Social Theory* 17:313–330.
Faught, Jim
1980   "Presuppositions of the Chicago School in the Work of Everett Hughes."
            American Sociologist 15:72–82.
Featherstone, Mike
1991   "Georg Simmel: An Introduction." *Theory, Culture and Society* 8:1–16.
Femia, Joseph
1995   "Pareto's Concept of Demagogic Plutocracy." *Government and Opposition*
            30:370–392.
Fendrich, Michael
1984   "Wives' Employment and Husbands' Distress: A Meta-Analysis and a
            Replication." *Journal of Marriage and the Family* 46:871–879.
Fenton, Steve
1984   *Durkheim and Modern Sociology.* Cambridge: Cambridge University Press.
Ferguson, Kathy E.
1980   *Self, Society and Womankind: The Dialectic of Liberation.* Westport, Conn.:
            Greenwood Press.
Ferry, Luc, and Renaut, Alain
1985/1990   *French Philosophy of the Sixties: An Essay on Antihumanism.* Amherst:
            University of Massachusetts Press.
Fine, Gary
1990   "Symbolic Interactionism in the Post-Blumerian Age." In G. Ritzer (ed.),
            Frontiers of Social Theory: The New Syntheses. New York: Columbia
            University Press: 117–157.
1995   "A Second Chicago School? The Development of a Postwar American
            Sociology." In Gary Alan Fine (ed.), *A Second Chicago School? The
            Development of a Postwar American Sociology.* Chicago: University of
            Chicago Press: 1–16.
1996   *Kitchens: The Culture of Restaurant Work.* Berkeley: University of
            California Press.
Fine, Gary Alan, and Manning, Philip
forthcoming "Erving Goffman." In George Ritzer (ed.), *The Blackwell Companion to
            Major Social Theorists.* Oxford, England, and Cambridge, Mass.: Blackwell.
Fine, William F.
1979   *Progressive Evolutionism and American Sociology, 1890–1920.* UMI
            Research Press (*n.p.*).
Fischer, Norman
1984   "Hegelian Marxism and Ethics." *Canadian Journal of Political and Social
            Theory* 8:112–138.

Fish, Virginia Kemp
1981   "Annie Marion MacLean: A Neglected Part of The Chicago School."
            Journal of the History of Sociology 3:43–62.
Fiske, Donald W., and Shweder, Richard A. (eds.)
1986   *Metatheory in Social Science: Pluralisms and Subjectivities.* Chicago:
            University of Chicago Press.
Fitzpatrick, Ellen
1990   *Endless Crusade: Women Social Scientists and Progressive Reform.*
            New York: Oxford University Press.
Flexner, Eleanor
1959   *Century of Struggle: The Woman's Rights Movement in the United States.*
            Cambridge, Mass.: Belknap Press.
Foucault, Michel
1980   *The History of Sexuality.* Vol. 1, *An Introduction.* New York: Vintage.
Fox, Renee C.
1997   "Talcott Parsons, My Teacher." *American Scholar* 66:395–410.
Frank, André Gunder
1966/1974   "Functionalism and Dialectics." In R. S. Denisoff, O. Callahan, and
            M. H. Levine (eds.), *Theories and Paradigms in Contemporary Sociology.*
            Itasca, Ill.: Peacock: 342–352.
Frank, R. I.
1976   Translator's introduction to Max Weber, *The Agrarian Sociology of
            Ancient Civilizations.* London: NLB: 7–33.
Freeman, C. Robert
1980   "Phenomenological Sociology and Ethnomethodology." In J. D. Douglas
            et al. (eds.), *Introduction to the Sociologies of Everyday Life.* Boston:
            Allyn and Bacon: 113–154.
Freese, Lee
1994   "The Song of Sociobiology." *Sociological Perspectives* 37:337–373.
Freund, Julian
1968   *The Sociology of Max Weber.* New York: Vintage.
Friedheim, Elizabeth
1979   "An Empirical Comparison of Ritzer's Paradigms and Similar Metatheories:
            A Research Note." *Social Forces* 58:59–66.
Friedrichs, Robert
1970   *A Sociology of Sociology.* New York: Free Press.
1972a   "Dialectical Sociology: Toward a Resolution of Current 'Crises' in Western
            Sociology." *British Journal of Sociology* 13:263–274.
1972b   "Dialectical Sociology: An Exemplar for the 1970's." *Social Forces*
            50:447–455.
Frisby, David
1981   *Sociological Impressionism: A Reassessment of Georg Simmel's Social
            Theory.* London: Heinemann.
1984   *Georg Simmel.* Chichester, Eng.: Ellis Horwood.
1992   *Simmel and Since: Essays on Georg Simmel's Social Theory.* London:
            Routledge.
Frisby, David (ed.)
1994   *Georg Simmel: Critical Assessments.* 3 vols. London: Routledge.

Fuhrman, Ellsworth R
1980   *The Sociology of Knowledge in America: 1883–1915.* Charlottesville: University Press of Virginia.
Fuhrman, Ellsworth R., and Snizek, William
1990   "Neither Proscience nor Antiscience: Metasociology as Dialogue." *Sociological Forum* 5:17–31.
Fulbrook, Mary
1978   "Max Weber's 'Interpretive Sociology.' " *British Journal of Sociology* 29:71–82.
Furfey, Paul
1953/1965   *The Scope and Method of Sociology: A Metasociological Treatise.* New York: Cooper Square Publishers.
Gandy, D. Ross
1979   *Marx and History: From Primitive Society to the Communist Future.* Austin: University of Texas Press.
Gane, Mike
1988   *On Durkheim's Rules of Sociological Method.* London: Routledge.
Gane, Mike (ed.)
1992   *The Radical Sociology of Durkheim and Mauss.* London: Routledge.
Gane, Nicholas
1997   "Max Weber on the Ethical Irrationality of Political Leadership." *Sociology* 31:549–564.
Gans, Herbert J., and Marx, Gary T.
1992   "Sociological Amnesia: The Noncumulation of Normal Social Science." *Sociological Forum* 7:701–710.
Gardner, Carol Brooks
1991   "Stigma and the Public Self: Notes on Communication, Self, and Others." *Journal of Contemporary Ethnography* 20:251–262.
Garfinkel, Harold
1967   *Studies in Ethnomethodology.* Englewood Cliffs, N.J.: Prentice-Hall.
Garland, Anne Witte
1988   *Women Activists: Challenging the Abuse of Power.* New York: Feminist Press.
Gaziano, Emanuel
1996   "Ecological Metaphors as Scientific Boundary Work: Innovation and Authority in Interwar Sociology and Biology." *American Journal of Sociology* 101:874–907.
Gellner, David
1982   "Max Weber, Capitalism and the Religion of India." *Sociology* 16:526–543.
Gergen, Kenneth J.
1973   "Social Psychology as History." *Journal of Personality and Social Psychology* 26:309–320.
1986   "Correspondence versus Autonomy in the Language of Understanding Human Action." In D. W. Fiske and R. A. Shweder (eds.), *Metatheory in Social Science: Pluralisms and Subjectivities.* Chicago: University of Chicago Press: 136–162.
Gerth, Hans, and Bramstedt, Ernest K.
1950   "A Note on the Work of Karl Mannheim." In H. Gerth and E. K. Bramstedt (eds.), *Freedom, Power and Democratic Planning.* London: Routledge and Kegan Paul: vii–xv.

Gerth, Hans, and Mills, C. Wright
1953   *Character and Social Structure.* New York: Harcourt, Brace and World.
Gerth, Hans, and Mills, C. Wright (eds.)
1958   *From Max Weber.* New York: Oxford University Press.
Gerth, Nobuko
1993   "Hans H. Gerth and C. Wright Mills: Partnership and Partisanship."
              International Journal of Politics, Culture and Society 7:133–154.
Giddens, Anthony
1972   "Introduction: Durkheim's Writings in Sociology and Social Philosophy." In
              A. Giddens (ed.), *Emile Durkheim: Selected Writings.* Cambridge:
              Cambridge University Press: 1–50.
1979   *Central Problems in Social Theory: Action, Structure and Contradiction in
              Social Analysis.* Berkeley: University of California Press.
1982   *Profiles and Critiques in Social Theory.* Berkeley: University of
              California Press.
1984   *The Constitution of Society: Outline of the Theory of Structuration.*
              Berkeley: University of California Press.
1990   *The Consequences of Modernity.* Stanford, Calif.: Stanford University Press.
1991   *Modernity and Self-Identity: Self and Society in the Late Modern Age.*
              Stanford, Calif.: Stanford University Press.
1992   *The Transformation of Intimacy: Sexuality, Love and Eroticism in Modern
              Societies.* Stanford, Calif.: Stanford University Press.
Giddings, Paula
1984   *When and Where I Enter: The Impact of Black Women on Race and Sex in
              America.* New York: William Morrow.
Gilbert, Margaret
1994   "Durkheim and Social Facts," in W. S. F. Pickering and H. Martins (eds.),
              Debating Durkheim. London: Routledge: 86–109.
Gilman, Charlotte Perkins
1893/1973   *The Yellow Wall-Paper.* New York: Feminist Press.
1898/1966   *Women and Economics: A Study of the Economic Relation between Men and
              Women as a Factor in Social Evolution.* New York: Harper and Row.
1900   *Concerning Children.* Boston: Small and Maynard.
1903   *The Home: Its Work and Influences.* New York: Macmillan.
1904   *Human Work.* New York: McClure and Phillips.
1911   *The Man-Made World.* London: Fisher Unwin.
1923   *His Religion and Hers: A Study of the Faith of Our Fathers and the Work of
              Our Mothers.* New York: Century.
Glatzer, Wolfgang
1998   "The German Sociological Association: Origins and Developments." Paper
              presented at the meetings of the International Sociological Association,
              Montreal, Canada.
Goffman, Erving
1959   *Presentation of Self in Everyday Life.* Garden City, N.Y.: Anchor.
Goldman, Harvey
1988   *Max Weber and Thomas Mann: Calling and the Shaping of Self.* Berkeley:
              University of California Press.
1992   *Politics, Death, and the Devil: Self and Power in Max Weber and
              Thomas Mann.* Berkeley: University of California Press.

1993   "Contemporary Sociology and the Interpretation of Weber." *Theory and Society* 22:853–860.

1994   "From Social Theory to Sociology of Knowledge and Back: Karl Mannheim and the Sociology of Intellectual Knowledge Production." *Sociological Theory* 12:266–278.

Gordon, Linda
1994   *Pitied but Not Entitled: Single Mothers and the History of Welfare.* New York: Free Press.

Gorman, Robert A.
1975a   "Alfred Schutz: An Exposition and Critique." *British Journal of Sociology* 26:1–19.

1975b   "The Phenomenological 'Humanization' of Social Science: A Critique." *British Journal of Sociology* 26:389–405.

1977   *The Dual Vision: Alfred Schutz and the Myth of Phenomenological Social Science.* London: Routledge and Kegan Paul.

Gottdiener, Mark
1993   "Ideology, Foundationalism, and Sociological Theory." *Sociological Quarterly* 34:653–671.

Gould, Carol
1978   *Marx's Social Ontology: Individuality and Community in Marx's Theory of Social Reality.* Cambridge, Mass.: MIT Press.

Gouldner, Alvin
1959/1967   "Reciprocity and Autonomy in Functional Theory." In N. Demerath and R. Peterson (eds.), *System, Change and Conflict.* New York: Free Press: 141–169.

1970   *The Coming Crisis of Western Sociology.* New York: Basic Books.

Graham, Keith
1992   *Karl Marx, Our Contemporary.* Toronto: University of Toronto Press.

Grathoff, Richard (ed.)
1978   *The Theory of Social Action: The Correspondence of Alfred Schutz and Talcott Parsons.* Bloomington: Indiana University Press.

Greatbatch, David, and Dingwall, Robert
1997   "Argumentative Talk in Divorce Mediation Sessions." *American Sociological Review* 62:151–170.

Greisman, Harvey C.
1986   "The Paradigm That Failed." In R. C. Monk (ed.), *Structures of Knowing.* Lanham, Md.: University Press of America: 273–291.

Greisman, Harvey C., and Ritzer, George
1981   "Max Weber, Critical Theory and the Administered World." *Qualitative Sociology* 4:34–55.

Gronow, Jukka
1997   *The Sociology of Taste.* London: Routledge.

Gross, Llewellyn
1961   "Preface to a Metatheoretical Framework for Sociology." *American Journal of Sociology* 67:125–136.

Guba, Egon G., and Lincoln, Yvonna S.
1994   "Competing Paradigms in Qualitative Research." In Norman K. Denzin and Yvonna S. Lincoln (eds.), *Handbook of Qualitative Research.* Thousand Oaks, Calif.: Sage: 105–117.

Gurney, Patrick J.
1981   "Historical Origins of Ideological Denial: The Case of Marx in American
            Sociology." *American Sociologist* 16:196–201.
Gurvitch, Georges
1964   *The Spectrum of Social Time.* Dordrecht, Neth.: D. Reidel.
Habermas, Jurgen
1981   "Modernity versus Postmodernity." *New German Critique* 22:3–14.
1984   *The Theory of Communicative Action.* Vol. 1, *Reason and the
            Rationalization of Society.* Boston: Beacon Press.
1987a   *The Theory of Communicative Action.* Vol. 2, *Lifeworld and System:
            A Critique of Functionalist Reason.* Boston: Beacon Press.
1987b   *The Philosophical Discourse of Modernity: Twelve Lectures.* Cambridge,
            Mass.: MIT Press.
Hackett, Amy
1976   "Feminism and Liberalism in Wilhelmine Germany 1890–1918." In
            B. Carroll (ed.), *Liberating Woman's History.* Urbana: University of Illinois
            Press: 127–136.
Hage, Jerald
1994a   "Constructing Bridges between Sociological Paradigms and Levels: Trying
            to Make Sociological Theory More Complex, Less Fragmented, and
            Politicized." In J. Hage (ed.), *Formal Theory in Sociology: Opportunity or
            Pitfall?* Albany: State University Press of New York: 152–168.
Hage, Jerald (ed.)
1994b   *Formal Theory in Sociology: Opportunity or Pitfall?* Albany: State
            University Press of New York.
Haines, Valerie
1988   "Is Spencer's Theory an Evolutionary Theory?" *American Journal of
            Sociology* 93:1200–1223.
1992   "Spencer's Philosophy of Science." *British Journal of Sociology* 43:155–172.
Halfpenny, Peter
1982   *Positivism and Sociology: Explaining Social Life.* London: Allen and Unwin.
Hall, John R.
1992   "Where History and Sociology Meet: Forms of Discourse and
            Sociohistorical Inquiry." *Sociological Theory* 10:164–193.
Hall, Richard
1983   "Theoretical Trends in the Sociology of Occupations." *Sociological
            Quarterly* 24:5–23.
Halls, W. D.
1996   "The Cultural and Educational Influences of Durkheim, 1900–1945."
            Durkheimian Studies 2:122–132.
Hankin, Thomas L.
1979   "In Defense of Biography: The Use of Biography in the History of Science."
            History of Science 17:1–16.
Harley, Sharon
1978   "Anna J. Cooper: A Voice for Black Women." In S. Harley and R. Terborg-
            Penn (eds.), *The Afro-American Woman: Struggles and Images.*
            Port Washington, N.Y.: Kennikat Press.
Harper, Diane Blake, Sylvester, Joan, and Walczak, David
1980   "An Empirical Comparison of Ritzer's Paradigms and Similar Metatheories:
            Comment on Friedheim." *Social Forces* 59:513–517.

Hartsock, Nancy
1983   *Money, Sex and Power: Towards a Feminist Historical Materialism.*
            New York: Longman.
Harvey, David
1989   *The Condition of Postmodernity: An Enquiry into the Origins of Cultural
            Change.* Oxford: Basil Blackwell.
Harvey, Lee
1982   "The Use and Abuse of Kuhnian Paradigms in the Sociology of Knowledge."
            British Journal of Sociology 16:85–101.
1987   "The Nature of 'Schools' in the Sociology of Knowledge: The Case of the
            'Chicago School.'" *Sociological Review* 35:245–278.
Hawthorn, Geoffrey
1976   *Enlightenment and Despair.* Cambridge: Cambridge University Press.
Hays, Sharon
1994   "Structure and Agency and the Sticky Problem of Culture." *Sociological
            Theory* 12:57–72.
Heap, James L., and Roth, Phillip A.
1973   "On Phenomenological Sociology." *American Sociological Review*
            38:354–367.
Hearn, Frank
1997   *Moral Order and Social Disorder: The American Search for Civil Society.*
            New York: Aldine de Gruyter.
Heberle, Rudolph
1965   "Simmel's Methods." In L. Coser (ed.), *Georg Simmel.* Englewood Cliffs,
            N.J.: Prentice-Hall: 116–121.
Hegel, G. W. F.
1807/1967   *The Phenomenology of Mind.* New York: Harper Colophon.
1821/1967   *The Philosophy of Right.* Oxford: Clarendon Press.
Heilbron, Johan
1990   "Auguste Comte and Epistemology." *Sociological Theory* 8:153–162.
1995   *The Rise of Social Theory.* London: Polity.
Heins, Volker
1993   "Weber's Ethic and the Spirit of Anti-Capitalism." *Political Studies*
            41:269–283.
Hekman, Susan
1983   *Weber, the Ideal Type, and Contemporary Social Theory.* Notre Dame, Ind.:
            University of Notre Dame Press.
Heller, Agnes
1976   *The Theory of Need in Marx.* New York: St. Martin's.
Hennis, Wilhelm
1994   "The Meaning of 'Wertfreiheit': On the Background and Motives of Max
            Weber's 'Postulate.'" *Sociological Theory* 12:113–125.
Heritage, John
1984   *Garfinkel and Ethnomethodology.* Cambridge: Polity Press.
Hewitt, John P.
1984   *Self and Society: A Symbolic Interactionist Social Psychology.* 3rd ed.
            Boston: Allyn and Bacon.
Heyl, John D., and Heyl, Barbara S.
1976   "The Sumner-Porter Controversy at Yale: Pre-Paradigmatic Sociology and
            Institutional Crisis." *Sociological Inquiry* 46:41–49.

Hilbert, Richard A.
1986   "Anomie and Moral Regulation of Reality: The Durkheimian Tradition in
            Modern Relief." *Sociological Theory* 4:1–19.
1992   *The Classical Roots of Ethnomethodology: Durkheim, Weber and Garfinkel.*
            Chapel Hill: University of North Carolina Press.

Hill, Forrest
1958   "Veblen and Marx." In Douglas F. Dowd (ed.), *Thorstein Veblen: A Critical
            Reappraisal.* Ithaca, N.Y.: Cornell University: 129–149.

Hill, Lisa
1996   "Anticipations of Nineteenth and Twentieth Century Social Thought in
            the Work of Adam Ferguson." *Archives Europeenes de Sociologie*
            37:203–228.

Hill, Michael R.
1989   "Empiricism and Reason in Harriet Martineau's Sociology." Introduction to
            M. Hill (ed.), *How to Observe Morals and Manners* by Harriet Martineau.
            New Brunswick, N.J.: Transaction Books.

Hill, Michael R., and Hoecker-Drysdale, Susan
2000   *Harriet Martineau: Theoretical and Methodological Perspectives.*
            New York: Garland.

Himes, Joseph
1966   "The Functions of Racial Conflict." *Social Forces* 45:1–10.

Hinkle, Roscoe
1963   "Antecedents of the Action Orientation in American Sociology before 1935."
            American Sociological Review 28:705–715.
1980   *Founding Theory of American Sociology: 1881–1915.* London: Routledge
            and Kegan Paul.
1994   *Developments in American Sociological Theory, 1915–1950.* Albany:
            State University of New York Press.

Hinkle, Roscoe, and Hinkle, Gisela
1954   *The Development of American Sociology.* New York: Random House.

Hochschild, Arlie Russell
1997   *The Time Bind: When Work Becomes Home and Home Becomes Work.*
            New York: Metropolitan Books.

Hochschild, Arlie, with Machung, Anne
1989   *The Second Shift.* New York: Avon Books.

Hoecker-Drysdale, Susan
1994   *Harriet Martineau: First Woman Sociologist.* New York: Berg Press.
forthcoming "Harriet Martineau." In George Ritzer (ed.), *The Blackwell Companion to
            Major Social Theorists.* Oxford, England, and Cambridge, Mass.:
            Blackwell.

Hofstadter, Richard
1959   *Social Darwinism in American Thought.* New York: Braziller.

Hollinger, David
1980   "T. S. Kuhn's Theory of Science and Its Implications for History." In
            G. Gutting (ed.), *Paradigms and Revolutions.* Notre Dame, Ind.: Notre Dame
            University Press: 195–222.

Holmwood, John, and Stewart, Alexander
1994   "Synthesis and Fragmentation in Social Theory: A Progressive Solution."
            Sociological Theory 12:83–100.

Holton, Robert J., and Turner, Bryan S.
1986   "Reading Talcott Parsons: Introductory Remarks." In R. J. Holton and
              B. S. Turner (eds.), *Talcott Parsons on Economy and Society.* London:
              Routledge and Kegan Paul: 1–24.
Homans, George C.
1958   "Social Behavior as Exchange." *American Journal of Sociology*
              63:597–606.
1961   *Social Behavior: Its Elementary Forms.* New York: Harcourt, Brace
              and World.
1962   *Sentiments and Activities.* New York: Free Press.
1969   "The Sociological Relevance of Behaviorism." In R. Burgess and
              D. Bushell (eds.), *Behavioral Sociology.* New York: Columbia University
              Press: 1–24.
1984   *Coming to My Senses: The Autobiography of a Sociologist.* New Brunswick,
              N.J.: Transaction Books.
Hook, Sidney
1965   "Pareto's Sociological System." In J. H. Meisel (ed.), *Pareto and Mosca.*
              Englewood Cliffs, N.J.: Prentice-Hall: 57–61.
Horowitz, Irving L.
1962/1967   "Consensus, Conflict, and Cooperation." In N. Demerath and R. Peterson
              (eds.), *System, Change and Conflict.* New York: Free Press: 265–279.
1983   *C. Wright Mills: An American Utopian.* New York: Free Press.
Hoyningen-Huene, Paul
1993   *Reconstructing Scientific Revolutions: Thomas S. Kuhn's Philosophy of
              Science.* Chicago: University of Chicago Press.
Huaco, George
1986   "Ideology and General Theory: The Case of Sociological Functionalism."
              Comparative Studies in Society and History 28:34–54.
Hudelson, Richard
1993   "Has History Refuted Marxism?" *Philosophy of the Social Sciences*
              23:180–198.
Hughes, John A., Martin, Peter J., and Sharrock, W. W.
1995   *Understanding Classical Sociology: Marx, Weber and Durkheim.*
              London: Sage.
Humphery, Kim
1998   *Shelf Life: Supermarkets and the Changing Cultures of Consumption.*
              Cambridge: Cambridge University Press.
Hunter, J. E., and Schmidt, F. L.
1989   *Methods of Meta-Analysis: Correcting Error and Bias in Research Findings.*
              Newbury Park, Calif.: Sage.
Hunter, J. E., Schmidt, F. L., and Jackson, G. B.
1982   *Meta-Analysis: Cumulating Research Findings across Studies.*
              Beverly Hills, Calif.: Sage.
Israel, Joachim
1971   *Alienation: From Marx to Modern Sociology.* Boston: Allyn and Bacon.
Jackman, Mary R., and Jackman, Robert W.
1973   "An Interpretation of the Relation between Objective and Subjective Social
              Status." *American Sociological Review* 38:569–582.

Jacobs, Bruce A.
1992   "Drugs and Deception: Undercover Infiltration and Dramaturgical Theory."
            Human Relations 45:1293–1310.
Jaffee, David
1996   *Levels of Socio-Economic Development Theory.* Westport, Conn.: Praeger.
Jameson, Fredric
1984   "Postmodernism, or the Cultural Logic of Late Capitalism." *New Left
            Review* 146:53–93.
1991   *Postmodernism, or, The Cultural Logic of Late Capitalism.* Durham, N.C.:
            Duke University Press.
Janssen, Jacques, and Verheggen, Theo
1997   "The Double Center of Gravity in Durkheim's Symbol Theory: Bringing the
            Symbolism of the Body Back In." *Sociological Theory* 15:294–306.
Jaworski, Gary Dean
1991   "The Historical and Contemporary Importance of Coser's *Functions*."
            Sociological Theory 9:116–123.
1995   "Simmel in Early American Sociology: Translation as Social Action."
            International Journal of Politics, Culture and Society 8:389–417.
1997   *Georg Simmel and the American Prospect.* Albany: State University of
            New York Press.
Jay, Martin
1973   *The Dialectical Imagination.* Boston: Little, Brown.
1984   *Marxism and Totality: The Adventures of a Concept from Lukács to
            Habermas.* Berkeley: University of California Press.
1986   *Permanent Exiles: Essays on the Intellectual Migration from Germany to
            America.* New York: Columbia University Press.
Jedlowski, Paolo
1990   "Simmel on Memory." In M. Kaern, B. S. Phillips, and R. S. Cohen (eds.),
            Georg Simmel and Contemporary Sociology. Dordrecht, Neth.: Kluwer:
            131–154.
Jenkins, Thomas H.
1996   "The Sociologist as Public Planner: American, German and British
            Examples." *Sociological Imagination* 33:18–36.
Joas, Hans
1985   *G. H. Mead: A Contemporary Re-examination of His Thought.* Cambridge,
            Mass.: MIT Press.
Johnson, Doyle Paul
1981   *Sociological Theory: Classical Founders and Contemporary Perspectives.*
            New York: Wiley.
Johnston, Barry V.
1995   *Pitirim Sorokin: An Intellectual Biography.* Lawrence: University Press
            of Kansas.
Jones, Greta
1980   *Social Darwinism and English Thought: The Interaction between Biological
            and Social Theory.* Atlantic Highlands, N.J.: Humanities Press.
Jones, Harold B.
1997   "The Protestant Ethic: Weber's Model and the Empirical Literature."
            Human Relations 50:757–778.

Jones, Robert Alun
1983   "The New History of Sociology." *Annual Review of Sociology* 9:447–469.
1986   "Durkheim, Frazer, and Smith: The Role of Analogies and Exemplars in the Development of Durkheim's Sociology of Religion." *American Journal of Sociology* 92:596–627.
1994   "The Positive Science of Ethics in France: German Influences in *De la Division du Travail Social*." *Sociological Forum* 9:37–57.
Jones, Susan Stedman
1996   "What Does Durkheim Mean by 'Thing'?" *Durkheimian Studies* 2:43–59.
Kaern, Michael, Phillips, Bernard S., and Cohen, Robert S. (eds.)
1990   *Georg Simmel and Contemporary Sociology*. Dordrecht, Neth.: Kluwer.
Kalberg, Stephen
1980   "Max Weber's Types of Rationality: Cornerstones for the Analysis of Rationalization Processes in History." *American Journal of Sociology* 85:1145–1179.
1985   "The Role of Ideal Interests in Max Weber's Comparative Historical Sociology." In R. J. Antonio and R. M. Glassman (eds.), *A Weber-Marx Dialogue*. Lawrence: University Press of Kansas: 46–67.
1990   "The Rationalization of Action in Max Weber's Sociology of Religion." *Sociological Theory* 8:58–84.
1994   *Max Weber's Comparative-Historical Sociology*. Chicago: University of Chicago Press.
1996   "On the Neglect of Weber's *Protestant Ethic* as a Theoretical Treatise: Demarcating the Parameters of Postwar American Sociological Theory." *Sociological Theory* 14:49–70.
1997   "Max Weber's Sociology: Research Strategies and Modes of Analysis." In Charles Camic, (ed.), *Reclaiming the Sociological Classics: The State of Scholarship*. Oxford: Blackwell: 208–241.
forthcoming "Max Weber." In George Ritzer (ed.), *The Blackwell Companion to Major Social Theorists*. Oxford, England, and Cambridge, Mass.: Blackwell.
Kandal, Terry R.
1988   *The Woman Question in Classical Sociological Theory*. Miami: International Universities Press.
Kanter, Rosabeth Moss
1977   *Men and Women of the Corporation*. New York: Basic Books.
Kaplan, Norman
1958   "Idle Curiosity," in Douglas F. Dowd, ed., *Thorstein Veblen: A Critical Reappraisal*. Ithaca: Cornell University: 39–55.
Karady, Victor
1983   "The Durkheimians in Academe: A Reconsideration." In P. Besnard (ed.), *The Sociological Domain*. Cambridge: Cambridge University Press: 71–89.
Kasler, Dirk
1985   "Jewishness as a Central Formation-Milieu of Early German Sociology." *History of Sociology: An International Review* 6:69–86.
Kaye, Howard L.
1991   "A False Convergence: Freud and the Hobbesian Problem of Order." *Sociological Theory* 9:87–105.

Keith, Bruce
1991   "Charlotte Perkins Gilman 1860–1935." In Mary Jo Deegan (ed.), *Women in Sociology: A Bio-Bibliographical Sourcebook*. Westport, Conn.: Greenwood Press: 149–156.
Keller, Frances Richardson
1988   "Introductory Essay." In *Anna Julia Cooper, Slavery and the French Revolutionists 1788–1805*. Queenston, Ontario: Edwin-Mellon Press.
Kelley, Florence (ed.)
1887/1986   "The Need for Theoretical Preparation for Philanthropic Work." In K. K. Sklar (ed.), *Notes of Sixty Years—The Autobiography of Florence Kelley*. Chicago: Charles H. Kerr: 91–104.
1895   *Hull-House Maps and Papers*. Boston: Crowell.
1899   "Aims and Principles of the Consumers League." *American Journal of Sociology* 5:289–304.
1905/1969   *Some Ethical Gains through Legislation*. New York: Arno.
Kellner, Douglas
1993   "Critical Theory Today: Revisiting the Classics." *Theory, Culture and Society* 10:43–60.
1995   "Marxism, the Information Superhighway, and the Struggle for the Future." *Humanity and Society* 19:41–56.
Kellner, Douglas (ed.)
1989   *Postmodernism, Jameson, Critique*. Washington, D.C.: Maisonneuve Press.
Kent, Raymond A.
1981   *A History of British Empirical Sociology*. Aldershot, Hants, Eng.: Gower.
Kettler, David, and Meja, Volker
1993   "Their 'Own Peculiar Way': Karl Mannheim and the Rise of Women." *International Sociology* 8:5–55.
1994   " 'That Typically German Kind of Sociology Which Verges towards Philosophy': The Dispute about Ideology and Utopia in the United States." *Sociological Theory* 12:279–303.
1995   *Karl Mannheim and the Crisis of Liberalism*. New Brunswick, N.J.: Transaction Publishers.
Kettler, David, Meja, Volker, and Stehr, Nico
1982   "Introduction: Karl Mannheim's Early Writings on Cultural Sociology." In K. Mannheim, *Structures of Thinking*. London: Routledge and Kegan Paul.
1984   *Karl Mannheim*. Chichester, Eng.: Ellis Horwood; London: Tavistock.
Kimmel, Michael
1996   *Manhood in America: A Cultural History*. New York: Free Press.
Kimmerling, Baruch
1992   "Sociology, Ideology, and Nation-Building: The Palestinians and Their Meaning in Israeli Sociology." *American Sociological Review* 57:446–460.
Klagge, Jay
1997   "Approaches to the Iron Cage: Reconstructing the Bars of Weber's Metaphor." *Administration and Society* 29:63–77.
Knorr-Cetina, Karin
1981   "Introduction: The Micro-Sociological Challenge to Macro-Sociology: Towards a Reconstruction of Social Theory and Methodology." In K. Knorr-Cetina and A. Cicourel (eds.), *Advances in Social Theory and Methodology*. New York: Methuen: 1–47.

Kohn, Melvin L.
1976   "Occupational Structure and Alienation." *American Journal of Sociology* 82:111–127.

Kolb, William L.
1944   "A Critical Evaluation of Mead's 'I' and 'Me' Concepts." *Social Forces* 22:291–296.

Korenbaum, Myrtle
1964   Translator's preface to Georges Gurvitch. *The Spectrum of Social Time.* Dordrecht, Neth.: D. Reidel: ix–xxvi.

Korllos, Thomas S.
1994   "Uncovering Simmel's Forms and Social Types." *International Social Science Review* 69:17–22.

Kronman, Anthony
1983   *Max Weber.* Stanford, Calif.: Stanford University Press.

Kuhn, Thomas
1962   *The Structure of Scientific Revolutions.* Chicago: University of Chicago Press.
1970   *The Structure of Scientific Revolutions.* 2nd ed. Chicago: University of Chicago Press.

Kurzweil, Edith
1980   *The Age of Structuralism: Lévi-Strauss to Foucault.* New York: Columbia University Press.
1987   "Psychoanalysis as the Macro-Micro Link." In J. Alexander et al. (eds.), *The Micro-Macro Link.* Berkeley: University of California Press: 237–254.

Lachman, L. M.
1971   *The Legacy of Max Weber.* Berkeley, Calif.: Glendessary Press.

Laclau, Ernesto, and Mouffe, Chantal
1985   *Hegemony and Socialist Strategy: Towards a Radical Democratic Politics.* London: Verso.

Langsdorf, Lenore
1995   "Treating Method and Form as Phenomena: An Appreciation of Garfinkel's Phenomenology of Social Action." *Human Studies* 18:177–188.

Laslett, Barbara, and Thorne, Barrie
1992   "Considering Dorothy Smith's Sociology." *Sociological Theory* 10:60–63.

Lassman, Peter, and Velody, Irving
1989   "Max Weber on Science: Disenchantment and the Search for Meaning." In P. Lassman, I. Velody, with H. Martins (eds.), *Max Weber's "Science as a Vocation."* London: Unwin Hyman: 159–204.

Lefebvre, Henri
1968   *The Sociology of Marx.* New York: Vintage.

Lehman, Edward W.
1988   "The Theory of the State versus the State of Theory." *American Sociological Review* 53:807–823.

Lehmann, Jennifer M.
1993a   *Deconstructing Durkheim: A Post-Post-Structuralist Critique.* London: Routledge.
1993b   *Durkheim and Women: The Problematic Relationship.* Lincoln: University of Nebraska Press.

1995   *Deconstructing Durkheim: A Post-Post-Structuralist Critique.* Lincoln:
            University of Nebraska Press.

Lemert, Charles
1979   *Sociology and the Twilight of Man: Homocentrism and Discourse in
            Sociological Theory.* Carbondale: Southern Illinois University Press.
1990   "The Uses of French Structuralisms in Sociology." In G. Ritzer (ed.),
            Frontiers of Social Theory: The New Syntheses. New York: Columbia
            University Press: 230–254.
1992a   "Sociological Metatheory and Its Cultured Despisers." In G. Ritzer (ed.),
            Metatheorizing. Newbury Park, Calif.: Sage: 124–134.
1992b   "Subjectivity's Limit: The Unsolved Riddle of the Standpoint." *Sociological
            Theory* 10:63–72.
1994a   "The Canonical Limits of Durkheim's First Classic." *Sociological Forum*
            9:87–92.
1994b   "Social Theory at the Early End of a Short Century." *Sociological Theory*
            12:140–152.
1994c   "Anna Julia Cooper." Paper presented at the annual meetings of the
            American Sociological Association. Los Angeles, California, August.
1995   *Sociology After the Crisis.* Boulder, Colo.: Westview.

Lemert, Charles (ed.)
1981   *French Sociology: Rupture and Renewal since 1968.* New York: Columbia
            University Press.
1999   *Social Theory: The Multicultural and Classical Readings.* Boulder, Colo.:
            Westview Press.

Lemert, Charles, and Bahn, Esme (eds.)
1998   *The Voice of Anna Julia Cooper.* Lanham, Md.: Rowman and Littlefield.

Lengermann, Patricia M.
1979   "The Founding of the *American Sociological Review.*" *American
            Sociological Review* 44:185–198.

Lengermann, Patricia M., and Niebrugge, Jill
1995   "Intersubjectivity and Domination: A Feminist Investigation of the Sociology
            of Alfred Schutz." *Sociological Theory* 13:25–37.

Lengermann, Patricia M., and Niebrugge-Brantley, Jill
1990   "Feminist Sociological Theory: The Near-Future Prospects." In G. Ritzer
            (ed.), *Frontiers of Social Theory: The New Syntheses.* New York:
            Columbia University Press: 316–344.

Lengermann, Patricia Madoo, and Niebrugge-Brantley, Jill
1998   *The Women Founders: Sociology and Social Theory, 1830–1930.* New York:
            McGraw-Hill.

Lengermann, Patricia M., and Wallace, Ruth A.
1985   *Gender in America: Social Control and Social Change.* Englewood Cliffs,
            N.J.: Prentice-Hall.

Lenzer, Gertrud (ed.)
1975   *Auguste Comte and Positivism: The Essential Writings.* Magnolia, Mass.:
            Peter Smith.

Lepenies, Wolf
1988   *Between Literature and Science: The Rise of Sociology.* Cambridge:
            Cambridge University Press.

Lerner, Gerda
1993   *The Creation of Feminist Consciousness.* New York: Oxford.

Lester, David (ed.)
1994   *Emile Durkheim, Le Suicide: One Hundred Years Later*. Philadelphia:
                Charles Press.

Levine, Donald
1971   "Introduction." In D. Levine (ed.), *Georg Simmel: Individuality and Social
                Forms*. Chicago: University of Chicago Press: ix–xiv.
1981a   "Rationality and Freedom: Weber and Beyond." *Sociological Inquiry*
                51:5–25.
1981b   "Sociology's Quest for the Classics: The Case of Simmel." In B. Rhea (ed.),
                The Future of the Sociological Classics. London: Allen and Unwin: 60–80.
1985   "Ambivalent Encounters: Disavowals of Simmel by Durkheim, Weber,
                Lukács, Park and Parsons." In D. Levine (ed.), *The Flight from Ambiguity:
                Essays in Social and Cultural Theory*. Chicago: University of Chicago
                Press: 89–141.
1989   "Simmel as a Resource for Sociological Metatheory." *Sociological Theory*
                7:161–174.
1991a   "Simmel and Parsons Reconsidered." *American Journal of Sociology*
                96:1097–1116.
1991b   "Simmel as Educator: On Individuality and Modern Culture." *Theory,
                Culture and Society* 8:99–118.
1995a   *Visions of the Sociological Tradition*. Chicago: University of Chicago Press.
1995b   "The Organism Metaphor in Sociology." *Social Research* 62:239–265.
1997   "Simmel Reappraised: Old Images, New Scholarship." In Charles Camic
                (ed.), *Reclaiming the Sociological Classics: The State of Scholarship*.
                Oxford: Blackwell: 173–207.

Levine, Donald, Carter, Ellwood B., and Gorman, Eleanor Miller
1976a   "Simmel's Influence on American Sociology—I." *American Journal of
                Sociology* 81:813–845.
1976b   "Simmel's Influence on American Sociology—II." *American Journal of
                Sociology* 81:1112–1132.

Levy-Bruhl, Lucien
1903/1973   *The Philosophy of Auguste Comte*. Clifton, N.J.: A. M. Kelley.

Lewis, J. David, and Smith, Richard L.
1980   *American Sociology and Pragmatism: Mead, Chicago Sociology, and
                Symbolic Interaction*. Chicago: University of Chicago Press.

Lewis, Reba Rowe
1991   "Forging New Syntheses: Theories and Theorists." *American Sociologist*
                Fall/Winter:221–230.

Lichtblau, Klaus, and Ritter, Mark
1991   "Causality or Interaction? Simmel, Weber and Interpretive Sociology."
                Theory, Culture and Society 8:33–62.

Lilla, Mark
1994   "The Legitimacy of the Liberal Age." In M. Lilla (ed.), *New French
                Thought: Political Philosophy*. Princeton, N.J.: Princeton University Press:
                3–34.

Lindbekk, Tore
1992   "The Weberian Ideal-Type: Development and Continuities."
                Acta Sociologica 35:285–297.

Lindner, Rolf
1996   *The Reportage of Urban Culture: Robert Park and the Chicago School.*
               Cambridge: Cambridge University Press.
Lipovetsky, Gilles
1987/1994   *The Empire of Fashion: Dressing Modern Democracy.* Princeton, N.J.:
               Princeton University Press.
Liska, Allen E.
1990   "The Significance of Aggregate Dependent Variables and Contextual
               Independent Variables for Linking Macro and Micro Theories." *Social
               Psychology Quarterly* 53:292–301.
Liska, Allen E., and Warner, Barbara
1991   "Functions of Crime: A Paradoxical Process." *American Journal of
               Sociology* 96:1441–1463.
Loader, Colin
1985   *The Intellectual Development of Karl Mannheim.* Cambridge: Cambridge
               University Press.
1997   "Free Floating: The Intelligentsia in the Work of Alfred Weber and
               Karl Mannheim." *German Studies Review* 20:217–234.
Loader, Colin, and Alexander, Jeffrey C.
1985   "Max Weber on Churches and Sects in North America: An Alternative Path
               toward Rationalization." *Sociological Theory* 3:1–6.
Lockwood, David
1956   "Some Remarks on *The Social System.*" *British Journal of Sociology*
               7:134–146.
Lodahl, Janice B., and Gordon, Gerald
1972   "The Structure of Scientific Fields and the Functioning of University
               Graduate Departments." *American Sociological Review* 37:57–72.
Lodge, Peter
1986   "Connections: W. I. Thomas, European Social Thought and American
               Sociology." In R. C. Monk (ed.), *Structures of Knowing.* Lanham, Md.:
               University Press of America: 135–160.
Lohmann, Georg, and Wilkes, Geoff
1996   "The Adaptation of Inner Life to the Inner Infinity of the Metropolis: Forms
               of Individualization in Simmel." *Thesis Eleven* 44:1–11.
Longhurst, Brian
1988   *Karl Mannheim and the Contemporary Sociology of Knowledge.* New York:
               St. Martin's.
Lovejoy, Arthur
1948   *Essays in the History of Ideas.* Baltimore: Johns Hopkins University Press.
Lovell, David W.
1992   "Socialism, Utopianism and the 'Utopian Socialists.'" *History of European
               Ideas* 14:185–201.
Lowy, Michael
1996   "Figures of Weberian Marxism." *Theory and Society* 25:431–446.
Luhmann, Niklas
1982   *The Differentiation of Society.* New York: Columbia University Press.
Lukács, Georg
1922/1968   *History and Class Consciousness.* Cambridge, Mass.: MIT Press.
1991   "Georg Simmel." *Theory, Culture and Society* 8:145–150.

Lukes, Steven
1972   *Emile Durkheim: His Life and Work.* New York: Harper & Row.
1977   "Power and Structure." In S. Lukes, *Essays in Social Theory.* London:
                Macmillan: 3–29.
Luxenberg, Stan
1985   *Roadside Empires: How the Chains Franchised America.* New York:
                Viking.
Lyman, Stanford, and Scott, Marvin
1970   *A Sociology of the Absurd.* New York: Appleton-Century-Crofts.
Lyotard, Jean-François
1984   *The Postmodern Condition: A Report on Knowledge.* Minneapolis:
                University of Minnesota Press.
MacCrae, Donald G.
1974   *Max Weber.* Harmondsworth, Eng.: Penguin.
1992   "Karl III's Uneasy Reign." *New Statesman and Society* 217:v–vi.
MacIver, Robert
1931   *Society: Its Structure and Changes.* New York: Long and Smith.
1942   *Social Causation.* Boston: Ginn.
MacKinnon, Catherine
1979   *Sexual Harassment of Working Women.* New Haven: Yale University Press.
MacLean, Annie Marion
1899   "Two Weeks in Department Stores." *American Journal of Sociology*
                21:721–741.
Maines, David R.
1977   "Social Organization and Social Structure in Symbolic Interactionist
                Thought." In A. Inkeles, J. Coleman, and N. Smelser (eds.), *Annual Review
                of Sociology,* Vol. 3. Palo Alto, Calif.: Annual Reviews: 259–285.
Maines, David, Bridger, Jeffrey C., and Ulmer, Jeffery T.
1996   "Mythic Facts and Park's Pragmatism: On Predecessor-Selection and
                Theorizing in Human Ecology." *Sociological Quarterly* 37:521–549.
Manent, Pierre
1994/1998   *The City of Man.* Princeton, N.J.: Princeton University Press.
Mann, Michael
1986   *The Sources of Social Power,* Vol. 1. New York: Cambridge University
                Press.
Mann, Susan A., Grimes, Michael D., and Kemp, Alice Abel
1997   "Paradigm Shifts in Family Sociology? Evidence from Three Decades of
                Family Textbooks." *Journal of Family Issues* 18:315–349.
Mannheim, Karl
1925/1971   "The Problem of a Sociology of Knowledge." In K. H. Wolf (ed.), *From
                Karl Mannheim.* New York: Oxford University Press: 59–115.
1926/1971   "The Ideological and the Sociological Interpretation of Intellectual
                Phenomena." In K. H. Wolff (ed.), *From Karl Mannheim.* New York:
                Oxford University Press: 116–131.
1928–1929/   "The Problem of Generations." In Karl Mannheim, *Essays on the Sociology
1952   of Knowledge.* New York: Oxford University Press: 276–320.
1929/1936   *Ideology and Utopia.* New York: Harcourt, Brace and World.
1929/1971   "Problems of Sociology in Germany." In K. H. Wolff (ed.), *From
                Karl Mannheim.* New York: Oxford University Press: 262–270.

1931/1936   "The Sociology of Knowledge." In K. Mannheim, *Ideology and Utopia.* New York: Harcourt, Brace and World: 264–311.

1932/1993   "The Sociology of Intellectuals." *Theory, Culture and Society* 10:69–80.

1935/1940   *Man and Society in an Age of Reconstruction.* New York: Harcourt, Brace and World.

1943   *Diagnosis of Our Time: Wartime Essays of a Sociologist.* London: Routledge and Kegan Paul.

1944/1971   "Education, Sociology and the Problem of Social Awareness." In K. H. Wolff (ed.), *From Karl Mannheim.* New York: Oxford University Press: 367–384.

1950   *Freedom, Power and Democratic Planning,* H. Gerth and E. K. Bramstedt (eds.). London: Routledge and Kegan Paul.

1952/1971a   "On the Interpretation of *Weltanschauung.*" In K. H. Wolff (ed.), *From Karl Mannheim.* New York: Oxford University Press: 8–58.

1952/1971b   "Competition as Cultural Phenomenon." In K. H. Wolff (ed.), *From Karl Mannheim.* New York: Oxford University Press: 223–261.

1953a   *Essays in the Sociology of Culture.* London: Routledge and Kegan Paul.

1953b   *Essays on Sociology and Social Psychology.* London: Routledge and Kegan Paul.

1953/1971   "Conservative Thought." In K. H. Wolff (ed.), *From Karl Mannheim.* New York: Oxford University Press: 132–222.

1956/1971   "The Democratization of Culture." In K. H. Wolff (ed.), *From Karl Mannheim.* New York: Oxford University Press: 271–346.

1957   *Systematic Sociology: An Introduction to the Study of Society.* J. S. Eros and W. A. C. Stewart (eds.). New York: Philosophical Library.

1982   *Structures of Thinking.* David Kettler, Volker Meja, and Nico Stehr (eds. and trans.). London: Routledge and Kegan Paul.

Mannheim, Karl, and Stewart, W. A. C.
1962   *An Introduction to the Sociology of Education.* London: Routledge and Kegan Paul.

Manning, Philip
1991   "Drama as Life: The Significance of Goffman's Changing Use of the Theatrical Metaphor." *Sociological Theory* 9:70–86.

1992   *Erving Goffman and Modern Sociology.* Stanford, Calif.: Stanford University Press.

Manuel, Frank E.
1962   *The Prophets of Paris.* Cambridge, Mass.: University Press.

1992   "A Requiem for Karl Marx." *Daedalus* 121:1–19.

Markus, Gyorgy
1991   "Concepts of Ideology in Marx." *Canadian Journal of Political and Social Theory* 15:87–106.

Martineau, Harriet
1822   "Female Writers on Practical Divinity." *Monthly Repository* 17:593–596.

1830/1836   "Letter to the Deaf." In H. Martineau, *Miscellanies,* Vol. 1. Boston: Hilliard Gray: 248–265.

1832   "Demerara." In H. Martineau, *Illustrations of Political Economy.* London: Charles Fox: 1–129.

1832/1836   "Essays on the Art of Thinking." In H. Martineau, *Miscellanies,* Vol. 1. Boston: Hilliard Gray: 122–179.

1832–1834   *Illustrations of Political Economy.* London: Charles Fox.

1836	*Miscellanies.* Boston: Hilliard Gray.
1836/1837	*Society in America.* 2 vols. New York: Saunders and Otley.
1837/1962	*Society in America.* Garden City, N.Y.: Doubleday Anchor.
1838a	"Domestic Service." *London and Westminster Review* 29:405–432.
1838b	*How to Observe Morals and Manners.* London: Charles Knight.
1838/1989	*How to Observe Manners and Morals.* New Brunswick, N.J.: Transaction Books.
1848	*Eastern Life: Present and Past.* London: Edward Moxon.
1853	*The Positive Philosophy of Auguste Comte, freely translated and condensed by Harriet Martineau.* London: John Chapman.

Marx, Karl

1842/1977	"Communism and the *Augsburger Allegemeine Zeitung.*" In D. McLellan (ed.), *Karl Marx: Selected Writings.* New York: Oxford University Press: 20.
1847/1963	*The Poverty of Philosophy.* New York: International Publishers.
1852/1963	*The Eighteenth Brumaire of Louis Bonaparte.* New York: International Publishers.
1857–1858/ 1964	*Pre-Capitalist Economic Foundations,* Eric J. Hobsbawm (ed.). New York: International Publishers.
1857–1858/ 1974	*The Grundrisse: Foundations of the Critique of Political Economy.* New York: Random House.
1859/1970	*A Contribution to the Critique of Political Economy.* New York: International Publishers.
1862–1863/ 1963	*Theories of Surplus Value,* Part 1. Moscow: Progress Publishers.
1862–1863/ 1968	*Theories of Surplus Value,* Part 2. Moscow: Progress Publishers.
1867/1967	*Capital: A Critique of Political Economy,* Vol. 1. New York: International Publishers.
1932/1964	*The Economic and Philosophic Manuscripts of 1844,* Dirk J. Struik (ed.). New York: International Publishers.

Marx, Karl, and Engels, Friedrich

1845/1956	*The Holy Family.* Moscow: Foreign Language Publishing House.
1845–1846/ 1970	*The German Ideology,* Part 1, C. J. Arthur (ed.). New York: International Publishers.
1848/1948	*Manifesto of the Communist Party.* New York: International Publishers.

Maryanski, Alexandra

| 1994 | "The Pursuit of Human Nature in Sociology and Evolutionary Sociology." *Sociological Perspectives* 37:375–389. |

Maryanski, Alexandra, and Turner, Jonathan H.

| 1992 | *The Social Cage: Human Nature and the Evolution of Society.* Stanford, Calif.: Stanford University Press. |

Masterman, Margaret

| 1970 | "The Nature of a Paradigm." In I. Lakatos and A. Musgrove (eds.), *Criticism and the Growth of Knowledge.* Cambridge: Cambridge University Press: 59–89. |

Matthews, Fred H.

| 1977 | *Quest for an American Sociology: Robert E. Park and the Chicago School.* Montreal: McGill University Press. |

Matthews, Glenna
1992   *Women's Power and Women's Place in the United States 1630–1970.* New York: Oxford University Press.
Mayer, Tom
1994   *Analytical Marxism.* Thousand Oaks, Calif.: Sage.
Mazlish, Bruce
1984   *The Meaning of Karl Marx.* New York: Oxford University Press.
McCann, Stewart J. H.
1997   "Threatening Times and the Election of Charismatic U.S. Presidents: With and Without FDR." *Journal of Psychology* 131:393–400.
McCaughey, Martha
1997   *Real Knockouts: The Physical Feminism of Women's Self-Defense.* New York: New York University Press.
McDonald, Lynne
1994   *The Women Founders of the Social Sciences.* Ottawa, Canada: Carleton University Press.
McKinney, John C.
1966   *Constructive Typology and Social Theory.* New York: Appleton-Century-Crofts.
McLellan, David
1973   *Karl Marx: His Life and Thought.* New York: Harper Colophon.
McLellan, David (ed.)
1971   *The Thought of Karl Marx.* New York: Harper Torchbooks.
McMurty, John
1978   *The Structure of Marx's World-View.* Princeton, N.J.: Princeton University Press.
McPhail, Clark, and Rexroat, Cynthia
1979   "Mead vs. Blumer." *American Sociological Review* 44:449–467.
Mead, George H.
1907/1964   "Concerning Animal Perception." In A. J. Reck (ed.), *Selected Writings.* Indianapolis: Bobbs-Merrill.
1934/1962   *Mind, Self and Society: From the Standpoint of a Social Behaviorist.* Chicago: University of Chicago Press.
1936   *Movements of Thought in the Nineteenth Century.* Chicago: University of Chicago Press.
1938/1972   *The Philosophy of the Act.* Chicago: University of Chicago Press.
1959   *The Philosophy of the Present.* LaSalle, Ill.: Open Court Publishing.
1982   *The Individual and the Social Self: Unpublished Work of George Herbert Mead.* Chicago: University of Chicago Press.
Mehan, Hugh, and Wood, Houston
1975   *The Reality of Ethnomethodology.* New York: Wiley.
Meisenhelder, Tom
1991   "Toward a Marxist Analysis of Subjectivity." *Nature, Society, and Thought* 4:103–125.
1997   "Pierre Bourdieu and the Call for a Reflexive Sociology." *Current Perspectives in Social Theory* 17:159–183.
Meja, Volker, and Stehr, Nico (eds.)
1990   *Knowledge and Politics: The Sociology of Knowledge Dispute.* London: Routledge.

Menzies, Ken
1977   *Talcott Parsons and the Social Image of Man.* London: Routledge and
               Kegan Paul.
Merton, Robert
1941/1957   "Karl Mannheim and the Sociology of Knowledge." In R. Merton (ed.),
               Social Theory and Social Structure. Rev. and enl. ed. New York: Free Press:
               489–508.
1949/1968   "Manifest and Latent Functions." In R. Merton, *Social Theory and Social
               Structure.* New York: Free Press: 73–138.
1968   *Social Theory and Social Structure.* New York: Free Press.
1975   "Structural Analysis in Sociology." In P. Blau (ed.), *Approaches to the Study
               of Social Structure.* New York: Free Press: 21–52.
1980   "Remembering the Young Talcott Parsons." *American Sociologist* 15:68–71.
1989   "The Sorokin-Merton Correspondence on 'Puritanism, Pietism and Science,'
               1933–34." *Science in Context* 3:291–298.
Mestrovic, Stjepan G.
1988   *Emile Durkheim and the Reformation of Sociology.* Totowa, N.J.: Rowman
               and Littlefield.
1992   *Durkheim and Postmodern Culture.* New York: Aldine de Gruyter.
1998   *Anthony Giddens: The Last Modernist.* London: Routledge.
Mészáros, István
1970   *Marx's Theory of Alienation.* New York: Harper Torchbooks.
Meyrowitz, Joshua
1995   "New Sense of Politics: How Television Changes the Political Drama."
               Research in Political Sociology 7:117–138.
Mill, John Stuart
1961   *Auguste Comte and Positivism.* Ann Arbor: University of Michigan Press.
Miller, David
1973   *George Herbert Mead: Self, Language and the World.* Austin: University of
               Texas Press.
1982a   "Introduction." In G. H. Mead, *The Individual and the Social Self:
               Unpublished Work of George Herbert Mead.* Chicago: University of
               Chicago Press: 1–26.
1982b   Review of J. David Lewis and Richard L. Smith, *American Sociology and
               Pragmatism. Journal of the History of Sociology* 4:108–114.
1985   "Concerning J. David Lewis' Response to My Review of *American
               Sociology and Pragmatism." Journal of the History of Sociology*
               5:131–133.
Miller, James
1993   *The Passion of Michel Foucault.* New York: Anchor Books.
Miller, W. Watts
1993   "Durkheim's Montesquieu." *British Journal of Sociology* 44:693–712.
Mills, C. Wright
1951   *White Collar.* New York: Oxford University Press.
1956   *The Power Elite.* New York: Oxford University Press.
1959   *The Sociological Imagination.* New York: Oxford University Press.
1960   *Listen Yankee: The Revolution in Cuba.* New York: McGraw-Hill.
1962   *The Marxists.* New York: Dell.

Milovanovic, Dragan
1995 "Dueling Paradigms: Modernist versus Postmodernist Thought." *Humanity and Society* 19:19–44.

Mitroff, Ian
1974 "Norms and Counter-Norms in a Select Group of the Apollo Moon Scientists: A Case Study of the Ambivalence of Scientists." *American Sociological Review* 39:579–595.

Mitroff, Ian, and Kilmann, Ralph
1978 *Methodological Approaches to Social Science.* San Francisco: Jossey-Bass.

Mitzman, Arthur
1970 *The Iron Cage.* New York: Universal Library.

Miyahara, Kojiro
1983 "Charisma: From Weber to Contemporary Sociology." *Sociological Inquiry* 55:368–388.

Molm, Linda D., and Cook, Karen S.
1995 "Social Exchange and Exchange Networks." In K. S. Cook, G. A. Fine, and J. S. House (eds.), *Sociological Perspectives on Social Psychology.* Boston: Allyn and Bacon: 209–235.

Mommsen, Wolfgang J.
1974 *The Age of Bureaucracy.* New York: Harper & Row.

Moore, Merritt H.
1936 "Introduction." In G. H. Mead, *Movements of Thought in the Nineteenth Century.* Chicago: University of Chicago Press: xi–xxxvii.

Morgan, Robin (ed.)
1970 *Sisterhood Is Powerful: An Anthology of Writings from the Women's Liberation Movement.* New York: Vintage.

Morris, Monica B.
1977 *Excursion into Creative Sociology.* New York: Columbia University Press.

Morrow, Raymond A.
1994 "Critical Theory, Poststructuralism, and Critical Theory." *Current Perspectives in Social Theory* 14:27–51.

Morse, Chandler
1961 "The Functional Imperatives." In M. Black (ed.), *The Social Theories of Talcott Parsons.* Englewood Cliffs, N.J.: Prentice-Hall: 100–152.

Morton, Donald
1996 "The Politics of Queer Theory in the (Post)Modern Moment." In Mary F. Rogers (ed.), *Multicultural Experiences, Multicultural Theories.* New York: McGraw-Hill: 90–98.

Mouzelis, Nicos
1997 "In Defence of the Sociological Canon: A Reply to David Parker." *Sociological Review* 97:244–253.

Mueller-Vollmer, Kurt
1985 "Language, Mind and Artifact: An Outline of Hermeneutic Theory since the Enlightenment." In K. Mueller-Vollmer (ed.), *The Hermeneutics Reader.* New York: Continuum: 1–53.

Muller, Hans-Peter
1994 "Social Differentiation and Organic Solidarity: The *Division of Labor* Revisited." *Sociological Forum* 9:73–86.

Mullins, Nicholas
1973   *Theories and Theory Groups in Contemporary American Sociology.*
            New York: Harper & Row.
1983   "Theories and Theory Groups Revisited." In R. Collins (ed.), *Sociological
            Theory—1983.* San Francisco: Jossey-Bass: 319–337.
Münch, P. A.
1975   "'Sense' and 'Intention' in Max Weber's Theory of Action." *Sociological
            Inquiry* 45:59–65.
Münch, Richard
1981   "Talcott Parsons and the Theory of Action. I. The Structure of the Kantian
            Core." *American Journal of Sociology* 86:709–739.
1982   "Talcott Parsons and the Theory of Action. II. The Continuity of the
            Development." *American Journal of Sociology* 87:771–826.
1987   "The Interpenetration of Microinteraction and Macrostructures in a Complex
            and Contingent Institutional Order." In J. Alexander et al. (eds.), *The Micro-
            Macro Link.* Berkeley: University of California Press: 319–336.
1991   "American and European Social Theory: Cultural Identities and Social
            Forms of Theory Production." *Sociological Perspectives* 34:313–336.
Nafassi, Mohammed R.
1998   "Reframing Orientalism: Weber and Islam." *Economy and Society*
            27:97–118.
Nash, Bradley, Jr., and Wardell, Mark
1993   "The Control of Sociological Theory: In Praise of the Interregnum."
            Sociological Inquiry 63:276–292.
Nass, Clifford I.
1986   "Bureaucracy, Technical Expertise, and Professionals: A Weberian
            Approach." *Sociological Theory* 4:61–70.
Natanson, Maurice
1973a   "Introduction." In A. Schutz, *Collected Papers I: The Problem of Social
            Reality.* The Hague: Martinus Nijhoff: xxv–xlvii.
1973b   *The Social Dynamics of George H. Mead.* The Hague: Martinus Nijhoff.
Nedelmann, Birgitta
1990   "Georg Simmel as an Analyst of Autonomous Dynamics: The Merry-Go-
            Round of Fashion." In M. Kaern, B. S. Phillips, and R. S. Cohen (eds.), *Georg
            Simmel and Contemporary Sociology.* Dordrecht, Neth.: Kluwer: 225–241.
1991   "Individualization, Exaggeration and Paralysation: Simmel's Three Problems
            of Culture." *Theory, Culture and Society* 8:169–194.
Nedelmann, Birgitta, and Sztompka, Piotr
1993   "Introduction." In B. Nedelmann and P. Sztompka (eds.), *Sociology in
            Europe: In Search of Identity.* Berlin: Walter de Gruyter: 1–23.
Nemedi, Denes
1995   "Collective Consciousness, Morphology, and Collective Representations:
            Durkheim's Sociology of Knowledge, 1894–1900." *Sociological
            Perspectives* 38:41–56.
Nicolaus, Martin
1974   "Foreword." In K. Marx, *The Grundrisse.* New York: Random House:
            7–63.
Nisbet, Robert
1959   "Comment." *American Sociological Review* 24:479–481.

1967   *The Sociological Tradition.* New York: Basic Books.
1974   *The Sociology of Emile Durkheim.* New York: Oxford University Press.
Noblit, George W., and Hare, R. Dwight
1988   *Meta-Ethnography: Synthesizing Qualitative Studies.* Newbury Park, Calif.:
            Sage.
Nolan, Barbara E.
1988   *The Political Theory of Beatrice Webb.* New York: AMS Press.
Oakes, Guy (ed.)
1984   *Georg Simmel on Women, Sexuality and Love.* New Haven: Yale
            University Press.
Oakes, Len
1997   *Prophetic Charisma: The Psychology of Revolutionary Religious
            Personalities.* Syracuse: N.Y.: Syracuse University Press.
Ogburn, William Fielding
1922/1964   *Social Change.* New York: Viking.
Oliver, Ivan
1983   "The 'Old' and the 'New' Hermeneutic in Sociological Theory."
            British Journal of Sociology 34:519–553.
Ollman, Bertell
1976   *Alienation.* 2nd ed. Cambridge: Cambridge University Press.
Olson, Richard
1993   *The Emergence of the Social Sciences, 1642–1792.* New York: Twayne.
O'Neill, William L.
1971   *A History of Feminism in America.* Chicago: Quadrangle Books.
Ono, Michikuni
1996   "Collective Effervescence and Symbolism." *Durkheimian Studies* 2:79–98.
Orr, Catherine M.
1997   "Charting the Currents of the Third Wave." *Hypatia* 12:29–43.
Ossio, Juan M.
1997   "Cosmologies." *International Social Science Journal*, 49:549–562.
Osterberg, Dag
1988   *Metasociology: An Inquiry into the Origins and Validity of Social Thought.*
            Oslo: Norwegian University Press.
Outhwaite, William
1994   *Habermas: A Critical Introduction.* Stanford, Calif.: Stanford University Press.
Owen, David (ed.)
1997   *Sociology after Postmodernism.* London: Sage.
Pareto, Vilfredo
1935   *A Treatise on General Sociology.* 4 vols. New York: Dover.
Park, Robert E.
1927/1973   "Life History." *American Journal of Sociology* 79:251–260.
Parker, David
1997   "Why Bother with Durkheim?" *Sociological Review* 45:122–146.
Parsons, Talcott
1934–1935   "The Place of Ultimate Values in Sociological Theory." *International
            Journal of Ethics* 45:282–316.
1937   *The Structure of Social Action.* New York: McGraw-Hill.
1942   "Some Sociological Aspects of the Fascist Movements." *Social Forces*
            21:138–147.

1947   "Certain Primary Sources and Patterns of Aggression in the Social Structure of the Western World." *Psychiatry* 10:167–181.

1949   *The Structure of Social Action.* 2nd ed. New York: McGraw-Hill.

1951   *The Social System.* Glencoe, Ill.: Free Press.

1954a   "The Prospects of Sociological Theory." In T. Parsons, *Essays in Sociological Theory.* New York: Free Press: 348–369.

1954b   "The Present Position and Prospects of Systematic Theory in Sociology." In T. Parsons, *Essays in Sociological Theory.* New York: Free Press: 212–237.

1960   "A Sociological Approach to the Theory of Organizations." In T. Parsons (ed.), *Structure and Process in Modern Societies.* New York: Free Press: 16–58.

1961   "Some Considerations on the Theory of Social Change." *Rural Sociology* 26:219–239.

1966   *Societies.* Englewood Cliffs, N.J.: Prentice-Hall.

1970a   *Social Structure and Personality.* New York: Free Press.

1970b   "On Building Social System Theory: A Personal History." *Daedalus* 99:826–881.

1971   *The System of Modern Societies.* Englewood Cliffs, N.J.: Prentice-Hall.

1975   "Social Structure and the Symbolic Media of Interchange." In P. Blau (ed.), *Approaches to the Study of Social Structure.* New York: Free Press: 94–100.

1977a   "General Introduction." In T. Parsons (ed.), *Social Systems and the Evolution of Action Theory.* New York: Free Press: 1–13.

1977b   "On Building Social System Theory: A Personal History." In T. Parsons (ed.), *Social Systems and the Evolution of Action Theory.* New York: Free Press: 22–76.

1990   "Prolegomena to a Theory of Social Institutions." *American Sociological Review* 55:319–333.

1998   "The 'Fragment' on Simmel [From Draft *Chapter XVIII (Structure of Social Action): Georg Simmel* and *Ferdinand Toennies:* Social Relationships and the Elements of Action." *American Sociologist* 29:21–30.

Parsons, Talcott, and Platt, Gerald
1973   *The American University.* Cambridge, Mass.: Harvard University Press.

Parsons, Talcott, and Shils, Edward A. (eds.)
1951   *Toward a General Theory of Action.* Cambridge, Mass.: Harvard University Press.

Paulsen, Micheal B., and Feldman, Kenneth A.
1995   "Toward a Reconceptualization of Scholarship: A Human Action System with Functional Imperatives." *Journal of Higher Education* 66:615–640.

Pearce, Frank
1989   *The Radical Durkheim.* London: Unwin Hyman.

Peel, J. D. Y.
1971   *Herbert Spencer: The Evolution of a Sociologist.* New York: Basic Books.

Pels, Dick
1993   "Missionary Sociology between Left and Right. A Critical Introduction to Mannheim." *Theory, Culture and Society* 10:45–68.

1996   "Karl Mannheim and the Sociology of Scientific Knowledge: Towards a New Agenda." *Sociological Theory* 14:30–48.

Perrin, Robert
1976   "Herbert Spencer's Four Theories of Social Evolution." *American Journal of Sociology* 81:1339–1359.
Perry, Wilhelmia E., Abbott, James R., and Hutter, Mark
1997   "The Symbolic Interactionist Paradigm and Urban Sociology." *Research in Urban Sociology* 4:59–92.
Phillips, Derek
1973   "Paradigms, Falsifications and Sociology." *Acta Sociologica* 16:13–31.
1975   "Paradigms and Incommensurability." *Theory and Society* 2:37–62.
Pickering, Mary
1993   *Auguste Comte: An Intellectual Biography.* Vol. 1. Cambridge: Cambridge University Press.
1997   "A New Look at Auguste Comte." In Charles Camic (ed.), *Reclaiming the Sociological Classics: The State of Scholarship.* Oxford: Blackwell: 11–44.
forthcoming "Auguste Comte." In George Ritzer (ed.), *The Blackwell Companion to Major Social Theorists.* Oxford, England, and Cambridge, Mass.: Blackwell.
Pierce, Jennifer
1995   *Gender Trials: Emotional Lives in Contemporary Law Firms.* Berkeley: University of California Press.
Pilcher, Jane
1994   "Mannheim's Sociology of Generations: An Undervalued Legacy." *British Journal of Sociology* 45:481–495.
Poggi, Gianfranco
1993   *Money and the Modern Mind: Georg Simmel's Philosophy of Money.* Berkeley: University of California Press.
1996   "Three Aspects of Modernity in Simmel's *Philosophie des Geldes:* Its Epiphanic Significance, the Centrality of Money and the Prevalence of Alienation." In Richard Kilminster and Ian Varcoe (eds.), *Culture, Modernity and Revolution: Essays in Honour of Zygmunt Bauman.* London: Routledge: 42–65.
Polit, Denise F., and Falbo, Toni
1987   "Only Children and Personality Development: A Quantitative Review." *Journal of Marriage and the Family* 49:309–325.
Pollner, Melvin
1991   "Left of Ethnomethodology: The Rise and Decline of Radical Reflexivity." *American Sociological Review* 56: 370–380.
Pope, Whitney
1973   "Classic on Classic: Parsons' Interpretation of Durkheim." *American Sociological Review* 38:399–415.
1975   "Durkheim as Functionalist." *Sociological Quarterly* 16:361–379.
1976   *Durkheim's Suicide: A Classic Analyzed.* Chicago: University of Chicago Press.
Pope, Whitney, and Cohen, Jere
1978   "On R. Stephen Warner's 'Toward a Redefinition of Action Theory: Paying the Cognitive Element Its Due.'" *American Journal of Sociology* 83:1359–1367.
Pope, Whitney, Cohen, Jere, and Hazelrigg, Lawrence E.
1975   "On the Divergence of Weber and Durkheim: A Critique of Parsons' Convergence Thesis." *American Sociological Review* 40:417–427.

Pope, Whitney, and Johnson, Barclay D.
1983   "Inside Organic Solidarity." *American Sociological Review* 48:681–692.
Postone, Moishe
1993   *Time, Labor, and Social Domination: A Reinterpretation of Marx's Critical
            Theory.* Cambridge: Cambridge University Press.
Powers, Charles H.
1986   *Vilfredo Pareto.* Newbury Park, Calif.: Sage.
Prendergast, Christopher
1986   "Alfred Schutz and the Austrian School of Economics." *American Journal
            of Sociology* 92:1–26.
Pressler, Charles A., and Fabio Dasilva
1996   *Sociology and Interpretation: From Weber to Habermas.* Albany: State
            University of New York Press.
Procter, Ian
1978   "Parsons's Early Voluntarism." *Sociological Inquiry* 48:37–48.
Prus, Robert
1996   *Symbolic Interaction and Ethnographic Research: Intersubjectivity and
            the Study of Human Lived Experience.* Albany: State University of
            New York Press.
Psathas, George
1989   *Phenomenology and Sociology: Theory and Research.* Lanham, Md.:
            University Press of America.
Puner, Helen Walker
1947   *Freud: His Life and His Mind.* New York: Dell.
Quadagno, Jill S.
1979   "Paradigms in Evolutionary Theory: The Sociobiological Model of Natural
            Selection." *American Sociological Review* 44:100–109.
Radnitzky, Gerard
1973   *Contemporary Schools of Metascience.* Chicago: Henry Regnery.
Radway, Janice
1984   *Reading the Romance: Women, Patriarchy and Popular Literature.*
            Chapel Hill: University of North Carolina Press.
Rammstedt, Otthein
1991   "On Simmel's Aesthetics: Argumentation in the Journal *Jugend,*
            1897–1906." *Theory, Culture and Society* 8:125–144.
Rattansi, Ali
1982   *Marx and the Division of Labour.* London: Macmillan.
Rawls, Anne Warfield
1996   "Durkheim's Epistemology: The Neglected Argument." *American Journal
            of Sociology* 102:430–482.
forthcoming "Harold Garfinkel." In George Ritzer (ed.), *The Blackwell Companion to
            Major Social Theorists.* Oxford, England, and Cambridge, Mass.:
            Blackwell.
Reedy, W. Jay
1994   "The Historical Imaginary of Social Science in Post-Revolutionary France:
            Bonald, Saint-Simon, Comte." *History of the Human Sciences* 7:1–26.
Reinharz, Shulamit
1992   *Feminist Methods in Social Research.* New York: Oxford
            University Press.

Reinharz, Shulamit (ed.)
1993   *A Contextualized Chronology of Women's Sociological Work.* Waltham,
            Mass.: Brandeis University Press.
Remmling, Gunter
1967   *Road to Suspicion: A Study of Modern Mentality and the Sociology of
            Knowledge.* New York: Appleton-Century-Crofts.
·1975   *The Sociology of Karl Mannheim.* Atlantic Highlands. N.J.: Humanities Press.
Rhoades, Lawrence J.
1981   *A History of the American Sociological Association.* Washington, D.C.:
            American Sociological Association.
Rich, Adrienne
1976   *Of Woman Born: Motherhood as Experience and Institution.* New York:
            Bantam.
Riesman, David
1953/1995   *Thorstein Veblen.* New Brunswick, N.J.: Transaction Publishers.
Ringer, Fritz
1997   *Max Weber's Methodology: The Unification of the Cultural and Social
            Sciences.* Cambridge, Mass.: Harvard University Press.
Ritzer, George
1975a   *Sociology: A Multiple Paradigm Science.* Boston: Allyn and Bacon.
1975b   "Sociology: A Multiple Paradigm Science." *American Sociologist*
            19:156–167.
1975c   "Professionalization, Bureaucratization and Rationalization: The Views of
            Max Weber." *Social Forces* 53:627–634.
1977   *Working: Conflict and Change.* 2nd ed. Englewood Cliffs, N.J.:
            Prentice-Hall.
1979   "Toward an Integrated Sociological Paradigm." In W. Snizek et al. (eds.),
            Contemporary Issues in Theory and Research. Westport, Conn.:
            Greenwood Press: 25–46.
1980   *Sociology: A Multiple Paradigm Science.* Rev. ed. Boston: Allyn and
            Bacon.
1981a   *Toward an Integrated Sociological Paradigm: The Search for an Exemplar
            and an Image of the Subject Matter.* Boston: Allyn and Bacon.
1981b   "Paradigm Analysis in Sociology: Clarifying the Issues." *American
            Sociological Review* 46:245–248.
1983   "The McDonaldization of Society." *Journal of American Culture* 6:100–107.
1985   "The Rise of Micro-Sociological Theory." *Sociological Theory* 3:88–98.
1987   "The Current State of Metatheory." *Sociological Perspectives: The Theory
            Section Newsletter* 10:1–6.
1988   "Sociological Metatheory: Defending a Subfield by Delineating Its
            Parameters." *Sociological Theory* 6:187–200.
1989   "Of Levels and 'Intellectual Amnesia.'" *Sociological Theory* 7:226–229.
1990a   "Micro-Macro Linkage in Sociological Theory: Applying a Metatheoretical
            Tool." In G. Ritzer (ed.), *Frontiers of Social Theory: The New Syntheses.*
            New York: Columbia University Press: 347–370.
1990b   "The Current Status of Sociological Theory: The New Syntheses." In
            G. Ritzer (ed.), *Frontiers of Social Theory: The New Syntheses.* New York:
            Columbia University Press: 1–30.
1990d   "Metatheorizing in Sociology." *Sociological Forum* 5:3–15.

1991a   *Metatheorizing in Sociology.* Lexington, Mass.: Lexington Books.
1991b   "The Recent History and the Emerging Reality of American Sociological
             Theory: A Metatheoretical Interpretation." *Sociological Forum* 6:269–287.
1992b   "Metatheorizing in Sociology: Explaining the Coming of Age." In G. Ritzer
             (ed.), *Metatheorizing.* Newbury Park, Calif.: Sage: 7–26.
1993   *The McDonaldization of Society.* Thousand Oaks, Calif.: Pine Forge Press.
1995   *Expressing America: A Critique of the Global Credit Card Society.*
             Thousand Oaks, Calif.: Pine Forge Press.
1996   *The McDonaldization of Society.* Revised ed. Thousand Oaks, Calif.:
             Pine Forge Press.
1997   *Postmodern Social Theory.* New York: McGraw-Hill.
1998   *The McDonaldization Thesis.* London: Sage.
1999   *Enchanting a Disenchanted World: Revolutionizing the Means of
             Consumption.* Thousand Oaks, Calif.: Pine Forge Press.
Ritzer, George (ed.)
1990c   "Symposium: Metatheory: Its Uses and Abuses in Contemporary Sociology."
             Sociological Forum 5:1–74.
1991c   "Recent Explorations in Sociological Metatheorizing." *Sociological
             Perspectives* 34:237–390.
1992a   *Metatheorizing.* Newbury Park, Calif.: Sage.
Ritzer, George, and Bell, Richard
1981   "Emile Durkheim: Exemplar for an Integrated Sociological Paradigm?"
             Social Forces 59:966–995.
Ritzer, George, and Gindoff, Pamela
1992   "Methodological Relationism: Lessons for and from Social Psychology."
             Social Psychology Quarterly 55:128–140.
1994   "Agency-Structure, Micro Macro, Individualism-Holism-Relationism:
             A Metatheoretical Explanation of Theoretical Convergence between the
             United States and Europe." In P. Sztompka (ed.), *Agency and Structure:
             Reorienting Social Theory.* Amsterdam: Gordon and Breach: 3–23.
Ritzer, George, and LeMoyne, Terri
1991   "Hyperrationality: An Extension of Weberian and Neo-Weberian Theory." In
             G. Ritzer, *Metatheorizing in Sociology.* Lexington, Mass.: Lexington Books:
             93–115.
Ritzer, George, and Trice, Harrison
1969   *An Occupation in Conflict: A Study of the Personnel Manager.* Ithaca, N.Y.:
             ILR Press.
Ritzer, George, and Walczak, David
1986   *Working: Conflict and Change.* 3rd ed. Englewood Cliffs, N.J.:
             Prentice-Hall.
1988   "Rationalization and the Deprofessionalization of Physicians."
             Social Forces 67:1–22.
Robbins, Derek
1991   *The Work of Pierre Bourdieu.* Boulder, Colo.: Westview Press.
Rocher, Guy
1975   *Talcott Parsons and American Sociology.* New York: Barnes and Noble.
Rock, Paul
1979   *The Making of Symbolic Interactionism.* Totowa, N.J.: Rowman and
             Littlefield.

Roemer, John E.
1982   "Methodological Individualism and Deductive Marxism." *Theory and Society* 11:513–520.
1986   *Analytical Marxism.* Cambridge: Cambridge University Press.
Rogers, Mary
forthcoming "Alfred Schutz." In George Ritzer (ed.), *The Blackwell Companion to Major Social Theorists.* Oxford, England, and Cambridge, Mass.: Blackwell.
Rogers, Mary (ed.)
1996   *Multicultural Experiences, Multicultural Theories.* New York: McGraw-Hill.
1998   *Contemporary Feminist Theory.* New York: McGraw-Hill.
Rojek, Chris
1995   "Veblen, Leisure and Human Need." *Leisure Studies* 14:73–86.
Rollins, Judith
1985   *Between Women: Domestics and Their Employers.* Philadelphia: Temple University Press.
Rosenau, Pauline Marie
1992   *Post-Modernism and the Social Sciences: Insights, Inroads, and Intrusions.* Princeton, N.J.: Princeton University Press.
Rosenberg, Alexander
1988   *Philosophy of Social Science.* Boulder, Colo.: Westview Press.
Rosenberg, Bernard
1956   *The Values of Veblen: A Critical Appraisal.* Washington, D.C.: Public Affairs Press.
1963   "Introduction." In Bernard Rosenberg (ed.), *Thorstein Veblen.* New York: Crowell: 1–14.
Rosenberg, Morris
1989   "Self-Concept Research: A Historical Review." *Social Forces* 68:34–44.
Rosenberg, Rosalind
1982   *Beyond Separate Spheres: Intellectual Roots of Modern Feminism.* New Haven: Yale University Press.
Ross, Dorothy
1991   *The Origins of American Social Science.* Cambridge: Cambridge University Press.
Rossi, Alice
1974   *The Feminist Papers: From Adams to de Beauvoir.* New York: Bantam.
Rossi, Alice (ed.)
1973   *The Feminist Papers.* New York: Bantam.
Roth, Guenther
1968   "Introduction." In G. Roth and C. Wittich (eds.), *Max Weber, Economy and Society,* Vol. 1. Totowa, N.J.: Bedminster Press: xxvii–civ.
1971   "Sociological Typology and Historical Explanations." In G. Roth and R. Bendix (eds.), *Scholarship and Partisanship: Essays on Max Weber.* Berkeley: University of California Press: 109–128.
1976   "History and Sociology in the Work of Max Weber." *British Journal of Sociology* 27:306–318.
1990   "Marianne Weber and Her Circle." *Society* 127:63–70.
Rubinstein, David
1986   "The Concept of Structure in Sociology." In M. L. Wardell and S. P. Turner (eds.), *Sociological Theory in Transition.* Boston: Allen and Unwin: 80–94.

Rueschemeyer, Dietrich
1994   "Variations on Two Themes in Durkheim's *Division du Travail:* Power,
            Solidarity, and Meaning in Division of Labor." *Sociological Forum* 9:59–71.
Runciman, W. G.
1972   *A Critique of Max Weber's Philosophy of Social Science.* London:
            Cambridge University Press.
Ryan, Mary
1990   *Women in Public: From Barriers to Ballots 1825–1880.* Baltimore:
            Johns Hopkins University Press.
Ryan, William
1971   *Blaming the Victim.* New York: Pantheon.
Ryndbrandt, Lynne
1999   *Caroline Bartlett Crane and Progressive Reform: Social Housekeeping and
            Sociology.* New York: Garland.
Sadri, Ahmad
1992   *Max Weber's Sociology of Intellectuals.* New York: Oxford University Press.
Salomon, A.
1945   "German Sociology." In G. Gurvitch and W. F. Moore (eds.), *Twentieth
            Century Sociology.* New York: Philosophical Library: 586–614.
1963/1997   "Georg Simmel Reconsidered." In Gary D. Jaworski, *Georg Simmel and
            the American Prospect.* Albany: State University of New York Press:
            91–108.
Sanday, Peggy Reeves
1990   *Fraternity Gang Rape: Sex, Brotherhood and Privilege on Campus.*
            New York: New York University Press.
1996   *A Woman Scorned: Acquaintance Rape on Trial.* New York: Doubleday.
Scaff, Lawrence
1988   "Weber, Simmel, and the Sociology of Culture." *Sociological Review*
            36:1–30.
1989   *Fleeing the Iron Cage: Culture, Politics, and Modernity in the Thought of
            Max Weber.* Berkeley: University of California Press.
forthcoming "Georg Simmel." In George Ritzer (ed.), *The Blackwell Companion to
            Major Social Theorists.* Oxford, England, and Cambridge, Mass.: Blackwell.
Scharff, Robert C.
1995   *Comte after Positivism.* New York: Cambridge.
Scharnhorst, Gary
1985   *Charlotte Perkins Gilman: A Bibliography.* Metuchen, N.J.: Scarecrow
            Press.
Schegloff, Emmanuel A.
1992   "Repair after Next Turn: The Last Structurally Provided Defense of
            Intersubjectivity in Conversation." *American Journal of Sociology*
            97:1295–1345.
Schluchter, Wolfgang
1981   *The Rise of Western Rationalism: Max Weber's Developmental History.*
            Berkeley: University of California Press.
1996   *Paradoxes of Modernity: Culture and Conduct in the Theory of Max Weber.*
            Stanford, Calif.: Stanford University Press.
Schmaus, Warren
1994   *Durkheim's Philosophy of Science and the Sociology of Knowledge:
            Creating an Intellectual Niche.* Chicago: University of Chicago Press.

Schmidt, Neal, Gooding, Richard Z., Noe, Raymond A., and Kirsch, Michael
1984   "Meta-Analyses of Validity Studies Published between 1964 and 1982 and the
            Investigation of Study Characteristics." *Personnel Psychology* 37:407–422.
Schmitt, Raymond L., and Schmitt, Tiffani Mari
1996   "Community Fear of AIDS as Enacted Emotion: A Comparative
            Investigation of Mead's Concept of the Social Act." *Studies in Symbolic
            Interaction* 20:91–119.
Schneider, Louis
1967   *The Scottish Moralists: On Human Nature and Society.* Chicago: University
            of Chicago Press.
1971   "Dialectic in Sociology." *American Sociological Review* 36:667–678.
Schneider, Mark A.
1993   *Culture and Disenchantment.* Chicago: University of Chicago Press.
Schroeter, Gerd
1985   "Dialogue, Debate, or Dissent? The Difficulties of Assessing Max Weber's
            Relation to Marx." In R. J. Antonio and R. M. Glassman (eds.), *A Weber-
            Marx Dialogue.* Lawrence: University Press of Kansas: 2–19.
Schulin, Ernst
1981   "German 'Geistesgeschichte,' American 'Intellectual History,' and French
            'Histoire des Mentalities' since 1900: A Comparison." *History of European
            Ideas* 1:195–214.
Schutz, Alfred
1932/1967   *The Phenomenology of the Social World.* Evanston, Ill.: Northwestern
            University Press.
1973   *Collected Papers I: The Problem of Social Reality.* The Hague:
            Martinus Nijhoff.
1975   *Collected Papers III: Studies in Phenomenological Philosophy.* The Hague:
            Martinus Nijhoff.
1976   *Collected Papers II: Studies in Social Theory.* The Hague: Martinus Nijhoff.
Schutz, Alfred, and Luckmann, Thomas
1973   *The Structure of the Life World.* Evanston, Ill.: Northwestern University Press.
Schwanenberg, Enno
1971   "The Two Problems of Order in Parsons' Theory: An Analysis from Within."
            Social Forces 49:569–581.
Schweber, Silvan S.
1991   "Auguste Comte and the Nebular Hypothesis." In R. T. Bienvenu and
            M. Feingold (eds.), *In the Presence of the Past: Essays in Honor of
            Frank Manuel.* Dordrecht, Neth.: Kluwer: 131–191.
Schwendinger, Julia, and Schwendinger, Herman
1974   *Sociologists of the Chair.* New York: Basic Books.
Scimecca, Joseph
1977   *The Sociological Theory of C. Wright Mills.* Port Washington, N.Y.:
            Kennikat Press.
Sciulli, David
1986   "Voluntaristic Action as a Distinct Concept: Theoretical Foundations of
            Societal Constitutionalism." *American Sociological Review* 51:743–766.
Sciulli, David, and Gerstein, Dean
1985   "Social Theory and Talcott Parsons in the 1980s." *Annual Review of
            Sociology* 11:369–387.

Scott, Joan Firor
1964   "Introduction to *Democracy and Social Ethics* by Jane Addams."
            Cambridge, Mass.: Harvard University Press.
Scott, John Finley
1963   "The Changing Foundations of the Parsonian Action Schema." *American
            Sociological Review* 28:716–735.
Scully, Diana
1980   *Men Who Control Health: The Miseducation of Obstetrician-Gynecologists.*
            Boston: Houghton Mifflin.
1990   *Understanding Sexual Violence: A Study of Convicted Rapists.* Boston:
            Unwin Hyman.
Searle, John
1972   "Chomsky's Revolution in Linguistics." *New York Review of Books*
            18:16–24.
Seckler, David
1975   *Thorstein Veblen and the Institutionalists.* Boulder, Colo.: Colorado
            Associated University Press.
Seidman, Steven
1983   *Liberalism and the Origins of European Social Theory.* Berkeley: University
            of California Press.
1994a   *Contested Knowledge: Social Theory in the Postmodern Age.* Oxford:
            Blackwell.
1994b   "Symposium: Queer Theory/Sociology: A Dialogue." *Sociological Theory*
            12:166–177.
Seligman, Adam B.
1993   "The Representation of Society and the Privatization of Charisma."
            Praxis International 13:68–84.
Sellerberg, Ann-Mari
1994   *A Blend of Contradictions: Georg Simmel in Theory and Practice.*
            New Brunswick, N.J.: Transaction Publishers.
Selvin, Hanan C.
1958   "Durkheim's *Suicide* and Problems of Empirical Research." *American
            Journal of Sociology* 63:607–619.
Shalin, Dmitri
1986   "Pragmatism and Social Interactionism." *American Sociological Review*
            51:9–29.
Shamir, Ronen
1993   "Formal and Substantive Rationality in American Law: A Weberian
            Perspective." *Social and Legal Studies* 2:45–72.
Shaw, Linda L.
1991   "Stigma and the Moral Careers of Ex-Mental Patients Living in Board and
            Care." *Journal of Contemporary Ethnography* 20:285–305.
Sherlock, Steve
1997   "The Future of Commodity Fetishism." *Sociological Focus* 30:61–78.
Shilling, Chris
1997a   "Emotions, Embodiment and the Sensation of Society." *Sociological Review*
            45:195–219.
1997b   "The Undersocialised Conception of the Embodied Agent in Modern
            Sociology." *Sociology* 31:737–754.

Shilling, Chris, and Mellor, Philip A.
1996   "Embodiment, Structuration Theory and Modernity: Mind/Body Dualism
             and the Repression of Sensuality." *Body and Society* 2:1–15.
Shils, Edward
1995   "Karl Mannheim." *American Scholar* 64:221–235.
1996   "The Sociology of Robert E. Park." *American Sociologist* 27:88–106.
Shirazi-Mahajan, Faegheh
1995   "A Dramaturgical Approach to Hijab in Post-Revolutionary Iran."
             Critique 7:35–51.
Shreve, Anita
1989   *Women Together, Women Alone: The Legacy of the Consciousness Raising
             Movement.* New York: Viking.
Shweder, Richard A., and Fiske, Donald W.
1986   "Introduction: Uneasy Social Science." In D. W. Fiske and R. A. Shweder
             (eds.), *Metatheory in Social Science.* Chicago: University of Chicago
             Press: 1–18.
Sica, Alan
1986   "Hermeneutics and Axiology: The Ethical Content of Interpretation." In
             M. L. Wardell and S. P. Turner (eds.), *Sociological Theory in Transition.*
             Boston: Allen and Unwin: 142–157.
1988   *Weber, Irrationality and Social Order.* Berkeley: University of
             California Press.
Sijuwade, Philip O.
1995   "Counterfeit Intimacy: A Dramaturgical Analysis of Erotic Performance."
             Social Behavior and Personality 23:369–376.
Silber, Ilana Friedrich
1993   "Monasticism and the 'Protestant Ethic': Asceticism, Rationality and Wealth
             in the Medieval West." *British Journal of Sociology* 44:103–123.
Simmel, Georg
1903/1971   "The Metropolis and Mental Life." In D. Levine (ed.), *Georg Simmel.*
             Chicago: University of Chicago Press: 324–339.
1904/1971   "Fashion." In D. Levine (ed.), *Georg Simmel.* Chicago: University of
             Chicago Press: 294–323.
1906/1950   "The Secret and the Secret Society." In K. Wolff (ed. and trans.),
             The Sociology of Georg Simmel. New York: Free Press: 307–376.
1907/1978   *The Philosophy of Money,* Tom Bottomore and David Frisby (eds. and
             trans.), London: Routledge and Kegan Paul.
1908/1950a "Subordination under a Principle." In K. Wolff (ed. and trans.),
             The Sociology of Georg Simmel. New York: Free Press: 250–267.
1908/1950b "Types of Social Relationships by Degrees of Reciprocal Knowledge of the
             Participants." In K. Wolff (ed. and trans.), *The Sociology of Georg Simmel.*
             New York: Free Press: 317–329.
1908/1955   *Conflict and the Web of Group Affiliations.* New York: Free Press.
1908/1959a "How Is Society Possible?" In K. Wolff (ed.), *Essays in Sociology,
             Philosophy and Aesthetics.* New York: Harper Torchbooks: 337–356.
1908/1959b "The Problem of Sociology." In K. Wolff (ed.), *Essays in Sociology,
             Philosophy and Aesthetics.* New York: Harper Torchbooks: 310–336.
1908/1971a "Group Expansions and the Development of Individuality." In D. Levine
             (ed.), *Georg Simmel.* Chicago: University of Chicago Press: 251–293.

1908/1971b   "The Stranger." In D. Levine (ed.), *Georg Simmel.* Chicago: University of Chicago Press: 143–149.

1908/1971c   "The Poor." In D. Levine (ed.), *Georg Simmel.* Chicago: University of Chicago Press: 150–178.

1908/1971d   "Domination." In D. Levine (ed.), *Georg Simmel.* Chicago: University of Chicago Press: 96–120.

1918/1971   "The Transcendent Character of Life." In D. Levine (ed.), *Georg Simmel.* Chicago: University of Chicago Press: 353–374.

1921/1968   "The Conflict in Modern Culture." In K. P. Etzkorn (ed.), *George Simmel.* New York: Teachers College Press, Columbia University: 11–25.

1950   *The Sociology of Georg Simmel,* Kurt Wolff (ed. and trans.). New York: Free Press.

1984   *On Women, Sexuality and Love,* Guy Oakes (trans.). New Haven: Yale University Press.

1991   "Money in Modern Culture." *Theory, Culture and Society* 8:17–31.

Simonds, A. P.

1978   *Karl Mannheim's Sociology of Knowledge.* Oxford: Clarendon Press.

Skinner, B. F.

1971   *Beyond Freedom and Dignity.* New York: Knopf.

Sklar, Kathryn Kish

1995   *Florence Kelley and the Nation's Work 1830–1900.* New Haven, Conn.: Yale University Press.

Skocpol, Theda

1979   *States and Social Revolutions.* Cambridge: Cambridge University Press.

1986   "The Dead End of Metatheory." *Contemporary Sociology* 16:10–12.

Skog, Ole-Jorgen

1991   "Alcohol and Suicide—Durkheim Revisited." *Acta Sociologica* 34:193–206.

Slater, Don

1997   *Consumer Culture and Modernity.* Cambridge: Polity Press.

Smelser, Neil

1987   "Depth Psychology and the Social Order." In J. Alexander et al. (eds.), *The Micro-Macro Link.* Berkeley: University of California Press: 267–286.

1988   "Sociological Theory: Looking Forward." *Perspectives: The Theory Section Newsletter* 11:1–3.

1997   *Problematics of Sociology: The Georg Simmel Lectures, 1995.* Berkeley: University of California Press.

Smith, Cyril

1997   "Friedrich Engels and Marx's Critique of Political Economy." *Capital and Class* 62:123–142.

Smith, David Norman

1998   "Faith, Reason, and Charisma: Rodolf Sohm, Max Weber, and the Theology of Grace." *Sociological Inquiry* 68:32–60.

Smith, Dorothy

1974   "Women's Perspective as a Radical Critique of Sociology." *Sociological Inquiry* 44:7–13.

1975   "An Analysis of Ideological Structures and How Women Are Excluded: Consideration for Academic Women." *Canadian Review of Sociology and Anthropology* 12:353–369.

1978	"A Peculiar Eclipsing: Women's Exclusion from Man's Culture." *Women's Studies International Quarterly* 1:281–295.
1979	"A Sociology for Women." In J. A. Sherman and E. T. Beck (eds.), *The Prism of Sex: Essays in the Sociology of Knowledge.* Madison: University of Wisconsin Press.
1987	*The Everyday World as Problematic: A Feminist Sociology.* Boston: Northeastern University Press.
1990	*The Conceptual Practices of Power: A Feminist Sociology of Knowledge.* Boston: Northeastern University Press.
1990b	*Text, Facts and Femininity: Exploring the Relations of Ruling.* London: Routledge and Kegan Paul.
1992	"Sociology from Women's Experience: A Reaffirmation." *Sociological Theory* 10:88–98.
1993	"High Noon in Textland: A Critique of Clough." *Sociological Quarterly* 34:183–192.

Smith, Norman Erik

1979	"William Graham Sumner as an Anti-Social Darwinist." *Pacific Sociological Review* 22:332–347.

Smith, T. V.

1931	"The Social Philosophy of George Herbert Mead." *American Journal of Sociology* 37:368–385.

Snitow, Ann, Stansell, Christine, and Thompson, Sharon

1983	*Powers of Desire: The Politics of Sexuality.* New York: Monthly Review Press.

Snizek, William E.

1976	"An Empirical Assessment of 'Sociology: A Multiple Paradigm Science.'" *American Sociologist* 11:217–219.

Snizek, William E., Fuhrman, Ellsworth R., and Miller, Michael K. (eds.)

1979	*Contemporary Issues in Theory and Research.* Westport, Conn.: Greenwood Press.

So, Alvin Y., and Suwarsono

1990	"Class Theory or Class Analysis? A Reexamination of Marx's Unfinished Chapter on Class." *Critical Sociology* 17:35–55.

Sorokin, Pitirim

1928	*Contemporary Sociological Theories.* New York: Harper.
1937–1941	*Social and Cultural Dynamics.* 4 vols. New York: American Book.
1956	*Fads and Foibles in Modern Sociology and Related Sciences.* Chicago: Regnery.
1963	*A Long Journey: The Autobiography of Pitirim Sorokin.* New Haven, Conn.: College and University Press.

Spencer, Herbert

1850/1954	*Social Statics.* New York: Robert Schalkenbach Foundation.
1864/1883/ 1968	*Reasons for Dissenting from the Philosophy of M. Comte and Other Essays.* Berkeley, Calif.: Glendessary Press.
1873/1961	*The Study of Sociology.* Ann Arbor: University of Michigan Press.
1883	*Recent Discussions in Science, Philosophy and Morals.* New York: Appleton.
1892/1965	*The Man versus the State.* Caldwell, Idaho: Caxton.
1897/1978	*The Principles of Ethics.* 2 vols. Indianapolis: Liberty Classics.

1902/1958   *First Principles.* New York: DeWitt Revolving Fund.
1904a   *An Autobiography,* Vol. 1. New York: Appleton.
1904b   *An Autobiography,* Vol. 2. New York: Appleton.
1908a   *The Principles of Sociology,* Vol. 1. New York: Appleton.
1908b   *The Principles of Sociology,* Vol. 2. New York: Appleton.
1908c   *The Principles of Sociology,* Vol. 3. New York: Appleton.
Spender, Dale
1982   *Women of Ideas (And What Men Have Done to Them).* London: Routledge and Kegan Paul.
Spender, Dale (ed.)
1983   *Feminist Theorists: Three Centuries of Key Women Thinkers.* New York: Random House.
Spykman, Nicholas
1925/1966   *Social Theory of Georg Simmel.* Chicago: Aldine.
Srubar, Ilja
1984   "On the Origin of 'Phenomenological' Sociology." In K. H. Wolff (ed.), *Alfred Schutz: Appraisals and Developments.* Dordrecht, Neth.: Martinus Nijhoff: 57–83.
Staats, Arthur W.
1976   "Skinnerian Behaviorism: Social Behaviorism or Radical Behaviorism?" *American Sociologist* 11:59–60.
Stacey, Judith, and Thorne, Barrie
1985   "The Missing Feminist Revolution in Sociology." *Social Problems* 32:301–316.
1996   "Is Sociology Still Missing Its Feminist Revolution?" *Perspectives: The ASA Theory Section Newsletter* 18:1–3.
Standley, Arline R.
1981   *Auguste Comte.* Boston: Twayne.
Stanfield, Ron
1974   "Kuhnian Scientific Revolutions and the Keynesian Revolution." *Journal of Economic Issues* 8:97–109.
Sterling, Dorothy
1979   *Black Foremothers: Three Lives.* New York: The Feminist Press.
Strauss, Anselm
1996   "Everett Hughes: Sociology's Mission." *Symbolic Interaction* 19:271–283.
Strenski, Ivan
1997   *Durkheim and the Jews of France.* Chicago: University of Chicago.
Swartz, David
1997   *Culture and Power: The Sociology of Pierre Bourdieu.* Chicago: University of Chicago Press.
Swedberg, Richard
1998   *Max Weber and the Idea of Economic Sociology.* Princeton: Princeton University Press.
Sweezy, Paul
1958   "Veblen on American Capitalism." In Douglas F. Dowd (ed.), *Thorstein Veblen: A Critical Reappraisal.* Ithaca, N.Y.: Cornell University: 177–197.
Symbolic Interaction
1988   Special issue on Herbert Blumer's legacy. 11:1–160.

Szacki, Jerzy
1979   *History of Sociological Thought.* Westport, Conn.: Greenwood Press.
Szmatka, Jacek, and Mazur, Joanna
1996   "Theoretical Research Programs in Social Exchange Theory." *Polish Sociological Review* 3:265–288.
Sztompka, Piotr
1991   *Society in Action: The Theory of Social Becoming.* Chicago: University of Chicago Press.
Sztompka, Piotr (ed.)
1994   *Agency and Structure: Reorienting Social Theory.* Amsterdam: Gordon and Breach.
Tabboni, Simonetta
1995   "The Stranger and Modernity: From Equality of Rights to Recognition of Difference." *Thesis Eleven* 43:17–27.
Takla, Tendzin, and Pope, Whitney
1985   "The Force Imagery in Durkheim: The Integration of Theory, Metatheory and Method." *Sociological Theory* 3:74–88.
Terkel, Studs
1974   *Working.* New York: Pantheon.
Thomas, J. J. R.
1985   "Rationalization and the Status of Gender Divisions." *Sociology* 19:409–420.
Thomas, Paul
1991   "Critical Reception: Marx Then and Now." In T. Carver (ed.), *The Cambridge Companion to Marx.* Cambridge: Cambridge University Press: 22–54.
Thomas, William I., and Thomas, Dorothy S.
1928   *The Child in America: Behavior Problems and Programs.* New York: Knopf.
Thomason, Burke C.
1982   *Making Sense of Reification: Alfred Schutz and Constructionist Theory.* Atlantic Highlands, N.J.: Humanities Press.
Thompson, Kenneth
1975   *Auguste Comte: The Foundation of Sociology.* New York: Halstead Press.
Thompson, William E., and Harred, Jackie L.
1992   "Topless Dancers: Managing Stigma in a Deviant Occupation." *Deviant Behavior* 13:291–311.
Thomson, Ernie
1994   "The Sparks That Dazzle Rather than Illuminate: A New Look at Marx's 'Theses on Feuerbach.' " *Nature, Society and Thought* 7:299–323.
Thorlindsson, Thorolfur, and Bjarnason, Thoroddur
1998   "Modeling Durkheim on the Micro Level: A Study of Youth Suicidality." *American Sociological Review* 63:94–110.
Tijssen, Lietake van Vucht
1991   "Women and Objective Culture: George Simmel and Marianne Weber." *Theory, Culture and Society* 8:203–218.
Tilman, Rick
1984   *C. Wright Mills: A Native Radical and His American Intellectual Roots.* University Park: Pennsylvania State University Press.
1992   *Thorstein Veblen and His Critics, 1891–1963: Conservative, Liberal, and Radical Perspectives.* Princeton, N.J.: Princeton University Press, 1992.

Tiryakian, Edward A.
1979   "The Significance of Schools in the Development of Sociology." In
            W. Snizek, E. Fuhrman, and M. Miller (eds.), *Contemporary Issues in
            Theory and Research.* Westport, Conn.: Greenwood Press: 211–233.
1981   "The Sociological Import of Metaphor." *Sociological Inquiry* 51:27–33.
1986   "Hegemonic Schools and the Development of Sociology: Rethinking the
            History of the Discipline." In R. C. Monk (ed.), *Structures of Knowing.*
            Lanham, Md.: University Press of America: 417–441.
1992   "Pathways to Metatheory: Rethinking the Presuppositions of
            Macrosociology." In G. Ritzer (ed.), *Metatheorizing.* Beverly Hills, Calif.:
            Sage: 69–87.
1994   "Revisiting Sociology's First Classic: *The Division of Labor in Society* and
            Its Actuality." *Sociological Forum* 9:3–16.
1995   "Collective Effervescence, Social Change and Charisma: Durkheim, Weber
            and 1989." *International Sociology* 10:269–281.
Titunik, Regina F.
1997   "A Continuation of History: Max Weber and the Advent of a
            New Aristocracy." *The Journal of Politics* 59:680–700.
Toby, Jackson
1977   "Parsons' Theory of Societal Evolution." In T. Parsons, *The Evolution of
            Societies.* Englewood Cliffs, N.J.: Prentice-Hall: 1–23.
Tole, Lise Ann
1993   "Durkheim on Religion and Moral Community in Modernity." *Sociological
            Inquiry* 63:1–29.
Torrance, John
1995   *Karl Marx's Theory of Ideas.* Cambridge: Cambridge University Press.
Touraine, Alain
1977   *The Self-Production of Society.* Chicago: University of Chicago Press.
1995   *Critique of Modernity.* Oxford: Blackwell.
Travers, Andrew
1992   "The Conversion of Self in Everyday Life." *Human Studies* 15:169–238.
Tribe, Keith
1989   "Introduction." In K. Tribe (ed.), *Reading Weber.* London: Routledge: 1–14.
Tseelon, Efrat
1992   "Is the Presented Self Sincere? Goffman, Impression Management and the
            Postmodern Self." *Theory, Culture and Society* 9:115–128.
Tucker, Robert C. (ed.)
1970   *The Marx-Engels Reader.* New York: Norton.
Turner, Bryan S.
1974   *Weber and Islam: A Critical Study.* London: Routledge and Kegan Paul.
1981   *For Weber: Essays in the Sociology of Fate.* Boston: Routledge and Kegan
            Paul.
1985   *The Body and Society: Explorations in Social Theory.* Oxford: Blackwell.
1986   "Simmel, Rationalization and the Sociology of Money." *Sociological
            Review* 34:93–114.
1995   "Karl Mannheim's *Ideology and Utopia.*" *Political Studies* 43:718–727.
Turner, Jonathan
1973   "From Utopia to Where? A Strategy for Reformulating the Dahrendorf
            Conflict Model." *Social Forces* 52:236–244.

1985a   "In Defense of Positivism." *Sociological Theory* 3:24–30.

1985b   *Herbert Spencer: A Renewed Appreciation.* Beverly Hills, Calif.: Sage.

1986   *The Structure of Sociological Theory.* 4th ed. Homewood, Ill.:
             Dorsey Press.

1989a   "Introduction: Can Sociology Be a Cumulative Science?" In J. Turner (ed.),
             Theory Building in Sociology: Assessing Theoretical Cumulation.
             Newbury Park, Calif.: Sage: 8–18.

1990a   "The Past, Present, and Future of Theory in American Sociology." In
             G. Ritzer (ed.), *Frontiers of Social Theory: The New Syntheses.* New York:
             Columbia University Press: 371–391.

1990b   "The Misuse and Use of Metatheory." *Sociological Forum* 5:37–53.

1991a   "Developing Cumulative and Practical Knowledge through Metatheorizing."
             Sociological Perspectives 34:249–268.

1991b   *The Structure of Sociological Theory.* 5th ed. Belmont, Calif.: Wadsworth.

1994   "The Failure of Sociology to Institutionalize Cumulative Theorizing." In
             J. Hage (ed.), *Formal Theory in Sociology: Opportunity or Pitfall?* Albany:
             State University Press of New York: 41–51.

forthcoming "Herbert Spencer." In George Ritzer (ed.), *The Blackwell Companion to
             Major Social Theorists.* Oxford, England, and Cambridge, Mass.:
             Blackwell.

Turner, Jonathan (ed.)
1989b   *Theory Building in Sociology: Assessing Theoretical Cumulation.*
             Newbury Park, Calif.: Sage.

Turner, Jonathan, and Beeghley, Leonard
1974   "Current Folklore in the Criticisms of Parsonsian Action Theory."
             Sociological Inquiry 44:47–63.

Turner, Jonathan, and Maryanski, A. Z.
1988   "Is 'Neofunctionalism' Really Functional?" *Sociological Theory* 6:110–121.

Turner, Stephen Park
1983   "Weber on Action." *American Sociological Review* 48:506–519.

1993   "Introduction: Reconnecting the Sociologist to the Moralist." In S. P. Turner
             (ed.), *Emile Durkheim: Sociologist and Moralist.* London: Routledge: 1–22.

1995   "Durkheim's *The Rules of Sociological Method:* Is It a Classic?"
             Sociological Perspectives 38:1–13.

1998   "Who's Afraid of the History of Sociology?" *Schwezerische Zeistschrift fur
             Soziologie* 24:3–10.

Turner, Stephen Park, and Factor, Regis A.
1994   *Max Weber: The Lawyer as Social Thinker.* London: Routledge.

Turner, Stephen Park, and Turner, Jonathan H.
1990   *The Impossible Science: An Institutional Analysis of American Sociology.*
             Newbury Park, Calif.: Sage.

Udehn, Lars
1981   "The Conflict between Methodology and Rationalization in the Work of
             Max Weber." *Acta Sociologica* 24:131–147.

Ullmann-Margalit, Edna
1997   "The Invisible Hand and the Cunning of Reason." *Social Research*
             64:181–198.

Urry, John
1995   *Consuming Places.* London: Routledge.

van den Berghe, Pierre
1963   "Dialectic and Functionalism: Toward Reconciliation." *American Sociological Review* 28:695–705.

Veblen, Thorstein
1899/1994   *The Theory of the Leisure Class.* New York: Penguin Books.
1899/1900/   "The Preconceptions of Economic Science." In Wesley Mitchell (ed.), *What*
1964   *Veblen Taught: Selected Writings of Thorstein Veblen.* New York: Augustus M. Kelley: 39–150.
1904   *The Theory of the Business Enterprise.* New York: Charles Scribner's Sons.
1906/1963   "The Socialist Economics of Karl Marx and His Followers." In Bernard Rosenberg (ed.), *Thorstein Veblen.* New York: Crowell: 58–73.
1909/1964   "The Limitations of Marginal Utility." In Wesley Mitchell (ed.), *What Veblen Taught: Selected Writings of Thorstein Veblen.* New York: Augustus M. Kelley: 151–175.
1915/1942   *Imperial Germany and the Industrial Revolution.* New York: Viking.
1918/1965   *The Higher Learning in America: A Memorandum on the Conduct of Universities by Business Men.* New York: Augustus M. Kelley.
1919/1964   *The Vested Interests and the Common Man.* New York: Augustus M. Kelley.
1921   *The Engineers and the Price System.* New York: Viking.
1922/1964   *The Instinct of Workmanship and the State of the Industrial Arts.* New York: Augustus M. Kelley.
1923   *Absentee Ownership and Business Enterprise in Recent Times: The Case of America.* New York: Viking.

Venable, Vernon
1945   *Human Nature: The Marxian View.* New York: Knopf.

Vetter, Betty M., Babco, Eleanor, and Jensen-Fisher, Susan
1982   *Professional Women and Minorities: A Manpower Resource Service.* Washington, D.C.: Scientific Manpower Commission.

Vidler, Anthony
1991   "Agoraphobia: Spatial Estrangement in Georg Simmel and Siegfried Kracauer." *New German Critique* 54:31–45.

Wacquant, Loïc J. D.
1992   "Toward a Social Praxeology: The Structure and Logic of Bourdieu's Sociology." In P. Bourdieu and L. J. D. Wacquant (eds.), *An Invitation to Reflexive Sociology.* Chicago: University of Chicago Press: 2–59.

Wagner, Helmut
1964   "Displacement of Scope: A Problem of the Relationship between Small Scale and Large Scale Sociological Theories." *American Journal of Sociology* 69:571–584.
1983   *Alfred Schutz: An Intellectual Biography.* Chicago: University of Chicago Press.

Wagner, Peter
1994   *A Sociology of Modernity: Liberty and Discipline.* London: Routledge.

Wallace, Ruth A. (ed.)
1989   *Feminism and Sociological Theory.* Newbury Park, Calif.: Sage.

Wallace, Walter
1988   "Toward a Disciplinary Matrix in Sociology." In N. Smelser (ed.), *Handbook of Sociology.* Newbury Park, Calif.: Sage: 23–76.

Wallerstein, Immanuel
1974   *The Modern World-System: Capitalist Agriculture and the Origins of the European World Economy in the 16th Century.* New York: Academic Press.
1980   *The Modern World-System II: Mercantilism and the Consolidation of the European World-Economy, 1600–1750.* New York: Academic Press.
1986   "Marxisms as Utopias: Evolving Ideologies." *American Journal of Sociology* 91:1295–1308.
1989   *The Modern World-System III: The Second Era of Great Expansion of the Capitalist World-Economy, 1730–1840.* New York: Academic Press.
Wallimann, Isidor
1981   *Estrangement: Marx's Conception of Human Nature and the Division of Labor.* Westport, Conn.: Greenwood Press.
Wallwork, Ernest
1972   *Durkheim: Morality and Milieu.* Cambridge, Mass.: Harvard University Press.
Ward, Kathryn
1993   "Reconceptualizing World System Theory to Include Women." In P. England (ed.), *Theory on Gender/Feminism on Theory.* New York: Aldine de Gruyter.
Warner, Michael (ed.)
1993   *Fear of a Queer Planet: Queer Politics and Social Theory.* Minneapolis: University of Minnesota Press.
Warriner, Charles
1969   "Social Action, Behavior and Verstehen." *Sociological Quarterly* 10:501–511.
Warsh, David
1990   "Modern Thinkers Merge Sociology, Economics to Explain Today's World." *Washington Post* Aug. 15:D3.
Wartenberg, Thomas E.
1982   "'Species-Being' and 'Human Nature' in Marx." *Human Studies* 5:77–95.
Wax, Murray
1967   "On Misunderstanding Verstehen: A Reply to Abel." *Sociology and Social Research* 51:323–333.
Webb, Beatrice Potter
1887   "The Dock Life of East London." *Nineteenth Century,* 22:301–314.
1891   *The Co-operative Movement in Great Britain.* London: Swan, Sonnenschein and Company.
1926   *My Apprenticeship.* New York: Longman, Green.
Weber, Marianne
1905/1919   "Jobs and Marriage." In M. Weber, *Frauenfrage und Frauengedanke.* Tübingen, Ger.: J. C. B. Mohr: 20–37.
1907   *Ehefrau und Mutter in der Rechtsentwicklung.* Tübingen: J. C. B. Mohr.
1912/1919a "Authority and Autonomy in Marriage." In M. Weber, *Frauenfrage und Frauengedanke.* Tübingen, Ger.: J. C. B. Mohr: 67–79.
1912/1919b "The Valuation of Housework." In M. Weber, *Frauenfrage und Frauengedanke.* Tübingen, Ger.: J. C. B. Mohr: 80–94.
1912a/1919/ "Authority and Autonomy in Marriage." Elizabeth Kirchen (trans.) in
1998   Patricia Lengermann and Jill Niebrugge-Brantley, *The Women Founders: Sociology and Social Theory, 1830–1930.* New York: McGraw-Hill. (Originally published in *Frauenfragen und Frauengedanken.* Tübingen: J. C. B. Mohr: 67–79.)

1912b/1919/ "On the Valuation of Housework." Elizabeth Kirchen (trans.) in
1998   Patricia Lengermann and Jill Niebrugge-Brantley, *The Women Founders:*
             Sociology and Social Theory, 1830–1930. New York: McGraw-Hill.
             (Originally published in *Frauenfragen und Frauengedanken.* Tübingen,
             Ger.: J. C. B. Mohr: 80–94.)
1913/1919   "Women and Objective Culture." In M. Weber, *Frauenfrage und*
             Frauengedanke. Tübingen, Ger.: J. C. B. Mohr: 95–134.
1918/1919/   "Women's Special Cultural Tasks." Elizabeth Kirchen (trans.) in Patricia
1998   Lengermann and Jill Niebrugge-Brantley, *The Women Founders: Sociology*
             and Social Theory, 1830–1930. New York: McGraw-Hill. (Originally
             published in *Frauenfragen und Frauengedanken.* Tübingen, Ger.: J. C. B.
             Mohr: 238–261.)
1919   *Frauenfrage und Frauengedanke* ("Reflections on Women and Women's
             Issues"). Tübingen, Ger.: J. C. B. Mohr.
1926/1975   *Max Weber: A Biography.* New York: Wiley.
1935   *Frauen und Liebe* ("Women and Love"). Koonigestein in Taunus, Ger.:
             K. B. Langewissche.
1975   *Max Weber: A Biography,* Harry Zohn (ed. and trans.). New York: Wiley.
Weber, Max
1896–1906/   *The Agrarian Sociology of Ancient Civilizations.*
1976   London: NLB.
1903–1906/   *Roscher and Knies: The Logical Problems of Historical Economics.*
1973   New York: Free Press.
1903–1917/   *The Methodology of the Social Sciences,* Edward Shils and Henry Finch
1949   (eds.). New York: Free Press.
1904–1905/   *The Protestant Ethic and the Spirit of Capitalism.* New York:
1958   Scribner's.
1906/1985   "'Churches' and 'Sects' in North America: An Ecclesiastical Socio-Political
             Sketch." *Sociological Theory* 3:7–13.
1915/1958   "Religious Rejections of the World and Their Directions." In H. H. Gerth
             and C. W. Mills (eds.), *From Max Weber: Essays in Sociology.* New York:
             Oxford University Press: 323–359.
1916/1964   *The Religion of China: Confucianism and Taoism.* New York: Macmillan.
1916–1917/   *The Religion of India: The Sociology of Hinduism and Buddhism.* Glencoe,
1958   Ill.: Free Press.
1921/1958   *The Rational and Social Foundations of Music.* Carbondale: Southern
             Illinois University Press.
1921/1963   *The Sociology of Religion.* Boston: Beacon Press.
1921/1968   *Economy and Society.* 3 vols. Totowa, N.J.: Bedminster Press.
1922–1923/   "The Social Psychology of the World Religions." In H. H. Gerth and
1958   C. W. Mills (eds.), *From Max Weber: Essays in Sociology.* New York:
             Oxford University Press: 267–301.
1927/1981   *General Economic History.* New Brunswick, N.J.: Transaction Books.
Weigert, Andrew
1981   *Sociology of Everyday Life.* New York: Longman.
Weingartner, Rudolph H.
1959   "Form and Content in Simmel's Philosophy of Life." In K. Wolff (ed.),
             Essays on Sociology, Philosophy and Aesthetics. New York: Harper
             Torchbooks: 33–60.

Weinstein, Deena, and Weinstein, Michael A.
1992   "The Postmodern Discourse of Metatheory." In G. Ritzer (ed.),
            Metatheorizing. Newbury Park, Calif.: Sage: 135–150.
1993   *Postmodern(ized) Simmel.* London: Routledge.
1998   "Simmel-Eco vs. Simmel-Marx: Ironized Alienation." *Current Perspectives
            in Social Theory* 18:63–77.
Wells, Gordon C., and Baehr, Peter
1995   "Editors' Introduction." In Max Weber, *The Russian Revolutions.*
            Ithaca, N.Y.: Cornell University Press.
Wells-Barnett, Ida B.
1894/1969   *On Lynchings.* New York: Arno.
1970   *Crusade for Justice: The Autobiography of Ida B. Wells,* Alfreda M. Duster
            (ed.). Chicago: University of Chicago Press.
Werbner, Pnina, and Basu, Helene
1998   *Embodying Charisma: Modernity, Locality and the Performance of Emotion
            in Sufi Cults.* London: Routledge.
White, Hayden
1973   *The Historical Imagination in Nineteenth-Century Europe.* Baltimore:
            Johns Hopkins University Press.
Whitehead, Alfred North
1917/1974   *The Organization of Thought, Educational and Scientific.* Westport, Conn.:
            Greenwood Press.
Whitmeyer, Joseph M.
1994   "Why Actor Models Are Integral to Structural Analysis." *Sociological
            Theory* 12:153–165.
Whyte, William F.
1961   "Parsons' Theory Applied to Organizations." In M. Black (ed.), *The Social
            Theories of Talcott Parsons.* Englewood Cliffs, N.J.: Prentice-Hall:
            250–267.
Wiggershaus, Rolf
1994   *The Frankfurt School: Its History, Theories, and Political Significance.*
            Cambridge, Mass.: MIT Press.
Wilde, Lawrence
1991   "Logic: Dialectic and Contradiction." In T. Carver (ed.), *The Cambridge
            Companion to Marx.* Cambridge: Cambridge University Press: 275–295.
Wiley, Norbert
1979   "The Rise and Fall of Dominating Theories in American Sociology." In
            W. Snizek, E. Fuhrman, and M. Miller (eds.), *Contemporary Issues in
            Theory and Research.* Westport, Conn.: Greenwood Press: 47–79.
1986   "Early American Sociology and *The Polish Peasant.*" *Sociological Theory*
            4:20–40.
1988   "The Micro-Macro Problem in Social Theory." *Sociological Theory*
            6:254–261.
1989   "Response to Ritzer." *Sociological Theory* 7:230–231.
Williams, Robin
1980a   "Talcott Parsons: The Stereotypes and the Reality." *American Sociologist*
            15:64–66.

1980b   "Pitirim Sorokin: Master Sociologist and Prophet." In R. Merton and M. W. Riley (eds.), *Sociological Traditions from Generation to Generation.* Norwood, N.J.: Ablex: 93–107.

Wilner, Patricia
1985   "The Main Drift of Sociology between 1936 and 1982." *History of Sociology: An International Review* 5:1–20.

Wiltshire, David
1978   *The Social and Political Thought of Herbert Spencer.* London: Oxford University Press.

Winterer, Caroline
1994   "A Happy Medium: The Sociology of Charles Horton Cooley." *Journal of the History of the Behavioral Sciences* 30:19–27.

Woldring, Henk E. S.
1986   *Karl Mannheim: The Development of His Thought.* Assen/Maastricht, Neth.: Van Gorcum.

Wolf, Frederic M.
1986   *Meta-Analysis: Quantitative Methods for Research Synthesis.* Beverly Hills, Calif.: Sage.

Worsley, Peter
1982   *Marx and Marxism.* Chichester, Eng.: Ellis Horwood.

Wright, Erik Olin
1985   *Classes.* London: Verso.
1987   "Toward a Post-Marxist Radical Social Theory." *Contemporary Sociology* 16:748–753.

Wright, Erik Olin, and Martin, Bill
1987   "The Transformation of the American Class Structure, 1960–1980." *American Journal of Sociology* 93:1–29.

Wrong, Dennis
1994   *The Problem of Order: What Unites and Divides Society.* New York: Free Press.

Yates, Gayle Graham
1985   *Harriet Martineau on Women.* New Brunswick, N.J.: Rutgers University Press.

Yeatman, Anna
1987   "Women, Domestic Life and Sociology." In C. Pateman and E. Gross (eds.), *Feminist Challenges: Social and Political Challenges.* Boston: Northeastern University Press: 157–172.

Zeitlin, Irving M.
1981   *Ideology and the Development of Sociological Theory.* 2nd ed. Englewood Cliffs, N.J.: Prentice-Hall.
1990   *Ideology and the Development of Sociological Theory.* 4th ed. Englewood Cliffs, N.J.: Prentice-Hall.
1994   *Ideology and the Development of Sociological Theory.* 5th ed. Englewood Cliffs, N.J.: Prentice-Hall.
1996   *Ideology and the Development of Sociological Theory.* 6th ed. Englewood Cliffs, N.J.: Prentice-Hall.

Zhao, Shanyang
1991   "Metatheory, Metamethod, Meta-Data-Analysis." *Sociological Perspectives* 34:377–390.

1993   "Realms, Subfields, and Perspectives: Differentiation and Fragmentation of Sociology." *American Sociologist* Fall/Winter, 5–14.

forthcoming "Metatheorizing in Sociology." In George Ritzer and Barry Smart (eds.), *Handbook of Social Theory.* London: Sage.

Znaniecki, Florian

1934   *Method of Sociology.* New York: Farrar and Rhinehart.

Zurcher, Louis A.

1985   "The War Game: Organization Scripting and the Expression of Emotion." *Symbolic Interaction* 8:191–206.

NAME INDEX

Abbott, Edith, 302, 304, 309–310
Abbott, Grace, 302, 309
Aboulafia, Mitchell, 400
Abraham, Gary, 227
Abrams, Philip, 31–32
Addams, Jane, 5, 9, 52, 290, 298, 302–309, 313, 391
Adorno, Theodor, 41, 59
Alexander, Jeffrey C., 42, 75, 198, 235, 242, 457–458
Althusser, Louis, 42
Amsterdamska, Olga, 46
Archer, Margaret S., 76
Arditi, Jorge, 277
Aristotle, 90, 182
Aron, Raymond, 266
Aronson, Ronald, 71
Arthur, C. J., 457

Bacon, Francis, 110
Bailey, Kenneth D., 456–457
Baker, Patrick L., 456
Balch, Emily G., 303
Baldwin, Alfred, 441, 450
Baldwin, John C., 387, 392
Ball, Terence, 154
Barbalet, 163
Barber, Bernard, 447
Baudrillard, Jean, 44, 75, 79, 82
Bauer, Bruno, 457
Beck, Ulrich, 77–78
Becker, Howard, 62
Beeghley, Leonard, 438
Benjamin, Jessica, 73
Berger, Peter, 42, 68–69, 406, 411
Bergson, Henri, 410, 412, 427
Berki, 167
Berlin, Isaiah, 108
Bierstedt, Robert, 410–412
Blau, Peter, 42, 64, 467
Blumer, Herbert, 41, 58, 66, 386, 395
Boas, Franz, 438
Booth, Charles, 319

Bottomore, Tom, 261, 275
Bourdieu, Pierre, 76–77, 458–460
Bourricaud, Francois, 446
Bramstedt, Ernest K., 378
Braverman, Harry, 42
Breckinridge, Sophonisba, 302, 309–310
Breuer, Joseph, 30
Brinton, Crane, 44
Brubaker, Rogers, 235, 240
Bulmer, Martin, 46–47
Burger, Thomas, 220, 224
Burgess, Ernest W., 48
Button, Graham, 69

Cabet, Etienne, 457
Charcot, Jean M., 30
Chodorow, Nancy, 73
Cohen, G. A., 176
Coleman, James S., 42, 70, 75
Collins, Randall, 37, 65, 67, 198
Comte, Auguste, 3–4, 8, 10–11, 14–15, 19, 22, 29, 31–33, 35, 40, 43, 87–115, 117, 120–121, 149, 182–183, 259, 289, 291–295, 304–305, 312, 378, 382, 403
Cooley, Charles H., 41, 44, 49–51, 59, 436
Cooper, Anna J., 5, 9, 52, 290, 312–315
Coser, Lewis, 64, 70, 271–272, 457
Cottrell, Leonard, 390
Cronk, George, 407
Curtis, Charles, 55

Dahrendorf, Ralf, 42, 64
Darwin, Charles, 32, 117, 142, 301, 324–325, 404
Davis, Kingsley, 54, 61, 431
de Bonald, Louis, 5, 13, 15, 201

Deegan, Mary J., 304
de Maistre, Joseph, 7, 13, 15, 201
DeQuincey, Thomas, 305
Descartes, Rene, 12, 110
Dewey, John, 50, 308, 324, 387–388, 391
Dilthey, Wilhelm, 220
Dreyfus, Alfred, 188–189
Durkheim, Emile, 3–4, 8–11, 14–19, 22, 27, 29, 31, 33–37, 41, 43, 47, 52, 54, 60–69, 76, 78, 82, 95, 97, 107, 113, 148–149, 167, 181–213, 229, 252, 259, 271, 282, 295–296, 301, 305, 358, 388, 403, 431, 433–434, 450, 457, 463–464, 466–467

Elias, Norbert, 30, 75
Elster, Jon, 164
Emerson, Richard, 42, 66
Engels, Friedrich, 35, 152–153, 156, 161, 171, 316, 457
Etzkorn, K. Peter, 264

Faris, R. E. L., 388, 391, 436
Ferguson, Adam, 15, 405
Ferry, Luc, 82
Feuerbach, Ludwig, 7, 20–21, 457, 466
Fine, Gary A., 58, 66
Fitzhugh, George, 40
Foucault, Michel, 42, 74–75, 80
Fourier, Charles, 457
Freud, Sigmund, 30, 41, 74, 438, 450
Freund, Julian, 249
Friedrichs, Robert, 460
Frisby, David, 261, 265, 275
Fromm, Erich, 59
Fuhrman, Ellsworth, 40, 43
Fulbrook, Mary, 228
Furfey, Paul, 458

Gadamer, Hans-Georg, 220
Garfinkel, Harold, 7, 42, 68,
    70, 411
Gerth, Hans, 62–63, 229, 378
Giddens, Anthony, 42, 70,
    76–78, 191
Giddings, Franklin, 49, 426
Gilman, Charlotte P., 4–5, 9,
    52, 290, 296–302, 308,
    314, 316, 318
Gindoff, Pamela, 458
Goffman, Erving, 7, 42,
    66–67
Gorman, Robert, 411
Gouldner, Alvin, 61
Grathoff, Richard, 410
Gross, Llewellyn, 458
Gurvitch, Georges, 467–468

Habenstein, Robert, 58
Habermas, Jurgen, 42, 59, 71,
    76–78, 220, 434, 457
Hall, Richard, 455
Hankin, Thomas, 462
Harrington, James, 6
Heap, James L., 412, 429
Heberle, Rudolph, 272
Hegel, G. W. F., 7, 19–21,
    23–25, 35–36, 94, 149,
    157, 173, 241, 388, 404,
    457–458, 466
Heidegger, Martin, 220
Heilbron, Johan, 92–93, 109
Hekman, Susan, 221, 223
Henderson, Lawrence J., 55
Hilbert, Richard A., 68
Hinkle, Roscoe, 40, 43, 46,
    436
Hobbes, Thomas, 12, 326
Hofstadter, Richard, 43, 116
Holton, Robert J., 434
Homans, George, 42, 55–57,
    65–66, 77, 205
Horkheimer, Max, 41, 59
Horowitz, Irving, 61
Huaco, George, 61–62
Hughes, Everett, 49, 58
Husserl, Edmund, 41, 68, 410,
    412–414, 419–421,
    426–427, 429
Huxley, T.H., 111

Ibn-Khaldun, Abdel R., 5, 10

Jackman, Mary, 467
Jackman, Robert, 467
James, William, 305, 388
Jameson, Fredric, 78–79
Jaworski, Gary D., 457
Jay, Martin, 36
Jung, Carl, 30

Kalberg, Stephen, 25, 223,
    225, 227, 239, 242, 245
Kant, Immanuel, 7, 22, 25,
    259
Kautsky, Karl, 7, 35, 41
Kelley, Florence, 9, 290, 298,
    302, 308–311
Kellor, Frances, 302,
    309–310
Kohlberg, Lawrence, 210
Kuhn, Manford, 41, 58
Kuhn, Thomas, 381, 460–462

Lachman, L.M., 221, 223
Lamarck, Jean B., 404
Lassman, Peter, 216
Lathrop, Julia, 302, 309
Laughlin, A. Laurence, 338
Lazarsfeld, Paul F., 62
Lefebvre, Henri, 71, 148, 156
Lemert, Charles, 183, 211
Levi-Strauss, Claude, 41, 74
Levine, Donald, 77, 239, 263,
    267, 269
Levy, Marion, 431
Lewis, J. David, 388
Lewis, Reba R., 469
Lilla, Mark, 82
Lipovetsky, Gilles, 82
Liska, Allen, 75
Loader, Colin, 235
Locke, John, 12
Lockwood, David, 61
Longhurst, Brian, 353, 381
Luckmann, Thomas, 42,
    68–69, 406, 411, 418
Luhmann, Niklas, 42, 78
Lukacs, Georg, 5, 29, 36, 41,
    60, 168, 174, 219, 362

Lukes, Steven, 208
Lyman, Stanford, 43
Lyotard, Jean F., 78

MacLean, Anna M., 302,
    309–310
Manent, Pierre, 82
Mannheim, Karl, 4, 41,
    60–61, 353–384
Manning, Philip, 66
Marcuse, Herbert, 59
Marshall, Alfred, 324, 327,
    434, 457
Martineau, Harriet, 5, 9, 32,
    290–296, 304
Marx, Karl, 3–5, 8–9, 11–12,
    15, 16–17, 19–25,
    27–31, 34–35, 37, 43,
    47, 54, 55, 59, 60, 63,
    71–72, 74, 78, 81,
    93–94, 99, 101–102, 113,
    145, 147–179, 201–202,
    215, 221, 226, 232, 241,
    250, 252, 259, 262–265,
    275–276, 289–291, 297,
    301, 305, 316, 320,
    323–325, 343, 353–356,
    358, 363, 365, 382, 388,
    403, 405–407, 422, 429,
    434, 457–458, 466–467,
    471
Masterman, Margaret, 461
Matthews, Fred H., 51
Mauss, Marcel, 209, 211
McLellan, David, 172
McMurty, 158
Mead, George H., 4, 11, 41,
    45, 49–50, 58, 77, 266,
    297, 301, 304–306,
    385–409, 429, 436, 457
Mehan, Hugh, 409, 411
Menzies, Ken, 432
Merton, Robert, 42, 54, 57,
    61, 77, 353–354,
    380–381, 431, 435, 465
Mestrovic, Stjepan G., 36, 78
Michels, Alfred, 219
Michels, Robert, 219
Mill, James, 457
Mill, John S., 89–90, 109
Miller, David, 388, 395

Miller, W. Watts, 182
Mills, C. Wright, 42, 61–64, 71, 148, 229
Mitzman, Arthur, 252
Miyahara, Kojiro, 232
Montesquieu, Charles, 7, 12, 110, 182, 188
Moore, Wilbert, 54, 61, 431
Morris, Monica, 410, 411
Morse, Chandler, 441
Munch, P. A., 221, 433

Nash, Bradley Jr., 465
Natanson, Maurice, 385, 406
Nedelmann, Birgitta, 77, 281
Nietzsche, Friedrich, 7, 25
Nisbet, Robert, 203, 206, 260

Oakes, Guy, 271
Ogburn, William F., 331
Ollman, Bertell, 157, 159–160, 172
Owen, Robert, 457

Pareto, Vilfredo, 5, 27, 34–35, 54–55, 148, 434, 457
Park, Robert, 28, 33, 41, 44, 47–51, 58, 297, 301, 305–306, 436
Parsons, Talcott, 4, 8, 10, 16–17, 27, 30, 34, 37, 41, 44, 53–54, 56–57, 61–64, 65, 69, 77, 148, 181, 189, 215, 268, 290, 409, 429, 431–454, 457
Peirce, Charles, 387
Prendergast, Christopher, 410, 427
Piaget, Jean, 210
Plato, 182
Pope, Whitney, 194
Proudhon, Pierre, 457–458

Remmling, Gunter, 361
Renaut, Alain, 82
Ricardo, David, 7, 21, 457–458

Rich, Adrienne, 73
Rickert, Heinrich, 226
Ritzer, George, 37, 458, 460, 462–463, 469–470
Robinson, Virginia, 302, 309
Roscher, Wilhelm, 217
Rose, Arnold, 58
Rosenau, Pauline M., 79
Ross, E. A., 43, 44, 436
Roth, Guenther, 228
Roth, Philip A., 412, 429
Rousseau, Jean J., 7, 12, 100–101
Rubinstein, David, 455
Runciman, W.G., 221
Ryan, William, 31

Saint-Simon, Claude H., 7, 14, 19, 92, 102, 182
Sartre, Jean P., 41
Say, Jean B., 457
Scheler, Max, 358
Schneider, Mark, 242
Schutz, Alfred, 4, 11, 41, 67–70, 215, 229, 358, 409–430
Schwendinger, Herman, 40
Schwendinger, Julia, 40
Scott, John F., 438
Seidman, Steven, 12, 14, 19–20, 80
Sheldon C. Joanna, 317
Sherwood, Steven J., 242
Shils, Edward A., 449
Simmel, Georg, 4, 7, 8, 10, 19, 24, 27–29, 37, 43, 47, 49, 51–52, 54, 58, 60, 78, 82, 113, 145, 148–149, 219, 259–287, 296, 301, 305–306, 316–317, 372, 380, 388, 463
Skinner, B. F., 41, 58, 65, 467
Small, Albion, 28, 42, 48, 304, 436
Smelser, Neil, 431
Smith, Adam, 7, 15, 21, 30, 324, 327, 457–458
Smith, Dorothy, 290, 305
Smith, Philip, 242
Smith, Richard L., 388

Snizek, William, 464
Sorokin, Pitirim, 41, 53, 56–57, 435
Spencer, Anna G., 302, 309
Spencer, Herbert, 3–4, 7, 9, 11, 15–16, 32–35, 40, 43, 113–146, 149, 182–183, 259, 289, 291–295, 301, 305, 312, 319, 324–325, 403, 445
Srubar, Ilja, 413
Starr, Ellen G., 302–303
Stone, Gregory, 58
Strauss, Anselm, 58
Sumner, William G., 40, 44–45, 324–325, 338
Swartz, David, 458, 460
Sweezy, Paul M., 42, 325
Sztompka, Piotr, 77

Taft, Jessie, 302, 309
Talbot, Marion, 302, 309
Tarde, Gabriel, 193
Thomas, Dorothy, 47
Thomas, Paul, 149
Thomas, W. I., 47, 49–50, 58, 306, 436
Tiryakian, Edward A., 36, 46
Toby, Jackson, 444
Turner, Bryan S., 434
Turner, Jonathan H., 16, 113, 133, 145, 438

Udehn, Lars, 228

Veblen, Thorstein, 4, 41, 45–46, 82, 323–352
Velody, Irving, 216
Venable, Vernon, 166
Vico, Giovanni, 110
Vidich, Arthur, 43
Voltaire, 100

Wagner, Helmut, 414, 420
Wallerstein, Immanuel, 35, 43
Wallwork, Ernest, 188, 207, 210

Ward, Lester, 41, 44, 436
Wardell, Mark L., 465
Washington, Booker T.,
    48–49
Watson, John B., 385–386
Wax, Murray, 221
Webb, Beatrice P., 5, 9, 52,
    290, 298, 302, 308,
    318–320
Weber, Marianne, 5, 9, 52,
    290, 298, 302, 308,
    316–318, 362
Weber, Max, 4, 7–11, 19,
    24–29, 31, 34, 37, 43,
    47, 52, 54, 59, 68–69,
78, 82, 94, 113, 124, 145,
    148–149, 162, 215–257,
    259, 261, 263, 265,
    275–276, 282, 290, 296,
    301–302, 305, 316, 353,
    357, 361–362, 367–368,
    372, 374–375, 380, 382,
    388, 403, 410, 412, 415,
    417, 427–429, 431,
    433–434, 436, 440, 457,
    463, 464
Weil, Felix J., 59
Weinstein, Deena, 37
Weinstein, Michael A., 37

Wells-Barnett, Ida, 5, 9, 52,
    290, 302, 312–315
Whitehead, Alfred N., 87
Whyte, William F., 440
Wiley, Norbert, 47, 51, 75
Williams, Robin, 431
Wolf, Frederick, 456
Wood, Houston, 409, 411
Worsley, Peter, 176
Wundt, Wilhelm, 188

Zeitlin, Irving, 11–13, 34
Znaniecki, Florian, 47

SUBJECT INDEX

Accumulation, in capitalism,
177–178
Acts, as units of study, 66,
386, 389–395
  four stages of, 389–392,
  406
    consummation, 392
    impulse, 389–390
    manipulation, 392
    perception, 390–391
  social, 386, 392, 397
  unit, 437, 449
Action(s) 167, 410, 428, 440,
468
  affectual, 225, 230
  collective, 309
  economic, 229
  individual, 28, 168, 181,
  309, 427, 468
  and interaction, 211
  meaning of, 230
  nonrational, 435
  political, 157
  rational, 373, 415
  reasonable, 415
  scientific subjective theory
  of, 410
  sensible, 415
  social, 229–230, 428, 436,
  464
  systems, 56, 432, 443–451,
  453
    behavioral organism,
    432, 441–442,
    450–451
    cultural system, 432,
    442–443, 448
    personality system,
    432, 439, 442,
    449–450
    social system, 432,
    442, 445–448, 450,
    453
  theory, 54, 230, 432,
  435–441, 457, 464
    Weberian, 433
  thought and, 36
  traditional, 230
  types of, 440

expressive, 440
instrumental, 440
intellectual, 440
moral, 440
valuerational, 440
Actor(s), 66, 156, 167–168,
181, 220, 266, 389,
409, 412, 436,
448–449, 468
  common-sense, 414–415
  consciousness of, 161
  Durkheim and, 203–211
  dependent variables,
  208–209
  individual, 168, 170, 441
  intentionality and, 412
Adaptive upgrading, 451
After Marxism, 72
Agency-structure integration,
42, 75–77, 227, 462
  dualism vs. duality, 76
  habitus and field
  (Bourdieu), 76
AGIL scheme (Parsons),
441–444, 447
  adaptation, 441
  goal attainment, 441
  integration, 441
  latency, 441
"Aims and Principles of the
Consumers' League",
311
Alienation of workers, 23,
162–166, 171, 234,
312
  components of, 163–164
  distortions resulting from,
  163–166
  from other workers, 164
Altruism, 95–96, 98, 101,
107, 132, 194
Ameliorism, 29, 31–32
American Economic
Association, 327, 339
American Federation of
Labor (AFL), 341, 343
American Journal of
Sociology, 46, 51, 56,
299, 310–311, 338

American Sociological
Association (ASA),
46, 70–71, 434
American Sociological
Review, 51, 58, 70, 299
American Sociological
Society (ASS), 45–46,
49, 51, 58, 301
Annals of the American
Academy of Political
and Social Science,
299
Anomie, 190, 194, 196, 201,
466–467
Anti-Semitism, 17, 188–189
Assembly line
  automobile, 79, 163–164
Association(s), 263, 266–271
  democratic, 309
  discretion, 284
  employer, 202
  forms of, 265
  friendship, 284
  marriage, 284–285
  (see also Interaction)
Authority
  legal, 232–235
  systems, 26, 231–239
    charismatic, 26, 232,
    236–239
    rational-legal, 26, 232,
    238 240
    traditional, 12, 26, 232,
    235–236, 238
"Authority and Autonomy in
Marriage", 316
Autonomy, 210, 317

Bankruptcy, 343
Behavior, 65, 436
  interpersonal, 262
  reinforcement, 65
  social, 463–465, 467, 469
Behaviorism, 385–387,
436
  Skinner's, 65
  Social, 464, 471
Beliefs, 231

Bourgeoisie, 151, 155, 159, 172, 174, 255
British sociology, the development of, 7, 29–34
Bureaucracy(ies), 18, 25–26, 69, 151, 223–224, 226, 228, 232, 234–235, 240–241, 372, 427, 466, 470
  ideal-typical, 233–234, 237
  structures of, 234
  university, 348
Bureaucratization, 14, 26, 224, 233–235
  expansion of, 235
  process of, 26
Bureaucrats, 235, 242
  ideal-typical, 233

Calvinism, 26, 224, 242, 250–254, 256
  predestination, 253
  salvation, 250–251
  signs in, 253
Capital, 173, 177, 353
Capital: A Critique of Political Economy, 151, 153, 163, 169–170, 173–174, 458
Capitalism, 22–23, 26, 40, 45, 69, 81, 94, 99, 149, 159–160, 162, 165–166, 168, 171, 174–178, 228, 236, 241, 264, 275, 318, 325, 429
  adventurer type, 252
  in China structural barriers, 254–255
  contradiction within, 155
  economic structures, 150, 471
  economy in, 28, 241, 319
  in India, 256–257
  Marx's theory of, 25, 457
  Modern, 154, 232, 234, 248

nature of, 174
oppressiveness of, 23
rise of, 7–8
spirit of, 24, 173, 222, 251–254
structures of, 21, 155–156, 160, 162–163, 166, 173
Western, 252
(See also *Division of labor; Money; Private property*)
Capitalist societies, 27, 30, 151, 162, 166, 168, 276, 451, 466
  cultural aspects of, 173–176
  economic structure of, 74, 173
  structure(s) of, 167–173
Carriers, 245
Caste system, 244, 256
Catholic Church, 13, 238, 378
Causality, 221–222, 229
  adequate, 222
  multiple, 222
Chaos theory, 456
Character and Social Structure, 63
Charisma
  as revolutionary force, 237
  routinization of, 225, 237–239
Chicago, The University of, 28, 45–46, 302
Chicago school, 10, 28, 46–52, 58–66
  Second, 59
  and social work, 82
  waning of, 51–52, 58–59
  the women of, 302–312
Choice(s), individual, 437
"Churches' and `Sects' in North America: An Ecclesiastical Socio-Political Sketch", 235
City(ies), 110, 272–274, 375
  sociology of, 48

Clan(s), 199–200, 243–244, 272, 403
Class and Class Conflict in Industrial Society, 64
Class and Class Consciousness, 36
Classless society, 155, 368
Collective conscience 18, 185, 187, 190–192, 194–195, 197, 200, 202, 208, 211
  content, 191
  intensity, 191
  rigidity, 191
  volume, 191
Collective effervescence, 200–201, 211
Collective representations, 185, 187, 191–192, 194
Collectivity(ies), 14, 191, 230, 295, 330, 426, 439, 445, 447, 466
Commodities, 168, 172–173, 176,
  circulation of, 170
    Commodities-Money-Commodities, 170
    Money-Commodities-Money, 170
  fetishism of, 168–169, 264
Communication, 280, 294
  theory, 457
Communism, 94, 103, 145, 148, 157, 159–160, 162, 164, 167, 172, 174, 201, 363
  preconditions for,148
  spread of,103
Communist Manifesto, 153
Communist revolution, 201
Communist societies, 37, 99, 144, 148, 155, 167
Concerning Children, 299
Condition of the Working Class in England, The, 152, 311
Conduct, 373, 385
Conflict theory, 42, 64–65, 71, 82, 215, 262, 464

Confucianism, 26, 249,
    255–256
Conscience, individual, 265
Consciousness, 20–21, 36,
    50–51, 65, 67,
    157–158, 162, 164,
    173, 204–205,
    207–210, 388,
    396–397, 412–413,
    421, 426–429, 437,
    440
  basic structures of, 412
  bifurcated, 305
  class, 174–175, 466
  creative, 265
  deep, 427
  false, 174–175, 360, 466
  human, 386
  individual, 174–175,
    191–192, 203, 209,
    265–266, 427
  of a period, 174
  self, 162, 404
  social, 173, 184
Consumer Society, 82
Consuming Places, 82
Consumption, 46, 327
  acts of, 279
  conspicuous, 46, 82, 323,
    334–335, 347
  food, 279
  new means of, 463
    casino-hotels, 463
    cruise lines, 463
    cybermalls, 463
    home shopping
      television, 463
    megamalls, 463
    superstores, 463
    theme parks, 463
  sociology of, 463
  theories of, 42, 82
*Contemporary Sociological
    Theories,* 56
*Contribution to the Critique
    of Political Economy,*
    458
Control, administrative, 373
*Cooperative Movement in
    Great Britain, The,*
    319

*Cours de Philosophie
    Positive,* 93
Creativity, 160–162, 403
  musical, 248–249
Credit economy, 285
Critical school, 41, 59, 71
Critical theory, 36, 59, 76,
    215, 363
Cultural ambivalence, 281
Cultural borrowing, 331–332
Cultural creativity, 281
Cultural determinism, 411,
    448
Cultural lag, 331
Cultural malaise, 281
Cultural products, 364, 382
Cultural sociology, 382
Cultural studies, 198, 211
Culture, 18, 29, 220–221,
    184, 196–197, 448,
    470
  and agency integration, 76
  disintegration of, 378
  individual, 279
  objective, 263–264,
    272–274, 278–279
  popular, 73, 294
  production, 317
  sociology of, 211
  subjective, 263–264
  tragedy of, 82, 273, 277,
    279–282

Deconstruction, 36
Democracy(ies), 232
*Democracy and Social
    Ethics,* 303, 308
Democratization, 378
Deviance, 433
Dial, The, 339
Dialectic(s), 142, 150–156,
    388, 405–407, 420
  actors and structures,
    155–156
  being and conceiving, 282
  conflict and contradiction
    in, 155, 407
  fact and value, 151, 226
  and Hegel, 19–21
  Hegelian, 466

"I" and "me", 406–407
  and Marx 21, 174, 221,
  past, present, and future,
    154
  reciprocal relations in,
    150–151,
  and Simmel, 262–265
  thesis, antithesis, synthesis
    model, 154–155
Dialectical materialism, 21
Differentiation, 118, 127,
    137, 139, 186, 451
  functional, 126
  structural, 126
Disciplinary matrix, 458
Distinction, 459
Division of labor, 18, 69, 82,
    97, 122, 126, 139, 160,
    169, 171–173,
    185–192, 278–279,
    308
  anomic, 190
  between the sexes, 140
  causes of, 139–140
  criticisms of, 172
  forced, 97
  pathologies of, 18, 201
  structural, 190
*Division of Labor in Society,
    The,* 18, 185–192,
    198, 201, 206,
    208, 211
Domination, 232, 270, 294,
    312, 314–315, 317,
    355
  male, 300
  traditional, 225
Dramaturgical analysis,
    66–67
  back stage, 67
  front stage, 67
Durkheimian theory, 36
Dyad, 29, 268
Dynamic density, 186–187,
    191, 193

Eastern Life: Present and
    Past, 296
Eastern Sociological Society,
    51

Economic(s):
  classical, 433
  determinism, 7, 24, 35, 41
  history, 427
  institutions, 136
  laws, 35
  marginal utility, 327–328
  Marx's theory of, 176–178
Economic and Philosophic Manuscripts of 1844, The, 153, 457
Economist, The, 116
Economy(ies), 6, 10, 24–25, 241, 294, 297, 315, 355, 447
  Money, 29, 173, 275–278, 280, 285
    and cynicism, 278
  private, 300
  public, 300
  rational capitalistic, 244
  structural components of, 169
Economy and Society, 216, 219, 224, 227–228, 241, 353
Education, 294, 300–301, 315, 379, 403
  graduate, 345
  higher, 345
    competition in, 347
    faculty in, 347–348
    and professional schools, 348
    and tenure, 348
    university administration, 346–347
  undergraduate, 345–346
    accountancy, 346
    control in, 345
    efficiency of, 345
    quantification of, 345
    standardization of, 345–346
    surveillance in, 345–346
    uniformity, 346
  women's, 296
Efficiency, 26, 233, industrial, 350

Egoism, 95–96, 98, 101, 107, 194, 202
"Eighteenth Brumaire of Louis Bonaparte", "The", 154
Elementary Forms of Religious Life The, 18, 188, 198
Emergence, 262, 403–404, 433
Enchanting a Disenchanted World: Revolutionizing the Means of Consumption, 82, 463
Enlightenment, the, 7, 11–12, 15–16, 19, 22
  Conservative reaction to, 7, 12–14
  Philosophy, 34
"Essays on the Art of Thinking", 294
Ethic(s), 259
  of conviction, 235
  and politics, 141–145
  of responsibility, 235
Ethnomethodology, 42, 68–70, 215, 229, 409–410, 429, 464, 467
Everyday life, sociologies of, 67–70
Evolutionary theory, 7, 15, 32–34, 117–119, 125, 185, 325, 451
  and Hegel, 20
  and Comte's law of the three stages, 15–16, 33, 90–91, 104, 110
    metaphysical stage, the, 15, 90–91, 100
    positivistic stage, the, 15, 90–91, 99
    theological stage, the, 15–16, 90–91, 99–100, 104
Exchange, 262
  relationships, 274
  theory, 42, 58, 70, 77, 260, 464
    birth of, 65–66
    (See also *Behaviorism*)

Exchange and Power in Social Life, 66
Existential sociology, 42
Existentialism, 464
Exploitation, 80, 174, 253
  of workers, 21, 155, 169–170, 176–177
Expressing America: A Critique of the Global Credit Card Society, 463

Factories, 8, 151, 244, 296, 331
Fads and Foibles in Modern Sociology and Related Sciences, 53
Family, 14, 33, 95–96, 130, 171, 191, 196, 272, 294, 296, 300, 315, 400, 403, 447, 468
  adultery, 132
  arrangements, 120
  bigamy, 132
  future of, 132
  monogamous, 13, 132
  primitive, 186
  promiscuity, 131–132
  structure(s), 130, 209
Fascism, 364, 377, 381
Fashion, 82, 263–264
  tyranny of, 296
"Female Writers on Practical Divinity", 296
Feminism, 9, 76, 290, 312
  African-American, 315
  cultural, 306
  radical, 314
  Third Wave, 73
    of motherhood, 73
  of work, 73
Feminist Studies, 73
Feminist theory, 36–37, 72–74, 77, 83
Fetishism, 90, 100
Feudalism, 99, 236, 243, 248
Fiduciary system, 447
First Principles, 142
Forerunner, The, 298–299

Frankfurt school, 61, 363
  Institute of Social
    Research, 59, 363
Freedom, 204,
  Individual, 141, 278
French Revolution, 6, 13, 15,
  22, 91, 100, 370–371
French sociology 7, 11–12,
  17–19, 29
  conservative, 18
  development of, 14–19
Freudian theory, 60, 63
*Functions of Social Conflict,
  The,* 457
Functionalism, 438, 445

Gender, 52, 73, 295–296,
  300, 302, 315,
  identity, 291, 302
  inequality, 297
  stratification, 297, 299
Gender and Society, 73
Generalized media of
  interchange, 452–453
Generalized other, the, 308,
  400–401
German historicism, 358–359
German Ideology, The,
  152–153, 457
German Sociological Society,
  27, 219, 226
German sociology, the
  development of, 7, 12,
  19–29
Gerontocracy, 236
Gestures, 392–394
  conversation of, 393, 395
  nonsignificant, 393–394
  physical, 393
  significant, 393
  vocal, 393
Grand theory, 63, 69, 148,
  353, 433
Group(s), 33, 400, 466, 468
  primary, 50
  social psychology of, 389
  socialist, 43
Group mind concept, 188,
  196–198
Grundrisse, 458

Habitus, 76
Harvard University:
  Department of Social
    Relations, 56–57, 432,
    434
  the rise of, 53
Hedonism, 202
Hermeneutic(s), 220, 382
  German, 357
Heterosexuality, 80–81
  enforced, 73
Higher learning, 345–348
Hinduism, 26, 249
  and capitalism, 256
His Religion and Hers, 299
*Holy Family: Against Bruno
  Bauer and Co., The,*
  152, 457
Home, The, 299
Homo Academicus, 459
Homo duplex, 205
Homo sociologicus,
Homosexuality, 80–81
*How to Observe Morals and
  Manners* 292, 295–296
*Hull-House Maps and
  Papers,* 310
Human nature, 94, 107, 137,
  140, 145, 158,
  328–330
  assumptions about,
    204–205
  duality of, 205
  emulation, 330, 334
  grand theory of, 89
  idle curiosity, 329–330
  instincts, 328–329, 334
  parental bent, 329
  passions, 204–205
Human potential, 156–162
  165, 324
  activity, 158, 160–162
  perception, orientation, and
    appropriation,
    159–161
  powers and needs, 157, 162
  natural, 157
  species, 157
  (See also *Consciousness*)
Human rights, 82
Human Work 299

Idea systems, 60
  ideology, 61
  utopia, 61
Ideal types, 217, 222–225
  228, 410, 416–417,
  422
  action, 225
  constructing, 416–417
  general sociological, 224
  historical, 224
  structural, 225
Idealism, 434
  German, 466
  and Hegel, 19, 94
  subjective, 20
Ideology, 60, 175–176,
  365–367, 371
  death of, 369
  disenchantment with, 369
  particular, 366
  theory of, 354–356
  total, 366
Ideology and Utopia, 363,
  365, 372, 381
*Illustrations of Political
  Economy,* 291, 293
Imitation theory, 193
*Imperial Germany and the
  Industrial Revolution,*
  349
Independent, The, 299
Individual(s), 95–96, 122
  cult of, 202–203
  evolution of, 326
  and facts, 210
  powerlessness of, 275
  psychology of, 389
  representations of, 205
  rights, 101
Individualism, 141, 202,
  307
  moral, 205, 191
Individuality, 403
Industrial arts, 324, 326–331,
  345
Industrial institutions,
  139–141
Industrial reserve army,
  177–178
Industrial Revolution, 8, 10,
  13, 22, 82, 302, 319,

Industrial society(ies), 30, 33, 79, 128–130, 133, 135, 141, 375
Industrialization, 14, 41, 44, 47, 240 375
Instinct of Workmanship and the State of the Industrial Arts, The, 339
Integrated sociological paradigm, 149, 432, 458, 464–471
Integration, 118, 125
  evolutionary, 135
  mal-, 450
  and order, 442
  political, 135
  for society, 451
  of theory and practice, 108
Intellectual revolution, 370
Intellectual stimulation, 280
Intelligence, 395–396
  practical, 418
  reflective, 396
  unreasoning, 395
Intelligentsia, 361–365
  socially unattached (free), 361, 363, 369
Interactants types of, 28–29, 416
  adventurer, 262, 270
  competitor, 262
  coquette, 262
  miser 28, 262, 270
  nobleman, 270
  prostitute, 28
  spendthrift, 28, 262, 270
  stranger, 28, 262 270, 416–417
Interaction(s), 65, 220, 301, 421, 438, 448, 468
  and distance, 269–270
  face-to-face, 423
  forms of, 28–29, 262, 265, 266–271
    acquaintanceship, 284
    confidence, 283
    conflict, 262, 270
    exchange, 262, 270
      prostitution, 270

sociability, 262, 270
subordination, 262, 265, 267, 270–271
superordination, 262, 265, 267, 270–271
and group size, 268–269
  (See also *Dyad; Triad*)
individual, 28
social, 67, 266–271
types, 267–271
  (See also *Action; Thought*)
Internalization, 265, 446
  of morality, 206
  of norms, 210
Intersubjectivity, 68, 420–422, 427
Introduction to Pareto, An, 55
Introduction to the Science of Sociology, An, 48
Irrationality:
  functional, 374
  Mannheim's, 372–376
  rational control over, 377
  types of, 373–376
Italian sociology, the development of, 7, 34–35

Jane Addams and the Men of the Chicago School, 304
"Jobs and Marriage", 317
Journal of Political Economy, 304, 338

Knowledge, 421
  existential, 226
  and generations, 355–356
  idiographic, 222, 216
  nomothetic, 222, 216
  normative, 226
  and politics, 356
  private components of, 421–422
  of skills, 420
  social distribution of, 421
  social origin of, 421

sociology of, 60
  empirical nature of, 357
  Mannheim's, 354–365
  rise of, 359
  systems of, 60
  useful, 420

L'annee sociologique, 189
Labor, 31, 161–162, 164, 315
  commodification of, 169
  movements, 43
  power, 177
  regulation of, 141
    communal, 141
    paternal, 141
    patriarchal, 141
  time, 151
  unions, 202, 341
Language, 97, 279, 393, 445, 470
Law(s), 18, 187–190, 198, 203, 241, 252, 294, 331, 344, 447, 466, 468, 470
  abstract, 90
  institutionalized, 17
  primitive, 246
  rationalization of, 246–247
  restitutive, 187
  sociology of, 19
  specialization within, 139
  training in,
    academic legal, 247
    craft, 247
Law of the three stages (see *Evolutionary theory and Comte's law of the three stages*)
Leadership, charismatic, 46, 236
Leisure:
  class, 48, 326, 333–337, 346
  conspicuous, 46, 334–335
  studies, 323
Liberalism and conservatism in sociology, 40, 144, 370–372, 382

Life and Labour of the People of London, The, 319
Life-world, 70, 419–420
  basic characteristics of, 419
  colonization of, 76–77
  rationalization of, 79
  they relations, 68, 425–426
  versus science, 414–416
  we relations, 68, 423–424
Listen Yankee: The Revolution in Cuba, 63
Long Road of Women's Memory, The, 303, 309
Lynching, 312–315

Macrosociology, 47, 95,
Man and Society in an Age of Reconstruction, 373, 381
Man-Made World or Our Androcentric Culture, The, 299
Market(s), 31, 168, 176, 224, 252, 276, 300
  foreign, 350
  free, 8
Marriage, 294–295, 316–317, 347
  and the law, 296
Marriage and Motherhood in the Development of Law, 316
Marxian sociology, 22, 73
  rise and fall of, 71–72
Marxian theory, 14, 22, 24–25, 27, 35, 63–65, 71, 77, 82, 147–179, 324–325, 358 367, 451, 463
  developments in, 59
  early and late, 150
  economic, 149,
  rejection of, 34
Marxism 189, 367
  deterministic, 35
  economic, 42
  European, 35–36
  Hegelian, 7, 35–36, 41, 59

historical, 42
  post, 77
  postmodern, 77
  structural, 42
  Weberian, 60
  Western, 36
Marxist Studies, 71
Marxists, The, 63
Material base, 175
Max Weber: A Biography, 316
McDonaldization of society, 37, 79, 463
  and credit cards, 37, 463
  (See also *Fordism*)
McDonaldization of Society, The, 463
McDonaldization Thesis, The, 463
Meaning(s), 397, 426–429
Mechanical solidarity, 185–187, 191, 208
Mechanization, 177
Men and Society in an Age of Reconstruction, 363
Mental processes, 167, 173, 197, 203, 229, 386, 388, 427
  and the mind, 395–398
MetaAnalysis, 456
Meta-data-analysis, 456
Metamethods, 455–456
Metasociology:
  neodialectical, 458
  positivistic, 458
Metatheorizing, 455–460
  external-intellectual, 456–457, 459
  external-social, 457, 459
  internal-intellectual, 456–457, 459–460
  internal-social, 456–457, 459–460
Metatheorizing, 463
Metatheorizing in Sociology, 463
Methodological holism, 458
Methodological individualism, 122, 125, 141, 458

Methodological relationism, 458
"Metropolis and Mental Life", "The", 260, 273
Micromacro theory, 42, 77–78, 227, 462
  and agencystructure linkage, 227
Microsociology, and Simmel, 260, 274
Militant society(ies), 33, 128–130, 132–134, 136–137, 140–141
Mind, the, 53, 90, 357, 397–398,
  neighborhood, 308
  sociology of, 380
Mind Self and Society: From the Standpoint of a Social Behaviorist, 50–51, 388, 390–391, 402, 409
  and the priority of the social, 388–389
Modern society(ies), 10, 136, 190–191, 198, 315, 334, 377, 404, 452
Modernism, 36
Modernity, 375
  defenders of, 78–79
  industrialism and, 134
  theories of, 44, 78–80,
  (See also *Organic solidarity*)
Modernization, 273
Monarchy(ies), 13, 372
Money, 82, 160, 165, 170, 252, 269–270, 273–274, 280, 285, 345, 453
  economy, 273, 275–278, 280, 285
  rationalization of, 276–278
  reification of, 276–278
  and value, 275–276
Monotheism, 90, 100
Moral disorder, 189
Moral education, 188, 206–208

Morality, 101, 104–105, 185, 187–189, 446
  collective/common, 18, 187, 189–191, 198, 200, 202, 204–208
  social, 206–207
More-life, 263–265
More-than-life, 263–265
Motives, 426–429
  "because", 428
  "in-order-to", 428
Multicultural social theory, 42, 80–81, 83
  Afrocentric theory, 81
  Native American theory, 81
  theories of masculinity, 81
Multidimensional sociology (Alexander), 75
  Action, 75
  levels of analysis:
    collective-idealist, 75
    collective-materialist, 75
    individual-idealist, 75
    individual-materialist, 75
  order, 75
My Apprenticeship, 319–320

National Women's Studies Association (NWSA), 73
Natural rhythm, 280
Natural selection, 32, 45
Nazism, 349–350, 363, 376–378, 381, 411
Need-dispositions, 438–439, 443, 446, 449–450
"Need for Theoretical Preparation for Philanthropic Work", "The", 311
Neoevolutionary sociological theory, 34
Neofunctionalism, 42, 68, 83, 457
NeoMarxian theory, 70, 82, 148
Network theory, 42
New Homes for Old, 310

New School for Social Research, 68, 339, 410–411
Newer Ideals of Peace, 303
Norms, 173, 184, 196–197, 231, 246–247, 252, 265, 325, 433, 435, 437, 439, 445–446–448, 466, 468, 470
  cultural system of, 181–182

Objectification, 160–162, 168
Occupational associations, 201–202
"On Female Education", 296
On Lynching, 313
On the Origin of the Species, 142
Oppression, 312, 314–315
Organic solidarity, 185–187, 191, 208
Organization(s), 234, 443, 466, 468
  bureaucratic, 241
  charismatic, 237–238
  ecclesiastical, 135–139
Origins of the Family, The, 299

Paradigm(s), 381, 460–462
  integrated sociological, 75, 460
  multiple, 460–464
  postmodern, 465
Parsonsian theory, 57, 65
Patriarchy, 13, 318,
Patrimonialism, 236
Pattern variables, 440–441, 451
  affectivity-affective neutrality, 440
  ascription-achievement, 440
  self-collectivity, 440
  specificity-diffuseness, 440
  universalism-particularism, 440

Peace and Bread in Times of War, 303
Phenomenology, 69–70, 358–359, 409, 411–412, 414, 421, 427, 464, 467
Phenomenology of the Social World, The, 67, 69, 409–410
Philosophy of Money, The, 28–29, 259–260, 269, 273–282
  negative effects of, 278–279
Planning, 376–379
  democratic, 377–378
  for freedom, 377
Polish Peasant in Europe and America, The, 47
Political economy:
  English, 7, 30–31, 152, 291
  Marx's theory of, 21–22
Political institutions, 119, 134–136, 138
Political revolution(s), 6, 8
"Politics and the Woman's Movement", 316
"Politics as a Vocation", 235, 302
Polity, 6, 137, 241, 247–248, 447, 468
  development of, 248
Polytheism, 90, 100
"Poor", "The", 270
Positive philosophy (see Positivism)
Positive Philosophy, The, 291–292
Positivism, 15–16, 87–89, 98, 100–105, 109, 114–115, 216, 357–358, 434–435
  invariant laws and, 88–89, 109
  as a religion, 105–106, 111, 114–115
  and the search for order and progress, 91–94
  and sex, 106
  weakness of, 358
Positivistic sociology, 16, 43

Postmodern social theory, 36, 42, 79, 81–82, 259, 463
Post, 42, 81–82
Postmodern society, 82
Postmodernism, 80, 211
  Disneyland, 79
  post-, 82
  simulations, 79
Postmodernity, 79
  theories of, 78–80
Poststructuralism, 42, 211
Poverty 28, 31, 299
  causes of, 319
  and Simmel, 270
Power, 25
  illegitimate, 317
  legitimate, 317
  typology of, 317
Power Elite, The, 63
Pragmatism, 304, 310, 387–388
  nominalist, 125, 388
  philosophical realism, 125, 388
Praxis, 21
  theory and, 167
Presentation of Self in Everyday Life, 66
Primary patriarchalism, 236
Primitive society(ies), 10, 18, 23, 121, 127, 132–133, 137, 159, 185–186, 198, 199, 248, 333, 402, 452
  amity, 137
  enmity, 137
Principles of Ethics, The, 141
Principles of Sociology, The, 125
Private property, 145, 160, 165, 171, 173, 334, 346
Production, 46, 323, 355
  acts of, 172, 279
  means of, 177, 234, 244
  owners of, 151, 154, 159, 163, 171
  private ownership of, 171

process of, 23, 160, 177, 307
Profane, 18
Professional institutions, 138–139
Profit, 177
Progressivism, 304
Proletariat, 81, 94, 106, 151, 154–155, 159, 162, 166–167, 172, 174–175, 177–178, 368
  class-consciousness, 23, emancipation of, 166–167
  exploitation of, 150, 175
Prophets, 245–246 255
  ethical, 245
  exemplary, 245
Protestant ethic, 222,
Protestant Ethic and the Spirit of Capitalism, The, 24, 37, 219, 222, 241, 251–252
Protestantism, 24, 43, 100, 222, 249–252
  ascetic, 250–251
Psychological behaviorism, 51, 58, 65, 385, 464
Psychological facts, 184
Publications of the American Sociological Society, 299

Quakers, 235

Race, 52, 73, 193, 295, 315, 328
  relations, 48
  and society, 313
Rational choice theory, 42, 75, 78, 83
Rationality, 32, 60, 78–80, 248
  formal, 25, 79, 236–237, 240, 242, 273, 374, 376
    calculability, 242, 273
    control, 242
    efficiency of, 26, 242

  in fastfood restaurants, 26
  irrationality of, 242, 375
  nonhuman vs. human technologies in, 242
  predictability of, 242
  functional, 373–374
  iron cage of, 79, 241, 263, 275
  irrationalities of, 242
  of lifeworld, 78
  Mannheim's, 372–376
    application of, 376
  meansends, 230, 239
  practical, 239–240
  of priesthood, 245–246
  substantial, 373
  substantive, 240, 242
  system, 78
  theoretical, 240
  types of, 131–132, 373–376
  value, 230 239
  Weberian theory of, 236, 238–239, 463
Rationalization, 26–28, 217, 225, 233, 235, 239–249, 276–277, 345, 372–373, 463
  of art forms, 248–249
  bureaucratic, 79, 240, 463
  of the city, 248
  of economic institutions, 243–244
  of fast-food restaurants, 26, 79, 463
    drive-through window, the, 26
  functional, 375
  iron cage of, 239
  of law, 246–247
  of medicine, 463
  process, 25, 241, 373
  of religion, 244–246
  self, 374–375
  substantial, 375
  structural barriers to, 250
  theory, 37
  (See also *City(ies); Law; Religion*)

Realms of the social world,
422–426
consociates, 423
folgewelt, 422–423
mitwelt, 422–426
umwelt, 422–425
vorwelt, 422–423
Reason, 12
"Reasons for Dissenting from
the Philosophy of M.
Comte", 114
Recipes, 417–420, 424
*Reflections on Women and
Women's Issues,* 316
Reflexivity, 398
Reformation, 200
Reification, 169, 252
of money, 276–278
of social structures, 169
Relationism, 360–361
Relativism, 360–361, 381
Religion(s), 10, 18–20, 26,
43, 46, 97, 115–116,
138, 196, 198–201,
207, 211, 241, 294,
296, 315, 468
anthropomorphization of
gods, 245
beliefs, 199
ceremony, 14, 120
in China, 254–256
church, 199
dynamogenic quality of,
198
in India, 256–257
irrational examples, 26
modern, 198–199
monotheism, 245
primitive, 198
and rise of capitalism,
249–257
ritual, 14, 120, 211
sociology of, 227, 427
symbols, 211
totemism, 18, 199–200,
211
worship, 14
(See also *Religiosity*)
Religiosity:
ascetism,
innerworldly, 250

otherworldly, 250
mysticism,
innerworldly, 250
worldrejecting, 250
Religious change, 7, 10–11
Renaissance, the, 200, 249
Rethinking Marxism, 71
Risk society, 79
*Risk Society: Towards a New
Modernity,* 77
"Risking Enchantment", 242
Role expectations, 450
*Rules of Sociological
Method, The,* 17–18,
183, 188, 192,
295, 463

Sacred vs. profane, 199–201,
211
Science, 17, 43, 115–116,
198, 331, 344,
404–405
growth of, 7, 11
and the social world,
414–417
of society, 357
"Science as a Vocation", 302
Scientific determinism, 35
Scientific objectivity, 226,
360
Scientific reporting, 48
Scientific sociology, 145
Scottish Enlightenment, 30
Scottish Moralists, 15, 30
*Second Twenty Years at Hull-
House, The,* 303
Secrecy, 282–286
betrayal and, 285
Self, the, 398–402, 406–407
childhood development of,
399–400
game stage, 399–400
play stage, 399
"I" and "Me", 401–404,
406–407
looking-glass, 50
as a mental process, 398
Self-actualization, 318
Self-observation, 375
Sensatism, 53

Sexism, 304
Sexuality, 80, 299, 302, 314
*Shelf Life: Supermarkets and
the Changing Cultures
of Consumption,* 82
Signs, 73
Simmelian theory, 36
postmodernized version of,
37
Sibs, 254
Slavery, 141, 243
*Slavery and the French
Revolutionists,* 313
Sociability, 161–162
(See also *Interaction, forms
of*)
Social amelioration, 47, 52,
291, 310
Social analysis:
levels of, 432, 443,
465–467
micro and macro,
465–466 468
a model of, 467–471
objectivesubjective
continuum,
466–468, 469–470
Simmel's, 28
Ritzer's theory, 467–471
macro objectivity, 75,
469
macro subjectivity, 75,
471
micro objectivity, 75,
469, 471
micro subjectivity, 75
Wiley's theory, 75
culture, 75
interaction, 75
self, 75
social structure, 75
*Social and Cultural
Dynamics,* 53
"Social Behavior as
Exchange", 65
*Social Behavior: Its
Elementary Forms,* 65
Social change, 15–16, 40–46,
53, 64, 101, 107, 125,
154, 407, 451–452
cyclical theory of, 35, 53

Social change—*Cont.*
elite theory of, 34
Pareto's theory of, 34
Social class(es), 52, 73, 110,
127, 172–173,
230–231, 296, 302,
315, 320, 324, 335,
356, 368, 466
conflict, 298, 307
distinctions, 120
relationships, 315
ruling, 354–355
stratification, 314–315,
317–318, 335, 355
as structures, 172
struggle, 40
Social conflict, 442
functions of, 64
Social construction of reality,
173, 465, 468, 470
*Social Construction of
Reality, The,* 68–69
Social control, 310, 376 402,
445–447
Social currents, 185,
187–188, 192–198
Social Darwinism, 32, 41,
44–45, 304, 325, 327
Social definitionism,
463–465, 467, 469,
471
Social disorder, 16–17, 92
Social disorganization, 47
Social dynamics, 15, 98–101,
104, 107, 114–115
Social equilibrium, 62, 94,
119, 444
Social evolution, 29, 32, 125,
138, 143, 404–405,
436, 451–452
compound societies, 33,
128, 134–135
doubly-compound
societies, 33, 128, 134
intermediate, 452
modern, 452
primitive, 452
trebly-compound societies,
33, 128, 134
Social facts, 17–18, 151, 167,
181–185, 193, 195,

201, 203, 206–207,
210, 252 301, 466
coercive, 211, 183
external, 183
material, 18, 184–185, 187,
191, 193, 208, 358,
466
nonmaterial, 18, 184–185,
187, 191–194,
196–198 205,
207–208, 358, 466
paradigm, 463–465, 469,
471
Social forms, 270–271
conflict, 270
exchange, 270
prostitution, 270
sociability, 270
Social geometry, 268–270,
282
numbers, 268
position, 268
self-involvement, 268
symmetry, 268
valence, 268
Social inequality, 40, 52, 61,
73, 291, 315
Social institutions, 10, 14, 18,
32, 47, 54, 65, 97,
119–120, 122, 125,
133, 137, 297,
325–326, 328, 403,
419, 467
ceremonial, 133–135
fashion, 134
forms of address, 134
mutilations, 133
obeisances, 133–134
presents, 133
titles, 134
trophies, 133
visits, 133
domestic, 130–132
monogamy, 132
polyandry, 131
polygyny, 131–132
evolution of, 130–141
political, 133
religious, 133
Social integration, 194–195
Social location, 355–356

Social mentalities, 53
idealistic, 53
ideational, 53
sensate, 53
Social mobility, 359
horizontal, 359
vertical, 359
Social Mobility, 56
Social order, 8, 434, 442
and progress, 91–94
Social physics, 15
Social reality:
construction of, 410, 412
levels of, 262, 184–185
mental construction of,
427–428
reification of, 69, 266
Social reform, 17, 31–32, 34,
47–48, 52
Social reformism, 16–17,
201–203
Social regulation, 194
Social revolution, 17–18,
102, 216, 335, 368,
370
Social Statics, 114, 116,
141–142
Social statics, 94–98, 104,
107, 114–115
Social status, 308, 467
Social structure(s), 14–16,
107, 120, 126, 167,
264, 271–272, 320,
437, 467
Deep, 74
dynamic equilibrium of,
54
large-scale, 17, 25, 29, 31,
54, 65, 156, 167–169,
172–173, 181, 209,
228
Social system(s), 69, 94, 432,
439
actors and, 446–448
status-role, 437–438,
445
sub, 94
Social System, The, 54, 434,
437, 443
Social theory, 46
Social types, 270

Socialism, 22–23, 141, 145, 149, 152, 154–155, 189, 201, 275
British Fabian, 319–320
expansion of, 141
French, 152
inevitability of, 154
rise of, 7–9
transition to, 156
Socialist societies, 23, 27, 144, 167, 234, 264
Socialization, 68, 206–208, 446–448
dialectics of, 446
gender, 301
process of, 13, 450
Societal community, 447
Societies, 438
Society, 120, 122, 271, 402–404, 407, 447
distributing system of, 127
external matters, 127
internal matters, 127
evolution of, 99, 125–130
hybrid, 130
ideal-typical, 95
mass, 375
as organism, 33, 126
regulative structures of, 127
size of, 33
sustaining structures of, 127
Society in America, 292, 295–296
Socioanalysis, 459
Sociobiology, 78, 451
Sociological Imagination, The, 62–63
personal troubles and public issues, 63
Sociological Inquiry, 73
Sociological methods, 122–125
abstract theorizing, 108, 182, 215
biases in, 123–124
class, 123–124
educational, 123
of patriotism and antipatriotism, 123

political, 124
theological, 124
comparative research, 16, 89, 99, 107, 124–125, 226
empirical research, 10, 12, 14, 31, 67, 70, 71, 88, 94, 124–125, 182, 193, 215, 268, 295, 319–320, 357–358, 413, 459
ethnographic studies, 51
experimentation, 16, 89, 99, 107
field studies, 31
historical, 89, 99, 107, 124–125, 154, 215–220, 226
observation, 16, 48, 88–89, 99, 107, 226
participant observation, 48, 59
questionnaires, 59
statistical techniques, 31, 51,
sympathetic introspection, 50, 59, 386
Sociological Society of London, 29
Sociological theory:
classical, 17
development of, intellectual forces in, 11–38
social forces in, 6–11
early years of, 3–38
early American, 40–52
feminist, 42, 80, 291, 297
from midcentury, 61–75
later years of, 39–84
queer, 80–83
recent developments in, 75–78
scientific, 148
synthetic, 44, 382
value-free, 149, 225, 227
Sociologists for Women in Society (SWS), 73
Sociology:
applied, 45, 108
behavioral, 464

and biology, 121
of the body, 451
conservative, 18
difficulties facing, 122–124
feminist, 295, 299
general theoretical logic for, 458
of gender, 296, 317
historical, 109, 217
institutionalization of, 46, 356
legitimizing, 120–121
meta, 455 459
metatheorizing in, 455–460
a multiple paradigm science, 462–464
occupational, 455
phenomenological, 42, 67, 411, 413, 426, 429
philosophical, 264
political, 427
and psychology, 121–122
pure, 45, 262
radical, 42, 63–64, 71
reflexive, 459–460
science of, 33, 119–122
scientific conception of, 35, 46
sociology of, 459
Sociology: A Multiple Paradigm Science, 462
Sociology of Marx, The, 71
Sociology of Sociology, A, 460
Some Ethical Gains through Legislation, 311
Specialization, 97, 126, 171–172, 186, 199, 279, 379, 393
destructive effects of, 172
of workers, 307
Species-being (see *Human potential*)
Standpoint theories, 81
State, the, 32, 169, 185, 191, 196, 272, 320, 344, 403, 468
role of, 27
Status, 25, 230–231
Studies in Ethnomethodology, 69–70

"Stranger", "The", 269
Stratification, 61, 241, 324
  class, 355
  economic dimension of, 25
  Marx's theory of, 24
  system, 253, 265, 467
  Weber's theory of,
    230–231
Structural functionalism, 35,
    42, 52–58, 64, 70–71,
    94, 97, 107, 130, 181,
    185, 211, 215, 221,
    438, 444, 458, 464
  functions and dysfunctions,
    61
  Parsons, 68
  peak and decline of, 61–63
Structuralism, 42, 211, 445
  French, 74
Structuration theory
    (Giddens), 76
Structure of Social Action,
    The, 35, 54, 189, 409,
    431–432, 434–435,
    437–438, 442–443
Structure of Scientific
    Revolutions, The,
    460–461
Subjective-objective culture,
    263–264, 271–275,
    277
Subjectivism, 216
Subjectivity, 51, 82, 114, 306,
    427
Suicide, 17, 37, 192–198, 208
  causes of, 193
  rates, 17, 192–194, 203,
    211, 467
  types of, 194–196
    altruistic, 195–196, 467
    anomic, 196, 190, 467
    egoistic, 194–195 467
    fatalistic, 196
Suicide, 17, 188, 190,
    192–193, 196, 198,
    206, 208, 210–211,
    463, 466,
Survival-of-the-fittest, 32, 34,
    44, 115, 121, 131,
    142–143
Sweatshops, 320

Symbols, significant,
    393–395
Symbolic interactionism, 28,
    41, 47, 49–52, 58, 66,
    77, 221, 229, 233, 260,
    266, 215, 395, 464,
    467, 471
  Iowa school of, 658
Symbolic media of exchange,
    453
Symbolic media of
    interchange, 453
Systeme de Politique
    Positive, 93
System(s) theory, 42, 78, 464
Systematic Sociology: An
    Introduction to the
    Study of Society, 353

Taoism, 26, 249, 255–256
Tariffs, 349–350
Technology, 324, 331, 470
  industrial, 29
Teleology, 241, 325, 327
Television, 79
Telos, 71
Tenements of Chicago, The,
    310
Theoretical Logic in
    Sociology, 458
Theoretical syntheses, 75,
    77–78, 462
Theories of Surplus Value,
    458
Theory and practice, 98,
    101–105, 108, 167
Theory and Society, 71
Theory of the Leisure Class,
    The, 46, 338
Thought(s), 104–105
  democratization of, 359
  individual, 181, 468
  system, 371
Totalitarianism, 377
Toward an Integrated
    Sociological
    Paradigm, 462
Trade union(s), 141, 272, 320
Traditionalism, 244
Trained incapacity, 344–345

"Transcendent Character of
    Life", "The", 264
Triad, 29, 268
Truth, copy theory of, 88
Twenty Years at Hull-House,
    303, 305
"Two Weeks in Department
    Stores", 310
Typifications, 416–420,
    423–424
  self-, 418

Unanticipated consequences,
    162, 166, 252
Urban ecology, 48
Urban ethnology, 48
Urbanization, 7, 9–10, 14, 41,
    47
Utilitarianism, 433, 435
Utopia, 365–369, 371
  conservative, 368
  disenchantment with, 369
  liberalhumanitarian, 368
  orgiastic chiliasm, 368
  socialistcommunist, 368
Utopian socialists, 155

"Valuation of Housework",
    "The", 318
Value, 269, 274
  integration, 443
  orientations, 438–439, 446,
    448
  system, 452
Values, 173, 182, 184,
    196–197, 225–227,
    231, 252, 265, 325,
    435, 437, 439, 443,
    445–448, 466, 468,
    470
  crisis of, 378
  exchange, 168, 176
  generalization of, 452
  internalized, 449
  judgments, 226–227, 406
  Marx's labor theory of, 21,
    176
  production of, 168
  relevance, 226

Values—*Cont.*
  and research, 226–227
  surplus, 21, 177
  and teaching, 225–226
  use, 168, 170, 176
Verstehen, 215, 219–221,
      229, 305, 436–438
Violence, 31
  by men against women,
      296
  symbolic, 460
"Vision of Sudden Death",
      "The", 305
Voice from the South by a
      Black Woman from the
      South, A, 312–313
Voluntarism, 433–435,
      437–439, 449

Warfare, 33, 129, 134–136,
      299
Waste, 335–336
Weberian theory, 24, 26,
      36–37, 63, 75,
      215–257, 410, 463
Weltanschauung, 364–365,
      367
White Collar, 63
Women, 102–103, 108, 294
  in early sociology, 52
  studies, 73
  subordination of, 300
Women and Economics, 298,
      300
Women and Love, 317
Women in Industry, 310
Work, 160–162

Worker(s), 16, 29, 82, 151,
      163, 174, 176, 202,
      244, 343
  productivity of, 162
Working class, 102, 152, 148,
      324, 340
  exploitation of, 149
  morality of, 102–103
  revolt, 155
Workshop the development
      of, 244
Worldsystem(s), 466, 468

Yellow WallPaper, The, 298
Young Hegelians, 7, 19–20,
      152, 457